THE NASSI · LEVY
SPANISH
THREE YEARS

WORKBOOK EDITION

Second Edition

Stephen L. Levy
Former Head, Foreign Language Department
Roslyn (New York) Public Schools

Robert J. Nassi
Former Teacher of Spanish
Los Angeles Valley Junior College
Los Angeles, California

AMSCO

AMSCO SCHOOL PUBLICATIONS, INC.
315 Hudson Street / New York, N.Y. 10013

With grateful acknowledgment to the coauthors,
Bernard Bernstein
Theodore F. Nuzzi

A la memoria de mis queridos padres por su inspiración, su apoyo y su amor.
S.L.L.

Cover and Text Design by A Good Thing, Inc.
Cover photograph of street scene in Barrio de Triana with
Santa Ana Church. Seville, Andalusia, Spain © INMAGINE
Composition by Compset, Inc.

Please visit our Web site at:
www.amscopub.com

When ordering this book, please specify *either* **R 4700 W** *or*
NASSI • LEVY SPANISH THREE YEARS Workbook

ISBN 978-1-56765-806-4
NYC ITEM: 56765-806-3

Printed in the United States of America

4 5 6 7 8 9 10   10 09 08 07

Preface

The NASSI/LEVY SPANISH THREE YEARS, Second Edition is designed to give students a comprehensive review and thorough understanding of the elements of the Spanish language and the highlights of Hispanic culture. The book was designed to incorporate and reflect the National Standards for Foreign Languages Learning in the 21st Century, also known as the 5 C's: communication, cultures, connections, comparisons, and communities. Abundant and varied exercises help students master each phase of the work.

ORGANIZATION

For ease of study and reference, the book is divided into seven Parts. Parts One to Four are organized around related grammar topics. Part Five covers the culture of Spain and Part Six the culture of Spanish America. Both cultural parts treat language, geography, history, life-styles, science, literature, music, art, and architecture. Part Seven provides materials for comprehensive practice and testing of the communication modes: interpersonal, interpretive, and presentational.

GRAMMAR

Each grammatical chapter deals fully with one major grammatical topic or several closely related ones. Explanations of structure are brief and clear. All points of grammar are illustrated by many examples, in which the key elements are typographically highlighted.

A book intended for third-level review of Spanish assumes that students have completed a basic sequence. Care has been taken, however, especially in the critical Part One: Verbs, to avoid the use of complex structural elements that are treated in other parts of the book. To enable students to concentrate on the structural practice, the vocabulary has been carefully controlled and systematically recycled throughout the grammatical chapters.

The scope of the book has been enriched by the inclusion of a number of grammatical elements not usually found in books of this type. Among these elements are common expressions with verbs (Chapter 16), common expressions with prepositions (in Chapter 20), common adverbial expressions (Chapter 21), and fractions (in Chapter 23).

EXERCISES

For maximum efficiency in learning, the exercises directly follow the points of grammar to which they apply. Carefully graded, the exercises proceed from simple assimilation to more challenging and open-ended manipulation of elements and communication. To provide functional continuity of a grammatical topic, the exercises are set in contexts or situations. Many are also personalized to stimulate student response and interaction with classmates.

While the contents of the exercises afford opportunities for extensive oral practice, the book's format also encourages reinforcement through written student responses, including extended written discourse. The grammatical chapters conclude with Mastery Exercises, in which all grammatical aspects in the chapter are again practiced in recombinations of previously covered elements. All directions to exercises are in Spanish.

FLEXIBILITY

The topical organization and the integrated completeness of each chapter permit the teacher to follow any sequence suitable to the objectives of the course and the needs of the students. This flexibility is facilitated by the detailed table of contents at the front of the book and the comprehensive grammatical index at the back. Teachers as well students will also find the book useful as a reference source.

CULTURE

The cultural chapters in Parts Five and Six are entirely in Spanish. Every effort was made to keep the narratives clear and readable. In addition to their wealth of cultural information, these narratives provide extensive reinforcement of structural and syntactical elements reviewed in Parts One through Four. To encourage students to read for comprehension with minimal interference from footnote references, footnoted meanings have been limited to unusual words and idioms. These footnotes are keyed by number to the text line in which the footnoted element occurs. Each cultural chapter includes exercises designed to test comprehension.

OTHER FEATURES

The Appendix features complete model verb tables and the principal parts of common irregular verbs, along with basic rules of Spanish punctuation and syllabication. Spanish-English and English-Spanish vocabularies and a comprehensive index complete the book.

   With its comprehensive coverage of the elements of Spanish, clear and concise explanations, extensive practice materials, functional vocabulary, and readable cultural narratives, this revised and updated edition of the NASSI/LEVY SPANISH THREE YEARS will help students strengthen their skills in the Spanish language. As students pursue proficiency, they will also gain valuable insights into the cultures of the Hispanic world.

Contents

Part One
Verbal Structures

Part Two
Nouns; Pronouns; Prepositions

Part Three
Adjectives; Adverbs; Numbers

Part Four
Other Structures

Part Five
Civilization: Spain

Part Six
Civilization: Spanish America

Part Seven
Comprehensive Testing: Speaking, Listening, Reading, Writing

Part One
Verbal Structure

Chapter 1
Present Tense

[1] REGULAR VERBS

The present tense of regular verbs is formed by dropping the infinitive ending (–ar, –er, –ir), and adding the following endings.

cantar:	cant	-o, -as, -a, -amos, -áis, -an
vender:	vend	-o, -es, -e, -emos, -éis, -en
recibir:	recib	-o, -es, -e, -imos, -ís, -en

EJERCICIO A   La familia Gómez cuenta lo que hace cuando es el cumpleaños de alguien en México. Escriba lo que ellos dicen.

EJEMPLO: ellos / tocar un disco   **Ellos tocan** un disco.

1. yo / comprar una tarjeta _____

2. los tíos / mandar flores _____

3. la madre / preparar un pastel _____

4. nosotros / buscar un regalo _____

5. tú / cantar *Las mañanitas* _____

6. los amigos / llamar por teléfono _____

7. la abuela / organizar una cena _____

EJERCICIO B   Los niños hablan de lo que hacen en la escuela. Escriba lo que dicen. Siga el ejemplo del Ejercicio A.

1. yo / abrir las ventanas _____

2. María / no correr en el patio _____

3. los alumnos / comer en la cafetería _____

4. tú / recibir buenos informes _____

5. nosotros / aprender la lección _____

6. la maestra / dividir la clase en grupos _____

7. nosotros / escribir la tarea _____

| EJERCICIO C | En su casa todos ayudan con los quehaceres. Escriba lo que hace cada persona, usando las sugerencias. |

SUGERENCIAS: pasar la aspiradora   usar el lavaplatos
lavar las ventanas   arreglar las camas
sacudir los muebles   sacar la basura
barrer el piso

1. Mi madre _____.

2. Mi padre _____.

3. Mis abuelos _____.

4. Mi hermana _____.

5. Yo _____.

6. Mis hermanos y yo _____.

[2] VERBS IRREGULAR IN THE PRESENT TENSE

The following verbs are irregular only in the first-person singular of the present tense:

caber (*to fit, to be room for*): *quepo,* cabes, cabe, cabemos, cabéis, caben

caer (*to fall*): *caigo,* caes, cae, caemos, caéis, caen

conocer (*to know, to be acquainted with*): *conozco,* conoces, conoce, conocemos, conocéis, conocen

Like **conocer:**

aborrecer *to hate, to loathe*	**desconocer** *to be ignorant of*	**ofrecer** *to offer*
agradecer *to thank*	**establecer** *to establish*	**parecer** *to seem*
aparecer *to appear*	**estremecerse** *to shudder*	**permanecer** *to remain*
carecer *to lack*	**merecer** *to deserve*	**pertenecer** *to belong*
crecer *to grow*	**nacer** *to be born*	**reconocer** *to recognize*
desaparecer *to disappear*	**obedecer** *to obey*	

dar (*to give*): *doy,* das, da, damos, dais, dan

hacer (*to make, to do*): *hago,* haces, hace, hacemos, hacéis, hacen

Like **hacer:**

deshacer *to undo*   **satisfacer** *to satisfy*

poner (*to put, to set*): *pongo,* pones, pone, ponemos, ponéis, ponen

Like **poner:**

componer *to compose*	**imponer** *to impose*
disponer *to dispose*	**oponer(se)** *to oppose*
exponer *to expose*	**proponer** *to propose*

saber (*to know*): *sé,* sabes, sabe, sabemos, sabéis, saben

salir (*to go out*): *salgo,* sales, sale, salimos, salís, salen

traducir (*to translate*): *traduzco,* traduces, traduce, traducimos, traducís, traducen

Like **traducir:**

conducir *to conduct, to lead*   producir *to produce*   reducir *to reduce*

traer (*to bring*): *traigo,* traes, trae, traemos, traéis, traen

Like **traer:**

atraer *to attract*

valer (*to be worth*): *valgo,* vales, vale, valemos, valéis, valen

ver (*to see*): *veo,* ves, ve, vemos, veis, ven

NOTE: Most verbs ending in **-cer** or **-cir** and having a vowel directly before the **c**, change the **c** to **zc** in the first-person singular (see conocer and traducir).

EXCEPTIONS: decir (digo), hacer (hago), cocer (cuezo)

IMPORTANT: Irregular verbs that change **c** to **zc** are identified in the vocabulary lists by **zc** in parentheses after the verb: **conocer (zc).**

EJERCICIO D **Usted trata de recordar lo que oyó en varios diálogos breves. En cada diálogo, complete las frases, usando la forma correcta del verbo de la primera frase.**

EJEMPLO: —Yo **voy** al cine.

—¿**Va** Alicia al cine contigo?

—Sí, ¿**vas** tú también?

1. —¿**Traen** Concha y Federico sus discos?

—Sí, y yo _____ mis discos también.

—Tú siempre _____ los mismos discos.

2. —¿Qué **hacen** Uds. esta noche?

—Yo no _____ nada, pero Alicia _____ la tarea.

—¡Tú nunca _____ nada!

3. —¿Dónde **ponemos** las maletas?

—Yo siempre las _____ en la alcoba.

—Enrique las _____ cerca de la puerta.

4. —¿Dónde **establecen** Uds. su casa?

—Yo _____ mi casa en Los Angeles.

—Y nosotros _____ la nuestra en Chicago.

5. —¿**Sabe** Ud. a qué hora termina la película?

—Yo no _____ a qué hora termina.

—Entonces nosotros no _____ si debemos entrar.

6. —¿**Da** Ud. una propina al mozo?

—Yo siempre le _____ una propina.

—Casi todos nosotros le _____ propinas.

7. —¿**Conoces** a ese chico?

—No, yo no lo _____ .

—Nosotros no lo _____ tampoco.

8. —¿Quién **propone** esta fiesta?

—El que la _____, necesita dinero.

—Pues, yo no _____ nada.

9. —Nosotros **obedecemos** las leyes siempre.

—¡Ja! Tú nunca _____ las leyes.

—Antes no, pero ahora sí, yo las _____ .

10. —¿Cuánta gente **cabe** en tu carro?

—Creo que _____ seis personas.

—Si no van dos personas, entonces _____ yo.

EJERCICIO E   Ud. recibió esta carta de un amigo que está estudiando en Chile. Complete la carta con la forma correcta de los verbos dados en paréntesis.

Querido amigo/Querida amiga:

Yo _____ mucho tu carta. Aquí te cuento algunas noticias mías. Ahora yo _____
        1. (agradecer)   *2.* (pertenecer)
a un club deportivo. Varios amigos míos _____ al mismo club también y me
                                          3. (pertenecer)
_____ que voy a divertirme mucho. El club _____ muchas actividades
    4. (parecer)   *5.* (ofrecer)
y _____ abierto hasta muy tarde todos los días. Yo _____ de las escuela a las
   6. (permanecer)   *7.* (salir)
dos y media y voy al club. Yo me _____ ropa deportiva y _____ muchos
                                  8. (poner)   *9.* (hacer)
ejercicios. Ya _____ a muchos jóvenes y ahora nosotros _____ planes para
                10. (conocer)   *11.* (hacer)
ir a Viña del Mar. Cuando regreso a casa yo _____ las tareas. Yo _____ que
                                             12. (hacer)   *13.* (saber)
te gustaría esta vida. Yo no _____ de nada y me _____ cuando recuerdo mi
                             14. (carecer)   *15.* (estremecer)
apatía antes de hacer el viaje. Es una experiencia que _____ la pena. Hasta pronto y saludos.
                                                        16. (valer)

[3] OTHER VERBS WITH IRREGULAR FORMS IN THE PRESENT TENSE

decir (*to say, to tell*):   *digo, dices, dice,* decimos, decís, *dicen*

estar (*to be*):   *estoy, estás,* estamos, estáis, *están*

haber (*to have*):   *he, has, ha,* hemos, habéis, *han*

ir (*to go*):   *voy, vas, va,* vamos, vais, van

oír (*to hear*):   *oigo, oyes, oye,* oímos, oís, *oyen*

ser (*to be*):   *soy, eres, es,* somos, sois, *son*

tener (*to have*):   *tengo, tienes, tiene,* tenemos, tenéis, *tienen*

NOTE: Like tener:

contener *to contain*   entretener *to entertain*   obtener *to obtain*

detener *to detain*   mantener *to maintain*   sostener *to sustain*

venir (*to come*):   *vengo, vienes, viene,* venimos, venís, *vienen*

EJERCICIO F   **Después de ver una película de horror, Ud. y varios amigos creen oír ruidos. Escriba lo que dicen.**

EJEMPLO: tú / oír gritos   **Tú dices** que **oyes** gritos.

1. Sarita / oír disparos   _____

2. Carlos y yo / oír pasos   _____

3. los hermanos / oír voces   _____

4. yo / oír suspiros   _____

5. tú / oír música   _____

6. Elena y Clara / oír una sirena   _____

EJERCICIO G   **Escriba lo que estas personas dicen que tienen y lo que van a hacer.**

EJEMPLO: Pedro / tener hambre / ir a comer
Pedro tiene hambre y **va** a comer.

1. Claudia / tener sed / ir a tomar un refresco

_____

2. ellos / tener sueño / ir a dormir

_____

3. tú / tener dolor de cabeza / ir a tomar una aspirina

_____

4. mi hermano y yo / tener calor / ir a nadar

_____

5. yo / tener suerte / ir a jugar la lotería

_____

| EJERCICIO H | Ud. regresa de un viaje a la América del Sur y ayuda al agente de inmigración en el aeropuerto. Ud. le dice de dónde son los turistas que llegan. Escriba de dónde son estas personas.

EJEMPLO: este señor / ser de Colombia
Este señor es de Colombia.

1. yo / ser de los Estados Unidos

_____

2. estos niños / ser de Chile

_____

3. esta señora / ser de Bolivia

_____

4. el joven / ser de México

_____

5. esta muchacha y yo / ser de los Estados Unidos

_____

| EJERCICIO I | Hay una fiesta en el gimnasio de la escuela. Escriba a qué hora viene cada persona al gimnasio.

EJEMPLO: Silvia / 6:30   **Silvia _viene_ a las seis y media.**

1. Pablo / 8:00   _____

2. tú / 7:15   _____

3. Carmen y Ana / 7:45   _____

4. yo / 6:00   _____

5. Roberto y yo / 6:25   _____

6. ustedes / 8:10   _____

| EJERCICIO J | Escriba dónde están sus amigos durante el verano.

EJEMPLO: Alfredo / en el campo   **Alfredo está** en el campo.

1. Ricardo / en España   _____

2. yo / en la ciudad   _____

3. tú / en el mar

_____

4. Paula y Esteban / en la escuela

_____

5. los hermanos López / en la granja

_____

EJERCICIO K | **Ud. cuida a dos niños mientras sus padres salen. Usando las sugerencias, escriba cinco frases para describir lo que pasa.**

SUGERENCIAS:
yo	oír los gritos de los niños
los niños	venir a las once
sus padres	no tener sueño
los vecinos	estar en la sala
la niña	ser bueno(a)
los niños y yo	ir a mirar la televisión

1. _____

2. _____

3. _____

4. _____

5. _____

EJERCICIO L | **Ud. habla con un alumno extranjero en la escuela. Conteste las preguntas que él le hace.**

1. ¿Adónde van tú y tus amigos los fines de semana?

_____

2. ¿Qué tienes ganas de hacer esta noche?

_____

3. ¿Qué haces cuando estás aburrido?

_____

4. ¿Por qué dices que tus amigos son simpáticos?

_____

5. ¿Cuál es el primer ruido que oyes por la mañana?

_____

6. ¿A qué hora vienen tus amigos?

_____

7. ¿Dónde están ellos ahora?

_____

[4] USES OF THE PRESENT TENSE

a. The present tense may have the following meanings in English.

Pablo *sale*.	*Pablo leaves (is leaving).*
Van a casa.	*They go (are going) home.*
¿Estudia Ud. español?	*Do you study Spanish?*
No *hablo* español.	*I do not speak Spanish.*

b. The present tense is often used instead of the future to ask for instructions or to refer to an action that will take place in the immediate future.

¿Lo *pongo* aquí?	*Shall I put it here?*
¿Qué *hacemos* ahora?	*What shall we do now?*
Llamo más tarde.	*I'll call later.*
Después *comemos*.	*We'll eat afterwards.*

c. The construction **hace** + *time expression* + **que** + *present tense* is used to express an action or event that began in the past and continues in the present. In such situations, the question is expressed by **¿Cuánto tiempo hace que...?** + *the present tense* or **¿Hace cuánto tiempo que...?** + *the present tense.*

Hace un año que *vivo* aquí.	*I have been living here for a year.*
Hace una hora que *esperamos*.	*We have been waiting for an hour.*
¿Cuánto tiempo hace que Ud. *trabaja*?	*How long have you been working?*

NOTE: The *present tense* + **desde hace** + *time expression* is also used to express a past action or event that continues in the present. In such situations, the question is expressed by **¿Desde cuándo . . .?** + *the present tense.*

Vivo aquí desde hace un año.	*I have been living here for a year.*
¿Desde cuándo *trabaja* Ud.?	*How long have you been working?*

EJERCICIO M   Ud. le cuenta a un amigo desde cuándo Ud. hace o no hace varias cosas. Escriba las frases según los ejemplos.

EJEMPLOS: montar a caballo (seis años)   no ir a un museo (dos meses)
Hace seis años que monto a caballo.   **No voy** a un museo **desde hace dos meses.**
Monto a caballo **desde hace seis años.**   **Hace dos meses que no voy** a un museo.

1. estudiar el español (cuatro años)

_____   _____

2. aprender a conducir (tres meses)

_____   _____

3. no jugar con el equipo de béisbol (dos años)

_____   _____

4. no pasar la Navidad en Puerto Rico (cinco años)

_____   _____

5. vivir en esta casa (diez años)

_____   _____

6. salir con esos amigos (dos semanas)

_____   _____

| EJERCICIO N | A Ud. no le gusta hacer las cosas inmediatamente. Escriba cuándo va a hacer estas cosas, usando las expresiones siguientes. |

hoy por la tarde (noche, mañana)   más tarde

esta noche (tarde, mañana)   después

mañana

EJEMPLO: ir a la biblioteca   **Voy** a la biblioteca **más tarde.**

1. arreglar el cuarto   _____

2. preparar la tarea   _____

3. ayudar a su hermano   _____

4. leer una novela   _____

5. estudiar para el examen   _____

6. devolver los libros a la biblioteca   _____

| EJERCICIO O | Ud. pasa el verano en un campamento, donde acaba de conocer a unos jóvenes. Escriba las preguntas que Ud. les hace para saber desde cuándo hacen varias cosas. |

EJEMPLO: venir a este campamento
    ¿Cuánto tiempo hace que Uds. **vienen** a este campamento?
    ¿Desde cuándo vienen Uds. a este campamento?

1. saber remar   _____

_____

2. pescar   _____

_____

3. practicar el esquí acuático   _____

_____

4. conocer a estas muchachas   _____

_____

5. salir juntos   _____

_____

6. ser amigos _____

_____

7. hacer excursiones _____

_____

EJERCICIO P Conteste las preguntas que le hace un primo acerca de la escuela.

1. ¿Saludan Uds. al profesor al entrar en la clase?

_____

2. ¿Dónde pones tus libros en la escuela?

_____

3. ¿A qué hora salen Uds. de la escuela?

_____

4. ¿Tienes que trabajar después de las clases?

_____

5. ¿Eres un buen alumno (una buena alumna)?

_____

6. ¿Qué haces el día antes de un examen?

_____

7. ¿Cuánto tiempo hace que no preparas una tarea?

_____

8. ¿Qué hacen Uds. cuando el profesor está ausente?

_____

EJERCICIO Q Ud. está en una fiesta y ve que un amigo suyo está agitado porque la persona que él invitó a la fiesta no le hace caso. Escriba las preguntas que Ud. hace, según las respuestas dadas.

EJEMPLO: **¿Cuánto tiempo hace que sales con ella?**
Hace diez días que salgo con ella.

1. _____

Están juntos desde hace dos horas.

2. _____

Hace una hora y media que bailan juntos.

3. _____

Yo la conozco desde hace un mes.

4. _____

Hace dos días que él tiene interés en conocerla.

5. _____

Estoy agitado desde hace una hora más o menos.

EJERCICIO R   **Los jóvenes siempre gozan de las vacaciones escolares. Trabajando con un(-a) compañero(-a), hablen de las actividades que generalmente practican durante las vacaciones escolares. Incluya información sobre adónde va, con quién(-es) va, por qué, cuánto tiempo pasa allí, lo que hace, etc. Saque apuntes sobre lo que su compañero(-a) contesta.**

EJERCICIO S   **Al terminar el Ejercicio R, y usando los apuntes que Ud. sacó, escriba un resumen de cómo su compañero(-a) pasa las vacaciones.**

_____

_____

_____

_____

_____

_____

_____

_____

_____

EJERCICIO T   **Hace una hora que Ud. espera a un amigo en la puerta de su casa pero no él llega. Escriba una nota que Ud. le deja en la puerta, en la cual le dice lo siguiente:**

> how long you have been waiting for him/her
>
> you do not understand why he/she is not there
>
> he/she always arrives on time
>
> how you feel (angry, upset, furious)
>
> you do not deserve this
>
> will he/she call you to explain
>
> when you will be at home

_____
_____
_____
_____
_____
_____
_____

| EJERCICIO U | **Lea el artículo que sigue y conteste las preguntas.**

Hablar español: habilidad vital para los políticos

Con la esperanza de ganar puntos entre la minoría más grande de los Estados Unidos y conscientes de que el español es de suma importancia para su supervivencia política, los candidatos, tanto demócratas como republicanos, toman cursos intensivos en este idioma.

Ahora la comunidad hispana cuenta con el 13 por ciento de la población y según los últimos comicios su creciente poder político y económico la pone firmemente en el radar de los políticos y de las grandes empresas. Como ejemplo de este conocimiento, el Partido Demócrata intenta llevar a cabo seis debates en inglés y en español entre los precandidatos de ese partido que anhelan ser el candidato demócrata en las próximas elecciones presidenciales. Como prueba de la creciente popularidad del bilingüismo, el primer debate será transmitido por una emisora hispana cuya programación se dirige al público hispanohablante.

Todo indica que saber español no es una moda pasajera. Lo que los legisladores quieren lograr es comunicarse de manera más directa con sus contribuyentes, aunque al principio lo hacen con frases chapurreadas. Y para poder hacer eso, muchos aprovechan las vacaciones de verano para repasar lecciones de vocabulario y gramática, tomar un curso intensivo o sumergirse en la lengua y la cultura hispana al pasar tiempo en un país hispano. También hay un programa creado exclusivamente para ellos, que es administrado por el Departmento de Agricultura.

Naturalmente el asunto no es puramente lingüístico, sino que también existen motivos políticos. Los republicanos quieren cambiar la imagen de su partido, buscar un mayor acercamiento con las minorías y mostrar que les interesan los asuntos que son importantes para los hispanos, como la educación, la vivienda, salud y creación de empleos. Los demócratas reconocen que aunque el voto hispano ha sido suyo en el pasado, no pueden descansar y es importantísimo utilizar la lengua de sus constituyentes para comunicarse con ellos.

1. ¿Por qué toman los políticos cursos intensivos de español?
   1. Desean asegurar su futuro político.
   2. Piensan visitar países hispanos.
   3. Deben satisfacer unos requisitos del gobierno.
   4. Necesitan explicar las nuevas leyes a sus constituyentes.

2. Los debates de los precandidatos serán transmitidos por televisión hispana porque
   1. varios candidatos son de origen hispano.
   2. reconocen la importancia y el poder del voto hispano.

    3. quieren atraer a un público homogéneo.

    4. la emisora hispana les regala el tiempo.

3. ¿Cómo desean comunicarse los políticos con sus constituyentes hispanos?

    1. Por medio de traductores e intérpretes.

    2. Salpicando sus charlas con expresiones en español.

    3. Conversando directamente con ellos en español.

    4. Usando una nueva tecnología de traducción.

4. ¿Con qué fin van a usar los políticos su bilingüismo?

    1. Para aclarar el propósito del partido.

    2. Para mostrar su habilidad en el idioma español.

    3. Para afirmar los asuntos que ellos apoyan.

    4. Para hablar mal de sus adversarios.

Chapter 2
Present Tense of Stem-Changing Verbs

[1] STEM-CHANGING VERBS ENDING IN -AR AND -ER

Stem-changing verbs ending in **-ar** or **-er** change the stem vowel in the present tense as follows.

> **e** to **ie**
> **o** to **ue**
> in all forms except for those for **nosotros** and **vosotros**

pensar (*to think*):   *pienso, piensas, piensa, pensamos, penséis, piensan*

Like **pensar:**

acertar *to hit the mark, to guess right*	**encerrar** *to lock in; to contain*
apretar *to tighten, to squeeze; to be tight*	**gobernar** *to govern*
atravesar *to cross*	**helar** *to freeze*
cerrar *to close*	**nevar** *to snow*
comenzar *to begin, to commence*	**quebrar** *to break*
confesar *to confess*	**remendar** *to patch, to mend*
despertar(se) *to awaken; (to wake up)*	**sentar(se)** *to seat, (to sit down)*
empezar *to begin*	

querer (*to want, to love, to wish*):   **quiero, quieres, quiere, queremos, queréis, quieren**

Like **querer:**

ascender *to ascend; to promote*	**encender** *to light; to ignite*
defender *to defend*	**entender** *to understand*
descender *to descend*	**perder** *to lose*

mostrar (*to show*):   **muestro, muestras, muestra, mostramos, mostráis, muestran**

Like **mostrar:**

acordarse (de) *to remember*	**jugar (*u* to *ue*)★** *to play (games, sports)*
acostar(se) *to put to bed, (to go to bed)*	**recordar** *to remember*
almorzar *to eat lunch*	**renovar** *to remodel, to renew*
contar *to count; to tell*	**tronar** *to thunder*
costar *to cost*	**volar** *to fly*
encontrar *to find, to meet*	

★ The verb **jugar** is conjugated as follows: *juego, juegas, juega, jugamos, jugáis, juegan.*

volver (*to return, to come or go back*):   vuelvo, vuelves, vuelve, volvemos, volvéis, vuelven

Like volver:

conmover   *to move (emotionally)*   oler (*o to hue*)   *to smell*
devolver   *to return, to give back*   poder   *to be able*
doler   *to pain, to ache*   resolver   *to solve; to resolve*
llover   *to rain*   soler   *to be in the habit of, to be accustomed to*
mover   *to move*

EJERCICIO A   ¿Qué hace su familia? Escriba lo que hace cada persona.

EJEMPLO: mi mamá / despertar a mi papá
Mi mamá despierta a mi papá.

1. mi papá / leer el periódico

_____

2. mis hermanos / cerrar las puertas

_____

3. yo / empezar a estudiar

_____

4. mi abuelo / contar su dinero

_____

5. nosotros / descender al comedor

_____

6. tú / contar un chiste

_____

EJERCICIO B   ¿Qué hacen estas personas? Escriba lo que hace cada persona.

EJEMPLO: Raúl / atravesar la calle   **Raúl atraviesa** la calle.

1. el jefe / ascender a los empleados   _____

2. los jóvenes / almorzar en la cafetería   _____

3. tú y yo / resolver el problema   _____

4. Sarita / encontrar una novela buena   _____

5. tú / devolver el regalo   _____

6. Rafael y yo / defender a los niños   _____

7. yo / comenzar a trabajar   _____

8. los actores / conmover al público   _____

| EJERCICIO C | Ud. llama al Cine Real para obtener información. Complete las frases con la forma correcta del verbo. |

SEÑORITA: Buenas tardes, Cine Real. ¿En qué _____ ayudarle?
1. (poder)

USTED: Buenas tardes. ¿ _____ Ud. darme alguna información, por favor?
2. (poder)

SEÑORITA: Sí, cómo no. ¿Qué _____ Ud. saber?
3. (querer)

USTED: ¿A qué hora _____ la función?
4. (comenzar)

SEÑORITA: La función _____ a las 5:10, las 7:30 y las 9:50.
5. (empezar)

USTED: ¿Y cuánto _____ las entradas?
6. (costar)

SEÑORITA: Cada entrada _____ cuatro pesos.
7. (costar)

USTED: ¿Y a qué hora _____ la taquilla?
8. (cerrar)

SEÑORITA: La taquilla _____ quince minutos después de la última función.
9. (cerrar)

USTED: Debemos apresurarnos. Nosotros _____ llegar tarde.
10. (soler)

SEÑORITA: Sí, deben apresurarse. Es una lástima si Uds. se _____ esta película. Mucha
11. (perder)

gente _____ verla y a veces la cola _____ a formarse una hora
12. (querer)   13. (comenzar)

antes. Pero Uds. _____ comprar las entradas para cualquier función.
14. (poder)

USTED: Gracias, señorita. Yo _____ su consejo muy útil.
15. (encontrar)

SEÑORITA: De nada. Adiós.

| EJERCICIO D | Conteste las preguntas que le hace un joven chileno que visita su escuela. |

1. ¿Atraviesas varias calles para llegar a la escuela?

_____

2. ¿Juegan Uds. al ajedrez?

_____

3. ¿A qué hora te despiertas los sábados?

_____

4. ¿Dónde almuerzan tú y tus amigos todos los días?

_____

5. ¿Suelen Uds. ir al cine?

_____

6. ¿Entiendes el francés?

_____

7. ¿Recuerdas mi número de teléfono?

_____

8. ¿Dónde te encuentro el sábado?

_____

[2] STEM-CHANGING VERBS ENDING IN -*IR*

Stem-changing verbs ending in **-ir** change the stem vowel in the present tense as follows:

> **e** to **ie**
> **o** to **ue**   in all forms except for those for **nosotros** and **vosotros**
> **e** to **i**

consentir (*to consent*):   consiento, consientes, consiente, consentimos, consentís, consienten

Like consentir:

advertir *to notify, to warn*	**preferir** *to prefer*
convertir *to convert*	**referir** *to recount; to refer*
divertirse *to enjoy oneself, to have a good time*	**sentir** *to regret, to feel sorry*
hervir *to boil*	**sentirse** *to feel (well, ill)*
mentir *to lie*	

NOTE: The verb **adquirir** (*to acquire*) is like **consentir:** adquiero, adquieres, adquiere, adquirimos, adquirís, adquieren.

dormir (*to sleep*):   duermo, duermes, duerme, dormimos, dormís, duermen

Like dormir:

dormirse *to fall asleep*   **morir(se)** *to die*

pedir (*to ask for, to request*):   pido, pides, pide, pedimos, pedís, piden

Like pedir:

despedirse (de) *to take leave (of), to say goodbye (to)*	**medir** *to measure*
gemir *to groan, to moan*	**reír(se)** *to laugh*
impedir *to prevent*	**reñir** *to quarrel, to scold*

repetir *to repeat*	sonreír(se) *to smile*
servir *to serve*	vestir(se) *to dress (oneself)*

NOTE: The verb **reír** (and **sonreír**) has an accent mark over the letter **i** in all forms: **río, ríes, ríe, reímos, reís, ríen.**

EJERCICIO E   Escriba el pasatiempo preferido de cada persona.

EJEMPLO: Manuel / el béisbol   Manuel **prefiere** el béisbol.

1. Sofía / el tenis _____

2. tú / el fútbol _____

3. Eduardo y Carlos / el voleibol _____

4. yo / la natación _____

5. Luz y yo / las damas _____

6. Ricardo / el ajedrez _____

7. mi padre / el dominó _____

EJERCICIO F   ¿Dónde duermen estas personas? Escriba dónde duerme cada persona.

EJEMPLO: yo / en casa de mi amigo   Yo **duermo** en casa de mi amigo.

1. mi madre / en el sofá _____

2. Lola / en la hamaca _____

3. mi abuelo / en el sofá _____

4. los niños / en el coche _____

5. yo / en la sala _____

6. tú / en el comedor _____

7. Rafael y yo / en el patio _____

EJERCICIO G   Escriba a quién riñe cada persona.

EJEMPLO: los padres / a sus hijos   **Los padres riñen** a sus hijos.

1. yo / a mi hermanito _____

2. la profesora / a los alumnos _____

3. el jefe / a los trabajadores _____

4. tú / a tu perro _____

5. nosotros / a nuestros amigos _____

6. Clara y Luis / a su gato _____

EJERCICIO H | ¿Cómo reaccionan las personas? Escriba lo que hacen, usando la forma correcta del verbo indicado.

EJEMPLO: Pablo y Lourdes no entienden la tarea. (pedir ayuda al profesor)
   Por eso Pablo y Lourdes **piden** ayuda al profesor.

1. María quiere comprar tela para hacer cortinas nuevas. (medir las ventanas)

_____

2. Yo preparo té para mi mamá. (hervir el agua)

_____

3. Los señores están en México y necesitan pesos, pero sólo traen dólares. (convertir los dólares en pesos)

_____

4. La policía está en la esquina porque hay un accidente automovilístico. (impedir el paso)

_____

5. Carlos habla con su abuelo pero él no oye bien. (repetir las frases)

_____

6. Tú preparas la cena y toda tu familia está en la mesa. (servir la cena)

_____

7. Tú quieres usar el auto pero tus padres dicen que no. (reñir con ellos)

_____

8. Todo el mundo escucha el chiste que Rafael cuenta. (reír a carcajadas)

_____

9. Encontramos a un ladrón en casa. (advertir a la policía)

_____

10. Alfonso quiere pasar la noche en casa de un amigo. (pedir permiso a sus padres)

_____

11. El payaso es muy bueno. (divertir mucho a los niños)

_____

12. El señor Pérez lee el termómetro. La temperatura es 20°F. (sentir frío)

_____

13. La fiesta termina y los jóvenes se van a casa. (decir adiós)

_____

Content

14. Mi padre está muy cansado y hay un programa aburrido en la televisión. (dormirse en el sillón)

_____

15. La madre mira el reloj y dice que van a llegar tarde. (vestir a su hijito rápidamente)

_____

[3] VERBS ENDING IN -UIR

In verbs ending in **-uir** (except **-guir***) a **y** is inserted after the **u** in all forms except those for **nosotros** and **vosotros**.

huir (*to flee*):   huyo, huyes, huye, huimos, huís, huyen

Like huir:

concluir *to conclude, to end*   distribuir *to distribute*
construir *to construct*   incluir *to include*
contribuir *to contribute*   influir *to influence, to have influence*
destruir *to destroy*   sustituir *to substitute*

| EJERCICIO 1 | Escriba lo que pasa en cada dibujo. Use los verbos *concluir, construir, contribuir, distribuir* y *destruir*. |

EJEMPLO: **Carlos construye** una casa de muñecas.

1. Los obreros_____   **2.** La señora_____

_____   _____

---

* See Chapter 3, page 28.

3. La película _____

_____

4. Carmen _____

_____

5. Elías _____

_____

6. El niño _____

_____

EJERCICIO J La emisora WABO pide contribuciones para los pobres. Escriba las respuestas que da el locutor en una entrevista.

1. ¿Qué contribuye Ud.?

_____

2. ¿Qué contribuye el público?

_____

3. ¿Quién distribuye las cosas?

_____

4. ¿Sobre quiénes influyen Uds.?

_____

5. ¿Cuándo concluye este proyecto?

_____

[4]   VERBS ENDING IN *-IAR* AND *-UAR*

Some verbs ending in **-iar** or **-uar** stress the **i** or the **u** (**í, ú**) in all forms except those for **nosotros** and **vosotros**. In the **vosotros** form the **a** takes an accent mark.

enviar (*to send*):   envío, envías, envía, enviamos, enviáis, envían

Like **enviar**:

confiar (en) *to rely (on), to confide (in)*	guiar *to guide*
espiar *to spy*	resfriarse *to catch cold*
fiarse (de) *to trust*	variar *to vary*

continuar (*to continue*):   continúo, continúas, continúa, continuamos, continuáis, continúan

Like **continuar**:

actuar   *to act*   graduarse   *to graduate*

NOTE: All stem-changing verbs are identified in the end vocabulary by the type of change (**ie, ue, i, y, í, ú**) after the verb: **pensar (ie)**.

EJERCICIO K   **En una reunión familiar, las tías hablan de sus hijos. Escriba lo que ellas dicen.**

EJEMPLO: Roberto / graduarse de la secundaria
Roberto se gradúa de la secundaria.

1. Clarisa / graduarse de la primaria

_____

2. los gemelos / graduarse de la universidad

_____

3. Pilar / graduarse de la preparatoria

_____

4. Elena /graduarse de la escuela de belleza

_____

5. Jorge y Javier / graduarse de la Facultad de Leyes

_____

EJERCICIO L   **En el consultorio del médico, Ud. responde a las preguntas que le hace el médico.**

1. ¿En qué estación se resfría Ud. más fácilmente? (en el invierno)

_____

2. ¿De qué tipo de medicina se fía Ud.? (las aspirinas)

_____

3. ¿Cuándo varía Ud. su dieta? (los fines de semana)

_____

4. ¿Adónde envía Ud. estas formas? (a la compañía de seguros)

_____

5. ¿En quién confía Ud.? (en los buenos amigos)

_____

M A S T E R Y   E X E R C I S E S

EJERCICIO M   **Usted va a presentar este anuncio en una emisora. Complete las frases con la forma correcta de los verbos.**

¿ _____ Ud. una comida sabrosa que no _____ mucho? Si Ud.
    1. (querer)   *2.* (costar)

_____ al Restaurante Dos Caminos, Ud. y sus invitados _____ todo lo
  3. (venir)   *4.* (encontrar)

mejor. Una comida completa _____ sólo ciento cincuenta pesos e _____
                         5. (costar)   *6.* (incluir)

el café y la propina. En el Restaurante Dos Caminos nosotros _____ la comida desde
                                                  7. (servir)

la una y media y la cocina no _____ hasta las cinco todos los días. Ud. no
                                   8. (cerrar)

_____ encontrar un lugar mejor. Nuestros meseros _____ a los clientes
  9. (poder)   *10.* (atender)

con cortesía y _____ la comida rápidamente. Uds. _____ bien cuando
             11. (servir)   *12.* (acertar)

_____ al Restaurante Dos Caminos, que _____ en la esquina de la Calle
  13. (venir)   *14.* (encontrarse)

Dolores y la Avenida Juárez. Uds. no _____ reservación.
                         15. (requerir)

EJERCICIO N   **Usted está en una zapatería y se prueba varios zapatos. Conteste las preguntas que le hace el dependiente.**

DEPENDIENTE: ¿Le puedo mostrar algo?

UD: (*Tell him that you want to try on these black shoes.*)

_____

DEPENDIENTE: ¿Qué número calza Ud.?

Ud: (*Tell him to measure your foot.*)

_____

DEPENDIENTE: ¿Cómo los siente?

UD: (*Tell him that they are tight.*)

_____

DEPENDIENTE: ¿Le muestro otro par de zapatos?

UD: (*Ask him to show you the blue pair.*)

_____

DEPENDIENTE: ¿Se refiere Ud. a éstos?

UD: (*Tell him that yes, you want to try those on.*)

_____

DEPENDIENTE: ¿Cuál de los dos prefiere Ud.?

UD: (*Tell him which pair you prefer.*)

_____

DEPENDIENTE: ¿Quiere Ud. otra cosa?

UD: (*Ask him the price.*)

_____

DEPENDIENTE: Cincuenta y cinco dólares.

UD: (*Tell him that you prefer a less expensive pair.*)

_____

DEPENDIENTE: Lo siento. Ahora no tenemos nada más barato.

UD: (*Thank him and tell him that you will return next week.*)

_____

EJERCICIO O   Ud. tiene un(-a) amigo(-a) por correspondencia que vive en Costa Rica. En sus cartas, Uds. suelen compartir información sobre la vida en sus países. Usando tantos verbos de este capítulo como pueda, escríbale una carta en que Ud. le describe el clima en diferentes zonas de los Estados Unidos. Incluya en su carta:

  the type of weather (heat, rain, snow, ice, etc.) in different regions
  how the people react to the weather
  how the weather affects daily activities
  how the different landscapes look at different times of the year
  activities that are popular in the different seasons and areas
  what you prefer
  where you want to live when you graduate
  ask for his/her recommendations or suggestions

Chapter 3
Verbs With Spelling Changes in the Present Tense

Verbs with changes in spelling are not truly irregular. The spelling change occurs before certain letters in order to preserve the original sound in accordance with the rules for Spanish pronunciation.

[1] VERBS ENDING IN *-CER* OR *-CIR*

In verbs ending in **-cer** or **-cir, c** changes to **z** before **o** or **a.**

> vencer (*to conquer, to overcome*):   ven*z*o, vences, vence, vencemos, vencéis, vencen

Like vencer: convencer   *to convince*   ejercer   *to exert, to exercise, to practice (a profession)*

[2] VERBS ENDING IN *-GER* OR *-GIR*

In verbs ending in **-ger** or **-gir, g** changes to **j** before **o** or **a.**

> dirigir (*to direct*):   diri*j*o, diriges, dirige, dirigimos, dirigís, dirigen

Like dirigir:

afligir *to afflict, to grieve*	**fingir** *to pretend*
coger *to seize, to grasp, to catch*	**proteger** *to protect*
escoger *to choose, to select*	**recoger** *to gather, to pick up*
exigir *to demand, to require*	

[3] VERBS ENDING IN *-GUIR*

In verbs ending in **-guir, gu** changes to **g** before **o** or **a.**

> distinguir (*to distinguish*):   distin*g*o, distingues, distingue, distinguimos, distinguís, distinguen

Like distinguir: extinguir   *to extinguish*

NOTES:

1. Some verbs with spelling changes also have stem changes. (See Chapter 2, pages 16 and 19.) Some verbs of this type are:

> cocer (*to cook*):   *cuezo, cueces, cuece,* cocemos, cocéis, *cuecen*

Like cocer: torcer   *to twist, to turn*

> corregir (*to correct*):   *corrijo, corriges, corrige,* corregimos, corregís, *corrigen*

Like **corregir:**   **elegir**   *to elect, to choose*

seguir (*to follow, to continue*):   *sigo,* **sigues, sigue,** seguimos, seguís, *siguen*

Like **seguir:**   **conseguir**   *to get, to obtain, to succeed in*
perseguir   *to pursue, to persecute*
proseguir   *to continue, to proceed*

2. Verbs ending in **–car, –gar,** and **–zar** have no spelling changes in the present tense. Changes occur only in the preterit (see Chapter 4), in commands (see Chapter 16), and in the present subjunctive (see Chapter 13).

3. Verbs with spelling changes are identified in the end vocabulary by the type of change (**z, j, g**) in parentheses after the verb: **vencer (z).**

EJERCICIO A   **Usando las sugerencias, escriba a quién convencen las siguientes personas.**

SUGERENCIAS: a los niños   a mis padres
a su jefe   al juez
al enfermo   a tu hermano
a los alumnos   a nuestros amigos

EJEMPLO: El médico   El médico **convence a los enfermos.**

1. El abogado   _____

2. Yo   _____

3. Los padres   _____

4. Roberto y yo   _____

5. El maestro   _____

6. Tú   _____

EJERCICIO B   **Escriba la profesión que ejercen varias personas, usando las sugerencias.**

SUGERENCIAS: salvavidas / abogado / dentista / profesor / carpintero / dependiente / enfermera

EJEMPLO: María cuida a los enfermos en el hospital.
María ejerce la profesión de enfermera.

1. Yo trabajo en un almacén y vendo ropa de niños.

   Yo _____.

2. Mi padre enseña a los alumnos.

   Mi padre _____.

3. Elena defiende a los criminales en la corte.

   Elena _____.

4. Mi tío arregla los dientes de muchas personas.

Mi tío _____ .

5. Pablo y yo cuidamos a los nadadores en la playa.

Pablo y yo _____ .

6. Tú construyes muchas cosas de madera.

Tú _____ .

EJERCICIO C | **Algunos amigos están en una tienda de deportes. Mire cada dibujo y escriba lo que escogen las personas.**

EJEMPLO: **Pilar escoge un guante de béisbol.**

1. Alberto _____

_____

2. Tú _____

_____

3. Elena y Ana _____

_____

4. Yo _____

_____

5. Sarita y yo _____

_____

EJERCICIO D | **¿Qué hacen las personas cuando no quieren hacer algo? Escriba lo que fingen estas personas en cada situación.**

EJEMPLO: David no quiere sacar la basura. (estar ocupado)
David finge estar ocupado.

1. Luis no quiere ir a la escuela hoy. (estar enfermo)

   Luis _____.

2. Yo no quiero bailar con esa persona. (estar cansado)

   Yo _____.

3. La niña no quiere cantar para los invitados. (tener dolor de garganta)

   La niña _____.

4. Tú no quieres ayudar a tu papá a las ocho de la mañana. (estar dormido)

   Tú _____.

5. Mi abuelo no me contesta cuando le pido dinero. (ser sordo)

   Mi abuelo _____.

6. Lisa y yo no contestamos cuando nuestros amigos nos llaman. (estar distraídos)

   Lisa y yo _____.

EJERCICIO E | **¿Es todo igual? En cada frase escriba la forma correcta de *distinguir* para mostrar si todo es igual o no.**

EJEMPLO: ¿De qué color es esa blusa? **Yo no distingo los colores.**

1. Rafael le habla de «tú» a la profesora de español.

   Él no _____ entre «tú» y «Ud.».

2. ¿Ves bien cuando no hay luz?

   No, en la oscuridad yo no _____ nada.

3. ¿Es éste un suéter verde o marrón?

   Nosotros no _____ los colores.

4. En ese cine el precio de las entradas es igual para todo el mundo.

   Ellos no _____ entre los adultos y los niños.

5. Mis hermanitos son gemelos.

   Nadie _____ quién es Ramón y quién es Raúl.

EJERCICIO F | **Conteste las preguntas que le hacen sobre sus impresiones de su escuela para un artículo en el periódico escolar.**

1. ¿Quién corrige las faltas en su clase de español?

    _____

2. ¿Quién convence a los estudiantes para que estudien más?

    _____

3. ¿Distinguen los profesores entre los alumnos preparados y los que no están preparados?

    _____

4. ¿Eliges tú los cursos que sigues?

    _____

5. ¿Cómo consiguen Uds. sacar buenas notas?

    _____

6. ¿Exigen los profesores mucho a sus alumnos?

    _____

7. ¿Finges tú estar distraído cuando no quieres contestar en una clase?

    _____

8. ¿Escogen Uds. a sus profesores?

    _____

9. ¿Quién protege los derechos de los estudiantes?

    _____

10. ¿Quién dirige esta escuela?

    _____

M A S T E R Y   E X E R C I S E S

| EJERCICIO G | En la clase de cocina, Silvia siempre quiere hacer lo mismo que hacen los otros alumnos. Escriba lo que ella dice: |

EJEMPLO: Tú cueces legumbres hoy.
           Yo cuezo legumbres también.

1. Javier recoge las habas.

    _____

2. Elena extingue el fuego.

    _____

3. Uds. siguen las instrucciones.

    _____

4. Nosotros corregimos la receta.

_____

5. Carolina y Luis consiguen platos limpios.

_____

6. Arturo escoge otra receta.

_____

7. La profesora exige mucho cuidado en la cocina.

_____

EJERCICIO H	Trabajando con un(a) compañero(-a), identifique a los trabajadores municipales y discuta el trabajo que ellos desempeñan para mantener la ciudad limpia, cómoda y segura. Por ejemplo, los policías, los bomberos, los basureros, el alcalde, los jueces, los maestros, etc. Saque apuntes sobre su discusión para usarlos en el siguiente ejercicio.

EJERCICIO I	Escriba una composición en la cual Ud. describe quiénes son los trabajadores municipales de su ciudad y lo que ellos hacen al ejercer su profesión. Use verbos como coger, distinguir, exigir, instruir, juzgar, proteger, recoger, etc.

_____

_____

_____

_____

_____

_____

_____

_____

_____

_____

_____

Chapter 4
Preterit Tense

[1] REGULAR VERBS

The preterit tense of regular verbs is formed by dropping the infinitive ending (–ar, –er, –ir), and adding the following endings.

invitar:	invit	-é, -aste, -ó, -amos, -asteis, -aron
correr:	corr	} -í, -iste, -ió, -imos, -isteis, -ieron
admitir:	admit	

 **EJERCICIO A** Escriba esta descripción de una llamada telefónica que hizo Amelia.

EJEMPLO: yo / llamar por teléfono a Clara
Yo llamé por teléfono a Clara.

1. Clara / contestar el teléfono

_____

2. yo / saludar a Clara

_____

3. nosotros / hablar de la fiesta del sábado pasado

_____

4. Enrique y Carlos / invitar a muchas personas

_____

5. sus padres / preparar muchas cosas para comer

_____

6. todo el mundo / pasar un buen rato allí

_____

7. tú / cantar y bailar mucho

_____

8. yo / regresar a casa tarde

_____

todo

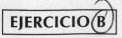 **EJERCICIO B** Describa cómo pasó el sábado cada persona, usando las siguientes sugerencias.

SUGERENCIAS: lavar el carro   limpiar la casa
preparar una cena especial   visitar un museo

trabajar en el jardín   estudiar en la biblioteca
mirar la televisión   contestar unas cartas
guardar la ropa de verano

EJEMPLO: **Sarita visitó un museo.**

1. Yo _____.

2. Mis hermanitos _____.

3. Mi madre _____.

4. Mi padre _____.

5. Mis hermanos y yo _____.

6. Tú _____.

EJERCICIO C   **Jorge le cuenta a Carlos sobre el lugar donde él y su amigo Eduardo trabajaron durante el verano. Conteste las preguntas que Carlos le hace a Jorge.**

1. ¿Dónde trabajaron Uds.? (en el supermercado)

_____

2. ¿Cuánto tiempo pasaron Uds. trabajando allí? (yo/20 horas a la semana; Eduardo/15 horas)

_____

3. ¿Cuánto dinero ganaste tú? (80 dólares)

_____

4. ¿Qué compraste con el dinero? (una bicicleta)

_____

5. ¿Quién más trabajó allí contigo? (Raquel)

_____

6. ¿A qué hora regresaron Uds. a casa anoche? (10:00 P.M.)

_____

7. ¿Les gustó el trabajo? (sí)

_____

EJERCICIO D   **Escriba lo que dicen que pasó el sábado pasado.**

EJEMPLO: Claudia / aprender un baile nuevo
               Claudia aprendió un baile nuevo.

1. Manuel y Pablo / no asistir a la fiesta

_____

2. Rosita / recibir un carro de sus padres

_____

3. tú / salir con tus primos

_____

4. mis padres / vender el automóvil

_____

5. llover / todo el día

_____

6. yo / conocer a la novia de mi hermano

_____

7. Rocío y yo / correr en una carrera

_____

8. Juan cumplir dieciséis años

_____

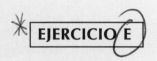 **EJERCICIO E**   **Complete la carta que Rogelio escribe sobre su amigo Víctor.**

Querido Alberto:

Cuando mi amigo Víctor _____ a pasar el verano en la playa, él _____ invitarme
                                    1. (salir)   _2. (prometer)_
a pasar unos días allí con él. Víctor _____ de repente ir a la playa por dos meses.
                                                3. (decidir)
Él _____ su motocicleta para tener dinero con qué vivir. Unos amigos suyos
        4. (vender)
le _____ alojamiento con ellos. Víctor _____ a esos amigos el año pasado cuando
    5. (prometer)   _6. (conocer)_
él _____ a una reunión de motociclistas. Víctor me _____ una carta y cuando yo
    7. (asistir)   _8. (escribir)_
la _____ _____ en seguida. Víctor _____ con su palabra. Yo
    9. (recibir)   _10. (responder)_   _11. (cumplir)_
no _____ tiempo. _____ mi ropa en una maleta y _____
    12. (perder)   _13. (meter)_   _14. (salir)_
en seguida. _____ sólo una vez durante mi visita y _____ a muchas personas.
                15. (llover)   _16. (conocer)_
También yo _____ por toda la playa. Entonces yo _____ por qué le gusta a Víctor
            17. (correr)   _18. (comprender)_
la vida de la playa.

Tu amigo,
Rogelio

EJERCICIO F *No*   Conteste las preguntas que le hace un amigo sobre su accidente.

1. ¿Cuándo ocurrió el accidente? (hace tres días)

_____

2. ¿Dónde sucedió? (cerca del estadio)

_____

3. ¿Qué perdiste en el accidente? (mis llaves)

_____

4. ¿Cuándo saliste del hospital? (ayer)

_____

5. ¿Sufriste mucho después del accidente? (un poco)

_____

6. ¿Vendieron tus padres tu bicicleta? (sí)

_____

EJERCICIO G *No*   ¿Conoce Ud. a alguna persona que haga muchísimas cosas en un día? Escriba lo que hizo esa persona ayer, usando los verbos indicados.

EJEMPLO: despertar   **Mi mamá *despertó* a la familia a las cinco de la mañana.**

1. preparar _____ .

2. limpiar _____ .

3. trabajar _____ .

4. salir _____ .

5. asistir _____ .

6. volver _____ .

7. escribir _____ .

8. meter _____ .

9. mirar _____ .

10. cerrar _____ .

EJERCICIO H   Un(-a) amigo(-a) suyo(-a) asistió a una fiesta de sorpresa anoche. Ud. no asistió. Primero, prepare las preguntas que Ud. quiere hacerle sobre la fiesta. Luego, hágale las preguntas a un(-a) compañero(-a) y escriba las respuestas.

TEMAS SUGERIDOS: la hora, el propósito de la fiesta, los regalos, los invitados, la comida, las diversiones

VERBOS SUGERIDOS: llegar, entrar, cumplir, recibir, asistir, preparar, comer, conocer, regresar, llamar

_____

_____

_____

_____

_____

_____

_____

_____

_____

_____

_____

_____

_____

_____

_____

_____

_____

_____

[2]   VERBS THAT CHANGE *I* TO *Y* IN THE PRETERIT

Verbs ending in **-er** or **-ir,** and containing a vowel immediately before the ending, change in the third-person singular from **-ió** to **-yó** and in the third-person plural from **-ieron** to **-yeron.** The **i** has an accent mark in all the other forms:

caer:	ca	
creer:	cre	
leer:	le	*-í, -íste, -yó, -ímos, -ísteis, -yeron*
oír:	o	
poseer:	pose	

NOTES:

1. Exceptions: **traer, atraer,** and all verbs ending in **-guir.**

2. Verbs that end in **-uir (construir, contribuir, distribuir, huir, incluir,** and others) also belong in this group, but no accent appears in the endings **-uiste, -uimos,** and **-uisteis.**

 **EJERCICIO I** Escriba lo que Ud. ve en estos dibujos, usando los verbos *construir, distribuir, huir, incluir, leer* y *oír* en el pretérito.

EJEMPLO: El niño **se cayó** de la bicicleta.

1. Carmen _____

2. Los jóvenes _____

3. El ladrón _____

4. El hombre rico _____

5. Los señores _____

_____

6. La cuenta _____

_____

EJERCICIO ~~J~~ No   Escriba las preguntas que Ud. haría en una entrevista con un científico famoso que acaba de recibir un premio. Use los verbos *concluir, contribuir, creer, influir, leer* y *oír.*

EJEMPLO: ¿Dónde *oyó* Ud. la noticia?

1. _____

2. _____

3. _____

4. _____

5. _____

[3] VERBS ENDING IN *-CAR, -GAR,* AND *-ZAR*

Verbs ending in **-car, -gar,** and **-zar** change in the first-person singular of the preterit as follows:

c changes to **qu**

g changes to **gu**

z changes to **c**

atacar (*to attack*):   ataqué, atacaste, atacó, atacamos, atacasteis, atacaron

Like **atacar:**

acercarse *to approach*	**educar** *to educate*
aplicar *to apply*	**embarcarse** *to embark*
arrancar *to root out, to pull out*	**equivocarse** *to be mistaken*
buscar *to look for, to seek*	**explicar** *to explain*
colocar *to place, to put*	**fabricar** *to make, to manufacture*
comunicar *to communicate*	**indicar** *to indicate*
dedicar *to dedicate, to devote*	**marcar** *to designate, to mark*

masticar *to chew*	sacrificar *to sacrifice*
pescar *to fish*	significar *to mean*
publicar *to publish*	suplicar *to beg, to implore*
replicar *to reply; to contradict (argue)*	tocar *to touch, to play (music)*
sacar *to take out*	

pagar (*to pay[for]*): pagué, pagaste, pagó, pagamos, pagasteis, pagaron

Like **pagar:**

agregar *to add*	entregar *to deliver, to hand over*
ahogarse *to drown*	jugar *to play (games, sports)*
apagar *to put out, to extinguish*	llegar *to arrive*
cargar *to load*	madrugar *to rise early*
castigar *to punish*	negar *to deny*
colgar *to hang*	obligar *to obligate, to compel*
encargar *to put in charge; to entrust; to order (goods)*	pegar *to stick, to beat*
	rogar *to ask, to beg*

cruzar (*to cross*): crucé, cruzaste, cruzó, cruzamos, cruzasteis, cruzaron

Like **cruzar:**

abrazar *to embrace, to hug*	empezar *to begin*
alcanzar *to reach, to overtake*	gozar *to enjoy*
almorzar *to eat lunch*	lanzar *to throw*
amenazar *to threaten*	realizar *to fulfill*
avanzar *to advance*	rezar *to pray*
comenzar *to begin, to commence*	tropezar *to stumble*
deslizarse *to slip, to glide*	

EJERCICIO K Escriba lo que estas personas dicen que hicieron anoche.

EJEMPLO   yo / pescar en el río
           Yo pesqué en el río.

1. yo / colocar mi ropa en el armario

_____

2. yo / buscar mis zapatos rojos

_____

3. yo / tocar la guitarra

_____

4. yo / comunicar la noticia a mis padres

_____

5. yo / fabricar un avión de plástico

_____

6. yo / explicar una película a mi hermanito

_____

7. yo / sacar la basura

_____

EJERCICIO L ~~NO~~   Su hermana busca unos discos compactos en la casa. Escriba las respuestas a las preguntas que Ud. le hace.

1. ¿Dónde colocaste los discos compactos? (en el estante)

_____

2. ¿Los buscaste allí? (sí)

_____

3. ¿Quién los tocó? (yo)

_____

4. ¿Cuándo los sacaste del estuche? (anoche)

_____

5. ¿Indicaste qué discos compactos perdiste? (no)

_____

6. ¿Cuánto tiempo dedicaste a buscarlos? (toda la mañana)

_____

7. ¿Los marcaste con tu nombre? (no)

_____

EJERCICIO M   Esteban explica cómo pasó el día de ayer. Escriba lo que él dice.

EJEMPLO: madrugar ayer
            Yo madrugué ayer.   -qué

1. colgar mi ropa del día anterior

_____

2. llegar a la escuela temprano

_____

3. cargar muchos libros

_____

4. entregar el trabajo en la clase de inglés

_____

5. encargar a Rosa de la reunión del comité

_____

6. jugar al tenis

_____

EJERCICIO N Conteste las preguntas que le hace un amigo acerca de una excursión en que él no participó.

1. ¿A qué hora llegaste a la escuela? (7:30 A.M.)

_____

2. ¿Quién se encargó de la excursión? (Roberto)

_____

3. ¿Quiénes cargaron la comida en el autobús? (nosotros)

_____

4. ¿A quién le entregaste el boleto? (al chofer)

_____

5. ¿Dónde colgaste tu saco? (en el autobús)

_____

6. ¿Cuánto pagaste por la excursión? ($25)

_____

7. ¿Quién se negó a pagar? (tú)

_____

EJERCICIO O Amelia siempre dice que ella hace lo mismo que sus amigas. Escriba lo que Amelia dice.

EJEMPLO: Claudia empezó una clase de yoga.
Yo también **empecé** una clase de yoga.

1. Sarita abrazó a su abuelo al verlo.

_____

2. Patricia se deslizó en el hielo.

_____

3. Carlota e Inés almorzaron en el restaurante nuevo.

_____

4. Carmen realizó su sueño en el viaje.

_____

5. Lourdes avanzó mucho en el curso.

_____

6. Pilar y tú alcanzaron a nadar cien metros.

_____

7. Yo empecé a leer una novela muy interesante.

_____

8. Mis primas gozaron de la visita.

_____

EJERCICIO P ~~No~~ **David quiere conocer mejor a un amigo nuevo de Venezuela. Conteste las siguientes preguntas.**

1. ¿Con quién almorzaste ayer?

_____

2. ¿Qué clases comenzaste a tomar?

_____

3. ¿Avanzaste mucho en el estudio del inglés?

_____

4. ¿Realizaste un sueño al venir aquí?

_____

5. ¿Empezaste a acostumbrarte a nuestro modo de vivir?

_____

EJERCICIO Q _Todo_ **Complete la siguiente carta que Javier les escribió a sus padres desde el campamento de verano.**

Queridos padres:

No comprendo por qué Uds. me _____ a venir a este campamento. Yo _____
　　　　　　　　　　　　　　　　　1. (obligar)　　　　　　　　　　　　　　　　2. (rogar)

mucho, pero eso no me _____ . El consejero que _____ de mi grupo es
　　　　　　　　　　　　3. (ayudar)　　　　　　　　　　4. (encargarse)

muy antipático. Cuando yo _____ mis cosas junto a mi cama, él me _____ .
　　　　　　　　　　　　　5. (colocar)　　　　　　　　　　　　　　　6. (castigar)

Cuando yo _____ mi ropa, él la _____ .
　　　　　　　　7. (colgar)　　　　　　　8. (descolgar)

　Mis compañeros son más o menos simpáticos. Pero ellos ya _____ a aburrirme. Ayer
　　　　　　　　　　　　　　　　　　　　　　　　　　　　　　　9. (empezar)

Juan y yo _____ al voleibol y _____ el partido. El domingo pasado unos
　　　　　　10. (jugar)　　　　　　　　11. (perder)

compañeros y yo _____ en una cafetería cerca del campamento. Entre los pocos pasatiempos
         12. (almorzar)

a que _____ , me _____ má la pesca. Anteayer Rafael y yo _____
     13. (dedicarse)   *14. (gustar)*   *15. (pescar)*

en el lago y él _____ tres peces grandes. Yo sólo _____ uno chiquito.
          16. (pescar)   *17. (pescar)*

  Yo sé que Uds. _____ un sueño y _____ mucho al mandarme aquí.
                    18. (realizar)   *19. (sacrificarse)*

Sin embargo, yo _____ cuando _____ este lugar. Tengo que despedirme
             20. (equivocarse)   *21. (escoger)*

porque el consejero ya _____ las luces.
                  22. (apagar)

Su hijo,

Javier

[4] STEM-CHANGING VERBS ENDING IN -IR

Verbs ending in **-ir** that have a stem change in the present tense also have a stem change
in the preterit. In the preterit tense, the stem vowel changes in the third-person singular
and plural, from **e** to **i** or from **o** to **u**.

  convertir (*to convert*): convertí, convertiste, convirtió, convertimos, convertisteis,
               convirtieron

  servir (*to serve*): serví, serviste, sirvió, servimos, servisteis, sirvieron

  dormir (*to sleep*): dormí, dormiste, durmió, dormimos, dormisteis, durmieron

NOTES:

 1. The verbs **reír** and **sonreír** are conjugated in the preterit as follows:

     reí, reíste, rió, reímos, reísteis, rieron

     sonreí, sonreíste, sonrió, sonreímos, sonreísteis, sonrieron

 2. Verbs ending in **-ir** that have **ñ** directly before the ending (**ceñir, gruñir, reñir**) drop the **i**
   of the ending in the third-person singular and plural (**riñó, riñeron**). Note that, because of
   the **ñ,** the sound of the ending is still regular.

| **EJERCICIO R** | ¿Qué hicieron ellos cuando oyeron la noticia? Escriba lo que hizo cada persona cuando oyó la noticia. |

EJEMPLO: María / sonreír
      María **sonrió.**

 1. los padres / reñir a los hijos

_____

 2. Gabriel / mentir a su madre

_____

3. Susana / repetir la noticia

_____

4. tú / preferir no estar allí

_____

5. yo / sentirse mal

_____

6. Beto y Raúl / servir la cena

_____

7. Juan y yo / vestirse rápidamente

_____

8. el abuelo / gruñir

_____

9. mi tío / dormirse en el sofá

_____

10. Uds. / advertir a los demás

_____

| EJERCICIO S | **Escriba cuál de sus parientes hizo una de estas cosas ayer durante una reunión en su casa. Use las siguientes sugerencias.** |

SUGERENCIAS: divertirse mucho   reírse mucho
                servir los refrescos   medir la terraza
                reñir a los nietos   sonreír dos veces
                despedirse de nosotros   dormirse en la hamaca

1. Mi madre _____.

2. Mis padres _____.

3. Mi tía _____.

4. Mis abuelos _____.

5. Mi primo _____.

6. Yo _____.

7. Mis primos _____.

8. Todos mis parientes _____.

[5] Verbs Irregular in the Preterit

a. The following verbs have an irregular stem in the preterit. The endings for these verbs are: **-e, -iste, -o, -imos, -isteis, -ieron** (**-eron** if **j** precedes the ending).

andar:	*anduve, anduviste, anduvo, anduvimos, anduvisteis, anduvieron*
caber:	*cupe, cupiste, cupo, cupimos, cupisteis, cupieron*
estar:	*estuve, estuviste, estuvo, estuvimos, estuvisteis, estuvieron*
haber:	*hube, hubiste, hubo, hubimos, hubisteis, hubieron*
hacer:	*hice, hiciste, hizo, hicimos, hicisteis, hicieron*
poder:	*pude, pudiste, pudo, pudimos, pudisteis, pudieron*
poner:	*puse, pusiste, puso, pusimos, pusisteis, pusieron*
querer:	*quise, quisiste, quiso, quisimos, quisisteis, quisieron*
saber:	*supe, supiste, supo, supimos, supisteis, supieron*
tener:	*tuve, tuviste, tuvo, tuvimos, tuvisteis, tuvieron*
venir:	*vine, viniste, vino, vinimos, vinisteis, vinieron*
decir:	*dije, dijiste, dijo, dijimos, dijisteis, dijeron*
producir:	*produje, produjiste, produjo, produjimos, produjisteis, produjeron*
traer:	*traje, trajiste, trajo, trajimos, trajisteis, trajeron*

b. The verbs **dar, ser,** and **ir** are also irregular in the preterit. **Dar** takes the endings of regular **-er, -ir** verbs; **ser** and **ir** have the same forms in the preterit.

dar:	*di, diste, dio, dimos, disteis, dieron*
ser: ⎫ ir: ⎭	*fui, fuiste, fue, fuimos, fuisteis, fueron*

NOTES:

1. The third-person singular of **hacer** is spelled **hizo.** The **c** changes to **z** to avoid the **k** sound.

2. All compounds of **poner** (**proponer,** etc.), **tener** (**detener,** etc.), **hacer** (**satisfacer,** etc.), **venir** (**convenir,** etc.), and **traer** (**atraer,** etc.) are conjugated in the same manner as the basic verb.

3. All verbs ending in **-ducir** are conjugated like **producir.**

   conducir (*to lead, to drive*):   *conduj*e, -iste, -o, -imos, -isteis, -eron

   traducir (*to translate*):   *traduj*e, -iste, -o, -imos, -isteis, -eron

4. The accent mark is omitted in the preterit forms of **dar, ver, ser,** and **ir.**

EJERCICIO T   **Después de tener un día libre durante una excursión a Madrid, los compañeros de excursión cuentan cómo pasaron el día. Escriba lo que dijeron.**

EJEMPLO   yo / andar por El Retiro
Yo anduve por El Retiro.

1. los señores Castro / ir a una corrida de toros

2. Graciela / hacer una excursión a Toledo

_____

3. los parientes de Ana / venir a visitarla

_____

4. yo / estar en la Plaza Mayor

_____

5. tú / querer visitar El Prado

_____

6. Nosotros / poder ver una tuna

_____

7. la señorita Álvarez / andar por la Gran Vía

_____

8. Micaela / ver una zarzuela

_____

9. Elena / querer ir al Valle de los Caídos

_____

10. el guía / ponerse a descansar

_____

EJERCICIO Ⓥ *NO* Ud. acaba de volver a casa después de pasar el fin de semana en casa de un amigo que vive en otra ciudad. Escriba siete frases, usando las sugerencias, que describan sus actividades durante el fin de semana.

SUGERENCIAS: ir al cine (teatro, circo, etc.)   poder ver un desfile
hacer empanadas   dar una fiesta
andar por la ciudad   tener ganas de ver una película
estar en el centro   conducir un carro
poner tarjetas postales

1. _____
2. _____
3. _____
4. _____
5. _____
6. _____
7. _____

[6] USES OF THE PRETERIT TENSE

The preterit tense expresses a particular single action or event completed at a specific time in the past:

Comenzó a leer el libro **ayer**.	*He began to read the book yesterday.*
Cesó de llover **a las cuatro**.	*It stopped raining at 4 o'clock.*
Carlos me *visitó* **el mes pasado**.	*Carlos visited me last month.*

NOTE: The verbs **conocer** (*to know, to be acquainted with*), **saber** (*to know*), **tener** (*to have*), **querer** (*to want*), and **poder** (*to be able*) often have a different meaning in the preterit:

Lo conocí en México.	*I met him in Mexico.* (began to know)
¿Cuándo **supieron** la verdad?	*When did they find out (learn) the truth?* (began to know)
Tuve carta de él esta mañana.	*I received a letter from him this morning.* (it came into my possession)
No **quiso** hacerlo.	*He refused to do it.* (final decision)
Pude convencerle.	*I managed to convince him.* (finally was able)

EJERCICIO V Un político de su pueblo (ciudad) acaba de regresar de un congreso internacional sobre el medio ambiente. Ud. lo entrevista para un artículo en el periódico de su escuela. Escriba seis preguntas que Ud. va a hacerle. Use las siguientes sugerencias:

 *5 frases*

SUGERENCIAS: cuándo, quién(es), (de) dónde, adónde, por qué, cuánto(s)

ir, hacer, pasar, visitar, conocer, andar, saber, estar, poder, poner, querer, venir, tener, empezar

EJEMPLOS: **¿Cuánto tiempo pasó Ud. en el congreso?**
¿Quiénes fueron con Ud.?

1. _____

2. _____

3. _____

4. _____

5. _____

6. _____

EJERCICIO W Imagínese que Ud. es ese político y conteste las preguntas del Ejercicio V.

EJEMPLOS: **Yo pasé una semana en el congreso.**   *5 respuestas*
Varios científicos fueron conmigo.

1. _____

2. _____

3. _____

4. _____

5. _____

6. _____

7. _____

8. _____

9. _____

10. _____

MASTERY EXERCISES

EJERCICIO X   Cuando Ud. llega de la escuela, su mamá no está en la casa. Encuentra una lista en la que ella escribió lo que tenía que hacer ese día. Escriba lo que ella hizo.

1. _____

2. _____

3. _____

4. _____

5. _____

6. _____

7. _____

8. _____

9. _____

10. _____

11. _____

12. _____

| **EJERCICIO Y** | Sus abuelos acaban de regresar de un viaje al extranjero. Conteste las preguntas que un amigo le hace acerca de ellos. |

1. ¿Cuánto tiempo estuvieron ellos fuera?

   _____

2. ¿Te trajeron muchos regalos?

   _____

3. ¿Tuviste que ir al aeropuerto cuando llegaron?

   _____

4. ¿Cómo supiste que el avión se demoró?

   _____

5. ¿Llegaste al aeropuerto a tiempo?

   _____

6. ¿Quién fue contigo al aeropuerto?

   _____

7. ¿Condujiste tú el carro?

   _____

8. ¿Cuándo empezaste a conducir en la ciudad?

   _____

9. ¿Pudiste estacionar el carro cerca de la terminal?

   _____

10. ¿Tuvieron ellos alguna dificultad en la aduana?

    _____

11. ¿Quién los vio cuando salieron de la aduana?

    _____

12. ¿Les dio gusto verte?

    _____

13. ¿Cargaste tú las maletas al carro?

_____

14. ¿A qué hora se despidieron Uds. de ellos?

_____

| EJERCICIO Z | Ud. compró un juguete para regalárselo a su primo, pero el juguete salió defectuoso. Escriba una carta a la tienda donde lo compró. Incluya los siguientes detalles. |

> the nature of the problem
> when you bought the toy
> what happened when you got it home
> the steps you took to exchange it
> who helped you at the store
> the reaction of the clerk
> how much you paid
> what you want
> why you want a fast resolution, etc.

_____

_____

_____

_____

_____

_____

_____

_____

_____

_____

_____

_____

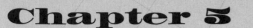

Chapter 5
Imperfect Tense

[1] REGULAR VERBS

The imperfect tense of regular verbs is formed by dropping the infinitive ending (-ar, -er, -ir), and adding the following endings.

tomar:	tom	-aba, -abas, -aba, -ábamos, -abais, -aban
leer:	le	} -ía, -ías, -ía, -íamos, -íais, -ían
subir:	sub	

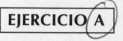 **EJERCICIO A** Su amigo Héctor habla de la vida de su pueblo. Escriba lo que dice.

EJEMPLO: nosotros / cenar a las diez.
Nosotros cenábamos a las diez.

1. yo / comprar un helado por cinco centavos

_____

2. todo el mundo / bañarse en el lago

_____

3. nosotros / almorzar a las dos

_____

4. los niños / cantar villancicos en la calle

_____

5. las personas / celebrar todas las fiestas

_____

6. mis amigos y yo / jugar al fútbol en la calle

_____

7. mis padres / andar por el parque todos los domingos

_____

8. el circo / llegar a mi pueblo en abril

_____

9. los muchachos y las muchachas / no caminar juntos

_____

10. tú / comprar todo en el mercado

_____

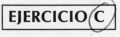 **EJERCICIO B**   **Algunos jóvenes recuerdan cosas que ellos o sus parientes hacían. Escriba lo que dicen.**

EJEMPLO: yo / dormir hasta las dos de la tarde.
             Yo dormía hasta las dos de la tarde.

1. mis amigos y yo / subir a los árboles

_____

2. Carmen / escribir poemas románticos

_____

3. Elías / vestirse de gaucho

_____

4. mi hermanito / repetir lo que todos / decir

_____

5. tú / seguir a tu hermana mayor

_____

6. yo / compartir todo lo que yo / tener

_____

7. Uds. / construir castillos de arena

_____

8. Beto / volver con la cara sucia

_____

9. yo / beber la leche con una pajita

_____

10. Sarita / tener miedo de la oscuridad

_____

EJERCICIO C   **Escriba seis frases en que Ud. cuenta lo que Ud. u otra persona hacía regularmente. Use las siguientes sugerencias.**

SUGERENCIAS: jugar   comer   vivir
               trabajar   perder   dormir(se)
               arreglar   poner   abrir

EJEMPLO: **Yo ponía la mesa todos los días.**

1. _____

2. _____

3. _____

4. _____

5. _____

6. _____

Todo

| **EJERCICIO D** | Ud. le hace varias preguntas a su abuela. Escriba sus respuestas. |

1. ¿Dónde vivías de niña?

   _____

2. ¿Con quién jugabas?

   _____

3. ¿Tenías muchos novios?

   _____

4. ¿Trabajaban tú y tus hermanos por la tarde?

   _____

5. ¿Te castigaban mucho tus padres?

   _____

6. ¿Qué hacías los sábados?

   _____

7. ¿Leías novelas románticas?

   _____

8. ¿Asistían tú y tus amigas a muchas fiestas?

   _____

[2] VERBS IRREGULAR IN THE IMPERFECT TENSE

There are three verbs irregular in the imperfect tense. They are:

ir:	*iba, ibas, iba, íbamos, ibais, iban*
ser:	*era, eras, era, éramos, erais, eran*
ver:	*veía, veías, veía, veíamos, veíais, veían*

EJERCICIO E   **Escriba adónde iban las siguientes personas los domingos.**

EJEMPLO: Carlos / al estadio
           Carlos iba al estadio.

1. las hermanas / al cine

_____

2. yo / a la iglesia

_____

3. Rafael y Juan / a la corrida de toros

_____

4. tú / al parque

_____

5. Elena y yo / a la piscina

_____

6. Ud. / a casa de sus abuelos

_____

EJERCICIO F   **Indique de qué país eran las siguientes personas que se conocieron en una fiesta.**

EJEMPLO: Ud. / de Colombia
           Ud. era de Colombia

1. yo / de España

_____

2. Pedro / de Puerto Rico

_____

3. las señoritas / de México

_____

4. nosotros / de Costa Rica

_____

5. tú / de Guatemala

_____

6. Nilda / de Bolivia

_____

NO

EJERCICIO G   **Escriba dónde dicen estas muchachas que veían a un señor todos los días. Use las siguientes sugerencias.**

SUGERENCIAS: en la parada del autobús
en la estación del metro
en el ascensor
en la cafetería
en la entrada de su oficina
en la esquina de su casa
en un taxi

EJEMPLO: María
María lo veía en un taxi todos los días.

1. Carlota _____ .

2. Ana y Pilar _____ .

3. Yo _____ .

4. Mi jefa _____ .

5. Alicia y yo _____ .

6. Tú _____ .

Todo

EJERCICIO H   **Exprese lo que hacían las personas a continuación. Use las siguientes sugerencias.**

SUGERENCIAS: lavar el carro los sábados
ir al supermercado todos
   los días
visitar a los abuelos los
   domingos
jugar al béisbol los sábados
   por la mañana
ver a los amigos los viernes por
   la noche
ir al campamento cada verano
ponerse furioso cuando los
   padres salían
ver una película los sábados

1. Mis padres _____ .

2. Mi hermanito _____ .

3. Mis amigos _____ .

4. Mi hermano _____ .

5. Mi abuela _____ .

6. Mi padre _____ .

7. Yo _____ .

8. Mis hermanos y yo _____ .

[3] USES OF THE IMPERFECT TENSE

The imperfect tense expresses continuous or repeated past actions, events, or situations. It is also used to describe the circumstances surrounding a past action or event.

a. The imperfect is used to describe what was happening, used to happen, or happened repeatedly in the past.

Los pájaros **cantaban**.	*The birds were singing.*
Vivíamos en esta calle.	*We used to live on this street.*
Tomás **llegaba** tarde a menudo.	*Thomas would often arrive (arrived) late.*

b. The imperfect is used to describe persons or things in the past.

Pedro **era** rubio y **tenía** los ojos azules.	*Peter was blond and had blue eyes.*
La sala **estaba** llena de gente.	*The living room was full of people.*

c. The imperfect expresses a state of mind in the past with the verbs **creer, pensar, querer,** and **saber.**

Creían (Pensaban, Sabían) que era importante.	*They believed (thought, knew) that it was important.*
Queríamos comprar un coche nuevo.	*We wanted to buy a new car.*

d. The imperfect expresses the time of day in the past.

Eran **las ocho.**	*It was eight o'clock.*

e. The imperfect is used to describe a situation that was going on in the past when another past single action or event expressed in the preterit occurred.

Comíamos **cuando nos llamó.**	*We were eating when he called us.*

EJERCICIO I Ud. habla de las fiestas de su juventud. Conteste las preguntas que le hace un amigo.

1. ¿Dónde eran las fiestas? (en casa de Raquel)

_____

2. ¿Quiénes estaban allí? (todo el mundo)

_____

3. ¿Quién servía los refrescos? (Raquel)

_____

4. ¿Qué clase de vestido llevaba ella puesto? (un vestido de fiesta)

_____

5. ¿Qué clase de aretes usaba ella? (de oro)

_____

6. ¿Dónde estaba ella mientras llegaban los invitados? (en la puerta)

_____

7. ¿Qué clase de música tocaban? (música latina)

_____

8. ¿A qué hora empezaba a irse la gente? (a las doce)

_____

EJERCICIO J   **Ud. acaba de visitar una casa modelo. Conteste las preguntas para describir la casa.**

1. ¿De cuántos pisos era la casa?

_____

2. ¿Cuántos cuartos tenía?

_____

3. ¿Había muebles bonitos?

_____

4. ¿De qué color era la alfombra?

_____

5. ¿De qué color estaban pintadas las paredes?

_____

6. ¿Cuántos dormitorios había?

_____

7. ¿Era grande la cocina?

_____

8. ¿Qué clase de muebles tenía?

_____

9. ¿Había muchas flores en el jardín?

_____

10. ¿Cobraban por entrar?

_____

NO

EJERCICIO K   **Imagínese que Ud. presenció un robo y ahora Ud. describe al ladrón. Escriba su descripción.**

EJEMPLO: **Eran las seis de la tarde. Era un joven alto. Medía seis pies y pesaba unas doscientas libras.**

_____

_____

_____

_____

_____

_____

_____

_____

Todo

EJERCICIO L   **Exprese lo que hacían varias personas cuando se fue la luz. Use las siguintes sugerencias.**

SUGERENCIAS: preparar la cena   hacer las tareas
              bañar a los niños   hablar por teléfono
              dormir la siesta   comer el almuerzo
              escribir una carta   jugar a los naipes

1. Ernesto _____.

2. Los padres _____.

3. Yo _____.

4. Enrique y tú _____.

5. Sarita y yo _____.

6. Mi abuelo _____.

7. La tía Lourdes _____.

8. Don Álvaro _____.

[4] *HACÍA* + TIME EXPRESSION + *QUE* + THE IMPERFECT TENSE

The construction **hacía** + an expression of time + **que** + the imperfect tense is used to describe an action or event that began in the past and continued in the past. In such situations the question is expressed by **¿Cuánto tiempo hacía que...?** + the imperfect tense or **¿Hacía cuánto tiempo que...?** + the imperfect tense.

Hacía un mes que *viajaban.*   *They had been traveling for a month.*

¿Cuánto tiempo hacía que *dormían?*   *How long had they been sleeping?*

NOTE: The imperfect tense + **desde hace** + an expression of time is also used to describe an action or event that began in the past and continued in the past. In such situations, the question is expressed by **¿Desde cuándo...?** + the imperfect tense.

Viajaban desde hacía un mes.   *They had been traveling for a month.*

¿Desde cuándo *dormían?*   *How long had they been sleeping?*

EJERCICIO M Pedro quiere saber desde cuándo sus amigos hacían varias cosas. Escriba las preguntas que hace Pedro, usando las expresiones *¿Cuánto tiempo hacía que...?* y *¿Desde cuándo...?*.

EJEMPLO: María / tocar el violín
¿Cuánto tiempo hacía que María **tocaba** el violín?
¿Desde cuándo tocaba María el violín?

1. Jorge / trabajar en el banco

_____

_____

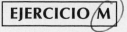

_____

_____

_____

_____

_____

_____

5.

_____

6. Alicia / vivir con sus abuelos

_____

_____

7. Uds. / no ir a trabajar los sábados

_____

_____

EJERCICIO N Escriba las respuestas a las preguntas del Ejercicio M, usando la información entre paréntesis.

EJEMPLO: (cinco años)
Hacía cinco años que María **tocaba** el violín.
María **tocaba** el violín **desde hacía cinco años.**

1. (tres meses)

_____

_____

2. (una semana)

_____

_____

3. (un año)

_____

_____

4. (dos años)

_____

_____

5. (15 años)

_____

_____

6. (un mes)

_____

_____

7. (4 semanas)

_____

_____

MASTERY EXERCISES

 **Usando las expresiones dadas, describa los dibujos para expresar lo que hacían estas personas.**

EXPRESIONES: todos los días   todas las noches   a menudo
               cada fin de semana   cada sábado

EJEMPLO: Arturo y Juan
           Arturo y Juan jugaban al tenis cada fin de semana.

1. El señor Ramos _____

_____

3. Roberto _____

_____

5. Los niños _____

_____

2. Sarita y María _____

_____

4. Los hermanos García _____

_____

6. Mi madre _____

_____

EJERCICIO P **Conteste las preguntas que le hace un periodista a un escritor célebre.**

1. ¿Qué edad tenía Ud. al llegar a este país?

_____

2. ¿En qué ciudad vivía Ud.?

_____

3. ¿Sabía Ud. hablar inglés al llegar a este país?

_____

4. ¿Estudiaba Ud. mucho?

_____

3. (Eran, Fueron) ya las cuatro de la tarde. Ramón y Elena (estaban, estuvieron) sentados en la sala. De las otras habitaciones (se oía, se oyó) el lejano rumor de voces, de gente que (hablaba, habló) en tono animado. Elena (se levantaba, se levantó) y (se acercaba, se acercó) a la ventana. (Miraba, Miró) afuera y (veía, vio) que todavía (llovía, llovió). (Experimentaba, Experimentó) una sensación de tristeza.

EJERCICIO B Escriba la forma correcta del pretérito o del imperfecto de los verbos entre paréntesis.

1. Alrededor de la mesa la familia _cenaba_ (cenar); chicos y mayores comiendo, riendo y hablando a la vez. De repente _sonó_ (sonar) la campana del pueblo. ¡Fuego! Todos _dejaron_ (dejar) la mesa y _se echaron_ (echarse) a correr hacia la plaza. Allí _vieron_ (ver) una escena horrible: _ardía_ (arder) la casa de un vecino. Por todas partes _se encontraba_ (encontrarse) gente que _gritaba_ (gritar) y _hacía_ (hacer) esfuerzos inútiles para extinguir el fuego. De pronto _apareció_ (aparecer) en una ventana la figura de una mujer.

2. Él _iba_ (ir) camino de la estación cuando _tropezó_ (tropezar) con un amigo que lo _detuvo_ (detener) para charlar un momento. Al llegar a la estación, _notó_ (notar) que el tren ya _estaba_ (estar) allí. _Se dio_ (darse) prisa pero _llegó_ (llegar) tarde. _Comenzó_ (comenzar) a pasearse por el andén, impaciente, lleno de enojo. _Miró_ (mirar) el reloj. Las nueve menos veinte. Le _quedaban_ (quedar) solamente veinte minutos para llegar a la oficina y seguramente no llegaría a tiempo.

3. Hernán Cortés _fue_ (ser) el conquistador de México. Cuando _llegaron_ (llegar) los españoles, los indios nunca habían visto caballos y _creían_ (creer) que hombre y caballo _eran_ (ser) una sola persona. También _creían_ (creer) que Cortés mismo _era_ (ser) su antiguo dios, que _volvió_ (volver) para gobernarlos. Con 400 soldados españoles, varias tribus y con la ayuda de Marina, una india que _hacía_ (hacer) de guía e intérprete, Cortés _pudo_ (poder) conquistar la capital azteca, Tenochtitlán (que es hoy la Ciudad de México).

EJERCICIO C Ud. está muy desilusionado(a) porque nadie fue a una fiesta que Ud. organizó. Conteste las preguntas que le hace un primo.

1. ¿A cuántas personas invitaste?

_____

2. ¿Les dijiste la fecha correcta?

_____

3. ¿Sabían tu dirección y número de teléfono?

_____

4. ¿Por qué dabas la fiesta?

_____

5. ¿Esperabas recibir regalos?

_____

6 ¿Qué hiciste al ver que nadie llegaba?

_____

7. ¿Qué descubriste?

_____

EJERCICIO D Conteste las preguntas que le hace su padre sobre una ventana rota en casa de un vecino.

1. ¿Dónde estabas tú esta tarde?

_____

2. ¿Con quién jugabas?

_____

3. ¿A qué jugaban?

_____

4. ¿Viste cuando la pelota pasó por la ventana?

_____

5. ¿Qué hicieron Uds. entonces?

_____

6 ¿Por qué no me dijiste nada cuando yo llegué a casa?

_____

7. ¿Quién rompió la ventana?

_____

8. ¿De quién era la pelota?

_____

EJERCICIO E *No*

Diez años después de graduarse de la escuela secundaria, Ud. va a una reunión. Escriba lo que Ud. hizo durante esos diez años.

EJEMPLO: Cuando me gradué de la escuela, me matriculé en la universidad.
Quería llegar a ser ingeniero.

_____

_____

_____

_____

_____

_____

_____

_____

_____

_____

_____

_____

_____

_____

EJERCICIO F

Muchas veces las personas hacen ciertas cosas porque tienen otra intención. Exprese lo que estas personas hicieron e indique por qué Ud. cree que lo hicieron.

EJEMPLO: Elsa / ir a la reunión escolar
Elsa fue a la reunión escolar porque tenía ganas de ver a su novio.

1. Larry / estudiar en México

_____

_____

2. Elena / participar en un concurso de baile

_____

_____

3. la señora / tomar una clase de coser

_____

_____

4. Roberto / trabajar después de las clases

_____

_____

5. Jenny / ahorrar su dinero

_____

_____

6. Natalia / ir a una universidad pequeña

_____

_____

| EJERCICIO G | **Todo el mundo recuerda un acontecimiento de su vida que lo afectó de una manera u otra. Escriba una composición en la cual Ud. describe un acontecimiento y cómo lo afectó a Ud. Incluya:** |

when it occurred	your reaction
what the event was	the effect it had
the people involved	what you learned from it
what happened	

_____

_____

_____

_____

_____

_____

_____

_____

_____

_____

_____

Chapter 7
Future Tense and Conditional

[1] FUTURE TENSE OF REGULAR VERBS

The future tense of regular verbs is formed by adding the following endings to the infinitive:

> ayudar:
> aprender: } -é, -ás, -á, -emos, -éis, -án
> escribir:

NOTES:
1. All future endings except **–emos** have an accent mark.
2. Verbs that have an accent mark in the infinitive (**oír, reír,** etc.) drop that accent in the future (**oiré, reiremos,** etc.).

EJERCICIO A   Exprese lo que las siguientes personas van a hacer mañana.

EJEMPLO: Luz / asistir a una conferencia
Luz asistirá a una conferencia.

1. Pedro / trabajar en el taller

    _____

2. mi madre / ir de compras

    _____

3. Petra / visitar a sus amigas

    _____

4. los amigos / jugar al tenis

    _____

5. yo / descansar todo el día

    _____

6. tú / comer en el centro

    _____

7. Eduardo y yo / defender el título del equipo de fútbol

    _____

8. Raquel y María / aprender otra canción española

    _____

9. mi abuelo / cortar la hierba

_____

10. los niños / vender limonada en la esquina

_____

| EJERCICIO B | Use las sugerencias y escriba cuándo Ud. va a hacer las siguientes actividades. |

SUGERENCIAS: graduarse de la escuela   en dos años
              viajar al extranjero   el año que viene
              trabajar en una oficina   el verano próximo
              casarse   mañana
              comprar su propio carro   en diez años
              escalar una montaña   en seis meses

EJEMPLO: **Yo viajaré al extranjero el verano próximo.**

1. _____

2. _____

3. _____

4. _____

5. _____

6. _____

[2] VERBS WITH IRREGULAR FUTURE

a. Verbs like **poder** drop the **e** of the infinitive, add an *r*, and then add the endings of the future tense.

> **poder:** *podr* –é, –ás, –á, –emos, –éis, –án

Like **poder: caber, haber, querer, saber**

b. In verbs like **poner**, the **e** (or **i**) of the infinitive is replaced by a **d** and the endings of the future tense are added:

> **poner:** *pondr* –é, –ás, –á, –emos, –éis, –án

Like **poner: salir, tener, valer, venir**

c. The verbs **decir** and **hacer** are irregular in the future tense:

> **decir:** *dir* –é –ás, –á, –emos, –éis, –án
>
> **hacer:** *har* –é, –ás, –á, –emos, –éis, –án

NOTE: Compound forms of the above irregular verbs are also irregular.

disponer, *dispondré*; **contener,** *contendrán*; **convenir,** *convendrá*; **satisfacer,** *satisfaremos*; **contradecir,** *contradirá*; and others.

EJERCICIO C **Exprese la forma correcta del futuro de los verbos en este mensaje electrónico que Enrique escribe a unos amigos que lo visitarán.**

Queridos amigos:

Yo _____ ir a la estación por ustedes. Sé que todos ustedes _____ ir juntos
       1. (poder)   *2.* (querer)

en mi carro, pero todo el mundo no _____ a la vez. Yo _____ que hacer
                                                      3. (caber)   *4.* (tener)

dos viajes a la estación. Mientras tanto, los demás _____ esperar en un café cerca de la
                                                                       5. (poder)

estación. Yo _____ todo lo posible por llevarlos a la fiesta rápidamente. Yo
                    6. (hacer)

_____ de mi casa temprano. Según el horario, ustedes _____ en el tren de
       7. (salir)   *8.* (venir)

las 7:35. Creo que todas las maletas _____ en el carro también. Si no, Roberto y
                                                9. (caber)

yo _____ volver a la estación por ellas. _____ muchas personas en la fiesta.
       10. (poder)   *11.* (haber)

Creo que su viaje _____ la pena. Sé que Elena _____ mucho gusto de ver-
                           12. (valer)   *13.* (tener)

los y tanto ella como yo _____ todo lo posible para que se diviertan. Después Uds.
                                   14. (hacer)

nos _____ cómo les fue.
       15. (decir)

Saludos,

Enrique

EJERCICIO D **Imagínese que Ud. y varios amigos van a vender cosas en el mercado de pulgas el sábado próximo. Use las sugerencias y escriba lo que cada persona hará.**

SUGERENCIAS: yo   tener que estar allí temprano
                       mis amigos y yo   hacer los carteles
                       usted   poner los precios
                       ellos   poner todo en orden
                       ustedes   querer ser el cajero
                       tú   decir los precios
                       todos nosotros   querer vender
                                                     salir al mediodía
                                                     poder atender a los clientes
                                                     querer irse temprano

1. _____

2. _____

3. _____

4. _____

5. _____

6. _____

7. _____

EJERCICIO E	Conteste las preguntas que le hace un(a) amigo(a) sobre una cita que Ud. tendrá con un(a) joven desconocido(a).

1. ¿Dónde se encontrarán el viernes por la noche?

   _____

2. ¿A qué hora llegará él (ella)?

   _____

3. ¿Adónde irán Uds.?

   _____

4. ¿Qué clase de ropa tendrás que llevar?

   _____

5. ¿Qué harán Uds. después?

   _____

6. ¿Podrás invitarlo(la) a la fiesta de Javier?

   _____

7. ¿Me dirás cómo te fue?

   _____

[3] USES OF THE FUTURE TENSE

a. The future tense is used in Spanish, as in English, to express future time.

Vendremos mañana.	*We will come tomorrow.*
¿Cuándo **irán Uds.?**	*When will you go?*

b. The future is used to express wonderment or probability at the present time and is often equivalent to English *I wonder, probably, must be, and can.*

¿Cuántos años *tendrá?*	*I wonder how old he is.* (*How old can he be?*)
¿Qué hora *será?*	*I wonder what time it is.* (*What time can it be?*)
Serán **las dos.**	*It is probably (It must be) two o'clock.*
Estará **cansado.**	*He must be (He is probably) tired.*

NOTE: The expression **deber de** followed by an infinitive may also be used to express probability at the present time:

Deben de estar cansados.	*They must be tired.*
Debe de ser la una.	*It is probably one o'clock.*

| EJERCICIO F | **Exprese cuándo las siguientes personas harán varias cosas.** |

EJEMPLO: Ramón / aprender a esquiar / el año próximo
Ramón aprenderá a esquiar el año próximo.

1. Carmen / sacar la basura / más tarde

_____

2. Elena y yo / visitar a los abuelos / la semana que viene

_____

3. tú / poder hablar español / después del verano

_____

4. Lina / tener que trabajar / los fines de semana

_____

5. Uds. / venir a comer / por la noche

_____

| EJERCICIO G | **Conteste las preguntas que le hace un compañero de viaje durante una excursión en autobús por la ciudad de Wáshington.** |

1. ¿Qué edificio será ése? (el Capitolio)

_____

2. ¿Dónde estarán todos los políticos hoy? (en casa; es sábado)

_____

3. ¿A qué hora comeremos? (a las doce)

_____

4. ¿Qué hora será ahora? (las diez y media)

_____

5. ¿Cuántas paradas haremos en esta excursión? (tres)

_____

6. ¿Cuál será la próxima parada? (la Casa Blanca)

_____

7. ¿Le gustará hacer al guía la misma excursión todos los días? (sí)

_____

8. ¿Qué clase de regalos venderán en la tienda de recuerdos? (vasos y camisetas)

_____

9. ¿Cuántas personas habrá en este autobús? (cuarenta y siete)

_____

10. ¿Cuándo podremos dormir la siesta? (por la tarde)

_____

M A S T E R Y   E X E R C I S E S — F U T U R E   T E N S E

| EJERCICIO H | ¿Cómo será el mundo cuando Ud. tenga 35 años? Conteste las siguientes preguntas. |

1. ¿En qué año tendrá Ud. 35 años?

_____

2. ¿Dónde vivirá Ud.?

_____

3. ¿Cómo se ganará Ud. la vida?

_____

4. ¿Estarán los miembros de su familia en la misma ciudad?

_____

5. ¿Habrá paz en el mundo?

_____

6. ¿Qué clase de música estará de moda?

_____

7. ¿Qué usarán Uds. para pagar las cuentas?

_____

8. ¿Qué clase de edificios se construirán?

_____

| EJERCICIO I | Ud. va a hacer un viaje a México, donde visitará a unos primos. Escríbales una carta para darles información sobre su viaje y hacerles algunas preguntas. Incluya: |

when you will leave your house   who will meet you

how you will get to the airport   the length of your visit

the probable departure and arrival time   what places you will visit together

what you will have with you

_____

_____

_____

_____

_____

_____

_____

_____

_____

_____

_____

_____

_____

[4] CONDITIONAL OF REGULAR VERBS

The conditional of regular verbs is formed in the same way as the future tense. The following endings are added to the infinitive:

ayudar:	
aprender:	*-ía, -ías, -ía, -íamos, -íais, -ían*
escribir:	

NOTE: Verbs that have an accent mark in the infinitive (**oír, reír,** etc.) drop that accent in the conditional (**oiría, reiríamos,** etc.).

EJERCICIO J   Unas amigas quieren hacer un viaje al extranjero durante el verano. Escriba lo que ellas harían en el viaje.

EJEMPLO: Elena / visitar las iglesias
           Elena visitaría las iglesias.

1. Gabriela / comer tapas en España

_____

2. Josefina y Graciela / ir a acampar

_____

3. Beatriz y yo / ir de compras todos los días

_____

4. tú / asistir a todas las excursiones

_____

5. yo / conocer a muchos jóvenes

_____

6. Clara y Anita / encontrar las discotecas

_____

| **EJERCICIO K** | **Ud. no sabe el pronóstico del tiempo para mañana. Use las sugerencias y escriba las cosas que haría o no haría en las circunstancias dadas.** |

SUGERENCIAS: mirar la televisión   dar un paseo por el parque
ir al cine   jugar al tenis
ir a la playa   estudiar para un examen
limpiar su cuarto   nadar en la piscina
leer una revista   dormir hasta el mediodía
montar en bicicleta   jugar al baloncesto

1. Si hiciera buen tiempo, **yo no iría al cine. Yo nadaría en la piscina.**

_____

_____

_____

_____

_____

2. Si hiciera mal tiempo, **yo no montaría en bicicleta. Yo limpiaría mi cuarto.**

_____

_____

_____

_____

_____

[5]   VERBS IRREGULAR IN THE CONDITIONAL

a. Verbs like **poder** drop the e of the infinitive and then add the endings of the conditional:

poder: *podr* –ía, –ías, –ía, –íamos, –íais, –ían

Like **poder: caber, haber, querer, saber**

b. In verbs like **poner,** the **e** (or **i**) of the infinitive is dropped and replaced by a **d** and the endings of the conditional are added:

poner: *pondr* –ía, –ías, –ía, –íamos, –íais, –ían

Like **poner: salir, tener, valer, venir**

c. The verbs **decir** and **hacer** are irregular in the conditional.

decir:	*dir*	}	-ía, -ías, -ía, -íamos, -íais, -ían
hacer:	*har*		

NOTE: Compounds of the irregular verbs are also irregular.

disponer, *dispondría*; contener, *contendría*; satisfacer, *satisfaríamos*, etc.

EJERCICIO L   **Varios compañeros de clase no comprendieron lo que dijo el profesor. Escriba lo que cada alumno cree que dijo el profesor.**

EJEMPLO: él / poner los ejemplos en la pizarra
Él pondría los ejemplos en la pizarra.

1. no haber clases el viernes

_____

2. los alumnos / poder salir temprano

_____

3. unos alumnos / tener que quedarse hasta las cuatro

_____

4. el director / venir a la clase el viernes

_____

5. Ricardo y yo / no decir nada

_____

6. tú / salir en una excursión el viernes

_____

7. valer la pena estudiar mucho

_____

8. la clase / querer una fiesta el viernes

_____

9. yo / hacer los preparativos para la fiesta

_____

10. todo el mundo / no caber en el autobús

_____

11. nadie / saber la respuesta a las preguntas

_____

12. mis compañeros y yo / poner los libros debajo de las sillas

_____

EJERCICIO M	Escriba lo que Ud. haría con un millón de dólares. Puede usar las sugerencias o pensar en otras.

SUGERENCIAS: ponerlo en el banco   poder comprar una casa
               hacer donaciones   querer compartirlo con sus parientes
               salir al extranjero   tener que ayudar a sus...

1. _____

2. _____

3. _____

4. _____

5. _____

6. _____

EJERCICIO N	Escriba lo que Ud. haría en estas circunstancias.

EJEMPLO: Tu mamá espera invitados a cenar y necesita ayuda.
           (poner la mesa) **Yo pondría** la mesa.

1. Tu amigo te presenta a una prima suya que acaba de llegar de Caracas.
(decirle: «mucho gusto»)_____

2. Tienes planes para salir con unos amigos pero hace mal tiempo.
(no salir con ellos)_____

3. Tu abuela no puede hacer las compras hoy porque está enferma.
(hacer las compras por ella)_____

4. Tus padres te dicen que debes venir a la casa antes de las diez.
(venir a la casa temprano)_____

5. Tus padres van a una boda y no quieren dejar a tu hermanita sola.
(tener que cuidarla)_____

[6] USES OF THE CONDITIONAL

a. The conditional is generally used as in English.

Ana no lo **pondría** allí.	*Ana would not put it there.*
Me gustaría verlo.	*I would like to see it.*
¿Podría Ud. mostrármelo?	*Would you be able to (Could you) show it to me?*

NOTES:

1. When *would* has the sense of *used to*, the imperfect tense is used in Spanish.

   Arturo nos **visitaba a menudo.**   *Arthur would often (used to) visit us.*

2. When *would* has the sense of *to be willing* (*to want*), the preterit tense of **querer** is used in Spanish.

   No **quiso** pagar la cuenta.   *He wouldn't (wasn't willing to, refused to) pay the bill.*

b. The conditional is used to express wonderment or probability in past time and is often equivalent to English *I wonder, probably, must have, could,* etc.:

¿Qué hora sería cuando salió?	*I wonder what time it was when he went out. (What time could it have been when he went out?)*
Serían las dos.	*It was probably (It must have been) two o'clock.*

NOTE: The expression **deber de** in the imperfect followed by an infinitive may also be used to express probability in past time.

Debían de estar cansados.	*They must have been tired.*
Ella debía de tener veinte años.	*She must have been twenty years old.*

EJERCICIO O	Varios amigos leen el periódico para buscar trabajo para el verano. Escriba qué clase de trabajo harían estas personas, según los anuncios.

> Se busca
> vendedor de ropa de niños.
> Preséntese en Galerías Gómez,
> Calle Mayor, 3.

EJEMPLO: **Yo vendería ropa de niños.**

> Se busca
> persona para tomar
> recados telefónicos.
> Llame al 625-15-55.

> Familia busca
> persona responsable
> para cuidar tres niños
> durante la mañana
> Sra. Flores, 516-59-18

1. Elena _____

_____

2. Roberto _____

_____

Se necesita
joven responsable
para entregar flores a domicilio.
Florería Naturaleza,
Calle del Jardín, 18.

Se buscan
dos señoritas para cajeras
en la taquilla del cine Roble.
Preséntese en persona,
Lunes de 9 a 11.

---

3. Jorge _____

_____

4. Dolores y María _____

_____

Se buscan
jóvenes fuertes y corteses
para servir mesas.
Restaurante de Oro,
Calle Principal, 104.

---

5. Javier y Octavio _____

_____

EJERCICIO P   **Conteste las preguntas que le hace un agente de viajes.**

1. ¿Adónde le gustaría ir a Ud.?

_____

2. ¿Cuándo podría salir la familia?

_____

3. ¿Y en qué fecha volverían Uds.?

_____

4. ¿Cuántos días pasaría la familia allí?

_____

5. ¿Haría Ud. el viaje solo(a)?

_____

6. ¿Cuánto dinero querría gastar Ud. en el viaje?

_____

7. ¿Harían Uds. excursiones allí?

_____

8. ¿Tendría Ud. que alquilar un coche allí?

_____

9. ¿Preferiría la familia quedarse en un hotel o en una casa de huéspedes?

_____

10. ¿Cómo pagaría Ud. la cuenta, al contado o con tarjeta de crédito?

_____

MASTERY EXERCISES — CONDITIONAL

EJERCICIO Q | **Complete esta carta que Raquel le escribió a una amiga. Escriba los verbos entre paréntesis en el modo potencial.**

Querida Amelia:

León me escribió que _____ a visitarme. Dijo que me _____ antes de
                            1. (venir)   _2. (llamar)_

venir. Le aseguré que _____ en casa y le prometí que no _____ otra cosa.
                       3. (estar)   _4. (hacer)_

A eso de las cuatro de la tarde él llamó para decirme que no _____ venir. Él
                                                              5. (poder)

_____ que posponer la visita para otra fecha y le _____ venir el domingo
6. (tener)   _7. (gustar)_

próximo. Quería saber si yo _____ libre ese día porque _____ invitarme al
                            8. (estar)   _9. (querer)_

cine. Nosotros _____ a ver el último estreno en el cine Azteca.
               _10. (ir)_

EJERCICIO R | **El año escolar acaba de terminar. Escriba cinco cosas que Ud. haría de manera diferente el año que viene.**

EJEMPLO: **Me levantaría más temprano todos los días.**

1. _____

2. _____

3. _____

4. _____

5. _____

EJERCICIO S | **Por primera vez un amigo suyo va a tener su propio cuarto. Ud. está ayudándole a decorarlo y amueblarlo. Escriba las sugerencias que Ud. le daría. Incluya sugerencias sobre:**

room color	decorations
furniture	storage
placement of the furniture	special ideas

_____

_____

_____

_____

_____

_____

_____

_____

_____

_____

_____

_____

_____

Chapter 8
Gerundio; Progressive Tenses

The **gerundio** is generally equivalent to the English present participle.

[1] GERUNDIOS OF REGULAR VERBS

The **gerundio** of regular verbs is formed by dropping the infinitive endings (**-ar, -er, -ir**) and adding **-ando, -iendo**.

cantar:	can*tando*	*singing*
comer:	com*iendo*	*eating*
abrir:	abr*iendo*	*opening*

[2] GERUNDIOS ENDING IN *-YENDO*

The **gerundio** of **-er** and **-ir** verbs with stems ending in a vowel is formed by adding **-yendo**.

caer:	ca*yendo*
creer:	cre*yendo*
leer:	le*yendo*
oír:	o*yendo*
traer:	tra*yendo*

[3] IRREGULAR GERUNDIOS

a. In the **gerundio**, stem-changing **-ir** verbs change the stem vowel from **e** to **i** and from **o** to **u**.

decir:	*diciendo*	pedir:	*pidiendo*
dormir:	*durmiendo*	sentir:	*sintiendo*
morir:	*muriendo*	venir:	*viniendo*

b. Other irregular **gerundios**

ir:	*yendo*	poder:	*pudiendo*

NOTE: In reflexive verbs, reflexive pronouns are usually added to the **gerundio** and a written accent is required: **vestirse:** *vistiéndose;* **reírse:** *riéndome;* **bañarse:** *bañándonos;* and so on.

[4] *GERUNDIO* IN PROGRESSIVE TENSES

The **gerundio** is used with forms of the verbs **estar, seguir, continuar,** and with verbs of motion, to stress that an event is (was or will be) in progress or is continuing at the moment indicated. These tenses are called progressive tenses.

Los niños están jugando.	*The children are playing.*
Él salió llorando.	*He went out crying.*
Los tiempos van cambiando.	*Times are changing.*
Siga Ud. leyendo.	*Keep on reading.*
Continuarán estudiando.	*They will continue studying.*
	(They will continue to study.)
Venían corriendo.	*They came running.*

NOTE: The **gerundios** of **estar, ir,** and **venir** are not used to form the progressive tenses of these verbs. Instead, the simple tenses are used.

Ella viene aquí.	*She is coming here.*
Rosa iba al parque.	*Rose was going to the park.*

[5] OTHER USES OF THE *GERUNDIO*

The **gerundio** is often the equivalent of *by* + an English present participle.

Viajando se aprende mucho.	*By traveling one learns much.*
Estudiando saldrás bien en los exámenes.	*By studying you will pass the examinations.*

 Escriba lo que están haciendo las personas en los siguientes dibujos.

EJEMPLO: **Arturo y Homero están jugando al tenis.**

1. Pepe _____

   _____

2. Elena y Esteban _____

   _____

3. La señora _____

   _____

4. Los señores Cabal _____

   _____

5. Sarita _____

   _____

6. Carlos _____

   _____

7. El niño _____

   _____

8. Las muchachas _____

   _____

EJERCICIO B   Ud. está en la cola para entrar en el cine. Escriba cómo salieron del cine las siguientes personas.

EJEMPLO: María / bailar   **María salió bailando.**

1. los niños / temblar   _____

2. Eduardo / reír   _____

3. la señora Tomás / llorar   _____

4. tú / pensar   _____

5. Daniel y Fernando / correr   _____

6. Leonardo / gritar   _____

EJERCICIO C   Describa lo que Ud. vio cuando entró en su casa el sábado por la tarde.

EJEMPLO: Cuando entré en la casa, mi mamá **estaba cosiendo** un vestido nuevo. Mi hermana **estaba tocando** el piano y el perro **estaba cantando.** Mi padre **estaba tratando de dormir** la siesta.

_____

_____

_____

_____

_____

_____

_____

_____

EJERCICIO D   *Todo*   Ud. va a pasar las vacaciones en el pueblo de sus abuelos. Escriba lo que su abuelo le cuenta de las personas del pueblo. Use los verbos *estar, seguir* o *continuar,* según el caso.

EJEMPLO: El señor Vargas / vender trigo   El señor Vargas **sigue vendiendo** trigo.

1. los hermanos Pinto / estudiar   _____

2. el señor Rangel / cortar leña   _____

3. Don Arturo / ser el banquero   _____

4. Rosita / cuidar a sus hermanitos   _____

5. el hermano de Pedro / decir mentiras _____

6. el pobre anciano / pedir limosna _____

7. tu abuelita / oír ruidos _____

8. el tío Octavio / perder las llaves _____

EJERCICIO E *Todo* **Es el Año Nuevo y Ud. está trabajando en una emisora de televisión. Ud. está describiendo cómo las personas están pasando la noche en un restaurante popular. Complete las frases siguientes, usando el gerundio de uno de los verbos dados (cada verbo debe usarse solamente una vez).**

comenzar	divertirse
caer	tirar
tocar	comer
celebrar	cantar
besar	bailar

1. La orquesta está _____ muchas canciones populares.

2. En una mesa un grupo de diez personas está _____ la cena tradicional.

3. Varias personas están _____ el Año Nuevo con champaña.

4. Los jóvenes continúan _____ .

5. Ahora los globos están _____ del techo.

6. La gente está _____ la canción tradicional.

7. Todo el mundo está _____ a comer las doce uvas.

8. Todos los esposos están _____ a sus esposas.

9. Muchas personas siguen _____ serpentinas.

10. Parece que todo el mundo está _____ .

EJERCICIO F **Ud. y su familia acaban de cenar. Escriba lo que está haciendo cada miembro de su familia. Use los verbos *estar, seguir* o *continuar* con gerundios.**

EJEMPLO: **Mi abuelo está mirando la televisión.**

1. Mi madre _____ .

2. Mi padre _____ .

3. Mi hermano _____ .

4. Mi hermana _____ .

5. Yo _____ .

Todo

EJERCICIO G Exprese en español lo que una profesora les dijo a sus estudiantes al terminar las clases.

EJEMPLO: estudiar a diario / recibir buenas notas
Estudiando a diario recibirán buenas notas.

1. viajar / ver cosas interesantes

_____

2. trabajar en el verano / ganar bastante dinero

_____

3. leer mucho / aumentar su vocabulario

_____

4. ayudarse el uno al otro / sentir mucha satisfacción

_____

5. seguir las reglas / no cometer errores

_____

EJERCICIO H Trabajando solo o con un(-a) compañero(-a), escriba cinco proverbios originales basados en sus experiencias.

1. _____

2. _____

3. _____

4. _____

5. _____

MASTERY EXERCISES

EJERCICIO I Escriba lo que el médico aconseja a los enfermos, usando los verbos *beber, comer, dormir, fumar, hacer* y *tomar* (cada verbo debe usarse solamente una vez).

1. Continúe _____ ocho horas cada noche.

2. Siga _____ la misma medicina.

3. Siga _____ mucha fruta fresca.

4. Siga _____ mucho ejercicio.

5. Continúe _____ cinco vasos de agua al día.

6. Siga _____ menos.

| EJERCICIO J | Unos amigos lo han invitado a pasar el fin de semana con ellos. Ud. no puede aceptar la invitación porque estará haciendo los preparativos para una reunión familiar en su casa. Escríbales y explíqueles lo que Ud. y sus parientes estarán haciendo. Incluya: |

> the purpose of the celebration
> when the guests will be arriving
> your responsibilities
> the responsibilities of your relatives
> what will be happening at the celebration

_____

_____

_____

_____

_____

_____

_____

_____

_____

| EJERCICIO K | Describa lo que Ud. estará haciendo en veinte años (su trabajo, su familia, sus pasatiempos, etc.). |

_____

_____

_____

_____

_____

_____

Chapter 9
Past Participle; Compound Tenses

[1] PAST PARTICIPLES

a. Past participle of regular verbs

The past participle of regular verbs is formed by dropping the infinitive ending and adding **–ado** or **–ido.**

tomar:	**tomado**	taken
comer:	**comido**	eaten
sufrir:	**sufrido**	suffered

b. Past participles ending in **–ído**

The past participles of **–er** and **–ir** verbs with stems ending in a vowel have an accent mark.

caer:	**caído**	**oír:**	**oído**
creer:	**creído**	**reír:**	**reído**
leer:	**leído**	**traer:**	**traído**

c. Irregular past participles

The following verbs and compounds of these verbs have irregular past participles.

abrir:	**abierto** opened	**morir:**	**muerto** died
cubrir:	**cubierto** covered	**poner:**	**puesto** put
decir:	**dicho** said	**resolver:**	**resuelto** resolved, solved
escribir:	**escrito** written	**romper:**	**roto** broken
hacer:	**hecho** done	**ver:**	**visto** seen
imprimir:	**impreso** printed	**volver:**	**vuelto** returned

Also, **descubrir** (*descubierto*), **deshacer** (*deshecho*), **imponer** (*impuesto*), **devolver** (*devuelto*), and others.

EJERCICIO A Complete esta carta que Sofía le escribió a Clara, usando los participios pasados de los verbos indicados.

Querida Clara:

¿No has _____ mis dos últimas cartas? ¿Por qué no me has _____ ?
      1. (recibir)   *2.* (escribir)

He _____ de llamarte por teléfono, pero nadie ha _____ . Ya he
      3. (tratar)   *4.* (contestar)

_____ de mi viaje y también te he _____ varias tarjetas postales de las
      5. (regresar)   *6.* (mandar)

ciudades que he _____ .
               7. (visitar)

    ¡Ya han _____ las vacaciones! ¡Qué lástima! Pero Rafael y yo hemos
                8. (terminar)

_____ de un viaje estupendo. Ya hemos _____ al trabajo, pero no
      9. (disfrutar)   *10.* (volver)

hemos _____ los días que hemos _____ en la Costa del Sol. ¿Tú nunca
        11. (olvidar)   *12.* (pasar)

has _____ allí, verdad? Desde que hemos _____ a casa, hemos
      13. (estar)   *14.* (llegar)

_____ ese viaje a todos nuestros amigos. Rafael y yo hemos _____ que
    15. (recomendar)   *16.* (decir)

jamás hemos _____ playas más bonitas. Y todo el mundo ha _____ tan
        17. (ver)   *18.* (ser)

simpático. Ya hemos _____ en hacer otro viaje allí pronto.
             19. (pensar)

    Me sorprendió no haber _____ noticias tuyas. Sé que has _____ a casa
                      20. (tener)   *21.* (ir)

de tu hermana y que has _____ cuidando a tus sobrinos mientras que tu hermana
                   22. (estar)

ha _____ un viaje a París. ¿Se han _____ bien los niños? ¿Ha
     23. (hacer)   *24.* (portar)

_____ mucho trabajo, verdad?
    25. (ser)

Hasta pronto,
Sofía

[2] COMPOUND TENSES

The past participle is used with the various tenses of the verb **haber** (*to have*) to form the compound tenses.

a. Present perfect tense

The present perfect tense is used to describe an action that began in the past and continues up to the present or an action that took place in the past but is connected with the present. It is formed with the present tense of **haber** and the past participle.

I have entered (eaten, lived) here lately.

he		hemos	
has	**entrado (comido, vivido)**	**habéis**	**entrado (comido, vivido)**
ha	**aquí últimamente**	**han**	**aquí últimamente**

b. Pluperfect (past perfect) tense

The pluperfect tense is used to describe an action that was completed in the past before another action took place. It is formed with the imperfect tense of **haber** and the past participle.

I had entered (eaten, lived) here before.

había		habíamos	
habías	entrado (comido, vivido)	habíais	entrado (comido, vivido)
había	aquí antes	habían	aquí antes

c. Preterit perfect tense

The preterit perfect tense is used mainly in literary style to indicate that the action or event had just ended. It usually follows such expressions as **cuando** (*when*); **apenas** (*scarcely, hardly*); **después (de) que** (*after*); **luego que, en cuanto, así que, tan pronto como** (*as soon as*). In conversation and informal writing, the preterit perfect is replaced by the preterit or the pluperfect tense. The preterit perfect is formed with the preterit tense of **haber** and the past participle.

I had entered (eaten, lived)

hube		hubimos	
hubiste	entrado (comido, vivido)	hubisteis	entrado (comido, vivido)
hubo		hubieron	

LITERARY: **Apenas hube llegado** cuando me llamó.
INFORMAL: **Apenas había llegado** cuando me llamó.
I had scarcely arrived when he called me.

LITERARY: **En cuanto hubo entrado,** todos se levantaron.
INFORMAL: **En cuanto entró,** todos se levantaron.
As soon as he had entered everyone got up.

d. Future perfect tense

The future perfect tense is used to describe an action or event that will have been completed in the future. It is formed with the future tense of **haber** and the past participle.

I shall (will) have entered (eaten, lived), etc.

habré		habremos	
habrás	entrado (comido, vivido)	habréis	entrado (comido, vivido)
habrá		habrán	

NOTES:

1. The future perfect may be used to express probability in past time.

¿Lo **habrá terminado?**	*I wonder if he has finished it.* (*Can he have finished it?*)
Habrán perdido las llaves.	*They (have) probably lost the keys.* (*They must have lost the keys.*)

2. The expression **deber de** followed by the perfect infinitive may be substituted for the future perfect in expressing probability in past time.

| **Deben de haber perdido** las llaves. | *They must have lost the keys.* |
| **Debe de haber tomado** el libro. | *He must have taken the book.* |

e. Conditional perfect tense

The conditional perfect tense is used to describe an action or event that would have been completed in the past. It is formed with the conditional tense of **haber** and the past participle.

I would have entered (eaten, lived), etc.

habría			habríamos		
habrías	}	**entrado (comido, vivido)**	habríais	}	**entrado (comido, vivido)**
habría			habrían		

NOTE: The conditional perfect is used to express probability in past time.

¿Lo **habría terminado?**   *I wonder if he had finished it.*
                                    (Could he have finished it?)

Habrían perdido las llaves.   *They had probably lost the keys.*

f. Perfect infinitive

The perfect infinitive is formed with the infinitive of **haber** and the past participle.

haber entrado (comido, vivido) *to have entered (eaten, lived)*

g. Perfect participle

The perfect participle is formed with the **gerundio** of **haber** and the past participle.

habiendo entrado (comido, vivido) *having entered (eaten, lived)*

EJERCICIO B   **Escriba lo que han hecho estas personas para un picnic en el parque.**

EJEMPLO: Arturo / comprar el pan
              Arturo ha comprado el pan.

1. Graciela / preparar la ensalada

2. tú / traer una manta

3. Elena y Roberto / sacar fotos

4. Javier / encender el fuego

5. yo / cocinar las salchichas

6. Sarita / poner la mesa

7. Jorge y yo / llevar una canasta de fruta

8. Ricardo / buscar dónde comprar los refrescos

_____

9. Beatriz / organizar unos juegos

_____

10. todo el mundo / contribuir dinero

_____

EJERCICIO C	Es sábado y Ud. ha dormido hasta el mediodía. Escriba lo que los otros miembros de su familia han hecho mientras Ud. dormía. Use las sugerencias o piense en otras.

SUGERENCIAS: limpiar la sala   sacar al perro
             lavar el carro   cortar la hierba del jardín
             ir de compras   hacer los ejercicios físicos
             arreglar el cuarto

1. Mi padre _____.

2. Mi madre _____.

3. Mi hermana _____.

4. Mis hermanos _____.

5. _____.

6. _____.

EJERCICIO D	Conteste las preguntas que le hace un joven colombiano.

1. ¿Ha visto Ud. muchos partidos de béisbol?

_____

2. ¿Han terminado ya las clases para este año?

_____

3. ¿Ha decidido Ud. cómo va a pasar las vacaciones?

_____

4. ¿Ha ido Ud. a los conciertos al aire libre durante el verano?

_____

5. ¿Le han gustado esos conciertos?

_____

6. ¿Ha buscado Ud. trabajo?

_____

7. ¿Ha visitado Ud. Colombia?

_____

8. ¿Han hecho Ud. y sus amigos algún viaje al extranjero?

_____

9. ¿Ha escuchado Ud. las noticias del día?

_____

10. ¿Ha jugado Ud. al dominó alguna vez?

_____

| EJERCICIO E | Escriba lo que estas personas habían hecho antes de la llegada de los invitados a la fiesta. |

EJEMPLO: Anita / decorar el cuarto
Anita había decorado el cuarto.

1. Raúl / traer los refrescos

_____

2. Gabriel y Alfonso / poner las mesas

_____

3. Marta / cortar la carne

_____

4. yo / comprar los platos de papel

_____

5. tú / preparar los refrescos

_____

6. Carlos / arreglar las sillas

_____

7. mi madre / cocinar una paella

_____

8. David y yo / escoger los discos

_____

9. mi papá / bajar el tocadiscos

_____

10. Gloria / apagar el televisor

_____

EJERCICIO F   **Escriba qué comodidades encontró la señora Cajal en su último viaje.**

EJEMPLO: Cuando llegamos al cuarto del hotel,
el botones / subir las maletas
El botones ya había subido las maletas.

1. Cuando llegamos al cuarto del hotel,

   (*a*)   la camarera / limpiar el cuarto

     _____

   (*b*)   el gerente / poner flores frescas

     _____

   (*c*)   el guía / mandar una botella de vino al cuarto

     _____

2. Cuando íbamos a los restaurantes,

   (*a*)   el guía / hacer la reservación

     _____

   (*b*)   el mesero / poner pan y mantequilla en la mesa

     _____

   (*c*)   el capitán / pedir agua mineral

     _____

3. Cuando visitábamos los museos,

   (*a*)   el guía / conseguir las entradas

     _____

   (*b*)   el chofer / estacionar cerca de la puerta de salida

     _____

EJERCICIO G   **Es el último día de su clase de español. Escriba cinco cosas que Ud. no había hecho hasta este año. Use las sugerencias o piense en otras.**

SUGERENCIAS: declamar un poema en español   hacer un viaje a España
comer en un restaurante español   preparar una piñata
escribir una carta comercial   leer una obra de teatro

1. _____

2. _____

3. _____

4. _____

5. _____

EJERCICIO H   **Escriba quién(es) habrá(n) hecho las siguientes travesuras durante una excursión al parque.**

EJEMPLO: Jaime / quitar las flores   **Jaime habrá quitado** las flores.

1. Ramón / romper la ventana   _____

2. tú / dejar la basura en el suelo   _____

3. mi hermanito / perder el guante de béisbol   _____

4. Rosa / caerse al lago   _____

5. los niños / esconder la comida   _____

6. nosotros / llenar los globos de agua   _____

7. Uds. / chocarse con otros barcos en el lago   _____

EJERCICIO I   **Escriba lo que habrán pensado sus padres cuando Ud. salió con unos amigos por un fin de semana.**

EJEMPLO: llevar un suéter
   ¿Habrá llevado un suéter?

1. llevar un paraguas

_____

2. tener bastante dinero

_____

3. comer bien

_____

4. comprar el boleto de vuelta

_____

5. nadar en la piscina

_____

6. jugar al tenis

_____

7. conocer a muchos jóvenes

_____

8. darles propina a los meseros

_____

9. gastar todo el dinero

_____

10. olvidar llamarnos por teléfono

_____

EJERCICIO J   **Escriba lo que Ud. habría hecho en estas circunstancias.**

EJEMPLO: Dos carros chocaron en la esquina. (llamar a la policía)
            Yo habría llamado a la policía.

1. Un anciano se cayó en la calle. (ayudarle a levantarse)

_____

2. Se le olvidó a su madre comprar leche. (ir a la tienda a comprarla)

_____

3. Un amigo estuvo en el hospital por cinco días. (visitarlo en el hospital)

_____

4. Su padre no quería hablar con alguien por teléfono. (decir que no estaba en casa)

_____

5. Su hermanito tenía mucha hambre. (prepararle un sandwich)

_____

6. Ayer fue el cumpleaños de una amiga suya. (darle flores)

_____

7. Un amigo suyo no tenía dinero para ir al cine con Ud. (prestarle 10 dólares)

_____

EJERCICIO K   **Escriba lo que Ud. habría hecho en estas circunstancias.**

1. No pudo cerrar la llave del baño.

_____

2. Oyó ruidos extraños en la casa por la noche.

_____

3. Olió gas en la cocina.

_____

4. Perdió todo su dinero y no pudo subir al autobús.

_____

5. Ud. rompió un florero valioso de su mamá.

_____

6. Su perro mordió a un niño en la calle.

_____

EJERCICIO L   **Escriba lo que hicieron estas personas habiendo terminado estas cosas.**

EJEMPLO: Carlos escribió una carta. (ponerla en un sobre)
Habiendo escrito la carta, **Carlos la puso** en un sobre.

1. María acostó a su hijito. (apagar la luz)

_____

2. Ellos comieron la merienda. (lavar los platos)

_____

3. Lourdes y yo salimos del cine. (volver a casa)

_____

4. Mi hermana lavó la ropa. (ponerla en la secadora)

_____

5. Los amigos jugaron una partida de ajedrez. (tomar un refresco)

_____

6. Tú compraste ropa nueva. (guardarla en el armario)

_____

7. Yo cerré el libro. (dejarlo en la mesa)

_____

EJERCICIO M   **El director de la escuela presentó unos premios a varios estudiantes de intercambio de países hispanos. Exprese por qué ellos recibieron los premios.**

EJEMPLO: Gladys recibió un certificado / estudiar mucho
Gladys recibió un certificado por **haber estudiado** mucho.

1. Marco recibió un trofeo / ganar muchas carreras

_____

2. Lisa recibió una medalla / dibujar el mejor cartel

_____

3. Verónica recibió un libro de poesías / escribir el mejor poema

_____

4. Lázaro recibió un certificado / ayudar a los otros

_____

5. Vicente recibió un cheque / construir el mejor tren

_____

6. Nilda recibió un diccionario / aprender más inglés

_____

7. Nelson y Ricky recibieron un certificado / preparar las mejores escenas breves

_____

M A S T E R Y   E X E R C I S E S

EJERCICIO N

Describa lo que Ud. y un amigo han hecho antes de salir de viaje al extranjero. Use las sugerencias o piense en otras.

SUGERENCIAS: sacar el pasaporte   hacer la maleta
                           comprar el boleto   lavar la ropa
                           hacer la reservación   leer las guías turísticas
                           escribir a los hoteles   visitar la oficina de turismo
                           cambiar dinero   hablar con otras personas
                           confirmar la reservación del vuelo   sacar dinero del banco

1. _____

2. _____

3. _____

4. _____

5. _____

6. _____

7. _____

8. _____

EJERCICIO O

Este año Ud. ha pensado mucho en las universidades. Escriba una composición en la que Ud. describe lo que ha hecho para informarse y prepararse para la universidad. Incluya:

      the research you have done (Internet, letters, etc.)

      with whom you have spoken

      school visits

      preparation of applications

      inquiries regarding scholarships

      why you have limited your search

      the assistance you have received from parents, family, friends

_____

_____

Chapter 10
Ser and *Estar*

[1] USES OF *SER*

Ser is used:

(*a*) to express an inherent quality or characteristic of the subject.

> Este vino *es de España.*
> La casa *es de madera.*
> Felipe *es bueno.*

(*b*) to describe or identify the subject.

> María *es alta* (*joven*).
> Mi hermano *es médico* (*fuerte*).
> El coche *es nuevo* (*blanco*).
> Juana *es rica* (*feliz*).
> ¿Quién *es? Soy* yo (*es* él).

(*c*) to express time, dates, and where an event takes place.

> ¿Qué *hora es ? Son las dos.*
> *¿Dónde es* el concierto? El concierto *es en el parque.*
> Hoy *es el treinta de enero.*

(*d*) with impersonal expressions.

> *Es necesario* estudiar.
> *Es importante* llegar a tiempo.

(*e*) to express a passive action with the past participle (see Chapter 12, page 125).

> Las ventanas *fueron cerradas* por el profesor.
> La puerta *fue abierta* por el niño.

NOTE: The forms of **ser** are summarized in the section on irregular verbs in the Appendix, page 496.

| EJERCICIO A |

Conteste las preguntas que le hace un amigo nuevo.

1. ¿Quién es usted?

_____

2. ¿De dónde es usted?

_____

3.   ¿Cuál es su nacionalidad?

_____

4.   ¿Cómo es usted?

_____

5.   ¿De qué es su casa?

_____

6.   ¿De qué color es su casa?

_____

7.   ¿Es usted un(a) estudiante aplicado(a)?

_____

8.   ¿Quién es el hijo mayor de su familia? ¿El hijo menor?

_____

9.   ¿Son simpáticos sus hermanos?

_____

10.   ¿Cómo es su cuarto?

_____

11.   ¿Cuáles son sus pasatiempos favoritos?

_____

12.   ¿Quién en su mejor amigo(a)?

_____

13.   ¿Es importante estudiar, verdad?

_____

14.   ¿Cuál es la fecha de hoy?

_____

15.   ¿Qué hora es?

_____

EJERCICIO B   **Ud. acaba de recibir una carta de una nueva amiga que vive en México. Complete las frases con la forma apropiada del verbo _ser_.**

Querido amigo/Querida amiga:

Yo _____ Gloria Caraballo. Ahora vivo en México pero no _____ mexi-
        1.   2.

cana. _____ de España y vivimos en México porque mi padre _____ el
        3.   4.

cónsul de España y le toca trabajar en México por dos años. Nosotros _____ una familia
                                                                                5.

grande y unida. Mis dos hermanos, Jorge y Víctor, _____ mayores y mi hermana Pilar
6.

_____ menor que yo. Mi mamá no trabaja pero como _____ la esposa de un
7. 8.

diplomático, _____ importante que ella vaya con mi padre a muchas funciones del gobierno.
9.

    La casa en que vivimos _____ muy grande. _____ de ladrillo.
10. 11.

Las casas de México no _____ de madera porque _____ más frescas cuando
12. 13.

hace calor si _____ de piedra. Esta casa _____ de un señor rico. Hay muchos
14. 15.

cuartos. Mi dormitorio _____ pequeño pero lindo. Da al jardín y _____
16. 17.

agradable sentarme allí por la tarde. Mi hermana _____ celosa y siempre me dice: «Oye,
18.

tú _____ la preferida de esta familia porque tu cuarto _____ el más
19. 20.

bonito.» También mi hermana y yo _____ buenas amigas. Ahora _____ las
21. 22.

cuatro y media de la tarde y debo despedirme de ti porque _____ la hora de mi clase de
23.

piano. Tocar un instrumento musical _____ lindo, ¿verdad? En tu carta cuéntame de
24.

tus amigos y dime cuáles _____ tus pasatiempos preferidos. _____ muy in-
25. 26.

teresante tener amistades de otros países, ¿verdad?

Hasta pronto.

[2] USES OF *ESTAR*

Estar is used:

(*a*) to express the location, position, or situation of the subject.

Madrid *está en España.*

¿Dónde está **la casa?**

Felipe *está delante de la bibilioteca.*

(*b*) to indicate a state or condition of the subject.

María *está cansada (sentada).*

El coche *está lleno (sucio).*

Ellos *están alegres (tristes).*

Luis *está enfermo (bien).*

La puerta *está abierta (cerrada).*

El gato *está vivo (muerto).*

(*c*) to form the progressive tenses (with the **gerundio**).

Están cantando.

Estaban jugando.

NOTES:

1. A condition may be a phase: **Juan está enfermo (triste);** a temporary state: **Está cansado (sentado);** or the results of an action: **La puerta está cerrada.** Note that a condition does not identify, describe, or express a characteristic.

2. The forms of **estar** are summarized in the section on irregular verbs in the Appendix, page 494.

(*d*) in certain common expressions:

estar a punto de + infinitive   *to be just about to*

estar para + infinitive   *to be about to*

estar por   *to be in favor of*

estar por + infinitive   *to be inclined to*

estar conforme, estar de acuerdo (con)   *to be in agreement (with), to agree*

estar de vuelta   *to be back*

Espérame, *estoy a punto de* **terminar.**	*Wait for me, I'm just about to finish.*
Estoy para **salir.**	*I'm about to leave.*
Estoy por **el nuevo candidato.**	*I am in favor of the new candidate.*
Estoy por **ir de compras.**	*I am inclined to go shopping.*
No *está de acuerdo* **conmigo.**	*He doesn't agree with me.*
No *estoy conforme* **con su opinión.**	*I am not in agreement with your opinion.*

EJERCICIO C   **Usted presenció un accidente. Conteste las preguntas que le hace un policía.**

1. ¿Dónde estaba Ud. cuando los vehículos chocaron? (en la esquina)

_____

2. ¿Estaban sentados o de pie los pasajeros del autobús? (sentados y de pie)

_____

3. ¿Estaba lleno el autobús? (Sí)

_____

4. ¿Dónde estaba el autobús? (parado en el semáforo)

_____

5. ¿Dónde estaba el coche? (detrás del autobús)

_____

6. ¿Cómo estaba la puerta del autobús (abierta)

_____

7. ¿Estaban bajándose del autobús algunos pasajeros? (Sí, tres personas)

_____

8. ¿Quién estaba conduciendo el coche? (un señor)

_____

9. ¿Qué estaban haciendo los pasajeros del coche? (hablando)

_____

10. ¿Quién estaba sentado detrás del chofer del coche? (un niño)

_____

11. ¿Qué estaba haciendo este niño? (jugando)

_____

12. En su opinión, ¿cómo estaba el chofer del coche? (distraído)

_____

EJERCICIO D   David no se siente bien y va la oficina de la enfermera de la escuela. Complete este diálogo con las formas apropiadas de *estar*.

DAVID: Buenas tardes.

ENFERMERA: Buenas tardes, David. ¿Cómo _____ tú hoy?
1.

DAVID: Yo no _____ bien. _____ enfermo. Me duele todo el cuerpo.
2.   3.

ENFERMERA: Sí, tú _____ muy pálido. ¿Desde cuándo _____ tú así?
4.   5.

DAVID: Hoy por la mañana yo _____ bien. Luego, cuando yo _____ en la
6.   7.

clase de inglés. me empezó la tos.

ENFERMERA: ¿_____ tus padres en casa ahora?
8.

DAVID: No. Mi padre _____ trabajando y mi madre _____ visitando
9.   10.

a mis abuelos porque mi abuelo _____ en el hospital. Ella no
11.

_____ de vuelta hasta las cinco.
12.

ENFERMERA: ¿_____ tu padre en su oficina ahora?
13.

DAVID: No lo creo. Él debe _____ en la oficina de uno de sus clientes. Él
14.

_____ a punto de salir para allá cuando yo llamé.
15.

ENFERMERA: ¿Dónde _____ tus hermanos?
                                16.

DAVID: Uno _____ estudiando en la universidad y los otros dos _____
                        17.   18.

     trabajando. Ellos _____ lejos de aquí.
                                    19.

ENFERMERA: ¿Dónde _____ situada la oficina de tu médico?
                                20.

DAVID: Su oficina _____ en la Calle Madero, pero él no va a _____
                            21.   22.

     allí hasta las seis.

ENFERMERA: Aqui hace frío porque las ventanas _____ abiertas. Tú deberías
                                                                        23.

     _____ en casa.
                    24.

DAVID: Yo _____ de acuerdo. Mis tíos _____ en casa ahora y su casa
                        25.   26.

     _____ cerca de la escuela.
                    27.

ENFERMERA: Voy a llamarlos. Si ellos no _____ ocupados, tú puedes ir a su casa.
                                                                28.

[3] ADJECTIVES USED WITH *SER* OR *ESTAR*

a. Some adjective may be used with either **ser** or **estar,** but the meaning of an adjective used with **ser** will differ from its meaning when used with **estar.**

Julio *es bueno* (malo).	*Julio is good (bad).*	(characteristic)
La sopa *está buena* (mala).	*The soup is good (bad).*	(condition)
Es listo.	*He is clever (smart).*	(characteristic)
Está listo.	*He is ready.*	(condition)
Es pálido.	*He is pale-complexioned.*	(characteristic)
Está pálido.	*He is pale.*	(condition)
Es seguro.	*It is safe (reliable).*	(description/characteristic)
Está seguro.	*He is sure.*	(condition/state of mind)
Él es vivo.	*He is sharp (quick).*	(characteristic)
Él está vivo.	*He is alive.*	(state/phase)
Es viejo (joven).	*He is old (young).*	(description)
Está viejo (joven).	*He looks old (young).*	(condition)
Él es aburrido.	*He is boring.*	(characteristic)
Él está aburrido.	*He is bored.*	(condition/state)

b. Adjectives used with **ser** and **estar** agree with the subject in gender and number.

Alicia está ocupada.	*Alicia is busy.*
Eran pobres.	*They were poor.*

EJERCICIO E   Complete esta descripción que Arturo hace de un domingo de primavera, usando las formas apropiadas de *ser* o *estar*.

Hoy _____ domingo. _____ el dos de mayo y empieza a hacer buen
        1.   2.

tiempo porque nosotros _____ en primavera. _____ las ocho de la mañana
                              3.   4.

cuando me levanto. Las ventanas de mi cuarto _____ abiertas y el aire que entra
                                                      5.

_____ fresco.
        6.

_____ un buen día para _____ en el parque. Mis amigos _____
        7.   8.   9.

de acuerdo, pero ellos _____ trabajando y no pueden acompañarme. No me gusta
                              10.

_____ solo, pero la única persona que _____ dispuesta a pasar el día conmigo
        11.   12.

_____ mi hermano menor. Mi hermana mayor _____ lista e interesante,
        13.   14.

pero hoy ella _____ muy preocupada. No le gusta su trabajo. Ella _____
                  15.   16.

buscando un trabajo nuevo y va a _____ ocupada hoy porque _____
                                        17.   18.

escribiendo cartas a varias compañías. Yo _____ seguro de que mis padres van
                                                  19.

a _____ furiosos si no quiero llevar a mi hermano menor. _____ cansado
      20.   21.

de salir con él porque siempre me _____ haciendo muchas preguntas. Él _____
                                        22.   23.

un chico bueno, pero él nunca _____ satisfecho. Le gusta _____ sentado
                                    24.   25.

delante de la casa y hablar con las personas que _____ caminando por la calle. No quiero
                                                        26.

_____ malo, pero voy a decirles a mis padres que hoy yo voy a _____ fuera
        27.   28.

hasta muy tarde. Entonces no tendré que _____ cuidando a mi hermano menor. Yo
                                              29.

_____ muy listo, ¿verdad?
        30.

EJERCICIO F   Teresa le cuenta a su madre de una familia que conoció en España. Complete las frases con las formas correctas de *ser* o *estar*.

1. Elena _____ cubana pero ahora ella y su familia _____ viviendo en
España.

2. Su hermano Lionel _____ muy listo en la escuela pero nunca _____
listo para salir a tiempo.

3. Su padre _____ médico y por eso _____ en el hospital la mayor parte del día.

4. El museo _____ enfrente de su casa.

5. El tío de Elena, señor Vargas, _____ ingeniero. Sus hijos siempre _____ jugando en el patio.

6. Los vestidos de la señora Vargas _____ de colores muy vivos y siempre _____ limpios.

7. El señor Vargas les dice a sus hijos que _____ importante honrar a sus padres.

8. Las ventanas _____ abiertas y los muebles _____ llenos de polvo.

9. Comíamos en un restaurante que _____ cerca de casa, pero la sopa nunca _____ caliente.

10. Mamá, tú todavía _____ pálida de la sorpresa.

EJERCICIO G   **Usted ha conocido a alguien por medio de una carta. Conteste las preguntas que le hizo a Ud. en la carta.**

1. ¿De dónde es Ud.?

    _____

2. ¿Dónde está Ud. ahora?

    _____

3. ¿Cómo está Ud. hoy?

    _____

4. ¿Quién está al lado de Ud.?

    _____

5. ¿Qué está haciendo Ud. ahora?

    _____

6. ¿Qué quiere ser Ud. algún día?

    _____

7. ¿Cómo es Ud.: alto/alta o bajo/baja; rubio/rubia o moreno/morena; gordo/gorda o delgado/delgada?

    _____

8. ¿Es Ud. un amigo/una amiga fiel?

    _____

9. ¿Dónde está situada su casa?

    _____

10. ¿Es su casa de piedra, de madera o de ladrillos?

    _____

11. ¿Está rodeada de árboles su escuela?

_____

12. ¿Está Ud. atento/atenta cuando hablan sus profesores?

_____

13. ¿Está Ud. de acuerdo con lo que dicen?

_____

14. ¿Quién fue elegido presidente de los Estados Unidos?

_____

15. ¿Está Ud. conforme con las ideas de nuevo presidente?

_____

16. ¿Por quién estuvo Ud.?

_____

17. ¿Estaba Ud. ocupado/ocupada ayer?

_____

18. ¿Qué estaba Ud. haciendo?

_____

19. ¿Es Ud. un estudiante/una estudiante ejemplar?

_____

20. ¿Dónde están sus amigos/amigas ahora?

_____

21. ¿Qué hace Ud. cuando está cansado/cansada?

_____

22. ¿Es Ud. una persona perezosa?

_____

23. ¿Por qué está Ud. alegre hoy?

_____

24. ¿A qué hora está Ud. de vuelta en su casa por las tardes?

_____

MASTERY EXERCISES

EJERCICIO H   **Escoja la forma correcta de *ser* o *estar* para completar los siguientes párrafos.**

1. (Estaban, Eran) las tres de la tarde. (Estaba, Era) un día de agosto hermoso. Los árboles (estaban, eran) cargados de frutas que más tarde (estarían serían) recogidas por niños y mayores. El aire (estaba, era) lleno del rumor de pájaros e insectos que se aprovechaban de luz del sol. En los campos de trigo y de maíz, los agricultores (estaban, eran) trabajando entre gritos y risas. El cielo (estaba, era) completamente libre de nubes. (Estaba, Era) una escena de belleza ideal. «Esto (está, es) vivir» pensaba el turista, respirando fuerte. La tristeza que había sentido antes iba cambiando. Ahora (estaba, era) alegre.

2. Luisito (está, es) un muchacho de trece años. (Está, Es) alto y tiene una sonrisa de angel. (Está, Es) bueno, listo y simpático, pero bastante pícaro y atrevido. Ayer se subió a un manzano y comió un par de manzanas verdes. Ahora (está, es) enfermo con fiebre y tiene que (estar, ser) en cama todo el día. Lo visité esta mañana y (estaba, era) pálido. Le pregunté: «¿Cómo (estás, eres)?» Me contestó con voz muy débil: «(Estoy, Soy) muy mal hoy.» El médico dice que la enfermedad no (está, es) grave y que dentro de dos o tres días yo (estaré, seré) tan bien como antes.

3. Los aztecas (estaban, eran) dueños del Valle de México. Su capital (estaba, era) Tenochtitlán, [que hoy día (está, es) la Ciudad de México]. (Estaba, Era) situada en un lago y (estaba, era) completamente rodeada de agua. Para llegar allí, (estaba, era) necesario cruzar por medio de uno de los numerosos puentes. En el centro de la ciudad (estaba, era) el palacio del emperador. (Estaban, Eran) una raza fuerte y agresiva y se habían hecho propietarios de mucho terreno ajeno. Cuando llegó Cortés, muchas naciones (estaban, eran) sujetas al poder de los aztecas. Su gobierno (estaba, era) severo y cruel, y practicaban el culto del sacrificio humano en los altares de sus templos.

4. El director de la expedición (estuvo, fue) el Sr. Suárez. (Estaba, Era) un hombre de mucha experiencia, de origen gallego, que había (estado, sido) navegante y que había (estado, sido) en muchos puertos. (Estaba, Era) martes, el treinta de enero, cuando salimos y nos dirigimos al África, donde, según él, (estaba, era) el tesoro. El mar (estaba, era) tranquilo. Una noche (estábamos, éramos) sentados en el salón, cuando uno de los compañeros de la empresa le preguntó si (estaba, era) seguro de que el mapa (estaba, era) genuino. Lleno de risa, se levantó de su asiento.

5. El Sr. Torres (estaba era) de España. (Estaba, Era) español de nacimiento. Había venido a Buenos Aires para (estar, ser) administrador del negocio de su padre, en la industria de la lana. (Estaba, Era) viudo y vivía con sus hijas y sus nietos. Su trabajo (estaba, era) fácil y tenía muchas horas libres. Su casa (estaba era) situada en la avenida principal de la ciudad y (estaba, era) de buena construcción, de ladrillos. Tenía una biblioteca que también (estaba, era) un despacho, con gran número de libros, cuadros y curiosidades. (Estaba, Era) muy aficionado a la lectura y prefería obras de historia. La puerta siempre (estaba, era) abierta para los amigos y conocidos.

EJERCICIO I   **Lea este cuento sobre un viaje que hicieron Roberto y Luis. Complete cada frase con la forma correcta de *ser* o *estar*.**

Roberto y Luis _____ 1. _____ viajando en automóvil. _____ 2. _____ de noche. El cielo _____ 3. _____ muy oscuro y _____ 4. _____ lleno de nubes. Los jóvenes _____ 5. _____ para atravesar un puente. El puente parecía _____ 6. _____ muy viejo. Ellos querían _____ 7. _____ seguros de que el puente _____ 8. _____ muy seguro. Roberto _____ 9. _____ manejando el coche. El coche _____ 10. _____ detenido delante de la entrada al puente. Luis _____ 11. _____ leyendo un letrero que decía: «El puente _____ 12. _____ inspeccionado por las autoridades hace un mes.» Los jóvenes _____ 13. _____ decididos a llegar a su destino antes del amanecer. Roberto _____ 14. _____ preocupado, pero Luis le dijo que no debía _____ 15. _____ preocupado porque el puente _____ 16. _____ seguro.

EJERCICIO J

Su hermano(-a) menor va a seguir el mismo curso que Ud. siguió el verano pasado en México y quiere vivir con la misma familia. Escriba una carta a la familia con quien Ud. vivió en México para presentarles a su hermano(-a). Incluya en la carta:

the purpose of the letter/why you are writing

introduce your sibling

a description (physical and personality) of your sibling

your similarities and differences

your reaction to and support of his/her decision

_____

_____

_____

_____

_____

_____

_____

_____

_____

_____

_____

_____

Chapter 11
Reflexive Verbs

[1] REFLEXIVE CONSTRUCTIONS IN SIMPLE AND COMPOUND TENSES

The reflexive pronouns (**me, te, se, nos, os, se**) generally precede the verb in the simple and compound tenses.

PRESENT TENSE

(yo) *me* lavo	(nosotros, -as) *nos* lavamos
(tú) *te* lavas	(vosotros, -as) *os* laváis
(Ud., él, ella) *se* lava	(Uds., ellos, -as) *se* lavan

PRETERIT

me lavé, te lavaste, etc.

IMPERFECT

me lavaba, te lavabas, etc.

FUTURE

me lavaré, te lavarás, etc.

CONDITIONAL

me lavaría, te lavarías, etc.

PRESENT PERFECT TENSE

(yo) *me* he lavado	(nosotros, -as) *nos* hemos lavado
(tú) *te* has lavado	(vosotros, -as) *os* habéis lavado
(Ud., él, ella) *se* ha lavado	(Uds., ellos, -as) *se* han lavado

PLUPERFECT

me había lavado, te habías lavado, etc.

FUTURE PERFECT

me habré lavado, te habrás lavado, etc.

CONDITIONAL PERFECT

me habría lavado, te habrías lavado, etc.

NOTE: The reflexive pronoun is another form of object pronoun, either direct or indirect. It indicates that the subject and the object of the verb are the same person or thing.

Nosotros levantamos el baúl.	*We lift the trunk.*
Nosotros *nos* levantamos.	*We stand up. (We lift ourselves.)*
Pongo el sombrero en la mesa.	*I put the hat on the table.*
***Me* pongo el sombrero.**	*I put on my hat. (I put the hat on myself).*

EJERCICIO A   **Escriba quién hace estas cosas por la mañana en su casa.**

yo	bañarse rápidamente	peinarse por quince minutos
mi madre	afeitarse	despertarse solo
mi padre	cepillarse los dientes	no desayunarse
mi hermano	vestirse de prisa	levantarse con dificultad
mis hermana	despedirse con un beso	
mis hermanos		

EJEMPLO: **Yo me visto de prisa.**

1. _____

2. _____

3. _____

4. _____

5. _____

6. _____

7. _____

8. _____

EJERCICIO B   **Ud. es consejero/consejera de un grupo de niños en un campamento de verano. Escriba cuál de los niños ha hecho estas cosas.**

EJEMPLO: Roberto / encerrarse en el baño
            Roberto se ha encerrado en el baño.

1. Clara y Sarita / dormirse en el cine

_____

2. Javier / acostarse debajo de un árbol

_____

3. los gemelos / quedarse en la piscina

_____

4. Eduardo / esconderse en el bosque

_____

5. Carlos / irse sin permiso

_____

6. Gabriel y Raúl / negarse a comer

_____

7. otro consejero y yo / enfadarse

_____

8. Yo / ponerse nervioso(a)

_____

EJERCICIO C	Escriba lo que pasó en estas circunstancias. Use las sugerencias o piense en otras.

SUGERENCIAS:

quedarse	enfadarse	resfriarse
casarse	escaparse	pararse
quejarse	pasearse	mojarse
enojarse	desmayarse	ahogarse
despertarse	esconderse	bañarse
asustarse	irse	

EJEMPLO: Nevó ayer y yo **me quedé en casa.**

1. Llovió ayer durante el partido y los jugadores de béisbol _____.

2. Mi papá no oyó el despertador por la mañana y él _____.

3. Las niñas vieron un ratoncito y ellas _____.

4. Pedro y Graciela fueron novios por un año. Ayer en la iglesia ellos _____.

5. Tú usaste mi blusa nueva. Yo _____.

6. El médico le puso una inyección a mi hermanito. Él _____ del dolor.

7. Elena y yo fuimos al parque donde nosotros _____.

8. Yo atrapé una rana pero la rana _____ de la caja en que la tenía.

9. La señora Pérez oyó malas noticias y ella _____.

10. El perro no pudo nadar en el río y _____.

[2] REFLEXIVE COMMANDS

The reflexive pronouns in affirmative commands follow the verb and are attached to it. In a negative command, the reflexive pronoun precedes the verb.

¡lá**ve**se!	¡lá**ven**se!
¡lá**va**te!	¡lava**os**!

¡no *se* lave! ¡no *se* laven!

¡no *te* laves! ¡no *os* lavéis!

NOTE: When the reflexive pronoun is attached to the affirmative command, there is an accent mark on the stressed vowel of the verb of the **tú, Ud.** and **Uds.** forms.

EJERCICIO D Escriba cinco órdenes que sus padres le dan a Ud. por la mañana. Use las sugerencias o piense en otras.

SUGERENCIAS: despertarse ahora   levantarse rápidamente

bañarse primero   cepillarse los dientes

lavarse el pelo   vestirse ahora mismo

desayunarse bien   peinarse antes de salir

EJEMPLO: **¡Despiértate ahora!**

1. _____

2. _____

3. _____

4. _____

5. _____

EJERCICIO E Alfredo y su hermano nunca hacen lo que su madre quiere. Escriba las órdenes que ella les da.

EJEMPLO: quedarse en la cama   **¡No se queden en la cama!**

1. tardarse en el baño _____

2. quejarse del desayuno _____

3. irse sin despedirse _____

4. cepillarse el pelo en la sala _____

5. olvidarse de preparar la tarea _____

6. acostarse en el sofá _____

7. quitarse los zapatos _____

EJERCICIO F Usando la sugerencia dada en paréntesis, escriba la orden que Ud. daría a cada persona indicada en cada situación.

EJEMPLO: *Tu hermano* va a salir de la casa con tu raqueta de tenis. (irse)
           ¡No te vayas con mi raqueta de tenis!

1. Ud. está cuidando *a dos niños* y ellos ya tienen mucho sueño. (acostarse)

_____

2. Tú y *tu hermana* están sentados en la sala cuando suena el teléfono. Tú no quieres contestar el teléfono. (levantarse)

_____

3. *Una amiga de su mamá* llama a la puerta. Ud. la invita a entrar en la sala para esperar a su mamá. (sentarse)

_____

4. *Su amigo* acaba de arreglar su bicicleta y Uds. van a comer. (lavarse las manos)

_____

5. Ud. y *un amigo* acaban de llegar a la piscina y van a tirarse al agua. Su amigo lleva gafas de sol. (quitarse las gafas)

_____

6. *A su madre* no le parece que un amigo la acompañe a Ud. al centro. (enfadarse)

_____

7. Ud. no salió bien en un examen y va a decírselo *a sus padres.* (ponerse furiosos)

_____

8. Ud. está en el parque de diversiones y va a subir a la montaña rusa con *un amigo* miedoso. (asustarse)

_____

[3] REFLEXIVE CONSTRUCTIONS WITH INFINITIVES AND THE GERUNDIO

When used with an infinitive or a **gerundio,** the reflexive pronoun may follow the verb and be attached to it or it may precede the conjugated form of the verb.

INFINITIVE: Voy a **peinar*me*** ahora.   *Me* voy a **peinar** ahora.
Acabamos de **desayunar*nos*.**   *Nos* acabamos de **desayunar.**

GERUNDIO: María **está lavándo*se*** la cara.   María *se* **está lavando** la cara.
Tú **estabas lavándo*te*** el pelo.   Tú *te* **estabas lavando** el pelo.

NOTE: With the **gerundio,** an accent mark is placed on the stressed vowel of the verb if the reflexive pronoun is attached to it.

Estamos **lavándonos.**   Estaba **desayunándome.**

EJERCICIO G   Complete, con la forma apropiada de los verbos dados, este diálogo telefónico entre Carmen y Luz sobre una fiesta que tendrá lugar el sábado.

CARMEN: ¿Piensas _____ en la fiesta de Rosa?
1. (divertirse)

LUZ: Claro que sí. Y quiero _____ allí hasta muy tarde.
2. (quedarse)

CARMEN: ¿Hasta qué hora te dejarán tus padres _____ en la fiesta?
3. (quedarse)

ing4587

LUZ: Hasta medianoche. Si llego después, ellos van a _____ .
4. (enfadarse)

CARMEN: ¿Qué piensas _____ ?
5. (ponerse)

LUZ: Todas las chicas van a _____ blusa y falda. Pero yo prefiero _____ un
6. (ponerse)   7. (ponerse)

vestido nuevo que acabo de comprar.

CARMEN: ¿Podré _____ en tu casa? Trabajo el sábado y tendré que _____
8. (vestirse)   9. (apresurarse)

para llegar a la fiesta a tiempo. Si debo volver a casa a _____ antes de ir a la
10. (cambiarse)

fiesta, no llegaré nunca. También así podrás ayudarme a _____ .
11. (peinarse)

LUZ: ¡Por supuesto que puedes _____ aquí! Así tendremos tiempo para decidir en
12. (vestirse)

quiénes debemos _____ en la fiesta.
13. (fijarse)

CARMEN: Bueno, debo _____ ahora porque tengo mucho que hacer. Y gracias, porque
14. (irse)

ahora podré _____ .
15. (tranquilizarse)

LUZ: De nada. Hasta el sábado.

CARMEN: Adiós.

EJERCICIO H Usando los verbos dados a continuación, escriba una frase para explicar por qué ciertas personas a quienes Ud. conoce, van a, deben, pueden, quieren, o prefieren hacer la acción del verbo.

EJEMPLO: acostarse **Cuando mi padre tiene sueño, prefiere acostarse enseguida.**

1. quejarse _____

2. preocuparse _____

3. lavarse _____

4. enojarse _____

5. apresurarse _____

6. resfriarse _____

7. afligirse _____

8. alegrarse _____

9. fijarse _____

10. despertarse _____

[4]   SUMMARY OF THE POSITION OF REFLEXIVE PRONOUNS

SIMPLE TENSE	*Se* lava.	*He washes himself.*
COMPOUND TENSE	*Nos* hemos lavado.	*We have washed ourselves.*
INFINITIVE	Quiero lavar*me*. or *Me* quiero lavar	*I want to wash myself.*
GERUNDIO	Estamos lavándo*nos*. or *Nos* estamos lavando.	*We are washing ourselves.*
COMMANDS	Lávense Uds. (affirmative) but No *se* laven Uds. (negative)	*Wash yourselves.* *Don't wash yourselves.*

[5]   USES OF REFLEXIVE VERBS

a. Some verbs have special meanings when used reflexively:

BASIC MEANING	REFLEXIVE MEANING
aburrir *to bore*	**aburrirse** *(to bore oneself) to become bored*
acostar *to put to bed*	**acostarse** *(to put oneself to bed) to go to bed*
bañar *to bathe (someone)*	**bañarse** *(to bathe oneself) to take a bath*
cansar *to tire*	**cansarse** *(to tire oneself) to become tired*
colocar *to place (something)*	**colocarse** *to place oneself; to get a job*
engañar *to deceive*	**engañarse** *to deceive oneself; to be mistaken*
esconder *to hide (something)*	**esconderse** *to hide (oneself)*
parar *to stop (something)*	**pararse** *to stop oneself, to stop*
poner *to put (something)*	**ponerse** *to place oneself; to put (something) on; to become*
sentar *to seat*	**sentarse** *(to seat oneself) to sit down*

b. Some verbs are always used reflexively in Spanish but not usually in English:

acordarse (de) *to remember*
apoderarse (de) *to take possession (of)*
apresurarse (a) *to hurry*
aprovecharse (de) *to avail oneself (of); to profit (by); to take unfair advantage (of)*
arrepentirse (de) *to repent, to regret*
atreverse (a) *to dare (to)*
burlarse (de) *to make fun (of)*
desayunarse *to have breakfast*
desmayarse *to faint*

escaparse (de) *to escape (from)*
fiarse (de) *to trust*
figurarse *to imagine*
fijarse (en) *to stare (at), to notice*
irse *to go away*
negarse (a) *to refuse (to)*
olvidarse (de) *to forget*
parecerse (a) *to resemble*
pasearse *to stroll*
quejarse (de) *to complain*

empeñarse (en) *to insist (on)*	**reírse (de)** *to laugh (at), to make fun (of)*
enterarse (de) *to find out about*	**tratarse (de)** *to concern, to be a question (of)*

c. Reflexive verbs express reciprocal action corresponding to English *each other, one another.*

Nos escribimos.	*We write to each other.*
Pepe y Elena se aman.	*Pepe and Elena love one another.*

NOTE: **Uno a otro (Una a otra)** or **el uno al otro (la una a la otra)** may be added to clarify or reinforce the meaning of the reflexive pronoun:

Las muchachas se miran.	*The girls look at each other (or look at themselves).*
Las muchachas se miran *una a otra (**la una a la otra**).*	*The girls look at each other.*
Pepe y Elena se aman *uno a otro (**el uno al otro**).*	*Pepe and Elena love each other.*

d. Reflexive verbs are often used to express a passive action when the subject is a thing (not a person) and when the agent (doer) is not indicated (see page 128).

Aquí *se habla* **español.**	*Spanish is spoken here.*
Estos libros *se venderán* **hoy.**	*These books will be sold today.*

EJERCICIO I	Manolo y sus amigos hablan de un concierto al que asistieron. Escriba las frases siguientes, usando el pretérito de los verbos dados.

EJEMPLO: la policía / colocar / barricadas en la entrada
La policía colocó barricadas en la entrada.

1. los policías / colocarse delante de ellas

_____

2. unos muchachos / sentar / a la gente

_____

3. ellos / sentarse / en los pasillos

_____

4. Roberto / esconder / una grabadora en su mochila

_____

5. él / esconderse / cerca del foro

_____

6. tres personas / desmayarse

_____

7. la primera parte del concierto / cansar al público

_____

8. en la segunda parte / el público / no cansarse de aplaudir

_____

9. nadie / apresurarse / a salir

_____

10. los policías / empeñarse / en mantener el orden

_____

11. muchas personas / quejarse / del calor

_____

12. varios policías / parar / un disgusto entre dos aficionados

_____

13. yo / pararse / para ver la escena

_____

14. nosotros / acordarse / del primer concierto de este grupo

_____

15. los comerciantes / aprovecharse / del público

_____

| EJERCICIO J | Conteste estas preguntas que le hace Rafael a Carmen sobre su novio. Conteste usando la forma recíproca. |

EJEMPLO: ¿Desde cuándo lo conoces? (hace 2 años)
Nosotros nos conocemos desde hace dos años.

1. ¿Dónde lo conociste? (en una fiesta)

_____

2. ¿Con qué frecuencia le escribes? (cada semana)

_____

3. ¿Cuándo hablas con él por teléfono? (todos los domingos)

_____

4. ¿Cuándo lo ves? (durante las vacaciones)

_____

5. ¿Lo amas mucho? (Sí)

_____

| EJERCICIO K | Ricardo está preparando los carteles para una fiesta que el Círculo Español va a ofrecer el sábado. Ayúdele a escribir los carteles. |

EJEMPLO: entrar / por aquí
Se entra por aquí.

1. aquí / cambiar / dinero

   _____

2. aquí / sacar / fotos

   _____

3. aquí / comprar / las entradas

   _____

4. vender / refrescos / aquí

   _____

5. vender / helado / aquí

   _____

6. prohibir / entrar / por aquí

   _____

7. salir / por aquí

   _____

8. oír / discos allí

   _____

MASTERY EXERCISES

EJERCICIO L   **Conteste estas preguntas que le hace un alumno de intercambio en su escuela.**

1. ¿Se ponen Uds. tristes cuando terminan las vacaciones?

   _____

2. ¿Se quejan Uds. cuando el profesor les da muchas tareas?

   _____

3. ¿Por qué se enfada el profesor a veces con Ud.?

   _____

4. ¿Se callan los alumnos mientras está hablando el profesor?

   _____

5. ¿Admite Ud. su error cuando se equivoca?

   _____

6. ¿Se enfadan sus padres cuando Ud. llega a casa tarde?

   _____

7. ¿Cuándo se graduará Ud. de esta escuela?

   _____

8. ¿En qué universidad se matriculará Ud.?

_____

9. ¿Qué quiere Ud. hacerse?

_____

10. ¿Cómo se divierte Ud. cuando está con sus amigos?

_____

EJERCICIO M Ud. acaba de volver a casa después de pasar un mes en un campamento de verano. Escriba una carta a un(-a) amigo(-a) en la que Ud. le describe sus experiencias en el campamento. Incluya en la carta:

your daily routine (morning routines, afternoon activities, evening events, etc.)
new experiences you had
information about the new friends you made
your reaction to camp life

_____
_____
_____
_____
_____
_____
_____
_____
_____
_____
_____

Chapter 12
Passive Constructions

In the active voice, the subject generally performs some action. In the passive voice, the subject is acted upon:

ACTIVE: **El alumno** *compró* **el libro.**　　*The student bought the book.*

PASSIVE: **El libro** *fue comprado por* **el alumno.**　　*The book was bought by the student.*

[1] FORMATION AND USE OF THE PASSIVE

If the agent (doer) is mentioned or implied, the passive construction in Spanish is similar to English: subject + form of **ser** + past participle + **por** + agent (doer):

Estas carreteras *fueron construidas por* **el gobierno.**	*These highways were built by the government.*
Todos mis amigos *han sido invitados por* **Carlos.**	*All my friends have been invited by Charles.*
La fiesta *será celebrada por* **los habitantes.**	*The festival will be celebrated by the inhabitants.*
Colón salió de España el 3 de agosto; América *fue* **descubierta el 12 de octubre.** (doer, Columbus, implied)	*Columbus left Spain on August 3; on October 12, America was discovered.*

NOTES:

1. In the passive, the past participle is used like an adjective and agrees with the subject in gender and number.
2. The agent is preceded by **por**. If the past participle expresses feeling or emotion, rather than action, **por** may be replaced by **de.**

Es amado (respetado, admirado) *de* **todos.**	*He is loved (respected, admired) by all.*
Era temido (odiado, envidiado) *de* **la gente.**	*He was feared (hated, envied) by the people.*

EJERCICIO A　　Hilda está muy orgullosa del papel que desempeñó su familia en el desarrollo de la ciudad. Escriba lo que Hilda le muestra a una amiga nueva durante un paseo por la ciudad. Use los verbos *construir, dedicar, pagar, plantar, regalar, terminar.*

EJEMPLO:　**Este rascacielos fue construido por mi abuelo.**

125

1. _____
   _____
   _____

2. _____
   _____
   _____

3. _____
   _____
   _____

4. _____
   _____
   _____

5. _____
   _____
   _____

6. _____
   _____
   _____

7. _____
   _____
   _____

8. _____
   _____
   _____

EJERCICIO B   En una fiesta, Gabriela cuenta quién preparó cada cosa. Escriba lo que dijo.

EJEMPLO: Manolo compró los refrescos.
Los refrescos fueron comprados por Manolo.

1. Estela preparó el pastel.

_____

2. Javier y Eduardo cocinaron la carne.

_____

3. Vicente colgó los adornos.

_____

4. Isabel puso la mesa.

_____

5. Sergio consiguió las tortillas.

_____

6. Luis escogió los discos.

_____

7. Raquel y yo hicimos los preparativos.

_____

8. Mi mamá pagó las cuentas.

_____

EJERCICIO C   Leonardo está leyendo un articulo en el periódico sobre la tormenta de anoche y quiere explicárselo a Jorge. Exprese lo que Leonardo dice, cambiando las frases a la voz pasiva.

1. Anoche una tormenta sorprendió a los habitantes.

_____

2. Las lluvias destruyeron muchos árboles.

_____

3. Un relámpago apagó todas las luces de la ciudad.

_____

4. El río inundó las calles.

_____

5. Las autoridades cerraron las escuelas.

_____

[2] SUBSTITUTE CONSTRUCTIONS FOR THE PASSIVE

a. If the agent (doer) is not mentioned or implied and the subject is a thing, the reflexive construction is preferred in Spanish. In such constructions, the subject usually follows the verb:

Aquí *se habla* español.	*Spanish is spoken here.*
Aquí *se hablan español y francés.*	*Spanish and French are spoken here.*
¿A qué hora *se cierran* las tiendas?	*At what time are the stores closed?*
Se publicó el libro.	*The book was published.*
Se perdieron los documentos.	*The documents were lost.*
Desde aquí *se pueden* ver los monumentos.	*From here the monuments can be seen.*

EJERCICIO D | El Círculo Español está preparando una cena. Escriba en qué tienda(s) se vende o se compra lo que van a necesitar.

carne molida	tortillas	queso
tomates	lechuga	rábanos
aceite	vinagre	cebollas
crema	servilletas	platos de papel
tenedores	cuchillos	

EJEMPLO: **En la lechería se vende crema.**
En la lechería se venden crema y queso.

_____

_____

_____

_____

_____

_____

EJERCICIO E | Es su primer día de trabajo en una oficina. Escriba lo que le dice su jefe.

EJEMPLO: llegar temprano a la oficina
Se llega temprano a la oficina.

1. contestar el teléfono en seguida

_____

2. recibir el correo por la mañana

_____

3. leer las cartas con cuidado

_____

4. escribir las cartas en la computadora

_____

5. tomar una hora de almuerzo

_____

6. llevar las cartas al correo

_____

7. comprar sellos en el correo

_____

8. archivar la correspondencia a diario

_____

9. poner los recados en los escritorios

_____

10. salir de la oficina a las cinco

_____

EJERCICIO F **Conteste las preguntas que le hace un primo que está de visita en su casa.**

1. ¿A qué hora se cerrarán las tiendas el sábado?

_____

2. ¿Cuándo se estrenará otra película en el cine?

_____

3. ¿Dónde se podrá encontrar una raqueta de tenis?

_____

4. ¿Cuándo se oirá el pronóstico del tiempo para mañana?

_____

5. ¿Dónde se comprarán regalos baratos?

_____

6. ¿Qué se venderá en la tienda de la esquina?

_____

7. ¿Dónde se podrá recibir el mejor tipo de cambio?

_____

8. ¿Cuánto se cobrará por entrar en el parque de diversiones?

_____

b. The pronoun **se** may also be used as an indefinite subject. In such constructions, **se** is not reflexive and is used only with the third person singular of the verb.

se dice:	*it is said, one says, people say, they say, you say*
se cree:	*it is believed, one believes, people believe, they believe, you believe*
se sabe:	*it is known, one knows, people know, they know, you know*

The forms **dicen** (they say), **creen** (they believe), and **saben** (they know) are used without **se:**

$$\left.\begin{array}{l}\textbf{Se dice}\\\textbf{Dicen}\end{array}\right\} \text{que es muy rico.} \quad \left.\begin{array}{l}\textit{It is said}\\\textit{They say}\end{array}\right\} \textit{that he is very rich.}$$

c. The indefinite **se** may be used to express the passive when the doer is indefinite (not mentioned or implied) and a person is acted upon.

Se **mató** *al hombre.*	*The man was killed.* *(Someone killed the man.)*
Se le **mató.**	*He was killed.* *(Someone killed him.)*
Se **mató** *a los hombres.*	*The men were killed.* *(Someone killed the men.)*
Se les **mató.**	*They were killed.* *(Someone killed them.)*
Se **castigará** *a la niña.*	*The child will be punished.* *(Someone will punish the child.)*
Se la **castigará.**	*She will be punished.* *(Someone will punish her.)*
Se **castigará** *a las niñas.*	*The children will be punished.* *(Someone will punish the children.)*
Se las **castigará.**	*They will be punished.* *(Someone will punish them.)*

NOTE: Although the person acted upon is a direct object, the forms **le** and **les** (instead of **lo** and **los**) are used for the masculine.

d. Instead of the indefinite **se** construction, the active third-person plural is often preferred.

Mataron al hombre (a los hombres).	*They killed the man (the men).* (indefinite)
Lo (los) mataron.	*They killed him (them).* (indefinite)
Castigarán a la niña (a las niñas).	*They will punish the child (the children).* (indefinite)
La (las) castigarán.	*They will punish her (them).* (indefinite)

[*3*] SUMMARY OF PASSIVE AND SUBSTITUTE CONSTRUCTIONS

	AGENT (DOER) EXPRESSED	AGENT (DOER) NOT EXPRESSED
	PASSIVE CONSTRUCTION SIMILAR TO ENGLISH	REFLEXIVE
THING	**Las camisas *serán vendidas por* el dependiente.**	***Se venderán* las camisas.**
		INDEFINITE
PERSON	**El alcalde *fue elegido por* el pueblo.**	***Se eligió* al alcalde. (*Se le* eligió.)** ***Eligieron* al alcalde. (*Lo eligieron.*)**

EJERCICIO G   Una madre da una lección a su hijo. Complete las frases con la forma necesaria del verbo apropiado. Escríbalas de dos maneras.

VERBOS: cruzar   saber   pagar
             comer   subir   aprender
             pasar   necesitar   decir
             entrar   poner

EJEMPLO: _____ gracias.
        Se dice gracias. **Dicen** gracias.

1. _____ por la escalera. _____ por la escalera.

2. _____ estudiando. _____ estudiando.

3. _____ la calle en la esquina. _____ la calle en la esquina.

4. _____ la mesa antes de comer. _____ la mesa antes de comer.

5. _____ por la puerta. _____ por la puerta.

6. _____ por favor. _____ por favor.

7. _____ que para comprar algo _____ dinero.

    _____ que para comprar algo _____ dinero.

8. _____ en el comedor. _____ en el comedor.

9. En el autobús _____ al entrar. En el autobús _____ al entrar.

EJERCICIO H   Paco es un niño que siempre repite lo que todos dicen. Escriba lo que él repitió cuando su mamá hablaba por teléfono.

EJEMPLO: Nombraron de jefe al Sr. Gómez.
        Se nombró de jefe al Sr. Gómez.
        Se le nombró de jefe.

1. Cogieron al hombre que robó la plata.

2. Acusaron al hombre del crimen.

3. Encerraron al ladrón en la cárcel.

4. Castigaron al ladrón.

5. Condenarán mañana al acusado.

M A S T E R Y   E X E R C I S E S

EJERCICIO I   El hermanito de Felipe hace muchas preguntas. Conteste las preguntas que él le hace mientras Ud. espera a su hermano.

1. ¿Cómo se dice «railroad» en español?

2. ¿A qué hora se cena en su casa?

3. ¿Qué se lee en un periódico?

4. ¿En dónde se compran medicinas?

5. ¿A quiénes se cura en un hospital?

6. ¿En dónde se encierra a los criminales?

7. ¿En qué países se habla portugués?

8. ¿Es respetado el presidente de la gente?

9. ¿Qué se dice cuando uno recibe un regalo?

10. ¿Por quién fue firmada la Declaración de Independencia?

EJERCICIO J   Escriba una carta a un(a) amigo(a) que vive en Lima, en la que Ud. describe una fiesta local que se celebra en su ciudad (pueblo, barrio). Piense en estas cosas.

cuándo se celebra; cómo se celebra; si se cierran los negocios o no;

qué actividades se ofrecen; por quién(es) es organizada la celebración; etc.

_____

_____

_____

_____

_____

_____

_____

EJERCICIO K   Describa una fiesta a la que Ud. asistió. Use formas de la voz pasiva donde sea possible.

EJEMPLO: La fiesta fue dada por mi amiga Alba. Se celebraba el cumpleaños de su novio, Jaime. Se invitó a todos los amigos de Jaime y de Alba. Se comenzó la celebración a las dos de la tarde . . . .

_____

_____

_____

_____

_____

_____

_____

_____

_____

_____

_____

Chapter 13
Subjunctive

FRANCIA

PORTUGAL ESPAÑA

○ Madrid Barcelona •

ITALIA

Islas Baleares

• Sevilla

[1] SUBJUNCTIVE IN SPANISH

Chapters 1 through 12 in this book deal with verb constructions in the indicative mood. The term *mood* describes the form of the verb showing the subject's attitude. In this and the next chapter, you will see how the subjunctive mood enables speakers of Spanish to express a variety of attitudes through different verb forms and constructions.

a. The indicative and the subjunctive

The indicative mood states facts and expresses certainty or reality. The subjunctive mood expresses uncertainty, doubt, wishes, desires, conjecture, supposition, and conditions that are unreal or contrary to fact. The subjunctive occurs much more frequently in Spanish than in English.

b. Use of the subjunctive

In Spanish, the subjunctive normally occurs in dependent clauses introduced by a conjunction or a relative pronoun.

[2] FORMS OF THE SUBJUNCTIVE

a. Present subjunctive of regular verbs

The present subjunctive of most verbs is formed by dropping the ending **-o** of the first person singular (yo form) of the present indicative and adding the following endings:

-ar verbs: *-e, -es, -e, -emos, -éis, -en*
-er
-ir } verbs: *-a, -as, -a, -amos, -áis, -an*

INFINITIVE	PRESENT INDICATIVE YO FORM	PRESENT SUBJUNCTIVE
tomar	tom*o*	tom*e*, tom*es*, tom*e*, tom*emos*, tom*éis*, tom*en*
comer	com*o*	com*a*, com*as*, com*a*, com*amos*, com*áis*, com*an*
escribir	escrib*o*	escrib*a*, escrib*as*, escrib*a*, escrib*amos*, escrib*áis*, escrib*an*

caber	que*po*	que*pa*, –*as*, –*a*, etc.
coger	co*jo*	co*ja*, –*as*, –*a*, etc.
conocer	cono*zco*	cono*zca*, –*as*, –*a*, etc.
destruir	destru*yo*	destru*ya*, –*as*, –*a*, etc.
distinguir	distin*go*	distin*ga*, –*as*, –*a*, etc.
salir	sal*go*	sal*ga*, –*as*, –*a*, etc.

b. Spelling changes in the present subjunctive

In the present subjunctive of verbs ending in –**car**, –**gar**, and –**zar**, **c** changes to **qu**, **g** to **gu**, and **z** to **c**. These spelling changes are the same as those that occur in the **yo** form of the preterit (see page 40).

INFINITIVE	PRETERIT YO FORM	PRESENT SUBJUNCTIVE
bus**car**	bus**qué**	bus**que**, -**es**, -**e**, etc.
pa**gar**	pa**gué**	pa**gue**, -**es**, -**e**, etc.
al**zar**	al**cé**	al**ce**, -**es**, -**e**, etc.

NOTE: In the verb **averiguar**, the **u** changes to **ü** before an **e** in order to keep the sound of the **u**, which otherwise would be silent.

PRETERIT: **averigüé**
PRESENT SUBJUNCTIVE: **averigüe**

c. Stem-changing verbs in the present subjunctive

(1) Stem-changing –**ar** and –**er** verbs have the same stem changes in the present subjunctive as in the present indicative (**e** to **ie**, **o** to **ue**).

cerrar: c*ie*rre, c*ie*rres, c*ie*rre, cerremos, cerréis, c*ie*rren
volver: v*ue*lva, v*ue*lvas, v*ue*lva, volvamos, volváis, v*ue*lvan

(2) Stem-changing –**ir** verbs have the same stem changes in the present subjunctive as in the present indicative (**e** to **ie**, **o** to **ue**, **e** to **i**). In the **nosotros** and **vosotros** forms, the stem vowel **e** changes to **i** and the stem vowel **o** changes to **u**.

sentir: s*ie*nta, s*ie*ntas, s*ie*nta, s*i*ntamos, s*i*ntáis, s*ie*ntan
dormir: d*ue*rma, d*ue*rmas, d*ue*rma, d*u*rmamos, d*u*rmáis, d*ue*rman
pedir: p*i*da, p*i*das, p*i*da, p*i*damos, p*i*dáis, p*i*dan

(3) Some verbs ending in –**iar** or –**uar** have an accent mark on the **i** or the **u** (**í**, **ú**) in all forms except those for **nosotros** and **vosotros**.

enviar: env*í*e, env*í*es, env*í*e, enviemos, enviéis, env*í*en
continuar: contin*ú*e, contin*ú*es, contin*ú*e, continuemos, continuéis, contin*ú*en

d. Present subjunctive of irregular verbs

The following verbs have irregular forms in the present subjunctive:

dar: *dé*, **des**, *dé*, **demos**, **deis**, **den**
estar: *esté*, *estés*, *esté*, **estemos**, **estéis**, *estén*
haber: *haya*, *hayas*, *haya*, *hayamos*, *hayáis*, *hayan*

ir:	*vaya, vayas, vaya, vayamos, vayáis, vayan*
saber:	*sepa, sepas, sepa, sepamos, sepáis, sepan*
ser:	*sea, seas, sea, seamos, seáis, sean*

NOTE: The subjunctive form **vaya** is used colloquially to express *what a*.

¡*Vaya* **lío en que estoy metido!**	*What a mess I am involved in!*
¡*Vaya* **memoria la suya!** Sabe todas las fechas históricas.	*What a memory he has! He knows all the historical dates.*

e. Imperfect subjunctive

The imperfect subjunctive of all verbs is formed by dropping the **–ron** ending of the third-person plural of the preterit tense and adding either the **–ra** or **–se** endings.

–ra, –ras, –ra, ´–ramos, –rais, –ran

–se, –ses, –se, ´–semos, –seis, –sen

INFINITIVE	PRETERIT THIRD PLURAL	IMPERFECT SUBJUNCTIVE
llegar	**llega***ron*	**llega***ra,* **llega***ras,* **llega***ra,* **llegá***ramos,* **llega***rais,* **llega***ran* *or* **llega***se,* **llega***ses,* **llega***se,* **llegá***semos,* **llega***seis,* **llega***sen*
vender	**vendie***ron*	**vendie***ra,* **vendie***ras,* **vendie***ra,* **vendié***ramos,* **vendie***rais,* **vendie***ran* *or* **vendie***se,* **vendie***ses,* **vendie***se,* **vendié***semos,* **vendie***seis,* **vendie***sen*
dormir	**durmie***ron*	**durmie***ra,* **durmie***ras,* etc., *or* **durmie***se,* **durmie***ses,* etc.
pedir	**pidie***ron*	**pidie***ra,* etc., *or* **pidie***se,* etc.
decir	**dije***ron*	**dije***ra,* etc., *or* **dije***se,* etc.
ir, ser	**fue***ron*	**fue***ra,* etc., *or* **fue***se,* etc.
creer	**creye***ron*	**creye***ra,* etc., *or* **creye***se,* etc.

NOTE: The **nosotros** form of the imperfect subjunctive is the only form that has an accent mark (on the vowel immediately before the ending).

f. Perfect subjunctive and pluperfect subjunctive

(1) The perfect subjunctive consists of the present subjunctive of **haber** plus a past participle.

haya		hayamos	
hayas	entrado	hayáis	entrado
haya		hayan	

(2) The pluperfect subjunctive consists of the imperfect subjunctive of **haber** plus a past participle.

hubiera (hubiese)		hubiéramos (hubiésemos)	
hubieras (hubieses)	dicho	hubierais (hubieseis)	dicho
hubiera (hubiese)		hubieran (hubiesen)	

[3] USES OF THE SUBJUNCTIVE

The subjunctive in dependent clauses is introduced by the conjunction **que**.

a. The subjunctive is used after verbs and expressions of advice, command, demand, desire, hope, permission, preference, prohibition, request, and suggestion.

aconsejar *to advise*	**insistir (en)** *to insist (on)*	**preferir** *to prefer*
decir *to tell (to order)*	**mandar** *to command, to order*	**prohibir** *to forbid, to*
dejar *to let, to allow*	**¡ojalá (que)... !** *I wish (hope)*	*prohibit*
desear *to wish, to want*	*that... ! If only... !*	**querer** *to wish, to want*
esperar *to hope*	**pedir** *to request, to ask for*	**rogar** *to beg, to request*
exigir *to require, to demand*	**permitir** *to permit, to allow*	**sugerir** *to suggest*
hacer *to make, to cause*	**suplicar** *to beg, to plead*	

Le aconsejaron que *saliera* **en seguida.**	*They advised him to leave at once.*
Les digo que *entren.*	*I tell them to enter (that they should enter).*
Quieren que *lleguemos* **temprano.**	*They want us to arrive early.*
¡Ojalá que Uds. no *se enfermen***!**	*I hope (that) you don't become ill!*
Espero que *se queden* **aquí.**	*I hope (that) they remain here.*
El profesor no permite que los alumnos *hablen* **en la clase.**	*The teacher does not permit the pupils to speak in class.*
Mis padres prefieren que yo no *mire* **ese programa de televisión.**	*My parents prefer that I do not watch that television program.*
Te ruego que *vengas.*	*I beg you to come.*

NOTES:

1. In all of the examples above, the verb in the main clause and the verb in the dependent clause have different subjects. If the subjects in both clauses are the same, **que** is omitted and the infinitive is used instead of the subjunctive.

Ellos quieren *ir* **a la fiesta.**	*They wish to go to the party.*
Mis hermanos prefieren *ver* **esa película.**	*My brothers prefer to see that movie.*

2. The verbs **dejar, hacer, mandar, permitir,** and **prohibir** may be followed by either the subjunctive or the infinitive.

Me manda que *salga.* ⎫
Me manda *salir.* ⎬ *He orders me to leave.*

Déjele que *hable.* ⎫
Déjele *hablar.* ⎬ *Let him speak.*

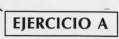

EJERCICIO A   Escriba el comentario que hace Roberto sobre estas personas.

mi madre	aconsejar	yo	pintar el cuarto
mi padre	decir	mi hermano(a)	lavar el coche
mis padres	desear	mis hermanos	estudiar más
el profesor	esperar	mis hermanos y yo	acostarse temprano
mi tío	exigir	tú	no salir por la noche
tú	hacer		buscar trabajo

yo	insistir (en)	descansar después de cenar
	pedir	ir de compras
	preferir	llegar temprano
	rogar	quedarse en casa

EJEMPLO: **Mi padre *insiste* en que mi hermana no *salga* por la noche.**

1. _____

2. _____

3. _____

4. _____

5. _____

6. _____

7. _____

8. _____

9. _____

10. _____

b. The subjunctive is used after verbs and expressions of feeling or emotion, such as fear, joy, sorrow, regret, surprise.

alegrarse (de) *to be glad*   **temer** *to fear*

sentir *to be sorry, to regret*   **tener miedo (de)** *to fear, to be afraid*

sorprenderse (de) *to be surprised*

Temían que no *volviera*.	*They were afraid that he would not return.*
Me alegro de que Uds. lo *hayan visto*.	*I am glad that you have seen it.*
Sentimos que ellos no *puedan* hacer el viaje con nosotros.	*We regret (We are sorry) that they cannot make the trip with us.*
¿Se sorprenden Uds. de que *haya* examen hoy?	*Are you surprised that there is an examination today?*

EJERCICIO B   **Unos parientes de Rosa acaban de llegar de Quito. Escriba lo que dice Rosa.**

EJEMPLO: yo / sorprenderse / ellos / saber hablar inglés
               Yo me sorprendo de que ellos sepan hablar inglés.

1. yo / alegrarse / ellos / haber venido

_____

2. yo / alegrarse / ellos / quedarse aquí por un mes

_____

3. yo / temer / ellos / no tener bastante dinero

_____

4. yo / tener miedo / ellos / ir a aburrirse

_____

5. yo / sentir / ellos / no poder quedarse aquí por más tiempo

_____

6. yo / lamentar / nosotros / no haberlos conocido hasta ahora

_____

| EJERCICIO C | Escriba la reacción de estas personas en cada circunstancia. Use los verbos dados entre paréntesis. |

EJEMPLO: Adolfo acaba de recibir una carta de sus primos en que dicen que aceptan
su invitación. (alegrarse)
Adolfo se alegra de que sus primos hayan aceptado su invitación.

1. Los jardineros cortaron el árbol favorito de la señora Leña. Ella está muy triste. (sentir)
La señora Leña _____.

2. Robaron en la casa de mi abuela. Ahora ella está muy asustada. (lamentar)
Mi abuela _____.

3. Al salir del examen final, Rafael le cuenta a un amigo que el examen fue muy fácil. (alegrarse)
Su amigo _____.

4. Los padres de Rocío le regalaron un coche. Ella no puede creerlo. (sorprenderse)
Rocío _____.

| EJERCICIO D | Escriba lo que sienten estas personas al saber lo siguiente: |

todo el mundo	alegrarse
mi padre	sorprenderse
los trabajadores	temer
los dueños	tener miedo de
yo	sentir
mis amigos y yo	

EJEMPLO: Cancelan muchos vuelos a causa de la neblina.
**Todo el mundo tiene miedo de que cancelen muchos vuelos a causa de
la neblina.**

1. El gobierno ha aumentado los impuestos.

_____

2. Ahora hay más trabajos.

_____

3. Se han acabado las huelgas.

_____

4. Cada empleado recibirá un aguinaldo bueno.

_____

5. Van a mejorar el servicio de correos.

_____

6. Habrá escasez de agua potable en las ciudades del norte.

_____

7. Las universidades rechazan mil solicitudes de estudiantes.

_____

8. Un cantante popular dará un concierto especial.

_____

9. Los «Azules» han ganado el campeonato mundial.

_____

10. Los campesinos no producen bastante trigo.

_____

EJERCICIO E   Ud. acaba de cambiar de escuela. Escriba cinco frases en las que Ud. describe sus emociones al entrar en la nueva escuela. Use uno de los verbos siguientes en cada frase: *alegrarse (de), sentir, sorprenderse (de), temer* o *tener miedo (de).*

EJEMPLO: **Yo temo que nadie me hable.**

1. _____

2. _____

3. _____

4. _____

5. _____

EJERCICIO F   Cambie las frases que Ud. escribió en el Ejercicio E al pasado del subjuntivo.

EJEMPLO: Yo **temía** que nadie me **hablara (hablase).**

1. _____

2. _____

3. _____

4. _____

5. _____

c. The subjunctive is used after verbs and expressions of doubt, disbelief, denial.

dudar *to doubt*   no creer *not to believe*   negar *to deny*

Dudamos que lo *sepan.*	*We doubt that they know it.*
No creo que Pedro lo *halle.*	*I don't believe that Peter will find it.*
Niegan que esto *sea* importante.	*They deny that this is important.*

NOTES:

1. The verb **creer,** when used interrogatively, indicates uncertainty and is usually followed by the subjunctive.

    ¿Cree Ud. que *vengan?*   *Do you believe that they are coming?*

2. **Creer, no dudar,** and **no negar** indicate belief or certainty and are usually followed by the indicative.

    Creo (No dudo, No niego) que Pedro   *I believe (I don't doubt, I don't deny)*
    lo **hallará.**   *that Pedro will find it.*

EJERCICIO G   **Su hermanito nunca cree lo que Ud. le cuenta. Escriba lo que dice su hermanito, usando *no creo* o *dudo.***

EJEMPLO: Yo conozco a Michael Jackson.
             Dudo que tú conozcas a Michael Jackson.

1. Nosotros te regalaremos una bicicleta.

_____

2. Eduardo juega al tenis todos los días.

_____

3. Este anillo vale más de mil dólares.

_____

4. Hay un programa interesante en la televisión.

_____

5. Tú y yo prepararemos la cena hoy.

_____

6. Estela tiene dieciséis años.

_____

7. Yo salgo con mis amigos esta noche.

_____

8. Mis padres te van a castigar.

_____

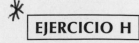

EJERCICIO H   **Escriba quién duda o no cree lo siguiente (yo, tú, mis amigos, mis padres, mi profesor).**

1. Rafael se graduará con su clase.

_____

2. Yo saco buenas notas en los exámenes.

_____

3. Mis hermanos y yo nos acostamos temprano hoy.

_____

4. Sofía busca otro trabajo.

_____

5. Nosotros vamos a la playa el sábado.

_____

6. Tú me prestas tu carro nuevo.

_____

7. Carlos trae sus discos compactos favoritos a la fiesta.

_____

EJERCICIO I	**Escriba quién niega estas cosas.**

EJEMPLO: La casa está terminada. (el ingeniero)
           El ingeniero niega que la casa esté terminada.

1. Los impuestos son altos. (el presidente)

_____

2. Yo trabajo bien aquí. (mi jefe)

_____

3. El examen es difícil. (la profesora)

_____

4. Los niños pueden romper la ventana. (la madre)

_____

5. Roberto hace muchas llamadas personales. (la telefonista)

_____

EJERCICIO J	**Escriba lo que piensa Carlos mientras escucha el pronóstico del tiempo. Use** *dudar, no creer* **o** *negar* **en cada frase.**

EJEMPLO: La tormenta puede causar muchos daños.
           Dudo que la tormenta pueda causar muchos daños.

1. La tormenta comenzará a eso de las siete.

_____

2. Los vientos serán muy fuertes.

_____

3. Uds. no deben salir de su casa.

_____

4. Habrá muchos relámpagos y truenos.

_____

5. Las autoridades ayudarán a las personas.

_____

6. Las lluvias inundarán las calles.

_____

7. Habrá muchos heridos.

_____

8. Perderemos el servicio de teléfonos.

_____

9. El desastre durará varias horas.

_____

10. Se apagará la luz.

_____

d. The subjunctive is used after impersonal expressions of possibility, doubt, uncertainty, necessity, emotion, and the like. If the impersonal expression indicates certainty, the indicative is used.

es dudoso *it is doubtful*	**es menester**
es importante *it is important*	**es necesario** } *it is necessary*
es imposible *it is impossible*	**es preciso**
es una lástima *it is a pity*	**es posible** *it is possible*
es mejor } *it is better*	**es probable** *it is probable*
más vale	**es importante** *it is important*

Es preciso **que** yo lo *compre.* — It is necessary that I buy (for me to buy) it.
Era *importante* **que** lo *viéramos.* — It was important that we see (for us to see) it.
Más vale **que** *llegues* temprano. — It is better for you to arrive early.
Es probable **que** *vayan.* — It is probable that they will go.
Es posible **que** Juan *esté* enfermo. — It is possible that Juan is sick.
But:
Es cierto **que** *irán.* — It is certain that they will go.
Es evidente **que** él no lo *sabe.* — It is evident that he does not know it.

Es verdad que Juan *está* enfermo.   *It is true that John is sick.*
No cabe duda que llegan (llegarán)   *There is no doubt they will arrive tomorrow.*
mañana.

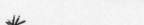

EJERCICIO K   Ud. y un amigo hablan de una fiesta que Ud. va a dar en su casa. Escriba lo
que Uds. dicen.

EJEMPLO: es probable / Rodolfo / no querer cantar
Es probable que Rodolfo no quiera cantar.

1. es preciso / mi mamá / ir al supermercado

_____

2. es dudoso / Elena / traer algunos discos compactos

_____

3. es importante / tú / estar aquí temprano

_____

4. es mejor / los hermanos Soto / no venir

_____

5. es imposible / Sarita / tener otro compromiso

_____

6. es necesario / nosotros / preparar comida para veinte personas

_____

7. es menester / yo / ayudarle a mi mamá

_____

8. mas vale / todo el mundo / divertirse

_____

EJERCICIO L   Juan trabaja de asistente de vuelo y habla con los pasajeros. Escriba lo que
dice.

es necesario	el capitán	hacer un anuncio
es importante	los pasajeros	seguir las instrucciones de seguridad
es dudoso	los niños	obedecer la señal de abrocharse el cinturón de seguridad
es mejor	todo el mundo	tomar su asiento en seguida
es posible	nosotros	permanecer sentado(s)
	yo	poner sus cosas debajo del asiento
		llegar a tiempo
		ayudar a los otros pasajeros
		prestar mucha atención

EJEMPLO: **Es probable que nosotros evitemos una tempestad.**

1. _____
2. _____
3. _____
4. _____
5. _____
6. _____
7. _____
8. _____

EJERCICIO M   Escriba siete cosas que Ud. cree necesarias o importantes para mejorar las condiciones de la ciudad en que Ud. vive. Use una expresión impersonal en cada frase.

EJEMPLOS: **Es importante que los ciudadanos obedezcan las leyes.**

Es menester que los parques estén limpios.

1. _____
2. _____
3. _____
4. _____
5. _____
6. _____
7. _____

EJERCICIO N   Mientras Ud. estaba de vacaciones un vecino cuidó sus plantas. Usando la expresión impersonal dada en cada frase, escriba su respuesta al comentario de su vecino.

EJEMPLO: Es menester que esta planta tenga sombra. (Es claro)
Es claro que esta planta tiene sombra.

1. Es evidente que yo he regado las plantas. (Es dudoso)

_____

2. Es necesario que las plantas estén al sol. (Es verdad)

_____

3. Es posible que yo haya cortado esta planta. (Es claro)

_____

4. Es una lástima que esta planta haya muerto. (Es cierto)

_____

5. Es dudoso que yo haya dañado las plantas. (No cabe duda)

_____

[4] SEQUENCE OF TENSES

The tense of the subjunctive depends on the form of the main verb.

VERB IN MAIN CLAUSE	VERB IN DEPENDENT CLAUSE
Present Indicative **Present Perfect** **Future** **Command**	**Present Subjunctive** *or* **Perfect Subjunctive**
Imperfect **Preterit** **Conditional** **Pluperfect**	**Imperfect Subjunctive** *or* **Pluperfect Subjunctive**

No { **permite** (present) **permitirá** (future) **ha permitido** (present perfect) **permita Ud.** (command) } que los jóvenes **entren.** (present subjunctive)

He does not permit / He will not permit / He has not permitted / Do not permit } the youngsters to enter (that the youngsters enter).

No { **permitía** (imperfect) **permitió** (preterit) **permitiría** (conditional) **había permitido** (pluperfect) } que los jóvenes **entraran (entrasen).** (imperfect subjunctive)

He did not permit / He did not permit / He would not permit / He had not permitted } the youngsters to enter (that the youngsters enter).

Dudo que lo *hayan visto.*
(present) (perfect subjunctive)

I doubt that they have seen it.

Dudaba que lo *hubieran (hubiesen) visto.*
(imperfect) (pluperfect subjunctive)

I doubted that they had seen it.

✳ | EJERCICIO O | **Complete estos cuentitos con la forma correcta de los verbos dados en paréntesis.**

1. La madre de Juan espera visita esta noche. Ella desea que Juan le ___ayude___ . Le dice a
 ‎ *1.* (ayudar)

Juan que ___ponga___ la mesa primero. Después es necesario que Juan ___vaya___
 ‎ ‎ ‎ ‎ ‎ ‎ *2.* (poner) ‎ *3.* (ir)

al mercado. Juan quiere ___usar___ su bicicleta pero su madre le prohibió que
 ‎ *4.* (usar)

___vaya___ allí en bicicleta. Es una lástima que Juan no ___pueda___ ir en bicicleta
 ‎ ‎ ‎ ‎ *5.* (ir) ‎ *6.* (poder)

porque su madre quiere ___tener___ todo listo y los invitados llegan en quince minutos.
 ‎ ‎ ‎ ‎ ‎ ‎ ‎ ‎ ‎ ‎ ‎ ‎ ‎ ‎ ‎ ‎ ‎ *7.* (tener)

2. Hoy es un día horrible para Rafael. Sus padres mandaron que él ___vaya___ a la peluquería.
 ‎ *1.* (ir)

No cabe duda de que Rafael ___cumpla___ porque si no, sus padres no van a permitir que
 ‎ *2.* (cumplir)

él ___acompañe___ a sus amigos al campo el domingo. ¡Pobre Rafael! Él no creía que la
 ‎ ‎ ‎ ‎ ‎ ‎ ‎ ‎ *3.* (acompañar)

peluquería ___esté___ cerrada aquel día. No buscó otra porque temía que otro peluquero
 ‎ ‎ ‎ ‎ ‎ ‎ ‎ ‎ ‎ ‎ ‎ *4.* (estar)

le ___corte___ mal el pelo. Ahora es probable que Rafael ___pase___ todo el día
 ‎ ‎ ‎ ‎ *5.* (cortar) ‎ *6.* (pasar)

en casa. ¡Ojalá que no ___espere___ tanto la próxima vez!
 ‎ ‎ ‎ ‎ ‎ ‎ ‎ ‎ ‎ ‎ ‎ *7.* (esperar)

3. Ayer pasé un día interesante en la corte. El juez prohibió que el preso ___proteste___ contra el
 ‎ *1.* (protestar)

castigo. Pero no cabía duda de que el preso ___se crea___ inocente. Su abogado le había
 ‎ *2.* (creerse)

aconsejado que ___diga___ la verdad. Era evidente que el jurado no le ___cree___
 ‎ ‎ ‎ ‎ ‎ ‎ ‎ *3.* (decir) ‎ *4.* (creer)

cuando dio su declaración. Según el veredicto, es necesario que el preso ___permanezca___ en la
 ‎ *5.* (permanecer)

cárcel por cinco años, por lo menos. Es dudoso que ___haya___ otro juicio porque el abo-
 ‎ *6.* (haber)

gado teme que el fiscal ___llame___ a otros testigos.
 ‎ ‎ ‎ ‎ ‎ ‎ ‎ ‎ ‎ ‎ *7.* (llamar)

4. Es posible que el primer día de clases no le ___agrade___ a Luis. Este año hicieron que él
 ‎ *1.* (agradar)

___tome___ unas materias muy difíciles. El año pasado el profesor exigió que sus estudiantes
 ‎ ‎ ‎ *2.* (tomar)

_____ muchos trabajos y era difícil que muchos alumnos _____ una
 ‎ ‎ *3.* (hacer) ‎ *4.* (sacar)

buena nota. Sus amigos le aconsejaron que no _____ nunca a la clase porque
 ‎ *5.* (faltar)

el profesor no aprueba que los alumnos _____ su clase. Es seguro que Luis
 ‎ *6.* (perder)

_____ que estudiar mucho este año.
 ‎ ‎ *7.* (tener)

5. Esperaban que la nieve _____ los montes con un manto blanco. Los amigos deseaban
1. (cubrir)

_____ a esquiar y para hacerlo, era preciso que _____ mucho. Joaquín
2. (ir)   *3.* (nevar)

pidió que su padre le _____ cien dólares para la excursión. Su padre sabía que era
4. (prestar)

dudoso que Joaquín le _____ el dinero, pero quería que su hijo _____ .
5. (devolver)   *6.* (divertirse)

Sólo le suplicó que _____ cuidado porque era probable que los montes
7. (tener)

_____ cubiertos de hielo por la lluvia del otro día. Al despedirse de los jóvenes el
8. (estar)

padre murmuró: «¡Ojalá que yo _____ ir a esquiar también! Es evidente que estos
9. (poder)

jóvenes _____ divertirse».
10. (saber)

EJERCICIO P   **Escriba la forma correcta de los verbos entre paréntesis para completar los comentarios de un profesor a sus alumnos en un examen.**

1. ¿Es posible que Ud. *quiera* decir otra cosa? (querer)

2. Exijo que tú *estudies* más. (estudiar)

3. Prefiero que no lo *diga* de esta manera. (decir)

4. Me sorprendí de que Ud. _____ eso. (pensar)

5. Es lástima que Ud. no lo *aprenda* aún. (aprender)

6. Dudo que alguien te *comprenda* . (comprender)

7. Me alegré de que tú _____ el final del cuento. (adivinar)

8. Nadie pide que yo se lo *explique* otra vez. (explicar)

9. Es verdad que tú *escribes* muy claramente. (escribir)

10. Sería mejor que tú _____ después de la clase para recibir ayuda especial. (venir)

M A S T E R Y E X E R C I S E S

EJERCICIO Q   **Usando las expresiones dadas, escriba ocho frases que formarán una carta en la que Ud. acepta la invitación de un(a) amigo(a).**

1. Me alegré de _____

_____

2. No creía _____

_____

3. Insisto en _____

_____

4. Es dudoso _____

_____

5. Sentí _____

_____

6. Quería _____

_____

7. Será necesario _____

_____

8. Espero _____

_____

| EJERCICIO R | **Ud. va a graduarse de la universidad y tiene ganas de mudarse a vivir a una ciudad grande. Sus padres siempre lo (la) han consentido mucho y Ud. debe convencerlos de los méritos de sus ideas. Prepare las cosas que Ud. mencionará para convencerles. Use verbos y expresiones como esperar, querer, rogar, dudar, temer, permitir, decir, es necesario (importante, mejor, una lástima, etc.) para expresar sus ideas.** |

_____

_____

_____

_____

_____

_____

_____

_____

_____

_____

_____

_____

_____

Chapter 14
Subjunctive (Continued)

FRANCIA
PORTUGAL
ESPAÑA
Barcelona
Madrid
Islas Baleares
ITALIA
Sevilla

[1] SUBJUNCTIVE IN DEPENDENT ADVERB CLAUSES

Adverb clauses are introduced by certain conjunctions and questions that state or imply *when?, where?, why?,* and similar question words.

a. The subjunctive is used in dependent clauses that express uncertainty, doubt, purpose, anticipation, or proviso. Such clauses are usually introduced by the following conjunctions:

a fin de que ⎫
para que ⎭ *in order that, so that*

a menos que *unless*

antes (de) que *before*

con tal que *provided that*

en caso de que *in case (that)*

sin que *without*

Terminaré el trabajo **antes de que** ellos **vuelvan**.	*I will finish the work before they return* [whenever that may be].
Leyó el artículo despacio **para que pudiéramos** entenderlo.	*He read the article slowly so that we could understand it.* [We may or may not have understood it.]
Salió **sin que** yo lo *supiera*.	*He left without my knowing it* [in such a way that I would not know it].

EJERCICIO A   Conteste las preguntas que Ud. le hace a una amiga a quien no le gusta hacer nada sin Ud.

EJEMPLO: ¿Deseas ir a la fiesta?
Iré a la fiesta con tal que tú vayas también.

1. ¿Deseas jugar al tenis?

_____

2. ¿Deseas ir de compras?

_____

3. ¿Deseas asistir a la reunión?

_____

4. ¿Deseas visitar a María?

_____

5. ¿Deseas ver una película?

_____

✳ | **EJERCICIO B** | Conteste las preguntas que Ud. le hace a una hermana menor que no hace nada sola.

EJEMPLO: ¿Vas a comer?
No comeré a menos que tú comas también.

1. ¿Vas a almorzar? _____

2. ¿Vas a dormir la siesta? _____

3. ¿Vas a arreglar tu cuarto? _____

4. ¿Vas a ayudarle a mamá? _____

5. ¿Vas a dar un paseo? _____

| **EJERCICIO C** | Conteste las preguntas que un amigo le hace usando la expresión *sin que*.

EJEMPLO: ¿Viste a Tomás?
No, él se fue sin que yo lo viera.

1. ¿Hablaste con Carlos?

_____

2. ¿Le diste el dinero a Jaime?

_____

3. ¿Le mostraste la foto a Pedro?

_____

4. ¿Le leíste la carta a Alfonso?

_____

5. ¿Invitaste a Gloria?

_____

| **EJERCICIO D** | Complete los comentarios que su tía le hace a su mamá mientras preparan la visita de unos primos. Complete cada frase con una conclusión final lógica usando una de las siguientes expresiones: *antes de que, con tal que, en caso de que o a menos que.*

EJEMPLO: Saldremos para el aeropuerto a las 10...
Saldremos para el aeropuerto a las 10, a menos que quieras salir antes.

1. Mi hija Alicia nos podrá acompañar al aeropuerto _____ .

2. El avión llegará a las 12 _____ .

3. De todos modos, yo te llamaré _____ .

4. Los primos piensan marcharse el viernes _____ .

5. Me gustaría invitarlos a cenar una noche _____ .

EJERCICIO E Escriba una pregunta como respuesta a las preguntas que le hace un amigo con quien Ud. va a salir el domingo.

EJEMPLO: ¿Va a nevar?
¿Qué haremos en caso de que nieve?

1. ¿Va a llover?

_____

2. ¿Va a hacer frío?

_____

3. ¿Va a costar mucho?

_____

4. ¿Vas a llegar tarde?

_____

5. ¿Vas a tener que trabajar?

_____

EJERCICIO F Ud. va a viajar por España con un pariente que visita España por primera vez. Escriba lo que Uds. van hacer.

EJEMPLO: Alquilaremos un carro / para que / tú / conocer los pueblos
Alquilaremos un carro **para que tú conozcas** los pueblos.

1. Iremos a la Costa del Sol / con tal que / no costar mucho

_____

2. Mandaré tarjetas postales / antes de que / yo / gastar todo el dinero

_____

3. Llevaré mi cámara / en caso de que / no vender fotos

_____

4. No iré a Barcelona / a menos que / tú / acompañarme

_____

5. Visitaremos El Prado / a menos que / tú / aburrirse

_____

6. Pasaremos tiempo en El Retiro / para que / tú / remar en el lago

_____

7. Te llevaré al Palacio Real / a fin de que / nosotros / ver los tesoros

_____

8. Nos quedaremos en Granada / con tal que / no hacer mucho calor

_____

EJERCICIO G	Escriba por qué un millonario ha comprado las cosas indicadas. Use una expresión diferente en cada frase: *para que, a fin de que, a menos que, antes (de) que, con tal que, en caso de que,* o *sin que.*

EJEMPLO: un avión

          Compró un avión para que su mujer pudiera viajar más fácilmente.

1. un televisor plasma

_____

2. tres entradas para el partido de fútbol

_____

3. una casa grande

_____

4. un carro lujoso

_____

5. un reloj de oro

_____

6. una casa en la playa

_____

7. una grabadora de video

_____

    b. The following conjunctions require the subjunctive if uncertainty, doubt, anticipation, or indefiniteness is implied. Otherwise, the indicative is used.

aunque *although, even though, even if*

cuando *when*

de manera que ⎫

de modo que ⎬ *so that*

después (de) que *after*

en cuanto ⎫

luego que ⎪

tan pronto como ⎬ *as soon as*

así que ⎪

hasta que *until*

mientras *while*

SUBJUNCTIVE	INDICATIVE
Aunque cueste **mucho dinero, lo comprar****é.**	*Aunque costó* **mucho dinero, lo compré.**
Although it may cost a lot of money, I'll buy it. [I don't know how much it costs.]	*Although it cost a lot of money, I bought it.* [It did cost a lot of money.]
Espere Ud. *hasta que* **ellos** *vengan.*	**Esperó** *hasta que* **ellos** *vinieron.*
Wait until they come [whenever that may be].	*He waited until they came.* [They did arrive.]
Te llamaré *cuando llegue* **a casa.**	**Siempre me llama** *cuando llega* **a casa.**
I will call you when I arrive home [whenever that may be].	*He always calls me when he arrives home* [his normal custom].

Leyó despacio, *de modo que* ellos *pudieran* entender.
He read slowly, so that they would be able to understand. [It's not known if they understood.]

Leyó despacio, *de modo que* ellos *pudieron* entender.
He read slowly, so that they were able to understand. [They understood.]

Dijo que lo haría *así que le pagáramos*.
He said he would do it as soon as we paid him.

Lo hizo *así que le pagamos*.
He did it as soon as we paid him.

NOTE: If the subjects of the main and the dependent clauses are the same, **que** is usually omitted and the infinitive is used.

Terminaré el trabajo *antes de volver*.
I will finish the work before I return (before returning).

Espere Ud. *hasta volver* a casa.
Wait until you return home (until returning home).

Leyó el artículo despacio *para entenderlo*.
He read the article slowly in order to understand it.

Salió *sin decir* adiós.
He left without saying good-bye.

EJERCICIO H   Escriba lo que Miguel dice que no va hacer ahora que no habla con su hermano.

EJEMPLO: cuidarlo / tener tiempo
No voy a cuidarlo aunque yo tenga tiempo.

1. ayudarle / necesitar ayuda

_____

2. comprarle un regalo / ser su cumpleaños

_____

3. prestarle el guante de béisbol / querer usarlo

_____

4. darle de comer / tener hambre

_____

5. devolverle la cámara / ser suya

_____

EJERCICIO I   Escriba lo que cuenta Adela de cómo ayuda a unas amigas.

EJEMPLO: Prometen avisarme / cuando / ellas / estar listas
Prometen avisarme **cuando ellas estén** listas.

1. Sé que les gustará el apartamento / luego que / ellas / verlo

_____

2. Revisan los muebles / de modo que / el dueño / no enojarse

_____

3. Deciden mudarse / en cuanto / ellas / firmar el contrato

_____

4. No les entregará el apartamento / hasta que / ellas / pagar el alquiler

_____

5. Tomarán el apartamento / aunque / no ser muy grande

_____

| EJERCICIO J | Escriba las frases del Ejercicio I, cambiándolas al pasado. |

EJEMPLO: Prometieron avisarme / cuando / ellas / estar listas
Prometieron avisarme **cuando estuvieran** listas.

1. Sabía que les gustaría el apartamento / que / ellas / verlo

_____

2. Revisaron los muebles / de modo que / el dueño / no enojarse

_____

3. Decidieron mudarse / en cuanto / ellas / firmar el contrato

_____

4. No les entregaba el apartamento / hasta que / ellas / pagar el alquiler

_____

5. Tomaban el apartamento / aunque / no ser muy grande

_____

| EJERCICIO K | Lola es la directora de un teatro de aficionados. Conteste las preguntas que le hace un miembro del grupo. |

EJEMPLO: ¿Cuándo se cerrará la puerta? (después de que / todos / llegar)
La puerta se cerrará después de que lleguen todos.

1. ¿Cuándo se quitarán el abrigo los señores? (así que/ ellos/ entrar en / el teatro)

_____

2. ¿Se callará el público? (en cuanto / alzarse el telón)

_____

3. ¿Cómo arreglaremos los asientos? (de modo que / el público / poder ver la función)

_____

4. ¿Cuándo se apagarán las luces? (tan pronto como / el locutor / aparecer en el escenario)

_____

5. ¿Se presentará la función si no hay público? (aunque / haber sólo dos personas)

_____

6. ¿Cuándo se limpiará el escenario? (después de que / la gente / salir del teatro)

_____

    c. The subjunctive is used after compounds of **–quiera** and similar indefinite expressions.

    dondequiera   _wherever_
    cualquier(a) (pl. **cualesquiera**)   _whatever, any_
    quienquiera (pl. **quienesquiera**)   _whoever_
    cuandoquiera   _whenever_
    por + adj. or adv. + **que**   _however, no matter how_

No se lo daré, _quienquiera que sea._	_I will not give it to him, whoever he may be._
Aceptaré _cualquier_ **puesto que** Ud. me ofrezca.	_I will accept any job (that) you offer me._
Por difícil que sea, lo haré.	_However (No matter how) difficult it may be, I will do it._

EJERCICIO L   **Conteste las preguntas que alguien le hace a Ud. sobre otro amigo.**

EJEMPLOS: ¿Cuándo irá?
Cuandoquiera que vaya, no importa.

¿Quién será?
Quienquiera que sea, podrá entrar.

¿Es interesante?
Por interesante que sea, no lo invitaré.

1. ¿Dónde viajará él?

_____, hará nuevos amigos.

2. ¿Es largo el viaje?

_____, él lo aguantará.

3. ¿Cuándo llegará?

_____, será bien recibido.

4. ¿Quién lo verá?

_____, se asombrará.

5. ¿Es valiente Vicente?

_____, tendrá que acostumbrarse.

6. ¿Qué hotel escogerá?

_____, le parecerá caro.

7. ¿Dónde vivirá?

_____, se quejará.

EJERCICIO M   Después de leer las dos frases, combínelas en una sola, usando *cuandoquiera, dondequiera, quien(es)quiera, cual(es)quiera o por... que.*

EJEMPLO: No sé quién lo hará. Todo el mundo puede hacerlo bien.
Quienquiera que lo haga, lo hará bien.

1. No sé a qué hora ellos vendrán. Los esperamos de todos modos.

_____

2. No sabemos cuánto pesa la mesa. Sólo sabemos que necesitarán cuatro hombres para moverla.

_____

3. No sé qué blusa vas a escoger. Todas te quedarán bien.

_____

4. No sé por qué trabajas tanto. Recibirás el mismo sueldo.

_____

5. No sabemos quién comprará este televisor. Será una verdadera ganga.

_____

[2] SUBJUNCTIVE IN RELATIVE CLAUSES

The subjunctive is used in relative clauses if the person or thing in the main clause is indefinite, nonexistent, or desired but not yet attained.

SUBJUNCTIVE	INDICATIVE
Busca un apartamento que *sea* cómodo y barato. *She is looking for an apartment that is comfortable and cheap.* [She may never find one.]	**Tiene un apartamento que *es* cómodo y barato** *She has an apartment that is comfortable and cheap.* [She has one.]
¿Conoce Ud. a alguien que *quiera* trabajar? *Do you know anyone who wants to work?* [indefinite]	**Conoce a alguien que *quiere* trabajar.** *He knows someone who wants to work.* [definite person]
No encuentro a nadie que *pueda* ayudarme. *I can't find anyone who can help me.* [nonexistent]	**Encontré a un hombre que *puede* ayudarme.** *I found a man who can help me.* [There is such a person.]

EJERCICIO N   Escriba lo que buscaban varias vecinas en las casas que compraron.

EJEMPLO: tener tres baños
Buscábamos una casa que tuviera tres baños.

1. tener / un comedor grande

2. estar / cerca de las escuelas

_____

3. ser / espaciosa y cómoda

_____

4. no costar / demasiado dinero

_____

5. tener / un sistema de seguridad

_____

6. no necesitar / muchos arreglos

_____

EJERCICIO O	Tomás está dirigiendo una campaña política. Escriba lo que él dice que van a hacer sus compañeros.

EJEMPLO:　Claudia / un señor / sacar fotos
Claudia busca un señor que saque fotos.

1. Fernando / alguien / hablar español

_____

2. Javier / varios jóvenes / llenar sobres

_____

3. Graciela / personas / repartir folletos

_____

4. tú / una muchacha / conocer este programa informático

_____

5. yo / alguien / poder hacer llamadas telefonicas

_____

6. María y Pablo / dos jóvenes / saber conducir bien

_____

EJERCICIO P	Escriba lo que contesta el señor Lobos cuando sus amigos le recuerdan lo que dijo antes de hacer un viaje al extranjero.

EJEMPLO:　Querías encontrar a un chofer que condujera bien.
No encontré a ningún chofer que condujera bien.

1. Buscabas un guía que conociera bien la ciudad.

_____

2. Deseabas encontrar un restaurante barato donde sirvieran buenas comidas.

_____

3. Querías hablar con alguien que hubiera hecho el mismo viaje.

_____

4. Buscabas un guía turístico que tuviera un plano claro de la ciudad.

_____

5. Querías encontrar gente que quisiera hacer una excursión a la costa.

_____

[*3*] CONDITIONAL SENTENCES

A conditional sentence consists of a condition (**si** clause) and a result (result clause). There are two basic types of conditions, "real" conditions and "unreal" or "contrary-to-fact" conditions.

[*4*] REAL CONDITIONS

Real conditions describe situations that are likely, certain, or factual. The indicative is used in both the **si** clause and the result clause to express a real condition:

Si estudias **más,** *sacarás* **mejores notas.** *If you study more, you will receive better grades.*
[You will almost certainly receive them.]

Si me telefoneó **ayer, no** *estaba* **en casa.** *If he called me yesterday, I was not at home.*
[He did call, and I was out.]

[*5*] CONTRARY-TO-FACT CONDITIONS

a. The imperfect and pluperfect subjunctives are used in contrary-to-fact conditions, as follows:

	SI-CLAUSE	RESULT CLAUSE
PRESENT TIME	Imperfect Subjunctive, **-se** or **-ra** form	Conditional (preferred in simple tenses) *or* Imperfect Subjunctive, **-ra** form only
PAST TIME	Pluperfect Subjunctive, **-se** or **-ra** form	Conditional Perfect *or* Pluperfect Subjunctive, **-ra** from only

Si tú *estudiases (estudiaras)* **más,** | *If you studied more, you would*
sacarías (sacaras) mejores notas. | *receive better grades.* [You don't receive good grades.]

Si tú *hubieses (hubieras) estudiado* | *If you had studied more, you would*
más, *habrías (hubieras)* **sacado** | *have received better grades.* [You
mejores notas. | didn't receive good grades.]

NOTE: The present subjunctive is never used in a **si** clause.

EJERCICIO Q   **Lea las frases en que Eduardo dice lo que hará. Luego cámbielas para decir lo que él haría en esas circunstancias.**

EJEMPLO: Si necesito dinero, se lo pido a mi padre.
Si **necesitase (necesitara)** dinero, se lo **pediría** a mi padre.

1. Si nos levantamos tarde, no llegaremos a tiempo.

_____

2. Si me ofrecen un puesto, lo aceptaré.

_____

3. Si trabajo allí, ganaré mucho dinero.

_____

4. Si me das el dinero, lo comparé.

_____

5. Si vienen tarde, no los esperaré.

_____

6. Si hace mal tiempo, nos quedaremos en casa.

_____

7. Si vemos a Jorge, se lo contaremos.

_____

EJERCICIO R   **Escriba qué haría Ud. en estas circunstancias.**

EJEMPLO: ir de compras
Si fuera de compras, compraría un regalo para mis padres.

1. visitar un museo

_____

2. hacer un viaje

_____

3. gastar mucho dinero

_____

4. escrbir una novela

_____

5. conocer a un actor (una actriz)

_____

6. construir una casa

_____

7. ganar la lotería

_____

8. ser médico

_____

EJERCICIO S	**Escriba lo que su abuelo dice que hubiera hecho de manera diferente y cuál hubiera (habría) sido el resultado.**

EJEMPLO: vivir en la ciudad
Si hubiera vivido en la ciudad, habría (hubiera) ido al teatro a menudo.

1. ahorrar dinero

_____

2. practicar un deporte

_____

3. tener su propio negocio

_____

4. seguir un curso en la universidad

_____

5. no vender la casa

_____

6. aprender a pintar

_____

7. viajar al extranjero

_____

b. The imperfect and pluperfect subjunctives are also used after **como si** (*as if*):

Ud. lo trata **como si** *fuera* un niño.   *You treat him as if he were a child*
                                                 [but he isn't].

Me miró **como si** yo *hubiera cometido*   *He looked at me as if I had committed a crime*
un crimen.   (but I didn't).

| EJERCICIO T | Escriba los comentarios que hace un dependiente sobre los clientes que entran en el almacén, usando *como si*. |

EJEMPLO: ese señor / hablar / ser el dueño
Ese señor habla **como si fuera** el dueño.

1. esa señora / hablar / nosotros / vender cosas defectuosas

_____

2. aquel joven / comprar / ser millonario

_____

3. esos niños / gritar / estar en su propia casa

_____

4. aquella señora / mirarme / yo / poner los precios

_____

5. este hombre / quejarse / ser un niño

_____

6. esas ancianas / verstirse / ser jóvenes

_____

7. este muchacho / hacer preguntas / no saber nada

_____

c. The **-ra** forms of the imperfect subjunctive of **querer, poder,** and **deber** may be used instead of the conditional of these verbs to express a polite request or statement.

Quisiera comprarlo.	*I would like to buy it.*
¿Pudiera Ud. hacerlo hoy?	*Could you do it today?*
Debiéramos verlo.	*We should (ought to) see it.*

| EJERCICIO U | Escriba la forma correcta de los verbos dados entre paréntesis en este mensaje electrónico que Carolina le envía a su amiga Lola. |

Hola Lola,

Yo _____ invitar a ti y a tu hermana a una fiesta. Tú _____ pensarlo bien
     1. (querer)   2. (deber)

porque Raúl va a asistir. Tú y Gloria _____ tomar el autobús que llega aquí a las seis y
                                           3. (poder)

media. Mi mamá y yo _____ ir a esperarlas en la terminal, pero estaremos muy ocupadas.
                              4. (querer)

Voy a hablarle a José para ver si él _____ ir a la terminal. Mientras tanto, Uds.
                                         5. (poder)

_____ decidir si vendrán o no. ¿ _____ tú llamarme por teléfono en
     6. (deber)   7. (poder)

cuanto recibas este mensaje? Gracias.

Carolina

| EJERCICIO V | Teresa y Norma van a ir compras. Ensayan lo que le van a decir al dependiente. Complete las frases con la forma correcta de *querer*, *poder* o *deber*, según el caso. |

1. Buenas tardes. Nosotras _____ comprar unos regalos.

2. ¿ _____ Ud. mostrarnos un anillo?

3. No _____ ser muy caro.

4. Yo _____ ver algo más económico y no _____ tener piedras.

5. ¿ _____ (nosotras) ver esos aretes?

6. ¿ _____ Ud. envolverlos como regalo? Gracias.

M A S T E R Y   E X E R C I S E S

| EJERCICIO W | Escriba la forma correcta de los verbos dados entre paréntesis en los cuentitos que siguen. |

1. Quería _____ un regalo especial que le _____ a su esposa. Pasó días
　　　　　　　　　1. (encontrar)　　　　　　　　　　　　　　　2. (gustar)

buscándolo en las tiendas. Por fin vio un alfiler precioso con cadena de oro. Era muy caro. «Por

mucho que _____ , lo compraré» dijo. «Ahora es necesario que lo _____
　　　　　　　3. (costar)　　　　　　　　　　　　　　　　　　　　　　4. (esconder)

para que ella no lo _____ , porque no quiero que _____ nada de esto
　　　　　　　　　5. (ver)　　　　　　　　　　　　6. (saber)

antes de la Navidad». Entró en casa con cara risueña y buscó un lugar que _____ seguro,
　　　　　　　　　　　　　　　　　　　　　　　　　　　　　　　　7. (ser)

pero sin éxito. Su esposa lo miraba con expresión extraña.

　　—¿Por qué me miras como si _____ un criminal?— gritó él, con enojo.
　　　　　　　　　　　　　　8. (ser)

　　— _____ que no me _____ — contestó ella.
　　　　9. (querer)　　　　　　　　　　10. (gritar)

2. El médico le aconsejó que _____ cama porque tenía un catarro. No quería
　　　　　　　　　　　　　　1. (guardar)

_____ todo el día en casa; no obstante, su madre insistió en que lo _____ .
　　2. (pasar)　　　　　　　　　　　　　　　　　　　　　　　　　　　　3. (hacer)

Pasó un día desagradable. Sintió no _____ ver a sus amigos. A la mañana siguiente,
　　　　　　　　　　　　　　　　4. (poder)

apenas se despertó, le dijo a su madre que _____ bien y que tenía el propósito fijo de
　　　　　　　　　　　　　　　　　　5. (estar)

salir. Pero ella le prohibió que _____ hasta que no _____ el médico.
　　　　　　　　　　　　　　6. (salir)　　　　　　　　　　7. (llegar)

　　—¡Ojalá que _____ pronto! Porque si no _____ saldré aún sin su
　　　　　　　　8. (venir)　　　　　　　　　　9. (venir)

permiso— dijo.

—No creo que _____ eso— le contestó su madre con calma, pero en tono firme.

10. (hacer)

3. Colón negaba que el mundo _____ llano. Pidió a su majestad la reina Isabel que

1. (ser)

le _____ a realizar su sueño:

2. (ayudar)

—Si yo _____ unas naves, _____ encontrar una nueva ruta occi-

3. (tener)   4. (poder)

dental que me _____ a las Indias.

5. (conducir)

Además de las naves, buscó unos navegantes que no _____ miedo de

6. (tener)

_____ al mar infinito. Pero no había nadie que _____ a confiarse a la

7. (salir)   8. (atreverse)

furia y violencia de los elementos. Sin embargo, Colón no se resignó al fracaso total de su proyecto.

Tenía el espíritu firme.

«Aunque _____ que buscarlos en las cárceles, los encontraré» se dijo «y cuando

9. (tener)

los _____ , podremos embarcarnos».

10. (encontrar)

4. Si _____ español, iré a España. Quienquiera que _____ hecho tal viaje

1. (aprender)   2. (haber)

dice que es un país encantador. No dudo que _____ razón. Es probable

3. (tener)

que _____ en la primavera. Espero _____ un viaje directo, en avión,

4. (ir)   5. (hacer)

con tal que _____ bastante dinero. Así que _____ allí, trataré de ver

6. (tener)   7. (llegar)

las diversas cosas que tiene la España actual. Después de unos días en Madrid, recorreré el país de

un extremo a otro sin descanso. Adondequiera que _____ , estoy seguro de

8. (ir)

_____ sacar muchas fotos para mostrárselas más tarde a mis amigos íntimos. Es una

9. (poder)

lástima que ellos no _____ acompañarme.

10. (poder)

5. Antes de que _____ el sol, ya corrían a través de los campos. Importaba que

1. (salir)

_____ a su destino, un pueblo cercano, a una distancia de diez millas de allí, de modo

2. (llegar)

que _____ reunirse con los otros.

3. (poder)

—Luego que _____ , podremos descansar—dijo el jefe.

4. (llegar)

—Por rápidamente que _____ nuestros caballos—dijo un soldado con amargura—

5. (correr)

es imposible que _____ allí a tiempo.

6. (estar)

—En todo caso—dijio el jefe con ira—es necesario _____ en un milagro, hacer
7. (creer)

esfuerzos como si _____ posible. Hay que andar sin tardanza, sin que el enemigo
8. (ser)

_____ cuenta.
9. (darse)

Cuando _____ , vieron con emoción a sus compañeros esperando debajo de los
10. (llegar)

árboles.

EJERCICIO X   **Es tiempo de las elecciones estudiantiles en su escuela. Ud. no es candi-dato(-a), pero le gusta expresarse sobre lo que dicen y prometen los candidatos. Escriba un ensayo en que Ud. hace saber sus pensamientos, opiniones y comentario sobre la campaña de los candidatos. Incluya lo siguiente:**

- what each candidate promises
- your reaction to their promises
- the issues with which you agree and/or disagree
- what you believe the issues should be
- what you would address if you if were a candidate
- how you would get your position across to the voters, etc.

_____
_____
_____
_____
_____
_____
_____
_____
_____
_____
_____
_____
_____
_____

Chapter 15
Commands

Treasure Hunt

[1] FORMAL COMMANDS

Formal commands with **Ud.** and **Uds.**, both affirmative and negative, are always expressed by the present subjunctive (see the Appendix, page 489).

tomar		*tome (Ud.)*		*tomen (Uds.)*		take
volver		*vuelva (Ud.)*		*vuelvan (Uds.)*		return
venir	(no)	*venga (Ud.)*	(no)	*vengan (Uds.)*	*(don't)*	come
ir		*vaya (Ud.)*		*vayan (Uds.)*		go
dar		*dé (Ud.)*		*den (Uds.)*		give

NOTE: With reflexive verbs, the reflexive pronoun is attached to the affirmative command and there is an accent mark on the next-to-last syllable of the verb. If the verb has only one syllable, it does not carry an accent mark: **dese.** In negative commands, the reflexive pronoun precedes the verb.

lavarse	*lávese*	*lávense*
	no se lave	*no se laven*
despedirse	*despídase*	*despídanse*
	no se despida	*no se despidan*

EJERCICIO A Escriba las instrucciones para hacer una llamada de un teléfono público en México.

EJEMPLO: descolgar el auricular
Descuelgue el auricular.

1. escuchar el tono antes de marcar

_____

2. poner la moneda

_____

3. marcar el número

_____

4. esperar hasta que alguien conteste

_____

5. oprimir el botón de la moneda

_____

6. hablar con la persona

_____

7. colgar el auricular

_____

8. comunicarse con la telefonista si hay algún problema

_____

| EJERCICIO B | **Escriba lo que deben hacer los buenos ciudadanos.** |

EJEMPLO: leer el periódico todos los días
           Lean el periódico todos los días.

1. escuchar las noticias todos los días

_____

2. no dejar de votar en las elecciones

_____

3. participar en las actividades de su comunidad

_____

4. ofrecer ayuda a los menos afortunados

_____

5. contribuir a las obras de caridad

_____

6. conocer a sus vecinos

_____

7. respetar los derechos de otros

_____

8. ser honrados

_____

9. escribir cartas al gobierno

_____

10. elegir a sus representantes

_____

Uds.

| EJERCICIO C | **Escriba lo que la señora Perales les dice a sus hijos cuando los deja con una niñera.** |

EJEMPLOS: portarse bien   no pelearse
            Pórtense bien.   **No se peleen.**

1. no salir a la calle

_____

2. no acercarse a la piscina

_____

3. bañarse a las siete

_____

4. no olvidarse de cepillarse los dientes

_____

5. ponerse la bata después de bañarse

_____

6. acostarse temprano

_____

7. dormirse rápidamente

_____

8. no levantarse de la cama

_____

[2] INDIRECT COMMANDS

a. Indirect commands are also expressed by the present subjunctive and are usually introduced by **que.**

Que hable **él (ella).**	*Let (Have) him (her) speak.*
Que oigan **la verdad.**	*Let (Have) them hear the truth.*
Que sean **felices.**	*May they be happy.*
Que lo haga **Juana.**	*Let (Have) Juana do it.*

EJERCICIO D Ud. es el (la) director(a) de una obra de teatro en su escuela. Escriba lo que debe hacer todo el mundo.

EJEMPLO: Enrique / pintar el decorado
Que Enrique pinte el decorado.

1. Sarita / hacer el vestuario

_____

2. Jorge y Arturo / arreglar las luces

_____

3. Carlos / hacer el papel del payaso

_____

4. Clara / ser la locutora

_____

5. ellos / poner las sillas

_____

6. Pepe / bajar y alzar el telón

_____

7. Laura e Inés / recoger los boletos

_____

8. Miguel / tocar el piano

_____

EJERCICIO E	**Beto es un niño a quien no le gusta hacer nada. Escriba quién debe hacer estas cosas, según él.**

EJEMPLO: No quiero sacar al perro. (mi hermano)
Que lo saque mi hermano.

1. No quiero ir a la tienda. (Conchita)

_____

2. No quiero hacer la tarea. (la maestra)

_____

3. No quiero comer los guisantes. (los perros)

_____

4. No quiero poner la mesa. (mi mamá)

_____

5. No quiero ayudarte. (tus amigos)

_____

b. Let us (Let's)

    (1) **The first-person plural of the present subjunctive is used to express _Let us_.**

**Esperemos** **un momento.**	_Let us wait a moment._
**Salgamos** **ahora.**	_Let us leave now._

    (2) _Let us go_ **is expressed by vamos. In the negative, the regular subjunctive form vayamos is used.**

**Vamos** **al teatro hoy.**	_Let us go to the theater today._
**No vayamos** **al teatro hoy.**	_Let us not go to the theater today._

    (3) **Vamos a** + infinitive may also be used to express _Let us_.

**Vamos a** **cantar** (or **Cantemos**).	_Let us sing._
**Vamos a** **aprender** (or **Aprendamos**) **la lección para mañana.**	_Let us learn the lesson for tomorrow._

    (4) **In expressing the affirmative _Let us_ with reflexive verbs, the final –s of the verb ending is dropped before adding the reflexive pronoun nos. An accent is placed on the stressed syllable.**

Sentémonos (= Sentemos + nos).   *Let's sit down.*
Vámonos (= Vamos + nos).   *Let's go (away).*

EJERCICIO F   **Escriba cómo Ud. y un amigo/una amiga piensan celebrar el cuatro de julio. Su amigo(a) está de acuerdo con sus sugerencias.**

EJEMPLO: dar una fiesta
         Demos una fiesta.
         Sí, vamos a dar una fiesta.

1. levantarse temprano _____

2. irse al centro _____

3. marchar en el desfile _____

4. comprar cohetes _____

5. reunirse con otros amigos _____

6. inflar muchos globos _____

7. colgar la bandera _____

8. divertirse mucho _____

EJERCICIO G   **Su amigo es muy indeciso. Escriba lo que dice cuando Ud. le sugiere algo durante un viaje al centro.**

EJEMPLO: ¿Nos paramos en las tiendas?
         Sí, parémonos en las tiendas, pero no nos paremos ahora.

1. ¿Nos sentamos en el parque? _____

2. ¿Nos desayunamos en ese restaurante? _____

3. ¿Nos quejamos del servicio?

_____

_____

4. ¿Nos acercamos al parque zoológico?

_____

_____

5. ¿Nos vamos pronto?

_____

_____

[3] FAMILIAR COMMANDS

a. Regular verbs

(1) The singular (**tú**) form of the familiar affirmative command is the same as the third-person singular of the present indicative.

(2) The plural (**vosotros**) form of the familiar affirmative command is formed by changing the **–r** ending of the infinitive to **–d**.

(3) The negative familiar command forms are all expressed by the present subjunctive.

	AFFIRMATIVE	NEGATIVE
mirar	_mira_ (tú) _mirad_ (vosotros)	_no mires_ (tú) _no miréis_ (vosotros)
correr	_corre_ (tú) _corred_ (vosotros)	_no corras_ (tú) _no corráis_ (vosotros)
dormir	_duerme_ (tú) _dormid_ (vosotros)	_no duermas_ (tú) _no durmáis_ (vosotros)

NOTE: The familiar plural forms (**vosotros, –as**) are rarely used in Spanish America. Formal plural commands (**ustedes**) are used instead.

EJERCICIO H _No_   **Escriba lo que la maestra les dice a los alumnos.**

EJEMPLO: (hablar) Niños, **hablad** español en la clase; no **habléis** inglés.

1. (terminar) Alumnos, _____ la tarea; no _____ la práctica.

2. (continuar) Niños, _____ la lectura; no _____ la conversación.

3. (empezar) Niños, _____ el examen; no _____ la tarea.

4. (dibujar)   Alumnos, _____ un castillo; no _____ una granja.

5. (escribir)   Alumnos, _____ un cuento; no _____ una novela.

EJERCICIO I   **La señora Peña tiene problemas con sus hijos. Escriba lo que dijo el señor Peña al enterarse de estos problemas.**

EJEMPLO: Carlos no se sienta a la mesa.
            Carlos, **siéntate** a la mesa; **no te sientes** en el escritorio.

1. Inés no se lava la cara.

   Inés, _____ la cara; no _____ el pelo.

2. Jorge no se despierta temprano.

   Jorge, _____ temprano; no _____ al mediodía.

3. Juan no se acerca a los libros.

   Juan, _____ a los libros; no _____ al refrigerador.

4. Pablo no se viste en seguida.

   Pablo, _____ en seguida; no _____ tan despacio.

5. Alicia no se pasea cuando hace sol.

   Alicia, _____ cuando hace sol; no _____ cuando llueve.

EJERCICIO J   **Su hermanito cree que es muy listo. Escriba lo que él les aconsejó a unos amigos.**

EJEMPLO: José no lee su libro.
            José, **lee** tu libro; **no leas** la revista.

1. Rosa no obedece a su madre.

   Rosa, _____ a tu madre; no _____ a tu amiga.

2. Pedro no cierra la boca.

   Pedro, _____ la boca; no _____ los ojos.

3. Alfredo no busca a su gato.

   Alfredo, _____ a tu gato; no _____ al perro.

4. Carolina no vuelve a su asiento.

   Carolina, _____ a tu asiento; no _____ a la pizarra.

5. Alberto no trae su cámara.

   Alberto, _____ tu cámara; no _____ tu tocacintas.

b.   Irregular verbs

The only irregular commands occur in the affirmative singular (**tú**). All other familiar commands are regular.

decir	*di*	decid	no digas	no digáis
hacer	*haz*	haced	no hagas	no hagáis
ir	*ve*	id	no vayas	no vayáis
poner	*pon*	poned	no pongas	no pongáis
salir	*sal*	salid	no salgas	no salgáis
ser	*sé*	sed	no seas	no seáis
tener	*ten*	tened	no tengas	no tengáis
valer	*val*	valed	no valgas	no valgáis
venir	*ven*	venid	no vengas	no vengáis

EJERCICIO K   **Antes de participar en una competencia, la madre de Micaela le dice lo que debe hacer. Escriba la forma correcta de los verbos dados entre paréntesis.**

EJEMPLO: (tener)   ¡No **tengas** prisa!
(ir)   ¡**Ve** con Dios!

  1. (hacer)   ¡_____ lo mejor que puedas!

  2. (decir)   ¡No _____ tonterías!

  3. (tener)   ¡_____ paciencia!

  4. (decir)   ¡_____ la verdad!

  5. (ser)   ¡No _____ perezosa!

  6. (poner)   ¡_____ mucha atención a las reglas!

  7. (tener)   ¡_____ cuidado!

  8. (ser)   ¡_____ buena!

  9. (salir)   ¡_____ en seguida!

 10. (ir)   ¡No _____ a llegar tarde!

 11. (venir)   ¡_____ a casa en cuanto termines!

 12. (hacer)   ¡No _____ caso a tus amigas!

 13. (tener)   ¡No _____ miedo!

 14. (ser)   ¡_____ muy lista!

 15. (hacer)   ¡_____ muchas preguntas!

EJERCICIO L   **Escriba lo que dirían estas personas en las circunstancias siguientes.**

EJEMPLO: ANITA: Ya son la once y media y tengo una cita a las doce.
SU AMIGA: (no tener prisa) ¡**No tengas prisa!**

1. ROBERTO: Mira, tu perro anda en el otro jardín.

   TÚ: (venir acá) _____

2. CARLOS: Yo no rompí la lámpara. Ésta no es mi pelota.

   SU MADRE: (no decir mentiras) _____

3. SARITA: ¡Ay! Hay un ratoncito allí.

   SU AMIGO: (no tener miedo) _____

4. PILAR: No sé si debo ir al baile con Ernesto.

   LUZ: (no ser tonta / ir con él) _____

5. PABLO: ¿Dónde debo poner el dinero?

   PAPÁ: (poner el dinero en un lugar seguro) _____

[4] OBJECT PRONOUNS WITH COMMANDS

a. Object pronouns (including reflexive pronouns) are attached to affirmative commands. An accent mark is required if the original stress was on the next-to-last syllable. In negative commands, object pronouns precede the verb.

Ayúd*ele*.	**No *le* ayude.**
Tráigan*lo*.	**No *lo* traigan.**
Hagámos*lo*.	**No *lo* hagamos.**
Levánta*te*.	**No *te* levantes.**
Aprended*lo*.	**No *lo* aprendáis.**
Di*les* el secreto.	**No *les* digas el secreto.**

b. With indirect commands introduced by **que**, the object pronoun always precedes the verb.

Que *lo* haga Juana.	**Que no *lo* haga Juana.**
Que *se* vayan en seguida.	**Que no *se* vayan en seguida.**

c. In the affirmative **vosotros** form of reflexive verbs, the final **–d** is dropped before adding the reflexive pronoun **os**.

***Sentaos* (= Sentad + os).**	*Sit down.*
***Divertíos* (= Divertid + os).**	*Enjoy yourselves.*
Exception:	
Idos	*Go away*

EJERCICIO M   **Escriba lo que este padre les dijo a sus hijos.**

EJEMPLO: Los niños no se divierten mucho.
            Niños, ***divertíos*** un poco; no ***os divertáis*** demasiado.

1. Los niños no se portan bien.

   Niños, _____ bien; no _____ mal.

2. Sus hijos no se ríen de tonterías.

   Hijos, _____ de tonterías; no _____ de la verdad.

3. Las chicas no se reúnen en el salón.

   Chicas, _____ en el salón; no _____ en el jardín.

4. Pablo e Inés nunca se ponen serios.

   Pablo e Inés, _____ serios, pero no _____ tristes.

5. Sus hijos no se dedican a la caridad.

   Hijos, _____ a la caridad; no _____ a los placeres.

EJERCICIO N   **Conchita es una hermanita celosa. Escriba lo que ella y su hermana Elsa dicen cuando su madre quiere hacer algo por Elsa.**

EJEMPLO: ¿Quieres que te prepare el desayuno?
       ELSA: **Sí, prepáramelo, mamá.**
       CONCHITA: **No se lo prepares.**

1. ¿Quieres que te envuelva el regalo?

   ELSA: _____

   CONCHITA: _____

2. ¿Prefieres que yo lave tu ropa hoy?

   ELSA: _____

   CONCHITA: _____

3. ¿Deseas que yo cambie el programa?

   ELSA: _____

   CONCHITA: _____

4. ¿Necesitas que yo te ayude?

   ELSA: _____

   CONCHITA: _____

5. ¿Quieres que tú y yo busquemos el vestido hoy?

   ELSA: _____

   CONCHITA: _____

6. ¿Prefieres que yo compre los refrescos?

ELSA: _____

CONCHITA: _____

7. ¿Deseas que tu papá y yo te acompañemos?

ELSA: _____

CONCHITA: _____

M A S T E R Y   E X E R C I S E S

EJERCICIO O Uds.
Escriba las reglas que deben seguirse en caso de un huracán.

EJEMPLO: tener cuidado y no estar nerviosos
Tengan Uds. cuidado y **no estén** nerviosos.

1. comprar bastante comida para una semana

_____

2. conservar una linterna a la mano

_____

3. preparar un aparato de radio portátil

_____

4. poner cinta o tablas en las ventanas

_____

5. quedarse dentro de la casa

_____

6. cerrar todas las ventanas

_____

7. correr las cortinas

_____

8. no acercarse a las ventanas durante la tormenta

_____

9. llenar la bañera de agua

_____

10. hervir el agua antes de tomarla

_____

11. no abrir el refrigerador a menudo

_____

12. escuchar las noticias

_____

13. no congestionar las líneas telefónicas

_____

14. no dejar nada en la terraza ni en el patio

_____

15. no salir hasta que la tormenta haya pasado

_____

EJERCICIO P   **Escriba las instrucciones que Juan le da a un amigo para llegar a la playa.**

EJEMPLO: tomar el Camino Real
            Toma el Camino Real.

1. ir hacia el norte

_____

2. seguir de frente

_____

3. en el quinto semáforo, dar vuelta a la derecha

_____

4. atravesar el puente

_____

5. mantenerse en el carril izquierdo

_____

6. pararse en el semáforo

_____

7. doblar a la izquierda

_____

8. continuar derecho

_____

9. empezar a buscar dónde estacionar el carro

_____

10. caminar una cuadra

_____

EJERCICIO Q Un amigo suyo quiere mandarle una copia de un documento que recibió en un mensaje electrónico, pero no sabe hacerlo. Escríbale un mensaje electrónico en el que Ud. le explica cómo adjuntar el documento y mandárselo a Ud. por el Internet. Use el imperativo. Incluya todos los pasos que debe hacer para mandarle el documento.

_____

_____

_____

_____

_____

_____

_____

_____

_____

_____

_____

Chapter 16
Common Expressions With Verbs

Many Spanish verbs are used idiomatically in certain expressions. A list of common expressions follows.

[1] EXPRESSIONS WITH *ACABAR*

acabar de + infinitive   *to have just*
acabar por + infinitive   *to end by, to finally*

Acabo de volver de la escuela.	*I have just returned from school.*
Se enfermó gravemente y *acabó por morir.*	*He became seriously ill and finally died.*

[2] EXPRESSIONS WITH *DAR*

dar a   *to face, to look out upon*
dar un abrazo   *to embrace*
dar con   *to come upon, to run into, to find*
dar cuerda (a)   *to wind*
dar de beber (comer) a   *to give a drink to (to feed)*
dar en   *to strike against, to hit*
dar las gracias (a)   *to thank*
dar gritos (voces)   *to shout*
dar la hora   *to strike the hour*
dar un paseo   *to take a walk; to go for a ride*
dar por + past participle   *to consider*
dar recuerdos (a)   *to give regards (to)*
dar una vuelta   *to take a stroll*
darse cuenta de   *to realize*
darse la mano   *to shake hands*
darse prisa   *to hurry*

Las ventanas *dan a* la avenida.	*The windows face the avenue.*
Al llegar, le *dio un abrazo* a su madre.	*On arriving, he embraced his mother.*
Dimos con Juan en el cine anoche.	*We ran into John at the movies last night.*
Cada mañana le *doy cuerda* a mi reloj.	*Each morning I wind my watch.*
Pedro le *dio de beber* a su perro.	*Peter gave his dog a drink.*
La pelota *dio en* el techo.	*The ball hit the ceiling.*
Le *di las gracias* por el regalo.	*I thanked him for the gift.*
Los niños *dieron gritos* de alegría.	*The children shouted with joy.*
Dio voces, pidiendo ayuda.	*He shouted, asking for help.*
El reloj *dio la una.*	*The clock struck one.*
Dimos un paseo en su carro.	*We took a ride in his car.*
El profesor *dio por terminada* la lección.	*The teacher considered the lesson ended.*
Dale mis recuerdos a tu padre.	*Give my regards to your father.*
Por la tarde, *doy una vuelta* por el parque.	*In the afternoon I take a stroll in the park.*
No se *dio cuenta* de su error.	*He did not realize his mistake.*

Al encontrarse, *se dieron la mano.*   *Upon meeting, they shook hands.*
¡*Dense prisa*! Ya son las ocho.   *Hurry! It is already eight o'clock.*

| **EJERCICIO A** | Julio cuenta lo que le pasó en el centro. Usando una expresión con *dar(se)* o *acabar,* exprese lo mismo que dice Julio. |

EJEMPLO: Yo paseaba por la Avenida Juárez.
             Yo **daba un paseo** por la Avenida Juárez.

1. Alfredo y yo andábamos por el centro.

_____

2. Nos encontramos con el papá de Gloria y nos saludamos.

_____

3. Él había dejado a Gloria en la biblioteca hacía un momento.

_____

4. Eran las doce en el reloj de la torre.

_____

5. El papá de Gloria no sabía que su reloj se había parado.

_____

6. Él arregló su reloj para que anduviera.

_____

7. Unos niños que gritaban en la esquina finalmente se callaron.

_____

8. Una pelota que tiraron cayó contra una ventana y quebró el vidrio.

_____

9. El papá de Gloria nos abrazó al despedirse.

_____

10. Mandé saludos a su familia y él me agradeció los saludos.

_____

| **EJERCICIO B** | Después de una fiesta en casa de Rogelio, su mamá le hace unas preguntas. Contéstelas, usando las sugerencias entre paréntesis. |

1. ¿Dónde estabas cuando dieron las doce? (acabar de salir de la fiesta)

_____

2. ¿Cuántas veces le diste de comer al perro ayer? (dos)

_____

3. ¿Cómo saludaste a los señores Roldán? (darse la mano)

_____

4. ¿Por qué llegaste tan tarde a casa? (dar un paseo en carro)

_____

5. ¿Por qué se dieron prisa tus primos? (era tarde)

_____

6. ¿Por qué le diste las gracias a Miguel? (el regalo)

_____

7. ¿De qué te diste cuenta? (todos se divirtieron mucho)

_____

8. ¿Qué piensas hacer esta mañana? (dar una vuelta con mis amigos)

_____

[3] EXPRESSIONS WITH *DEJAR*

dejar caer   *to drop*
dejar de + infinitive   *to fail to, to stop, to neglect to*

> **Juanito *dejó caer* el vaso de leche.**   *Juanito dropped the glass of milk.*
> ***Dejó́lde estudiar* y cerró el libro.**   *He stopped studying and closed the book.*

[4] EXPRESSIONS WITH *ECHAR*

echar(se) a   *to start to*   **echar la culpa**   *to blame*
echar al correo   *to mail*   **echar de menos**   *to miss*

> **Al ver al policía, el ladrón *se echó a* correr.**   *On seeing the policeman, the thief started to run.*
>
> **No te olvides de *echar* las cartas *al correo*.**   *Don't forget to mail the letters.*
> **Le *echó la culpa* a su hermana.**   *He blamed his sister.*
> **Los niños *echaron de menos* a su vecino.**   *The children missed their neighbor.*

[5] EXPRESSIONS WITH *HABER*

hay   *there is, there are*   **habrá**   *there will be*
hubo ⎫   **habría**   *there would be*
había ⎭ *there was, there were*   **ha habido**   *there has (have) been*
haber de + infinitive   *to be (supposed) to, to have to*
haber que + infinitive   *to be necessary*
haber (mucho) lodo   *to be (very) muddy*
haber luna   *to be moonlight*
haber neblina   *to be foggy, misty*
haber (mucho) polvo   *to be (very) dusty*
haber sol   *to be sunny*

He de **salir a las nueve.**	*I am to leave at nine o'clock.*
Habrá que **salir temprano.**	*It will be necessary to leave early.*
Después de la lluvia *había lodo.*	*After the rain it was muddy.*
Anoche *hubo luna.*	*There was moonlight last night.*
Esta mañana *había neblina.*	*This morning it was foggy.*
Hay mucho polvo **por el camino.**	*It is very dusty on the road.*
No *hubo sol* **ayer y llovió.**	*It wasn't sunny yesterday and it rained.*

  Ofelia está de vacaciones y le escribe a su amiga Rosita. Complete la carta con las expresiones dadas.

Querida Rosita:

Por fin llegamos al hotel. El viaje fue terrible. _____ en el camino y _____

          1. (haber polvo)   *2.* (haber lodo)

a lo largo del río. Por la mañana, cuando salimos, _____ . El portero _____

                           3. (haber neblina)   *4.* (dejar caer)

mi maleta y _____ a un pobre perro que se le atravesó. Se enojó conmigo, porque yo no

           5. (echar la culpa)

pude controlarme y _____ reír. _____ mucha gente buscando cuarto en el

                6. (echarse a)   *7.* (haber)

hotel. No sabían que _____ hacer reservaciones con anticipación. Voy a aprovechar

                    8. (haber que)

que _____ ahora para nadar en la piscina. Pero antes quiero _____ esta carta

      9. (haber sol)   *10.* (echar al correo)

para que la recibas pronto. _____ escribirme. Ya te _____ mucho.

               11. (no dejar de)   *12.* (echar de menos)

Tu amiga,

Ofelia

(6) EXPRESSIONS WITH *HACER*

hacer + time expression + **que** + preterit	
preterit + **hace** + time expression	} *ago*

hace poco *a little while ago*
hacer buen (mal) tiempo *to be good (bad) weather*
hacer (mucho) frío (calor) *to be (very) cold (warm)*
hacer (mucho) viento *to be (very) windy*
hacer caso *to pay attention, to heed, to notice*
hacer de *to work as, to act as*
hacer el papel de *to play the role of*
hacer pedazos (añicos) *to break to pieces, to tear to shreds, to smash*
hacer una pregunta *to ask a question*
hacer una visita *to pay a visit*
hacer un viaje *to take a trip*
hacerse + noun *to become*
hacerse tarde *to become (grow) late*
hacer(se) daño *to harm, to damage, to hurt (oneself)*

Hace una semana que vino **a verme.**	
Vino **a verme** *hace una semana.*	} *He came to see me a week ago.*

El tren salió *hace poco.*	*The train left a little while ago.*
Ayer *hizo buen tiempo.*	*Yesterday the weather was good.*
En el invierno *hace frío.*	*It is cold in the winter.*
Ayer no salí porque *hacía viento.*	*Yesterday I didn't go out because it was windy.*
Ese muchacho no *hizo caso* de mis consejos.	*That boy didn't heed my advice.*
Diego *hizo de* capitán en el juego.	*In the game, Diego acted as captain.*
La actriz se negó a *hacer el papel de condesa.*	*The actress refused to play the role of countess.*
El muchacho *hizo pedazos* el papel.	*The boy tore the paper to shreds.*
Me *hizo una pregunta,* pero no contesté.	*He asked me a question, but I didn't answer.*
Anoche le *hice una visita* a mi amigo.	*Last night I paid a visit to my friend.*
Hice un viaje a México el año pasado.	*I took a trip to Mexico last year.*
Para *hacerse médico,* es necesario estudiar mucho.	*In order to become a doctor, it is necessary to study a lot.*
Se hicieron muy buenos amigos.	*They became very good friends.*
Se hizo tarde y tuvimos que marcharnos.	*It became very late and we had to leave.*
El frío *hizo daño* a los árboles.	*The cold damaged the trees.*
Se cayó y *se hizo daño.*	*He fell and hurt himself.*

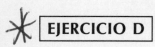

EJERCICIO D | La emisora de su escuela transmite las noticias todos los días. Hoy Ud. va a dar las noticias sobre un huracán. Usando correctamente una de las expresiones dadas, complete el reporte siguiente.

En el noticiero de hoy yo _____ locutor del boletín meteorológico. _____
          1. (hacer de)   *2. (hacer)*

unos minutos me dieron este reporte sobre un huracán que está pasando por el sur de los Estados Unidos.

Hoy por la mañana _____ en los pueblos de la costa. De repente, a eso de las dos de la
              3. (hacer buen tiempo)

tarde, empezó a _____ . _____ y todo lo que no estaba amarrado voló.
              4. (hacer mal tiempo)   *5. (hacer mucho viento)*

Estos objetos volantes _____ las ventanas de tiendas y casas. Muchos habitantes no
                    6. (hacer pedazos)

_____ los avisos que pasaron tanto por la radio como por la televisión. El huracán también
   7. (hacer caso de)

_____ en los pueblos del interior. _____ un momento, el alcalde
   8. (hacer mucho daño)   *9. (hacer)*

_____ a uno de los pueblos e _____ sobre los daños causados por el
   10. (hacer una visita)   *11. (hacer preguntas)*

huracán. Un anciano dijo que _____ cincuenta años que no veía un huracán tan fuerte.
                     12. (hacer)

EJERCICIO E | Conteste las preguntas siguientes que Pablo le hace a un amigo.

1. ¿Cuándo harás un viaje al exterior?

_____

2. ¿Cuánto tiempo hace que no viajas en avión?

_____

3. ¿Quién hará el viaje contigo?

_____

4. ¿Quién hará de guía?

_____

5. ¿Te hace daño a los oídos viajar en avión?

_____

6. ¿Qué tiempo hace ahora en la costa de España?

_____

7. ¿A quién quieres hacerle una visita?

_____

8. ¿Te gusta viajar cuando hace mal tiempo?

_____

[7] EXPRESSIONS WITH *PERDER*

echarse a perder   *to be spoiled, to be ruined*
perder cuidado   *not to worry*
perder de vista   *to lose sight of*

La leche *se echó a perder.*   The milk was spoiled.
Pierda cuidado; todo saldrá bien.   Don't worry; everything will turn out right.
Lo siguieron, pero pronto *lo*   They followed him, but they soon lost sight of him.
  perdieron de vista.

[8] EXPRESSIONS WITH <u>*PONERSE*</u>

ponerse + adjective   *to become, to turn*
ponerse a + infinitive   *to begin to, to set about*
ponerse de acuerdo   *to come to an agreement*

Al oír la noticia, el niño *se puso pálido.*   On hearing the news, the child became pale.
El día *se puso gris.*   The day turned grey.
La alumna *se puso a llorar.*   The pupil began to cry.
Por fin *se pusieron de acuerdo.*   Finally, they came to an agreement.

[9] EXPRESSIONS WITH *TENER*

tener (mucho) calor (frío)   *to be (very) warm (cold)*
tener cuidado   *to be careful*
tener dolor de cabeza (estómago, etc.**)**   *to have a headache (stomach ache, etc.)*
tener éxito   *to be successful*
tener ganas de   *to feel like*
tener (mucha) hambre (sed)   *to be (very) hungry (thirsty)*

> **tener la culpa (de)**   *to be to blame (for)*
> **tener lugar**   *to take place*
> **tener miedo de**   *to be afraid of*
> **tener por**   *to consider*
> **tener prisa**   *to be in a hurry*
> **tener que ver con**   *to have to do with*
> **tener razón (no tener razón)**   *to be right (to be wrong)*
> **tener (mucho) sueño**   *to be (very) sleepy*
> **tener (mucha) suerte**   *to be (very) lucky*
> **tener vergüenza (de + infinitive)**   *to be ashamed (of)*

Tenía calor y se quitó el sobretodo.	*He was warm and took off his overcoat.*
Tengan cuidado al cruzar la calle.	*Be careful when crossing the street.*
Ayer *tuve dolor de estómago.*	*Yesterday I had a stomach ache.*
Él *tiene éxito* en todo lo que hace.	*He is successful in everything he does.*
A veces *tengo ganas de* bailar.	*At times I feel like dancing.*
Cuando *tengo sed*, tomo agua.	*When I am thirsty I drink water.*
El muchacho *tiene la culpa* de lo que pasó.	*The boy is to blame for what happened.*
¿Cuándo *tendrá lugar* la fiesta?	*When will the party take place?*
El niño *tiene miedo de* la oscuridad.	*The child is afraid of the dark.*
Lo tengo por persona honrada.	*I consider him an honest person.*
Tenía prisa y no pude detenerme a charlar.	*I was in a hurry and could not stop to chat.*
No *tengo nada que ver con* eso.	*I have nothing to do with that.*
¿*Tengo razón?*—No, *no tienes razón*.	*Am I right?—No, you are wrong.*
María *tenía sueño* y se acostó.	*Mary was sleepy and went to bed.*
No *tuvo suerte* y perdió el dinero.	*He wasn't lucky and lost the money.*
¿No *tienes vergüenza?*	*Aren't you ashamed?*

EJERCICIO F   **Carolina lee una revista y se fija en las figuras que aparecen en los anuncios. Escriba lo que piensa Carolina al verlas.**

EJEMPLO: Una señora lleva un abrigo grueso, una gorra, una bufanda y guantes.
Ella **tendrá mucho frío.**

1. Se ve la cabeza de un señor. Tiene las manos en las sienes y una mirada de dolor.

El señor _____.

2. Es una noche oscura. Un niño acaba de despertarse en su cama y tiene una mirada de pavor.

El niño _____.

3. Una pareja está sentada en el mostrador de un café. Miran el menú y hablan.

Ellos _____.

4. Una señora se ve muy contenta. Tiene un cheque de la lotería en la mano.

Ella _____.

5. Un joven está con sus padres delante de una universidad. Es el día en que el joven se gradúa.

El joven _____.

6. Hay un letrero en la carretera. El símbolo representa la forma de una «S».

Los conductores _____.

7. Un participante en un programa de la televisión acaba de acertar la respuesta correcta.

   El participante _____.

8. Un señor corre para alcanzar un autobús. Mira su reloj.

   El señor _____.

9. Un niño se estira y bosteza delante del televisor.

   El niño _____.

10. En un restaurante elegante un niño volcó una copa de vino tinto y manchó el vestido de su mamá. La mamá está furiosa.

    El niño _____.

| EJERCICIO G | Enrique no se siente bien. Escriba lo que le dice a su mamá. Use una expresión con *tener, ponerse* o *perder* en cada frase. |

1. MAMÁ: ¿Qué tienes, hijo?

   ENRIQUE: _____

2. MAMÁ: ¿Por qué te pusiste el suéter?

   ENRIQUE: _____

3. MAMÁ: ¿Quieres tomar una sopa caliente?

   ENRIQUE: _____

4. MAMÁ: ¿Tomaste la leche que te dejé anoche?

   ENRIQUE: _____

5. MAMÁ: ¿Por qué te acostaste tan temprano anoche?

   ENRIQUE: _____

6. MAMÁ: Voy a medirte la fiebre.

   ENRIQUE: _____

7. MAMÁ: Sin embargo, no debes bajarte de la cama.

   ENRIQUE: _____

---

[10] EXPRESSIONS WITH *VOLVER*

volver a + **infinitive** *to… again*
volver en sí *to regain consciousness, to come to*
volverse + **adjective** *to become*

El cantante *volvió a cantar.*	*The singer sang again.*
El herido nunca *volvió en sí.*	*The wounded man never regained consciousness.*
Mi papá *se ha vuelto imposible.*	*My father has become impossible.*

[11] OTHER COMMON VERBAL EXPRESSIONS

encogerse de hombros *to shrug one's shoulders*
guardar cama *to stay in bed*
hacer saber *to inform, to let (someone) know*
llegar a ser *to become, to get to be*
llevar a cabo *to carry out, to carry through*
oír hablar de *to hear about*
oír decir que... *to hear that...*
pensar + infinitive *to intend to*
quedarse con *to keep, to hold on to*
quedar en que... (quedar en + infinitive) *to agree that, to agree to*
querer decir *to mean*
sacar una fotografía *to take a picture*
valer la pena *to be worthwhile*

Al oír la noticia, sólo *se encogió de hombros.*	*On hearing the news, he only shrugged his shoulders.*
Tenía fiebre y tuvo que *guardar cama* **por dos días.**	*He had a fever and had to stay in bed for two days.*
Me *hizo saber* **que no volvía hoy.**	*He let me know that he wouldn't return today.*
Después de muchos años de estudio, logró *llegar a ser* **médico.**	*After many years of study, he managed to become a doctor.*
El capitán *llevó a cabo* **las órdenes del general.**	*The captain carried out the general's orders.*
En la clase de historia *oímos hablar de* **Simón Bolívar.**	*In history class, we heard about Simon Bolivar.*
Oí decir que **te vas a Venezuela.**	*I heard that you are going to Venezuela.*
Pienso viajar **a España este verano.**	*I intend to travel to Spain this summer.*
Se quedó con **mi pluma.**	*He kept (walked off with) my pen.*
¿En qué quedaste **con Miguel?**	*What did you and Michael agree to?*
Quedamos en encontrarnos **aquí.**	*We agreed to meet here.*
¿Qué *quiere decir* **esta palabra?**	*What does this word mean?*
Me gusta *sacar fotografías.*	*I like to take pictures.*
A veces *vale la pena* **escuchar las noticias.**	*Sometimes it's worthwhile to listen to the news.*

EJERCICIO H   Varios amigos hacen comentarios sobre diversos asuntos. Escoja la expresión necesaria y escríbala en la forma correcta.

guardar cama	pensar	querer decir
hacer saber	perder cuidado	valer la pena
llegar a ser	ponerse a	volver a
oír hablar de	quedarse con	volver en sí

1. «El tiempo es oro» es un proverbio que _____ que no debemos malgastar el tiempo.

2. Mi hermana se desmayó al ver al ratoncito, pero a poco ella _____ .

3. María me parece una chica simpática. ¿Qué has _____ ella?

4. Yo voy a España durante las vacaciones. ¿Qué _____ hacer tú?

5. Cuando puedo, siempre asisto a conciertos de música clásica. Quiero _____ director de orquesta.

6. Mi tía no encontró el anillo la primera vez y _____ buscarlo.

7. Cuando fui a la feria con unos amigos, nos perdimos en el camino. Pero Jorge dijo: «_____ , tengo un mapa».

8. Después de las vacaciones, Adolfo _____ estudiar seriamente.

9. Sarita me pidió mi vestido blanco para ir a una fiesta y _____ con él.

10. Es una película fabulosa. _____ que la veas pronto.

11. Después de dar a luz, Juanita tuvo que _____ por una semana.

12. Ojalá me _____ a tiempo si vienen o no.

EJERCICIO I   Ud. acaba de volver de un viaje al extranjero. Conteste las preguntas que le hace un tío.

1. ¿Sacó Ud. muchas fotografías durante sus vacaciones?

   _____

2. ¿Quién se quedó con las fotos?

   _____

3. ¿Cree que vale la pena viajar al extranjero?

   _____

4. ¿Cuándo vuelve a hacer otro viaje?

   _____

5. ¿Se puso nervioso (nerviosa) al subir al avión?

   _____

6. ¿Qué piensa hacer el verano próximo?

   _____

7. ¿Vale la pena visitar los museos?

   _____

8. ¿Le gusta ver cuadros de los que ha oído hablar?

   _____

9. ¿En qué quedó con los amigos que conoció en el viaje?

   _____

10. ¿Pudo llevar a cabo todos sus planes para el viaje?

   _____

MASTERY EXERCISES

EJERCICIO J   **En la clase de composición, los alumnos aprenden a expresar sus ideas de otra forma. Escriba estas frases, sustituyendo correctamente la expresión subrayada con una expresión con *dar, haber, hacer* o *tener*.**

EJEMPLO: Quiero un apartamento con vista a los árboles y los bancos.
Quiero un apartamento **que dé** al parque.

1. La mamá se apresura porque desea preparar una comida especial para su familia.

2. El padre le agradeció al salvavidas por ayudar a su hijita.

3. Cada tarde los ancianos solían andar por la calle principal del pueblo.

4. Mañana es necesario que los niños se despierten a las cinco.

5. Cuando le tocaba al hermano menor hacer algo en la casa, siempre decía que le dolía la cabeza.

6. Al ver al joven con quien rehusó ir al baile, Elsa se apenó de no haberlo aceptado.

7. El baile será el sábado por la noche en el gimnasio del colegio.

8. Cuando el profesor devolvió los exámenes, Martín temió mirar el suyo.

9. El mes pasado el frío dañó la cosecha de los campesinos.

_____

_____

10. Cuando mis hermanitos juegan, Ricardo es el médico y Gloria es la enfermera.

_____

_____

| EJERCICIO K | **Complete la carta que Emilio les escribió a sus padres de la universidad, usando expresiones con *acabar, dar(se), dejar, echar(se), haber, hacer(se)* o *tener*.** |

Queridos padres:

Nunca sé la hora ni la fecha en que vivo. Anoche, al quitarme el reloj lo _____ *caer* al
                                                                        1.

suelo y se rompió definitivamente. Esta mañana me desperté de repente y _____
                                                                        2.

cuenta de que era tarde cuando el reloj de la iglesia _____ las nueve. Me pareció que
                                                        3.

_____ de dormirme. Había pasado una mala noche porque algo que comí me
      4.

_____ *daño* y _____ *dolor de estómago.* Me levanté rápidamente
      5.   6.

y _____ *prisa* porque las clases en la universidad habían comenzado _____
    7.   8.

una hora. Un amigo trató de _____ *una pregunta,* pero no pude detenerme. Cuando salí a
                              9.

la calle, _____ *viento.* Yo _____ *suerte* porque cuando iba a
          10.   11.

_____ *a correr,* otro amigo pasó en su carro. Queríamos llegar a la universidad rápida-
      12.

mente, pero _____ *que* _____ *cuidado* con la policía. Cuando llegué al
            13.   14.

laboratorio, _____ *miedo de* la reacción del profesor y también _____
              15.   16.

vergüenza de haber llegado tan tarde. Al entrar yo en la clase, el profesor _____ *de hablar* y
                                                                              17.

me miró tan fijamente que yo _____ *ganas de* dar media vuelta y salir corriendo. Después
                              18.

de la clase, mis compañeros _____ *a reír* cuando yo le pedí una disculpa al profesor.
                            19.

Yo sé que tengo que ser más responsable si quiero _____ un buen científico.
                                                    20.

¡_____ *mis saludos* a toda la familia! Yo los _____ *de menos* a todos.
  21.   22.

Su hijo,

Emilio

| EJERCICIO L | Complete el diálogo que oyó Pepe mientras esperaba en una oficina, usando correctamente una forma de las expresiones de la columna de la derecha. |

1. SECRETARIA: ¿En qué puedo servirle, señor?

   SEÑOR: Yo _____ verme con el Sr. Vargas aquí hoy.

1.

2. SECRETARIA: Lo siento, pero él _____ salir de la oficina.

1.

   SEÑOR: _____ una semana que _____ él

2.   3.

   en la calle y _____ para encontrarnos hoy.

4.

3. SECRETARIA: _____ señor. Yo le _____ que Ud.

1.   2.

   estuvo aquí.

   SEÑOR: Gracias, señorita, porque no tengo tiempo de _____

3.

   visitarlo hoy. _____ él _____ salir

4.   5.

   de viaje. ¿Es cierto?

4. SECRETARIA: Sí señor, _____ . El va a una conferencia que

1.

   _____ en Bogotá.

2.

   SEÑOR: ¡Qué _____ !

3.

quedar en
acabar de
hacer
dar con
ponerse de
  acuerdo
perder cuidado
hacer saber
volver a
oír decir que
pensar
tener razón
tener lugar
tener suerte

| EJERCICIO M | A Ramoncito le fascina hacer muchas preguntas sobre cualquier tema. Conteste las preguntas que él hace. |

1. ¿Qué tomas cuando tienes sed?

   _____

2. ¿Cuántas veces al día le das de comer a tu gato (perro)?

   _____

3. ¿Qué haces cuando tienes sueño?

   _____

4. Cuando hay mucho ruido en tu casa, ¿quién tiene la culpa generalmente?

   _____

5. Cuando tienes prisa, ¿te echas a correr?

   _____

6. ¿A quiénes les haces visita los domingos?

   _____

7. ¿Crees que tus padres tienen razón en lo que te aconsejan?

_____

8. ¿Les haces caso?

_____

9. ¿Qué haces cuando tienes dolor de muelas?

_____

10. Cuando pides prestado un lápiz, ¿lo devuelves o te quedas con él?

_____

11. ¿Sabes qué quiere decir «hacer cola»?

_____

12. ¿Crees que vale la pena estudiar español?

_____

13. ¿Te gusta volver a ver las buenas películas?

_____

14. Cuando sacas malas notas, ¿te pones triste o te pones bravo?

_____

15. Cuando te enfermas y tienes que guardar cama, ¿cómo se lo haces saber a tu escuela?

_____

EJERCICIO N | **Lo han invitado a Ud. a escribir una reseña de una película recién estrenada. Su reseña se publicará en una edición especial en español del periódico estudiantil. Use cuantas expresiones de este capítulo que pueda. Incluya en la reseña:**

- a brief summary of the film, including where and when it takes place, the principal characters, etc.
- what you thought of the acting
- something about the direction of the film
- your reaction to the setting, wardrobe, special effects, etc.
- your overall reaction/rating (favorable or unfavorable) with reasons
- your recommendation to the reader about seeing the film

_____

_____

_____

_____

_____

_____

Part Two
Nouns; Pronouns; Prepositions

ESPAÑA

Islas Baleares

Islas Canarias

MÉXICO

REPÚBLICA DOMINICANA

PUERTO RICO

CUBA

HONDURAS

NICARAGUA

GUATEMALA

EL SALVADOR

COSTA RICA

PANAMÁ

VENEZUELA

COLOMBIA

ECUADOR

PERÚ

BOLIVIA

PARAGUAY

CHILE

URUGUAY

ARGENTINA

Chapter 17
Nouns and Articles

[1] GENDER OF NOUNS

All nouns in Spanish are either masculine or feminine.

a. Nouns that refer to male beings are masculine. Nouns that refer to female beings are feminine.

MASCULINE	FEMININE
el hombre *man*	**la mujer** *woman*
el rey *king*	**la reina** *queen*
el príncipe *prince*	**la princesa** *princess*
el poeta *poet*	**la poetisa** *poet*

b. Nouns ending in –o are usually masculine. Nouns ending in –a are usually feminine.

MASCULINE	FEMININE
el hijo *son*	**la hija** *daughter*
el tipo *type*	**la distancia** *distance*
el zapato *shoe*	**la bota** *boot*

c. A few nouns ending in –o are feminine.

la mano *hand*	**la radio** *radio*
la foto★ *photo*	**la moto★★** *motorcycle*

d. Some nouns ending in –a are masculine.

el clima *climate*	**el planeta** *planet*
el día *day*	**el problema** *problem*
el drama *drama*	**el programa** *program*
el idioma *language*	**el telegrama** *telegram*
el mapa *map*	**el tranvía** *streetcar*

e. Nouns ending in –dad, –tad, –tud, –umbre, –ie, or ión are normally feminine.

la ciudad *city*	**la unión** *union*
la dificultad *difficulty*	
la juventud *youth*	Exceptions:
la certidumbre *certainty*	
la especie *species, kind*	**el avión** *airplane*
la excepción *exception*	**el camión** *truck*

★**La foto** is an abbreviation of **la fotografía.**
★★**La moto** is an abbreviation of **la motocicleta.**

f. Masculine nouns that refer to people and end in **-or, -és,** or **-n** add **a** for the feminine equivalents.

<table>
<tr><td align="center">MASCULINE</td><td align="center">FEMININE</td></tr>
<tr><td>**el escultor** *sculptor*</td><td>**la escultora** *sculptress*</td></tr>
<tr><td>**el francés** *Frenchman*</td><td>**la francesa** *Frenchwoman*</td></tr>
<tr><td>**el alemán** *German*</td><td>**la alemana** *German*</td></tr>
</table>

Exceptions:

<table>
<tr><td>**el emperador** *emperor*</td><td>**la emperatriz** *empress*</td></tr>
<tr><td>**el actor** *actor*</td><td>**la actriz** *actress*</td></tr>
</table>

NOTE: If a masculine noun bears an accent mark on the last syllable, the accent is dropped in the equivalent feminine form.

<table>
<tr><td>el fran*cés*</td><td>la fran*cesa*</td></tr>
<tr><td>el ale*mán*</td><td>la ale*mana*</td></tr>
</table>

g. Some nouns are either masculine or feminine depending on their meaning.

<table>
<tr><td align="center">MASCULINE</td><td align="center">FEMININE</td></tr>
<tr><td>**el capital** *capital (money)*</td><td>**la capital** *capital (city)*</td></tr>
<tr><td>**el cura** *priest*</td><td>**la cura** *cure*</td></tr>
<tr><td>**el guía** *guide (male)*</td><td>**la guía** *guidebook, guide (female)*</td></tr>
<tr><td>**el policía** *policeman*</td><td>**la policía** *police force, policewoman*</td></tr>
</table>

h. Some nouns referring to people do not change their form but distinguish their gender only by the article.

<table>
<tr><td>**el (la) artista** *artist*</td><td>**el (la) joven** *youth*</td></tr>
<tr><td>**el (la) dentista** *dentist*</td><td>**el (la) mártir** *martyr*</td></tr>
<tr><td>**el (la) testigo** *witness*</td><td>**el (la) modelo** *model*</td></tr>
</table>

i. Days of the week, months of the year, and names of rivers and oceans are masculine.

<table>
<tr><td>**el lunes** *Monday*</td><td>**(el) septiembre** *September*</td></tr>
<tr><td>**el Amazonas** *the Amazon (river)*</td><td>**el Pacífico** *the Pacific (ocean)*</td></tr>
</table>

j. The gender of other nouns must be learned individually.

EJERCICIO A   Ricardo cuida a su primo. Para entretenerlo, le hace identificar varias cosas. Escriba lo que responde el niño.

EJEMPLO: **el papel**

1. _____

2. _____

3. _____

4. _____

5. _____

6. _____

7. _____

8. _____

9. _____

10. _____

11. _____

12. _____

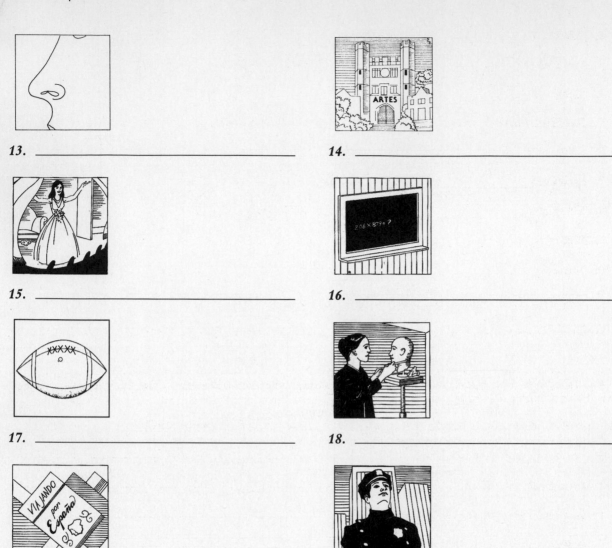

13. _____

14. _____

15. _____

16. _____

17. _____

18. _____

19. _____

20. _____

| EJERCICIO B | Dorotea ha hecho el árbol genealógico de su familia. Identifique a estas personas. |

Juan García—María Pérez de García

Sarita Vélez (de García)—Eduardo García   Luz García (de Montoya)—Carlos Montoya

Dorotea   Cándida   Jaime   Pablo   Raúl   Gabriel

EJEMPLO: María Pérez de García es **la madre** de Eduardo.

1. Juan García es _____ de Eduardo y Luz.

2. Eduardo es _____ de Sarita.

3. Dorotea es _____ de Jaime y Cándida.

4. Gabriel es _____ de Jaime.

5. María Pérez de García es _____ de Carlos y Sarita.

6. Carlos es _____ de Eduardo.

7. Sarita es _____ de Juan García.

8. Carlos es _____ de María Pérez de García.

9. Luz es _____ de Dorotea, Cándida y Jaime.

10. Jaime es _____ de Sarita y Eduardo.

11. Raúl es _____ de Eduardo.

12. María Pérez de García es _____ de Dorotea, Cándida y Jaime.

EJERCICIO C	Lolita va a participar en un concurso de vocabulario. Lea el significado y luego escriba la palabra apropiada.

EJEMPLO: un grupo de muchas personas   **la muchedumbre (la multitud)**

1. un representante de la iglesia   _____

2. un lugar como Chicago   _____

3. la persona que preside en la corte   _____

4. donde guardan a los prisioneros   _____

5. una obra representada en el teatro   _____

6. el hombre que escribe versos   _____

7. la parte temprana de la vida   _____

8. lo contrario de «la duda»   _____

9. el documento que contiene el
        sistema de leyes de una nación   _____

10. lo que habla una persona   _____

11. cuando las personas duermen   _____

12. un sinónimo de «el gusto»   _____

13. veinticuatro horas   _____

14. el hijo de un rey   _____

15. las oficinas centrales del gobierno federal   _____

16. el acto de repartir cosas

_____

17. lo que buscan para el cáncer

_____

18. un hábito de una cultura

_____

19. el símbolo de los enamorados

_____

20. lo que tiene una persona sana y justa

_____

[2] PLURAL OF NOUNS

a. Nouns ending in a vowel form the plural by adding **s.**

el líquido	*liquid*	**los líquidos**	*liquids*
la conquista	*conquest*	**las conquistas**	*conquests*
el hombre	*man*	**los hombres**	*men*

b. Nouns ending in a consonant (including **-y**) form the plural by adding **es.**

el papel	*paper*	**los papeles**	*papers*
el rey	*king*	**los reyes**	*kings, rulers*

NOTES:

1. Nouns ending in **-z** change the **-z** to **-c** before adding **es: el lápiz, los lápices; la actriz, las actrices.**

2. An accent mark is added or dropped to keep the original stress.

el joven	**los** *jóvenes*	**el francés**	**los franceses**
el examen	**los** ex*á*menes	**la reunión**	**las reuniones**

3. Except for nouns ending in **-és,** nouns ending in **s** do not change in the plural.

el (los) lunes	**el (los) paréntesis**
la (las) dosis	**la (las) síntesis**

4. In a mixed plural (masculine and feminine), the masculine plural form of the noun is used.

los hijos = **el hijo y la hija (los hijos y las hijas)**
los amigos = **el amigo y la amiga (los amigos y las amigas)**
los abuelos = **el abuelo y la abuela**
los señores Gómez = **el señor y la señora Gómez**

EJERCICIO D   Rosita fue de compras. Escriba lo que cuenta, usando la forma plural de los sustantivos dados.

Al terminar la época de las _____ navideñas, los _____ ofrecen muchas
                                    1. (fiesta)   *2.* (almacén)

_____ En todos los _____ hay _____ en rebaja. A mí me
     3. (ganga)   *4.* (departamento)   *5.* (cosa)

gusta ir de compras los _____ . El sábado pasado todos los _____ estaban en
                             6. (sábado)   *7.* (suéter)

rebaja; también los _____ de diversas _____ estaban a _____
                          8. (traje)   *9.* (tela)   *10.* (precio)

reducidos. Vi que muchos _____ compraron estas _____ de vestir.
11. (joven)   12. (prenda)

Entré en el departamento de los _____ de deporte porque necesito una raqueta de te-
13. (artículo)

nis nueva. Había allí muchas _____ , porque daban las pelotas gratis con la compra de una
14. (persona)

raqueta. Todos los _____ estaban ocupados y no pude esperar porque tenía que tomar dos
15. (vendedor)

_____ para llegar a casa. Sin embargo, mientras iba hacia la puerta de salida, no pude resistir
16. (autobús)

una ganga especial. Vendían _____ de _____ de unas _____
17. (lápiz)   18. (labio)   19. (marca)

europeas a tres por el precio de uno. Tuve que comprar dos _____ grandes para cargar to-
20. (bolsa)

dos mis _____ . En la cola del autobús encontré a los _____ Pareda, que
21. (paquete)   22. (señor)

habían comprado dos _____ a color para unos _____ suyos. Al subir al
23. (televisor)   24. (pariente)

autobús vi que había solamente dos _____ para sentarse, y la señora Pareda y yo nos sentamos.
25. (lugar)

---

[3] FORMS OF THE ARTICLES

a. There are four definite articles in Spanish corresponding to English *the:*

	SINGULAR	PLURAL
MASCULINE	**el**	**los**
FEMININE	**la**	**las**

NOTES:

1. Feminine nouns that begin with the stressed sound of **a** (**a-** or **ha-**) take the article **el** in the singular. In the plural, the article is **las.**

        el agua *water*   **las aguas** *waters*
        el alma *soul*   **las almas** *souls*
        el hacha *ax*   **las hachas** *axes*

        But:

        la amiga
        la alumna } initial **a** is not stressed

2. The masculine article **el** combines with the prepositions **de** and **a** to form **del** and **al.**

3. The neuter article **lo,** used with adjectives, does not vary in form.

        lo bueno *the good (that which is good)*

b. There are four indefinite articles in Spanish corresponding to English *a (an)*, *some*, *several*, *a few*.

	SINGULAR	PLURAL
MASCULINE	un	unos
FEMININE	una	unas

EJERCICIO E   El sobrino de Graciela va a cumplir un año. Escriba una lista de las cosas que ella debe comprar para su fiesta.

EJEMPLO: platos   **unos platos**

1. pastel _____

2. servilletas _____

3. juguete _____

4. helados _____

5. cucharas _____

6. tenedores _____

7. refrescos _____

8. adornos _____

9. premios _____

10. invitaciones _____

11. vela _____

12. mantel de papel _____

13. vasos _____

14. globos _____

15. litros de leche _____

EJERCICIO F   Mientras Leonardo camina por las calles de Salamanca, él identifica lo que ve.

EJEMPLO: farmacia   **una farmacia**

1. peluquería _____

2. café _____

3. restaurante _____

4. lavandería _____

5. iglesia _____

6. perfumería _____

7. almacén _____

8. hospital _____

9. museo _____

10. universidad _____

11. cuartel de bomberos _____

12. carnicería _____

13. escuela _____

14. parque _____

15. asilo de ancianos _____

16. supermercado _____

17. río _____

18. terminal de autobuses _____

19. plaza _____

20. jardín _____

EJERCICIO G   **Escriba lo que Gregorio saca de su maleta al llegar a casa de sus abuelos.**

Gregorio saca de su maleta _____

_____

_____

_____

_____

_____

_____

_____

[4] USES OF THE ARTICLES IN SPANISH

a. The definite article is used in Spanish before the names of languages, except after **hablar, en,** or **de.**

El español es importante hoy día.	*Spanish is important nowadays.*

But:

Mi amigo *habla francés.*	*My friend speaks French.*
Todo el libro está escrito *en alemán.*	*The whole book is written in German.*
La clase *de español* es interesante.	*The Spanish class is interesting.*

NOTES:

1. If an adverb occurs between **hablar** and a name of a language, the article may be used with the language.

Habla bien el español.	*He speaks Spanish well.*

2. Current everyday usage tends to omit the definite article after the verbs **estudiar, aprender, leer, escribir, enseñar,** and **saber.**

Yo estudio portugués.	*I study Portuguese.*
¿Sabes francés?	*Do you know French?*

b. The definite article is used before titles, except when addressing the person.

El señor Gómez salió ayer.	*Mr. Gómez left yesterday.*
¿Cómo está Ud., señora Álvarez?	*How are you, Mrs. Alvarez?*

NOTE: The article is omitted before **don (doña), Santo (San, Santa).**

c. The definite article is used instead of the possessive adjective with parts of the body or wearing apparel when the possessor is clear.

Ella se lava *el pelo.*	*She washes her hair.*
Se puso *el sombrero.*	*He put on his hat.*

d. The definite article is used with the time of day.

Es *la una.*	*It's one o'clock.*
Me acuesto a *las diez.*	*I go to bed at ten o'clock.*

e. The definite article is used before nouns used in a general or abstract sense.

El hombre es mortal.	*Man is mortal.*
La libertad es preciosa.	*Liberty is precious.*
Los diamantes son caros.	*Diamonds are expensive.*

f. The definite article is used before infinitives functioning as nouns. The article is often omitted, however, when the infinitive is the subject in a sentence. Infinitive nouns are always masculine.

(*El*) *mentir* **es un vicio.**	*Lying is a vice.*

g. The definite article is used with the names of seasons.

Me gusta *la primavera* (*el verano,* *el otoño, el invierno*).	*I like spring (summer, autumn, winter).*

NOTE: The article may be omitted after the preposition **en.**

Voy a España *en* (*el*) *verano.*	*I am going to Spain in the summer.*

h. The definite article is used with the days of the week, except after the verb **ser** when expressing dates.

Iré al teatro *el domingo.*	*I will go to the theater (on) Sunday.*
Los viernes **hay pruebas.**	*(On) Fridays there are tests.*
El examen fue *el lunes* **pasado.**	*The exam was last Monday.*

But:

Hoy *es jueves.*	*Today is Thursday.*
Se acordó que el día siguiente *era* *sábado* **y no había clases.**	*He remembered that the following day was Saturday and there were no classes.*

i. The definite article is used before names of rivers, oceans, and mountains.

los Andes	*the Andes*	**el Amazonas**	*the Amazon* (river)
los Alpes	*the Alps*	**el Orinoco**	*the Orinoco* (river)
el Pacífico	*the Pacific*	**el Mediterráneo**	*the Mediterranean*

j. The definite article is used before certain names of countries, states, and cities.

el Brasil	*Brazil*	**la Argentina**	*Argentina*
los Estados Unidos	*the United States*	**el Perú**	*Peru*
la Florida	*Florida*	**la Habana**	*Havana*
el Japón	*Japan*	**el Uruguay**	*Uruguay*
el Paraguay	*Paraguay*	**el Canadá**	*Canada*
el Ecuador	*Ecuador*	**el Cairo**	*Cairo*

NOTES:

1. Current everyday usage tends to omit the definite article before the names of countries.

Vivo en Estados Unidos desde hace dos años.

2. The definite article is used with geographical names that are modified.

América tiene muchas riquezas.	**España está en Europa.**
La **América del Sur tiene muchas riquezas.**	**Me interesa** *la* **España del siglo XV.**

k. The definite article is used before nouns of weight or measure. English uses the indefinite article.

un dólar *la libra*	*a dollar a pound*
diez centavos *la docena*	*ten cents a dozen*

| EJERCICIO H | Escriba la forma apropiada del artículo definido, si es necesario, en este diálogo entre Javier y un alumno de intercambio de su escuela. |

JAVIER: ¿De dónde eres?

TOMÁS: Soy de _____ Perú.
<u>1.</u>

JAVIER: ¿Hay montañas cerca de tu país?

TOMÁS: Sí, _____ Andes.
<u>2.</u>

JAVIER: ¿Vas allí a menudo?

TOMÁS: Sí, _____ esquiar es mi deporte favorito.
<u>3.</u>

JAVIER: ¿Qué estación te gusta más?

TOMÁS: Me gusta más _____ invierno.
<u>4.</u>

JAVIER: ¿Quién es ese señor?

TOMÁS: Es _____ señor Lobos. Es _____ profesor de _____ inglés.
<u>5.</u> <u>6.</u> <u>7.</u>

JAVIER: ¿Estudias _____ inglés?
<u>8.</u>

TOMÁS: Sí, puesto que vivo en _____ Estados Unidos _____ inglés es un idioma importante para mí.
<u>9.</u> <u>10.</u>

JAVIER: ¿Hablas otro idioma también?

TOMÁS: Yo no, pero mi mamá habla _____ francés.
<u>11.</u>

JAVIER: ¿Ves muchas películas?

TOMÁS: Sí, suelo ir a _____ cine _____ viernes por _____ noche.
<u>12.</u> <u>13.</u> <u>14.</u>

JAVIER: ¿Qué hora será?

TOMÁS: Son _____ doce y media. ¿Por qué?
<u>15.</u>

JAVIER: Tengo una cita con _____ señora Bello. Ella es mi consejera.
<u>16.</u>

TOMÁS: Debes apresurarte. _____ llegar tarde no es una buena idea.
<u>17.</u>

JAVIER: Ella es muy simpática. ¿La conoces? Ella tiene _____ pelo largo.
<u>18.</u>

TOMÁS: No la conozco. Mi consejero es _____ doctor Muñoz y él tiene _____ nariz larga.
<u>19.</u> <u>20.</u>

Hasta luego.

JAVIER: Sí, nos vemos después.

| EJERCICIO I | Conteste las preguntas que hace una alumna en una encuesta. |

1. ¿Qué día es hoy? (miércoles)

_____

2. ¿Qué hora es? (1:00)

_____

3. ¿En qué estación estamos? (primavera)

_____

4. ¿De qué color tiene tu mamá el pelo? (castaño)

_____

5. ¿Y los ojos? (verdes)

_____

6. ¿Cuándo vas al parque? (sábado)

_____

7. ¿Cuándo sales a cenar con tus padres? (martes)

_____

8. ¿Dónde viven tus abuelos? (Florida)

_____

9. ¿Quién es tu profesor de matemáticas? (señorita Castillo)

_____

10. ¿Qué lengua estudias? (alemán)

_____

11. ¿Cuál es tu ciencia favorita? (química)

_____

12. ¿A qué hora te acuestas? (11:00)

_____

13. ¿Cuál es tu deporte favorito? (béisbol)

_____

14. ¿Cuánto cuesta un refresco en la cafetería? (50 centavos)

_____

15. ¿Qué país te gustaría visitar? (Brasil)

_____

[5] NEUTER ARTICLE *LO*

a. The neuter article **lo** precedes an adjective used as a noun to express a quality or an abstract idea.

Lo nuevo **no es siempre mejor que** *lo viejo*.	*The new (That which is new) is not always better than the old (what is old).*
Pienso *lo mismo* **que Ud.**	*I think the same as you.*

b. **Lo** + adjective (or adverb) + **que** = how

Ya veo *lo simpático* (*simpática*) **que es.**	*I do see how nice he (she) is.*
Me sorprende *lo rápidamente que* **corre.**	*I am surprised how quickly he runs.*

NOTE: Since the article **lo** is neuter, it has no plural form. **Lo** is used whether the adjective is masculine or feminine, singular or plural.

EJERCICIO J   Escriba sus impresiones sobre los conceptos siguientes, usando *lo*.

SUGERENCIAS: disgustar   interesar   encantar
fascinar   molestar   fastidiar
importar   preocupar   impresionar

EJEMPLO: romántico   **Lo romántico me aburre.**

1. cómico _____

2. pintoresco _____

3. diferente _____

4. raro _____

5. peligroso _____

6. emocionante _____

7. imposible _____

8. bello _____

9. curioso _____

10. difícil _____

EJERCICIO K   Ud. acaba de volver de pescar en el lago. Usando *lo* y las sugerencias, escriba sus impresiones de la excursion.

SUGERENCIAS: cómico   divertido   interesante   major
dificil   peligroso   peor   impresionante

EJEMPLO: **Lo aburrido fue esperar.**

1. perder el pez _____

2. tocar los peces _____

3. no hablar _____

4. limpiar los pescados _____

5. sentarse a esperar _____

6. vender los pescados _____

| EJERCICIO L | Escriba sus impresiones de una novela que Ud. acaba de leer, usando *lo* + uno de los siguientes adjectives. |

emocionante	divertido	triste
romántico	mejor	aburrido
interesante	curioso	impresionante
cómico	raro	

EJEMPLO: **Lo romántico fue la boda.**

1. _____

2. _____

3. _____

4. _____

5. _____

6. _____

7. _____

[6] OMISSION OF THE ARTICLE

a. The article is omitted.

(1) Before nouns in apposition.

Madrid, *capital* de España, está en el centro del país. — *Madrid, the capital of Spain, is in the center of the country.*

Lope de Vega, *dramaturgo* español, escribió muchas comedias. — *Lope de Vega, a Spanish playwright, wrote many plays.*

(2) Before numerals expressing the numerical order of rulers.

Carlos Quinto — *Charles the Fifth*
Isabel Segunda — *Isabel the Second*

b. The indefinite article is omitted.

(1) Before predicate nouns denoting a class or group (social class, occupation, nationality, religion, etc.).

Es peluquero. — *He is a barber.*
Soy americano. — *I am (an) American.*
Quiero hacerme médico. — *I want to become a doctor.*

NOTE: If the predicate noun is modified, the indefinite article is expressed.

Era *un peluquero hábil*.   *He was a skillful barber.*
Quiero ser *un médico bueno*.   *I want to be a good doctor.*

(2) Before or after certain words that ordinarily have the article in English: **otro** (*another*), **cierto** (*a certain*), **ciento** (*a hundred*), **mil** (*a thousand*), **tal** ... (*such a* ...), **¡qué** ... ! (*what a* ... !).

otra carta *another letter*	**mil soldados** *one (a) thousand soldiers*
cierto día *a certain day*	**tal hombre** *such a man*
cien dólares *one (a) hundred dollars*	**¡Qué memoria!** *What a memory!*

EJERCICIO M   Escriba los recados que la secretaria le dejó a su jefe.

EJEMPLO: Pedro Cabal / presidente / Industrias Modernas / llamó
       Pedro Cabal, presidente de Industrias Modernas, llamó.

1. Elvira Soto / dueña / Fábrica Equis / canceló su cita

_____

2. General Vidal / director / Banco Nacional / aprobó su préstamo

_____

3. Sra. Moreno / esposa / Gabriel Moreno / llamó

_____

4. Esteban Núñez / ayudante / Sra. Amador / telefoneó dos veces

_____

5. Rodolfo Esteves / padre / su yerno / dejó otro número

_____

6. David Rivera / agente / la policía / devolvió su llamada

_____

7. Carlos / chofer / Sr. Asturias / dejó un paquete

_____

8. Sr. Cuevas / gerente / la compañía / quiere verlo mañana

EJERCICIO N   Conteste estas preguntas que le hace un aduanero en el aeropuerto de Barajas.

1. ¿Cuál es su nacionalidad?

_____

2. ¿Cuál es su profesión? (estudiante)

_____

3. ¿Qué clase de estudiante es Ud.?

_____

4. ¿Qué quiere Ud. hacerse?

_____

5. ¿En qué hotel se quedará Ud.? (Felipe II)

_____

6. ¿Por qué escogió Ud. ese hotel? (bueno)

_____

7. ¿Cuánto dinero piensa Ud. gastar en el viaje? ($1,000)

_____

EJERCICIO O **Complete este monólogo con el artículo apropiado, si es necesario, o con _otro_, _cien_, _cierto_, _mil_, _tal_ o _¡qué!_.**

Buenos das. Soy Patricia Bulnes y soy _____ actriz. Los críticos dicen que soy _____ actriz buena y
                                      1.   *2.*

popular. El público me manda más de _____ cartas al día. Ya he hecho _____ películas y mañana
                                            3.   *4.*

comienzo a trabajar en _____ película. ¡Y _____ película! Hago el papel de _____ mujer rica y ele-
                            5.   *6.*   *7.*

gante. _____ mujer se aburre rápidamente y pasa el tiempo viajando. La película comienza en París,
      8.

_____ capital de Francia. _____ día estamos en Londres, _____ capital de Inglaterra, porque la acción
  9.   *10.*   *11.*

también se desarrolla allí. La protagonista es _____ mujer caprichosa que se mete en muchos líos. Hay
                                             12.

_____ escena en que _____ hombres se visten de policía y la acompañan a _____ fiesta grandísima.
  13.   *14.*   *15.*

¡_____ segura me sentí cuando filmaron esa escena! _____ película va a costar más de cien mil dólares
  16.   *17.*

porque cada actor recibe _____ dólares al día. No me importa. Tengo _____ vida interesante y emocio-
                            18.   *19.*

nante. ¡_____ buena suerte tengo!
      20.

MASTERY EXERCISES

EJERCICIO P **Conteste estas preguntas, con las que Alicia practica para un examen.**

1. ¿Cuál es el río más grande de la América del Sur?

_____

2. ¿En qué país hispanoamericano vivían los incas?

_____

3. ¿Qué idioma hablan en el Uruguay?

_____

4. ¿Cuál es y dónde está la capital de España?

_____

5. ¿Qué país está al norte de los Estados Unidos?

_____

6. ¿Qué ciudad era popular para los turistas antes de Fidel Castro?

_____

7. ¿Quién fue un dramaturgo español que escribió muchas comedias?

_____

8. ¿Cómo se llama el río que está entre México y los Estados Unidos?

_____

9. ¿Cómo se llama la capital del Perú, que tiene mucha arquitectura colonial?

_____

10. ¿En qué país de Suramérica no se habla español?

_____

EJERCICIO Q **Cada familia tiene un modo especial de celebrar un evento especial (un cumpleaños, un aniversario, una fiesta, una temporada del año, etc.). Escoja un evento que su familia celebra en una forma especial y escriba un ensayo en el que Ud. describe detalladamente la celebración. Incluya lo siguiente:**

- the name of the event
- when it is celebrated
- where it takes place
- why it is celebrated
- the special way in which it is celebrated (when this tradition began, etc.)
- who participates in the celebration
- what you like or dislike about it, etc.
- what makes the celebration unique

_____

_____

_____

_____

_____

_____

_____

_____

_____

_____

_____

_____

_____

_____

_____

Chapter 18
Personal Pronouns

[1] SUBJECT PRONOUNS

	SINGULAR		PLURAL
yo	*I*	**nosotros, -as**	*we*
tú	*you* (familiar)	**vosotros, -as**	*you* (familiar)
usted (Ud.)	*you*	**ustedes (Uds.)**	*you*
él	*he*	**ellos**	*they* (masculine)
ella	*she*	**ellas**	*they* (feminine)

Subject pronouns are not used in Spanish as often as in English. Normally the verb ending indicates the subject. Spanish subject pronouns are used for clarity, emphasis, and politeness.

Él **leía mientras** *yo* **cantaba.**	*He was reading while I was singing.*
No hagas eso: *yo* **debo hacerlo.**	*Don't do that: I must do it.*
¡Pase *Ud.***! Tome** *Ud.* **asiento.**	*Enter! Take a seat.*

NOTES:

1. Even though subject pronouns are usually omitted, **usted** and **ustedes** are regularly used.

2. The **vosotros** form (familiar plural) is used in Spain but rarely in Spanish America, where the form **ustedes** is preferred.

3. The English pronoun *it* is not expressed as a subject in Spanish.

¿Dónde está? Está en el cajón.	*Where is it? It's in the drawer.*
¿Qué es? Es un libro.	*What is it? It's a book.*

EJERCICIO A   **En una fiesta, Víctor identifica a sus amigos y dice de dónde son. Escriba el pronombre apropiado en cada frase.**

EJEMPLO: Elena y Rosa son hermanas. Ellas nacieron en La Habana.

1. Jorge y Pedro son primos. _____ son de Bogotá.

2. Luz y Pilar son hermanas. _____ son de Cali.

3. Eduardo y yo somos amigos. _____ somos de Chicago.

4. Lola es la hermana de Carlos. _____ es de Caracas.

5. Esteban es el primo de Ricardo. _____ es de San José.

6. Rocío y María, ¿de dónde son _____ ? _____ soy de Panamá y _____ es de México.

7. Clara, ¿de dónde eres _____ ? _____ soy de San Juan.

8. Beto y Anita, ¿de dónde son _____ ? _____ somos de Buenos Aires.

9. Gustavo, ¿de dónde son tus padres? _____ son de Francia.

10. Beatriz y Sara, ¿dónde vivieron _____ antes de venir aquí? _____ vivimos cerca de la capital.

EJERCICIO B   Conteste las preguntas que le hace un vecino nuevo. Use los pronombres apropiados.

1. ¿Cómo te llamas?
   _____

2. ¿Dónde están tus padres?
   _____

3. ¿Quién es esa chica?
   _____

4. ¿Cómo se llama la escuela a que vas?
   _____

5. ¿Quiénes son esos señores?
   _____

6. ¿Podemos tú y yo jugar al tenis?
   _____

7. ¿Dónde juegan tú y tus amigos?
   _____

8. ¿Tienes otra raqueta?
   _____

9. ¿Es ese señor tu padre?
   _____

10. ¿Dónde podemos comprar leche?
   _____

[2] PREPOSITIONAL PRONOUNS

SINGULAR	PLURAL
mí *me*	**nosotros, -as** *us*
ti *you* (familiar)	**vosotros, -as** *you* (familiar)
usted (Ud.) *you*	**ustedes (Uds.)** *you*
él *him, it*	**ellos** *them* (masculine)
ella *her, it*	**ellas** *they* (feminine)
sí *yourself, himself, herself, itself*	**sí** *yourselves, themselves*

a. The prepositional pronoun is used as the object of a preposition and always follows the preposition.

No es para *mí*; es para *ellos*.   *It's not for me; it's for them.*

b. The pronouns *mí, ti,* and *sí* combine with the preposition *con* as follows:

conmigo   *with me*
contigo   *with you* (fam.)
consigo   *with you (yourself), with him(self), with her(self), with them(selves)*

NOTES:

1. The prepositional pronouns are identical with the subject pronouns, except for **mí, ti,** and **sí.**

2. The forms **conmigo, contigo,** and **consigo** do not change in gender and number.

3. The familiar plural form **vosotros, –as** is used in Spain but rarely in Spanish America, where the form **ustedes** is preferred.

c. Common prepositions

a   *to, at*
acerca de   *about*
además de   *besides*
alrededor de   *around*
ante   *before, in the presence of*
antes de   *before*
cerca de   *near*
con   *with*
contra   *against*
de   *of, from*
debajo de   *beneath, under*
delante de   *in front of*
dentro de   *within, inside*
desde   *from, since*
después de   *after*
detrás de   *behind*

durante   *during*
en   *in, on*
encima de   *above, on top of*
enfrente de   *in front of, opposite*
entre   *between, among*
frente a   *in front of*
fuera de   *outside of; aside from*
hacia   *toward*
hasta   *until*
lejos de   *far from*
para   *for, in order to*
por   *for, by, through*
según   *according to*
sin   *without*
sobre   *over, above*
tras   *after*

| EJERCICIO C | Su hermano le hace preguntas sobre sus compras. Escriba para quién(es) son estas cosas, usando el pronombre apropiado. |

EJEMPLO: ¿Son los guantes para mi abuelita?
Sí, son para ella.

1. ¿Es la pelota para Jorge?

_____

2. ¿Son los discos para nosotros?

_____

3. La blusa es para mamá, ¿verdad?

_____

4. ¿Es el sombrero para papá?

_____

5. Los dulces son para los niños, ¿verdad?

_____

6. ¿Son los aretes para Luz y Alba?

_____

7. El abrigo es para ti, ¿verdad?

_____

8. El guante de béisbol es para mí, ¿verdad?

_____

9. ¿Es el rebozo para la tía Conchita?

_____

10. Los calcetines son para Luis y Paco, ¿verdad?

_____

| EJERCICIO D | A Roberto no le gusta jugar con nadie. Escriba lo que dice cuando su mamá le hace sugerencias. Use los pronombres apropiados. |

EJEMPLO: Enrique va a jugar al baloncesto.
No quiero jugar con él.

1. Gloria va a jugar al voleibol.

_____

2. Pedro y Arturo van a jugar al fútbol.

_____

3. Gladys y Beatriz van a jugar al dominó.

_____

4. Tu papá y yo vamos a jugar a los naipes.

_____

5. Yo voy a jugar al tenis.

_____

6. Lupita va a jugar al béisbol.

_____

| EJERCICIO E | Conteste las preguntas que le hace un compañero de campamento, usando el pronombre apropiado. |

EJEMPLO: ¿Es la pulsera de Carmen?
           Sí, es de ella.

1. ¿Vives cerca del estadio?

_____

2. ¿Te gusta correr alrededor de la cancha de tenis?

_____

3. ¿Juegas contra tus hermanos?

_____

4. ¿Puedo ir contigo en el barco?

_____

5. ¿Según el consejero, a qué hora debemos apagar la luz?

_____

6. ¿Fuiste al cine sin tu tarjeta de identidad?

_____

7. Camino hacia el bosque para llegar a la piscina, ¿verdad?

_____

8. ¿Quién estaba delante de ti en la cola hoy?

_____

9. ¿Qué pusiste debajo de la cama de Raúl?

_____

10. ¿No te sentiste bien durante los ejercicios esta mañana?

_____

11. ¿Irás a la tienda por mí?

_____

12. ¿Plantaron flores detrás de la oficina?

_____

13. ¿Me vas a decir algo sobre la película?

_____

14. ¿Quiénes estaban allí además de Uds.?

_____

15. ¿Pusieron la bandera en la ventana?

_____

[3] OBJECT PRONOUNS

a. The object pronouns are as follows.

DIRECT	INDIRECT
SINGULAR	**SINGULAR**
me *me* **te** *you* (familiar) ~~**le** *you (masculine); him*~~ **lo** *you, him, it* (masculine) **la** *you* (feminine), *her, it* (feminine)	**me** (*to*) *me* **te** (*to*) *you* (familiar) **le** (*to*) *you,* (*to*) *him,* (*to*) *her,* (*to*) *it*
PLURAL	**PLURAL**
nos *us* ~~**os** *you (familiar)*~~ **los** *you, them* (masculine) **las** *you, them* (feminine)	**nos** (*to*) *us* **os** (*to*) *you* (familiar) **les** (*to*) *you,* (*to*) *them*

NOTES:

1. The forms **me, te, nos,** and **os** are both direct and indirect object pronouns. They are also reflexive pronouns (see page 114).

2. In Spanish America, **lo** is preferred to **le** as direct object.

3. Before an indirect–object pronoun, the prepositions *to, for,* or *from* are not expressed in Spanish.

Me dio el dinero.	*He gave the money to me.*
Me compró el libro.	*He bought me the book.*
Me cobró el dinero.	*He collected the money from me.*

b. Position of object pronouns.

(1) Object pronouns, direct or indirect, normally precede the verb.

Juan *me* ve.   *Juan sees me.*
El maestro *les* ha hablado.   *The teacher has spoken to them.*

(2) When the direct or indirect object pronouns are used with an infinitive, a **gerundio,** or an affirmative command, they may be attached to the verb.

Deseo enviar*lo*.
or
***Lo* deseo enviar.**   } *I want to send it.*

Estoy enviándo*lo*.
      or   } *I am sending it.*
***Lo* estoy enviando.**

Enví*elo*.   *Send it.*

But:

No *lo* envíe.   *Don't send it.*

NOTES:

1. The object pronouns may either be attached to the infinitive or the **gerundio** or precede the conjugated form of the verb.

2. When an object pronoun is attached to the **gerundio** or the affirmative command, an accent mark is normally required on the stressed vowel of the verb in order to keep the original stress. If the affirmative command has only one syllable (**pon**), no accent mark is required (**ponlo**).

| **EJERCICIO F** | Conteste las preguntas que le hace un amigo en una llamada telefónica. Use un pronombre en cada frase. |

1. ¿Buscaste la lista de los discos?

_____

2. ¿Compraste el disco que querías?

_____

3. ¿Viste a Carmen y a Gloria?

_____

4. ¿Escuchaste las noticias hoy?

_____

5. ¿Leíste el periódico de la mañana?

_____

6. ¿Miraste las fotos en la página tres?

_____

7. ¿Esperaste a tus padres en el centro?

_____

8. ¿Ayudaste a tu hermanito con la tarea?

_____

9. ¿Vas a ver la película a las ocho?

_____

10. ¿Invitaste a Tomás y a Luis a la fiesta?

_____

11. ¿Terminaste la tarea?

_____

12. ¿Aprendiste el poema de memoria?

_____

13. ¿Quién hizo el diseño?

_____

14. ¿Tienes los boletos para el teatro?

_____

15. ¿Pediste el carro prestado a tu papá?

_____

EJERCICIO G | **La abuela de Carmen es mexicana y va a preparar los platos favoritos de su familia. Escriba lo que ella le cuenta a su esposo y lo que él le responde.**

EJEMPLO: a mi hijo / enchiladas suizas
A mi hijo le voy a preparar enchiladas suizas.
Bueno, **¡prepárale** enchiladas suizas!

1. a Carmen / chiles rellenos

_____

_____

2. a Roberto y a Paco / tacos de pollo

_____

_____

3. a ti / tamales

_____

_____

4. a nosotros / flan

_____

_____

5. a mí / sopa de fideos

_____

_____

EJERCICIO H | **La mamá de Joaquín le pregunta si ha empacado las cosas que necesita para ir a acampar. Escriba lo que le contesta Joaquín.**

EJEMPLO: ¿Empacaste la manta? (Sí)   **Sí, la empaqué.**

1. ¿Y el suéter? (Sí)   _____

2. ¿Y la mochila? (No)   _____

3. ¿Y la tienda? (Sí) _____

4. ¿Y los platos de plástico? (Sí) _____

5. ¿Y los zapatos de tenis? (Sí) _____

6. ¿Y las botas? (No) _____

7. ¿Y el mapa? (Sí) _____

8. ¿Y las llaves? (Sí) _____

9. ¿Y el impermeable? (No) _____

10. ¿Y el cepillo de dientes? (Sí) _____

EJERCICIO I	Según Lourdes, uno de sus profesores habla muchos idiomas. Escriba lo que ella cuenta.

EJEMPLO: a José / inglés
            A José le habla en inglés.

1. a mí / español

   _____

2. a Pierre y a Claude / francés

   _____

3. a Sofía / italiano

   _____

4. a María y a mí / inglés

   _____

5. a Karl / alemán

   _____

6. a Cristóbal y a Melina / griego

   _____

7. a ti / ruso

   _____

8. a Uds. / portugués

   _____

EJERCICIO J	Escriba cuándo visita Ud. a estas personas.

EJEMPLO: su abuela   **La visito todos los domingos.**

1. sus primos _____

2. su mejor amigo / amiga _____

3. sus compañeros de clase _____

4. su vecino _____

5. su cura _____

6. su tía _____

7. su médico _____

EJERCICIO K La tía de Alfredo está enferma y hay una enfermera en la casa. Alfredo quiere saber lo que ella hace. Escriba las preguntas que él le hace a la enfermera.

EJEMPLO: poner inyecciones a mi tía
¿Le pone inyecciones a mi tía?

1. dar la medicina a mi tía

_____

2. bañar (a mi tía)

_____

3. preparar la comida a mis tíos

_____

4. arreglar el cuarto a ellos

_____

5. peinar (a mi tía)

_____

6. contestar el teléfono

_____

7. vestir (a mi tía)

_____

EJERCICIO L En la clase de costura María está cosiendo un vestido. Escriba las instrucciones que le da la maestra y el comentario que hacen unas compañeras.

EJEMPLO: cortar el patrón
MAESTRA: **Córtalo.**
AMIGA: **Va a cortarlo.**
OTRA AMIGA: **Está cortándolo.**

1. medir la tela

MAESTRA: _____

AMIGA: _____

OTRA AMIGA: _____

2. poner los alfileres

MAESTRA: _____

AMIGA: _____

OTRA AMIGA: _____

3. coser las mangas

MAESTRA: _____

AMIGA: _____

OTRA AMIGA: _____

4. coser los botones

MAESTRA: _____

AMIGA: _____

OTRA AMIGA: _____

5. planchar el vestido

MAESTRA: _____

AMIGA: _____

OTRA AMIGA: _____

6. colgar el vestido

MAESTRA: _____

AMIGA: _____

OTRA AMIGA: _____

[4] *GUSTAR* AND OTHER VERBS USED WITH INDIRECT-OBJECT PRONOUNS

a. The verb **gustar** expresses *to like.*

Me gusta **el vestido.**	*I like the dress.* (Literally: *The dress pleases me.*)
Te gustan **las flores.**	*You like the flowers.* (Literally: *The flowers please you.*)
Le gustaría **viajar a Europa.**	*He would like to travel to Europe.* (Literally: *To travel to Europe would please him.*)

b. **Gustar** is preceded by an indirect-object pronoun. Note that the form of **gustar** agrees with the subject, which generally follows it.

Te gustará *el libro.*	*You will like the book.*
Te gustarán *los libros.*	*You will like the books.*
Nos gustó *la novela.*	*We liked the novel.*
Nos gustaron *las novelas.*	*We liked the novels.*
Les gusta *cantar.*	*They like to sing.*

NOTE: If the thing liked is not a noun but an "action" (expressed by a verb or clause), **gustar** is used in the third-person singular.

Le gusta *cantar y bailar.*	*He likes to sing and dance.*
Me gustaría *que vinieras hoy.*	*I would like you to come today.*

c. The indirect-object noun normally precedes the indirect-object pronoun.

A María no **le gusta** leer.	*María doesn't like to read.*
A los niños **les gusta** ir al cine.	*The children like to go to the movies.*
A Roberto **le gustan** los dulces.	*Roberto likes sweets.*

d. Other verbs used like **gustar:**

agradar   *to be pleased with, to please*

Les agradó mi regalo.	*They were pleased with my gift.*
	(My gift was pleasing to them.)

bastar   *to be enough, to suffice*

Me bastan tres dólares.	*Three dollars are enough for me.*

doler   *to be painful, to cause sorrow*

Me duele el pie izquierdo.	*My left foot hurts (is painful to me).*

faltar
hacer falta } *to be lacking, to need*

Le faltan cincuenta centavos.	*He lacks fifty cents. (Fifty cents are lacking to him.)*
Le hace falta dinero.	*He needs money. (Money is lacking to him.)*

parecer   *to seem*

Me parece imposible.	*It seems impossible to me.*

placer   *to be pleasing, to be pleased*

Me place poder ayudarlo.	*I am pleased to be able to help you.*

quedar (a uno)   *to remain (to someone), to have left*

Nos queda un solo día.	*We have only one day left.*

sobrar   *to be left over, to have too much*

Me sobran tres cartas.	*I have three cards too many.*

tocar (a uno)   *to be one's turn*

A mí **me toca** lavar los platos.	*It is my turn to wash the dishes.*

EJERCICIO M   **Algunos amigos hablan de sus gustos. Escriba lo que dicen.**

EJEMPLO: a mí / gustar / los deportes
A mí me gustan los deportes.

1. a nosotros / gustar / la música popular

_____

2. a Elena / gustar / cantar mientras trabaja

_____

3. a ti / gustar / las ferias

_____

4. a Pedro y a Carlos / no gustar / patinar en el hielo

_____

5. a ustedes / gustar / ir al teatro

_____

6. a mí / gustar / las películas románticas

_____

7. a ellas / gustar / los bailes

_____

8. a Ramón / no gustar / el helado de fresa

_____

9. a ti y a mí / gustar / pasar un buen rato

_____

10. a Celia / no gustar / las bromas

_____

EJERCICIO N   **Unos amigos piensan hacer una fiesta de disfraces. Escriba un comentario para cada frase, usando la información dada.**

EJEMPLO: JAIME: Me invitaron a una fiesta de disfraces.
LOURDES: a mí / agradar / los disfraces
A mí me agradan los disfraces.

1. EDUARDO: Tenemos que comprar los refrescos. Cuestan doce dólares.
SILVIA: a mí / quedar / sólo cinco dólares

_____

2. ROSA: No tengo tela para hacer el disfraz que quiero usar.
GLORIA: a mi mamá / sobrar / tela

_____

3. GABRIEL y LUZ: ¿Quién va a llevar la comida?
ESTEBAN: a Alfonso / tocar / llevar la comida

_____

4. VICTORIA: Vamos a dar un premio por el mejor disfraz.

BETO Y FELIPE: a nosotros / parecer / una buena idea

_____

5. LOLA: Voy a comprar las máscaras. ¿Cuántas necesitamos?

MANUEL: a nosotros / bastar / veinte máscaras

_____

6. HÉCTOR: Voy a ir de compras al supermercado con Raúl.

VÍCTOR: a Raúl / doler / las piernas

_____

7. SARITA: Ya terminamos de decorar el salón.

TOMÁS: a ti / no faltar / imaginación

_____

8. PABLO: Va a ser una fiesta fabulosa. ¡Todos muestran tanto entusiasmo!

ADELA: a mí / placer / el entusiasmo de la gente

_____

9. DAVID y JAVIER: Vas a quedar muy impresionado con nuestro disfraz.

FERNANDO: Lo sé. a ustedes / gustar / lo absurdo

_____

10. MARÍA: Hemos invitado a diecinueve personas.

PILAR: a nosotras / hacer falta / invitar a otro chico

_____

EJERCICIO O | **Gloria hace una encuesta sobre los gustos de sus amigos. Escriba lo que ellos responden, usando (*no*) *gustar*, (*no*) *fascinar*, (*no*) *encantar*.**

EJEMPLO: ¿Bailas mucho?
Sí, me encanta bailar.

1. ¿Vas de compras a menudo?

_____

2. ¿Reciben Uds. muchos regalos?

_____

3. ¿Ven ellos muchas películas?

_____

4. ¿Juega Antonio muchos deportes?

_____

5. ¿Sabes conducir?

_____

6. ¿Cocinan Uds. de vez en cuando?

_____

7. ¿Leen ellas muchas novelas?

_____

8. ¿Coso yo mi propia ropa?

_____

9. ¿Sabe Carlos esquiar?

_____

10. ¿Montan Uds. en bicicleta?

_____

EJERCICIO P	**Roberto y Pedro han pasado un mes en un programa de intercambio en México. Conteste las preguntas que les hicieron sus amigos.**

1. ¿Les pareció buena la experiencia? (sí, muy buena)

_____

2. ¿A Uds. les agradó la familia con que vivieron? (mucho)

_____

3. Roberto, ¿te sobró dinero del viaje? (50 dólares)

_____

4. Pedro, ¿qué te hizo falta durante el viaje? (nada)

_____

5. ¿A quién le dolió el estómago en México? (a Pedro)

_____

6. ¿Les queda tiempo ahora para mostrar las fotografías que sacaron? (sí)

_____

7. ¿Cuánto tiempo les hace falta para terminar de mostrarlas? (15 minutos)

_____

8. ¿Qué les parecieron las playas que visitaron? (muy bonitas)

_____

9. ¿Qué les tocaba hacer en la casa? (arreglar las camas)

_____

10. ¿Qué les gusto de esta experiencia? (hacer nuevos amigos)

_____

[5] DOUBLE-OBJECT PRONOUNS

a. When a verb has two object pronouns, the indirect-object pronoun (usually a person) precedes the direct-object pronoun (usually a thing).

Juan *me lo* **da.**	*Juan gives it to me.*
Juan *te la* **da.**	*Juan gives it to you (fam.).*
Juan *se los* **da.**	*Juan gives them to you (him, her, them).*
Juan *nos las* **da.**	*Juan gives them to us.*

NOTES:

1. **Le** and **les** change to **se** before **lo, la, los, las.**

Juan *le* **da el libro.**	*Juan gives the book to you (him, her).*
Juan *se lo* **da.**	*Juan gives it to you (him, her).*

2. The various meanings of **se** may be clarified by adding **a Ud. (Uds.), a él (ella), a ellos (ellas).**

Su madre *se lo* **da** *a ella* **(*a ellos*).**   *Her mother gives it to her (to them).*

b. The position of double-object pronouns is the same as for single-object pronouns.

Me lo **da.**	*He gives it to me.*
Desea dár*melo*. or *Me lo* **desea dar.**	*He wants to give it to me.*
Está dándo*melo*. or *Me lo* **está dando.**	*He is giving it to me.*
¡Dé*melo*!	*Give it to me.*
But:	
¡No *me lo* **dé!**	*Don't give it to me.*

NOTE: When both object pronouns are attached to the verb, an accent mark is placed on the stressed syllable.

EJERCICIO Q   **Nicolás está muy contento porque su mamá le compró lo que necesita para su primer día de clases. Escriba lo que dice su mama.**

EJEMPLO: Voy a enseñarle el cuaderno a papá.
¡Enséñaselo!

1. los lápices _____

2. la mochila _____

3. las gomas _____

4. la regla _____

5. la pluma _____

6. el diccionario _____

| EJERCICIO R | La madre le dice a su esposo lo que ella tiene que comprarles a los hijos. Escriba las dos formas en que el señor puede responder. |

EJEMPLO: Tengo que comprarles suéteres a los niños.
Sí, debes comprárselos.
Sí, se los debes comprar.

1. Tengo que comprarle zapatos a Gregorio.

_____

_____

2. Tengo que comprarle una blusa a María.

_____

_____

3. Tengo que comprarle medias a Alicia.

_____

_____

4. Tengo que comprarles una corbata a los niños.

_____

_____

5. Tengo que comprarle un traje a Gregorio.

_____

_____

| EJERCICIO S | El jefe de Clara es muy indeciso. Un minuto quiere una cosa y luego no la quiere. Escriba las órdenes contradictorias que le da a Clara. |

EJEMPLO: darme el calendario
¡Démelo!
¡No me lo dé!

1. llevar estos documentos a la señora Guzmán

_____

_____

2. pedir ayuda a otra secretaria

_____

_____

3. cancelar el pedido a los señores Ruiz

_____

_____

4. darme las cartas para firmar

_____

_____

5. buscarme el otro archivo

_____

_____

6. contestarnos el teléfono

_____

_____

7. mandar un telegrama a mi socio

_____

_____

8. entregar el sueldo a los empleados

_____

_____

EJERCICIO T **Felipe estudia para un examen en que tiene que explicar varias profesiones. Escriba lo que dice su hermano cuando Felipe acierta las respuestas.**

EJEMPLO: Un cajero da dinero a las personas.
Sí, se lo da.

1. Un profesor enseña la lección a la clase.

_____

2. Un médico receta medicinas a los enfermos.

_____

3. Un juez dicta una sentencia al prisionero.

_____

4. Una criada limpia la casa a la señora.

_____

5. Un ladrón roba las joyas a las personas.

_____

6. Un locutor presenta a los artistas al público.

_____

7. Un ingeniero construye casas a la gente.

_____

8. Un mesero sirve el almuerzo a los clientes.

_____

9. Un dependiente vende cosas a los clientes.

_____

10. Un gerente da órdenes a los empleados.

_____

M A S T E R Y   E X E R C I S E S

| EJERCICIO U | Complete, con los pronombres apropiados, esta carta que Rocío le escribe a una amiga. |

Querida Dolores:

Fui de compras hoy con mi hermana. Es imposible ir de compras con _____ porque
                                                                    1.

_____ siempre da con algún conocido y se pone a charlar con _____ .
       2.   3.

_____ fuimos a un nuevo centro comercial. La avenida era ancha y caminando por
       4.

_____ vimos que estaba llena de chicas, y con _____ , sus novios.
       5.   6.

   ¿Te acuerdas _____ de los hermanos Castro? Hoy _____ encontramos en el cen-
                     7.   8.

tro comercial. _____ me acordaba de _____ , pero _____ no se acordaban de
                    9.   10.   11.

_____ . Juan es muy alto y _____ estudia en la universidad. Tiene su propio aparta-
     12.   13.

mento cerca de _____ . Manuel es mayor y _____ trabaja. Graciela es su novia y va a
                     14.   15.

casarse con _____ en junio. Tengo muchas ganas de ver las fotos. Espero que _____
                  16.   17.

_____ mandes en cuanto _____ tengas.
     18.   19.

   Otra noticia. Como sabes, a Estela _____ gusta montar en bicicleta. El sábado pasado
                                             20.

_____ recorrió toda la ciudad, montada en _____ y llevando con _____ una
     21.   22.   23.

guía. Anoche visité la casa de Rogelio. _____ entré en la casa y dentro de _____ estaba
                                              24.   25.

la familia: los padres, y además de _____ , los tres hijos. _____ hicieron sentir tan
                                          26.   27.

nerviosa.

_____ he contado muchas nuevas a _____ en esta carta. Ahora tú
                28.   29.

_____ debes una carta. ¡Escribe _____ pronto!
          30.   31.

Saludos de
Rocío

EJERCICIO V **Algunos amigos recuerdan escenas, que para ellos son inolvidables. Escriba cómo terminaron estas escenas.**

EJEMPLO: Al ver a los ciegos, el bondadoso doctor sacó una limosna.
          Se apresuró a **dársela**.

1. En la juguetería la niña insistía en que su padre comprara la muñeca.

Por fin el padre _____.

2. El matador no quería dedicar el toro, pero al recibir el aplauso del público, él _____.

3. Mi sobrino no se acuesta sin que alguien le lea un cuento. Tenía tanto sueño que se durmió antes de

que yo _____.

4. El primer día que Luz sacó su licencia de conducir, ella corrió un semáforo. Tuvo que enseñar la li-

cencia al policía cuando él le dijo: ¡ _____!

5. Cuando el novio de mi hermana llegó a la casa, escondía unos claveles detrás de él. Yo le dije: Juan,

_____.

6. Un chofer compraba un periódico mientras esperaba un semáforo durante las horas de punta. Tenía sólo un billete de cinco dólares y mientras esperaba su cambio, el tráfico empezó a moverse. El

vendedor se apresuró a _____.

7. Una señora encontró una cartera cerca de la jefatura. Ella recogió la cartera del suelo y siguió cami-

nando. Es seguro que ella _____.

8. Cuando el equipo de Hugo ganó el campeonato, él les repitió la noticia a todos sus amigos. Su padre

dijo: Otra vez está _____.

9. Antes de la Navidad se publicó una foto del alcalde visitando a los niños en el hospital. Va allí para

distribuir regalos. Otra vez el alcalde estaba _____.

10. Victoria iba a una fiesta, pero la blusa que iba a ponerse tenía una mancha. Su hermana, Elena, dijo

que tenía una blusa que Victoria podía usar. Elena dijo: _____.

EJERCICIO W **Los perros y los gatos son buenos animales caseros. Escriba un ensayo en el que Ud. describe a su animal casero o el de un pariente o amigo y explique por que Ud. le tiene tanto cariño. Incluya lo siguiente:**

- introduce your pet (name, breed, physical description, etc.)
- why you gave him/her that name
- his/her personality characteristics
- special qualities
- an interesting or humorous anecdote involving your pet
- what you tell him/her to do and his/her reaction
- the role of your pet in your family life

_____

_____

_____

_____

_____

_____

_____

Chapter 19
Relative Pronouns

[1] QUE

Que is the most frequently used relative pronoun. **Que** refers to both persons and things. After a preposition, however, **que** refers only to things; **quien(es)** refers to persons.

	NO PREPOSITION	PREPOSITION
PERSONS	el hombre *que* habló	la mujer *con quien* hablé
THINGS	el libro *que* leo	la pluma *con que* escribo

El libro *que* estoy leyendo es muy difícil.
The book (that) I am reading is very difficult.

Este libro, *que* es muy difícil, fue escrito en el siglo XV.
This book, which is very difficult, was written in the 15th century.

El hombre *que* fue elegido presidente es muy popular.
The man who was elected president is very popular.

Plácido Domingo, *a quien* escuché cantar el sábado, nació en España.
Placido Domingo, whom I heard singing on Saturday, was born in Spain.

Las circunstancias *en que* me encuentro son terribles.
The circumstances in which I find myself are terrible.

NOTES:

1. The relative pronoun is never omitted in Spanish, as it may be in English.

   Las señoras que esperábamos...   *The ladies we expected...*

2. In Spanish, a comma is used to set off non-restrictive relative clauses.

   Este diccionario, que es bastante malo, me lo regalaron ayer.
   This dictionary, which I received yesterday, is quite bad.

3. In Spanish, the preposition always precedes the relative pronoun.

   Las leyes a que estamos sujetos...   *The laws (which) we are subject to...*

EJERCICIO A   Escriba lo que dice el guía que acompaña a unos turistas en el Museo del Prado.

EJEMPLO: los colores / usar / el pintor
Fíjense en los colores que usó el pintor.

1. las líneas / crear / los escultores

---

2. las figuras / crear / el pintor

_____

3. el estilo / usar / el artista

_____

4. las sombras / pintar / los artistas

_____

5. los detalles / incluir / el pintor

_____

6. la sonrisa / captar / el artista

_____

7. el mensaje / expresar / el pintor

_____

| EJERCICIO B | Ud. le enseña una foto a un amigo e identifica a las personas que viajaron en su grupo a España. Escriba lo que Ud. dice de las personas en la foto. |

EJEMPLO: el joven / perder su dinero
           Éste es el joven que perdió su dinero.

1. la chica / gastar 500 dólares

_____

2. los chicos / hacernos bromas

_____

3. el chico / visitar a unos primos

_____

4. las chicas / alejarse del grupo

_____

5. el chico / no comer nada

_____

6. la señorita / dirigir el grupo

_____

7. los chicos / mandar cien tarjetas postales

_____

8. la chica / no visitar los museos

_____

EJERCICIO C Ud. ayuda a su mamá a limpiar el desván. Escriba lo que ella dice al encontrar unas cosas viejas en un baúl.

EJEMPLO: el vestido / en / casarme
Mira el vestido en que me casé.

1. las zapatillas / en / dar mi primer paso

_____

2. la pluma / con / escribir cartas a tu papá

_____

3. el cepillo / con / peinar a tu hermana

_____

4. el álbum / en / escribir versos

_____

5. el reloj / en / aprender a decir la hora

_____

6. el menú del restaurante / a / ir con los amigos

_____

7. la cámara / con / sacar muchas fotos

_____

EJERCICIO D Roberto ganó el premio en un concurso científico. Escriba lo que les dice a unas personas que lo visitan en el laboratorio.

EJEMPLO: los condiscípulos / con / trabajar
Éstos son los condiscípulos con quienes trabajé.

1. el laboratorio / en / hacer el estudio

_____

2. el profesor / a / pedir consejos

_____

3. la computadora / con / resolver los problemas

_____

4. el científico / por / enterarme del tema

_____

5. el cuaderno / en / anotar mis observaciones

_____

6. la biblioteca / en / pasar muchas horas

_____

7. la persona / a / dedicar el trabajo

_____

8. el catre / en / dormir la siesta

_____

9. los jueces / a / deber mi gratitud

_____

10. mis amigos / con / trabajar por un mes

_____

EJERCICIO E   **Gabriel se despierta en el hospital y no recuerda lo que le pasó. Escriba lo que le dice la enfermera, combinando las dos frases.**

EJEMPLO: Aquí está el médico. Lo llamé por la mañana.
            Aquí está el médico **a quien llamé** por la mañana.

1. Éste es el jarabe. Se lo dimos ayer.

_____

2. Éstas son las píldoras. El médico se las recetó.

_____

3. Trajeron la medicina. El médico la recetó anoche.

_____

4. Ese señor es el boticario. Él preparó la medicina.

_____

5. Este hombre es otro doctor. Ud. habló con él anoche.

_____

6. Soy la enfermera. Ud. se quejó de mí.

_____

7. Éste es el Hospital de Caridad. Lo trajeron aquí en una ambulancia.

_____

[2]   *QUIEN(ES)* AND ALTERNATE FORMS

Quien(es) is also used as subject to express *he (she, those, the one, the ones) who*. An alternate form is **el (la, los, las) que.**

Quien estudia, siempre aprende.	*He (She) who studies always learns.*
Los que estudian, siempre aprenden.	*Those who study always learn.*

EJERCICIO F | La abuela de Estela usa muchos refranes cuando habla. Complete los refranes que Estela trata de recordar.

EJEMPLO: **El que** no se atreve, no pasa el mar.

1. _____ busca, encuentra.

2. _____ va despacio y con tiento, hace dos cosas a un tiempo.

3. _____ mal anda, mal acaba.

4. _____ temprano se levanta tiene una hora más de vida y en su trabajo adelanta.

5. _____ a hierro matan, a hierro mueren.

6. _____ esperan, desesperan.

7. _____ la hace, la paga.

8. _____ mucho hablan, mucho yerran.

9. _____ mucho abarcan, poco aprietan.

10. _____ siembra amigos, cosecha amigos.

EJERCICIO G | Escriba lo que la maestra dice el primer día de clases, usando *quien, quienes, el que, la que, los que* o *las que*.

EJEMPLO: **Quienes** estudian reciben buenas notas.

1. _____ no falta a la clase, aprende más.

2. _____ se esfuerzan, tienen éxito.

3. _____ llega temprano, está listo para trabajar.

4. _____ preparan la tarea, están mejor preparados.

5. _____ prestan atención en la clase, comprenden más.

6. _____ participan en la lección, aprenden mejor.

[3] TWO ANTECEDENTS

If there are two antecedents, and there is need for clarification, **quien(es)** or **que** is used to indicate the nearer of the two. The more distant antecedent is indicated by a form of **el (la, los, las) cual(es)** or **el (la, los, las) que.**

El padre de **Felipe**, *quien (que)* está enfermo, lo cuida con cariño. (Felipe is ill.)	*The father of Felipe, who is ill, cares for him lovingly.*
El padre de Felipe, *el cual (el que)* está enfermo, no saldrá hoy. (The father is ill.)	*Felipe's father, who is ill, will not go out today.*

[4] RELATIVE PRONOUNS AFTER PREPOSITIONS

The relative pronouns **el (la, los, las) cual(es)** and **el (la, los, las) que** are used after all prepositions, regardless of the location of the antecedent. **Que** and **quien(es)** may be used after the prepositions **a, de, en,** and **con.**

Subió a la cumbre, **desde la cual (la que)** vio el valle.	He climbed to the mountain top, from which he saw the valley.
La casa **delante de la cual (la que)** estamos, es la antigua residencia del gobernador.	The house in front of which we are standing is the old residence of the governor.
Es un hombre **del que (de quien)** poco se sabe.	He is a man about whom little is known.
El apartamento **en (el) que** vivía era muy pequeño.	The apartment in which he lived was very small.

EJERCICIO H   Complete las frases con las que Jorge describió una visita a un pueblo en la Costa del Sol, usando el pronombre relativo apropiado en cada frase.

1. Fue un día glorioso en _____ llegamos.

2. Las nubes, detrás de _____ brillaba el sol, parecían de algodón.

3. El administrador del hotel abrió un cuaderno grande en _____ escribió nuestros nombres.

4. Nos acercamos a la iglesia, delante de _____ quedamos asombrados.

5. Los pescadores, entre _____ no se encontraba ninguna mujer, estaban en la playa.

6. El guía, con _____ yo hablé mucho, nos explicó las costumbres de los pescadores.

7. Las lanchas de los pescadores, delante de _____ había una red enorme, parecían de juguete.

8. Con aire misterioso los pescadores abrieron la red, dentro de _____ había más de doscientos pescados.

9. A la mañana siguiente salí al balcón del hotel, desde _____ podía ver la salida de los pescadores.

10. Tomamos el desayuno a las diez, después de _____ salimos del pueblo.

EJERCICIO I   Combine las frases siguientes para expresar los datos que apuntó un policía en su libreta para seguirle la pista a un ladrón.

EJEMPLO: Conozco a varios policías. Siento verdadero afecto por ellos.
Conozco a varios policías **por los cuales** siento verdadero afecto.

1. En la sala vi una cortina. El criminal se escondió detrás de ella.

_____

_____

2. Quería ver los dormitorios. Había otra puerta cerca de ellos.

_____

_____

3. Me fijé en la mesa del comedor. Encontré una colilla debajo de ella.

_____

_____

4. Me asomé al garaje. Encontré un coche abandonado dentro de él.

_____

_____

5. Traté de usar el teléfono. Había pintura fresca sobre él.

_____

_____

[5] *LO QUE*

a. **Lo que** is equivalent to the English relative pronoun *what* (*that which*).

Le di **lo que** me pidió.   *I gave him what he asked me for.*

b. **Lo que** and **lo cual** are equivalent to English *which* (*a fact; something*) if the antecedent is a clause or an idea.

Pepe llegó tarde, **lo que (lo cual)** no le gustó al maestro.   *Pepe arrived late, (something) which did not please the teacher.*

EJERCICIO J   **Exprese lo que piensan los pasajeros de un autobús al llegar a la primera parada de descanso. Use *lo que* con las sugerencias.**

SUGERENCIAS: tomar un refresco   comer una hamburguesa
                        llamar a casa   comprar un helado
                        lavarse las manos   buscar un periódico

EJEMPLO: **Lo que yo necesito es lavarme las manos.**

1. _____
2. _____
3. _____
4. _____
5. _____

EJERCICIO K   Escriba las preguntas que hace un guía turístico a los turistas.

EJEMPLO: encontrar / buscar
¿Encontró Ud. lo que buscaba?

1. comprar / necesitar

_____

2. hallar / esperar

_____

3. hacer / querer

_____

4. conocer / desear

_____

5. ver / interesarle

_____

6. experimentar / yo decirle

_____

EJERCICIO L   Exprese en una sola frase lo que comentan estos amigos.

EJEMPLO: El chico reparó en la señorita. Esto le molestó a ella.
El chico reparó en la señorita, **lo cual** le molestó a ella.

1. El policía puso una multa en el carro. Esto enfureció al señor.

_____

2. El mesero trajo el café en seguida. Esto no le agradó a la señora.

_____

3. Mi papá limpió el sótano de la casa. Esto dio gusto a mi mamá.

_____

4. El señor se cayó en el hielo. Esto causó risa a la niña.

_____

5. Mi hermanito perdió diez dólares. Mi mamá se esperaba esto.

_____

[6] *CUYO*

Cuyo (-a, -os, -as), meaning *whose,* refers to both persons and things. **Cuyo** is a relative adjective and agrees with the thing (or person) possessed, not with the possessor.

El muchacho **cuya corbata** llevo, es mi primo.

The boy whose tie I am wearing is my cousin.

EJERCICIO M **Exprese cómo identifica José a varias personas en una fiesta.**

| Aquel señor
Esa señora
Ese hombre
Aquella joven
Esa muchacha | cuyo (-a, -os, -as) | carro está delante de la casa
canción están tocando
chistes son aburridos
flores están en la mesa
novio baila solo
sombrero está en el piso | es | mi tío
mi jefe
mi abuela
mi prima
mi padre
mi hermana |

EJEMPLO: **Esa señora, cuyo carro está delante de la casa, es mi abuela.**

1. _____

2. _____

3. _____

4. _____

5. _____

MASTERY EXERCISES

EJERCICIO N **Escriba lo que Roberto le aconseja a un amigo en una carta. Use el pronombre relativo apropiado.**

Tú no estás al corriente. _____ debes hacer es mirar las noticias en la televisión. Hay un pro-
1.

grama de noticias _____ se llama «24 Horas». Es un programa _____ se transmite
2. 3.

desde México todos los días, por _____ te enterarás de las noticias del día. El locutor,
4.

_____ voz es conocida tanto en el extranjero como en su país, presenta todos los acontecimien-
5.

tos con claridad. ¿Recuerdas al hombre _____ te presenté en la fiesta de Marisol? Bueno, él es el
6.

sobrino del locutor a _____ me refiero. Mi tía Aurora, _____ vive en México, es su
7.   8.

vecina. Él tiene un rancho fuera de la ciudad en _____ tiene muchos caballos. Eran éstos los
9.

caballos de _____ te hablé después de mi último viaje. También, fue en su casa _____
10.   11.

mis padres pasaron el año nuevo. A ver si haces _____ te aconsejo para estar al día.
12.

Tu amigo,
Roberto

EJERCICIO O   **Escriba lo que cuenta Rafael de un amigo suyo. Junte las dos frases usando un pronombre relativo. El símbolo ★ indica el comienzo de la cláusula relativa.**

EJEMPLO: Voy a comprarme un carro modelo deportivo. ★Tengo muchas ganas de un carro deportivo.
Voy a comprarme un carro modelo deportivo, **del que (del cual) tengo muchas ganas.**

1. Voy a salir con unos amigos. ★Me gusta mucho salir con ellos.

    _____

    _____

2. Mi mejor amigo ★ha conseguido entradas para el para el partido de fútbol. Mi mejor amigo se llama Paco.

    _____

    _____

3. Paco tiene un tío. ★Su tío trabaja en el estadio.

    _____

    _____

4. Él tiene cinco entradas. ★Las entradas cuestan veinticinco dólares cada una.

    _____

    _____

5. Los primos de Paco ★no van a los partidos a menudo. Los primos consiguen las entradas.

    _____

    _____

EJERCICIO P   **Imagínese que Ud. trabaja en la oficina del alcalde durante una sequía. Ud. tiene que leerles a unos periodistas una declaración del alcalde sobre la escasez de agua. Escriba los pronombres relativos que faltan.**

Experimentamos una escasez de agua _____ tiene dos causas principales. Primero, aunque ha
1.

llovido mucho, las lluvias _____ cayeron no llenaron las represas de agua. Segundo, la falta de
2.

agua _____ existe, se debe también a la falta de nieve durante el invierno pasado. Debido a esto,
3.

_____ yo les aconsejo a todos los ciudadanos es _____ conserven el agua,
4.   5.

_____ ahora es tan valiosa como una joya. _____ los ciudadanos pueden hacer es no
6.   7.

malgastar el agua, no regar los céspedes y no lavar los carros. Estas advertencias, _____ son de
8.

máxima importancia, pueden ayudar a conservar el agua que nos queda. Los habitantes de nuestra ciudad,

en _____ tengo mucha confianza y a _____ estimo mucho, podrán disminuir el riesgo
9.   10.

_____ existe. Todo _____ digo es para nuestro bien y _____ no cooperen
11.   12.   13.

harán daño a los demás. Hay inspectores _____ vigilarán el consumo de agua por toda la ciudad.
14.

Ellos multarán a los ciudadanos _____ no obedezcan estas reglas.
15.

EJERCICIO Q   **Un grupo de estudiantes de intercambio acaba de regresar a España después de pasar un mes en su escuela. Escriba un artículo para la sección en español del periódico estudiantil en el que Ud. da un resumen y un comentario sobre la estancia de estos estudiantes españoles en su escuela. Escriba frases en que Ud. use pronombres relativos. Incluya lo siguiente:**

- the size of the group
- the length of their stay
- where they were from
- who accompanied them and something about this person
- the general impression of the students with whom you spoke during the exchange
- where they stayed and the reaction of these families
- special activities/events the school sponsored for them (dances, excursions, assembly programs, etc.)
- the reaction of your school mates to them
- special activities the exchange students planned for the school
- what they enjoyed most about the exchange

_____
_____
_____
_____
_____
_____
_____

Chapter 20
Prepositions

Prepositions relate two elements of a sentence (noun to noun, verb to noun, verb to infinitive, verb to pronoun, and the like).

Entra *en* **él.**	*He enters it.*
Comienza *a* **leer.**	*He begins to read.*

NOTE: For a list of common prepositions, see page 218.

[1] PREPOSITIONAL MODIFIERS

a. A preposition + noun modifying another noun is equivalent to an adjective.

un anillo *de oro*   *a gold ring (a ring of gold)*
un vaso *de agua*   *a glass of water*
un vaso *para agua*   *a water glass (a glass for water)*

b. A preposition + noun modifying a verb is equivalent to an adverb.

Sale *con frecuencia*.   *He goes out frequently (with frequency).*

EJERCICIO A   Identifique los objetos que Adela vio en un catálogo de regalos de Navidad.

EJEMPLO: **una taza para café**

1. _____

2. _____

3. _____

4. _____

5. _____

6. _____

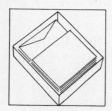

7. _____

8. _____

9. _____

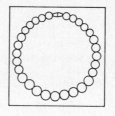

10. _____

EJERCICIO B   **Escriba lo que Elena y Carmen comentan de otra amiga, usando las sugerencias.**

SUGERENCIAS: vestirse   con (sin) cuidado
               peinarse   con (sin) atención
               ir al cine   con (sin) gusto
               visitarme   con (sin) frecuencia
               hablar   de prisa
               no hacernos caso   con (sin) intención

EJEMPLO: **Ella se viste sin gusto.**

1. _____

2. _____

3. _____

4. _____

5. _____

6. _____

[2] PREPOSITIONS USED WITH INFINITIVES

In Spanish, the infinitive is the only verb form that may follow a preposition.

El avión tardó **en aterrizar.** *The plane was delayed in landing.*
Acabo **de terminar de estudiar.** *I just finished studying.*
Se negó **a ayudarme.** *He refused to help me.*

a. Verbs requiring a before an infinitive

Verbs expressing beginning, motion, teaching, or learning, and a few other verbs, require the preposition a before an infinitive.

comenzar a ⎫	**acertar a** *to happen to (by chance)*
empezar a ⎬ *to begin to*	**acostumbrarse a** *to become accustomed to*
ponerse a	
principiar a ⎭	**aspirar a** *to aspire to*
acercarse a *to approach*	**atreverse a** *to dare to*
apresurarse a *to hasten (hurry) to*	**ayudar a** *to help to*
correr a *to run to*	**convidar a** *to invite to*
ir a *to go to*	**decidirse a** *to decide to*
regresar a *to return to (to ... again)*	**dedicarse a** *to devote oneself to*
salir a *to go out to*	**disponerse a** *to get ready to*
venir a *to come to*	**invitar a** *to invite to*
volver a *to return to (to ... again)*	**llegar a** *to succeed in*
enseñar a *to teach to*	**negarse a** *to refuse to*
aprender a *to learn to*	**obligar a** *to force, to compel to*
	resignarse a *to resign oneself to*

La niña *se puso a* **llorar.** *The girl started to cry.*
Salió a **comprar** pan. *He went out to buy bread.*
Estoy aprendiendo a **tocar** la guitarra. *I am learning to play the guitar.*
Lo *convidé a* **almorzar** conmigo. *I invited him to have lunch with me.*
¿Te *decidiste a* venir *a* **cenar?** *Did you decide to come for dinner?*
Me *obligaron a* **quedarme** en casa. *They forced me to stay home.*

b. Verbs requiring de before an infinitive

acabar de *to have just*	**dejar de** *to fail to, to stop*
acordarse de *to remember to*	**encargarse de** *to take charge of*
alegrarse de *to be glad*	**olvidarse de** *to forget to*
cesar de *to stop*	**tratar de** *to try to*

Acuérdate de **regresar** temprano.   *Remember to return early.*
Roberto *dejó de* **escribirme**.   *Roberto stopped writing to me.*
Trataré de **llegar** a tiempo.   *I will try to arrive on time.*
No te *olvides de* **llamar** a Pedro.   *Don't forget to call Pedro.*

c. Verbs requiring **en** before an infinitive

consentir en *to consent to, to agree*	**empeñarse en** *to be determined to; to insist on*
consistir en *to consist of*	**insistir en** *to insist on*
convenir en *to agree to*	**tardar en** *to delay in, to be long in*

Consintió en **ir** al baile conmigo.   *She agreed to go to the dance with me.*
Convenimos en **estudiar** juntos.   *We agreed to study together.*
Se empeña en **comprar** una bicicleta   *He insists on buying an expensive*
cara.   *bicycle.*
No creo que *tarde en* **llegar**.   *I don't believe he will be long in coming.*

d. Verbs requiring **con** before an infinitive

amenazar con *to threaten to*	**soñar con** *to dream of*
contar con *to count on, to rely on*	

Me *amenazó con* **contárselo** a mi   *He threatened to tell my mother.*
madre.
Cuento con **ganar** el premio.   *I count on winning the prize.*
Soñaba con **viajar** por el mundo.   *He dreamed of traveling around the world.*

EJERCICIO C   **Complete, con las preposiciones apropiadas, esta cartita que Jorge le escribió a un amigo.**

Acabo _____ presenciar una escena chistosa en la calle. Un señor altísimo se disponía
                1.

_____ casarse con una mujer muy baja. Los novios comenzaron _____ bajarse del
      2.   3.

carro delante de la iglesia, cuando un grupo de personas se acercó _____ saludarlos. La novia
                                                                          4.

trató _____ bajarse del carro, pero estas personas la obligaron _____ volver
            5.   6.

_____ sentarse. El novio se apresuró _____ ayudarle, porque no quería que la ceremonia
      7.   8.

tardara _____ comenzar. La novia se empeñaba _____ tratar _____ salir del
              9.   10.   11.

carro. Con eso un policía acertó _____ pasar por allí e insistió _____ correr a las
                                        12.   13.

personas. Pero el novio las invitó _____ entrar en la iglesia. Ellas consintieron _____
                                          14.   15.

hacerlo, y el policía se encargó _____ ayudarle a la novia _____ salir del carro. Parecía
                                        16.   17.

como si la pobre novia se hubiera resignado _____ quedarse en el carro. Los novios se
18.

decidieron _____ salir por otra puerta de la iglesia al concluir la ceremonia. Cuando terminó la
19.

ceremonia, empezó _____ llover.
20.

EJERCICIO D Ud. es periodista y acaba de entrevistar a un cantante famoso de España. Usando sus apuntes de la entrevista, escriba el artículo en frases completas. Tendrá que añadir las preposiciones y usar los tiempos correctos del verbo.

EJEMPLO: empeñarse / dar gusto a su público
Se empeña en dar gusto a su público.

1. el cantante / alegrarse / estar / los EE. UU.

_____

2. él / empezar / cantar / cuando / tener diez años

_____

3. su madre / enseñarle / tocar la guitarra

_____

4. él / dedicarse / entretener a la gente

_____

5. en sus conciertos / el público / obligarlo / cantar más

_____

6. él / siempre consentir / hacerlo

_____

7. desde chico / él / aspirar / ser famoso

_____

8. él / insistir / cantar canciones populares

_____

9. él / acabar / dar conciertos / quince ciudades

_____

10. él / volver / visitar / los EE. UU. pronto

_____

EJERCICIO E Margarita es una chica envidiosa. Escriba lo que les cuenta a sus padres, añadiendo las preposiciones necesarias.

EJEMPLO: el padre de Lourdes / enseñarle / conducir
El padre de Lourdes **le enseñó a** conducir.

1. los padres de Marta / consentir / mandarla al campamento de tenis

_____

2. los hermanos de Rocío / nunca / olvidarse / darle un regalo

_____

3. la madre de Luisa / ayudarle / escoger la ropa

_____

4. los padres de Beatriz / no insistir / acompañarla a todas partes

_____

5. la abuela de Rosa / encargarse / organizar una fiesta

_____

6. los padres de Susana / decidirse / comprarle un carro

_____

7. la mamá de Luz / acabar / hacerle un vestido nuevo

_____

[3] PREPOSITIONS USED BEFORE INFINITIVES

The following prepositions are commonly used before an infinitive. The equivalent English construction normally uses a present participle.

a *to, at*	**en** *in, on, of*
al + inf. *upon, on*	**en lugar de** ⎱ *instead of*
antes de *before*	**en vez de** ⎰
con *with* (sometimes *to* or *of*)	**hasta** *until*
de *of, to*	**sin** *without*
después de *after*	

Al entrar, vio a su hija.	*(On) Entering, he saw his daughter.*
Antes de salir, prepárese.	*Before going out, prepare yourself.*
Después de descansar un rato, se levantó.	*After resting a while, he got up.*
Se acostó **en vez de estudiar.**	*He went to bed instead of studying.*
Salió **sin decir** nada.	*He left without saying anything.*

NOTE: A verb + preposition + infinitive construction must have the same subject. If the subjects are different, **que** is required and a conjugated verb form is used instead of the infinitive. Compare:

Me alegro de estar aquí.	*I am glad to be here.*
Me alegro *de que* **Ud. esté** aquí.	*I am glad that you are here.*
Insiste en vender la casa.	*She insists on selling the house.*
Insiste *en que su marido venda* **la casa.**	*She insists that her husband sell the house.*

Se desayunó después de preparar el café.	*He ate breakfast after preparing the coffee.*
Se desayunó *después* **(***de***)** *que su* **madre preparó** el café.	*He ate breakfast after his mother prepared the coffee.*

EJERCICIO F   Escriba lo que Ud. o sus parientes hacen en estas circunstancias. Combine, en cualquier orden, expresiones de las cuatro columnas para expresarlo.

al	desayunarse	mi padre	cepillarse los dientes
antes de	entrar en la casa	yo	dar las gracias
después de	comer	mi madre	saludar a mis padres
en vez de	estudiar	mis padres	mirar la televisión
en lugar de	ayudar a mis hermanos	mi hermano	escuchar discos
sin	tomar el café	mi hermana	no hablar con nadie
	decir adiós		salir de la casa

EJEMPLO: **Al entrar en la casa, yo saludo a mis padres.**

1. _____

2. _____

3. _____

4. _____

5. _____

6. _____

7. _____

EJERCICIO G   Jaime cuenta lo que pasó durante una visita al despacho de su profesor de química. Añada las preposiciones al, antes de, después de, en vez de, o sin, según sea necesario.

Fui a ver a mi profesor de química en su despacho. _____ entrar en su despacho, vi que él estaba
1.

leyendo un mensaje electrónico. Tenía una mirada de sorpresa en la cara. Parece que él leía el mensaje

_____ creerlo. Estaba calificando unos exámenes _____ recibir el mensaje. Pasó un
2.   3.

rato largo mirando el mensaje y _____ leerlo varias veces, empezó a sonreír. De repente se le-
4.

vantó de la silla, se puso el abrigo y _____ decir ni una palabra, se marchó. Salió del despacho
5.

_____ ayudarme. _____ perder un momento, yo lo seguí al ascensor.
6.   7.

[4] VERBS USED WITHOUT PREPOSITION BEFORE AN INFINITIVE

deber *ought to, must*	**poder** *to be able, can*
dejar *to let, to allow*	**preferir** *to prefer*
desear *to wish, to desire*	**pretender** *to attempt*
esperar *to hope, to expect*	**prometer** *to promise*
hacer *to make, to have (something done)*	**querer** *to want, to wish*
lograr *to succeed in*	**saber** *to know how to*
necesitar *to need*	**soler** *to be accustomed to, usually*
oír *to hear*	**ver** *to see*
pensar *to intend*	

Debo ir a la escuela hoy.	*I ought to go to school today.*
No me **dejan salir**.	*They don't let me go out.*
Hizo construir una casa.	*He had a house built.*
Pienso comenzar mañana.	*I intend to begin tomorrow.*
Suele volver a las doce.	*He usually returns at twelve o'clock.*

EJERCICIO H   **Conteste las preguntas que le hace un(a) amigo(a) nuevo(a).**

1. ¿Qué sueles hacer durante el fin de semana?

_____

2. ¿Qué piensas hacer este fin de semana?

_____

3. ¿Qué prefieres, ir al cine o visitar el museo?

_____

4. ¿Con quién prometiste salir el viernes por la noche?

_____

5. ¿A quién esperas ver en el parque?

_____

6. ¿Podrás acompañarme al centro el sábado por la mañana?

_____

7. ¿Sabes conducir un carro?

_____

8. ¿Qué quehaceres debes hacer en casa?

_____

9. ¿Necesitas pedirles permiso a tus padres para salir?

_____

10. ¿Prometes llamarme por teléfono esta noche?

_____

EJERCICIO I   Ud. está trabajando de consejero(a) en un campamento de verano. Escriba lo que les diría a los chicos de ocho años de edad de su grupo el primer día. Use las expresiones sugeridas en las tres columnas.

yo	deber	prestar atención
Uds.	dejar	ayudarse el uno al otro
nosotros	desear	aprender muchas cosas
tú	esperar	ir a acampar
	lograr	obedecer las reglas del campamento
	necesitar	ser amables
	pensar	acostarse a la hora indicada
	poder	levantarse en seguida
	preferir	mantener todo en orden
	prometer	jugar al fútbol
	querer	no hacer bromas
	saber	dar premios cada semana
	soler	cooperar siempre
		respetarse el uno al otro
		divertirse mucho

EJEMPLOS: **Uds. deben prestarme atención.**
Pienso enseñarles muchas cosas este verano.

1. _____

2. _____

3. _____

4. _____

5. _____

6. _____

7. _____

8. _____

9. _____

10. _____

11. _____

12. _____

13. _____

14. _____

15. _____

[5] COMMON EXPRESSIONS WITH PREPOSITIONS

a causa de *because of*
No salió **a causa de** su resfrío.   *He didn't go out because of his cold.*

a eso de *about + time*
Nos reuniremos **a eso de** las cinco.   *We'll get together at about five o'clock.*

a fines de *at the end of*
La primavera comienza **a fines de**   *Spring begins at the end of March.*
marzo.

a fuerza de *by dint of (by persevering)*
A fuerza de estudiar, aprendió bien   *By (persevering in) studying, he*
la historia.   *learned history well.*

a la + adjective *in the style, in the manner*
Se viste **a la** antigua.   *She dresses in an old-fashioned manner.*
Sirvieron una comida **a la** mexicana.   *They served a meal in the Mexican style.*

a pie *on foot*
Fueron de Madrid a Toledo **a pie.**   *They went from Madrid to Toledo on foot.*

a principios de *at the beginning of, early in*
Pienso estar allí **a principios de** mayo.   *I intend to be there early in May.*

a tiempo *on time*
Si quieres comer, vuelve **a tiempo.**   *If you want to eat, return on time.*

a través de *through, across*
Supe la noticia **a través de** un amigo.   *I learned the news through a friend.*

al aire libre *outdoors, in the open air*
Le gusta nadar **al aire libre.**   *He likes to swim in the open air.*

de hoy en adelante *henceforth, from now on*
De hoy en adelante, estudiaré a diario.   *From now on I'll study every day.*

de otro modo *otherwise*
Pague Ud. ahora; **de otro modo** llamo   *Pay now; otherwise I'll call the police.*
a la policía.

de pie *standing*
El alumno se levantó y se quedó **de pie.**   *The pupil stood up and remained standing.*

de vez en cuando *from time to time*
De vez en cuando me gusta ir al cine.   *From time to time I like to go to the movies.*

desde luego (que no) *of course (not), naturally*
                                  (not)
Desde luego, el carro costó mucho.   *Of course the car cost a great deal.*

en cambio *on the other hand*
Juan es perezoso; **en cambio** su   *Juan is lazy; on the other hand, his*
hermano es diligente.   *brother is diligent.*

en cuanto a *as for, in regard to*
En cuanto a ti, ya sabes lo que te   *As for you, you know what awaits*
espera.   *you.*

en efecto *in fact, really; yes, indeed (as a response)*
En efecto, lo compré ayer.   *Yes, indeed, I bought it yesterday.*

(en) ocho días *(in) a week*
Se casan de hoy **en ocho días.**   *They are getting married a week from today.*

(en) quince días *(in) two weeks, (in) a fortnight*
Prometió regresar **en quince días.**   *He promised to return in two weeks.*

en vez de   *instead of*
   En vez de estudiar, se fue al cine.   *Instead of studying, he went to the movies.*

EJERCICIO J   Conteste las preguntas que le hace un alumno de intercambio, usando los modismos indicados.

1. ¿Cuándo comenzó a nevar anoche? (a eso de)

_____

2. ¿Por qué no fueron Uds. al cine? (a causa de)

_____

3. Si no hay autobús, ¿cómo podré ir a la escuela? (a pie)

_____

4. ¿Cómo lograste comprar la bicicleta nueva? (a fuerza de)

_____

5. ¿Cuándo terminan las clases aquí? (a fines de)

_____

6. ¿Y cuándo comienzan de nuevo? (a principios de)

_____

7. Durante el invierno, ¿nieva aquí con frecuencia? (en efecto)

_____

8. ¿Piensas trabajar durante el verano? (desde luego)

_____

EJERCICIO K   Gabi pasa el verano en España. Complete la carta que ella escribe a una prima con la expresión preposicional apropiada de la siguiente lista.

a eso de	a tiempo	desde luego
a fines de	a través de	de vez en cuando
al aire libre	de hoy en adelante	en cuanto a
a pie	de otro modo	en efecto
a principios de	de pie	en vez de

Saludos desde Madrid. El avión llegó _____ y _____ las ocho de la mañana
                                        1.   *2.*

ya estaba en la casa de huéspedes. Mi cuarto es amplio, bonito y limpio. _____ los árboles,
                                                                              3.

puedo ver la Plaza Mayor.

   La universidad queda cerca y puedo ir allí _____. Sin embargo, sé que
                                                  4.

_____ me despertaré tarde y tendré que tomar el metro. Cuando va muy lleno hay que
   5.

viajar _____.
6.

En la plaza mayor hay un café _____ y _____ pienso sentarme allí
7.　　　　　　　　　8.

todas las tardes. Las clases comienzan _____ la semana próxima y terminan
9.

_____ agosto. _____ la profesora, todavía no puedo contarte nada. Sólo sé
10.　　　　　　　　　11.

que tendré que estudiar mucho. _____ tendré que encerrarme en el cuarto por las noches
12.

_____ salir con mis amigos; _____ no aprenderé nunca español.
13.　　　　　　　　　14.

_____ encontraré la manera de divertirme también.
15.
Hasta pronto.

[6] PERSONAL A

The preposition **a** is used before the direct object of a verb if the direct object is:

a. A definite person or persons.

> Visita *a* su amigo (*a* sus padres, *a*　　　*He visits his friend (his parents,*
> Roberto, etc.).　　　　　　　　　　　*Robert, etc.).*

b. A domestic animal (pet, etc.).

> Quiere *a* su perrito (*a* Fido, *a* su gato,　*She loves her little dog (Fido, her cat,*
> etc.).　　　　　　　　　　　　　　*etc.).*

c. A pronoun referring to a person.

> Veo *a* alguien.　　　　　　　　　*I see someone.*
> No veo *a* nadie.　　　　　　　　　*I see no one.*

> NOTE:　The personal **a** is not used with the verb **tener**.
> **Tengo un amigo.**　　　　　　　　*I have a friend.*

EJERCICIO L　　**Raúl y su primo Carlos celebran el mismo cumpleaños. Escriba lo que la mamá de Raúl le dice que debe hacer.**

EJEMPLO:　amar / tu primo　　**Debes amar a** tu primo.

1. visitar / Carlos　　　　_____

2. llamar / tus abuelos　　_____

3. comprarle un regalo / tu primo　_____

4. invitar / sus amigos a la fiesta　_____

5. mandarle / una tarjeta / Carlos _____

6. felicitar / tu primo _____

EJERCICIO M **Gloria está estudiando en México durante el verano. Complete el mensaje electrónico que ella le va a mandar a su profesora de español. Use la «a personal» cuando sea necesario.**

Por fin llegué a estudiar y visitar _____ mis primos que viven en México. Son unos primos
                                        1.

_____ quienes quiero mucho. Tienen _____ un perro que me sigue por todas partes.
      2.   *3.*

Quiero mucho _____ este perro porque es muy cariñoso y juguetón. Extraño _____
                  4.   *5.*

mi familia, pero estoy aprendiendo mucho aquí. Llamé _____ la tía de Rocío la semana pasada y
                                                          6.

le dio mucho gusto _____ ella recibir sus saludos. Conocí _____ un joven que vive
                        7.   *8.*

cerca de la casa de mis primos. Él prometió comunicarse conmigo por correo electrónico cuando regrese

a los Estados Unidos. Él habla español e inglés y tiene _____ amigos. Veo _____ Juan
                                                              9.   *10.*

todos los días en la escuela. Él conoce _____ muchos personas de mi familia porque es amigo de
                                              11.

mi primo mayor. Llamo _____ mis padres una vez por semana.
                            12.

Al final del mes los otros estudiantes y yo pensamos visitar Acapulco. ¿Ha visto Ud. _____
                                                                                            13.

algunos de mis amigos? Si ve _____ alguien, favor de explicarle que he estado tan ocupada que
                                  14.

no he podido mandar tarjetas postales _____ nadie. Ahora debo escribirle _____
                                            15.   *16.*

Susana porque me ha mandado muchos mensajes electrónicos.

[7] PARA AND POR

Both **para** and **por** have similar basic meanings in English. Whether to use **para** or **por** depends on the Spanish context. Their meanings in English may vary with the context.

a. Para

(1) **Para** expresses purpose or goal.

Estudia **para médico**.	*He studies to be a doctor.*
Trabajé **para comprar un coche**.	*I worked in order to buy a car.*
Estudió **para pasar el examen**.	*He studied to pass the exam.*

(2) **Para** expresses the special use of an object.

Necesito un **cepillo para el pelo.**	*I need a hairbrush.*
Es una **caja para dulces.**	*It is a candy box (a box for candy).*

But:

Es una **caja de dulces.**	*It is a box of candy.*

(3) **Para** expresses destination or direction.

Ayer salió **para México.**	*Yesterday he left for Mexico.*
Esta carta es **para ti.**	*This letter is for you.*

(4) **Para** indicates a time or date in the future.

Estará listo **para el viernes.**	*It will be ready for (by) Friday.*
Estaré de regreso **para la una.**	*I will be back by one o'clock.*

(5) **Para** means *for* or *considering that*, when comparing a person, object, or situation with others of its kind.

Para un extranjero, habla bien el inglés.	*For a foreigner, he speaks English well.*
Se ve joven **para su edad.**	*He looks young, considering his age.*

(6) **Para** is used with the reflexive pronoun **sí** to mean *to* or *for himself* (*herself, them-selves*).

Abrió el libro y leyó **para sí.**	*He opened the book and read to himself.*
Lo quieren todo **para sí.**	*They want everything for themselves.*

> **b. Por**

- by means of
- time, duration
- exchange
- through, by along
- transportation
- reason/motive

(1) **Por** introduces the agent (doer) in a passive construction.

México fue conquistado **por Pizarro.**	*Mexico was conquered by Pizarro.*

(2) **Por** expresses "in exchange for".

Pagó un dólar por el cuchillo.	*He paid a dollar for the knife.*
Quiero cambiar este coche por uno más grande.	*I want to exchange this car for a larger one.*

(3) **Por** means *along, through, by,* and *around* after a verb of motion.

Entraron por el jardín.	*They came in through the garden.*
Me pasearé por esa calle.	*I will stroll along that street.*
Pasó por aquí a las tres.	*He came by here at three o'clock.*

(4) **Por** expresses the duration of an action.

Fue a Europa **por dos meses.**	*He went to Europe for two months.*
Tendrá que guardar cama **por una semana.**	*He will have to stay in bed for a week.*

(5) **Por** expresses indefinite time.

Por la tarde juego al tenis.	*In the afternoon I play tennis.*
¿Quieres venir mañana *por la mañana*?	*Do you want to come tomorrow morning?*

(6) **Por** means *for the sake of* and *on behalf of.*

Habló *por la clase.*	*He spoke on behalf of the class.*
Lo hago todo *por ti.*	*I do it all for your sake.*

(7) **Por** (meaning *for*) is used after the verbs **enviar, ir, luchar, mandar, preguntar, regresar, venir,** and **volver.**

Fue (Envió, Preguntó) *por* el médico.	*He went (sent, asked) for the doctor.*
Vino (Volvió, Regreso) *por* sus libros.	*He came (came back, returned) for his books.*

(8) **Por** expresses a reason or motive.

Trabaja *por* necesidad.	*He works out of necessity.*
Lo castigaron *por* llegar tarde.	*He was punished for arriving late.*

(9) **Por** expresses manner or means.

Lo pidieron *por* escrito.	*They asked for it in writing.*
Lo enviaron *por* avión.	*It was sent by plane.*

(10) **Por** is equivalent to English *per* or *by the*.

Gana cien dólares *por* semana.	*He earns a hundred dollars per (a) week.*
Es más barato *por* docena.	*It is cheaper by the dozen.*

(11) **Por** expresses opinion or estimation and is equivalent to English *for* or *as*.

Se le conocía *por* Pepe Navaja.	*He was known as Pepe Navaja.*
Se hace pasar *por* médico.	*He passes himself off as a doctor.*
Me tomaron *por* natural del país.	*They took me for a native.*

(12) **Por** is used in certain adverbial expressions.

> **por eso** *that's why, therefore, and so*
> **por lo común** ⎫
> **por lo general** ⎬ *generally*
> **por lo visto** *apparently*
> **por supuesto (que)** *of course, naturally*

Hace calor y humedad; **por eso** hay muchos insectos.	*It's hot and humid; that's why (and so) there are many insects.*
Por lo común llueve mucho en abril.	*Generally it rains a lot in April.*
Por lo visto todo está en orden.	*Apparently everything is in order.*
Por supuesto que vendrá hoy.	*Naturally he'll come today.*

NOTES:

1. **Por** or **para** are not used with the verbs **buscar** (*to look for, to seek*), **esperar** (*to wait for, to await*), and **pedir** (*to ask for, to request*). These verbs take a direct object in Spanish.

Buscaron un asiento.	*They looked for a seat.*
Esperó dos horas a su amiga.	*He waited two hours for his girlfriend.*
Quiero pedirle un favor.	*I want to ask a favor of you. (I want to ask you for a favor.)*

2. **En** is used instead of **por** to mean by a means of transportation for passengers.

Envió el paquete por avión.	*He sent the package by plane.*
But:	
Viajé por Europa en tren.	*I traveled through Europe by train.*

✳ *Para → Give reason*

EJERCICIO N	Escriba los consejos que da la abuelita de Miguel.

EJEMPLO: Las naranjas son buenas *para* la salud.

1. _____ iluminar la sala, hay que encender la luz.

2. Deben estudiar más _____ llegar a la universidad.

3. No dejen _____ mañana lo que puedan hacer hoy.

4. Deben tener una sonrisa _____ todo el mundo.

5. La leche es buena _____ los huesos.

6. Hay que poner los platos _____ sopa en la mesa primero.

7. Si hacen el trabajo ahora, _____ el fin de semana estarán libres.

8. _____ verme sólo tienen que llamarme.

9. _____ vieja, comprendo bien a los jóvenes.

10. En 1950 yo salí _____ España.

EJERCICIO O | **Complete, con *por* o *para*, lo que el abuelo de Pepe le contó sobre sus viajes.**

En la época que fui a España _por_ (1.) primera vez, se viajaba _por_ (2.) barco. Estuvimos en el mar _por_ (3.) seis días _por_ (4.) una tempestad terrible. Recuerdo que casi todos los pasajeros enviaron _por_ (5.) el médico y éste, _para_ (6.) ser tan dedicado a su trabajo, no durmió _por_ (7.) tres días. _Para_ (8.) ser un viaje tan difícil, mis hermanos y yo nos divertimos mucho. Podíamos correr _por_ (9.) todos los rincones del barco y parecía que teníamos el barco sólo _para_ (10.) nosotros. _Para_ (11.) comer, teníamos que ir al comedor. _Para_ (12.) mi mamá, esto no era fácil _por_ (13.) tener que vestir a tres niños. _Para_ (14.) entrar en el comedor pasábamos _por_ (15.) dos puertas grandísimas de vidrio. A mi hermanito Pablo le fascinaba poner las manos _por_ (16.) todo el vidrio. _Por_ (17.) más que tratara, mi mamá no podía detenerlo.

Mi último viaje a España fue _por_ (18.) avión. ¡Qué diferencia! Estuve en el avión sólo _por_ (19.) seis horas. Mi compañero de asiento era un joven español que estudiaba _para_ (20.) piloto. _Para_ (21.) ser español, hablaba bien el inglés. Caminé _por_ (22.) el avión, pero no era tan largo ni tan interesante como cuando caminaba _por_ (23.) el barco. La comida fue servida _por_ (24.) tres aeromozos agradables. Uno de ellos ha trabajado de aeromozo _por_ (25.) veinte años. Me dijo que sólo hace seis vuelos _por_ (26.) mes y _por_ (27.) lo general descansa _por_ (28.) unos cinco días entre los vuelos. El viajar _por_ (29.) avión es más rápido, pero ¡cuánto daría yo _por_ (30.) un viaje en barco!

EJERCICIO P   Escriba las respuestas de Doris a estas preguntas que le hizo una amiga después de un viaje a España.

1. ¿Cuántos días estuvieron Uds. en España? (15)

   _____

2. ¿Cuánto pagó Elena por la bolsa? ($50)

   _____

3. ¿Cómo mandaron Uds. las cartas desde España? (avión)

   _____

4. ¿Cuál es la mejor forma de viajar dentro del país? (autobús)

   _____

5. ¿Cuánto gastaste por día? ($100)

   _____

6. ¿Cuándo jugaban Uds. al tenis? (la tarde)

   _____

7. ¿Cuántas horas remaron Uds. en el Lago del Retiro? (3)

   _____

8. ¿Cómo entraron las moscas en el autobús? (la ventana)

   _____

MASTERY EXERCISES

EJERCICIO Q   Ud. quiere trabajar de asistente social. Conteste las preguntas que le hacen en la entrevista.

1. ¿Le gustaría a Ud. ayudar a las personas necesitadas?

   _____

2. ¿Cómo podría Ud. ayudar a esas personas?

   _____

3. ¿Ha hecho Ud. algo por los menos afortunados?

   _____

4. ¿Suele Ud. burlarse de las personas que tienen menos que Ud.?

   _____

5. ¿Tarda Ud. generalmente en hacer lo que le piden?

6. Para ser justo, ¿qué haría Ud.?

_____

7. ¿Para qué profesión estudió Ud.?

_____

8. ¿Visitaría Ud. a las personas en sus casas?

_____

9. ¿Para qué?

_____

10. ¿Cuánto espera Ud. ganar por mes?

_____

✳ | EJERCICIO R | **Lea este cuento y escriba la preposición que debe usarse en cada caso.**

El zapatero tropezó _____ el carnicero en la calle. Éste quería _____ saber
                     1. (con / en)   **2.** (a / —)

cómo le iba en el negocio. El zapatero le dijo que _____ más que trataba, no podía
                                                    3. (por / para)

_____ vender más de un par de zapatos _____ día. _____
4. (en / —)   **5.** (por / para)   **6.** (A / Al)

oír esto el carnicero se puso nervioso. Trató _____ darle una respuesta pero
                                               7. (de / en)

_____ contestar, el zapatero le dijo: « _____ comprar zapatos, la gente
8. (antes de / con)   **9.** (En vez de / Después de)

compra carne. Si nos hacemos socios, la gente no puede _____ negarse
                                                        10. (a / —)

_____ comprar zapatos también. _____ comenzar, vamos _____
11. (a / de)   **12.** (Por / Para)   **13.** (a / en)

regalar un par de zapatos _____ cada cincuenta dólares que compren de carne.
                           14. (por / para)

Acabo _____ leer en una revista que un comerciante puede _____ manejar
      15. (de / en)   **16.** (— / de)

mejor sus fondos si tiene _____ un socio». El carnicero tardó mucho _____
                           17. (a / —)   **18.** (en / a)

contestar. Pensó: «¿Por qué insiste este señor _____ tratar _____ arruinarme?
                                                19. (en / de)   **20.** (de / a)

Si le hago caso y convengo _____ juntarme con él, _____ la semana que
                            21. (en / con)   **22.** (por / para)

viene habré cesado _____ ganar dinero y vender carne». _____ no ser
                    23. (de / en)   **24.** (Por / Para)

descortés le preguntó al zapatero si él sabía _____ preparar la carne para los clientes. El
                                               25. (a / —)

zapatero, lleno de entusiasmo, le replicó _____ vacilar: «No, pero tú puedes _____
                                           26. (sin / de)   **27.** (a / —)

enseñarme _____ ser un carnicero próspero como tú». El carnicero suspiró y se dijo:
        28. (a / de)

« _____ ser un mal comerciante, sabe _____ resolver sus problemas».
  29. (Por / Para)   *30.* (a / —)

EJERCICIO S   **Cada año hay una feria en su ciudad o pueblo. Por primera vez, sus padres consintieron en darle permiso a asistir a la feria solo(-a) con unos amigos. Escriba un cuento en que Ud. relata cómo pasó el día en la feria con sus amigos. Incluya lo siguiente.**

- the reason for the fair
- when it generally takes place
- where it is held
- when you left for the fair
- when you arrived there
- traffic conditions
- who went with you
- how you travelled there
- what you did at the fair
- your reaction to the fair
- how it compares to previous years or other fairs you have attended, etc.

_____

_____

_____

_____

_____

_____

_____

_____

_____

_____

_____

_____

_____

_____

Part Three
Adjectives; Adverbs; Numbers

MÉXICO

CUBA
REPÚBLICA
DOMINICANA
PUERTO RICO
HONDURAS
GUATEMALA
NICARAGUA
EL SALVADOR
COSTA RICA
VENEZUELA
PANAMÁ
COLOMBIA
ECUADOR

PERÚ

BOLIVIA
PARAGUAY

CHILE
URUGUAY
ARGENTINA

ESPAÑA
Islas Baleares
Islas Canarias

Chapter 21
Adjectives and Adverbs

[*1*] ADJECTIVES

a. Gender of adjectives

(1) Adjectives ending in **–o** form the feminine by changing **o** to **a**. Most adjectives ending in a consonant form the feminine by adding **a**.

pequeño, pequeña *small, little*
feo, fea *ugly*
seco, seca *dry*
español, española *Spanish*

francés, francesa *French*
hablador, habladora *talkative*
trabajador, trabajadora *hard-working*

(2) Many adjectives have the same form for both the masculine and the feminine.

fácil, fácil *easy*
popular, popular *popular*
grande, grande *large*

agradable, agradable *pleasant*
agrícola, agrícola *agricultural*

b. Plural of adjectives

The plural of adjectives is formed by

(1) adding **s** when the singular form ends in a vowel.

secos, españolas, agradables

(2) adding **es** when the singular form ends in a consonant.

españoles, populares, fáciles.

NOTES:

1. Adjectives with singular forms ending in **–z** change **z** to **c** in the plural.

feliz, felices

2. Some adjectives add or drop an accent mark in order to keep the original stress.

joven, jóvenes *young*
francés, francesa, franceses, francesas *French*
inglés, inglesa, ingleses, inglesas *English*
alemán, alemana, alemanes, alemanas *German*
cortés, corteses *courteous, polite*

EJERCICIO A La señorita Ruiz habla de sus alumnos. Escriba cómo los describe, usando estos adjetivos.

inteligente	cortés	bondadoso	cómico
perezoso	puntual	juguetón	popular
diligente	cumplido	bonito	joven
trabajador	amable	hablador	dedicado

1. Los alumnos son _____

_____

2. Las alumnas son _____

_____

3. Todos los alumnos son _____

_____

| EJERCICIO B | Rogelio y Anita preparan una lista de los adjetivos que usarían para describirse a sí mismos. Escriba la lista que prepara cada uno. |

| ROGELIO | ANITA |

1. joven _____

2. español _____

3. trabajador _____

4. diligente _____

5. encantador _____

6. amable _____

7. guapo _____

8. cortés _____

9. leal _____

10. interesante _____

c. Position of adjectives

(1) Descriptive adjectives normally follow the nouns they modify.

un libro *interesante*   *an interesting book*
la casa *blanca*   *the white house*

(2) Descriptive adjectives may stand before the noun to emphasize the quality of the adjective or its inherent characteristic.

Admiré los árboles, con sus *verdes* **hojas.**   *I admired the trees, with their green leaves.*
El invierno me trae *malos* **recuerdos.**   *Winter brings me bad memories.*

NOTE: Some adjectives have different meanings, depending on their position.

Wáshington fue un *gran* **hombre.**   *Washington was a great man.*
But:

Mi tío es un **hombre** *grande,* casi un   *My uncle is a big man, almost a giant.*
gigante.

Common adjectives that may change their meaning with a change in position are:

	AFTER THE NOUN	BEFORE THE NOUN
antiguo, -a	*old* (ancient)	*old* (former), *old-time*
cierto, -a	*sure; true*	*a certain*
grande	*large, big*	*great*
mismo, -a	*him* (her, it)-*self*	*same*
nuevo, -a	*new*	*another, different*
pobre	*poor*	*unfortunate*
simple	*silly, simpleminded*	*simple, mere*

(3) Limiting adjectives (numbers, possessive and demonstrative adjectives, adjectives of quantity) usually precede the noun.

dos plumas   *two pens*   *aquel* hombre   *that man*
algún día   *some day*   *tal* cosa   *such a thing*
mis primos   *my cousins*   *menos* dinero   *less money*

Common adjectives of quantity are:

algunos (–as) *some*   **poco (–a, –os, –as)** *little, few*
cada *each, every*   **tanto (–a, –os, –as)** *so much, so many*
cuanto (–a, –os, –as) *as much*   **todo (–a, –os, –as)** *all, every*
más *more*   **unos (–as)** *some*
menos *less*   **unos (–as) cuantos (–as)** *a few*
ningunos (–as) *no, not any*   **varios (–as)** *several*
numerosos (–as) *numerous*

EJERCICIO C   **Arturo acaba de llegar a la ciudad de México y no habla bien el español. Ayúdelo a expresarse organizando las palabras que quiere usar en frases lógicas.**

EJEMPLO: antiguo / busco / Majestic / el / Hotel
Busco el antiguo Hotel Majestic.

1. cuarto / con / necesito / grandes / un / ventanas / muchas / grande

_____

2. aquí / pasar / pienso / cuantos / días / unos

_____

3. interesantes / a / voy / varias / hacer / excursiones

_____

4. mi / es / ésta / cámara / nueva

_____

5. buenas / amigos / quieren / mis / de / pirámides / las / fotos / muchas

_____

6. que / han / me / personas / ésta / numerosas / dicho / ciudad / gran / una / es

_____

7. amigos / con / varios / viajar / pobres / iba / amigos / a / trabajar / que / esos / tuvieron / pero

_____

| **EJERCICIO D** | A la mamá de Pablo siempre le gusta usar muchos adjetivos. Usando los adjetivos entre paréntesis, conteste las preguntas que le hace Pablo sobre una boda a la que ella asistió. |

EJEMPLO: ¿Cuántas **personas** había en la boda? (tanto, elegante)
¡Había **tantas personas elegantes** en la boda!

1. ¿Usó la novia el **vestido** de su abuela? (antiguo, blanco)

_____

2. ¿Qué clase de **cena** sirvieron? (uno, delicioso)

_____

3. ¿Con qué **amigos** se sentaron en la mesa? (uno, viejo, simpático)

_____

4. ¿Había **orquesta** en la fiesta? (dos, animado)

_____

5. ¿Qué **recuerdo** les dieron a los invitados? (barato, simple)

_____

6. ¿Viste a tus **primos**? (amable, algunos)

_____

7. ¿Con cuántas **parejas** bailaste? (varios, encantador)

_____

8. ¿Cómo es el **carro** del novio? (nuevo, amarillo)

_____

9. ¿Cómo eran los **regalos** que recibieron? (caro, numeroso)

_____

10. ¿Acompañó una **cantante** a la orquesta? (antipático, cierto)

_____

| **EJERCICIO E** | La señora Abanico describe las diferencias que existen entre sus dos hijos, Roberto y Sara. Use los adjetivos dados para expresar lo que ella dice. |

alegre	diligente	gordo	perezoso
ambicioso	divertido	independiente	quieto
cómico	encantador	melancólico	responsable
delgado	generoso	pensativo	serio

EJEMPLO: **Roberto es cómico y Sara es seria.**

1. _____
2. _____
3. _____
4. _____
5. _____
6. _____
7. _____
8. _____
9. _____
10. _____

EJERCICIO F   David tiene que conseguir los muebles para el escenario de una obra que va a presentarse en su escuela. Escriba lo que él debe obtener.

EJEMPLO: un sofá / verde   **un sofá verde**

1. dos butacas / viejo _____

2. una mesa / redondo _____

3. un ramo de flores / fresco _____

4. dos cortinas / azul _____

5. unos libros / antiguo _____

6. una alfombra / grueso _____

7. una caja / fuerte _____

8. tres lámparas / pequeño _____

9. una almohada / blando _____

10. una silla / cómodo _____

EJERCICIO G   Complete el cuento que escribió Ricardo, usando la forma apropiada de los adjetivos dados. Los adjetivos no están colocados en el orden que deben usarse.

Era una noche _____ y _____ de invierno. En la casa
              1.   2.

todo el mundo se sentía _____ por el calor que salía de la
                             3.

chimenea _____ en la cual ardían _____ leños
          4.   5.

_____ .
   6.

1–6
largo
tranquilo
uno
grande
oscuro
antiguo

El abuelo _____ estaba sentado en una silla _____ .
             7.   8.

En sus manos _____ y _____ tenía un libro.
                        9.   10.

Desde el piso, sus nietos miraban sus ojos _____ que reflejaban la
                                          11.

luz _____ y _____ del fuego. Les leía un cuento
      12.   13.

de las hazañas_____ y _____ de un héroe
              14.   15.

_____ . Mientras afuera soplaba un viento _____ ,
     16.   17.

los niños escuchaban con interés _____ las palabras _____
                              18.   19.

del anciano. Él _____ se divertía leyendo _____
                20.   21.

historias _____ a sus nietos_____ Poco a poco
         22.   23.

los ojos _____ de los niños empezaban a cerrarse. Una sonrisa
              24.

_____ llenaba la cara _____ del abuelo.
     25.   26.

7–13
rojo
cómodo
fuerte
simpático
claro
arrugado
caliente

14–19
famoso
intenso
fabuloso
señorial
amenazador
emocionante

20–26
este
querido
arrugado
brillante
mismo
interesante
satisfecho

d. Shortened forms of adjectives

(1) The following adjectives drop the final **-o** when used before a masculine singular noun.

uno *one, a, an*	***un* libro**	*one (a) book*	
bueno *good*	***un* buen caballo**	*a good horse*	
malo *bad*	***un* mal año**	*a bad year*	
primero *first*	**el *primer* día**	*the first day*	
tercero *third*	**el *tercer* piso**	*the third floor*	
alguno *some*	***algún* día**	*some day*	
ninguno *no, not any*	***ningún* objeto**	*no object*	

NOTES:

1. The adjectives **alguno** and **ninguno** require an accent mark when the **-o** is dropped: **alg*ú*n, ning*ú*n.**

2. If a preposition comes between the adjective and the noun, the full form of the adjective is used.
   ***uno* de los tres** *one of the three*
   el *tercero del* grupo *the third (one) of the group*

(2) **Santo** becomes **San** before the masculine name of a saint, except with names beginning with **To-** or **Do-**.

***San* Juan** *Saint John*
***San* Francisco** *Saint Francis*

    But:

***Santo* Tomás** *Saint Thomas*
***Santo* Domingo** *Saint Dominic*

(3) **Grande** becomes **gran** when used before a singular noun of either gender.

un *gran* poeta
una *gran* poetisa } *a great poet*

But:

un edificio *grande*   *a large building*
una casa *grande*   *a large house*

(4) **Ciento** becomes **cien** before a noun of either gender and before the numbers **mil** and **millones.** This short form is not used with multiples of **ciento (doscientos, trescientos,** etc.) or in combination with any other number **(ciento diez).**

cien libros (muchachas)   *one (a) hundred books (girls)*
cien mil años   *one (a) hundred thousand years*
cien millones de dólares   *one (a) hundred million dollars*

But:

cuatro**cientos** coches   *four hundred cars*
cuatro**cientas** personas   *four hundred people*
ciento veintisiete sillas   *one (a) hundred twenty-seven chairs*

EJERCICIO H   Gabriel y unos amigos hablan de las ciudades de los Estados Unidos que emplean la palabra Santo como parte de su nombre. Escriba los nombres de las ciudades que usan San, Santo o Santa.

EJEMPLO: **Santa Fe**

San	Santo	Santa
_____	_____	_____
_____	_____	_____
_____	_____	_____
_____	_____	_____

EJERCICIO I   Complete, con la forma apropiada del adjetivo, esta carta que Gloria le escribió a una amiga.

Querida Rosita:

Saludos desde Puerto Rico, donde estoy pasando unas _____ vacaciones. Estamos alojados
_____1. (bueno)_____

en un hotel _____ cerca de la playa, que se llama el _____ Hotel. Ayer fue
_____2. (grande)_____ _____3. (grande)_____

la _____ vez que no llovió por la tarde. Tengo _____ noticias:
_____4. (primero)_____ _____5. (bueno)_____

el _____ día del viaje conocí a un chico muy simpático. Lo conocí durante
_____6. (tercero)_____

mi _____ excursión al Viejo _____ Juan. Entré en _____
_____7. (tercero)_____ _____8. (Santo)_____ _____9. (alguno)_____

tiendas porque buscaba _____ regalo para mi hermano. Encontré _____
10. (uno)   11. (uno)

cinturón de cuero, pero costaba _____ dólares. No pude comprarlo, pero
12. (ciento)

_____ día espero tener bastante dinero para hacerlo.
13. (alguno)

Roberto es de la República Dominicana. Él vive en la capital, _____
14. (Santo)

Domingo. _____ de sus amigos conoce nuestra _____ ciudad
15. (Ninguno)   16. (grande)

de _____ Francisco. A Roberto le gusta viajar. Él tiene parientes que viven
17. (Santo)

en _____ Fe, Nuevo México.
18. (Santo)

Roberto es de ascendencia española. Hace más de _____ años su familia llegó de
19. (ciento)

España. Su abuelo era el alcalde de una ciudad _____ y todos decían que era
20. (grande)

un _____ hombre.
21. (grande)

Nuestra habitación da al mar y estamos en el _____ piso. En el hotel
22. (tercero)

hay _____ cincuenta habitaciones. Tengo que levantarme temprano porque hay menos
23. (ciento)

de _____ sillas en la playa, y trato de ser la _____ persona que llega a la
24. (ciento)   25. (primero)

playa para conseguir un _____ lugar cerca de las palmas. Pasado mañana será
26. (bueno)

un _____ día porque terminan estos _____ días de descanso. Saldremos en
27. (malo)   28. (bueno)

el _____ avión de la mañana.
29. (primero)

Tu _____ amiga,
30. (bueno)
Gloria

[2]   ADVERBS

a. **Adverbs are formed regularly by adding –mente to the feminine singular form of an adjective.**

un hombre **rico** *a rich man*
un hombre **ricamente** vestido   *a richly dressed man*

Es un trabajador **hábil**.   He is a skillful worker.
Lo fabricó **hábil**mente.   He made it skillfully.

NOTE: In a series of two or more adverbs, the ending **–mente** is added only to the last one.

Pablo escribió **clara, rápida** y **fácil**mente.

Frank wrote clearly, rapidly, and easily.

b. Adverbial phrases may be formed by using **con** + noun.

La joven cantaba **con alegría** (*alegremente*).

The girls sang with happiness (happily).

Saludó a la dama **con cortesía** (*cortésmente*).

He greeted the lady with courtesy (courteously).

c. The words **más, menos, poco, mucho, mejor, peor,** and **demasiado** may be used either as adjectives or adverbs.

ADJECTIVE	ADVERB
Pablo tiene *menos* **dinero** que yo.	Él es *más* **pobre.**
Pablo has less money than I do.	*He is poorer.*
La Sra. Álvarez compra *demasiadas* **joyas.**	Ella es *demasiado* **rica.**
Mrs. Alvarez buys too many jewels.	*She is too rich.*
Mi **voz es** *peor* que la tuya.	Tú **cantas** *mejor* que yo.
My voice is worse than yours.	*You sing better than I.*

NOTE: As adjectives, **mucho, poco,** and **demasiado** vary in gender and number; as adverbs, they do not change.

d. Some adverbs have forms distinct from the adjective forms.

bueno *good* **bien** *well*
malo *bad* **mal** *badly*

Arturo es **un** *buen* **músico y toca** *bien* el piano.

Arturo is a good musician and plays the piano well.

Juan es un **muchacho** *malo;* **trata** *mal* a su hermana.

Juan is a bad boy; he treats his sister badly.

EJERCICIO J Escriba el adverbio que describe lo que Jorge dice de sus amigos después de un viaje.

EJEMPLO: Eduardo condujo _____ . (cuidadoso)
Eduardo condujo **cuidadosamente.**

1. Héctor volvió al carro _____ . (rápido)

2. Lorenzo pidió instrucciones _____ . (cortés)

3. Gabriel hizo todo _____ . (lento)

4. Eduardo condujo _____ . (hábil)

5. Los jóvenes hablaban _____ . (alegre)

EJERCICIO K Conteste las preguntas que le hace un alumno nuevo de la escuela.

1. ¿Quién juega al tenis mejor, tú o tu mejor amigo?

_____

2. ¿Cuál de tus profesores enseña mejor?

_____

3. ¿Estudias mucho antes de un examen?

_____

4. ¿Es demasiado difícil el español?

_____

5. ¿Por qué dices que este año es peor que el año pasado?

_____

6. ¿Cómo te sientes hoy, bien o mal?

_____

7. ¿Trabajas mucho o poco todos los días?

_____

8. ¿Cuánto gastas cuando sales con tus amigos, mucho, poco o demasiado?

_____

EJERCICIO L	**Lea este relato de Juan. Luego, hágalo más vivo, completando los espacios con adverbios. Forme los adverbios de los adjetivos dados. Use cada adjetivo solamente una vez.**

claro	dulce	rápido
completo	fácil	repentino
cortés	inmediato	total
desafortunado	malo	violento
desgraciado	profundo	

Mi hermana mayor siempre trata _____ a las personas que le hablan por teléfono. Ayer por
                                          _1._

la tarde ella dormía la siesta y estaba _____ dormida cuando _____ sonó
                                                    _2._   _3._

_____ el teléfono. Lo contestó _____ pero no reconoció _____
        _4._   _5._   _6._

la voz de la persona que llamaba. No contestó _____ porque no se había despertado
                                                          _7._

_____ . Era un extranjero que hablaba español _____ y _____ .
        _8._   _9._   _10._

Mi hermana no comprendió _____ lo que quería. _____ , la persona llamaba
                                      _11._   _12._

de un teléfono público. Cuando mi hermana comenzó a comprenderlo, _____ se le acabó
                                                                              _13._

el dinero y se cortó la comunicación _____ .
                                              _14._

EJERCICIO M	Claudio siempre confirma los comentarios de sus amigos después de salir de una ópera. Escriba lo que Claudio dijo usando la expresión adverbial *con + sustanivo*.

EJEMPLO: El público aplaudió enérgicamente.
El público aplaudió **con energía.**

1. Los cantantes cantaron alegremente.

_____

2. Los músicos tocaron entusiasmadamente.

_____

3. El conductor dirigió la orquesta hábilmente.

_____

4. Los bailarines bailaron torpemente.

_____

5. El cantante principal cantó claramente.

_____

6. Los aficionados aplaudieron frecuentemente.

_____

e. Some adverbial expressions are formed by combining prepositions with other words.

(1) preposition + noun

a fondo *thoroughly*
a la derecha (izquierda) *to the right (left)*
a la vez *at the same time*
al cabo (de) *at the end of*
al fin *finally*
de día *by day*
de memoria *by heart*
de noche *at night*
de repente *suddenly*
de rodillas *kneeling*
de veras *really, truly*
en seguida *immediately, at once*
por desgracia *unfortunately*
sin duda *undoubtedly*
sin embargo *nevertheless*

Pablo estudió el capítulo *a fondo.*	*Pablo studied the chapter thoroughly.*
Ahora tienes que doblar *a la derecha.*	*Now you must turn to the right.*
Puede escribir y hablar *a la vez.*	*He can write and speak at the same time.*
Regresó *al cabo de* **dos meses.**	*He returned at the end of two months.*
Al fin **consintió en que su hijo saliera.**	*Finally, he consented to his son's going out.*
De día **trabajo,** *de noche* **duermo.**	*By day I work, at night I sleep.*
Se sabe la poesía *de memoria.*	*He knows the poem by heart.*

De repente se oyó un gran ruido.	*Suddenly a loud noise was heard.*
Pidió perdón *de rodillas.*	*Kneeling, he asked for forgiveness.*
¿La quieres *de veras?*	*Do you really love her?*
Se marchó *en seguida.*	*He left immediately (at once).*
Por desgracia, mi reloj está roto.	*Unfortunately my watch is broken.*
Sin duda el clima es mejor allá.	*Undoubtedly the climate is better there.*
Estaba enfermo y, *sin embargo,* se levantó.	*He was sick; nevertheless, he got up.*

(2)   preposition + adjective

a menudo   *often*
a solas   *alone*
de nuevo   *again*
de pronto   *suddenly*
en general, por lo general   *generally*
por consiguiente   *consequently*
por supuesto   *of course*

Se encuentran en la calle *a menudo.*	*They often meet in the street.*
Al día siguiente tuvieron *de nuevo* un examen.	*On the following day, they had a test again.*
De pronto decidió irse.	*Suddenly he decided to leave.*
En general las joyas son muy caras.	*Generally jewels are very expensive.*
Estaba hablando y, *por consiguiente,* no oyó la pregunta del profesor.	*He was speaking, and, consequently, he didn't hear the teacher's question.*
Por supuesto, es necesario trabajar.	*Of course, it's necessary to work.*

(3)   preposition + adverb

al (a lo) menos   *at least*
en cuanto   *as soon as*

Esa señora tendrá *a lo menos* ochenta años.	*That lady must be at least eighty years old.*
Llámame *en cuanto* llegues.	*Call me as soon as you arrive.*

(4)   preposition + verb form

al amanecer   *at daybreak*
al anochecer   *at nightfall.*
al parecer   *apparently, seemingly*
por lo visto   *apparently, evidently*
por escrito   *in writing*

Se puso en marcha *al amanecer* y regresó *al anochecer.*	*He got started at daybreak and returned at nightfall.*
Al parecer no piensa regresar.	*Apparently he doesn't intend to come back.*
Por lo visto ya se acostó.	*Evidently he already went to bed.*
Preparen los ejercicios *por escrito.*	*Prepare the exercises in writing.*

(5)   preposition + adjective + noun

de buena gana   *willingly*
de mala gana   *unwillingly*
en ninguna parte   *not anywhere, nowhere*
en otra parte   *elsewhere*
en todas partes   *everywhere*

Me prestó el libro *de buena gana*, pero el dinero *de mala gana*.	He lent me the book willingly, but the money unwillingly.
No encontró la revista que quería *en ninguna parte*.	He didn't find the magazine he wanted anywhere.
La lluvia cayó *en otra parte*.	The rain fell elsewhere.
Había papeles regados *en todas partes*.	There were papers scattered everywhere.

EJERCICIO N   Escriba una frase para describir cada dibujo, empleando una expresión adverbial con preposición.

EJEMPLO: Arturo se puso **de rodillas** y le pidió a María que se casara con él.

1. Gabriel _____

_____

2. El Sr. Vargas _____

3. Julia _____

_____

4. Ernesto y Carlos _____

_____

5. _____

_____

6. _____

_____

EJERCICIO O   Eduardo y Edgardo son unos gemelos traviesos. Complete lo que su madre dice de ellos usuando la expresión apropiada.

a la derecha	al amanecer	en ninguna parte
a la izquierda	al anochecer	en seguida
a la vez	al fin	en todas partes
a menudo	de repente	por lo visto

¡No puedo creer lo que hacen mis hijos! Se despiertan muy temprano, _____,
                                                                          1.

y _____ comienzan a hacer travesuras. Es imposible comprenderlos porque los dos siempre
        2.

hablan _____ y discuten muy _____. Ayer salieron corriendo
          3.   4.

_____ y no pude encontrarlos _____ Los busqué _____,
      5.   6.   7.

pero no di con ellos. En la esquina, una vecina me dijo que los había visto doblar _____,
                                                                                            8.

pero otra dijo que los vio ir _____. _____ regresaron a casa
                                      9.   10.

_____. _____ habían estado jugando en la casa de un amigo.
      11.   12.

---

f. The following are common adverbial expressions formed with two or more words.

ahora mismo *right now*	**hoy (en) día** *nowadays*
a pesar de *in spite of*	**hoy mismo** *this very day*
cada vez más *more and more*	**junto a** *beside*
cuanto antes *as soon as possible*	**mientras tanto** *meanwhile*
de cuando en cuando *from time to time*	**rara vez** *seldom*
(abrir) de par en par *(to open) wide*	**sano y salvo** *safe and sound*
dentro de poco *shortly*	**tal vez** *perhaps*
fuera de sí *beside oneself*	**tan pronto como** *as soon as*
	ya no *no longer*

¡Acuéstate *ahora mismo*!   *Go to bed right now!*
***A pesar de* la tormenta, aterrizamos**   *In spite of the storm, we landed safe and*
  ***sanos y salvos*.**   *sound.*

El español se pone *cada vez más* difícil.	Spanish is becoming more and more difficult.
Escribe esa carta *cuanto antes*.	Write that letter as soon as possible.
Lo veo en la escuela *de cuando en cuando*.	I see him at school from time to time.
Las puertas estaban abiertas *de par en par*.	The doors were wide open.
Dentro de poco llegarán las vacaciones.	Vacation time will come shortly.
Al ver el error, se puso *fuera de sí*.	On seeing the mistake, he was beside himself.
Hoy día todo cuesta caro.	Nowadays everything is expensive.
Tienes que entregarme los documentos *hoy mismo*.	You have to hand me the documents this very day.
Estaba sentado *junto a* la ventana.	He was sitting beside the window.
Los niños jugaban; *mientras tanto*, su madre preparaba la cena.	The children were playing; meanwhile, their mother prepared supper.
Me escribe muy *rara vez*.	He writes to me very seldom.
Tal vez regrese mañana.	Perhaps he'll return tomorrow.
Tan pronto como recibió el dinero, se lo gastó.	As soon as he received the money, he spent it.
Ya no asiste a los conciertos de los domingos.	He no longer attends Sunday's concerts.

EJERCICIO P Conteste en español y en frases completas, las preguntas que le hace un amigo sobre sus clases.

1. ¿Qué materias te parecen más útiles hoy día?

_____

2. Si pudieras cambiar tus clases ahora mismo, ¿cuáles cambiarías?

_____

3. ¿Te gustan las matemáticas, a pesar de que son difíciles?

_____

4. ¿Cuál de tus clases se pone cada vez más difícil?

_____

5. Si fueras el (la) profesor(a), ¿cuándo darías exámenes, rara vez, de cuando en cuando o a menudo?

_____

6. ¿Cómo prefieres contestar preguntas en clase, oralmente o por escrito?

_____

7. ¿Prefieres estudiar de día o de noche?

_____

8. ¿Haces tus tareas de buena gana o de mala gana?

_____

| EJERCICIO Q | La mamá de Sarita le dejó un recado por escrito antes de salir a trabajar. Complete ese recado con la expresión apropiada. |

a pesar de   de cuando en cuando   mientras tanto
ahora mismo   de par en par   tal vez
cada vez más   dentro de poco   tan pronto como
cuanto antes   hoy mismo   ya no

¡_____ vas a limpiar tu cuarto! Se ve _____ desorganizado. Debes hacerlo
                1.   2.

_____ te levantes. Abres las ventanas _____ para airearlo y _____
        3.   4.   5.

recoges la ropa que _____ esté limpia. _____ es necesario hacer ciertas
                        6.   7.

cosas _____ que no te gusten. _____ comienzan las clases de nuevo y sería
            8.   9.

bueno que comenzaras a prepararte _____ . Salgo _____ de la casa y
                                        10.   11.

cuando regrese _____ salgamos de compras.
                    12.

M A S T E R Y   E X E R C I S E S

| EJERCICIO R | Conteste las preguntas que encontró Adolfo en un artículo del periódico sobre la personalidad. |

1. ¿Tiene Ud. pocos o muchos amigos?

   _____

2. ¿Toma Ud. baños fríos o calientes?

   _____

3. ¿Saluda Ud. cortésmente a sus conocidos?

   _____

4. ¿Es Ud. más o menos perezoso(-a) que sus hermanos?

   _____

5. ¿Le gusta a Ud. la compañía de gente culta?

   _____

6. ¿Hace Ud. ejercicios físicos todos los días?

   _____

7. ¿Prefiere Ud. una almohada dura o blanda?

   _____

8. ¿Escucha Ud. atentamente a las otras personas?

   _____

9. ¿Está Ud. orgulloso(-a) de todo lo que Ud. hace?

_____

10. ¿Hace Ud. las cosas lenta o rápidamente?

_____

11. ¿Se enoja Ud. fácil o difícilmente?

_____

12. ¿Trata Ud. a sus padres cariñosamente?

_____

13. ¿Trabaja Ud. bien o mal en compañía de sus amigos?

_____

14. ¿Tiene Ud. un gran sueño para el futuro?

_____

15. ¿Daría Ud. su último dólar a un pobre hombre?

_____

EJERCICIO S	**Complete el diálogo entre Rosa y Roberto, dos gemelos que hablan del futuro. Escoja la palabra necesaria y escríbala en su forma apropiada.**

ROSA: _____ día quiero casarme con _____
                 1.   2.

      señor _____ .
                  3.

ROBERTO: Yo pienso casarme con _____ mujer _____
                           4.   5.

      pero hay _____ cosas que quiero hacer _____ .
                  6.   7.

ROSA: Tú sabes _____ que al graduarme de la universidad quiero
                  8.

      tener _____ carrera _____ . Voy a ser
               9.   10.

      _____ diseñadora _____ .
          11.   12.

ROBERTO: A mí me gusta la vida _____ . Quiero hacer
                    13.

      _____ viaje _____ al Amazonas y
         14.   15.

      encontrar lo que _____ hombre haya descubierto todavía.
                  16.

ROSA: _____ sueños suenan _____ .
     17.   18.

1–7
alguno
bonito
otro
primero
rico
uno
uno

8–18
aventurero
bien
bien
bueno
famoso
largo
ninguno
nuestro
uno
uno
uno

ROBERTO: _____ personas nunca realizan sus sueños. Tenemos que
19.

trabajar _____ para realizarlos.
20.

ROSA: _____ tú y yo nos ayudamos.
21.

ROBERTO: Sí, tú y yo nos ayudamos el _____ por
22.

_____ .
23.

ROSA: Mi _____ hermano, te deseo _____ éxito
24.   25.

· en todo lo que hagas.

ROBERTO: Gracias. Igualmente.

19–25
alguno
afortunado
ciento
ciento
mucho
mucho
mucho
querido

EJERCICIO T | **Está lloviendo. Carlos y un amigo juegan un juego que consiste en completar una situación con un comentario apropiado. Escriba en español los comentarios para cada situación, usando la expresión dada.**

1. Arturo y sus amigos fueron a la playa. En menos de una hora están en casa. Arturo le dice a su mamá:

(por desgracia) _____

2. El niño tiene todos sus juguetes en el piso de la sala. Su mamá espera visita y le dice:

(ahora mismo) _____

3. Hoy es el quince de abril. Mi cumpleaños es el veinte y nueve de abril. Anita dice para sí:

(cuanto antes) _____

4. Rafael vio un accidente en la calle. Había sólo unos cuantos heridos:

(sano y salvo) _____

5. Los actores trabajaron bien en la obra, pero la escenografía no era muy buena. Roberto comentó:

(a pesar de) _____

6. El señor Cabral encontró una cartera en la calle con doscientos dólares. Quiere devolverla a su dueño:

(por supuesto) _____

7. Ud. no está bien y tiene mucha calentura.

(en seguida) _____

8. La señora Ramírez contesta el teléfono. Preguntan por alguien que no vive allí. Después hay otra llamada y piden lo mismo. Ella dice para sí:

(sin duda—de nuevo) _____

9. Jaime encontró un libro antiguo en el que pronostican que el hombre viajará al espacio. Piensa para sí:

(hoy día) _____

10. María está muy cansada. Todavía tiene una lista larga de cosas para hacer. Piensa para sí:

(cada vez más) _____

EJERCICIO U   **Ud. le regaló un aparato eléctrico o electrónico (walkman, teléfono celular, máquina de afeitar, segadora de césped, televisor con control remoto, un taladro, una sierra eléctrica, un ipod, una máquina de ejercicio, etc.) a su papá para el Día de los Padres. La primera vez que él lo usó, el aparato no funcionó. Ud. trató de devolverlo a la tienda donde lo compró, pero no querían aceptarlo. Escriba una carta al fabricante del aparato, en la cual Ud. explica todas las circunstancias. Use tantos adjetivos, adverbios y expresiones adverbiales como pueda e incluya lo siguiente:**

- the purpose of your letter
- when and where you made the purchase
- a description of what happened / the problem
- the immediate actions you took
- how they can assist you
- your desired outcome
- how they can contact you
- the need for a timely resolution of the problem

_____

_____

_____

_____

_____

_____

_____

_____

Chapter 22
Comparisons

[1] COMPARISON OF INEQUALITY

a. Adjectives are compared as follows:

POSITIVE	**bello(-a, -os, -as)**	*beautiful*
COMPARATIVE	**más (*menos*) bello(-a, -os, -as)**	*more (less) beautiful*
SUPERLATIVE	**el (*a, los, las*)...más (*menos*) bello(-a, -os, -as)**	*the most (least) beautiful*

Este monumento es *bello*.	*This monument is beautiful.*
Ése es *más (menos) bello que* éste.	*That one is more (less) beautiful than this one.*
Aquél es *el monumento más (menos) bello del* país.	*That one is the most (least) beautiful monument in the country.*
Aquella flor es *la más (menos) bella del* jardín.	*That flower is the most (least) beautiful (one) in the garden.*
Es *la mejor (peor) actriz del* mundo.	*She is the best (worst) actress in the world.*

NOTES:

1. In the superlative, the noun stands between the article (**el, la, los, las**) and the adjective.

    Sirven la comida más rica de la ciudad.   *They serve the most delicious meal in town.*

2. After the superlative, **de** means *in*.

EJERCICIO A   **Durante una excursión por la ciudad de Madrid, Xavier hace muchas comparaciones. Escriba las comparaciones que hace, usando *más* o *menos* por turnos en cada oración.**

EJEMPLO: esta iglesia / alto / la otra
Esta iglesia **es más alta que** la otra.

1. esta estatua / antiguo / las otras

_____

2. este edificio / alto / el otro

_____

3. aquel museo / conocido / éste

_____

4. ese barrio / interesante / éste

_____

5. estas tiendas / caro / las otras

_____

6. este puente / largo / aquél

_____

7. esta puerta / ancho / ésa

_____

EJERCICIO B Imagínese que alguien le ha hecho preguntas sobre los miembros de su familia. Escriba quién es el (la) más (menos)... de su familia.

EJEMPLO: tranquilo
Mi mamá es la más tranquila de la familia.

1. paciente

_____

2. bondadoso

_____

3. nervioso

_____

4. alegre

_____

5. divertido

_____

6. triste

_____

7. generoso

_____

8. amable

_____

9. ambicioso

_____

10. indeciso

_____

| EJERCICIO C | La señora Espejuelas compara a sus alumnos. Escriba lo que dice de ellos. Use *más* o *menos* por turnos en cada oración. |

EJEMPLO: Roberto es diligente. (Carmen)
Carmen es menos diligente que Roberto.

1. Luz es estudiosa. (Ramón)

_____

2. Carlos es hablador. (Héctor)

_____

3. Esteban es inteligente. (Ana)

_____

4. Beto es independiente. (Clara)

_____

5. Estela es nerviosa. (Beatriz)

_____

6. Jorge es atlético. (Víctor)

_____

7. María es seria. (Cristina)

_____

b. The comparative forms of **bueno, malo, grande,** and **pequeño** are irregular.

POSITIVE	COMPARATIVE	SUPERLATIVE
bueno(-a, -os, -as) *good*	**mejor(es)** *better*	**el (la) mejor** **los (las) mejores** *the best*
malo(-a, -os, -as) *bad*	**peor(es)** *worse*	**el (la) peor** **los (las) peores** *the worst*
grande(s) *great, big*	**mayor(es)** *greater; older*	**el (la) mayor** **los (las) mayores** *the greatest; the oldest*
	más grande(s) *larger*	**el (la) más grande** **los (las) más grandes** *the largest*
	menos grande(s) *less large*	**el (la) menos grande** **los (las) menos grandes** *the least large*
pequeño(-a, -os, -as) *small*	**menor(es)** *minor, lesser; younger*	**el (la) menor** **los (las) menores** *the least; the youngest*
	más pequeño(-a, -os, -as) *smaller*	**el (la) más pequeño(-a)** **los (las) más pequeños(-as)** *the smallest*

> **menos pequeño(-a, -os, -as)**   **el (la) menos pequeño(-a)**
> *less small*   **los (las) menos pequeños(-as)**
> *the least small*

NOTES:

1. **Mejor** and **peor** generally precede the noun. **Mayor** and **menor** generally follow the noun.

    mi *mejor* **amigo**   *my best friend*
    la **hermana** *mayor*   *the older (oldest) sister*

2. The regular and irregular comparative forms of **grande** and **pequeño** have different meanings. **Más grande** and **más pequeño** compare differences in size or height (physical meaning); **mayor** and **menor** compare differences in age or status (figurative meaning).

    mi **hermano** *más pequeño*   *my smaller (smallest) brother*
    mi **hermano** *menor*   *my younger (youngest) brother*
    de *menor* **importancia**   *of lesser importance*

EJERCICIO D   **Un amigo quiere saber su opinión sobre varias cosas. Escriba cuál, en su opinión, es la mejor y la peor de las cosas indicadas.**

EJEMPLO: película
«Lord of the Ring» es la mejor película. «Friday the Thirteenth» es la peor.

1. disco compacto

   _____

   _____

2. programa de televisión

   _____

   _____

3. beisbolista profesional

   _____

   _____

4. jugadora de tenis profesional

   _____

   _____

5. obra de teatro

   _____

   _____

6. equipo de fútbol americano

   _____

   _____

7. novela

_____

_____

8. grupo musical

_____

_____

9. comida

_____

_____

10. cantante

_____

_____

EJERCICIO E Su mamá comenta cómo Ud. y sus hermanos hacen los quehaceres de la casa. Escriba lo que ella dice, usando los comparativos por turnos.

EJEMPLO: lavar los platos
             Gloria lava los platos mejor (peor) que yo.

1. planchar

_____

2. usar la aspiradora

_____

3. limpiar el sótano

_____

4. lavar el carro

_____

5. regar el jardín

_____

6. cocinar

_____

7. cuidar al bebé

_____

8. pintar

_____

EJERCICIO F	Describa a un pariente mayor y a otro menor que Ud. Use los adjetivos *bueno, malo, grande* y *pequeño* para describirlos.

EJEMPLO: Arturito es mi hermano **menor**. Él es el **menor** de la familia y es el más **pequeño** también. Mis otros hermanos, Pedro y Linda, son **mayores** que él también. Él grita **mejor** que yo.

1. el pariente mayor

_____

_____

_____

_____

_____

2. el pariente menor

_____

_____

_____

_____

_____

c. Adverbs are compared as follows:

POSITIVE	**rápidamente**	*rapidly*
COMPARATIVE	**más (menos) rápidamente**	*more (less) rapidly*
SUPERLATIVE	**más (menos) rápidamente** (*menos*) **bello(-a, -os, -as)**	*more (less) rapidly than*

Este tren corre *rápidamente*.　　*This train runs rapidly.*
Este tren corre *más rápidamente*.　*This train runs more rapidly.*
Este tren corre *más rápidamente que*　*This train runs more rapidly than the*
　los otros.　　　　　　　　　　　　*others.*

NOTES:

1. The superlative of adverbs is not distinguished from the comparative.

2. The adverbial superlative formed with the neuter article **lo** is an absolute superlative and not a superlative of comparison. It is usually followed by a phrase expressing possibility.

Ese tren corre lo menos rápidamente　*That train runs the least rapidly*
　posible.　　　　　　　　　　　　　*possible.*
Ella llegó lo más temprano posible.　*She arrived the earliest possible.*

EJERCICIO G   La señora Valdés compara a los chicos y las chicas de su clase. Escriba lo que ella dijo de ellos al hablar con otra profesora de un proyecto que la clase llevó a cabo. Use *más* o *menos* + *adverbio* por turnos en cada frase.

EJEMPLO: Los chicos trabajaron _____. (cuidadoso)
Los chicos trabajaron **menos cuidadosamente.**
Las chicas trabajaron **más cuidadosamente.**

1. Los chicos decoraron el salón de clase _____. (rápido)

   _____

2. Las chicas cortaron los diseños _____. (hábil)

   _____

3. Los chicos crearon diseños _____. (fácil)

   _____

4. Las chicas hicieron preguntas _____. (frecuente)

   _____

5. Las chicas aceptaron los comentarios _____. (alegre)

   _____

EJERCICIO H   Los jueces de un concurso literario hablan de los participantes en el concurso. Escriba lo que dijeron, usando *más* o *menos* (por turnos) + *adverbio* + *que* en cada frase.

EJEMPLO: Lourdes / expresarse claramente / los demás
Lourdes **se expresó más claramente que** los demás.

1. Raúl / contestar rápidamente / Lourdes

   _____

2. Elena / escribir el ensayo fácilmente / Octavio

   _____

3. Gabriel / hablar fuertemente / Raúl

   _____

4. Clarita / portarse respetuosamente / los demás

   _____

5. Sara / recitar hábilmente / los otros

   _____

6. Octavio / pensar cuidadosamente / Clarita

   _____

d. **Que** (*than*) is used after a comparative.

Es **más alta** *que* yo.   *She is taller than I.*
Tienen **menos dinero** *que* yo.   *They have less money than I.*

De (*than*) replaces **que** before a number if the sentence is affirmative. If the sentence is negative, **que** is used.

Ganó **más (menos)** *de* ocho dólares.   *He earned more (less) than eight dollars.*

     But:

No ganó **más** *que* ocho dólares.   *He didn't earn but eight dollars.*
         (He didn't earn more than eight dollars.)

If the second part of the comparison is a clause with a **different** verb, **de** is used together with a form of **el (la, los, las) que**.

Gasta **más** dinero *del que* **gana** su padre.   *He spends more money than his father earns.*
Leyó menos libros *de los que* le **recomendó** el profesor.   *He read fewer books than the professor recommended.*

NOTE: In each of these sentences, the nouns **dinero** and **libros** are the objects of both verbs: **gasta—dinero, gana—dinero** (implied); **leyó—libros, recomendó—libros** (implied). If the noun is not the object of both verbs, or if an adjective or adverb is being compared, **de lo que** is used.

Gasta **más dinero** *de lo que* crees.   *He spends more money than you think.*
Habla **más rápidamente** *de lo que* escribe.   *He speaks more rapidly than he writes.*

The word **dinero** in the first example is not the object of both verbs (**gasta—dinero**, but **crees—que gasta**). In the second example, the adverb **rápidamente** is being compared.

EJERCICIO I   **María visita a unos primos y cada noche escribe en su diario. Complete las frases con *de, que, del que, de la que, de los que, de las que,* o *de lo que*.**

Estoy en un pueblo que tiene menos _____ 1. mil habitantes. Es más pequeño

_____ 2. el parque central de mi ciudad. En esta aldea hay más guardias _____ 3.

necesitan. Ayer mi tí me llevó a una tertulia en la que hubo más _____ 4. treinta personas.

Esta tía es mayor _____ 5. mi mamá.

No recuerdo cuántos años hace que ella vive aquí, pero lleva menos _____ 6. cinco años

en esta aldea. Durante la tertulia, mi tía tradujo lo que las personas decían, pero ellas hablaban más rápida-

mente _____ 7. ella podía traducir. Sirvieron café y unas galletitas, pero era menos

_____ 8. yo hubiera podido comer. Tenía más hambre _____ 9. una persona

que no hubiera comido en veinticuatro horas. Mi prima Adela come más _____ nadie
10.

pero no pesa más _____ cincuenta kilos.
11.

Cuando fui a la tienda, compré más tarjetas _____ podré usar. ¡Ojalá tuviera más
12.

dinero _____ encuentro en el bolsillo! Así podría comprar otros regalos. Todavía tengo
13.

menos regalos _____ voy a necesitar. Me alegro de haber venido aquí. Estoy divirtiéndome
14.

más _____ me imaginaba.
15.

[2] COMPARISON OF EQUALITY

a. **tan** + adjective or adverb + **como** (*as... as*)

Ella no es **tan pobre como** él.   *She is not as poor as he.*
Mi coche corre **tan rápidamente como**   *My car runs as fast as hers.*
el suyo.

EJERCICIO J | **Doña Alicia es la abuela de los gemelos Carlos y Martín. Para ella, los dos son iguales. Escriba lo que dice de ellos.**

EJEMPLO: alto
            Carlos es tan alto como Martín.

1. bonito

_____

2. serio

_____

3. inteligente

_____

4. vivo

_____

5. alegre

_____

6. risueño

_____

7. cómico

_____

EJERCICIO K	Ahora escriba cómo los nietos de doña Alicia hacen varias cosas.

EJEMPLO: llorar fuertemente
Carlos llora tan fuertemente como Martín.

1. caminar rápidamente

_____

2. hablar cortésmente

_____

3. jugar hábilmente

_____

4. reírse alegremente

_____

5. comer lentamente

_____

b. (1) **tanto (–a, –os, –as) + noun + como** (*as much / as many . . . as*) is used to compare quantities

   Esta vaca da *tanta leche como* ésa.   *This cow gives as much milk as that one.*
   Recibió *tantos juguetes como* pidió.   *He received as many toys as he asked for.*

   (2) **tanto (–a, –os, –as) (pronoun) + como** (*as much / as many . . . as*) is used to compare actions

   Leímos *tanto como* ellos.   *We read as much as they.*

EJERCICIO L	Luisa cree que es necesario hacer tanto como sus amigas. Escriba lo que ella hizo.

EJEMPLO: gastar
Ella gastó tanto como sus amigas.

1. correr   _____

2. comer   _____

3. trabajar   _____

4. dormir   _____

5. estudiar   _____

6. leer   _____

7. comprar   _____

8. hablar   _____

9. jugar _____

10. descansar _____

___

| EJERCICIO M | Clara y Rocío viajan juntas, pero nunca están de acuerdo. Escriba lo que Rocío dice después de una excursion. |

EJEMPLO: CLARA: Había muchos americanos en la excursión. (alemanes)
            ROCÍO: **No había tantos americanos como alemanes en la excursión.**

1. CLARA: Había muchas rosas en el jardín del palacio. (claveles)

ROCÍO: _____

2. CLARA: Vendían unas banderas bonitas. (tarjetas)

ROCÍO: _____

3. CLARA: Visitamos muchos museos. (iglesias)

ROCÍO: _____

4. CLARA: Comimos muchas tapas. (galletas)

ROCÍO: _____

5. CLARA: Gastamos muchos euros. (dólares)

ROCÍO: _____

6. CLARA: Entramos en muchos almacenes. (librerías)

ROCÍO: _____

7. CLARA: Hizo mucho calor al mediodía. (a las dos)

ROCÍO: _____

c. Expressions of comparison

cuanto antes
lo más pronto posible } *as soon as possible*
tan pronto como sea posible

cuanto (-a, -os, -as) más (menos)..., tanto (-a, -os, -as) más (menos)... } *the more (less)...,*
cuanto (-a, -os, -as) más (menos)..., más (menos)... } *the more (less)...*

Venga a verme **lo más pronto posible.**   *Come to see me as soon as possible.*
Cuanto más habla, (tanto) menos escucho.   *The more he talks, the less I listen.*

NOTE: **Tanto** may be omitted in the expression **cuanto más (menos)..., tanto más (menos).**

Comparisons 301

EJERCICIO N Escriba lo que una maestra dice de sus estudiantes. Use *cuanto (-a, -os, -as) más (menos)…, tanto (-a, -os, -as) más (menos)* por turnos.

EJEMPLO: estudiar / aprender
Cuanto menos estudian, tanto menos aprenden.

1. escuchar / saber

_____

2. trabajar / ganar

_____

3. dar / recibir

_____

4. tratar / lograr

_____

5. leer / aprender

_____

6. viajar / conocer

[3] ABSOLUTE SUPERLATIVE

a. To express an absolute superlative (when no comparison is involved), **-ísimo (-a, -os, -as)** is often added to the adjective. The meaning is the same as **muy** + adjective.

muy barato
baratísimo } *very cheap*

NOTES:
1. **Muchísimo** = *very much.*
2. Adjectives ending in a vowel drop that vowel before adding **-ísimo.**
3. Adjectives ending in **-co, -go,** or **-z** change **c** to **qu, g** to **gu**, and **z** to **c** before adding **-ísimo.**

fres**co**   fres**qu**ísimo
lar**go**   lar**gu**ísimo
fero**z**   fero**c**ísimo

b. To form adverbs from adjectives in **-ísimo**, add **-mente** to the feminine form of the adjective.
riquísimamente,   **lentísim**amente

EJERCICIO O Alberto tiene la costumbre de exagerar mucho cuando habla de su vida. Usando *-ísimo*, escriba cómo describe las cosas.

EJEMPLO: yo / vivir / casa / grande
Yo vivo en una casa grandísima.

1. yo / vivir / avenida / ancha

_____

2. yo / tener / perro / feroz

_____

3. mi coche / ser / lujoso

_____

4. mis primos / ser / ricos

_____

5. yo / dar / fiestas / elegantes

_____

6. mis padres / ser / generosos

_____

7. la piscina de mi casa / ser / larga

_____

8. yo / viajar / mucho

_____

| EJERCICIO P | **Conteste estas preguntas que le hace un amigo, usando la forma -*ísimo*.** |

1. ¿Estudió Ud. mucho anoche?

_____

2. ¿Es muy larga la distancia desde su casa a la escuela?

_____

3. ¿Vuelve Ud. rápidamente a casa al salir de la escuela?

_____

4. ¿Escucha Ud. muy atentamente en la clase?

_____

5. ¿Trabaja Ud. muy diligentemente todos los días?

_____

6. ¿Está Ud. muy cansado / cansada después de un día de trabajo?

_____

7. ¿Sabe Ud. cocinar muy ricamente?

_____

8. ¿Se divierte Ud. mucho con sus amigos?

_____

9. ¿Tiene Ud. un horario muy difícil?

_____

10. ¿Es Ud. muy animado / animada en una fiesta?

_____

M A S T E R Y   E X E R C I S E S

EJERCICIO Q Lázaro es un joven colombiano que acaba de inscribirse en su escuela. Conteste las preguntas que él le hace sobre su pueblo.

1. ¿Cae tanta lluvia en agosto como en abril?

_____

2. ¿Hace tanto calor en la primavera como en el verano?

_____

3. ¿Hay tantos insectos en diciembre como en julio?

_____

4. ¿Es más bella la primavera que el invierno?

_____

5. ¿Hay tantas hojas en los árboles en enero como en julio?

_____

6. ¿Fue ayer un día más claro que hoy?

_____

7. ¿Es septiembre mejor que enero?

_____

8. ¿Son los jardines tan verdes en marzo como en agosto?

_____

9. ¿Es éste el árbol menos alto del jardín?

_____

10. ¿Cuándo hay menos nieve, en el otoño o en el invierno?

_____

EJERCICIO R

Imagínese que Ud. trabaja en una agencia de publicidad donde preparan anuncios sobre ciertos productos para la televisión. Escriba un anuncio en el que Ud. describe las semejanzas y las diferencias entre un producto y otro y por qué su producto es mejor.

EJEMPLO: un radio portátil

Este radio portátil es mejor que los otros. Ud. puede escuchar tantas emisoras como en los otros, pero el precio es más económico que el de las otras marcas.

_____

_____

_____

_____

_____

_____

_____

EJERCICIO S

Ud. pasó el verano estudiando en Costa Rica donde participó en un programa especial. Al volver a la escuela, le piden que escriba un artículo sobre sus experiencias en Costa Rica para una edición en español del periódico estudiantil. Antes de comenzar a escribir el artículo busque información en el Internet sobre Costa Rica. Escriba el artículo en el que Ud. incluye lo siguiente:

- background information on the program you attended (language, ecology, etc.)
- when and where it was held
- the goal of the program
- the similiarities/differences you noted in daily life in Costa Rica
- a comparison of the values you observed (family, school, ecological, political, economic, etc.)
- your reflections on (comparison of) life in Costa Rica and life in your town/city
- what you enjoyed most/least about the experience

_____

_____

_____

_____

_____

_____

Chapter 23
Numbers; Times; Dates

[1] CARDINAL NUMBERS

0 cero	
1 uno	20 veinte
2 dos	21 veintiuno, -a, veintiún
3 tres	(veinte y uno, -a, un)
4 cuatro	22 veintidós (veinte y dos)
5 cinco	23 veintitrés (veinte y tres)
6 seis	24 veinticuatro (veinte y cuatro)
7 siete	25 veinticinco (veinte y cinco)
8 ocho	26 veintiséis (veinte y seis)
9 nueve	27 veintisiete (veinte y siete)
10 diez	28 veintiocho (veinte y ocho)
11 once	29 veintinueve (veinte y nueve)
12 doce	30 treinta
13 trece	31 treinta y uno, -a, un
14 catorce	40 cuarenta
15 quince	50 cincuenta
16 dieciséis (diez y seis)	60 sesenta
17 dieciocho (diez y siete)	70 setenta
18 dieciocho (diez y ocho)	80 ochenta
19 diecinueve (diez y nueve)	90 noventa
100 cien (ciento)	400 cuatrocientos, -as
101 ciento uno, -a, un	500 quinientos, -as
115 ciento quince	600 seiscientos, -as
116 ciento dieciséis	700 setecientos, -as
200 doscientos, -as	800 ochocientos, -as
300 trescientos, -as	900 novecientos, -as
1.000 mil	1.000.000 un millón (de)
2.000 dos mil	2.000.000 dos millones (de)
100.000 cien mil	100.000.000 cien millones (de)

NOTES:

1. Spanish uses periods rather than commas to separate digits.

   (Spanish) **1.376.426**   (English) *1,376,426*

2. In decimals, Spanish uses a comma where English uses a period.

   (Spanish) **$5,35**   (English) *$5.35*
   Cinco dólares (con) treinta y cinco   *Five dollars and thirty-five cents.*
   (centavos).

3. The conjunction **y** is used only between tens and units, that is, in numbers 31 to 99.

43 **cuarenta** *y* **tres**   56 **cincuenta** *y* **seis**
74 **setenta** *y* **cuatro**   99 **noventa** *y* **nueve**

But:

109 **ciento nueve**   304 **trescientos cuatro**

4. The numbers 16 to 19 and 21 to 29 are usually written as one word. In such compounds, the numbers 16, 22, 23, and 26 have an accent on the last syllable:

17 **diecisiete**   16 **diecis*éis***
21 **veintiuno**   22 **veintid*ós***

5. The only numerals that vary with gender are **uno (una, un)** and the compounds of **ciento (doscientos, -as; trescientos, -as;** and so on):

un **libro**   *a (one) book*
una **pluma**   *a (one) pen*
trescien*tos* hombres   *three hundred men*
cuatrocien*tas* mujeres   *four hundred women*
veintiún lápices   *twenty-one pencils*
cincuenta y *una* tarjetas   *fifty-one cards*

6. **Ciento** becomes **cien** before nouns and before the numbers **mil** and **millones.** In all other numbers, the full form **ciento** is used.

cien **botellas**   *cien* **mil soldados**
cien **buenos libros**   *cien* **millones de** habitantes

But:

ciento **veinticinco** dólares

7. **Un** is not used before **ciento** or **mil. Un** is used before the noun **millón.** If another noun follows **millón, de** is placed between **millón** and the other noun.

ciento dos alumnos   *un* **millón** *de* dólares
mil doscientos años

✳ EJERCICIO A Ud. está en un congreso que tiene lugar en un hotel de la ciudad de México. Ud. tiene las responsabilidad de contar el número de personas que hay en cada salón. Escriba los números que Ud. contó.

EJEMPLO: Salón Guanajuato   18 personas   **dieciocho (diez y ocho) personas**

1. Salón Acapulco   63 personas _____
2. Salón Veracruz   71 personas _____
3. Salón Guadalajara   15 personas _____
4. Salón Tampico   37 personas _____
5. Salón Oaxaca   126 personas _____
6. Salón Tijuana   54 personas _____
7. Salón Ixtapa   89 personas _____

8. Salón Querétaro   162 personas _____

9. Salón Torreón   41 personas _____

10. Salón Morelia   25 personas _____

EJERCICIO B   Ud está trabajando en el departamento internacional de un banco y le toca escribir la cantidad de los giros en letras. Escriba estos números:

1. 568 bolívares _____

2. 1.381 colones _____

3. 2.010 dólares _____

4. 30.432 sucres _____

5. 891 bolívares _____

6. 5.755,86 dólares _____

7. 12.967 quetzales _____

8. 184 euros _____

9. 1.989 pesos _____

10. 1.750.322 dólares _____

EJERCICIO C   Ud. piensa hacer un viaje a España. Antes de ir, Ud. va a la biblioteca para averiguar el número de habitantes de las ciudades que piensa visitar. ¿ Cuántos habitantes tiene cada ciudad? Exprese los números en letras en español.

1. Madrid   3.155.359 _____

2. Barcelona   1.593.075 _____

3. Sevilla   704.154 _____

4. Valencia   807.000 _____

5. Málaga   558.287 _____

EJERCICIO D   Ud. lee una lista que tiene el número de estudiantes que hay en sus clases. ¿Cuántos estudiantes hay en cada clase? ¿Cuántos son chicos? ¿Cuántas son chicas? Escriba los números en letras en español.

CLASE	NÚMERO DE ALUMNOS	NÚMERO DE CHICOS	NÚMERO DE CHICAS
Álgebra	28	16	12
Inglés	34	21	13
Español	25	11	14
Biología	30	19	11
Historia	27	6	21
Coro	76	31	45
Arte	18	8	10
Educación física	82	41	41

EJERCICIO E   Ud. ha conocido a muchas personas en un congreso. Antes de terminar el congreso, Ud. pide el número de teléfono de varias personas de los Estados Unidos. Escriba los números de teléfono en español.

EJEMPLO: Luz Armendáriz   212—375—2669
                dos doce—tres setenta y cinco—veinte y seis sesenta y nueve

1. Arturo López   609–832–5508

---

2. Sarita Claveles   202–541–8297

---

3. Gilberto Robles   305–422–1746

---

4. Gabriela Coles   513–668–7033

---

5. Javier Muñiz   815–342–4351

---

6. Blanca Flores   914–282–6625

7. Sergio Bulnes   717–951–1965

| EJERCICIO F | Conteste estas preguntas en español. Escriba los números en letras. |

1. ¿Cuántos habitantes hay en la ciudad en que Ud. vive?

---

2. ¿Cuántos alumnos hay en su escuela? ¿Cuántos chicos? ¿Cuántas chicas?

---

3. ¿Cuánto cuesta el automóvil que más le gusta a Ud.?

---

4. ¿Cuánto pagó Ud. por los zapatos que lleva ahora?

---

5. ¿Cuánto quiere Ud. ganar al año cuando empiece a trabajar?

---

6. ¿Cuál es su número de teléfono?

---

[2] ARITHMETIC EXPRESSIONS

The following expressions are used in arithmetic problems in Spanish.

y *plus* (+)
  Cuatro **y** nueve **son** trece.

menos *minus* (−)
  Veinte **menos** once **son** nueve.

por (*multiplied*) *by*, "*times*" (×)
  Ocho **por** siete **son** cincuenta y seis.

dividido por *divided by* (÷)
  Ciento cuarenta y cuatro **dividido por** doce **son** doce.

son *equals* (=)

| EJERCICIO G | Usted va a trabajar en una tienda durante el verano. Antes de darle el trabajo, el patrón quiere saber si Ud. puede expresar estos números en español. Escriba lo siguiente en letras en español. |

1. 414 − 363 = 51

---

2. $336 \times 12 = 4032$ _____

_____

3. $254 + 587 = 841$ _____

_____

4. $911 - 276 = 635$ _____

_____

5. $31{,}217 \div 31 = 1007$ _____

_____

6. $419 + 716 = 1135$ _____

_____

7. $1818 \div 18 = 101$ _____

_____

8. $345 + 577 = 922$ _____

_____

9. $864 \div 16 = 54$ _____

_____

10. $990 \div 9 = 110$ _____

_____

11. $93 \times 71 = 6603$ _____

_____

12. $119 \times 17 = 2023$ _____

_____

[*3*] ORDINAL NUMBERS

1st	**primero, –a (primer)**		*6th*	**sexto, –a**
2nd	**segundo, –a**		*7th*	**séptimo, –a**
3rd	**tercero, –a (tercer)**		*8th*	**octavo, –a**
4th	**cuarto, –a**		*9th*	**noveno, –a**
5th	**quinto, –a**		*10th*	**décimo, –a**

Ordinal numbers are usually used only through tenth; thereafter, cardinal numbers are used.

la **tercera** fila   *the third row*
la **Quinta** Avenida   *Fifth Avenue*
Carlos **Quinto**   *Charles V*
But:
el siglo **diecinueve**   *the 19th century*
la página (número) **doce**   *page 12*

NOTES:

1. A cardinal number used in place of an ordinal is always masculine, since **número** is understood.

2. The ordinals **primero** and **tercero** drop the final –o before a masculine singular noun.

el *primer* **día**
el *tercer* **edificio**
But:
la **primera** visita
el siglo **tercero**

3. Ordinal numbers are often printed as **1º, 1ᵉʳ (primero, primer); 2º (segundo); 5ª (quinta); 10ª (décima),** and so on.

| EJERCICIO H | Usted está hablando con unos amigos y discuten el número de veces que han hecho varias cosas. Indique el número de veces que Ud. ha hecho las actividades indicadas. |

EJEMPLO: visitar el museo de arte / 2
        Es la segunda vez que visito el museo de arte.

1. montar a caballo / 2

   _____

2. hacer un viaje en avión / 5

   _____

3. ver esta película / 3

   _____

4. ir a acampar / 6

   _____

5. regresar a esta tienda / 4

   _____

6. marcar su número de teléfono / 9

   _____

7. conocer a los padres de su amigo / 1

   _____

8. comer en un restaurante español / 8

   _____

9. repetir la respuesta / 10

_____

10. ir a esquiar / 7

_____

EJERCICIO I	Usted va de compras a un almacén y consulta el directorio de la tienda para saber en qué piso venden las cosas que quiere comprar. Escriba los pisos a que Ud. debe ir para comprar lo que tiene en su lista.

Artículos para Caballeros: trajes, sombreros, abrigos	2	Juguetes	10
		Libros	5
Artículos para Caballeros: camisas, ropa interior, corbatas	1	Loza—Cristalería—Plata	9
		Mantelería—Ropa de Cama	6
Artículos para casa: cortinas, lámparas, alfombras	7	Películas	1
		Restaurantes—Café	1
		—Patio	8
Boletos de Teatro	1	Salón de Belleza	11
		Sombreros—Damas	3
Cámaras	5	Telas	7
Carteras para Damas	1	Maletas	5

Centro Musical—Discos compactos
   Grabadoras,
   Radio, Televisión
	3	Vestuario—Damas	2,3,4

		Vestuario—Niños	4
Cosméticos	1	Zapatos—Caballeros	2
Servicios para Caballeros	4,7	Zapatos—Damas	6
Servicios para Damas	6,8	Zapatos—Niños	4
Guantes—Damas	1		
Impermeables, Paraguas	1		

EJEMPLO: **¿En qué piso venden…?**
          un sombrero para hombre **el segundo piso**

1. platos   _____

2. zapatos para niño   _____

3. una grabadora   _____

4. una lámpara   _____

5. una novela   _____

6. un juguete   _____

7. refrescos   _____

8. guantes para mujer   _____

9. toallas _____

10. maletas _____

[4] FRACTIONS

½	medio(-a), la mitad de	*(the/one) half*
⅓	**un tercio, la tercera parte de**	*(the/one) third*
¼	un cuarto, la cuarta parte de	*(the/one) fourth, quarter*
⅔	**dos tercios, las dos terceras partes de**	*(the) two thirds*
¾	tres cuartos, las tres cuartas partes de	*(the) three fourths, quarters*
⅘	**cuatro quintos, las cuatro quintas partes de**	*(the) four fifths*
⅒	**un décimo, la décima parte de**	*(the/one) tenth*

NOTES:

1. Except for **medio** and **tercio,** noun fractions are formed with ordinal numbers through tenth. Thereafter, the ending **–avo** is usually added to the cardinal number.

   ¹⁄₁₂ **un doceavo, la doceava parte de**   *(the/one) twelfth*

2. Fractions are masculine nouns.

   3⅓ **tres y un tercio**   *three and one third.*

   When the fraction precedes the thing divided, it may be used with the feminine noun **parte,** unless a unit of measure is expressed.

   una tercera parte (un tercio) del libro   *a third of the book*

      But:

   un tercio de libra   *a third of a pound*

3. The adjective **medio(-a)** means *half,* while the noun **la mitad** means *half of.*

   media docena de huevos   *half a dozen eggs*
   la mitad de la clase   *half of the class*

[5] MULTIPLES

Multiple numerals are used in the same manner as their English equivalents.

una vez *once*	**simple** *single, simple*	
dos veces *twice*	**doble** *double*	
tres veces *three times*	**triple** *triple*	

Lo llamé **dos veces.**	*I called him up twice.*
Vino a visitarme **una vez.**	*He came to visit me once.*
Comí **el doble** de lo que comiste tú.	*I ate twice as much as you.*

NOTES:

1. Numeral adverbs expressing the number of times of an occurrence are formed by a cardinal number and the feminine noun **vez** (*a time*).

   He visto la película **cuatro veces.**   *I have seen the film four times.*

2. Multiples like **doble, triple** may be either adjectives or nouns.

Es una máquina de *doble* acción.	*It's a double-action machine.*
Este cuadro vale hoy **el doble**.	*This painting is worth twice as much today.*

EJERCICIO J	**Exprese en letras los números indicados en español.**

1. la 5ª columna _____

2. la 8ª Avenida _____

3. el 9° día _____

4. Alfonso XIII _____

5. el 4° párrafo _____

6. el siglo XX _____

7. la 3ª fila _____

8. la 7ª serie _____

9. ⅓ de kilo _____

10. el 10° aniversario _____

11. el 2° edificio _____

12. el 3ᵉʳ capítulo _____

13. ⅖ _____

14. el tranvía 43 _____

15. ½ mes _____

16. de 1ª calidad _____

17. Carlos V _____

18. el 1ᵉʳ Congreso Panamericano _____

19. el 6° renglón _____

20. el 3ᵉʳ grado _____

[6] TIME

¿Qué hora es?	*What time is it?*
Es la una.	*It is one o'clock.*
Son las dos (tres, cuatro, etc.).	*It is two (three, four, etc.) o'clock.*
Son las diez y veinte.	*It is 10:20 (twenty after ten).*
Son las ocho y cuarto (quince).	*It is 8:15 (a quarter past eight).*
Son las seis y media (treinta).	*It is 6:30 (half past six).*

Son las doce menos veinte (dos, cuarto, etc.).	*It is 11:40 (11:58, 11:45, etc.).*
¿A qué hora salió Ud.?	*At what time did you leave?*
a(l) mediodía	*at noon*
a (la) medianoche	*at midnight*
a eso de las siete	*at about seven o'clock*
Dio la una (Dieron las dos).	*It struck one (It struck two).*

NOTES:

1. **Es** is equivalent to *it is* for one o'clock, **son** for the other hours; **a** expresses *at*.

2. The article **la** (for **la hora**) is always used with one o'clock; **las** (for **las horas**) is used with the other hours.

3. *After or past* is expressed by **y**; *to* or *of* by **menos**. After "half past," time may be expressed by the following hour minus (**menos**) the minutes or by the expression **faltar** + minutes + **para** + following hour.

| Son las tres *y* veinte y cinco. | *It is 3:25.* |
| Es la una *menos* diez. (Faltan diez *para* la una.) | *It is 12:50 (ten minutes to one).* |

   It is not uncommon to hear 12:50 expressed numerically: **Son las doce y cincuenta.**

4. **Media,** an adjective, agrees with **hora; cuarto,** a noun, does not vary.

5. The expressions **de la madrugada** and **de la mañana** correspond to English A.M. (morning). The former refers to the hours before daylight, the latter to the daylight hours. **De la tarde** (*afternoon*) and **de la noche** (*evening*) correspond to P.M. **En punto** means *sharp*.

a las tres *de la* madrugada	*at 3 A.M.*
a las ocho y media *de la* mañana	*at 8:30 A.M.*
a las cuatro *de la tarde*	*at 4 P.M.*
Eran las nueve *en punto de la noche.*	*It was 9 P.M. sharp.*

EJERCICIO K   Ud. le enseña a un primo a decir la hora en español. Exprese las horas indicadas en los relojes.

1. _____

2. _____

3. _____

4. _____

5. _____

6. _____

7. _____

8. _____

9. _____

10. _____

11. _____

12. _____

13. _____

14. _____

15. _____

16. _____

17. _____   18. _____

19. _____   20. _____

EJERCICIO L   Ud. tiene la costumbre de hacer ciertas cosas a la misma hora todos los días. Escriba la hora a la que Ud. suele hacer las cosas indicadas.

EJEMPLO: comer el almuerzo
           Yo **como** el almuerzo **a las doce (a mediodía).**

1. despertarse para ir a la escuela

   _____

2. mirar su programa favorito de televisión

   _____

3. cenar con su familia

   _____

4. ir a la clase de español

   _____

5. acostarse todos los días

   _____

6. llegar a la escuela

   _____

7. preparar las tareas

   _____

8. hablar por teléfono con un amigo

   _____

EJERCICIO M   Lea estos problemas y conteste las preguntas.

1. Ud. tiene que estar en la escuela a las siete y media todos los días. El viaje a la escuela en bicicleta dura veinte y ocho minutos. ¿A qué hora debe Ud. salir de su casa?

   _____

2. Su clase de matemáticas dura cuarenta y dos minutos. Comienza a las nueve y doce. ¿A qué hora termina?

   _____

3. Ud. estudia durante una hora y media para un examen. Cuando cierra los libros, son las once menos quince. ¿A qué hora comenzó Ud. a estudiar?

   _____

4. A Ud. le gusta hablar por teléfono. Ud. llama a su amigo a las ocho menos cinco y cuelga el teléfono cuarenta minutos después. ¿Qué hora es?

   _____

5. El viaje de su casa a la playa dura ochenta y nueve minutos. Ud. sale a las siete y media de la mañana. ¿Qué hora es cuando Ud. llega a la playa?

   _____

EJERCICIO N   Ud. lleva un diario donde escribe por las noches. Describa a qué hora hizo hoy diez actividades durante el día.

EJEMPLO: **Hoy me bañé a las siete de la mañana.**

1. _____
2. _____
3. _____
4. _____
5. _____
6. _____
7. _____
8. _____
9. _____
10. _____

[7] DATES

¿Cuál es la fecha de hoy? ⎫	*What is today's date?*
¿A cuántos estamos hoy? ⎭	
Es el primero de enero. ⎫	*It is January 1.*
Estamos a primero de enero. ⎭	
Es el dos (tres, cuatro) de marzo.	*It is March 2 (3, 4).*
Es el diez de febrero de dos mil cuatro.	*It is February 10, 2004.*
Salió el tres de agosto.	*He left on August 3.*

NOTES:

1. Cardinal numbers are used for all dates except **primero** (*first*).

2. The names of months are written with small letters in Spanish.

3. The years are expressed in thousands and hundreds, not in hundreds alone, as in English. 1400 = **mil cuatrocientos.**

4. With dates, **el** corresponds to *on*.

   Te veré *el* **lunes.**   *I will see you on Monday.*

EJERCICIO O   Ud. habla con un amigo de Venezuela sobre las fechas culturales importantes de los Estados Unidos. Escriba las fechas indicadas.

1. February 14 _____

2. July 4 _____

3. October 12 _____

4. December 25 _____

5. February 12 _____

6. January 1 _____

7. February 22 _____

8. November 11 _____

9. April 1 _____

10. October 31 _____

EJERCICIO P   Escriba en español, expresando los números en letras.

1. May 2, 1808 _____

2. December 20, 1910 _____

3. October 12, 1492 _____

4. December 7, 1941 _____

5. March 31, 1519 _____

6. February 22, 1732 _____

7. April 1, 1649 _____

8. September 16, 1810 _____

9. November 1, 1396 _____

10. April 12, 2001 _____

EJERCICIO Q   Ud. está preparando su «árbol genealógico». Escriba la fecha en que nacieron estas personas de su familia.

1. su abuelo paterno _____

2. su abuela paterna _____

3. su abuelo materno _____

4. su abuela materna _____

5. su padre _____

6. su madre _____

7. su hermano(-a) mayor _____

8. su hermano(-a) menor _____

9. su fecha de nacimiento _____

10. un tío o una tía _____

EJERCICIO R   Ud. acaba de entablar amistad con un amigo por correspondencia de Chile. Escriba una carta en la que le cuenta lo siguiente en español.

1. el país en que Ud. vive

2. el número de estados que hay en su país

3. la fecha en que su país ganó la independencia

4. el nombre del primer presidente de su país

5. la población de su ciudad o estado (aproximadamente)

6. el número de escuelas que hay en su barrio

7. el año de estudios en que Ud. está

8. su fecha de nacimiento

9. el horario de su escuela

10. la fecha de su último día de clases este año

_____

_____

_____

_____

_____

_____

_____

_____

_____

_____

_____

_____

| EJERCICIO S | **Ud. habla con un estudiante de Colombia que visita su clase de español y hace muchas preguntas sobre su escuela y la vida de los jóvenes norteamericanos. Conteste las preguntas.** |

1. EL COLOMBIANO: ¿Cuántos días a la semana vas a la escuela?

UD.: _____

2. EL COLOMBIANO: ¿Cuántos alumnos hay en tu año escolar?

UD.: _____

3. EL COLOMBIANO: ¿Cuántos minutos dura cada clase?

UD.: _____

4. EL COLOMBIANO: ¿A qué hora es tu primera clase?

UD.: _____

5. EL COLOMBIANO: ¿A qué distancia vives de la escuela?

UD.: _____

6. EL COLOMBIANO: ¿Cuánto tiempo necesitas para llegar a la escuela a tiempo?

UD.: _____

7. EL COLOMBIANO: ¿Por qué no hay clases el primer martes de noviembre?

UD.: _____

8. EL COLOMBIANO: ¿Cuántos años debes tener para poder votar?

Ud.: _____

9. EL COLOMBIANO: ¿Cuánto vale un buen diccionario de inglés?

Ud.: _____

10. EL COLOMBIANO: ¿En qué año piensas graduarte?

Ud.: _____

MASTERY EXERCISES

EJERCICIO T

Ud está ayudando a una vecina anciana de origen mexicano a contestar una carta en español que ella recibió de la oficina de servicios sociales de su ciudad. Para ayudarla a conseguir el seguro social, escriba una carta en la que Ud. incluye lo siguiente:

- for whom you are writing the letter
- her date of birth and social security number
- how much she earned last year
- the amount of money she has in the bank
- how much money she owes and to whom (credit card, etc.)
- the amount she pays in rent each month
- the year of the car she has
- the number of people that live in her home
- how many times she has visited the office
- the date she wants to receive the first check

_____

_____

_____

_____

_____

_____

_____

_____

_____

_____

_____

_____

_____

_____

_____

EJERCICIO U   Ud. tiene que preparar una presentación sobre un desastre natural que ocurrió recientemente en su barrio o en el mundo que presentará a la clase de español. Por ejemplo, un temblor, una inundación, una nevada, un tornado, etc. Si necesita información, haga una búsqueda en el Internet. Escriba lo que Ud. dirá en su presentación. Incluya lo siguiente:

- the nature of the disaster
- where it took place
- when it began and ended (dates and times)
- its effect on the population (injured, homeless, etc.)
- its effect on crops and animals
- the estimated amount of financial loss
- the number of people who participated in the rescue mission
- how many times this has occurred in the past
- how everyone can help those affected by the disaster

_____

_____

_____

_____

_____

_____

_____

_____

_____

_____

_____

_____

_____

Part Four

Other Structures

MÉXICO

REPÚBLICA
DOMINICANA
PUERTO RICO

CUBA
HONDURAS
NICARAGUA

GUATEMALA
EL SALVADOR

COSTA RICA
PANAMÁ

VENEZUELA

COLOMBIA

ECUADOR

PERÚ

BOLIVIA

PARAGUAY

CHILE

URUGUAY

ARGENTINA

ESPAÑA
Islas Baleares

Islas Canarias

Chapter 24
Interrogatives; Exclamations

[1] INTERROGATIVES

a. Common interrogative expressions

PRONOUNS	ADVERBS
¿quién(-es)? *who?*	**¿cómo?** *how?*
¿prep. + quién(-es)? . . . *whom?*	**¿para qué?** *why? (for what purpose?)*
¿qué? *what?*	**¿por qué?** *why? (for what reason?)*
¿cuál(-es)? *what, which* (one[s])?	**¿dónde?** *where?*
¿cuánto(-a)? *how much?*	**¿cuándo?** *when?*
¿cuántos(-as)? *how many?*	

ADJECTIVES
¿qué? *what?, which?*
¿cuánto(-a)? *how much?*
¿cuántos(-as)? *how many?*

NOTE: In Spanish, questions have an inverted question mark (¿) at the beginning and a normal one (?) at the end.

b. ¿Qué? and ¿cuál?

The pronoun **¿qué?** asks about a description, definition, or explanation; **¿cuál?** asks about a choice or selection.

¿Qué es esto?	*What is this?*
¿Cuál de los dos desea Ud.?	*Which (one) of the two do you want?*
¿Cuáles son los meses del año?	*What are the months of the year?*

As an adjective **¿qué?** is generally used instead of **¿cuál(-es)?**.

¿Qué libro desea Ud.?	*Which book do you want?*

c. ¿Por qué? and ¿para qué?

Both expressions are equivalent to English *why?* **¿Por qué?** asks about a reason. **¿Para qué?** asks about a purpose.

¿Por qué no viene Ud. con nosotros? —**Porque no quiero.**	*Why don't you come with us?* —*Because I don't want to.*
¿Para qué desea Ud. consultar ese libro? —**Para ver** las fotos.	*Why do you want to consult that book?* —*To see the photos.*

NOTES:

1. **¿Por qué?** is logically used in a question calling for a reply with **porque** (*because*); **¿para qué?** calls for a reply with **para.**

2. Interrogative words, whether in direct or indirect questions, have written accents. Indirect questions, however, do not have question marks.

   ¿Quién es?—No sé quién es.   *Who is he?—I don't know who he is.*

EJERCICIO A   **Orlando no presta mucha atención cuando sus amigos hablan y no oye quién(-es) hará(n) ciertas cosas. Escriba las preguntas que él hace para saber quién(-es) hará(n) lo siguiente.**

EJEMPLO: Roberto va a acampar.
            ¿Quién va a acampar?

1. Mis hermanas van de compras.

_____

2. Heriberto trabaja en el almacén.

_____

3. Mi abuelo piensa viajar a México.

_____

4. Nosotros compramos un televisor más grande.

_____

5. Ustedes escribirán la carta esta noche.

_____

6. Clara venderá su bicicleta.

_____

EJERCICIO B   **Ricardo y su hermanito estudian en el mismo cuarto. El hermanito encuentra muchas palabras que no comprende. Según las respuestas de Ricardo, escriba las preguntas que hizo el hermanito.**

EJEMPLO: **¿Qué es la vida?** La vida es un misterio.

1. _____   El acero es un metal.

2. _____   El béisbol es un deporte.

3. _____   La cabra es un animal.

4. _____   Un discípulo es un alumno.

5. _____   Un novelista es un escritor.

EJERCICIO C Estela lleva a su hermanita a la juguetería para ver qué juguete ella prefiere recibir de regalo de cumpleaños. Escriba las preguntas que hace Estela.

EJEMPLO: ¿Qué muñeca deseas?
Deseo esta muñeca.

1. _____

Me gusta más la muñeca gorda.

2. _____

Prefiero el vestido amarillo.

3. _____

La segunda muñeca es la más bonita.

4. _____

Estoy mirando la ropita que viene con la muñeca.

5. _____

También quiero una cuna para la muñeca.

EJERCICIO D Usted trabaja en una tienda de ropa, y atiende a una señora que quiere comprar un suéter. Escriba las preguntas que Ud. le hace para saber (1) lo que ella busca; (2) el color; (3) la talla; (4) el estilo; (5) el dinero que piensa gastar; y (6) el modo de pagar la cuenta.

1. _____
2. _____
3. _____
4. _____
5. _____
6. _____

EJERCICIO E Cuando Beto visitó a México, él quiso aprender lo máximo posible sobre el país. Según las respuestas dadas, escriba las preguntas que hizo Beto.

EJEMPLO: ¿Cuál es la comida de mediodía?
La comida de mediodía es el almuerzo.

1. _____

El jarabe tapatío es un baile regional.

2. _____

Los mariachis son los músicos típicos.

3. _____

El Distrito Federal es la ciudad más grande del país.

4. _____

Acapulco es un puerto muy bonito.

5. _____

El peso es la moneda nacional.

6. _____

Los colores de la bandera son verde, blanco y colorado.

7. _____

El metro es un medio de transporte dentro de la capital.

EJERCICIO F   Ud. tiene una entrevista con un escritor famoso que acaba de recibir un premio importante e ilustre. Escriba las preguntas que Ud. le hará, usando *¿qué?, ¿quién(-es)?, ¿cuál?, ¿dónde?, ¿cuándo?, ¿cuánto?, ¿por qué?, ¿para qué?* y *¿cómo?*

1. _____

2. _____

3. _____

4. _____

5. _____

6. _____

7. _____

8. _____

9. _____

EJERCICIO G   La primera vez que Alberto sacó el carro de su papá, un policía lo detuvo. Escriba las preguntas que hizo el policía, según las respuestas de Alberto.

1. POLICÍA: _____

ALBERTO: El carro es de mi papá.

2. POLICÍA: _____

ALBERTO: Mi nombre es Alberto Zuloaga.

3. POLICÍA: _____

ALBERTO: Tengo dieciocho años.

4. POLICÍA: _____

ALBERTO: Mi dirección es Avenida Reforma, 27.

5. POLICÍA: _____

ALBERTO: Estos jóvenes son mis amigos.

6. POLICÍA: _____

ALBERTO: Vamos al cine.

7. POLICÍA: _____

ALBERTO: Estacioné el carro aquí porque tenemos prisa.

8. POLICÍA: _____

ALBERTO: Recibí la licencia de conducir el mes pasado.

9. POLICÍA: _____

ALBERTO: Es la primera vez que me detiene un policía.

10. POLICÍA: _____

ALBERTO: Le diré a mi papá que aprendí una lección cara.

[2] EXCLAMATIONS

Exclamatory words, like interrogative words, have written accents. The most common exclamatory words are:

¡Qué... !   *What . . . ! What a . . . ! How . . . !*
¡Cuánto(-a)... !   *How much . . . !*
¡Cuántos(-as)... !   *How many . . . !*
¡Cuán... !   *How . . . !*

¡Qué día!	*What a day!*
¡Qué grande es!	*How large it is!*
¡Cuánto dinero tiene!	*How much money he has!*

NOTES:

1. Exclamatory sentences have an inverted exclamation mark (¡) at the beginning and a normal one (!) at the end.

2. If the noun is modified, the exclamation is made more intense by placing **tan** or **más** before the adjective.

    ¡Qué día *tan* (*más*) hermoso!   *What a beautiful day!*

3. Before an adjective or adverb, **¡qué... !** (*how . . . !*) may be replaced by **¡cuán... ! Cuán** occurs mainly in literary style:

    ¡Qué fácilmente lo hace! $\left.\right\}$
    ¡Cuán fácilmente lo hace!   *How easily he does it!*

| **EJERCICIO H** | Después de ver un ballet, unos amigos hablan de las bailarinas y de la producción. Escriba lo que dicen, usando *¡qué… !, ¡cuánto… !* o *¡cuántos… !*. |

EJEMPLO: gracia / tener / ellas
¡Cuánta gracia tenían ellas!

1. bonitas / ser / ellas

_____

2. energía / tener / ellas

_____

3. fácilmente / saltar / ellas

_____

4. vestuario / bonito

_____

5. ligeramente / moverse / ellas

_____

6. música / dulce

_____

7. músicos / tener / la orquesta

_____

8. estilo / clásico

_____

| **EJERCICIO I** | David y un amigo acaban de ver una película. Su amigo está de acuerdo con los comentarios que David hace sobre la película. Escriba lo que el amigo exclama al oír los comentarios de David. |

EJEMPLO: Era una película ridícula.
¡Qué película más (tan) ridícula!

1. Los actores trabajaron mal.

_____

2. La acción era muy lenta.

_____

3. El paisaje era muy bello.

_____

4. Mostraron muchas playas.

_____

5. El lenguaje era muy infantil.

_____

| **EJERCICIO J** | **Escriba lo que Ud. exclamaría al ver lo siguiente.** |

EJEMPLO: nota / buena
¡Qué nota más buena!

1. bicicleta / nueva

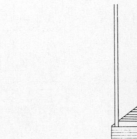

2. león / feroz

3. cola / larga

4. autobús / lleno

5. avión / veloz

6. pájaros / en el cielo

7. tráfico / en el centro

_____

_____

8. gente / en una caseta

_____

_____

9. partido / emocionante

_____

_____

10. casas / misteriosas

_____

_____

MASTERY EXERCISES

EJERCICIO K **Al salir de un examen, varios estudiantes hacen los comentarios siguientes. Subraye la forma admirativa correcta.**

1. ¡(Qué, Cuánta) desgracia! Salí mal en esta prueba.

2. ¡(Cuál, Qué) examen más difícil!

3. ¡(Cuán, Qué) memoria! Tú supiste todas las fechas históricas.

4. ¡(Qué, Lo que) prueba más larga!

5. ¡(Qué, Cuán) maestro tan estricto!

6. ¡(Cuántas, Cuán) preguntas más complejas había!

7. ¡(Cómo, Qué) aplicados debemos ser!

8. ¡(Qué, Cómo) lentamente trabajé!

9. ¡(Cuántos, Cómo) detalles pidió!

10. ¡(Cuán, Qué) mala suerte tengo!

EJERCICIO L Beto llama por teléfono a su amigo Luis, pero no lo encuentra en casa. Complete esta llamada telefónica, formulando las preguntas que Beto le hizo a la persona que contestó el teléfono. Las palabras subrayadas son las respuestas a las preguntas.

1. BETO: _____

   JOSÉ: Habla <u>José</u>.

2. BETO: _____

   JOSÉ: Creo que Luis fue <u>al teatro</u>.

3. BETO: _____

   JOSÉ: Salió <u>a eso de las siete</u>.

4. BETO: _____

   JOSÉ: Creo que volverá <u>tarde</u>.

5. BETO: _____

   JOSÉ: La función dura <u>dos horas y media</u>.

6. BETO: _____

   JOSÉ: Yo le diré que lo llame <u>mañana</u>.

7. BETO: _____

   JOSÉ: <u>El número</u> es el 525–67–85.

8. BETO: _____

   JOSÉ: Lo llamará antes de <u>las nueve</u>. Adiós.

EJERCICIO M Ud. va a hacer su primer viaje a España para visitar a un(-a) amigo(-a) español(-a) que pasó un año en su escuela. Ud. está muy emocionado(-a) del viaje y a la vez tiene muchas preguntas. Escríbale una carta a su amigo(-a) en la cual Ud. exprese o pide información sobre lo siguiente.

- your excitement about the trip
- the number of days remaining until the trip
- how you feel about seeing your friend and meeting his/her family and friends
- how far the airport is from their home
- who will meet you at the airport
- how much taxis charge
- how to find them at the airport
- his/her cell phone number
- how much money to bring
- the exchange rate
- what will you do together

- the meal times
- which are the best restaurants
- what you can bring the family
- your anticipation of the trip

_____

_____

_____

_____

_____

_____

_____

_____

_____

_____

_____

_____

_____

_____

| EJERCICIO N | Ud. tiene un amigo por correspondencia y los dos intercambian cintas. En la última cinta que Ud. recibió, no se grabó todo el mensaje de su amigo. Formule preguntas para hacerle a su amigo sobre lo que faltó en la cinta. El símbolo _____ indica que algo no se grabó. |

EJEMPLO: No recibí tu última _____.
    ¿Qué no recibiste?

Hola amigo,

Recibí tu cinta y tenía toda intención de contestarla en seguida, pero debido a _____ no lo hice.
1.

La semana pasada _____ me visitó. Nos divertimos mucho aunque no pudimos _____ .
2.   3.

Pensamos ir allí cuando _____ otra vez.
4.

El sábado fui al estadio para ver _____ . El equipo _____ ganó el partido. Fue un partido
5.   6.

muy _____ .Tuve suerte porque mi _____ me regaló el boleto.
7.   8.

Debes mandarme _____ cintas de las canciones más populares de tu país. _____ te mandan
9.   10.

muchos saludos.

Tu amigo,
Carlos

1. _____

2. _____

3. _____

4. _____

5. _____

6. _____

7. _____

8. _____

9. _____

10. _____

Chapter 25
Possession

[1] EXPRESSING POSSESSION

a. Possession is normally expressed in Spanish by **de** + the possessor.

el suéter *de* **Alberto**	*Alberto's sweater*
el coche *de* **los señores Molina**	*the Molinas' car*
los cuadernos *de* **los estudiantes**	*the students' notebooks*
los guantes *de* **mi hermana**	*my sister's gloves*

NOTE: To avoid repetition in a sentence, the noun representing the thing possessed is replaced by its definite article + **de.**

Este sombrero y **el de** Pedro son nuevos.	*This hat and Pedro's (that of Pedro) are new.*
Su opinión es diferente de **la de** su tío.	*His opinion differs from his uncle's (that of his uncle).*

b. **¿De quién(-es)?**, when followed by a form of **ser,** is equivalent to the English **interrogative** *whose?*.

¿De quién es el suéter verde?	*Whose green sweater is it?*
¿De quiénes es el coche nuevo?	*Whose new car is it?*
¿De quiénes son estos cuadernos?	*Whose notebooks are these?*
¿De quién son estos guantes?	*Whose gloves are these?*

c. The possessive relative **cuyo** (**-a, -os, -as**) is equivalent to the English relative *whose*. **Cuyo** agrees in gender and number with the person or thing possessed and not with the possessor. (See Chapter 19, page 244.)

El hombre *cuya* casa compré, vive ahora en Toledo.	*The man whose house I bought now lives in Toledo.*

EJERCICIO A | A Marta siempre le gusta prestar mucha atención a las acciones de sus amigos y hacerles preguntas. Según las respuestas, escriba las preguntas que Marta les hace a sus amigos.

EJEMPLO: Llevo la chaqueta de Rosa.
   ¿De quién es la chaqueta que llevas?

1. Estoy leyendo la revista de Susana.

_____

2. La profesora de Alberto está ausente hoy.

_____

3. Eché al correo las cartas del señor Gómez.

_____

4. Lavamos el coche de los señores Laredo ayer.

_____

5. Celebramos el aniversario de los padres de Arturo anoche.

_____

6. Volvimos a la casa de Roberto y Juan después del partido.

_____

7. Voy a la fiesta de Lourdes esta noche.

_____

8. Estoy copiando la tarea de Pablo.

_____

| EJERCICIO B | Juanito y Carmen han encontrado una caja que contiene muchas cosas. Juanito quiere saber de quién son las cosas. Carmen adivina de quién son. Escriba (1) las preguntas que hace Juanito y (2) las respuestas que da Carmen, según los ejemplos. |

EJEMPLOS: estos lápices / Alejandro
¿De quién son estos lápices?
Estos lápices son de Alejandro.

esta bandera verde, blanca y colorada / los mexicanos
¿De quiénes es esta bandera verde, blanca y colorada?
Esta bandera verde, blanca y colorada es de los mexicanos.

1. los guantes negros / la señora Álvarez

_____

_____

2. la mochila roja / un estudiante distraído

_____

_____

3. esta pluma de oro / el profesor

_____

_____

4. estos zapatos viejos / el presidente

_____

_____

5. las carteras nuevas / Alicia y Rocío

_____

_____

6. este cinturón grande / una persona gorda

_____

_____

7. las botas de vaquero / el chico guapo

_____

_____

8. esta regla rota / la maestra de geometría

_____

_____

9. estas camisas sucias / los jugadores

_____

_____

10. esta cámara cara / Enrique

_____

_____

EJERCICIO C   **Imagínese que Ud. y un amigo están en una feria en la que todos los países hispano-americanos están representados. Conteste las preguntas que le hace su amigo.**

EJEMPLO: ¿Prefieres la comida de Cuba o la de Puerto Rico?
Prefiero la de Puerto Rico.

1. ¿Te gusta más el arte de Venezuela o el de Guatemala?

_____

2. ¿Prefieres las costumbres de Bolivia o las de Costa Rica?

_____

3. ¿Cuál te interesa más, la poesía de la Argentina o la de Chile?

_____

4. ¿Te gustaría visitar las playas de la República Dominicana o las de México?

_____

5. ¿Cuál te parece más fácil de comprender, el dinero del Perú o el de Panamá?

_____

6. ¿Te interesa más la música de Puerto Rico o la de México?

_____

7. ¿Quiénes te parecen mejores futbolistas, los jugadores de la Argentina o los de Chile?

_____

[2] POSSESSIVE ADJECTIVES

SHORT FORM	LONG FORM	MEANINGS
mi, mis	mío, -a, -os, -as	*my*
tu, tus	tuyo, -a, -os, -as	*your* (familiar singular)
su, sus	suyo, -a, -os, -as	*your, his, her, its, their*
nuestro, -a, -os, -as		*our*
vuestro, -a, -os, -as		*your* (familiar plural)

a. The short forms of possessive adjectives precede the noun.

mi **abrigo**   *my overcoat*
su **reloj**   *his (your, her, its, their) watch*
nuestra **casa**   *our house*
tus **corbatas**   *your ties*
nuestros **sacos**   *our jackets*

NOTE: Possessive adjectives agree in gender and number with the person or thing possessed, not with the possessor.

b. The long forms of possessive adjectives follow the noun.

¡Dios *mío*!   *My God!*
una camisa *mía*   *a shirt of mine*
un primo *tuyo*   *a cousin of yours*
unos amigos *nuestros*   *some friends of ours*

NOTE: To avoid ambiguity, **su** (**sus**) and **suyo** (**suya, suyos, suyas**) may be replaced by the article plus **de Ud. (Uds.), de él (ella),** or **de ellos (ellas).**

Estaba esperando a **su** tía.   *He was waiting for his (her, your, their) aunt.*

Estaba esperando a **la** tía **de ella.**   *He was waiting for her aunt.*

c. The definite article is used instead of the possessive adjective with parts of the body or wearing apparel when the possessor is clear.

Pablo abrió *el* **paraguas.**   *Pablo opened his umbrella.*
El alumno levantó *la* **mano.**   *The pupil raised his hand.*
Juan se puso *los* **zapatos.**   *Juan put on his shoes.*
  But:
Juan se puso *mis* **zapatos.**   *Juan put on my shoes.*

EJERCICIO D   Ud. y un amigo preparan una lista de las cosas que Uds. y otros amigos van a llevar a una fiesta. Su amigo quiere saber de quién(-es) son las cosas. Escriba las respuestas a sus preguntas.

EJEMPLO: ¿De quién es la cámara que Raúl va a llevar a la fiesta?
Es su cámara.

1. ¿De quién es la grabadora que Gilberto va a llevar a la fiesta?

---

2. ¿De quiénes son los discos compactos que tú y Rafael van a llevar a la fiesta?

_____

3. ¿De quién son los adornos que María va a llevar a la fiesta?

_____

4. ¿De quién son los videos que Adela va a llevar a la fiesta?

_____

5. ¿De quiénes es el juego electrónico que Pedro y Luis van a llevar a la fiesta?

_____

6. ¿De quién es el juego nuevo que tú vas a llevar a la fiesta?

_____

7. ¿Sabes de quién es la guitarra que yo voy a llevar a la fiesta?

_____

EJERCICIO E   **A Guillermo le gusta usar la ropa de otras personas. Habla con un amigo que le espera mientras se viste para salir juntos. Escriba los adjetivos posesivos necesarios en cada frase.**

ROBERTO: Hoy llevas un suéter muy bonito. ¿Es _____ suéter nuevo?
1.

GUILLERMO: No, no es _____ suéter nuevo. Es de _____ hermano Pablo.
2.   3.

ROBERTO: ¿Siempre usas _____ cosas?
4.

GUILLERMO: Casi siempre. Me gustan _____ suéteres y _____ sombreros.
5.   6.

ROBERTO: Esta corbata es bonita. ¿Dónde la compraste?

GUILLERMO: No la compré. No es _____ corbata. Es de _____ hermano Eduardo.
7.   8.

Me gusta usar _____ corbatas.
9.

ROBERTO: ¿Qué más usas de _____ hermanos?
10.

GUILLERMO: A veces me pongo _____ calcetines y _____ abrigo.
11.   12.

ROBERTO: ¿No tienes _____ propio abrigo?
13.

GUILLERMO: Sí, pero _____ abrigo no es tan caliente como los de _____ hermanos.
14.   15.

ROBERTO: Bueno, vámonos. Ya es tarde.

GUILLERMO: Espera un momento. Tengo que buscar _____ cinturón negro.
16.

ROBERTO: Creo que está allí en la mesa pero me parece que es de _____ papá.
17.

GUILLERMO: Sí, es de él, pero como él y yo lo usamos, decimos que es _____ cinturón.
18.

ROBERTO: Tienes suerte. _____ hermanos no me dejan usar nada.
19.

GUILLERMO: Estoy listo. Vamos, porque _____ amigas nos esperan.
20.

EJERCICIO F Esteban es un joven distraído. Lea la descripción de lo que pasa en su casa todas las mañanas. Luego escriba debajo de cada oración la forma larga del adjetivo posesivo subrayado.

EJEMPLO: Esto pasa en su casa cada mañana.
la casa suya

1. Esteban nunca oye su reloj despertador.

_____

2. Por eso su mamá tiene que despertarlo cada mañana.

_____

3. Mientras Esteban se levanta y se viste, ella le dice: «Puse tu camisa y tus pantalones en la silla».

_____

4. Debes usar tu suéter nuevo hoy porque hace mucho frío.

_____

5. Debes darte prisa porque nuestra vecina va a llevarte a la escuela hoy en su coche.

_____

6. Recuerda que vas a su dentista hoy. Tu cita es a las tres y media.

_____

7. Mi horario es muy pesado hoy.

_____

8. Tengo que preparar una cena especial porque vienen nuestros amigos.

_____

9. ¿Dónde está tu gorra? ¿Y tus libros?

_____

10. ¡Ay, mi Dios! ¿Por qué será tan distraído mi hijo?

_____

EJERCICIO G   Sarita, una niña de cuatro años, le cuenta a su mamá lo que pasó en su clase hoy. Complete las frases con la palabra necesaria.

1. Roberto se quitó _____ zapatos.

2. Clara se lastimó _____ dedo.

3. Eduardo levantó _____ la mano para contestar.

4. La maestra abrió _____ paraguas cuando bajamos del autobús.

5. Luz se cortó _____ pelo con las tijeras.

6. Yo me lavé _____ manos después de pintar.

7. La enfermera se puso _____ guantes de goma cuando curó a Juan.

8. Pablo se rompió _____ nariz cuando se cayó.

9. Perdí _____ pañuelo en la escuela.

10. Después de jugar al fútbol, a Humberto le dolieron _____ piernas.

EJERCICIO H   Cuando los jóvenes están juntando sus cosas al terminar la fiesta, de repente se va la luz. Cuando la luz vuelve, se dan cuenta de que tienen cosas que no son de ellos. Usted y Héctor tratan de corregirlo. Escriba lo que usted dice.

EJEMPLO: HÉCTOR: Jorge tiene el abrigo de Pedro.
            USTED: **Tienes razón, no es el abrigo suyo; es el de Pedro.**

1. HÉCTOR: María tiene las botas de Adela.

   USTED: _____

2. HÉCTOR: Pablo tiene la gorra de béisbol de Enrique.

   USTED: _____

3. HÉCTOR: Anita se puso el suéter de Clara.

   USTED: _____

4. HÉCTOR: José tiene mis guantes.

   USTED: _____

5. HÉCTOR: Pilar y Ema tienen las revistas de Lourdes y Marisol.

   USTED: _____

6. HÉCTOR: Ricardo tiene el paraguas de Alejandro.

   USTED: _____

7. HÉCTOR: Juan y yo tenemos los discos compactos de Carlos.

USTED: _____

8. HÉCTOR: Tú tienes el video de Rosa.

USTED: _____

EJERCICIO I	Antes de salir de la casa por la mañana, la señora Ramos hace una serie de preguntas. Conteste las preguntas con la forma larga del adjetivo posesivo.

EJEMPLO: ¿Tienes tus llaves?
Sí, tengo las llaves mías.

1. ¿Apagaste tu computadora?

_____

2. ¿Prepararon sus tareas?

_____

3. ¿Llevó Rocío su almuerzo?

_____

4. ¿Dejé mi cartera en la mesa del comedor?

_____

5. ¿Diste de comer a tu perro?

_____

6. ¿Encendió Roberto la lámpara de su alcoba?.

_____

7. ¿Cerramos bien la puerta de nuestra casa?

_____

8. ¿Tienes tus anteojos?

_____

[3] POSSESSIVE PRONOUNS

el mío, la mía, los míos, las mías	*mine*
el tuyo, la tuya, los tuyos, las tuyas	*yours* (fam. sing.)
el suyo, la suya, los suyos, las suyas	*yours, his, hers, its, theirs*
el nuestro, la nuestra, los nuestros, las nuestras	*ours*
el vuestro, la vuestra, los vuestros, las vuestras	*yours* (fam. pl.)

a. Possessive pronouns consist of the definite article + the long form of the possessive adjective.

b. The possessive pronoun agrees in number and gender with the noun it replaces, not with the possessor.

Mi automóvil es más hermoso que *el* (= el automóvil) *suyo.* — *My automobile is more beautiful than yours.*

Esos libros y *los* (= los libros) *míos* son novelas. — *Those books and mine are novels.*

NOTES:

1. The specific meaning of **el suyo (la suya, los suyos, las suyas)** may be made clear by replacing the possessive with the expressions **de Ud. (Uds.), de él (ella),** or **de ellos (ellas)** after the article.

sus plumas y *las de Ud.* — *his pens and yours*
mis billetes y *los de ella* — *my tickets and hers*

2. After forms of **ser,** the article preceding the possessive pronoun is usually omitted.

Estas corbatas **son mías.** — *These ties are mine.*
Aquella corbata **es suya.** — *That tie is his.*

EJERCICIO J — Jorge es un niño de seis años. A Jorge le gusta decir que todo lo que él tiene es mejor que lo que tienen otras personas. Cambie las frases según el ejemplo.

EJEMPLO: Mi bicicleta es más nueva que la bicicleta de Raimundo.
Mi bicicleta es más nueva **que la suya.**

1. Mi hermano es más alto que el hermano de Elena.

_____

2. Mi uniforme es más lindo que tu uniforme.

_____

3. Su gato no es más grande que nuestro gato.

_____

4. Mis amigos son más fuertes que tus amigos.

_____

5. Sus abuelos son más pobres que nuestros abuelos.

_____

6. Las amigas de mi hermano son más bonitas que las amigas de Pablo.

_____

7. Tu casa es menos moderna que mi casa.

_____

8. Tu juego electrónico es menos interesante que el juego electrónico de mis hermanos.

_____

9. Mi mamá cocina mejor que tu mamá.

_____

10. El hermano de Alfredo es más cobarde que mi hermano.

_____

| **EJERCICIO K** | **Usted reflexiona sobre varias cosas. Escriba las frases según el ejemplo.** |

EJEMPLO: Mis impresiones del viaje y las impresiones de José son buenas.
Mis impresiones del viaje y **las suyas** son buenas.
Mis impresiones del viaje y **las de él** son buenas.

1. Mi coche y el coche de Alicia son del mismo color.

_____

2. Mis gustos y los gustos de Jorge son parecidos.

_____

3. Mi cumpleaños y el cumpleaños de los gemelos caen el primero de marzo.

_____

4. Los consejos de mis padres y los consejos de los padres de Raquel no son parecidos.

_____

5. Mis joyas y las joyas de ustedes son lindas.

_____

6. Nuestra idea y la idea de Jaime y Beto son interesantes.

_____

7. Tu fiesta y las fiestas de tus amigas son alegres.

_____

8. Las calificaciones de Ana y las calificaciones de Elena son altas.

_____

| **EJERCICIO L** | **Elsa y Beatriz son gemelas. Elsa siempre sabe dónde está todo. Beatriz, al contrario, nunca encuentra nada. Elsa siempre tiene que decirle dónde están las cosas que busca. Escriba las respuestas a las preguntas de Beatriz.** |

EJEMPLO: BEATRIZ: Busco la cámara de Alfredo. (en la mesa del comedor)
ELSA: **La suya está en la mesa del comedor.**

1. BEATRIZ: ¿Dónde está mi blusa verde? (en el armario)

ELSA: _____

2. BEATRIZ: Aquí está el reloj de mamá. No encuentro el reloj de papá. (en la cocina)

ELSA: _____

3. BEATRIZ: ¿Dónde dejé nuestros boletos para el teatro? (en tu mochila)

ELSA: _____

4. BEATRIZ: ¿Viste mi cepillo de pelo? (en el baño)

ELSA: _____

5. BEATRIZ: No encuentro mi cinturón rojo. ¿Puedo usar tu cinturón rojo? (en el cajón)

ELSA: _____

6. BEATRIZ: Busco las llaves de Alfredo. (en el escritorio)

ELSA: _____

7. BEATRIZ: Tengo que buscar tu disco compacto de Enrique Iglesias. (en el tocadiscos)

ELSA: _____

M A S T E R Y   E X E R C I S E S

EJERCICIO M   Bárbara tiene la costumbre de comparar sus cosas con las de sus amigas. Exprese en español los posesivos o expresión posesiva apropiados que corresponden a las personas indicadas.

EJEMPLO: Mi abrigo es verde. ¿De qué color es _____ ? _____ es negro.
            (tú)   (nosotras)
Mi abrigo es verde. ¿De qué color es **el tuyo** ? **El nuestro** es negro.

1. _____ joyas cuestan mucho. _____ son más caras. _____
   (ella)   (Clara)   (nosotras)
no valen nada.

2. El sombrero _____ es de paja. _____ es de felpa. _____
   (Pablo)   (Ernesto)   (yo)
es de lana.

3. He gastado todo _____ capital. ¿Qué has hecho con _____ ? _____
   (yo)   (tú)   (yo)
está en el banco.

4. La pluma verde es _____ . ¿ _____ es la pluma azul? Es _____ .
   (él)   (quién)   (Anna)

5. He perdido _____ paraguas. ¿ _____ es ése? Es _____ .
   (yo)   (quién)   (ellos)

EJERCICIO N   Sofía vive con una familia venezolana durante su visita a Caracas. Conteste las preguntas que ella le hace al hijo menor de la familia.

1. ¿Cuándo celebras tu cumpleaños?

_____

2. ¿Cuándo celebran tus padres el aniversario de su boda?

_____

3. ¿Te quitas o te pones los zapatos al salir de casa?

_____

4. ¿De quién son los juguetes que están en el cuarto de tu hermana?

_____

5. ¿Prefieres cenar en tu propia casa o en la de tus abuelos?

_____

6. ¿Eres más inteligente que tus hermanos?

_____

7. ¿Te lavas las manos antes de comer?

_____

8. ¿Cuál de estas muñecas es la tuya, la grande o la gorda?

_____

9. ¿Te gusta sacar fotos de tus amigos?

_____

10. La escuela de tus hermanos es la escuela Simón Bolívar, ¿cuál es la tuya?

_____

11. ¿Cómo saludas a tu maestro?

_____

12. ¿Es Arturito uno de tus amigos?

_____

13. ¿Acompañan Uds. a sus padres cuando van al cine?

_____

14. ¿Hasta qué hora te permiten tus padres mirar la televisión?

_____

15. ¿Oyes y comprendes bien mis palabras?

_____

16. ¿Son mejores las notas de los otros estudiantes que las tuyas?

_____

17. ¿Cuál es tu clase favorita?

_____

18. ¿Juegas con los amigos de tus hermanos?

_____

19. ¿Quién es el mayor de tus hermanos?

_____

20. ¿Te prestan tus hermanos sus juguetes?

_____

| EJERCICIO O | Ud. y un(-a) amigo(-a) hacen un viaje al Perú. Desgraciadamente, al reclamar el equipaje en Lima, Ud. no encontró el suyo. Ya han pasado dos días desde su llegada. Escriba una declaración a la aerolínea de lo ocurrido en la cual Ud. incluye lo siguiente. |

- when and where you checked your suitcase
- the baggage claim ticket number and flight number
- the contents of the suitcase and its value
- how the airline employees in Lima responded to your problem
- how you have coped with the situation (borrow/buy clothing, etc.)
- pertinent information on how the airline can contact you in Lima
- how you would like the problem resolved

_____

_____

_____

_____

_____

_____

_____

_____

_____

_____

Chapter 26
Demonstrative Adjectives and Pronouns

[1] DEMONSTRATIVE ADJECTIVES

MASCULINE	FEMININE	MEANING
este	esta	*this*
estos	estas	*these*
ese	esa	*that*
esos	esas	*those*
aquel	aquella	*that*
aquellos	aquellas	*those*

Demonstrative adjectives precede the nouns they modify and agree with them in number and gender.

este libro   *this book*
esas plumas   *those pens*

NOTES:

1. **Este** (**estos,** etc.) (*this* [*these*]) refers to what is near or directly concerns the speaker. **Ese** (**esos,** etc.) (*that* [*those*]) refers to what is not so near or directly concerns the person addressed. **Aquel** (**aquellos,** etc.) (*that* [*those*]) refers to what is remote from both the speaker and the person addressed or does not directly concern either.

Este lápiz es rojo.	*This pencil is red.*
Juan, déme Ud. *ese* **libro que tiene en la mano.**	*Juan, give me that book you have in your hand.*
Juan, déme Ud. *aquel* **libro.**	*Juan, give me that book over there.*

2. The adverbs **aquí** (*here*), **ahí** (*there*), and **allí/allá** ([*over*] *there*) correspond to the demonstratives **este, ese,** and **aquel.**

Deja {	*esta* mesa *aquí.*	**Leave** {	*this table here.*
	ese asiento *ahí.*		*that chair there.*
	aquel sofá *allí/allá.*		*that sofa over there.*

EJERCICIO A   Alicia acaba de comprar la ropa que va a llevar en un viaje que va a hacer. Su amiga quiere saber cuánto costó cada cosa. Escriba las preguntas que le hace la amiga.

EJEMPLOS: blusa
            ¿Cuánto costó esta blusa?

            guantes
            ¿Cuánto costaron estos guantes?

1. zapatos

_____

2. traje de baño

_____

3. impermeable

_____

4. falda

_____

5. bolso

_____

6. pantalones

_____

7. gafas de sol

_____

8. pijamas

_____

EJERCICIO B   Cuando Ramón fue a la corrida de toros, llevó sus binoculares para ver mejor desde su asiento. Escriba lo que dice al ver la corrida por los binoculares.

EJEMPLO: filosa / espada
¡Qué filosa es aquella espada!

1. valiente / torero

_____

2. fuertes / toros

_____

3. bonitas / capas

_____

4. larga / espada

_____

5. veloces / banderilleros

_____

6. impresionante / desfile

_____

7. elegante / traje de luces

_____

EJERCICIO C

En un mercado de frutas, Gloria desea comprar toda la fruta que ve. Escriba lo que va a comprar.

EJEMPLOS: melón / aquí
Va a comprar este melón.

uvas / ahí
Va a comprar esas uvas.

plátanos / allí
Va a comprar aquellos plátanos.

1. naranjas / aquí

_____

2. toronjas / allí

_____

3. piña / ahí

_____

4. melocotones / allí

_____

5. manzanas / aquí

_____

6. pera / ahí

_____

7. sandía / allá

_____

8. cerezas / ahí

_____

EJERCICIO D

Gilberto y sus amigos presencian un desfile. Escriba lo que dicen mientras se les acerca el desfile.

EJEMPLO: globos
Miren esos globos.

1. payaso

_____

2. caballo

_____

3. flores

_____

4. banderas

_____

5. luces

_____

6. cartel

_____

7. coches

_____

8. cohetes

_____

EJERCICIO E   **Alfonso hace preguntas sobre el pueblo que visita. Contéstelas, usando un adjetivo demostrativo.**

1. ¿Está abierta todo el día la librería de allí?

_____

2. ¿Son caros los restaurantes de ahí?

_____

3. ¿Venden sangría en los cafés de aquí?

_____

4. ¿Son viejos los árboles de allá?

_____

5. ¿Hay un lago en el parque de ahí?

_____

6. ¿Dan una buena obra en el teatro de aquí?

_____

7. ¿Venden tarjetas postales en la papelería de ahí?

_____

8. ¿Es posible nadar en el río de allí?

_____

[2] DEMONSTRATIVE PRONOUNS

MASCULINE	FEMININE	NEUTER	MEANING
éste **éstos**	**ésta** **éstas**	**esto**	*this (one)* *these*
ése **ésos**	**ésa** **ésas**	**eso**	*that (one)* *those*
aquél **aquéllos**	**aquélla** **aquéllas**	**aquello**	*that (one)* *those*

a. Demonstrative pronouns agree in number and gender with the nouns they replace.

este libro y **aquél** (= aquel libro)   *this book and that (one)*

b. (1) The neuter forms **esto, eso, aquello** do not refer to specific nouns but to statements, ideas, understood nouns, and the like. These forms do not vary in number and gender.

Pablo siempre llega tarde, y **eso** no le gusta al maestro.	*Paul always comes late, and the teacher doesn't like that.*
Su padre está enfermo, y **esto** lo pone triste.	*His father is ill, and this makes him sad.*

(2) The question **¿Qué es esto (eso, aquello)?** uses the neuter form because the noun is not known. After the noun has been mentioned, the form of the demonstrative adjective or pronoun must correspond to the noun.

¿Qué es **esto?**—Es una flor.	*What is this?—It is a flower.*
¿Es bonita **esta flor?**—Sí.	*Is this flower pretty?—Yes.*

NOTE: Demonstrative pronouns are distinguished from demonstrative adjectives by an accent mark. The neuter pronouns have no accent mark, since there are no corresponding neuter adjectives.

EJERCICIO F   **Cuando Esteban llegó al campamento de verano, encontró muchos anuncios pegados por dondequiera. Subraye la forma demonstrativa correcta.**

1. Coloque Ud. la maleta en este armario, no en _____.

(a) éste   (b) aquél   (c) ese   (d) esos

2. No se permite entrar por esa puerta, sino por _____.

(a) esto   (b) éste   (c) ésta   (d) aquél

3. Este horario marca las actividades, _____ no.

(a) ese   (b) ése   (c) aquello   (d) aquélla

4. Ponga Ud. los juguetes en este estante, no en _____.

(a) éste   (b) ése   (c) aquel   (d) esto

5. No apague Ud. esa luz, sino _____ .

    (a) aquella   (b) estas   (c) ésta   (d) ésa

EJERCICIO G   **Pablo y Jorge comparan cosas que su madre siempre les decía. Complete las oraciones con el pronombre demostrativo apropiado.**

EJEMPLO: *Esto* es bueno para la salud. Debes comerlo todo.

1. No debes hacer _____ porque tu papá se enojará.

2. _____ es importante para nosotros.

3. _____ no es bueno para ti.

4. Los niños no deben decir _____ .

5. _____ es algo bonito.

6. Un niño decente no haría _____ .

7. _____ me alegra mucho.

8. Si haces _____ , tendré que castigarte.

EJERCICIO H   **Conteste las preguntas que la mamá de Julia le hace cuando van de compras al almacén. Use el pronombre demostrativo apropiado.**

1. MAMÁ: ¿Te gusta este suéter o aquella blusa? (la blusa)

    JULIA: _____

2. MAMÁ: ¿Prefieres esa falda o este vestido? (el vestido)

    JULIA: _____

3. MAMÁ: ¿Deseas estas botas o aquellos zapatos? (las botas)

    JULIA: _____

4. MAMÁ: ¿Quieres esa gorra o este sombrero? (el sombrero)

    JULIA: _____

5. MAMÁ: ¿Debo comprar aquel abrigo o este impermeable? (el abrigo)

    JULIA: _____

6. MAMÁ: ¿Prefieres estos guantes de lana o esos guantes de piel? (los guantes de piel)

    JULIA: _____

c. The pronoun **éste** (**-a, -os, -as**) also means *the latter* (the latest, the most recently mentioned); **aquél** (**-la, -los, -las**) also means *the former* (the most remotely mentioned).

Juan es mayor que Pablo; **éste** tiene
seis años, **aquél** tiene nueve.

John is older than Paul; the former is
nine years old, the latter is six.

NOTE: In English, we usually say "the former and the latter." In Spanish, the order is reversed; **éste** (*the latter*) comes first.

EJERCICIO I	Después de su primer día de clases, Pepe hace varios comentarios. Complete cada oración con la forma apropiada de *éste* y *aquél*.

1. Eduardo y Rocío: _____ es alta, _____ es bajo.

2. Los juguetes y los rompecabezas: _____ son difíciles, _____ son viejos.

3. Gregorio y Beatriz: _____ es chistosa, _____ es serio.

4. Los niños y las niñas: _____ son habladoras, _____ son juguetones.

5. Las pinturas y los lápices: _____ son largos, _____ son brillantes.

EJERCICIO J	Carlos siempre repite lo que su hermana mayor dice. Escriba lo que Carlos dice, usando la forma correcta de *éste* y *aquél*.

EJEMPLO: ANA: Alicia es bonita pero Luz es más bonita.
CARLOS: **Sí, ésta es más bonita que aquélla.**

1. ANA: El señor Rivas es más estricto que la señorita Ramos.

CARLOS: _____

2. ANA: Gerardo es menos alto que sus hermanos Arturo y Beto.

CARLOS: _____

3. ANA: Clara es más aplicada que sus condiscípulos.

CARLOS: _____

4. ANA: Juan es gordo. Su amiga María es delgada.

CARLOS: _____

5. ANA: Mi bicicleta es nueva. La tuya es vieja.

CARLOS: _____

d. The definite article (**el, la, los, las**) followed by **de** (*that of, the one of*) or **que** (*the one that*) functions like a demonstrative pronoun.

el (la) de María   *that of (the one of) María*
los (las) de María   *those of (the ones of) María*
el (la) que está aquí   *the one that is here*
los (las) que están aquí   *the ones that are here*

El vestido de María es distinto **del**   *María's dress is different from Juana's; it*
de Juana; es muy parecido **al que**   *is very similar to the one Isabel*
lleva Isabel.   *is wearing.*

EJERCICIO K   Nicolás le escribió a Ud. una tarjeta postal de México. Escriba el pronombre demostrativo, empleando la forma correcta del articulo (*el, la, los, las*).

Pude planear mi propio itinerario pero no _____ de Roberto. Mi viaje es más interesante que _____ de
                                       1.   2.

mi primo. El clima mexicano es semejante a _____ de otras partes de Latinoamérica. La gente de
                                              3.

México y _____ de Guatemala hablan español. Los precios de este año son más altos que _____ del año
         4.   5.

anterior. Las montañas del norte son enormes, _____ del sur son más pequeñas. El nuevo guía es menos
                                               6.

interesante que _____ que se marchó. Será posible llevar a cabo mis planes y _____ de mis amigos.
                7.   8.

MASTERY EXERCISES

EJERCICIO L   Imagínese que Ud. está en un museo y hay pinturas, esculturas, tapices y otros objetos de arte a su alrededor. Describa cinco de los objetos de arte que Ud. ve, usando un adjetivo demostrativo.

SUGERENCIAS: pintura   cruz
               tapiz   figura
               escultura   cajita
               joya   modelo

EJEMPLOS: **Miren Uds. esos cofres antiguos.**
            Este cuadro de un ángel es hermoso.
            Me gusta aquel paisaje.

1. _____

2. _____

3. _____

4. _____

5. _____

EJERCICIO M **Mientras Sergio se baña y se viste, reflexiona sobre el viaje que está haciendo y lo que todavía quiere hacer. Complete el párrafo, usando un demostrativo apropiado.**

_____ tarde voy a ir a _____ tienda que vi ayer cuando pasamos por _____
   1.   2.   3.

calle angosta. Allí se venden _____ instrumentos musicales típicos de _____ país.
                                    4.   5.

_____ señora elegante del grupo dijo que _____ instrumentos cuestan mucho en los
   6.   7.

Estados Unidos. Voy a comprar _____ que sean fáciles de meter en _____ maleta de
                                   8.   9.

mano que tengo. Necesito buscar el regalo de mi papá y _____ de mi abuelo también. Si no
                                                            10.

encuentro nada en _____ almacén, iré a _____ de la esquina. _____ viaje me
                       11.   12.   13.

va a costar mucho porque los precios de los regalos y _____ de la comida son altos. Sin embargo,
                                                          14.

me he divertido mucho en _____ vacaciones; son más divertidas que _____ del año
                              15.   16.

pasado cuando pasé todo el tiempo en _____ hotel aislado en las montañas. _____ vez
                                          17.   18.

hay personas interesantes y simpáticas. Voy a recomendar _____ excursión a Rafael y a Alberto.
                                                              19.

A _____ le gusta ir de compras y a _____ le encanta conocer lugares nuevos. No debo
     20.   21.

olvidar _____ parque que está cerca del centro, donde saqué _____ fotos de la gente
            22.   23.

remando en _____ lago tranquilo. Todo _____ me da mucha alegría.
               24.   25.

EJERCICIO N **Rosa visita a su amiga Laura en el dormitorio de la universidad y le hace preguntas sobre lo que ve en el cuarto. Conteste las preguntas de Rosa.**

1. ¿Sacaste ese libro de la biblioteca?

_____

2. ¿Cuándo compraste aquella cinta?

_____

3. ¿Cuál de estos álbumes te gusta más, éste o aquél?

_____

4. ¿Es tuyo este vestido?

_____

5. De las dos estaciones que pasaste aquí, el otoño y el invierno, ¿te gustó más éste o aquél?

_____

6. ¿Cambiarías esta compañera de cuarto por la de Lourdes?

_____

7. ¿Es esa señora el ama de llaves del dormitorio?

_____

8. ¿Quién te regaló aquellos guantes?

_____

9. ¿Quieres prestarme esta falda o aquélla?

_____

10. ¿Es más fácil este semestre o el del otoño?

_____

EJERCICIO O   **Desde la niñez Ud. ha sido un coleccionista ávido. Escriba una presentación que Ud. dará a su clase de español en la cual Ud. explica y muestra ejemplos de este pasatiempo. Incluya lo siguiente:**

- what you collect (dolls, coins, stamps, baseball cards, rocks, etc.)
- when and how you began this hobby
- explain/describe your first acquisition and why it is important to you
- explain/describe several acquisitions and their value
- where you acquired different items
- an anecdote about one of the items in your collection
- how this hobby has affected your life
- what this collection means to you

_____

_____

_____

_____

_____

_____

_____

_____

_____

_____

_____

Chapter 27
Negation

[1] NEGATIVES

a. Principal negatives and their opposite affirmatives.

NEGATIVE	AFFIRMATIVE
no *no, not*	**sí** *yes*
nadie *no one, nobody, (not) anyone*	**alguien** *someone, somebody, anyone*
nada *nothing, (not) anything*	**algo** *something, anything*
nunca **jamás** } *never, (not) ever*	**siempre** *always*
tampoco *neither, not either*	**también** *also*
ninguno (-a) *no, none, (not) any*	**alguno (-a)** *some, any*
ni... ni *neither . . . nor; not . . . nor*	**o... o** *either . . . or*
sin *without*	**con** *with*

b. The most common negative is **no**, which always precedes the conjugated verb.

Ud. *no* sabe la lección.   *You don't know the lesson.*
¿*No* ha estudiado Ud.?   *Haven't you studied?*

c. If an object pronoun precedes the verb, the negative precedes the object pronoun.

Ud. *no* lo sabe.   *You don't know it.*

d. Spanish sentences may have two or more negatives. If one of the negatives is **no**, it precedes the verb. If **no** is omitted, another negative precedes the verb.

No veo a nadie nunca. }
Nunca veo a nadie.   *I never see anyone.*

No lo leyó tampoco. }   *He didn't read it either. (Neither did*
Tampoco lo leyó.   *he read it.)*

No usó ni papel ni lápiz. }   *He used neither paper nor pencil. (He*
Ni papel ni lápiz usó.   *didn't use either paper or pencil.)*

NOTES:

1. A negative preceded by a preposition retains that preposition when placed before the verb.

A nadie veo.

2. The negatives **nadie, nada, ninguno, nunca,** and **jamás** are used after comparatives.

Toca el piano **mejor que** *nadie.*	*He plays the piano better than anyone.*
Ahora lo creo **más que** *nunca.*	*Now I believe it more than ever.*
La niña desea una muñeca **más que** *nada.*	*The child wants a doll more than anything.*

3. The negatives **nadie, nada, ninguno, nunca,** and **jamás** are used in questions expecting negative answers.

¿Has visto **jamás** una película más aburrida?	*Have you ever seen a more boring film?*

4. The negatives **nadie, nada, ninguno, nunca,** and **jamás** are used in phrases beginning with **sin** and **antes (de** or **que).**

Salió *sin* decir *nada.*	*He left without saying anything.*
Antes de hacer *nada*, tienes que limpiar tu cuarto.	*Before doing anything, you must clean your room.*
Llegó **antes que** *nadie.*	*He arrived before anyone else.*

5. **Ninguno** as an adjective may be replaced by **alguno.** When so used, **alguno** follows the noun, and the negative is more emphatic.

No tengo *ninguna* amiga. ⎫	*I have no friend. (I don't have any*
No tengo amiga *alguna.* ⎬	*friend.)*

NOTE: **Ninguno** is almost always used in the singular form as an adjective.

¿Tiene Ud. algunos CDs de Enrique Iglesias?	*Do you have any CDs by Enrique Iglesias?*
No tengo ningun CD de Enrique Iglesias.	*No, I don't have any CDs by Enrique Iglesias.*

EJERCICIO A   **Javier es un joven de Acapulco y quiere conocerlo a Ud. mejor. Conteste las preguntas que él le hace, usando expresiones negativas.**

1. ¿Juega Ud. al fútbol los sábados?

_____

2. ¿Mira Ud. su programa favorito con alguien?

_____

3. ¿Cuándo va Ud. al museo?

_____

4. ¿Le gustan los tacos y los tamales?

_____

5. ¿Conoce Ud. a algunos mexicanos?

_____

6. A mí no me gusta la nieve. ¿Y a Ud.?

_____

7. ¿Preparó Ud. algo para la fiesta?

_____

8. ¿Dice Ud. algo cuando sale de la casa?

_____

EJERCICIO B   La mamá de Carmen siempre la contradice. Escriba lo que ella niega.

EJEMPLO: Mi hermana es fea.
             Tu hermana no es fea.

1. Jorge es aburrido.

_____

2. Luis y Daniel son futbolistas famosos.

_____

3. Mi papá es médico.

_____

4. Sarita tiene las muñecas de Elena.

_____

5. Rafael y Ernesto trabajan en la librería.

_____

EJERCICIO C   La señora Cabado tiene un problema porque sus hijos no le ayudan con los quehaceres de la casa. Escriba lo que le cuenta a su hermana.

EJEMPLO: sacar la basura
             Nadie saca la basura.

1. usar la aspiradora

_____

2. arreglar su cuarto

_____

3. lavar el carro

_____

4. sacar al perro

_____

5. planchar la ropa

_____

6. regar el jardín

_____

EJERCICIO D A Héctor le gusta presumir de lo atlético que es, pero su hermanito dice la verdad. Escriba lo que dice su hermanito.

EJEMPLO: Yo corro dos millas todos los días.
Tú nunca corres dos millas.

1. Yo levanto pesas cada mañana.

_____

2. Yo nado en la piscina todos los días.

_____

3. Yo siempre hago muchos ejercicios.

_____

4. Yo juego al tenis por la tarde.

_____

5. Yo juego al boliche cada semana.

_____

EJERCICIO E El señor Soto tiene antojo de postre, pero no hay nada en la casa. Escriba lo que le dice su esposa.

EJEMPLO: ¿Tenemos fruta?
No tenemos ninguna fruta.

1. ¿Tenemos helado?

_____

2. ¿Tenemos dulces?

_____

3. ¿Tenemos chocolate?

_____

4. ¿Tenemos galletas?

_____

5. ¿Tenemos bizcochos?

_____

6. ¿Tenemos torta de manzana?

_____

EJERCICIO F Ricardito es un niño problemático porque no le gusta hacer nada. Escriba lo que contesta.

EJEMPLO: ¿Te gusta correr o patinar?
No me gusta ni correr ni patinar.

1. ¿Te gusta hablar o callarte?

   _____

2. ¿Te gusta bailar o cantar?

   _____

3. ¿Te gusta pintar o dibujar?

   _____

4. ¿Te gusta jugar o descansar?

   _____

5. ¿Te gusta salir o quedarte en casa?

   _____

6. ¿Te gusta escuchar discos compactos o mirar la televisión?

   _____

EJERCICIO G   A César no le gusta contestar las preguntas que le hacen. Escriba las respuestas de César, según el ejemplo.

EJEMPLO: ¿Viste a alguien en la calle?
   Yo no vi a nadie en la calle.

1. ¿Bailaste con María en la fiesta?

   _____

2. ¿Hablaste con tus primos?

   _____

3. ¿Escribiste una carta a Gloria?

   _____

4. ¿Te acuerdas de los hermanos Silva?

   _____

5. ¿Viste a la novia de Roberto?

   _____

EJERCICIO H   La hermanita de Clarisa repite lo que dice su hermana. Escriba lo que dice.

EJEMPLO: Yo no voy al cine.
   Yo no voy al cine **tampoco.**

1. Yo no preparé la tarea anoche.

   _____

2. Mis amigas y yo no hablamos por teléfono.

   _____

3. Juanito no pidió helado de fresa.

_____

4. Mi prima no compró el regalo.

_____

5. Yo no visité a mis abuelos.

_____

[2] NEGATIVE EXPRESSIONS

Él no lo ve. **Ni** yo **tampoco.**	*He doesn't see it. Neither do I.*
Ya no tengo dinero.	*I no longer have money.*
No me quedan **más que** diez centavos. ⎫	*I have no more than ten cents left.*
No me quedan **sino** diez centavos. ⎭	*(I have only ten cents left.)*
¿Estás listo? **Todavía no.**	*Are you ready? Not yet.*
¿Puede Ud. pagarme? **Ahora no.**	*Can you pay me? Not now.*
Ni siquiera visita a su madre.	*He doesn't even visit his mother.*
¿Cómo van las cosas? **Sin novedad.**	*How are things going? Nothing new.*
	(The same as usual.)
¿Me prestas tu auto? ¡**De ninguna manera!**	*Will you lend me your car? Certainly not! (By no means.)*
Tenemos que esperar dos horas; **no hay remedio.**	*We have to wait two hours; it can't be helped.*
No cabe duda; la libertad es preciosa.	*There's no doubt; liberty is precious.*
No importa.	*It doesn't matter.*
No obstante mis esfuerzos, no pude llegar a tiempo.	*In spite of my efforts, I couldn't arrive on time.*

EJERCICIO I   **Complete estas situaciones, usando una de las expresiones siguientes.**

ya no	ahora no	ni... tampoco
no... más que	ni siquiera	todavía no
sin novedad	de ninguna manera	no importa

1. Hay mucha neblina. Su amigo oye el ruido de un avión y dice: —No puedo ver el avión.

Ud. responde: _____

2. Un amigo le dice: —Vamos a visitar a Carlos. Vive en esa casa verde.

Ud. responde: _____

3. Ud. va de compras con su mamá. Ella le pregunta si está listo(a).

Ud. responde: _____

4. Su hermanito pide que Ud. le ayude con su tarea de matemáticas. Ud. está ocupado(a).

Ud. responde: _____

5. Después de una cena enorme, Ud. y un amigo van al cine. Al pasar la dulcería en la entrada del cine, su amigo le dice: —Yo no puedo comer nada más.

Ud. responde: _____

6. Por casualidad, Ud. da con un amigo en la calle. El amigo le pregunta: —¿Cómo van las cosas?

Ud. responde: _____

7. Su papá le cuenta que el hijo de un amigo suyo ha ganado el campeonato de tenis. Ud. sabe que el chico no sabe jugar bien.

Ud. responde: _____

8. Después de un día en el parque de diversiones, Ud. y sus amigos tienen hambre. Buscan el dinero que les queda y no tienen suficiente. A Ud. le quedan veinticinco centavos.

Ud. responde: _____

9. Una amiga suya quiere pedirle prestada una falda morada. Ud. no la tiene.

Ud. responde: _____

10. Al salir de un concierto al aire libre, al que acudieron más de un millón de personas, su hermano dice que no volverá a esa clase de espectáculo.

Ud. responde: _____

[3] *PERO* AND *SINO*

Both **pero** and **sino** mean *but*. **Pero** is more general and may also mean *however;* **sino** is used only after a negative statement to express a contrast with a sense of "on the contrary," "but rather." Compare.

No llueve ahora, *pero* va a llover más tarde.	*It's not raining now but it's going to rain later.*
Tiene dinero, *pero* no es feliz.	*He has money but (however) he is not happy.*
No habla portugués, *sino* español.	*He doesn't speak Portuguese but (rather) Spanish.*
No llevaba camisa blanca, *sino* azul.	*He wasn't wearing a white shirt but (rather) a blue one.*

NOTES:
1. The comparison is always between two equivalent parts of speech (noun—noun, adjective—adjective, infinitive—infinitive).

No me gusta estudiar, *sino* ir al cine.	*I don't like to study but (on the contrary) to go to the movies.*
No compré zapatos blancos *sino* rojos.	*I didn't buy white shoes but red ones.*

2. If the contrasting verbs are not infinitives, **sino que** is used.

No cerró la puerta, *sino que* la dejó abierta.	*He didn't close the door but (on the contrary) left it open.*

| EJERCICIO J | **Manuel está enojado con su amiga, Rosalinda. Conteste las preguntas de su mamá usando *pero*.** |

1. MAMÁ: Rosalinda te invitó a su fiesta, ¿verdad? (No fui.)

MANUEL: _____

2. MAMÁ: ¿Le compraste un regalo? (No se lo di.)

MANUEL: _____

3. MAMÁ: ¿Te llamó ella por teléfono? (No contesté el teléfono.)

MANUEL: _____

4. MAMÁ: Ella es una chica inteligente. (antipática)

MANUEL: _____

5. MAMÁ: ¿Vas a llamar para disculparte? (No hablaré con ella.)

MANUEL: _____

| EJERCICIO K | **Alfredo ayuda a su hermanito a estudiar unas palabras nuevas. El hermanito no acierta ninguna de las palabras. Escriba lo que Alfredo dice.** |

EJEMPLO: Un hogar es una fábrica. (una casa)
Un hogar no es una fábrica sino una casa.

1. Un cirujano es un abogado. (un médico)

_____

2. Una guitarra es un deporte. (un instrumento musical)

_____

3. Un colegio es una universidad. (una escuela)

_____

4. Una butaca es un cuarto. (un mueble)

_____

5. La horchata es un pan. (una bebida)

_____

| EJERCICIO L | **Es la primera vez que Analuz cuida a los hijos de un vecino. Escriba lo que le cuenta a su mamá al volver a casa.** |

EJEMPLO: preparar la tarea / mirar la televisión
Los niños no prepararon la tarea sino que miraron la televisión.

1. lavar los platos / dejarlos en la mesa

_____

2. beber leche / tomar refresco

_____

3. comer en la cocina / cenar en la sala

_____

4. quedarse en casa / salir al patio

_____

5. estudiar la lección / hacer gimnasia

_____

EJERCICIO M **Gloria está de vacaciones en Madrid y escribe una carta a su hermana, después de un día de muchas frustraciones. Use *pero, sino,* o *sino que* para expresar lo que Gloria quiere decir.**

Querida Anita:

Estoy cansada, _____ quiero escribirte esta cartita. Hoy no hizo frío _____ llovió por
            1.   2.

la tarde, cuando íbamos a visitar el Parque del Buen Retiro. Por eso no fuimos al parque _____
             3.

al museo del Prado. Creí que conocía el arte español _____ me equivoqué muchas veces. El
                                       4.

cuadro «Las Meninas» no fue pintado por Goya _____ por Velázquez. Es muy bonito
                                       5.

_____ no pude pasar mucho tiempo estudiándolo porque había mucha gente en el museo.
      6.

Después de la visita al museo no fuimos a un café _____ regresamos al hotel, porque no paraba
                                  7.

de llover. A la hora de la cena no fui a un restaurante, _____ pedí la comida en mi cuarto. No
                                  8.

aproveché el tiempo para descansar _____ para escribir muchas tarjetas postales. Mañana no vis-
                      9.

itaré otros lugares famosos _____ las tiendas.
           10.

Hasta pronto,
Gloria

M A S T E R Y   E X E R C I S E S

EJERCICIO N **Conteste las preguntas que un(-a) amigo(-a) nuevo(-a) le hace, expresando en sentido negativo todo lo possible.**

1. ¿Le ha dado el maestro mucho trabajo?

_____

2. ¿Sabe Ud. hablar otras lenguas?

_____

3. ¿Duerme Ud. la siesta algunas tardes?

_____

4. ¿Tiene Ud. necesidad de algo?

_____

5. ¿Compró Ud. algo en el almacén ayer?

_____

6. ¿Cuál prefiere Ud., la música clásica o la música flamenca?

_____

7. ¿Prestó Ud. a alguien su cámara?

_____

8. ¿Hay algo que le molesta a Ud.?

_____

9. ¿Conoce Ud. a alguien que repare bicicletas?

_____

10. ¿Siempre trata Ud. a sus amigos igualmente?

_____

11. ¿Ha ido Ud. jamás a otra ciudad solo(a)?

_____

12. ¿Piensa Ud. ir al teatro esta noche también?

_____

13. Cuando hace mucho frío, ¿sale Ud. con gorra?

_____

14. ¿Alguien le ha engañado alguna vez?

_____

15. ¿Qué prefiere Ud. beber, jugo o refresco?

_____

EJERCICIO O   **Pilar hace comentarios de su viaje a España. Complete las oraciones con _pero_, _sino_, o _sino que_.**

1. España no es un país industrial, _____ agrícola.

2. El clima de La Mancha no es húmedo, _____ seco.

3. Visitamos a Toledo, _____ nos alojamos en Madrid.

4. No quería gastar mucho dinero, _____ tenía que comprar muchos regalos.

5. Conocí a muchos jóvenes, _____ ninguno me dio su dirección.

6. Quería pasar más tiempo en Segovia, _____ nos marchábamos al día siguiente.

7. No había perdido mi boleto de avión, _____ lo había guardado en otro bolsillo.

| EJERCICIO P | **Durante la temporada de fútbol (béisbol, baloncesto, etc.) recién pasada, el equipo de su escuela no ganó ningún partido. Escriba Ud. una carta al periódico estudiantil en la cual Ud. reflexiona sobre esta situación. Incluya lo siguiente en su carta.** |

- why you are writing this letter
- how you feel about the results
- your general impression of the season
- what you feel caused it (teamwork, coaching, injuries, etc.), with specific examples
- how the students reacted to it
- your suggestions for not allowing this to happen again

_____

_____

_____

_____

_____

_____

_____

_____

_____

_____

_____

_____

_____

_____

_____

_____

Part Five

Civilization: Spain

ESPAÑA

Islas Baleares

Islas Canarias

MÉXICO

REPÚBLICA
DOMINICANA
PUERTO RICO

CUBA
HONDURAS
NICARAGUA

GUATEMALA
EL SALVADOR
COSTA RICA
PANAMÁ

VENEZUELA

COLOMBIA

ECUADOR

PERÚ

BOLIVIA

PARAGUAY

CHILE

URUGUAY

ARGENTINA

Chapter 28
El Idioma Español

El idioma conocido como español es realmente el castellano, la lengua del reino de Castilla, que se convirtió en el idioma nacional de España y llegó al Nuevo Mundo con los conquistadores. La pro-
5 nunciación del español de América se parece a la de Andalucía y las Islas Canarias, donde no hay diferencias entre la **c** (en **ce** o **ci**), la **z** y la **s.**

El español es una lengua romance, o sea que es derivada del latín vulgar que hablaban los romanos
10 cuando llegaron a la Península Ibérica. Otras lenguas que se hablan en España son el vasco, el catalán y el gallego. El vasco o vascuence es una lengua de origen caucásico con influencias célticas. Se habla en el País Vasco, una región en el
15 norte de España. El catalán y el gallego son lenguas romances que derivan del latín. Se hablan en las regiones de Cataluña y Galicia respectivamente. En catalán, sobre todo, hay una rica tradición literaria.

En el castellano se notan, además del latín, in-
20 fluencias de los otros pueblos que vivieron en la península. La menor es la de los visigodos, porque éstos aprendieron el latín vulgar. Hay menos de un centenar de palabras en español de origen visigodo, y la mayoría son nombres propios como
25 **Fernando, Rodrigo** y **Álvaro.** Los griegos contribuyeron más vocabulario, aunque muchas de las palabras de origen griego llegaron al español a través del latín. Éstas se pueden reconocer fácilmente porque tienen las mismas raíces en inglés.
30 Algunos ejemplos son **la filosofía, la geometría, la química, la lógica, el alfabeto, la aritmética, la democracia, el teatro, el dragón, el poema, el problema** y **el programa.**

De todos los pueblos invasores, los árabes, que
35 estuvieron en España por ocho siglos, fueron los que más palabras contribuyeron al español. Más de 4.000 palabras del español de hoy fueron adaptadas del árabe. Entre ellas están **el arroz, el azúcar, azul, el ajedrez, el alcohol, el algodón, el al-
40 calde, el álgebra, ojalá** y **el marfil.**

En América, palabras indígenas enriquecieron el español. El vocabulario adoptado depende de las culturas y dialectos indígenas de cada región. De esos dialectos hay todavía dos que se hablan hoy en
45 día extensamente: el guaraní en el Paraguay y en el nordeste de la Argentina y el quechua en el Perú, Bolivia y zonas del Ecuador y de Chile. Estos dos dialectos han influido sobre todo en el español de las regiones donde se hablan, pero hay palabras que
50 han trascendido fronteras y se usan universalmente como **la papa, la pampa** y **el cóndor,** de origen quechua, y **el ananás, el jaguar (o yaguar), el tapir** y **la tapioca,** del guaraní. Además, aún idiomas indígenas que ya no se hablan, como el de
55 los aztecas, contribuyeron muchas palabras al español. Algunas de éstas han pasado al inglés, como **el tomate, el cacao, el chocolate, el chicle, el chile, el aguacate** y **el coyote.**

En este siglo, al surgir los Estados Unidos como
60 potencia económica mundial, y debido también a la proximidad geográfica, muchas palabras del inglés han pasado a formar parte del español familiar. Tenemos, por ejemplo, muchas palabras importantes como el fútbol, el béisbol, el basketball, el
65 match, el jogging o footing, el vagón, el film, el flash, el rock, el jazz, los jeans, el suéter, el picnic, el sandwich, el report, y el test entre otros. Hay que destacar también algunos verbos del inglés muy usados como parquear y chequear. De las nuevas
70 tecnologías, el español ha adquirido del inglés palabras como la computadora y el disco o el disquet y verbos como salvar, printear y chatear entre otros.

Aunque nos referimos en general al «idioma español», existen diferencias de uso y vocabulario
75 en los varios países en que lo hablan. La situación es semejante a la del inglés de los Estados Unidos y el de Inglaterra, con la diferencia que el español se habla en diez y nueve países autónomos, en Puerto Rico y en las grandes comunidades hispanas de los
80 Estados Unidos.

---

3   **convertirse en** to become
27 **a través de** through

50 **trascender fronteras** to spread beyond borders
59 **al surgir los Estados Unidos** when the U.S. emerged

| EJERCICIO A | ¿Cierto o falso? Indique si cada frase es cierta o falsa, cámbiela para que sea cierta. |

1. El catalán es otro nombre que se le da a la lengua española.

_____

2. La pronunciación del español de América se parece a la del sur de España.

_____

3. El español es una lengua germánica.

_____

4. En ciertas regiones de España la gente habla el vasco, el catalán y el gallego.

_____

5. Los visigodos tuvieron mucha influencia en el castellano.

_____

6. Las palabras en español derivadas del griego no aparecen en otras lenguas del mundo.

_____

7. Los árabes contribuyeron muchas palabras al español.

_____

8. Las civilizaciones indígenas de América no influyeron en la lengua española.

_____

9. El uso y el vocabulario de la lengua española son iguales dondequiera que ésta se hable.

_____

10. El español es un idioma que se habla en unos veinte países del mundo.

_____

| EJERCICIO B | Complete cada frase correctamente. |

1. El idioma español se conoce también como el _____ .

2. La pronunciación del español de América se parece a la de _____ .

3. El español se deriva del _____ .

4. Otras lenguas que se hablan en España son el _____ , el _____ y el _____ .

5. De los pueblos que vivieron en la península, _____ tuvieron la menor influencia en la lengua española.

6. Geometría, lógica y democracia son palabras españolas de origen _____ .

7. El pueblo invasor que más palabras contribuyó al español fue el _____ .

8. En América, la lengua española fue enriquecida por palabras _____ .

9. Dos dialectos indígenas que todavía se hablan en ciertas partes de América son

el _____ y el _____ .

10. Hoy en día se nota mucha influencia del _____ en el idioma español. Por ejemplo,

tenemos palabras relacionadas con las nuevas tecnologías como la _____ y

el _____ .

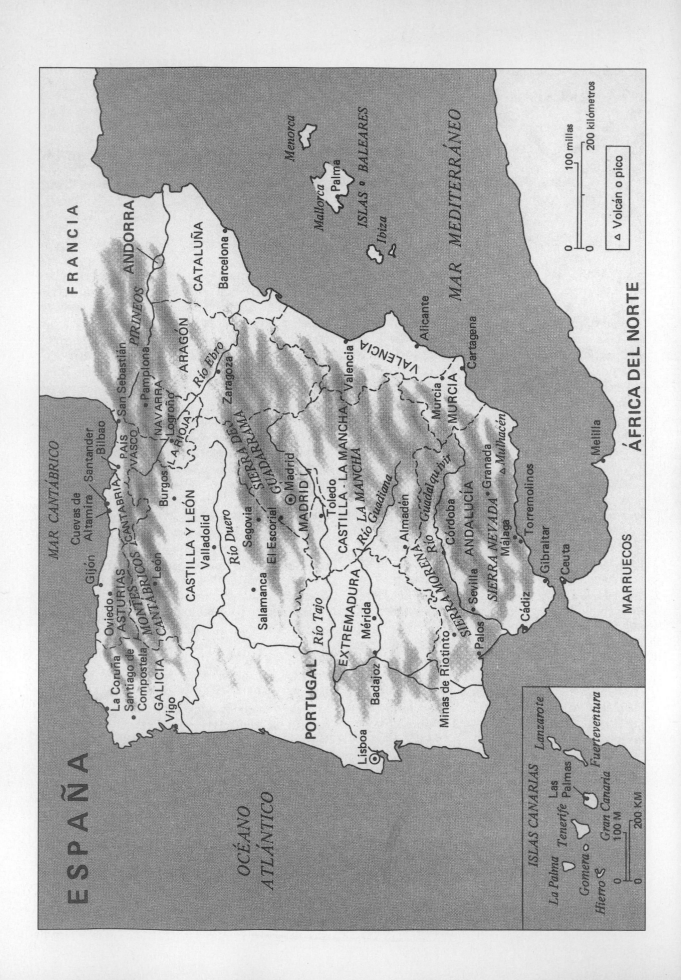

Chapter 29
La Geografía de España

Extensión, clima y población

España está situada al sudoeste del continente europeo, ocupando las cuatro quintas partes de la Península Ibérica. Limita con Portugal al oeste y
5 con Francia al nordeste. El resto del país está rodeado por las aguas del Mar Mediterráneo al este y las del Océano Atlántico al oeste. Al sur, el Estrecho de Gibraltar separa a España del continente africano. Políticamente, el territorio español
10 también abarca las Islas Baleares en el Mediterráneo, las Islas Canarias en el Atlántico y los puertos de Melilla y Ceuta sobre la costa mediterránea de Marruecos.

En total, unos 40 millones de habitantes viven
15 en un área algo menor que la del estado de Tejas, pero cuatro veces más grande que la del estado de Nueva York.

España se halla en la zona templada, pero las diferencias físicas que se notan en su territorio ha-
20 cen que el clima sea muy variado. A lo largo de la costa norte y en las montañas del noroeste, el clima es templado; ésta el la region más fría y lluviosa del país. En cambio en las tierras del sur y del este el clima es cálido. En la meseta central y en parte de
25 la costa sudeste predomina un clima de extremos: altísimas temperaturas y gran sequedad en el verano e intenso frío en el invierno. Por eso se ha dicho que Castilla tiene «seis meses de invierno y seis de infierno». Los cambios climáticos en los úl-
30 timos 15 años, debidos a la contaminación y a la capa de ozono, son drásticos y variables en toda España.

Cordilleras y ríos principales

España es el país más montañoso de Europa des-
35 pués de Suiza. Casi la mitad del interior del país está cubierta por una extensa altiplanicie llamada la meseta. Varias cadenas de montañas rodean esta meseta. Las Sierras de Guadarrama (al norte de Madrid) y Gredos la dividen en dos: al norte
40 Castilla y León y al sur Castilla-La Mancha, donde queda la extensa llanura de La Mancha, famosa en el mundo por la novela de Miguel de Cervantes,

«El ingenioso hidalgo Don Quijote de la Mancha». Al sur del país están la Sierra Morena, que separa la Mancha del valle del Guadalquivir, y la 45 Sierra Nevada, donde se encuentra el pico más alto de la península, el Mulhacén (3.478 metros), cerca de Granada.

Al noroeste están los Montes Cantábricos, con picos hasta de 2.600 metros, y al norte se extien- 50 den los Pirineos, que marcan la frontera con Francia y tienen cumbres de más de 3.300 metros.

Entre las cordilleras mencionadas se encuentran los ricos valles formados por los cinco ríos más grandes de España. En el norte el Ebro, llamado 55 antiguamente Iberus, le dio su nombre a la península. Este río pasa por la ciudad de Zaragoza y desemboca en el Mediterráneo. Los otros cuatro desembocan todos en el Atlántico. El río más largo es el Tajo, que pasa por la ciudad de Toledo y 60 atraviesa Portugal para desembocar cerca de Lisboa. El Duero, que nace cerca de Burgos en Castilla y León, pasa por Valladolid y entra en Portugal en su camino al Atlántico. El Guadiana, al sur del país, pasa por Mérida y Badajoz, dos an- 65 tiguos centros romanos. El Guadalquivir, en cuyas orillas se hallan las ciudades de Córdoba y Sevilla, es el río más navegable de España. Su nombre viene del árabe y quiere decir «río grande».

Minerales y productos principales
70

España es un país básicamente agrícola, pero se ha industrializado mucho en los últimos 40 años. En el norte abundan la madera y la pesca. En la parte central se cultivan el trigo, el maíz y otros cereales. 75 En el este se cultiva el arroz y en el sudeste hay cultivo de verduras en inmensos invernaderos. España es el tercer productor mundial de vino; la vid se cultiva por todas partes. Son célebres los vinos de Jerez, Málaga, La Rioja y el Penedés. España 80 es además el país con más olivares del mundo y produce y exporta aceitunas y aceite de oliva de gran calidad. España es también famosa por su fruta. En Lérida se cultivan las manzanas y las

---

3 **las cuatro quintas partes** four fifths
20 **a lo largo de** along

79 **el vino de Jerez** sherry (wine)

379

peras; en Valencia crecen las naranjas y los limones; y el sur es famoso por los dátiles y las frutas tropicales.

5   España es además muy rica en minerales. El más importante es el hierro, que se extrae en la provincia de Vizcaya, en el norte. En el sur del país están las minas de plomo de Linares y en el sudeste, las minas de cobre de Río Tinto. En la parte central del sur están las minas de mercurio de 10 Almadén, las más grandes del mundo.

En los últimos 50 años se han desarrollado la industria siderúrgica y la metalúrgica, particularmente la fabricación de automóviles. La industria textil se concentra en Cataluña, pero es importante 15 en todo el estado español. Regiones como Las Baleares y Valencia sobresalen por la fabricación de calzado y artículos de piel y cuero. En las dos últimas décadas se han desarrollado además la industria de la construcción y de servicios electrónicos a 20 cargo de pequeñas y medianas empresas.

Un producto natural de España es el sol y sus hermosas playas del Cantábrico, Atlántico y Mediterráneo. España es pues una interesante atracción turística durante casi todo el año. De hecho, el 25 crecimiento económico que ha producido España en los últimos años es de los primeros de la Comunidad Económica Europea.

División territorial del país

Históricamente, España tiene 50 provincias agru- 30 padas en 15 regiones. Cada una de ellas tiene sus propias tradiciones, cultura y en algunos casos su propia lengua. Administrativamente y desde mediados de los años ochenta (siglo XX), España se ha dividido en 17 comunidades autónomas*, cada 35 una de las cuales ha ido recibiendo competencias del gobierno central de manera desigual. Por ejemplo, Cataluña y el País Vasco tienen gobiernos autónomos hace más de 25 años y han elaborado Estatutos** que les permiten autogobernarse con 40 una cierta flexibilidad económica y social.

---

* Las comunidades autónomas son: Galicia, Asturias,
  Cantabria, País Vasco, Navarra, La Rioja, Aragón, Cataluña,
  Castilla-La Mancha, Castilla-León, Madrid, Valencia,
  Murcia, Extremadura, Andalucía, Las Baleares y Las
  Canarias. Ceuta y Melilla no son comunidades autónomas.
**Estatuto: Conjunto de leyes fundamentales de un gobierno
  en relación a la nacionalidad o al territorio.

EL NORTE

Las regiones del norte del país incluyen a Galicia, Asturias, Cantabria, el País Vasco, Navarra y La Rioja.

1. Galicia está al norte de Portugal, rodeada por 45 el Atlántico. Sus habitantes, los gallegos, son descendientes de los celtas, que llegaron del centro de Europa. Además del español hablan gallego, lengua derivada del latín que se parece al portugués. Los puertos principales de esta 50 región son Vigo y La Coruña.

2. Asturias está entre Galicia y Cantabria y es famosa por su industria minera. Allí se halla Covadonga, donde el héroe Pelayo venció a los moros en el año 718, iniciando así el 55 período conocido como la Reconquista. Las ciudades principales de esta región son Oviedo y Gijón.

3. Cantabria está al este de Asturias. Allí se halla la cueva de Altamira, famosa por sus pinturas 60 prehistóricas.

4. El País Vasco está cerca de los Pirineos, en la parte norte y central del país. Es montañoso, bien irrigado y hermoso. Además del español, sus habitantes hablan el vascuence, lengua de 65 origen caucásico con influencias célticas. Los vascos tienen un carácter independiente y emprendedor. Son importantes sus industrias siderúrgicas y metalúrgicas. También tienen un fuerte sentimiento religioso. San Ignacio de 70 Loyola, fundador de la Compañía de Jesús (o los jesuitas) [1] nació allí. En esta región vascongada se halla la célebre playa de San Sebastián llamada La Concha, de fama nacional y conocida también como el "Biarritz" 75 [2] o el Lido [3] de España.

5. Navarra es una región montañosa al este del País Vasco. Pamplona, su capital, es famosa por sus ferias anuales. Allí se celebra en julio la fiesta de San Fermín, que atrae a muchos turistas 80 de todo el mundo.

6. La Rioja es famosa por sus vinos de buena calidad, los vinos de Rioja. Su capital es Logroño.

EL CENTRO

En el centro del país están las regiones de Castilla, 85 Madrid y Extremadura.

7. Castilla, que ocupa la mayor parte de la Meseta Central, está dividida en Castilla y León al

---

11 **la industria siderúrgica** iron and steel works

norte y Castilla-La Mancha al sur. Tomó su nombre por los muchos castillos que se construyeron allí durante les guerras entre moros y cristianos. Su idioma, el castellano, es el idioma oficial de España. Ninguna otra región ha influido tanto en la vida nacional como Castilla, cuyos reyes jugaron un papel decisivo en la unificación de las varias regiones en una nación. La región de Castilla y León tiene además ricas minas de hierro y carbón.

8. Madrid es la capital de España y el principal centro político y económico del país. Es la residencia de la familia real y se encuentran aquí el gobierno central y las Cortes. Es también uno de los centros culturales más importantes de la Península Ibérica.

9. Extremadura, al sur de Castilla y León, está llena de montes. El río Guadiana corre por estas tierras, donde se hallan muchos monumentos de la época romana. Allí nacieron tres de los grandes conquistadores, Francisco Pizarro, Hernán Cortés y Vasco Núñez de Balboa.

EL SUR

10. Andalucía, la región del sur del país, recibió la influencia más profunda de la cultura árabe. Sus ciudades principales representan los distintos períodos de su historia. Cádiz, por ejemplo, fue el centro del comercio fenicio. Más tarde, durante la época musulmana, florecieron centros como Córdoba, Granada y Sevilla. En Andalucía se hallan las típicas casas españolas, pintadas de vivos colores, con patio en el centro y con rejas y balcones que dan a la calle.

EL ESTE

En la parte este del país están las regiones de Cataluña, Valencia, Murcia y Aragón.

11. Cataluña está situada al nordeste del país, en la costa mediterránea, y es la región más industrial de España. Su ciudad principal, Barcelona, es el puerto más grande del país. Los catalanes son bilingües, pues además del castellano hablan su propio idioma, el catalán, derivado también del latín. Los catalanes tienen, al igual que los vascos, un fuerte sentimiento nacionalista. En 1979 lograron restaurar «La Generalitat», su gobierno autónomo. Este

sigue hoy vigente con su propio estatuto y autogobierno.

12. Valencia, conocida por la fertilidad de su tierra y su excelente sistema de riego, está al sur de Cataluña. Es llamada «la huerta de España» a causa de sus numerosos productos agrícolas, entre los cuales son bien conocidas las deliciosas naranjas valencianas. El sistema de canales de irrigación que se usa allí fue introducido en España por los moros. Las costumbres de los valencianos, así como sus tradiciones, están bien representadas en algunas de las novelas del escritor Vicente Blasco Ibáñez (1867– 1928). En Valencia se habla, además del español, el valenciano, considerado como un dialecto del catalán.

13. Murcia, al sur de Valencia, es típicamente mediterránea. Es rica en minerales como el hierro y el cobre. Los productos principales de esta región son los dátiles, los limones y las naranjas.

14. Aragón está al nordeste del país. La industria ganadera es muy importante en esta región. Abarca la cría de ovejas, vacas, bueyes, cerdos y cabras. Zaragoza, su ciudad principal, deriva su nombre del emperador romano Julio César (Caesaraugusta) y fue de gran importancia militar durante la ocupación romana de España.

Posesiones extraterritoriales

España tiene todavía algunas posesiones extraterritoriales, residuos del gran imperio español.

1. Las Islas Baleares forman un archipiélago en el Mediterráneo. Las más conocidas son Mallorca, Menorca e Ibiza y sus respectivas capitales son Palma de Mallorca, Mahón e Ibiza. Su industria principal es el turismo. Mallorca y Menorca son importantes también por la fabricación de perlas y de calzado.

2. Las Islas Canarias forman un archipiélago de siete islas grandes en el Atlántico, frente a la parte sur de Marruecos. Las islas están divididas en dos provincias, Santa Cruz de Tenerife y Las Palmas. Desde 1982 las Canarias se constituyeron en Comunidad Autónoma.

3. Melilla y Ceuta son dos puertos en la costa de Marruecos que le pertenecen a España desde los siglos XV y XVII, respectivamente.

---

75 **extraterritorial** outside territorial limits
78 **el archipiélago** archipelago (a group of islands)
90 **Comunidad Autónoma** self-governing community

Ciudades principales

1. Madrid es la capital de España y la ciudad más grande del país, con cinco millones de habitantes. Situada en el centro del país, tiene muchos lugares históricos de interés. Entre ellos están el Museo del Prado, donde se encuentra una colección impresionante de las obras de los grandes pintores españoles como Velázquez, El Greco y Goya; el Palacio Real, uno de los palacios más grandes y lujosos del mundo: el Parque del Buen Retiro, el parque principal de la capital y antiguo campo de recreo de los nobles españoles; y la Puerta del Sol, la plaza principal de donde se dice que salen todas las carreteras de España.

Cerca de la capital está El Escorial, un enorme monasterio fundado por el rey Felipe II en 1563, cuya construcción duró 22 años. Es de estilo severo, clásico y majestuoso. El edificio contiene el Panteón de los Reyes, donde están enterrados muchos de los reyes de España. También hay una valiosa biblioteca, una iglesia y una rica colección de cuadros y tapices.

Otro monumento enorme cerca de la capital es el Valle de los Caídos, construido en memoria de los soldados que murieron en la Guerra Civil Española (1936–39) y dedicado en 1959. Encima de la ancha bóveda hay una cruz que tiene más de 125 metros de altura. Allí fue enterrado en 1975 el general Francisco Franco, dictador de España desde 1939 hasta su muerte.

2. Barcelona es la capital de Cataluña, una de las más grandes ciudades del país y el puerto principal de España. La ciudad tiene calles y avenidas famosas como El Paseo de Gracia y Las Ramblas, consideradas de las más hermosas de Europa. La Plaza Cataluña es el centro comercial y social de la ciudad. El barrio gótico, cerca del mar, tiene una importante catedral gótica y varias iglesias pequeñas de estilos románicos y góticos. En este barrio, de calles estrechas y pintorescas, se encuentran la plaza Real y el Palacio de la Generalitat.

Barcelona, también llamada «ciudad condal» y conocida por sus ferias y congresos, ha sido tradicionalmente y sigue siendo un gran centro artístico y cultural. Tiene museos de renombre nacional e internacional y muchas galerías de arte. Han vivido aquí muchos pintores, escritores, artistas y diseñadores de moda de fama mundial. Es de destacar el arquitecto modernista Antonio Gaudí cuya obra, extendida por toda la ciudad, es de una belleza única. En 1992 Barcelona fue la sede de los Juegos Olímpicos; la Villa Olímpica a orillas del mar y el complejo olímpico en la montaña de Montjuïc son hoy indispensables visitas turísticas. En las afueras de la ciudad se halla el famoso monasterio benedictino de Montserrat, visitado todos los años por miles de turistas y peregrinos.

3. Sevilla, a orillas del Guadalquivir, es la ciudad principal de Andalucía. Durante la época colonial era el único puerto de donde salían los buques para el Nuevo Mundo. La Catedral de Sevilla es la catedral gótica más grande del mundo y allí se encuentra la tumba de Cristóbal Colón. La Giralda, construida en el siglo XII, es la torre de la catedral y un admirable ejemplo de arquitectura árabe. En lo alto de la torre hay una estatua que hace de veleta y gira con el viento. Sevilla es una típica ciudad andaluza, cuya parte antigua posee calles estrechas y hermosos patios que adornan el interior de las casas.

4. Valencia es la capital de la región valenciana. Es un puerto a orillas del Mediterráneo y un gran centro agrícola, industrial y comercial. Son famosas sus fiestas falleras, de interés turístico internacional, que se celebran del 12 al 19 de marzo por San José. Se queman inmensas figuras en las plazas y barrios. Estas son construidas por los ciudadanos con materiales inservibles durante todo el año. En 2001 se inauguró la Ciudad de las Ciencias y de las Artes, diseñado por el famoso arquitecto valenciano, Santiago Calatrava. Es un complejo de cinco edificios destinados al desarrollo y a la divulgación del arte, las ciencias, la cultura y el ocio.

5. Granada está situada al pie de la Sierra Nevada. Fue la última fortaleza de los moros en España, conquistada por los Reyes Católicos en 1492. Entre los lugares de interés están el Albaicín, un pintoresco barrio donde viven los gitanos desde principios del siglo XVI; la Alhambra, antiguo palacio de los reyes moros, inmortalizado por el escritor norteamericano

---

20 **Panteón de los Reyes** burial place for kings   73 **hacer de** to act as

Washington Irving (1783–1859) en su libro
«The Alhambra», y donde están el famoso
Patio de los Leones y otros ejemplos del arte
musulmán; y el Generalife, otro palacio moro
que tiene fama por sus jardines encantadores y
por haber sido la residencia de verano de los
reyes moros.

6. Toledo está situada a orillas del río Tajo, a poca
distancia de Madrid. Fue capital de la España
visigoda y residencia de los reyes de España
hasta 1560. La ciudad ha quedado inmortalizada en los cuadros del gran pintor El Greco.
El famoso Alcázar de Toledo, un castillo moro
que fue destruido durante la Guerra Civil en
1936, ha sido totalmente reconstruido.

7. Cádiz es un puerto sobre el Atlántico. En
tiempos primitivos fue una colonia de los
fenicios.

8. Bilbao, capital de la provincia de Vizcaya, es el
centro de la industria minera del norte. Hizo
un papel muy importante durante las Guerras
Carlistas a la muerte de Fernando VII en 1833.
Está creciendo por su interés cultural ya que
en 1997 se inauguró allí el Museo Guggen-
heim, obra de Frank Gehry, de fama internacional.

9. Burgos es la antigua capital de Castilla y León.
Tiene una famosa catedral del mismo nombre
que es una de las maravillas de la arquitectura
gótica en España. Allí se halla la tumba del Cid
Campeador, el héroe nacional de España.

10. Santiago de Compostela es una ciudad gallega
visitada todos los años por miles de peregrinos
religiosos que hacen el tradicional Camino de
Santiago. Según la tradición, en esta ciudad se
encuentra la tumba del apóstol Santiago, patrón de España. Desde el descubrimiento de su
tumba en el siglo IX, peregrinos medievales y
modernos han hecho y siguen haciendo, desde
cualquier parte de España o de Europa, esta
ruta de peregrinación hasta Santiago de
Compostela. A esta ruta se la llama el tradicional Camino de Santiago.

11. Salamanca tiene una de las universidades más
viejas de Europa, la Universidad de Salamanca,
fundada en el siglo XIII. La ciudad conserva
una catedral románica del siglo XII y otra
gótica del siglo XVI, además de numerosos
edificios de los siglos XVI a XVIII.

12. Córdoba, a orillas del Guadalquivir, fue en los
siglos X y XI la capital del gobierno musulmán en España y el centro cultural más importante de toda Europa. Es una de las
ciudades más pintorescas de España. Su famosa
mezquita, hoy en día catedral, es un monumento árabe cuya construcción fue iniciada en
el año 786. Zaragoza, centro de la cultura
aragonesa, es famosa por la Basílica del Pilar.
Concentra además una fuerte industria auto-
movilística.

NOTES:

[1] **Compañía de Jesús o los jesuitas:** Catholic
religious order founded by San Ignacio de
Loyola in 1534. Almost from the beginning,
education, scholarship, and missionary work
became its principal activities. The society
grew rapidly and quickly assumed a promi-
nent role in the defense of Catholicism, emphasizing obedience to the Pope. The Jesuits
are today the largest order of male religious.
The order has continued work on all levels of
education and has played an important role
not only in Spain but also in Spanish America.

[2] **Biarritz:** famous French seaside resort on the
Atlantic Ocean.

[3] **Lido:** island close to Venice, Italy, famous for
its fashionable beaches.

21 **hacer un papel** to play a role

EJERCICIO A | Escriba la letra que indique la relación correcta con cada expresión de la columna de la izquierda.

1. montañas cerca de Madrid _____

2. río más navegable de España _____

3. pico más alto de España _____

4. vinos famosos _____

5. antiguo centro romano _____

6. montañas del sur de España _____

7. río más largo de España _____

8. frontera occidental _____

9. montañas del noroeste de España _____

10. montañas entre Francia y España _____

11. el mercurio _____

12. frontera oriental _____

13. el plomo _____

14. río que dio su nombre a la península _____

15. río que nace en Castilla _____

a. la Sierra de Guadarrama
b. Badajoz
c. el Ebro
d. el Guadiana
e. Linares
f. el Duero
g. Jerez y Málaga
h. Almadén
i. Portugal
j. la Sierra Morena
k. el Guadalquivir
l. el Tajo
m. los Pirineos
n. los Montes Cantábricos
o. el Mulhacén
p. el Mediterráneo

EJERCICIO B | ¿Cierto o falso? Indique si cada frase es cierta o falsa. Si es falsa, cámbiela para hacerla cierta.

1. Todos los ríos de España desembocan en el Mar Mediterráneo.

_____

2. Los Pirineos forman la frontera entre España y Portugal.

_____

3. España y Portugal forman la Península Ibérica.

_____

4. El río más navegable de España es el Guadiana.

_____

5. El Ebro es el único río que desemboca en el Océano Atlántico.

_____

6. El clima de España es muy variado.

_____

7. La cordillera que está en el norte de España es la Sierra de Guadarrama.

_____

8. El Río Tajo pasa por Toledo y Lisboa.

_____

9. La extensión de España es mayor que la del estado de Tejas.

_____

10. Las naranjas y otras frutas tropicales abundan en el norte de España.

_____

EJERCICIO C	**Escriba la letra que indique la relación correcta con cada expresión de la columna de la izquierda.**

1. Montserrat _____

2. Museo del Prado _____

3. Puerta del Sol _____

4. El Retiro _____

5. Bilbao _____

6. Santiago _____

7. Burgos _____

8. Granada _____

9. Toledo _____

10. Valle de los Caídos _____

11. la Catedral de Sevilla _____

12. Salamanca _____

13. Córdoba _____

14. la Plaza de Cataluña _____

15. Sevilla _____

a. plaza principal de Madrid

b. santo patrón de España

c. el Río Tajo

d. última fortaleza de los moros en España

e. monumento de la Guerra Civil

f. el Cid Campeador

g. parque público de Madrid

h. paseo moderno

i. grandes pintores españoles

j. catedral gótica más grande del mundo

k. mezquita iniciada en 786

l. centro comercial y social de Barcelona

m. tumba de Cristóbal Colón

n. una universidad antigua

o. monasterio famoso

p. centro de la industria minera del norte

EJERCICIO D	Escriba la letra que indique la relación correcta con cada expresión de la columna de la izquierda.

1. Ibiza _____

2. Valencia _____

3. San Sebastián _____

4. el vascuence _____

5. Santa Cruz de Tenerife _____

6. Pamplona _____

7. Covadonga _____

8. Andalucía _____

9. Barcelona _____

10. Galicia _____

a. región del centro del país
b. idioma de origen caucásico con influencias célticas
c. una de las Islas Baleares
d. Pelayo
e. La Coruña
f. «la huerta de España»
g. gran influencia árabe
h. ciudad principal de Cataluña
i. playa famosa
j. las Islas Canarias
k. monumentos romanos
l. capital de Navarra

EJERCICIO E	Complete las frases siguientes en español.

1. La Universidad de Salamanca fue fundada en el siglo _____ .

2. El Albaicín se halla en la ciudad de _____ .

3. El famoso Patio de los Leones está en _____ , un palacio construido por los moros.

4. El puerto principal de España es _____ .

5. La capital de España es _____ .

6. La Basílica del Pilar está en _____ .

7. Felipe II hizo construir _____ .

8. _____ , el hermoso castillo moro en Toledo, fue destruido durante la Guerra Civil española.

9. La tumba del Cid está en la catedral de _____ .

10. _____ pintó muchas escenas de la ciudad de Toledo.

EJERCICIO F	¿Cierto o falso? Indique si cada frase es cierta o falsa. Si es falsa, cámbiela para hacerla cierta.

1. Palma es la capital de las Islas Canarias.

_____

2. La sede de los Juegos Olímpicos de 1992 fue Sevilla.

_____

3. La Reconquista empezó con una batalla que tuvo lugar en Asturias.

_____

4. Las Islas Canarias se hallan en el continente de África.

_____

5. San Ignacio de Loyola fundó la Compañía de Jesús.

_____

6. Los puertos de La Coruña y Barcelona están en la provincia de Galicia.

_____

7. La capital de España está en Castilla-La Mancha.

_____

8. Málaga es el puerto más grande de España.

_____

9. Los sistemas de irrigación usados en Valencia fueron introducidos por los moros.

_____

10. Murcia está al norte de Valencia.

_____

11. Asturias recibió la influencia más profunda de la cultura árabe.

_____

12. Muchos extranjeros van a Pamplona en el mes de julio.

_____

13. El gallego es un idioma relacionado con el francés.

_____

14. La ciudad principal de Cataluña es Barcelona.

_____

15. Cádiz fue un gran centro comercial establecido por los romanos.

_____

EJERCICIO G   **Complete cada frase escribiendo el nombre de la region.**

1. _____ está directamente al norte de Portugal.

2. _____ es la región más industrial de España.

3. _____ es la «huerta de España».

4. _____ ha tenido la mayor influencia en la vida nacional.

5. _____ tiene una ciudad que fue nombrada por un emperador romano.

6. En _____ se inició la Reconquista.

7. Los habitantes de _____ hablan el español y una lengua derivada del latín, parecida al portugués.

8. _____ dio al mundo muchos conquistadores.

9. _____ todavía conserva mucho de la gran cultura árabe.

10. _____ es una región típicamente mediterránea.

11. Desde 1982 _____ se constituyeron en Comunidad Autónoma.

12. En _____ se encuentran ricas minas de carbón y de hierro.

13. La famosa playa de San Sebastián llamada La Concha se halla en _____ .

14. _____ tienen gobiernos autónomos desde hace casi 25 años.

15. En la capital de _____ se celebra la fiesta de San Fermín.

Época primitiva

La España de hoy es el producto de los diversos pueblos que la invadieron, trayendo consigo sus propias lenguas, costumbres y características.

5   Los iberos son el primer pueblo sobre el cual hay informes, aunque no se sabe mucho de su historia. Eran de origen mediterráneo y se extendieron por toda la región sudoriental de España.

    Los celtas, de origen centroeuropeo, entraron
10 en la península por el norte a eso del año 1.000 a. de J.C. Los iberos eran hombres bajos y morenos; en cambio los celtas eran rubios y más altos. De la unión de las dos razas se formó la raza celtíbera.

    Mientras tanto los fenicios, grandes navegantes y
15 comerciantes del norte de África, establecieron colonias en el sur de la península. Eran un pueblo de una cultura avanzada, que introdujeron en España el arte de escribir, el uso de la moneda y el arte de trabajar los metales. Los fenicios fundaron muchos centros
20 comerciales, entre ellos Cádiz y Málaga.

    En el siglo VII a. de J.C. los griegos, otro pueblo de comerciantes, establecieron algunas colonias en la costa oriental e introdujeron el cultivo de la uva y el olivo.

25   Los cartagineses entraron en la península en el siglo VI a. de J.C. para ayudar a los fenicios en sus guerras contra los celtíberos. Pronto, sin embargo, los cartagineses emplearon sus armas contra los fenicios, los vencieron, y se apoderaron de gran
30 parte de la península. Luego había de venir lógicamente el enfrentamiento con la otra potencia marítima del Mediterráneo, Roma.

    Los celtíberos lucharon tanto contra los cartagineses como contra los romanos. Celosos de su
35 independencia, preferían morir antes que rendirse. Un ejemplo de su heroísmo fue el sitio de Sagunto (219 a. de J.C.) que duró nueve meses. Cuando los cartagineses, bajo el mando de Aníbal, su famoso general, entraron por fin en la ciudad, no hallaron
40 más que muerte y ruinas.

    Las legiones romanas finalmente vencieron a los cartagineses en el año 202 a. de J.C. en las llamadas Guerras Púnicas. Entonces Roma pudo dedicarse a la conquista de la península, cuyos

habitantes, sin embargo, ofrecieron dura resistencia 45 a los romanos. El sitio de Numancia (133 a. de J.C.), que duró más de quince meses, fue otro ejemplo del heroísmo español.

    Los romanos permanecieron en España unos seis siglos, y esa época es sin duda una de las más 50 significativas en la formación de la cultura hispana. Los romanos dieron la base del idioma actual, un magnífico sistema de leyes, su estructura económica y social y muchas obras públicas, grandes carreteras, puentes y acueductos. Fundaron ciudades, 55 levantaron escuelas y construyeron teatros y anfiteatros al aire libre. El cristianismo, que había nacido dentro de los confines del imperio romano, se convirtió en una de las fuerzas permanentes de la sociedad hispanoromana. 60

    Hacia el siglo V d. de J.C., sin embargo, Roma se hallaba ya en decadencia. Los visigodos, una de las tribus germánicas del norte, invadieron a España, terminaron la dominación romana y establecieron su gobierno en Toledo. Pero a pesar de la domi- 65 nación visigoda, que duró casi cuatro siglos, la gran influencia romana continuó en la península. Los godos adoptaron la lengua hispanoromana, las leyes y las costumbres. El catolicismo triunfó definitivamente en España, y la iglesia llegó a tener un 70 enorme poder al lado de los reyes feudales.

Los moros y la reconquista

Los musulmanes (árabes, moros y beréberes) comenzaron a entrar por el sur en el año 711. En la batalla de Guadalete vencieron a los soldados del 75 rey Rodrigo, el último rey visigodo. Los moros lograron dominar toda la península, con excepción de algunas regiones del norte. En el año 718 Pelayo, con un pequeño ejército de visigodos, venció a los moros en Covadonga (Asturias). Así 80 comenzó la llamada Reconquista, una lucha constante entre moros y cristianos que duró casi ocho siglos, hasta 1492.

    Gracias en parte a la influencia árabe, España llegó a ser el país más avanzado y más culto de 85 toda Europa. Los moros trajeron su arquitectura, su

---

3   **traer consigo** to bring with them
10   **a. de J.C. (antes de Jesucristo)** B.C.
31   **potencia marítima** sea power

61   **d. de J.C. (después de Jesucristo)** A.D.

arte y sus sistemas de irrigación, que aún hoy se usan. De todas partes llegaban estudiantes a Córdoba (la capital de los moros) para estudiar matemáticas, ciencias y medicina. El rey cristiano
5 de León, Alfonso X, llamado el Sabio, reunió en su corte a muchos sabios, entre los cuales había árabes, cristianos y judíos. Allí estudiaron y enseñaron, y a ellos se debe mucho de lo que hoy sabemos de la España medieval.
10   Durante los tres primeros siglos de la dominación mora, se vivió mayormente en paz. Pero más tarde llegaron otros invasores del norte de África, y los reinos cristianos empezaron a unirse para reconquistar sus tierras. El Cid Campeador,
15 Rodrigo Díaz de Vivar, vivió en el siglo XI y se distinguió en las luchas entre moros y cristianos. Era muy temido de los moros, quienes le dieron el título de El Cid, que significa «señor» en árabe. En el año 1094 venció a los moros de la ciudad de
20 Valencia y gobernó esta ciudad hasta su muerte en 1099. Sobre sus hazañas se escribió un poema épico, el Poema del Cid, una de las obras maestras de la literatura española.
        La Reconquista no fue rápida porque los habi-
25 tantes de la península no estaban unidos y pensaban en términos regionales, no como una sola nación. En 1469 Isabel, princesa de Castilla, se casó con Fernando, príncipe de Aragón. Más tarde, cuando ella llegó a ser reina de Castilla y él rey de
30 Aragón, dos de los reinos más poderosos, la España cristiana quedó unificada por primera vez. Del gran imperio árabe sólo quedaba el reino de Granada, gobernado por Boabdil, el último rey moro. Fernando e Isabel, llamados los Reyes
35 Católicos, conquistaron a Granada en 1492, terminando así la Reconquista.
        Los Reyes Católicos entonces trataron de reunir bajo su corona las otras regiones independientes. Crearon la Santa Hermandad, una institución
40 encargada de proteger a la población rural, y reorganizaron la Inquisición [1], cuya misión era mantener la unidad religiosa. En 1492 expulsaron a todos los judíos de España.

Grandeza de España

45 Bajo el reinado de los Reyes Católicos, España llegó a ser la primera nación de Europa. Fue la reina Isabel quien recibió a Cristóbal Colón, un

navegante genovés, y resolvió ayudarle en su empresa, dándole tres barcos, la Pinta, la Niña y la Santa María. El día 3 de agosto de 1492, estos tres   50
barcos partieron de Palos, en el sur de España. El día 12 de octubre del mismo año, Colón y sus marineros pisaron tierra en una isla que llamaron San Salvador (hoy en día conocida por el nombre de Watling Island).   55
        Con el descubrimiento del Nuevo Mundo empezó el gran imperio español. Gonzalo Fernández de Córdoba, el «Gran Capitán», que había adquirido fama durante las guerras contra los moros, conquistó gran parte de Italia para los Reyes   60
Católicos.
        Durante el reinado de Carlos I de España (V de Alemania) (1517–1556), nieto de los Reyes Católicos, la nación española llegó a tener posesiones en Alemania, Austria, Italia, los Países Bajos, América,   65
el norte de África y el sur del Pacífico. Ésta fue la época de los grandes descubrimientos y conquistas.
        En 1556 Carlos I de España se retiró a un monasterio y entregó el poder a su hijo, Felipe II, quien reinó hasta 1598. Era un hombre inteli-   70
gente, pero austero y fanático. Desde el Escorial, soñaba con poner fin al protestantismo y hacer eterna la gloria de España. Durante su reinado tuvo lugar la famosa batalla de Lepanto contra los turcos, que acabó con el poder otomano en el   75
Mediterráneo. También ocurrió el mayor desastre naval sufrido por España, la destrucción de la Armada Invencible en 1558 a manos de Inglaterra, su rival religioso y político. Esta derrota inició la decadencia del imperio español.   80

Decadencia

Felipe II murió en 1598 y sus sucesores, Felipe III y luego Felipe IV, no fueron capaces de gobernar territorios tan grandes. España empezó a sufrir derrotas y a perder tierras. Además, el dominio del   85
mar ya no le pertenecía a España, sino a Inglaterra. Aunque la literatura y el arte seguían floreciendo, había mucha corrupción en los asuntos del gobierno, y el pueblo sufría mucha miseria. España experimentó la ruina económica a causa de las fre-   90
cuentes guerras, la emigración al Nuevo Mundo y la expulsión de los judíos y los moros.
        Durante el reinado de Carlos II la decadencia de la nación española llegó a ser casi completa. La

---

17 **ser temido de** to be feared by
29 **llegar a ser** to become

64 **llegar a tener** to succeed in having, to manage to have
65 **los Países Bajos** the Netherlands (Holland)
74 **tener lugar** to take place, to occur
90 **a causa de** on account of, because of

muerte del rey en 1700 marca el fin de la dinastía de los Habsburgos [2] en España y el comienzo de la dinastía de los Borbones [3], que dura hasta tiempos modernos.

5 En 1759 subió al poder Carlos III, bajo cuyo reinado se nacionalizó la enseñanza, se estableció el servicio de correos, se hicieron muchas reformas urbanas y se fomentaron la agricultura, la industria y el comercio.

Siglos XVIII a XXI

10 Desgraciadamente Carlos IV era tan débil que deshizo toda la obra de su padre, Carlos III. Durante su reinado, Napoleón invadió a España en 1808 y nombró rey a su hermano José. El dos de mayo del mismo año, los ciudadanos madrileños se rebelaron
15 contra los soldados franceses, y así comenzó la Guerra de Independencia que duró hasta 1813. Esta guerra ha quedado inmortalizada en las obras del gran pintor español Francisco Goya.

Con la ayuda de Inglaterra, España logró final-
20 mente expulsar a las tropas francesas de su terri-torio. Desde entonces, el dos de mayo se ha considerado como la fiesta nacional del país.

Después de la derrota de los franceses, subió
25 Fernando VII al poder, un monarca reaccionario que suprimió el espíritu liberal del país y gobernó como rey absoluto. Durante su reinado, España perdió casi todas sus colonias en el Nuevo Mundo.

Después de la muerte de Fernando VII en
30 1833, estalló una guerra civil entre los carlistas tradicionalistas (partidarios del príncipe Don Carlos, hermano de Fernando) y los liberales (partidarios de Isabel II, hija del rey y todavía menor de edad). Esta guerra es conocida como las Guerras Carlistas
35 que ocasionaron batallas e incidentes de 1833 a 1839, de 1855 a 1860 y de 1872 a 1876. La tercera guerra carlista fue ganada por los ejércitos liberales en 1876.

La primera república, que había sido estable-
40 cida en 1873, duró sólo once meses durante los cuales pasaron por el poder cuatro presidentes. Alfonso XII, hijo de Isabel II, volvió como rey en 1874, pero murió en 1885. Durante la regencia de su esposa, María Cristina, se acabó el resto del im-
45 perio español. Por el Tratado de París (1898), que terminó la guerra entre España y los Estados Unidos, España perdió a Cuba, Puerto Rico, las Filipinas y Guam.

En 1902 Alfonso XIII subió al trono, pero fue
50 expulsado en 1931 por haber permitido que el dictador Primo de Rivera gobernase a España de 1923 a 1930, y por haber actuado mal en la guerra de Marruecos.

La segunda república española fue declarada en
55 1931 pero duró solamente cinco años, a causa de las muchas luchas políticas. Bajo la república, España recibió una nueva constitución y muchas leyes liberales. Por desgracia, el gobierno no pudo mantenerse fuerte, y en 1936 estalló la Guerra
60 Civil. Después de muchas luchas sangrientas, el general Francisco Franco logró vencer las fuerzas de la República y estableció una dictadura en 1939, que duró hasta su muerte en 1975.

El gobierno actual de España es una monarquía
65 constitucional. En 1969, Franco y las Cortes (o el parlamento) nombraron como futuro rey y jefe del estado al príncipe Juan Carlos, nieto de Alfonso XIII, quien subió al trono en 1975. La monarquía española es hereditaria, pero el poder del rey es
70 sólo simbólico. Hay en España pues unas cámaras parlamentarias, elegidas cada cuatro años por sufra-gio universal, con un jefe de gobierno llamado primer ministro, que es la cabeza visible del go-bierno. En el parlamento o las Cortes están repre-
75 sentados los partidos políticos.

El rey Juan Carlos I supo rodearse de jefes de gobierno, como Arias Navarro y Adolfo Suárez, que lo ayudaron en la transición pacífica hacia la democracia. Adolfo Suárez estuvo al frente del par-
80 tido reformista UCD (Unión de Centro Demo-crático) y fue jefe de gobierno desde 1976 hasta 1982. Desde 1982 hasta 1996 el partido socialista PSOE (Partido Socialista Obrero Español) y su jefe, Felipe González, estuvieron al frente del go-
85 bierno español. La época socialista estuvo marcada por un fuerte apogeo económico al principio, pero luego los escándalos de corrupción y el paro fueron en aumento. En 1985 se aprobó la admisión de España a la Comunidad Económica Europea
90 [4].

En 1996 se produjo un cambio político en España al ganar las elecciones un partido conser-vador, el PP o Partido Popular. Al frente de este partido y como jefe de gobierno estaba José María
95 Aznar.

Al comienzo del siglo XXI, España tiene una democracia estable, forma parte de la comunidad económica europea y ha adoptado su moneda

---

15 **los ciudadanos madrileños** the citizens of Madrid
30 **estallar** to break out

única, el euro, desapareciendo así pues la peseta. Sin embargo, España sigue teniendo retos sociales por solucionar—el terrorismo político, el paro y una inmigración incontrolada—son los más importantes en estos momentos.

NOTES:

[1] la Inquisición: Tribunal established during the Middle Ages to try heretics and those suspected of converting only nominally to Christianity. This institution was particularly powerful in Spain in the late fifteenth century. It influenced and affected the religious policies of the Catholic monarchs, Ferdinand and Isabella, who expelled first all Jews who refused to be baptized and, later on, all Moors. The Inquisition became synonymous with horror, religious bigotry, and cruel fanaticism.

[2] los Habsburgos: Royal family from Germany, one of the principal sovereign dynasties of Europe from the fifteenth to the twentieth century. The dynasty started in Spain with Charles V, who became the most powerful of the Habsburgs.

[3] los Borbones: Royal family from France. With the exception of a few years, from 1868–1874, the House of Bourbon ruled in Spain from 1700 to 1931. It returned to the throne of Spain in 1975 with Juan Carlos I.

[4] la Comunidad Económica Europea: European Common Market. Comprised of Belgium, Denmark, France, Germany, Greece, Ireland, Italy, Luxembourg, the Netherlands, Portugal, Spain, and the United Kingdom. These nations aim to integrate their economies, coordinate social development, and bring about the political union of the democratic states of Europe.

EJERCICIO A   Escriba la letra que indique la relación correcta con cada expresión de la columna de la izquierda.

1. las Guerras Púnicas _____

2. el uso de monedas _____

3. Palos _____

4. Numancia _____

5. Boabdil _____

6. Rodrigo Díaz de Vivar _____

7. Pelayo _____

8. derrota de la Armada Invencible _____

9. Francisco Franco _____

10. Isabel II _____

a. Guerra Carlista
b. último rey de los moros
c. la segunda república española
d. la primera gramática española
e. Cristóbal Colón
f. los fenicios
g. invasión romana
h. Covadonga
i. derrota de los cartagineses
j. dictador
k. el héroe nacional de España
l. Felipe II

EJERCICIO B   ¿Cierto o falso? Indique si cada frase es cierta o falsa. Si es falsa la frase, cambie el elemento necesario para hacerla cierta.

1. Los habitantes primitivos del país fueron los celtíberos.

2. Los fenicios fundaron muchos centros comerciales.

3. El Sitio de Sagunto es un ejemplo del heroísmo de los cartagineses.

4. Los visigodos dieron la base del idioma actual de España.

5. Bajo la influencia romana, España llegó a ser el país más avanzado y más culto de Europa.

6. Pelayo es el héroe nacional de España.

7. La España cristiana se unificó con la boda de Fernando e Isabel.

8. La destrucción de la Gran Armada terminó el período de la decadencia de España.

9. La Guerra de Independencia comenzó el dos de mayo.

10. Al terminar la Guerra Civil española en 1939, el gobierno de España era una monarquía constitucional.

EJERCICIO C   **Identifique el personaje.**

1. El rey de España que perdió el trono en 1931.

2. Tomó el poder en 1939 y fue dictador hasta su muerte.

3. Conquistó gran parte de Italia para los Reyes Católicos.

4. Durante su reinado se estableció el servicio de correos.

5. Durante su reinado, la decadencia de España llegó a ser casi completa.

6. Se disputó el trono de España con Isabel II.

7. El actual presidente del gobierno español o primer ministro.

8. Los grandes descubrimientos y conquistas sucedieron durante su reinado.

_____

9. El rey actual de España.

_____

10. Durante su reinado, España perdió la mayor parte de sus colonias en América.

_____

EJERCICIO D — Complete las frases siguientes en español.

1. España tuvo el mayor número de posesiones durante el reinado de _____ .

2. _____ gobernó en España durante el reinado de Alfonso XIII.

3. Los _____ introdujeron el cultivo de la uva y el olivo en España.

4. Bajo Felipe II, España venció a los turcos en la batalla de _____ .

5. Un rey español muy progresista de la Casa de Borbón fue _____ .

6. El gobierno actual de España es _____ .

7. Napoleón invadió a España en el año _____ .

8. España está hoy dividida en _____ comunidades autónomas.

9. España logró expulsar a los franceses con la ayuda de _____ .

10. La dominación romana terminó en el siglo _____ .

EJERCICIO E — Indique el orden cronológico de las personas siguientes, escribiendo en orden ascendente los números 1–10 en los espacios correspondientes.

1. _____ Pelayo

2. _____ Carlos V

3. _____ Juan Carlos I

4. _____ Alfonso XII

5. _____ el rey Rodrigo

6. _____ Felipe II

7. _____ Fernando e Isabel

8. _____ Rodrigo Díaz de Vivar

9. _____ Isabel II

10. _____ Fernando VII

Chapter 31
La Literatura de España

Orígenes y Edad Media

Desde los tiempos antiguos, España ha estado bien representada en la literatura mundial. Los orígenes de la literatura española pueden encontrarse en pe-
5 queñas canciones líricas de tipo popular que datan del siglo XI. Estas canciones, llamadas jarchas, fueron escritas en dialecto español mozárabe y represen-tan la primera manifestación de lo que será más tarde el tipo de lírica tradicional española, el vi-
10 llancico.

El «Poema (o Cantar) de Mio Cid» es el más antiguo y mejor ejemplo de la poesía épica es-pañola. Cuenta las hazañas del héroe nacional de España, Rodrigo Díaz de Vivar, y está dividido en
15 tres partes o cantares que tratan de tres épocas dis-tintas de su vida. El poema, de autor anónimo, fue compuesto hacia el año 1140.

Alfonso X, el Sabio (1221–1284) es la figura más prominente de la literatura española de la
20 Edad Media. Bajo su reinado la literatura llegó a tener prestigio oficial. Además de escribir varias obras en prosa y en verso, reunió en su corte a los hombres más cultos de la época para estudiar, traducir y escribir textos en distintas áreas, desde
25 historia hasta astronomía. A él se deben «Las siete partidas», una vasta colección de leyes y costum-bres que reflejan la sociedad de la época.

En el siglo XIV empezaron a aparecer los libros de caballería, que fueron populares hasta finales del
30 siglo XVI. Se caracterizaban por su idealismo sen-timental, su atmósfera lírica y las aventuras sobre-naturales de sus héroes.

En el siglo XV comenzó una renovación de la poesía. Los romances, poemas narrativos épico-líri-
35 cos que se cantan, tuvieron su origen en ese siglo y han sobrevivido hasta hoy día. Tratan de temas heroicos, históricos o líricos, y se considera que re-flejan el alma y la tradición del pueblo español.

Jorge Manrique (1440–1479) es famoso por
40 sus «Coplas», un poema escrito para honrar la muerte de su padre. Se considera tal vez como la mejor obra de poesía lírica escrita durante la Edad Media. Fue traducida al inglés, en verso, por el poeta norteamericano Henry Wadsworth Longfellow
(1807–1882).
45
Antonio de Nebrija (1441–1522) es cono-cido por haber escrito la primera gramática caste-llana, publicada en 1492. Fue la primera gramática escrita sobre una lengua moderna.

Siglo de Oro
50
El llamado Siglo de Oro es la época más gloriosa de la literatura española. En este período de casi dos siglos, vivieron los autores considerados como clásicos por excelencia. Comienza durante la primera mitad del siglo XVI y termina hacia fines
55 del siglo XVII, con la muerte de Pedro Calderón de la Barca.

Garcilaso de la Vega (1501–1536), soldado y poeta, fue un verdadero representante del Renaci-miento. Introdujo en España nuevas formas de
60 poesía lírica y popularizó la forma poética llamada soneto. Con Garcilaso comienza la literatura es-pañola moderna.

En el siglo XVI surge un género de narración literaria de tipo realista y satírico que se llama la
65 novela picaresca. Ésta describe las aventuras de un pícaro, un personaje sin raíces, que sirve de criado, cambia con frecuencia de amo y ciudad y engaña para poder vivir. Sus comentarios son una ver-dadera sátira de la vida y la sociedad de la época.
70 La primera y más típica de las novelas de este género es el «Lazarillo de Tormes», de autor anón-imo, que apareció en 1554.

Miguel de Cervantes Saavedra (1547–1616) es conocido en todo el mundo como el au-
75 tor de «Don Quijote de la Mancha», uno de los li-bros más leídos en todos los idiomas. Siendo joven, Cervantes se distinguió como soldado en la Batalla de Lepanto [1], donde perdió el uso del brazo izquierdo. De allí su sobre-nombre de «el Manco
80 de Lepanto». Su vida personal fue una serie de fra-casos. Pasó cinco años cautivo de los piratas turcos. Luego tuvo mala suerte en los negocios y pasó al-gún tiempo en la cárcel. Tampoco tuvo éxito en su matrimonio. Como escritor dejó poesías, novelas,

---

1 **la Edad Media** the Middle Ages
3 **la literatura mundial** world literature
28 **el libro de caballería** romance of chivalry
41 **tal vez** perhaps

84 **tener éxito** to be successful

obras de teatro y una colección de doce novelas cortas, las «Novelas ejemplares».

En 1605 se publicó la primera parte de su obra maestra, «El ingenioso hidalgo don Quijote de la 5 Mancha». En 1615 se publicó la segunda parte. El libro trata de un hombre de edad avanzada que se imagina caballero y sale en su caballo, Rocinante, para buscar aventuras y combatir las injusticias del mundo, pero sin éxito. Lleva como escudero a 10 Sancho Panza, un labrador ignorante pero de mucho sentido común. Este libro, que Cervantes escribió para burlarse de los libros de caballería, está lleno de episodios ridículos. Pero, además del humorismo de las aventuras, hay una base filosófica, 15 el conflicto entre el idealismo y el materialismo. El libro es considerado como la obra maestra de la literatura española y una de las obras más importantes de la literatura universal de todos los tiempos.

20 **Francisco de Quevedo** (1580–1645) fue el escritor satírico por excelencia en la literatura española. «Los sueños», una serie de relatos, es su obra maestra en prosa. Escribió también una gran novela picaresca, «La vida del buscón», y dejó un 25 tesoro de poesía lírica.

Lope de Vega (1562–1635) fue un verdadero «monstruo de la naturaleza», como lo llamó Cervantes a causa de su gran producción literaria. Escribió toda clase de obras, pero su fama se debe 30 más a sus obras dramáticas, entre las que se cuentan más de mil comedias, todas en verso.

Se ha dicho que Lope de Vega es el padre de la comedia moderna y el creador del teatro nacional español. Expuso su teoría y técnica de escribir 35 comedias, afirmando que el teatro es una representación de la vida y que el escritor debe tener libertad total. Sus obras más famosas son las que tratan de la historia de España y de la dignidad humana. Se pueden mencionar entre éstas 40 «Fuenteovejuna» y «Peribáñez y el Comendador de Ocaña». En estas dos obras, la gente del pueblo lucha contra las injusticias de los nobles.

Juan Ruiz de Alarcón (1581–1639) nació en México de padres españoles. Escribió más de 45 veinte obras teatrales en las cuales castigaba el vicio y alababa la virtud. Entre las principales deben mencionarse «Las paredes oyen», contra la calumnia, y «La verdad sospechosa», contra la mentira.

Tirso de Molina (1584–1648) fue uno de los 50 más grandes dramaturgos españoles. Su verdadero

nombre era Fray Gabriel Téllez. Es famoso por haber creado el personaje de don Juan en su drama «El burlador de Sevilla». Desde la época de Tirso, la figura de don Juan ha inspirado la obra de muchos autores en diversos países. En la música, por ejem- 55 plo, el gran compositor Mozart usó el tema de don Juan en su ópera «Don Giovanni».

Pedro Calderón de la Barca (1600–1681) fue el último de los grandes dramaturgos del Siglo de Oro. El tema principal de sus obras es el honor. 60 Sus dos obras principales son «El alcalde de Zalamea» y «La vida es sueño». En la primera, un hombre del pueblo, elegido alcalde, manda matar a un noble para vengar el honor de su hija. La segunda contiene ideas filosóficas profundas sobre la 65 realidad y los sueños.

Siglos XVIII y XIX

El siglo XVIII es el siglo de la luces o de la razón. Este siglo es más importante por la filosofía que por la literatura. Las letras españolas estuvieron 70 enormemente influenciadas por los filósofos franceses. En 1713 se estableció la Real Academia Española, cuya tarea era y sigue siendo la de mantener la pureza del idioma español.

En 1833, a la muerte de Fernando VII, regre- 75 saron al país muchos españoles que habían salido durante su reinado. Éstos trajeron consigo las ideas liberales que habían aprendido en otros países. Así comenzó en España el romanticismo, movimiento literario que exaltaba al individuo, sus ideas y sus 80 sentimientos, sin preocuparse por las reglas literarias clásicas del siglo XVIII.

Ángel Saavedra, Duque de Rivas (1791– 1865) escribió «Don Álvaro o la fuerza del sino», un drama romántico que más tarde inspiró al com- 85 positor italiano Giuseppe Verdi para su ópera «La fuerza del destino».

José de Espronceda (1808–1842) fue un poeta romántico, cuyas obras principales son «El estudiante de Salamanca» y «Canto a Teresa». Se le ha 90 comparado, en su vida y en su obra, con el poeta inglés Lord Byron (1788–1824).

Mariano José de Larra (1809–1837) fue un ensayista y crítico importante. Escribió bajo varios seudónimos, uno de ellos «Fígaro», una colección 95 de «Artículos de costumbres» que son una sátira al modo de vivir de su tiempo.

---

12 **burlarse de** to make fun of
23 **la obra maestra** the masterpiece

José Zorrilla (1817–1893) escribió «Don Juan Tenorio», un drama basado en el tema de Don Juan, pero desde un punto de vista romántico. Esta obra se ha llevado al teatro español en multitud de ocasiones, siempre con el mismo éxito.

Gustavo Adolfo Bécquer (1836–1870) escribió «Rimas», una colección de unas setenta poesías líricas, algunas de las cuales son popularísimas.

El romanticismo fue seguido por un movimiento literario llamado realismo, que pretendía representar la «realidad» sin idealizarla. La novela del siglo XIX se caracteriza por su realismo y su regionalismo. Muchos autores escribieron acerca de la región donde habían nacido, su «patria chica».

Fernán Caballero es el seudónimo de Cecilia Böhl de Faber (1796–1877). Esta autora inició la novela costumbrista [2] en España. Describió las costumbres de su época y de su región, Andalucía, en un estilo sencillo y natural. Su obra principal es «La Gaviota».

Las novelas de **Juan Valera** (1824–1905) son una visión poética de la vida en Andalucía. Le interesaba la psicología de sus personajes, y su obra más famosa, «Pepita Jiménez», es un estudio psicológico sobre la vocación religiosa.

Benito Pérez Galdós (1843–1920), el novelista español más importante del siglo XIX, dejó una vasta producción literaria. Fue liberal y crítico violento de la intolerancia religiosa y de la injusticia social. Entre sus obras deben mencionarse la novela «Doña Perfecta», contra la intolerancia religiosa, y los «Episodios Nacionales», una serie de más de sesenta narraciones históricas sobre la España del siglo XIX.

Emilia Pardo Bazán (1852–1921) introdujo el naturalismo [3] en España y estableció contacto entre la vida literaria europea y la española. Escribió acerca de su región, Galicia. Sus novelas principales son «Los pazos de Ulloa» y «La madre naturaleza».

Armando Palacio Valdés (1853–1938) fue un novelista muy popular. Escribió «La hermana San Sulpicio», sobre la región de Andalucía, y «José», acerca de los pescadores de Asturias.

Vicente Blasco Ibáñez (1867–1928) fue muy popular, no sólo en España sino también en el extranjero. Su obra principal es «La barraca», que describe la vida de los campesinos valencianos. También escribió «Sangre y arena», sobre la corrida de toros, y «Los cuatro jinetes del Apocalipsis», que trata de la Primera Guerra Mundial. Fue un gran defensor de las ideas republicanas y de la libertad del individuo frente al Estado y estuvo muchas veces en la cárcel por sus ideas políticas.

La «Generación del '98» hasta nuestros días

Como resultado de la guerra de 1898 contra los Estados Unidos, España perdió lo poco que le quedaba de su imperio colonial. A raíz de este desastre, un grupo de intelectuales jóvenes españoles comenzó a examinar el estado cultural y espiritual de su país dentro del mundo moderno. Estos escritores se conocen hoy como la «Generación del '98» e incluyen ensayistas, novelistas, poetas y dramaturgos.

Francisco Giner de los Ríos (1839–1915) fue filósofo, profesor y el gran educador de los intelectuales. Su influencia se nota en los escritores de la «Generación del '98». Fundó la Escuela Libre de Enseñanza, centro de ideas liberales.

Miguel de Unamuno (1864–1936) es la figura dominante de la «Generación del '98», y su influencia sigue siendo importante. Fue filósofo, crítico, poeta y novelista. Su atractivo es la pasión y la violencia con que se muestra al lector. Su ensayo más conocido es «Del sentimiento trágico de la vida», que explora uno de sus temas favoritos, el abismo que existe entre la fe y la razón, entre la falta de fe y el deseo de inmortalidad.

Ramón del Valle-Inclán (1866–1936) fue famoso por la riqueza de su lenguaje. Su prosa puede casi llamarse poesía. Entre sus obras deben mencionarse las cuatro «Sonatas», de primavera, de estío, de otoño y de invierno, y la novela «Tirano Banderas».

En el teatro **Jacinto Benavente** (1866–1954) es un nombre bien conocido. Este dramaturgo ganó el Premio Nobel de Literatura en 1922. Sus obras más importantes son «La malquerida» y «Los intereses creados».

Ramón Menéndez Pidal (1869–1968) fue un erudito muy importante de la España del siglo XX. Hizo estudios profundos sobre la lengua y la literatura medievales de España, entre ellos «Los orígenes del español», «El romancero español» y «La España del Cid».

Pío Baroja (1872–1956) fue uno de los novelistas principales de la Generación del 98. En sus

---

47 **en el extranjero** abroad   60 **a raíz de** as a result of

novelas hay mucha fuerza y acción. Dos de las más importantes son «El árbol de la ciencia» y «Camino de perfección». La primera se considera una novela autobiográfica, en la que el autor expone sus ideas
5 inconformistas y los problemas sociales de su época.

José Martínez Ruiz, llamado **«Azorín»,** (1873–1967) escribió ensayos y novelas. En sus obras relacionó la España antigua con la moderna,
10 en un lenguaje muy sencillo y natural. Entre sus obras principales deben mencionarse «La voluntad», «Castilla» y «Los valores literarios». Se le considera el crítico literario más importante de la «Generación del '98».

15 **Antonio Machado** (1875–1939) fue uno de los mejores poetas de este siglo y uno de los más amados y respetados. Sus poemas son breves, pero tratan de temas fundamentales. Introdujo el modernismo de Rubén Darío en la poesía española,
20 pero sin dejarse influir totalmente por este estilo. Su obra «Campos de Castilla» tiene por tema el paisaje austero de su país.

Gregorio Martínez Sierra (1881–1947) logró crear notables personajes femeninos en sus
25 obras dramáticas. La más conocida es «Canción de cuna». Fue también autor del texto sobre el que de Falla compuso su ballet «El amor brujo».

José Ortega y Gasset (1883–1955) fue un filósofo y ensayista que buscó los valores espiri-
30 tuales de España en su tradición. Se le considera el maestro de toda una generación de escritores españoles e hispanoamericanos. Dos de sus obras principales son «La rebelión de las masas» y «Meditaciones del Quijote».

35 La época de la Guerra Civil en España (1936–39) afectó tanto la literatura como la vida diaria de los españoles. Muchos escritores se opusieron a la dictadura que estableció Franco al terminar la guerra y salieron del país para vivir en el extran-
40 jero. Otros fueron encarcelados o condenados a muerte.

Juan Ramón Jiménez (1881–1958), maestro del Modernismo, radicaba en Puerto Rico cuando ganó el Premio Nobel de Literatura en 1956.
45 Además de varias colecciones de poesías, escribió también libros en prosa. De éstos el más conocido es «Platero y yo», que describe los recuerdos de su juventud.

Federico García Lorca (1898–1936) fue un
50 notable poeta y dramaturgo andaluz que escribió en forma dramática sobre temas folklóricos y tradicionales. Su teatro trata en gran parte de las pasiones humanas. Entre sus obras deben mencionarse los dramas «Bodas de sangre» y «La casa de Bernarda Alba» y los poemas de su 55 «Romancero gitano». García Lorca murió en circunstancias trágicas durante la Guerra Civil.

Jorge Guillén (1893–1984) es el poeta de la llamada «poesía pura»; es decir, poesía que carece de anécdota y está hecha de conceptos y abstrac- 60 ciones. Hasta 1957 fue autor de un solo libro, «Cántico», que se publicó por primera vez en 1928 y llegó a incluir 500 poemas en su quinta edición. Su última colección de poemas, publicada en 1981, se titula «Final». Enseñó en muchas universi- 65 dades del mundo, entre ellas Harvard y Wellesley College en los Estados Unidos.

Vicente Aleixandre (1898–1984) fue un ensayista y poeta que recibió el Premio Nobel de Literatura en 1977. En su ensayo «Los encuentros», 70 el autor pinta con palabras, retratos de los grandes escritores españoles a quienes conoció. Su obra poética es surrealista y neoromántica a la vez; el tema central es el amor en su doble aspecto de fuerza destructora e ilusión de la vida. Entre esta 75 obra poética se distinguen «La destrucción o el amor» y «Sombras del paraíso».

Alejandro Casona (1900–1965) fue un dramaturgo que vivió muchos años en la Argentina después de la Guerra Civil. Escribió con mucha 80 fuerza dramática. Dos de sus obras principales son «La dama del alba» y «Los árboles mueren de pie».

Ramón J. Sender (1902–1982) abandonó España después de la Guerra Civil; vivió en Guatemala y México y luego se radicó en los 85 Estados Unidos. Es conocido por sus novelas «Requiem para un campesino español», sobre sus experiencias en la Guerra Civil, «Mr. Witt en el Cantón», «Crónica del alba» y «En la vida de Ignacio Morel». Por estas obras recibió varios pre- 90 mios literarios.

Después de la Guerra Civil, aparece en España una nueva generación de escritores. Muchos de ellos habían vivido sus años de juventud cara a cara con los horrores de esa guerra. Influidos por ella, 95 estos escritores se han preocupado por los problemas sociales y económicos que España ha afrontado desde la posguerra hasta hoy.

Mercé Rodoreda (1908–1983) fue la escritora catalana más importante de la posguerra es-

---

94 **cara a cara** face to face
98 **la posguerra** postwar (refers to the years after the Civil War)

pañola. Durante la dictadura de Franco tuvo que exiliarse a Francia y a Suiza para poder seguir escribiendo en catalán. Entre sus obras destacan «La plaza del diamante», «Aloma», «Veintidós cuentos», «La calle de las camelias», y «Espejo coto». En ellas escribe sobre la Guerra Civil Española, la sociedad de posguerra, y el papel de la mujer en la sociedad. Transforma la experiencia dolorosa de la vida y la muerte en amor y compasión. Sus obras han sido traducidas a otros idiomas. Desde 1998 se da en Cataluña el Premio Mercè Rodoreda a escritores catalanes que sobresalen por sus cuentos y sus narraciones.

Julián Marías (1914–2005) es un filósofo y ensayista contemporáneo, discípulo fiel de Ortega y Gasset. Ha hecho un examen sincero y veraz sobre los problemas que afectan a la sociedad española como la educación sentimental, la felicidad humana y la mujer del siglo XX, entre otros. Entre sus obras más conocidas están «Historia de la filosofía», «Introducción a la filosofía», «Los Estados Unidos en escorzo», «Los españoles», «España en nuestras manos» y «España ante la historia y ante si misma.» Con esta última obra recibió un premio importante en 1996.

Camilo José Cela (1916–2002) ha sido el más famoso de los novelistas contemporáneos. Fue un gran maestro del lenguaje y poseía un humor de tono burlón y coloquial. Con la novela, «La familia de Pascual Duarte» lamenta la falta de dignidad personal que se notaba en la España de la posguerra. Otras importantes obras suyas son: «La colmena», «Viaje a la Alcarria», «Mazurca para dos muertos» y «La cruz de San Andrés» entre muchas otras. En 1989 recibió el Premio Nobel de Literatura y sus «Obras completas» se han publicado en 25 volúmenes. Fue también miembro de la Real Academia de la Lengua Española.

Antonio Buero Vallejo (1916–2000) escribió obras dramáticas que dieron dignidad al teatro español y lo modernizaron. Trató de invadir la realidad humana, psicológica y social de nuestro tiempo, tanto de España como del resto del mundo. Sus obras más famosas incluyen «Las meninas», «En la ardiente oscuridad», e «Historia de una escalera». Fue miembro de la Real Academia de la Lengua Española y en 1999 recibió el Premio de Honor de los Max de las Artes Escénicas.

Miguel Delibes (1920–   ) es un novelista de estilo sobrio y sencillo que ha retratado la realidad de la sociedad española de la posguerra, en especial al hombre humilde. Entre sus novelas más conocidas están «El camino», «Diario de un cazador», «Las ratas», «Cinco horas con Mario», «Los santos inocentes», obra llevada al cine con gran éxito y «El hereje» entre muchas más. Con esta última recibió el Premio Nacional de Literatura Narrativa en 1999.

Carmen Laforet (1921–   ) causó una gran conmoción con la publicación de la novela «Nada» en 1946. Esta trata del vacío espiritual de la España de la posguerra y le valió un premio literario muy importante. Desde entonces ha ganado otros premios y ha publicado, entre otras, las novelas «La isla y los demonios», «La mujer nueva» y «Cuentos de este siglo».

José Hierro (1922–2002) es uno de los poetas más destacados de la posguerra por haber logrado una poesía honda, humana y apasionada con un mínimo de imágenes. Su obra poética incluye «Alegría», «Cuanto sé de mí», «Poesía del momento», «Agenda» y «Poemas de Nueva York». También se ha publicado su «Antología poética».

Ana María Matute (1926–   ) es una escritora que ha dado al mundo una producción literaria abundante y de primera calidad. Sus cuentos y novelas traen una delicada sensibilidad que no ciega su visión clara y perceptiva de la realidad. «Fiesta al noroeste», «Pequeño teatro», «Los hijos muertos»" y «Primera memoria» son novelas que le valieron premios nacionales. Entre sus obras más recientes destacan «Luciérnagas», «La oveja negra», «El verdadero final de la Bella Durmiente», «Casa de juegos prohibidos» y la colección de «Todos mis cuentos» publicada en el año 2000. Sus libros han sido traducidos a 23 lenguas. En 1996 ingresó como miembro de la Real Academia de la Lengua Española.

Alfonso Sastre (1926–   ) es un dramaturgo que escribe sobre la sociedad con el fin de dar un mensaje social a su público. «La mordaza» y «Escuadra hacia la muerte» son dos de sus obras conocidas. En 2003 se le otorgó el Premio de Honor de los Max de las Artes Escénicas.

Rafael Sánchez Ferlosio (1927–   ) es un narrador y ensayista español que recibió el Premio Nadal de narrativa en 1955 por su obra, «El Jarama». Otra importante obra suya es «Industrias y andanzas de Alfanhuí». Sus novelas mezclan la realidad con lo fantástico.

Antonio Gala (1930–   ) es un poeta y dramaturgo que discute temas actuales a través de

---

los ojos de personajes históricos. Entre sus obras más conocidas están «Anillos para una dama», «Noviembre y un poco de yerba», «Petra Regalada», «Carmen, Carmen», «La regla de tres» y «La pasión turca».
5 Esta última fue llevada al cine por Vicente Aranda. Gala recibió el Premio de Honor de los Max de las Artes Escénicas en 2001.

Juan Goytisolo (1931–   ) es un novelista contemporáneo que presenta los problemas y las
10 inquietudes de la sociedad española en obras como «Juegos de mano», «El circo», «Duelo en el paraíso», «Fiestas», «Revindicación del Conde Don Julián» «Juan sin tierra» y «Señas de identidad». Con esta última obra recibió el premio Europalia
15 en 1985.

En los últimos años hay en España una narrativa desenfadada, flexible y atrevida que refleja la realidad española de una democracia progresista, los avances de la tecnología, y los conflictos so-
20 ciales que afectan tanto España como Europa, Estados Unidos y el mundo internacional.

Manuel Vázquez Montalbán (1939–2003) fue periodista y escritor de novelas policíacas. Entre sus novelas más destacadas hay que citar «Yo maté a
25 Kennedy», «Historias de política ficción» «Tatuaje», «Roldán, ni vivo ni muerto» y «Los pájaros de Bangkok». Además, contribuyó con sus ensayos en muchos periódicos y revistas españoles e internacionales. Tiene un libro de ensayos titulado «Mis al-
30 muerzos con gente inquietante» en el cual hace un estudio de los personajes más destacables de la política y la sociedad española del momento.

Arturo Pérez-Reverte (1951–   ) escritor actual que plasma sus experiencias periodísticas en
35 su narrativa. Combina la ficción con la realidad periodística de una manera natural y fantástica. Desde 1973 hasta 1994 fue reportero de radio y de televisión, pero ahora se dedica exclusivamente a la literatura. Entre sus obras más destacadas están «El
40 maestro de esgrima», «La tabla de Flandes», «El club Dumas», «Las aventuras del capitán Alatriste» y «La carta esférica». Su obra ha sido traducida a veinte idiomas.

Terenci Moix (1952–2003) fue un escritor
45 catalán que escribió tanto en su lengua nativa como en español. Combina en su narrativa sus viajes fantásticos internacionales con una observación minuciosa de la realidad humana y de la sociedad de los años sesenta hasta nuestros días. Entre sus
50 obras más famosas hay que destacar «La torre de los vicios capitales», «El día que murió Marilyn» y «No digas que fue un sueño.» Se le otorgaron importantes premios de literatura catalana como el de Josep Pla y el Ramón Llull.

55 **José Luis García Montero** (1958–   ) es poeta, ensayista y columnista de opinión. Además, es profesor de literatura en la Universidad de Granada. Recibió el premio Cervantes de Poesía en 1999 y entre su obra poética hay que destacar
60 «Y ahora ya eres dueño del Puente de Brooklyn», «Tristia», «El jardín extranjero», «Las flores del frío» y «Completamente viernes».

NOTES:

[1] **la Batalla de Lepanto:** Battle of Lepanto
65 (1571, Lepanto, Greece). Naval battle between allied Christian forces, led by the king of Spain's brother, and the Ottoman Turks. The victory of the Christian forces had great impact in Europe.

[2] **la novela costumbrista:** A literary genre re-
70 ferring to novels with strong regional flavor that describe local customs and manners.

[3] **el naturalismo:** Naturalism, a theory in literature emphasizing the role of heredity and environment upon human life and character
75 development. It states that literature should conform to describing nature without idealization or avoidance of the ugly.

EJERCICIO A   **¿Cierto o falso? Indique si cada frase es cierta o falsa. Si es falsa, cámbiela para que sea cierta.**

1. Una de las óperas de Mozart está basada en un tema popular de una obra de Tirso de Molina.

_____

2. «Don Quijote de la Mancha» fue escrito para burlarse de los libros de caballería.

_____

3. Los siglos XVI y XVII se llaman también el Siglo de Oro.

_____

4. La vida de Espronceda fue semejante a la del poeta inglés Byron.

_____

5. Emilia Pardo Bazán introdujo el realismo en España.

_____

6. En su novela «Los cuatro jinetes del Apocalipsis», Blasco Ibáñez describe los desastres de la Primera Guerra mundial.

_____

7. La primera guerra carlista causó la formación de un grupo de intelectuales llamado la «Generación del '98».

_____

8. Azorín fue el crítico más conocido de la «Generación del '98».

_____

9. Camilo José Cela es un autor del siglo XIX.

_____

10. En su obra «Platero y yo», Juan Ramón Jiménez describe su juventud.

_____

11. Vicente Aleixandre fue un poeta que recibió el Premio Nobel de Literatura en 1977.

_____

12. Antonio Gala es el dramaturgo cuyas obras dramáticas dieron dignidad al teatro español.

_____

13. El modernismo de Rubén Darío fue introducido en la poesía española por Jorge Guillén.

_____

14. Los autores de la posguerra han escrito sobre los problemas sociales y económicos de la España de esa época.

_____

15. Julián Marías se distinguió en la literatura española como dramaturgo..

_____

EJERCICIO B **Escriba la letra que indique la relación correcta con cada expresión de la columna de la izquierda.**

1. El Cid   _____

2. Larra   _____

3. «Novelas ejemplares»   _____

4. «Episodios nacionales»   _____

5. Gustavo Adolfo Bécquer   _____

6. Blasco Ibáñez   _____

7. «Los intereses creados»   _____

8. «La vida es sueño»   _____

9. «Sonatas»   _____

10. Fernán Caballero   _____

a. Benavente

b. Calderón de la Barca

c. «La barraca»

d. «La Gaviota»

e. Rodrigo Díaz de Vivar

f. Valle-Inclán

g. «Fígaro»

h. Cervantes

i. «Rimas»

j. «Don Álvaro o la fuerza del sino»

k. Pérez Galdós

EJERCICIO C   **Subraye el nombre correcto.**

1. Dramaturgo del Siglo de Oro: Quevedo, Palacio Valdés, Tirso de Molina

2. Poeta romántico: Espronceda, Jorge Manrique, Fernán Caballero

3. Daba importancia al individuo: realismo, regionalismo, romanticismo

4. Ganó el Premio Nobel: Pérez Galdós, Juan Ramón Jiménez, Juan Valera

5. Escudero de don Quijote: Sancho Panza, Rocinante, Fígaro

6. Escribió acerca de la España de la posguerra: Laforet, Palacio Valdés, Unamuno

7. Dramaturgo español que vivió en la Argentina: Pío Baroja, Alejandro Casona, José Martínez Ruiz

8. El gran maestro de los intelectuales de la Generación del '98: Ortega y Gasset, Valle-Inclán, Giner de los Ríos

9. Erudito importante del siglo XX: Alfonso el Sabio, Menéndez Pidal, el Duque de Rivas

10. Escribió sobre el tema de «don Juan»: Duque de Rivas, Larra, Zorrilla

---

EJERCICIO D   **Identifique estos autores u obras de la literatura española.**

1. Soy el autor de «Las siete partidas».

   _____

2. Soy una serie de relatos que representan la obra maestra en prosa de Quevedo.

   _____

3. Fui el último gran dramaturgo del Siglo de Oro.

   _____

4. Escribí la primera gramática de la lengua española.

_____

5. Escribí más de mil comedias y expuse mis ideas sobre este género.

_____

6. Soy el más antiguo y mejor ejemplo de la poesía épica española.

_____

7. Fui soldado y poeta en el Siglo de Oro; popularicé el soneto en España.

_____

8. Soy una obra poética importantísima de Jorge Manrique.

_____

9. Fui llamado «el Manco de Lepanto».

_____

10. Me consideran el héroe nacional de España.

_____

| EJERCICIO E | Identifique las obras siguientes, escribiendo para cada una (a) el género de la obra (drama, poesía, novela, ensayo), (b) el autor y (c) la época (Siglo de Oro, Romanticismo, Realismo, Generación del '98, Posguerra). |

EJEMPLO: Don Quijote   **novela   Cervantes   Siglo de Oro**

1. Lazarillo de Tormes

_____

2. Nada

_____

3. Doña Perfecta

_____

4. Fiesta al noroeste

_____

5. Historia de la filosofía

_____

6. Los intereses creados

_____

7. La Gaviota

_____

8. En la ardiente oscuridad

_____

9. Don Juan Tenorio

_____

10. Del sentimiento trágico de la vida

_____

11. El árbol de la ciencia

_____

12. La familia de Pascual Duarte

_____

13. Fuenteovejuna

_____

14. El alcalde de Zalamea

_____

15. La rebelión de las masas

_____

16. Bodas de sangre

_____

17. El burlador de Sevilla

_____

18. Cántico

_____

19. Requiem por un campesino español

_____

20. La vida del buscón

_____

FRANCIA

PORTUGAL ESPAÑA

Barcelona

○ Madrid Islas Baleares ITALIA

● Sevilla

La música

España es un país muy rico en música folklórica. Un buen ejemplo de este género de música es el flamenco de la región de Andalucía. Sus orígenes
5 se encuentran en la música árabe, gitana, andaluza y judía del siglo XIV. El flamenco es un cante acompañado de música de guitarra y un baile improvisado. El llamado «cante jondo» (hondo o profundo) es muy triste y trata de temas como la
10 muerte y la angustia. El cante chico trata sobre temas alegres.

El instrumento típico y tradicional de España es la guitarra, en la que se toca tanto música clásica como popular. Para acompañamiento se tocan la
15 pandereta y las castañuelas. En la región de Galicia el instrumento típico es la gaita.

España ha dado al mundo un género de música llamado zarzuela. La zarzuela es una combinación de música, canto, diálogo hablado, coros y bailes. Es
20 un género entre la comedia musical de los Estados Unidos y la ópera. Uno de los mejores compositores de zarzuela fue **Francisco Asenjo Barbieri** (1823–1894). Sus obras más conocidas son «Pan y toros» y «El barberillo de Lavapiés». «La verbena de
25 la paloma», del compositor **Tomás Bretón** (1850–1923), es quizá la zarzuela más famosa.

Compositores, instrumentistas, cantantes

Los tres compositores españoles más conocidos son
30 Isaac Albéniz, Enrique Granados y Manuel de Falla. **Isaac Albéniz** (1860–1909) compuso una ópera y música para piano. Entre sus composiciones principales están «Iberia» y «El Albaicín». **Enrique Granados** (1867–1916) también compuso
35 puso música para piano. Su obra maestra, «Goyescas», está inspirada en la obra del pintor Francisco Goya. **Manuel de Falla** (1876–1946) fue el más célebre de los compositores españoles del siglo XX. Como Granados y Albéniz, también
40 de Falla se inspiró en temas folklóricos. Pero de Falla compuso principalmente música para orquesta.

En 1939, después de la Guerra Civil, de Falla se radicó en Argentina. **Joaquín Rodrigo** (1901– 1999) también es uno de los compositores contemporáneos de fama internacional. Es conocido 45 for su famoso «Concierto de Aranjuez».

Entre los instrumentistas se distinguen Pablo Casals, José Iturbi, Andrés Segovia y Alicia de Larrocha. **Pablo Casals** (1876–1973) fue uno de los mejores violonchelistas del mundo. Salió de 50 España en 1939, después de la Guerra Civil, porque se oponía a la dictadura de Franco. En 1956 se estableció en Puerto Rico, donde organizó un festival internacional de música que se sigue celebrando anualmente en su memoria. **José** 55 **Iturbi** (1895–1980) fue pianista y director de orquesta sinfónica. También actuó en varias películas de Hollywood en los años cuarenta. **Andrés Segovia** (1894–1987) fue uno de los maestros de la guitarra y se presentó en todas las salas de 60 concierto del mundo. Su fama se debe no sólo a su maestría, sino a que rehabilitó la guitarra como instrumento de música clásica en el siglo XX. Entre los guitarristas de flamenco más conocidos contemporáneos hay que citar a Paco de Lucía y a 65 Raimundo Amador de fama internacional. Sus conciertos, siempre esperados, son de gran estilo y calidad. **Alicia de Larrocha** (1923–   ) es una pianista contemporánea que ha ganado fama mundial, tanto por su interpretación de los grandes 70 compositores españoles, como por su interpretación de otros compositores clásicos mundiales.

Otros españoles se han destacado en el género operático. Son famosos, y han cantado en los grandes teatros de ópera del mundo, las sopranos 75 **Victoria de los Ángeles y Monserrat Caballé** y los tenores **Alfredo Krauss, Plácido Domingo y Juan Carreras.**

En la música popular hay cantantes que han logrado fama mundial por su interpretación de canciones de última onda. Entre ellos se hallan **Sara** 80 **Montiel, Lola Flores, Julio Iglesias, Raphael, Camilo Sesto, Rocío Jurado, Rocío Durcal, José Luis Perales, Lolita, Isabel Pantoja, Juan Manuel Serrat, Ana Belén y Victor Manuel.**

---

las bellas artes fine arts
6 **un cante** song, singing (used mostly in expressions related to flamenco music)

60 **la sala de concierto** concert hall
80 **canciones de la última onda** the latest popular songs

En los últimos diez años hay cantantes jóvenes españoles que están alcanzando éxitos internacionales. Entre ellos hay que mencionar a **Enrique Iglesias** y **Alejandro Sanz Rosario.**

5   Como representante de la canción andaluza hay que mencionar a **Carlos Cano** (1946–1996) que se hizo famoso por cantar coplas al estilo popular andaluz. Las coplas son antiguas canciones de historias populares cantadas por la gente de pueblo. 10 Cano reavivó una bonita tradición andaluza.

El baile

Casi todas las regiones de España tienen sus propios bailes, y hay grandes diferencias entre ellos. La región que tiene mayor variedad es Andalucía. De 15 allí vienen el bolero, el fandango, la seguidilla, el jaleo, la malagueña, la sevillana y el flamenco. Muchas veces el baile se acompaña con una pandereta y castañuelas. De Aragón viene la jota, un baile muy alegre que se baila en parejas, acom- 20 pañado de castañuelas y coplas cantadas. La sardana es el baile regional de Cataluña; se baila en grupo, en un gran círculo. El baile regional de Galicia es la muñeira, que se baila en parejas con musica de gaita.

25   A través de los años ha habido varios intérpretes famosos de baile flamenco, que lo han llevado a todos los rincones del mundo. Estos bailarines incluyen a **Vicente Escudero, Carmen Amaya, Antonio Gades, Lola Flores, Sara** 30 **Baras y Joaquín Cortés.** Otro baile típico español es la rumba. **Peret y Rosario** son reconocidos como cantantes y bailadores de rumba.

La arquitectura

35 Romanos, moros y españoles, todos dejaron en España ejemplos magníficos de su arquitectura. De los romanos existen todavía puentes y acueductos, como el acueducto de Segovia. De los moros quedan mezquitas, alcázares y el exquisito palacio 40 de la Alhambra, en Granada.

De la Edad Media se conservan muchas catedrales de estilo románico, como la de Santiago de Compostela, y de estilo gótico, como las catedrales de Burgos, Sevilla y Toledo.

45   De los tiempos posteriores debe mencionarse El Escorial, cuyo arquitecto principal fue **Juan de Herrera** (1530–1597). El estilo barroco fue introducido en España por **José de Churriguera**, un arquitecto famoso del siglo XVIII. El llamado «estilo churrigueresco» mezcla elementos góticos y 50 barrocos. **Antoni Gaudí** (1852–1926) fue un importante arquitecto modernista barcelonés de principios del siglo XX que ha alcanzado fama mundialmente. La mayoría de sus obras se encuentran esparcidas por toda la ciudad de Barcelona. 55 Sus edificios están marcados por líneas curvas y exhuberantes de piedra y de metal; además, están adornados con pintorescos frescos y mosaicos. Entre sus obras principales están «La sagrada familia», «La pedrera» y «El parque Güell».

La pintura
60

España ha tenido una tradición muy rica en la pintura. No hay prácticamente museo de importancia en el mundo que no tenga cuadros de los maestros españoles. El Prado, en Madrid, es el museo princi- 65 pal de España. Entre los pintores españoles de renombre internacional están los siguientes:

Doménico Theotocopulos (1541–1614), llamado **el Greco,** nació en Creta. Estudió varios años en Italia y pasó luego a España, establecién- 70 dose en Toledo. Allí vivió hasta su muerte. Su obra se caracteriza por lo religioso y por la originalidad de su dibujo, que alarga y estiliza las figuras. Entre sus cuadros más famosos están «El entierro del Conde de Orgaz» y «Vista de Toledo». 75

José de Ribera (1588–1652) nació en España, pero pasó la mayor parte de su vida en Italia. Su obra se caracteriza por su gran realismo y los efectos de luz y color. Su cuadro más famoso es «El martirio de San Bartolomé». 80

Francisco de Zurbarán (1598–1664) pintó cuadros religiosos en un estilo realista y sobrio. Su «Monje en meditación» es representativo de su obra artística.

Diego Velázquez (1599–1660) fue el pintor 85 más original y perfecto de la escuela española. Fue pintor de cámara del rey Felipe IV y pintó muchos cuadros de la familia real. Entre sus obras maestras están «Las meninas», «La rendición de Breda», conocida también por «Las lanzas», «Los borra- 90 chos», «Las hilanderas» y muchos retratos de nobles de la época.

Bartolomé Esteban Murillo (1617–1682) fue principalmente un pintor religioso y es famoso

---

87   **el pintor de cámara** court painter
88   **la familia real** the royal family

por sus cuadros de «La inmaculada concepción». Es conocido también como dibujante y pintó tipos populares de gran realismo.

Francisco de Goya y Lucientes (1746–1828) fue el pintor más famoso de su época y uno de los grandes precursores de la pintura moderna. Fue pintor de los reyes Carlos III y Carlos IV y autor de varios retratos satíricos de la familia real. Son famosos la colección de aguafuertes llamada «Caprichos», la serie de grabados sobre la Guerra de Independencia contra Napoleón «Los desastres de la guerra», y el cuadro «Los fusilamientos del tres de mayo». Entre sus obras más conocidas están también «La maja vestida» y «La maja desnuda»

Joaquín Sorolla (1863–1923) es el pintor de «sol y color». Muchos de sus cuadros se encuentran en la ciudad de Nueva York, en el Museo de la Sociedad Hispánica.

Ignacio Zuloaga (1870–1945) pintó muchos tipos españoles con gran realismo: toreros, pordioseros y gitanos, entre otros.

José María Sert (1876–1945) es famoso por sus murales y por una serie de cuadros que representan episodios del Quijote. Estos cuadros se hallan en el salón Sert del hotel Waldorf-Astoria en la ciudad de Nueva York.

Pablo Picasso (1881–1973) nació y fue educado en Málaga, pero pasó la mayor parte de su vida en Francia. Es famoso como iniciador del Cubismo, un estilo de pintura que rechaza la perspectiva tradicional, presentando objetos fragmentados cuyas partes se ven simultáneamente. Pero la obra total de Picasso muestra su genio en diversos medios y estilos. Su famoso cuadro «Guernica» representa la destrucción de ese pueblo vasco durante la Guerra Civil Española.

Picasso ha sido uno de los más grandes pintores del siglo XX. Sus pinturas sobre la Guerra Civil Española y la Segunda Guerra Mundial se han expuesto y siguen exponiéndose en todos los museos del mundo.

Joan Miró (1893–1983) es uno de los más grandes representantes del arte abstracto unido a la fantasía surrealista. Su obra se caracteriza por su sencillez y la riqueza de su imaginación. En 1950 pintó un mural para la Universidad de Harvard. Los cuadros de Miró, de colores vivos y formas raras, reflejan el firmamento, el cielo, las estrellas, el mar, los pájaros y la mujer. Su obra también es reconocida en el mundo entero y se exhibe en los museos de más renombre internacional.

Sus cuadros son provocativos y reflejan las ideas críticas y extravagantes del pintor, que algunos han caracterizado de paranoico y de irracional. Tiene fama mundial.

Salvador Dalí (1904–1989) pertenece a la escuela surrealista. Sus obras representan los pensamientos fantásticos de su subconsciente, con gran atención al detalle. Dalí mismo dijo que sus cuadros eran «fotografías de sueños pintadas a mano».

Científicos

España ha producido varios científicos de renombre. Entre ellos están **Santiago Ramón y Cajal** (1852–1934), quien ganó el Premio Nobel de Medicina en 1906 por sus muchos descubrimientos acerca de las funciones del sistema nervioso; **Juan de La Cierva** (1895–1936), quien inventó el autogiro, precursor del helicóptero; y **Severo Ochoa** (1905–1993) quien ganó el Premio Nobel de Medicina en 1959 por sus estudios sobre las enzimas.

---

60   **pintadas a mano** hand painted

EJERCICIO A   **¿Cierto o falso? Indique si cada frase es cierta o falsa. Si es falsa, cámbiela para que sea cierta.**

1. El cante jondo es un ejemplo de la música popular de España.

---

2. El instrumento típico de España es el piano.

---

3. La zarzuela es un género musical que combina la música, el canto, la danza y el diálogo hablado.

4. Manuel de Falla compuso principalmente música para piano.

_____

5. Andrés Segovia fue el mejor violonchelista del mundo.

_____

6. Raphael y Julio Iglesias son conocidos por sus pinturas.

_____

7. Los bailes tradicionales de España incluyen distintos bailes regionales.

_____

8. Monserrat Caballé y Plácido Domingo son dos cantantes de ópera muy famosos.

_____

9. Miró pintó el famoso cuadro «Guernica».

_____

10. La jota es un baile regional muy alegre que se baila en parejas.

_____

11. El museo más importante de España se llama el Museo del Prado.

_____

12. Murillo es un pintor conocido por la originalidad de su dibujo, que alarga y estiliza las figuras.

_____

13. El pintor más perfecto y original de la escuela española fue Sorolla.

_____

14. Zuloaga fue el pintor que captó escenas de la Guerra de Independencia contra Napoleón.

_____

15. Salvador Dalí es el pintor español que inició el cubismo.

_____

EJERCICIO B   **Subraye la palabra o expresión que complete correctamente cada frase:**

1. El compositor que escribió la música del ballet «El sombrero de tres picos» es

(a) Albéniz   (b) Granados   (c) Iturbi   (d) de Falla

2. Un baile regional de Aragón es

(a) la malagueña   (b) la sardana   (c) la jota   (d) el fandango

3. Un tipo de obra teatral que puede corresponder a la comedia musical de los Estados Unidos es

(a) la zarzuela   (b) la seguidilla   (c) la pandereta   (d) el ballet

4. De los siguientes, el que no se emplea como instrumento de música es

   (a) la gaita   (b) la guitarra   (c) el flamenco   (d) la pandereta

5. Un bailarín español muy conocido fue

   (a) Granados   (b) Victoria de los Ángeles   (c) Casals   (d) Escudero

6. Uno de los mejores violonchelistas del mundo fue

   (a) Iturbi   (b) Casals   (c) Segovia   (d) Albéniz

7. Un baile regional de Cataluña es

   (a) el flamenco   (b) la sardana   (c) la muñeira   (d) la sevillana

8. Un ejemplo de música folklórica es

   (a) el cante jondo   (b) la zarzuela   (c) el ballet   (d) Goyescas

9. El gran maestro de la guitarra fue

   (a) Segovia   (b) Escudero   (c) Granados   (d) Asenjo Barbieri

10. La música que acompaña la muñeira se toca con

   (a) la guitarra   (b) el piano   (c) la gaita   (d) las castañuelas

---

EJERCICIO C   **Complete correctamente estas frases.**

1. Un pintor español famoso por sus cuadros surrealistas fue _____ .

2. Un acueducto construido por los romanos está en la ciudad de _____ .

3. «El entierro del Conde de Orgaz» es una obra maestra del pintor _____ .

4. La construcción más famosa de los moros es _____ en Granada.

5. «Las meninas» es una obra maestra del pintor _____ .

6. El fundador del cubismo fue _____ .

7. El museo principal de España es el Museo _____ .

8. «Los fusilamientos del tres de mayo» es una obra de _____ .

9. El pintor español cuyas obras se hallan en un gran hotel de Nueva York

   es _____ .

10. El arquitecto principal del Escorial fue _____ .

EJERCICIO D   **Identifique qué o quién es (fue).**

1. el artista que creó «Los caprichos»

   _____

2. una bailarina conocida por sus interpretaciones del baile flamenco

_____

3. el músico que compuso el ballet «El amor brujo»

_____

4. una cantante de ópera española conocida internacionalmente

_____

5. un pintor extranjero que fue a España y se estableció en Toledo

_____

6. un pintor surrealista contemporáneo

_____

7. el músico que compuso «Iberia» y «El Albaicín»

_____

8. el pintor español del siglo XVII que pasó la mayor parte de su vida en Italia

_____

9. el científico conocido por sus estudios sobre las enzimas

_____

10. el compositor de música que se inspiró en las obras de Goya

_____

11. una obra teatral con música, diálogo hablado, coros y bailes

_____

12. el inventor del autogiro

_____

13. el pintor de «sol y color»

_____

14. el gran científico español que hizo estudios sobre el sistema nervioso

_____

15. el arquitecto que introdujo en España el estilo barroco

_____

16. un baile regional que se baila en un gran círculo

_____

17. la música gitana con influencia de música árabe

_____

18. el estilo de pintura que presenta objetos fragmentados y rechaza la perspectiva tradicional

_____

19. el pintor español, muchas de cuyas obras están en el Museo de la Sociedad Hispánica

_____

20. el pintor del siglo XVII que pintó «La rendición de Breda»

_____

Chapter 33
La Vida y las Costumbres

La vida diaria contemporánea en España se parece a la vida diaria contemporánea en los Estados Unidos. Sin embargo, cada país del mundo tiene algo de particular. En España hay muchas tradi-
5 ciones y costumbres interesantes y a la vez diferentes de las que tenemos en nuestro país.

La casa y la familia

LA CASA

Las casas de las ciudades grandes son semejantes a
10 las de las otras ciudades del mundo. Hay casas particulares y casas de apartamentos. Un 65% de las familias españolas viven en casas o apartamentos propios, y sólo un 35% de la población española vive en apartmentos de alquiler. En los pueblos de
15 España y en las ciudades antiguas, las casas suelen estar situadas en calles estrechas. Por lo general, suelen ser de dos o tres plantas, con balcones, ventanas con rejas y patios pintorescos. En muchas casas las paredes están cubiertas de azulejos.

20 NOMBRES Y APELLIDOS

Los nombres españoles son diferentes a los de los Estados Unidos. Además del nombre de pila, cada niño español lleva dos apellidos, el de su padre seguido del de su madre. A veces se pone «y» entre
25 los dos apellidos. Por ejemplo, el Sr. Carlos Pérez (y) Gómez se casa con doña María Vega (y) González. Tienen un hijo que se llama Juan Pérez (y) Vega. La hermana de Juan se llama Adela Pérez (y) Vega. Si Adela se casa con Leandro Fernández (y) Ál-
30 varez, ella se llamará doña Adela Pérez de Fernández. Esta manera de llamar a las personas se extiende a todos los países hispanos.

EL DÍA DEL SANTO

Los españoles generalmente llevan el nombre de
35 un santo y, además de su propio cumpleaños, celebran el día de ese santo.

Tipos pintorescos

Los gitanos viven principalmente en el sur de España. Sin embargo, han sido un pueblo nómada y siguen viajando por toda España. Están llenos de
40 vida y tienen fama de ser muy listos. Algunos de ellos se ganan la vida diciendo la fortuna. En los últimos 15 años los gitanos se han integrado en la vida social y comercial del país y muchos tienen un oficio remunerado. Se dedican a comprar y a
45 vender en los mercados ambulantes de las diferentes provincias españolas. Mantienen muchas de sus tradiciones, dentro de las que la música y el baile son las más importantes.

La tuna es un grupo de veinte músicos calle-
50 jeros que han sido parte de la vida estudiantil univeristaria de España desde antes del siglo XVI. Los tunos usan un traje tradicional de color negro y llevan una capa. Los instrumentos musicales que tocan incluyen el laúd, la bandurria, el requinto, la
55 guitarra y la pandereta. Antes las tunas estaban formadas por muchos más músicos, pero ahora los grupos son mucho más reducidos. Las principales universidades españolas siguen conservando su tuna como símbolo de la tradición medieval de los
60 trovadores españoles.

Actividades sociales
y costumbres

La vida social es muy importante para los españoles. Acostumbran a pasar mucho tiempo en las
65 cafeterías y los bares, charlando, comiendo y bebiendo con los amigos. Cenan tarde y, por consiguiente, se acuestan tarde.

Unos años atrás, todavía existía en muchas ciudades el ateneo, club intelectual donde se reunían
70 grupos literarios y científicos. Los ateneos hoy en día organizan actividades culturales y recreativas para todos, especialmente para los jóvenes y las personas de avanzada edad. Las tertulias y las re-

---

15 **soler** + infinitive to usually...
22 **nombre de pila** first name
24 **seguido de** followed by
42 **decir la fortuna** to tell someone's fortune
50 **los músicos callejeros** street musicians

55 **la bandurria** Spanish string instrument of the lute type
55 **el requinto** Spanish string instrument, similar to a small guitar with only four strings
67 **por consiguiente** therefore

uniones familiares son todavía muy comunes entre los españoles. Se juntan para charlar y divertirse.

La lotería está dirigida por el gobierno central, es muy popular y está en aumento. Hay varios sor-⁵ teos de lotería semanales muy populares entre la clase social trabajadora. Después están dos grandes sorteos nacionales: la lotería de Navidad y la lotería del Niño. El premio mayor se llama "el gordo." Cada año las familias galardonadas con este premio ¹⁰ hacen cambios considerables en sus vidas.

La siesta es la costumbre de acostarse por la tarde durante las horas de mayor calor. Se cierran las tiendas y las oficinas, y los trabajadores regresan a sus casas a comer y descansar o dormir la siesta. ¹⁵ Después de la siesta, las oficinas y tiendas se abren de nuevo y quedan abiertas hasta muy tarde. Ésta es una costumbre que también ha ido desapareciendo en las ciudades grandes.

Comidas y bebidas

²⁰ En España, como en los Estados Unidos, por lo general se comen tres comidas principales. La diferencia está en el horario, pues allá comen más tarde. El desayuno se toma alrededor de las ocho de la mañana y puede consistir en café con leche o ²⁵ chocolate y pan con mantequilla y mermelada o bollos. Tanto la comida, que se toma cerca de las dos de la tarde, como la cena, que se toma después de las ocho o nueve de la noche, son comidas completas. Un menú normal puede consistir en ³⁰ sopa, ensalada, carne con arroz o verduras y postre. Entre la comida y la cena, alrededor de las seis de la tarde, se toma la merienda, algo ligero como un sandwich o un bocadillo. Como aperitivo, antes de la comida o la cena, o para acompañar las bebidas ³⁵ alcohólicas, se acostumbra comer tapas, sabrosos bocados, presentados en platos diminutos, de variedades culinarias típicas de las regiones españolas.

La comida española es variada, sana, nutritiva y deliciosa. No es picante, como cree la gente. Entre ⁴⁰ los platos tradicionales está la paella, arroz con pollo o mariscos, bien sazonado con ajo, sal, pimiento, tomate y otras verduras como guisantes y judías verdes. La paella más conocida es la valenciana, de fama internacional. El cocido, conocido ⁴⁵ también como olla o puchero, es otro plato típico español. Es un potaje o sopa caliente que contiene una gran variedad de carnes y verduras. Cada región española hace un cocido diferente. El gaz-

pacho, sopa fría hecha de tomates, pimiento verde, pepino, cebolla, ajo, aceite de oliva y sal, es típico ⁵⁰ de la región andaluza, pero se toma en toda España como un plato veraniego muy refrescante.

Las bebidas más corrientes que toman los españoles incluyen el café, el té, la leche, el chocolate y todo tipo de refrescos y zumos de frutas natu-⁵⁵ rales. El vino, la cerveza y la sangría acompañan las comidas y los aperitivos. La sangría, bebida típica española, es refrescante y contiene vino tinto, agua, azúcar y trozos de naranja, manzana y limón. El cava, bebida usada en las fiestas y ocasiones espe-⁶⁰ ciales para brindar, es un vino suave con burbujas. Otra bebida tradicional es la horchata, hecha de almendras, agua y azúcar. Se toma fría en verano como refresco.

A los españoles, especialmente a los niños, les ⁶⁵ encanta el chocolate, que se prepara muy espeso y caliente y se toma con bizcochos, panecillos o churros. Estos se parecen a nuestros "donuts," pero son como palos largos y son más ricos cuando están calientes. El chocolate con churros es ideal ⁷⁰ para la merienda y las fiestas de cumpleaños.

La ropa

En general, la ropa de los españoles es semejante a la del resto de los europeos. Debido a los medios de comunicación—la televisión, el cine y el ⁷⁵ Internet—la influencia norteamericana es cada vez más visible en la manera de vestir de la juventud española.

Sin embargo, en España se conservan todavía algunas prendas tradicionales. La mantilla es un ⁸⁰ gran pañuelo de seda y encajes, que llevaba antiguamente la mujer para cubrirse la cabeza. Debajo de la mantilla se usaba un peine alto, ricamente adornado, llamado peineta. El mantón es un chal grande y bordado que sirve de adorno o de abrigo. ⁸⁵ Ambos se usan todavía en fiestas y celebraciones religiosas y tradicionales. También los lucen, con mucho orgullo, las bailadoras de flamenco, y así, conservan la tradición española.

En pueblos agrícolas y ganaderos, algunos an-⁹⁰ cianos todavía llevan boina, especialmente en otoño y en invierno. Es una gorra de lana redonda semejante al "beret" francés. Entre los campesinos se usan las alpargatas, sandalias de lona con suela de soga. Sin embargo, los españoles usan cada vez más, ⁹⁵ a cualquier edad, las zapatillas de deporte.

---

4 **el sorteo** drawing of numbers in a lottery
16 **de nuevo** again

Días de fiesta

RELIGIOSOS

España es un país católico desde hace siglos y las fiestas religiosas siguen siendo importantes. La
5 mayoría de los españoles son católicos y conservan y practican sus costumbres y tradiciones religiosas.

La Navidad cae el 25 de diciembre. En Nochebuena, la gente va a la iglesia para oír la «Misa de Gallo» y cantar villancicos. Muchas casas y estable-
10 cimientos públicos tienen su nacimiento expuesto. Es un conjunto de pequeñas figuritas, adornadas minuciosamente, que representan el nacimiento de Jesucristo. También se acostumbra a dar regalos, llamados aguinaldos, a las personas que han servido a
15 la familia durante el año (el cartero, la muchacha de la limpieza, la niñera, el jardinero y otros). Los niños reciben sus regalos el Día de los Reyes Magos, el 6 de enero. Los Reyes Magos son para los niños españoles lo que Santa Claus es para los
20 niños de los Estados Unidos.

El Carnaval es un período de diversión antes del Miércoles de Ceniza, que comienza la Cuaresma. El Carnaval en España se celebra con disfraces de manera informal entre amigos y parientes. La Cuaresma,
25 días de ayuno y penitencia, termina el Domingo de Resurección o Día de la Pascua Florida. Este domingo es un día festivo de alegría y diversión. La Semana Santa, que precede a la Pascua Florida, se celebra con cierta solemnidad aunque la devoción
30 se va perdiendo. El Día de Viernes Santo hay procesiones religiosas en muchos pueblos y ciudades. Cada pueblo tiene su santo patrón, cuyo día se celebra con una fiesta popular. La víspera hay una verbena, o sea una fiesta nocturna.
35 Santos muy populares en España son Santiago, patrón del país, San Isidro, patrón de Madrid, y San Jorge, patrón de Cataluña. Fuera de España es muy conocida la fiesta de San Fermín, santo patrón de Pamplona, que dura ocho días. Cada día de fiesta,
40 los toros que van a participar en las corridas se sueltan a correr por las calles, desde los corrales hasta la plaza de toros. Mucha gente trata de torearlos por las calles.

El 8 de diciembre se celebra la Inmaculada
45 Concepción, día dedicado a la Virgen María. Hay en las ciudades españolas muchas iglesias y basílicas dedicadas a la Virgen. Las vírgenes más veneradas por los españoles son la del Pilar, la Paloma Blanca del Rocío, la Macarena, la Almudena, la de Atocha,
50 la de Montserrat y la Merced.

El Día de los Difuntos, el 2 de noviembre, está dedicado a la memoria de los que han muerto. La gente visita los cementerios y adorna con flores las tumbas de parientes y amigos.

NACIONALES
55 Hay tres días festivos importantes hoy en España. El 6 de diciembre se celebra el Día de la Constitución. Fue en el Referéndum del 6 de diciembre de 1978 que los españoles votaron por la constitución que conduciría hoy a la democracia, después
60 de cuarenta años de dictadura.

El 12 de octubre es el Día de la Hispanidad, o el Día de la Raza, que corresponde a nuestro «Columbus Day» y se celebra en todo el mundo hispano. El 1 de mayo es el Día del Trabajo, que se
65 celebra en toda Europa.

Diversiones y deportes

La corrida de toros es un espectáculo de mucho colorido, muy típico de España. En las ciudades grandes, generalmente hay corridas los domingos por la tarde y los días de fiesta importantes. Esas
70 tardes las plazas se llenan de gente, sobre todo si los toreros son famosos. Antes de comenzar la corrida, todos los participantes desfilan por la arena, mientras se escucha la música de pasodobles.

La corrida tiene tres partes, que se llaman
75 suertes. En la primera suerte los picadores entran, montados a caballo. Llevan picas largas, con las cuales castigan al toro en la cerviz. En la segunda suerte entran los banderilleros, a pie, llevando las banderillas. Esperan la embestida del toro y, al pasar
80 éste, le ponen las banderillas en la cerviz. En la tercera suerte el matador, armado de una espada de acero muy fino, y llevando una pequeña muleta roja, exhibe su arte y su valor. Ejecuta varios pases con la muleta, hasta que llega el momento ideal
85 para matar al toro. Entonces, cara a cara con el adversario, le entierra la espada y lo mata. Lo que el público estima y aplaude más es la valentía y el arte del torero.

---

8   **la Misa de Gallo** Midnight Mass
17 **los Reyes Magos** the Three Wise Men
22 **Miércoles de Ceniza** Ash Wednesday
26 **la Pascua Florida** Easter

40 **se sueltan a correr** are let loose to run
74 **el pasodoble** a typical Spanish march
85 **la muleta** matador's stick with attached red cloth hanging

El jai-alai, también llamado pelota, es un juego vasco. Es muy popular en toda España, en algunos países hispanoamericanos y en la Florida. Se juega con una pelota dura en un gran frontón de tres paredes. Es semejante al «handball», pero en vez de tirar y coger la pelota con la mano, se emplea una cesta larga y estrecha, atada a la muñeca.

El fútbol es el deporte más popular en España, al igual que en el resto de Europa y en Latino- américa. Es pues el deporte nacional por excelen- cia en la mayoría los países hispanos. Además del fútbol, hay otros deportes, como el tenis, el ci- clismo, el basketball, el hándbol y el esquí, que han adquirido importancia en España en las últimas décadas. Todos estos deportes han dado figuras destacadas a nivel nacional e internacional.

EJERCICIO A   **En cada grupo escriba las dos palabras o expresiones relacionadas.**

1. santo, mantilla, peineta, banderilla

2. nacimientos, alpargatas, horchata, villancicos

3. siesta, premio gordo, lotería, tertulia

4. ateneo, olla, toros, cocido

5. gitanos, puchero, cuaresma, mercados

6. gazpacho, matador, muleta, santo

7. arroz con pollo, santo patrón, verbena, Reyes Magos

8. tuna, pandereta, siesta, sangría

9. Semana Santa, Día de la Raza, Pascua Florida, San Fermín

10. frontón, misa de gallo, picador, jai-alai

EJERCICIO B   **Complete las frases siguientes.**

1. Los niños españoles reciben sus regalos de Navidad el Día de _____.

2. El apellido paterno (del padre) de Juan Díaz y Pérez es _____.

3. En el mundo hispano el doce de octubre se celebra el Día de _____.

4. En la corrida de toros, el torero que va montado se llama _____.

5. El santo patrón de Madrid es _____.

6. El plato de arroz, pollo y mariscos se llama _____.

7. El Día de la Constitución se celebra el _____.

8. En la tercera suerte de la corrida de toros, el torero importante es _____.

9. Una bebida espesa y caliente que se toma en la merienda es _____.

10. El premio más grande de la lotería es _____.

EJERCICIO C   **Escoja la respuesta correcta y escríbala en el espacio correspondiente.**

1. En la corrida de toros, el picador _____.

(mata al toro, emplea una muleta, va montado a caballo, usa las banderillas)

2. La fiesta de San Fermín se celebra _____.

(en toda España, en Madrid, en Pamplona, en Barcelona)

3. La tuna es _____.

(un grupo de músicos, un baile, una canción, un instrumento musical)

4. El santo patrón de España es _____.

(San Juan, Santiago, Santo Tomás, San Isidro)

5. En el jai-alai, para tirar la pelota se emplea _____.

(una muleta, una espada, una peineta, una cesta)

6. Una boina se lleva en _____.

(la cabeza, los pies, las manos, el cuello)

7. La Semana Santa es un período _____.

(de diversión y alegría, que dura tres días, que precede a la Pascua Florida, que se llama también el Día de los Difuntos)

8. En la Navidad, los españoles ponen _____.

(un nacimiento, una mantilla, una verbena, una romería)

9. La bebida fría, hecha de almendras, es _____.

(el chocolate, la sangría, la horchata, el té)

10. Las tres partes de una corrida de toros se llaman _____.

(escenas, actos, jornadas, suertes)

| EJERCICIO D | **Escriba la letra que indique la relación correcta con cada expresión de la columna de la izquierda.** |

1. tertulia _____

2. tapas _____

3. gitano _____

4. ateneo _____

5. Montserrat _____

6. Nochebuena _____

7. merienda _____

8. puchero _____

9. siesta _____

10. alpargata _____

a. aguador

b. Virgen

c. comida ligera

d. descanso

e. reunión

f. sandalia

g. la buenaventura

h. villancicos

i. club literario

j. bocados

k. cocido

Part Six

Civilization: Spanish America

ESPAÑA

Islas Baleares

Islas Canarias

MÉXICO

REPÚBLICA DOMINICANA

PUERTO RICO

CUBA

HONDURAS

GUATEMALA

NICARAGUA

EL SALVADOR

COSTA RICA

VENEZUELA

PANAMÁ

COLOMBIA

ECUADOR

PERÚ

BOLIVIA

PARAGUAY

CHILE

URUGUAY

ARGENTINA

Chapter 34
La Geografía de Hispanoamérica

Al sur de los Estados Unidos, y ocupando una extensión mucho más grande que la de nuestro país, viven unos trescientos cincuenta millones de personas que constituyen la llamada América española, o sea lugares donde el idioma oficial es el español. La América Española comprende diecinueve países, situados en tres regiones distintas: (1) México y la América Central, (2) las Antillas y (3) la América del Sur.

México y la América Central

1. **México** se halla al sur de Norteamérica, limitado al norte por los Estados Unidos, al oeste por el Pacífico, al sur por Guatemala y Belice y al este por el Golfo de México. El Río Bravo del Norte (que nosotros llamamos el Río Grande) lo separa de Tejas.

     México es un país de contrastes. Dos cadenas de montañas, la Sierra Madre Oriental y la Sierra Madre Occidental, lo atraviesan de norte a sur, y desde el centro del país hasta el interior de los Estados Unidos se extiende una inmensa altiplanicie llamada la Mesa Mexicana. Por el contrario, en el este, la Península de Yucatán es un área baja, plana y selvática. En las montañas se hallan varios grandes volcanes, el más famoso de los cuales es el Popocatépetl. El país tiene además muchos ríos, lagos y lagunas.

     Una de las principales riquezas del país es la agricultura; con cultivos de maíz, trigo, arroz, frijoles, algodón, café, tomates y papas. La minería es también importante con minas de plomo, cobre y zinc. México es el primer productor de plata del mundo y uno de los mayores productores de gas natural y petróleo. Las industrias principales son las de conservas de productos alimenticios, productos químicos y la industria textil. También son importantes las industrias derivadas de la minería como las del hierro, acero, petróleo y gas natural. Finalmente, el turismo es una importante fuente de ingresos.

     La capital del país, Ciudad de México, está situada en la meseta central a una altura de más de 2.200 metros. Fue fundada por Hernán Cortés sobre las ruinas de Tenochtitlán, la antigua capital azteca conquistada por los españoles en 1521. Como muchas de las ciudades de la América Española, la Ciudad de México representa una mezcla impresionante de lo colonial y lo moderno. Allí se encuentra el Castillo de Chapultepec, un museo histórico que antes servía de residencia a los presidentes del país. Hay además muchos puntos de interés: (1) el Paseo de la Reforma, la avenida más elegante de la capital; (2) el Zócalo, la plaza mayor; (3) el Palacio de Bellas Artes, el teatro más grande de todo el país, que contiene también una magnífica colección de pinturas mexicanas; (4) el Museo de Antropología, donde se puede aprender la historia y admirar la cultura y el arte de las tribus indias de la región; (5) la Ciudad Universitaria; (6) la Basílica de Guadalupe, la iglesia más famosa del país, construida en honor de la Virgen de Guadalupe, patrona de México; (7) la Catedral; y (8) importantes ruinas arqueológicas como el Templo Mayor. Los famosos jardines flotantes de Xochimilco y los templos y pirámides de Teotihuacán se hallan a poca distancia de la capital.

     Otras ciudades importantes de México son: Guadalajara, segunda ciudad del país y el centro principal de la agricultura y la ganadería; Veracruz y Tampico, puertos importantes sobre el Golfo de México; Acapulco y Puerto Vallarta, puertos sobre el Pacífico, famosos por sus playas; Taxco, monumento nacional a la arquitectura colonial y centro de la industria de la plata; Mérida, en la península de Yucatán, centro de la producción de henequén; y Chichén-Itzá, antigua ciudad maya en el norte de Yucatán, donde hay notables ruinas mayas y toltecas.

2. **Guatemala,** al sur de México, es un país de montañas y de lagos. Gracias a sus niveles diferentes, tiene un clima variado que le ha permitido desarrollar una agricultura también muy variada. Sus productos principales son el café, las bananas, el chicle (del cual se hace la goma de mascar), las maderas finas, la caña de azúcar, el ganado de ovejas y cerdos, el petróleo, el níquel y el pescado. Guatemala también está en vías de desarrollo industrial. La industria textil y las industrias derivadas del azúcar, la goma, los muebles y los productos químicos

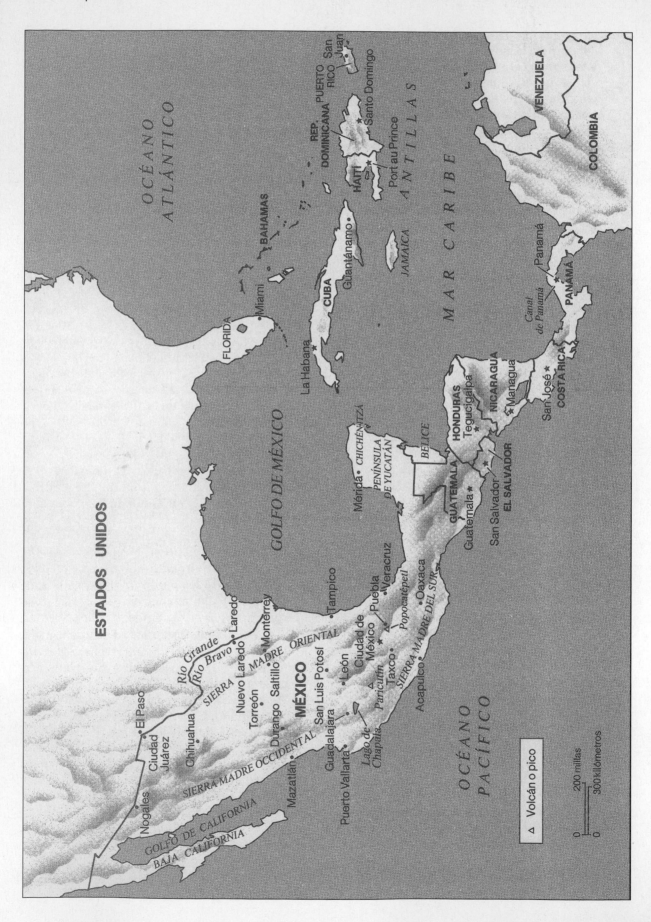

están en vías de desarrollo. Además, el turismo está creciendo en los últimos años. Guatemala es el país de mayor población de Centroamérica y el que tiene un porcentaje más alto de indígenas puros (54% de la población). Fue la sede de una de las civilizaciones más avanzadas, los mayas. La capital del país es la Ciudad de Guatemala.

3. **Honduras** es el país más montañoso de Centroamérica. Como los otros países de la región, tiene un clima muy variado. Es un país básicamente agrícola, cuyos productos principales son las bananas, el café, el tabaco, la caña de azúcar y las maderas finas. Los Estados Unidos compran el 90% de los productos de exportación que son el plátano, el oro y la plata. Otros recursos naturales del país son el plomo, el zinc, el hierro, el cobre y el carbón. La industria pesquera es importante. La capital es Tegucigalpa.

4. **El Salvador** es la nación mas pequeña de Centroamérica y además la única que no está bañada por el Atlántico. El país tiene más de 350 ríos y muchos lagos y lagunas muy hermosos. El café es su producto más importante, seguido por el algodón y la caña de azúcar. El petróleo y la energía hidroeléctrica son recursos naturales del país. Las industrias en vías de desarrollo incluyen las conservas, las bebidas o refrescos y los metales ligeros. La capital es San Salvador.

5. **Nicaragua** es el país más grande de la América Central. Es también agrícola y produce maíz, algodón, café, plátano, caucho y maderas preciosas. Es además el país más ganadero de Centroamérica. Otros importantes recursos naturales de este país son el oro, la plata, el cobre, el zinc y el plomo. Las industrias derivadas de los metales, los productos químicos, el algodón y el cuero son las que están creciendo. La capital es Managua.

6. **Costa Rica** es el único país centroamericano donde la mayoría de la población es de raza blanca. Es, también, el único país de América que no tiene ejército; una Guardia Civil mantiene el orden. Costa Rica ha sido tradicionalmente democrático y ha fomentado la educación pública. Sus principales productos de exportación son el café y los plátanos, aunque produce también cacao, caña de azúcar, papas y una gran variedad de frutas.

Además de un considerable aumento del turismo, el desarrollo industrial también es vigente. Hay que destacar las industrias de conservas, materiales para la construcción, productos plásticos, microprocesadores y la industria textil. La capital es San José.

7. **Panamá** está en el istmo del mismo nombre, que une las dos Américas. El famoso Canal de Panamá, que atraviesa el país, fue comenzado por un francés, Fernando de Lesseps, en 1881 y terminado por los Estados Unidos en 1914. Una gran parte de la población del país vive directa o indirectamente de las operaciones del Canal. La agricultura apenas comenzó a desarrollarse en los últimos veinte y cinco años, y su producto principal es el plátano. Además de los plátanos, se cultivan el arroz, la caña de azúcar, el maíz, el café y una gran variedad de verduras (o vegetales). Entre las industrias que están creciendo en los últimos años hay que mencionar los materiales para la construcción y las refinerías de petróleo. La capital del país es la Ciudad de Panamá y el puerto principal sobre la Zona del Canal es Balboa.

Las Antillas

Las Antillas son un grupo de islas en el Mar Caribe que incluyen a Cuba, Santo Domingo (o La Española, nombre dado por Cristóbal Colón a la isla) y Puerto Rico. Santo Domingo está compartida por Haití y la República Dominicana.

1. **Cuba,** la isla más grande de las Antillas, fue descubierta por Colón en su primer viaje. Debido a la fertilidad de su tierra y la belleza de su paisaje, se ha llamado «la Perla de las Antillas». Las industrias más destacadas son las del tabaco, azúcar, productos químicos, biotecnología, maquinaria agrícola y materiales para la construcción. La ganadería y la pesca son industrias importantes y el país es también rico en minerales. La capital es La Habana.

De gran interés histórico es el Castillo del Morro, situado en el puerto de La Habana, que sirvió de fortaleza para proteger la isla contra los piratas ingleses en el siglo XVI. En Guantánamo hay una base naval que pertenece a los Estados Unidos.

2. **La República Dominicana** ocupa las dos terceras partes de la isla de La Española, lla-

---

98 **las dos terceras partes** two thirds

MAR CARIBE

OCÉANO
ATLÁNTICO

Barranquilla
Cartagena
La Guaira
★ Caracas
Río Orinoco
LLANOS
Medellín
VENEZUELA
GUYANA
Río Magdalena
★ Bogotá
SURINAM
GUAYANA
FRANCESA
COLOMBIA

Quito ★
Cotopaxi
Chimborazo
Guayaquil
ECUADOR
Ecuador

LOS ANDES
Río Amazonas

PERÚ
Callao
Lima
Cuzco

BRASIL

Lago
Titicaca
★ La Paz
BOLIVIA
★ Brasilia

LOS ANDES
Desierto de Atacama
GRAN CHACO
Río Paraguay
Río de Janeiro

OCÉANO
PACÍFICO
Tucumán
PARAGUAY
Asunción ★
Iguazú

CHILE
Córdoba
Río Paraná
Aconcagua
URUGUAY
Viña del Mar
Valparaíso
Rosario
Buenos Aires ★
★ Montevideo
OCÉANO
ATLÁNTICO
Santiago
Río de la Plata

Islas Juan
Fernández
(Ch.)
PAMPAS

ARGENTINA

PATAGONIA

0   300 millas

0   500 kilómetros

△ Volcán o pico

Estrecho
De
Magallanes
Islas Malvinas
(Falkland Islands)
(Ing.)
Tierra del Fuego
Cabo de
Hornos

mada Quisqueya antes del Descubrimiento y bautizada La Española por Colón. Durante el período colonial, casi todas las expediciones conquistadoras del Nuevo Mundo partieron de esta isla.

La base de la economía es la agricultura, principalmente el cultivo de la caña de azúcar, el cacao, el café, el plátano y el maíz. La pesca está en pleno desarrollo al igual que las industrias derivadas del azúcar, el tabaco, el cemento, el oro, la plata y la industria textil. Además, el turismo es una fuente importantísima de riqueza.

La capital del país, Santo Domingo, es la ciudad más antigua de América, fundada en 1496. Allí se encuentra la Universidad más antigua del Nuevo Mundo, la Universidad de Santo Tomás de Aquino, fundada en 1538 y llamada hoy la Universidad de Santo Domingo.

3. **Puerto Rico** pasó a manos de los Estados Unidos en 1898 y es hoy en día un Estado Libre Asociado. Sus habitantes han tenido la ciudadanía estadounidense desde 1917. Los productos principales de la isla son el café, la caña de azúcar, el tabaco, el plátano y la piña. Las industrias más importantes son las de conservas, productos farmacéuticos y electrónicos. El turismo es una gran fuente de ingresos en la isla.

La isla, llamada Borinquén por los indígenas, fue descubierta por Colón en 1493. Su capital, San Juan, fue fundada en 1508 por Ponce de León, el primer gobernador de la isla. Es un puerto comercial muy activo y además aún conserva fortificaciones y hermosos edificios de la época colonial española.

La América del Sur

La mayor parte de Sudamérica está al sur del ecuador, y las estaciones del año caen en orden opuesto a las nuestras. Cuando nosotros estamos en invierno, allí tienen verano.

Volando en avión sobre la América del Sur, se ve que casi todos los países son montañosos. En el este están las tierras altas de las Guayanas y del Brasil. Al oeste la larga cordillera de los Andes, la mayor cadena del mundo, se extiende desde el Caribe hasta Antártica por más de 7.500 kilómetros. Estas montañas, con sus vastas mesetas, sus valles y sus picos majestuosos, han tenido gran influencia en el lento desarrollo del continente. Han hecho muy difícil y costosa la construcción de ferrocarriles y carreteras, impidiendo así el transporte y el comercio. Hasta cierto punto, el transporte aéreo ha mejorado las comunicaciones.

Las montañas tienen separados, no solamente a los diferentes países, sino también a veces a las regiones de un mismo país, como sucede en el Perú, el Ecuador y Colombia. Los Andes son ricos en minerales como el oro, la plata, el aluminio, el cobre, el platino, el hierro y el estaño. Las mesetas son muy saludables y allí se ha establecido la mayor parte de la población.

Tres vastas llanuras ocupan el interior del continente, extendiéndose hasta la costa del Atlántico. Éstas son las del Amazonas, el Chaco y la Pampa, donde están los valles de los ríos Orinoco, Amazonas, Paraná y Paraguay. Allí se encuentran selvas, bosques y pantanos.

PAÍSES DEL ESTE

1. **La Argentina** recibió su nombre, que quiere decir «de plata», porque los primeros conquistadores pensaron que la región era rica en minas de plata. Los indios que encontraron a lo largo del Río de la Plata llevaban hermosos ornamentos de plata, pero ésta provenía del Perú. La Argentina es el país más grande de habla hispana. Se extiende desde la región del Chaco en el norte, hasta la Tierra del Fuego y el Estrecho de Magallanes en el sur; y desde el Atlántico en el este, hasta los Andes. Por lo general, el país tiene un clima templado, aunque hay extremos de frío en el sur (Tierra del Fuego) y de calor y humedad en las selvas del Chaco. En el extremo nordeste, entre la Argentina y el Brasil, están las famosas cataratas del Iguazú, de 70 metros de altura. En la región andina se halla el Aconcagua, un pico que alcanza una altura de 6.959 metros y es el pico más alto de todo el hemisferio occidental. La mayor parte del país es una llanura extensa, llamada la Pampa, la tierra del gaucho y el centro de la agricultura y la ganadería. La Argentina es uno de los primeros productores de trigo del mundo y su riqueza ganadera es también una de las primeras del mundo. Otros importantes productos agrícolas son el limón,

9 **en pleno desarrollo** developed at full scale
22 **Estado Libre Asociado** Commonwealth

la vid, el girasol, el maíz y la soja. Como recursos naturales hay que mencionar el cobre, el hierro, el acero, el zinc, el manganeso, el uranio y el petróleo. Las industrias más desarrolladas son las de conservas de productos alimenticios, la textil, la metalúrgica y la de productos químicos y motocicletas.

La población es de raza blanca en su mayoría, mayormente descendientes de españoles e italianos. Buenos Aires, la capital, es la ciudad más grande de Sudamérica y su puerto figura entre los más activos del mundo. Es una ciudad moderna y cosmopolita, con grandes y elegantes avenidas, plazas, tiendas y teatros. Los habitantes de la ciudad se llaman porteños. La segunda ciudad en importancia es Rosario, puerto a orillas del río Paraná y centro industrial.

2. **El Uruguay,** llamado antes la Banda Oriental, es la nación hispana más pequeña de la América del Sur. Limita al norte con el Brasil, al oeste y al sur con la Argentina y al este con el Océano Atlántico. El clima del país es templado, sin calores ni fríos extremos. Por sus costas se extienden muchas playas elegantes, de gran interés turístico. Entre ellas está la de Punta del Este, donde tuvo lugar en 1961 la Conferencia Interamericana que ratificó el programa de la Alianza Para el Progreso.

La población del Uruguay es en su mayoría de origen europeo, principalmente español e italiano. El Uruguay ha sido un país progresista, donde hay muy poco analfabetismo. Las industrias principales se derivan de la ganadería, como la industria de la carne congelada y en conserva y la industria del cuero. La industria pesquera es también importante al igual que las de maquinaria eléctrica, los transportes, los productos químicos y la textil. Montevideo, capital y puerto principal de la nación, está al este de Buenos Aires, en la orilla opuesta del Río de la Plata.

3. **El Paraguay** es uno de los dos países de la América del Sur que no tienen puerto de mar, pero el Río Paraná le permite comunicarse con el Atlántico. El país se halla entre Bolivia, el Brasil y la Argentina. Al oeste, la región del Gran Chaco ocupa las dos terceras partes del país. Es una vasta llanura semiárida, cubierta por selvas espesas en el norte, por la cual lucharon Bolivia y el Paraguay desde 1932 hasta 1935. El resultado de la guerra fue que el Paraguay recibió las dos terceras partes del territorio, y Bolivia consiguió una salida al mar por medio del Río Paraguay. La famosa yerba mate, una especie de té, es un producto importante del Paraguay, así como también la madera de un árbol llamado quebracho, que se emplea para curtir el cuero. La agricultura de este país es rica en algodón, caña de azúcar, maíz, trigo, tabaco, soja, frutas y verduras. Hay tambien ganado vacuno y de cerdo. Las industrias más avanzadas incluyen, además de la textil, la de los productos derivados de la madera y el azúcar, las de bebidas y refrescos y las de materiales para la construcción. La capital del país, Asunción, es un puerto fluvial de considerable importancia.

PAÍSES ANDINOS

Los países andinos se encuentran en el oeste del continente y comprenden a Chile, Bolivia, el Perú, el Ecuador, Colombia y Venezuela. La cordillera de los Andes atraviesa casi todos estos países de norte a sur.

1. **Chile** se encuentra al extremo sudoeste, entre la Argentina y el Océano Pacífico. El país se extiende 4.270 kilómetros, desde la frontera con el Perú en el norte, hasta Tierra del Fuego en el sur, parte de la cual le pertenece a Chile. El país tiene una anchura media de 180 kilómetros y en algunas partes se vuelve mucho más estrecho. Es un país de mucha actividad sísmica y numerosos terremotos han destruido en el pasado regiones enteras. El Desierto de Atacama, en el norte, es uno de los desiertos más secos del mundo; a veces pasan años y no cae ni una gota de agua. Allí se encuentra la región minera más importante; Chile es el segundo productor mundial de cobre. Además del cobre, otros recursos naturales son los nitratos, los metales preciosos y la energía hidroeléctrica. La industria siderúrgica es importante al igual que las derivadas de los metales preciosos.

En el extremo sur el clima es polar. El valle central, en cambio, tiene un clima excelente y es el centro agrícola del país. Los productos principales son la vid (de la cual se ha desarrollado una importante industria de vinos) y

---

55 **por medio de** through, by (means of)
67 **un puerto fluvial** river port

los cereales. Otros productos agrícolas que se cultivan en Chile son las papas y las frutas. La pesca y el ganado vacuno y lanar aportan al país una riqueza considerable. En esta región se encuentran las ciudades más importantes del país: Santiago, la capital, y Valparaíso, el puerto principal. Viña del Mar, una playa muy famosa, queda cerca de Valparaíso. En el sur del país hay una región de grandes lagos que se llama la «Suiza chilena» por su extrema belleza e interés turístico para los deportes de invierno.

2. **Bolivia,** llamada así en honor de Simón Bolívar, se conocía en tiempos coloniales por Alto Perú. Aunque está en la zona tórrida, el país tiene un clima muy variado. En algunas partes es el país más frío del continente sudamericano, debido a su gran altura. Tiene fronteras con el Brasil al norte y al este, con el Paraguay al sudeste, con la Argentina al sur, con chile al sudoeste y con el Perú al noroeste. Como se ve, Bolivia no tiene salida al mar y depende de los países vecinos para exportar sus productos. La población de Bolivia es india en más de un cincuenta por ciento, y los grupos más numerosos son los aimaraes, los quechuas y los guaraníes. El país es muy rico en minerales. Potosí era conocido en tiempos coloniales como el centro más importante de la producción de plata del mundo. Hoy en día Bolivia es uno de los primeros productores de estaño. Tiene además cobre, cinc, plomo, azufre y oro. Los productos agrícolas que se cultivan en el país son el arroz, el maíz, el algodón, el tabaco, la coca, las papas y la soja. Entre las industrias más desarrolladas están las de productos alimenticios, la textil y las artesanías.

La capital del país, La Paz, es la capital más alta del mundo, situada a más de 3.600 metros sobre el nivel del mar. El lago Titicaca, entre Bolivia y Perú, es el lago navegable más alto del mundo; se encuentra a una altura de 3.800 metros.

3. **El Perú** es tres veces más grande que el estado de California. Está limitado al norte por el Ecuador y Colombia, al este por el Brasil y Bolivia, al sur por Chile y al oeste por el Pacífico. Los Andes dividen al país en tres regiones naturales: la costa pacífica, que es estrecha y desértica; la sierra, constituida por una altiplanicie y dominada por los Andes, donde vive más de la mitad de la población; y la selva hacia el Amazonas, un inmenso llano que cubre más de la mitad del país.

La agricultura es la actividad fundamental del país, pero la minería también ocupa un lugar importante en la economía. Casi toda la industria minera se concentra en Lima, la capital, y sus alrededores. La pesca ha tomado importancia debido a su abundancia y su variedad en las aguas peruanas. Las ovejas y, en las zonas más elevadas, animales como la alpaca, la llama y la vicuña producen lana para el consumo interno y también para la exportación. Los productos agrícolas más importantes son el maíz, el trigo, el arroz, el algodón, las papas, la caña de azúcar, los plátanos, el café y la coca. Los minerales más destacados son el cobre, la plata, el oro, el carbón, el fosfato y el potasio. Entre las industrias que se están desarrollando en los últimos años se encuentran la textil, las conservas, los metales preciosos y la construcción naval.

Antes de la llegada de los españoles, florecieron grandes civilizaciones en el Perú. La más avanzada y mejor conocida fue la de los incas, destruida por Francisco Pizarro en 1533. Su capital era Cuzco, que hoy es el centro arqueológico del país. Cerca de Cuzco se hallan las ruinas de Machu-Picchu, restos de una ciudad sagrada inca, que atrae muchos turistas. Lima, capital del país, es también el centro comercial y cultural. Pizarro la llamó «Ciudad de los Reyes», porque la fundó el 6 de enero, Día de los Reyes Magos. Allí se halla la Universidad de San Marcos, fundada en 1551. El Callao, a trece kilómetros de Lima, le sirve de puerto y es el primer puerto exportador de harina de pescado.

4. **El Ecuador** se llama así por la línea geográfica del mismo nombre que lo atraviesa. En este país se hallan dos volcanes que figuran entre los picos más altos del continente, el Chimborazo (de 6.300 metros) y el Cotopaxi (de 5.940 metros).

El Ecuador es un país agrícola, cuyo producto más importante hoy en día es el plátano, aunque hasta hace unos años el cacao constituía su riqueza principal. Produce también café, arroz, maderas finas, caucho, tagua (o marfil vegetal, que sirve para fabricar botones) y paja toquilla, con la cual se hacen los sombreros de jipijapa que nosotros llamamos

---

39 **sobre el nivel del mar** above sea level

«Panama hats». La pesca y el ganado vacuno y lanar son fuentes de riqueza de las que se han derivado algunas industrias alimenticias. Otras industrias están relacionadas con el petróleo, las maderas finas, el papel y los productos químicos.

Quito, la capital, está a una altura de 2.827 metros, al pie de un volcán. Por su altura tiene un clima bastante frío, a pesar de estar en el centro de la Zona Tórrida. La ciudad ha conservado mucho de su carácter colonial. Guayaquil es el puerto principal y el centro comercial del país.

5. Colombia está limitada al norte por el Mar Caribe, al sur por el Ecuador y el Perú, al oeste por el Pacífico y Panamá, y al este por Venezuela y el Brasil. Esta república, nombrada en honor de Colón, es el único país de la América del Sur que tiene puertos en dos mares, en el Caribe (Cartagena y Barranquilla) y en el Pacífico (Buenaventura). El territorio puede dividirse en tres regiones: la andina al oeste, donde vive la mayoría de la población y donde se encuentran nevados y volcanes de más de 5.400 metros; los llanos orientales y la selva del Amazonas. El país tiene grandes y caudalosos ríos, siendo el más importante el Magdalena, que atraviesa el país de sur a norte y es un importante medio de comunicación. Gracias a la diversidad del clima, hay toda clase de cultivos. Los productos principales de exportación son el café, los plátanos y el petróleo. El país es además rico en carbón, oro, plata, platino y esmeraldas. Entre las industrias más importantes hay que citar las conservas, la

textil, el calzado, los productos químicos, y los metales y piedras preciosas.

Bogotá, la capital, está en el interior y ha sido, desde su fundación en 1538, el centro principal del país. En sus alrededores se encuentra el salto de Tequendama, de 157 metros de alto, mucho más alto que el Niágara, pero menos ancho. Medellín es la segunda ciudad del país y el centro de la producción de café.

6. Venezuela, patria de Bolívar, el Libertador, está situada en el extremo norte de Sudamérica. El país está bañado por las aguas del Mar Caribe al norte y tiene fronteras con Colombia al oeste, con el Brasil al sur y con Guyana al este. La población está concentrada en las zonas montañosas del oeste y en las costas. El Orinoco, río principal de Venezuela, tiene más de 2.400 kilómetros de largo y sus llanos son un centro ganadero importante. El país también produce café y cacao de primera calidad, pero la base de su economía es el petróleo. Venezuela es uno de los mayores productores mundiales. Otros recursos naturales del país son el gas natural, la bauxita, el oro y el hierro. Las industrias principales derivan del petróleo, el acero y el aluminio. Están creciendo las industrias de materiales para la construcción y las de montar vehículos.

Caracas es la capital política y comercial de la nación. Es una ciudad modernísima, con grandes avenidas y hermosos y elegantes edificios públicos y residenciales. La Guaira, a veinticinco kilómetros, le sirve de puerto en el Caribe.

---

24 **el nevado** permanently snow-capped mountain
27 **caudaloso** having great volume of water

EJERCICIO A   Escriba la letra que indique la relación correcta con cada expresión de la columna de la izquierda.

1. Puerto Rico _____

2. Honduras _____

3. Xochimilco _____

4. Costa Rica _____

5. Río Bravo del Norte _____

a. gran teatro mexicano
b. plaza mayor de la Ciudad de México
c. museo histórico
d. Estado Libre Asociado
e. país sin ejército
f. base naval
g. «Perla de las Antillas»

6. Veracruz   _____

7. Nicaragua   _____

8. El Morro   _____

9. El Salvador   _____

10. La Española   _____

11. Santo Domingo   _____

12. Palacio de Bellas Artes   _____

13. Castillo de Chapultepec   _____

14. Cuba   _____

15. Guantánamo   _____

h. jardines flotantes

i. frontera con los Estados Unidos

j. país más grande de Centroamérica

k. puerto del Golfo de México

l. país más montañoso de Centroamérica

m. Haití y la República Dominicana

n. fortaleza del siglo XVI

o. ciudad más antigua de América

p. país más pequeño de Centroamérica

EJERCICIO B   **¿Cierto o falso? Indique si cada frase es cierta o falsa. Si es falsa, cámbiela para hacerla cierta.**

1. México forma parte de la América Central.

_____

2. El Río Bravo del Norte separa a México de Guatemala.

_____

3. Guatemala produce chicle, del cual se hace la goma de mascar.

_____

4. Cuba era llamada Borinquén por los indígenas.

_____

5. La universidad más antigua del Nuevo Mundo está en La Habana.

_____

6. El Zócalo es la plaza mayor de la Ciudad de México.

_____

7. Tampico y Veracruz son puertos mexicanos en el Océano Pacífico.

_____

8. Costa Rica es un país industrial.

_____

9. Guadalajara es la tercera ciudad de México.

_____

10. El Salvador importa mucho café.

_____

| EJERCICIO C | ¿Cierto o falso? Indique si cada frase es cierta o falsa. Si es falsa, cámbiela para que sea cierta. |

1. En la mayor parte de Sudamérica las estaciones caen en orden semejante a las de los Estados Unidos.

_____

2. Casi todos los países de la América del Sur son montañosos.

_____

3. La Cordillera de los Andes está en la parte este del continente.

_____

4. Bolivia y el Paraguay son los dos únicos países hispanoamericanos sin puertos de mar.

_____

5. Las Cataratas del Iguazú están entre la Argentina y el Uruguay.

_____

6. Venezuela es el segundo productor mundial de cobre.

_____

7. El Aconcagua es el pico más alto del hemisferio oriental.

_____

8. El Paraguay es la nación hispana más pequeña de la América del Sur.

_____

9. Punta del Este es una famosa playa de Colombia.

_____

10. El Paraguay se comunica con el Océano Atlántico por medio del Río de la Plata.

_____

| EJERCICIO D | Escriba la letra que corresponde a la capital de cada país. |

1. Honduras _____

2. Guatemala _____

3. Nicaragua _____

4. Puerto Rico _____

5. México _____

6. la República Dominicana _____

7. Costa Rica _____

8. El Salvador _____

a. San José
b. Tampico
c. Ciudad de México
d. Tegucigalpa
e. Ciudad de Panamá
f. Guantánamo
g. La Habana
h. Managua
i. San José
j. San Juan
k. Santo Domingo
l. Ciudad de Guatemala
m. San Salvador

9. Cuba _____

10. Panamá _____

EJERCICIO E   Escriba la letra que indique la relación correcta con cada expresión de la columna de la izquierda.

1. el Uruguay _____		*a.*	guerra entre Bolivia y el Paraguay
2. Quito _____		*b.*	industria ganadera
3. gaucho _____		*c.*	minerales
4. Bogotá _____		*d.*	grandes productores de petróleo
5. México y Venezuela _____		*e.*	capital del Ecuador
6. porteños _____		*f.*	Buenos Aires
7. Río de La Plata _____		*g.*	capital del Paraguay
8. Gran Chaco _____		*h.*	la Banda Oriental
9. la Argentina y el Uruguay _____		*i.*	La Pampa
10. Asunción _____		*j.*	Buenos Aires y Montevideo
		k.	capital de Colombia

EJERCICIO F   Escriba la letra que indique la relación correcta con cada expresión de la columna de la izquierda.

1. Cartagena _____		*a.*	puerto de Caracas
2. Viña del Mar _____		*b.*	desierto chileno
3. Titicaca _____		*c.*	sombreros
4. Machu-Picchu _____		*d.*	Venezuela
5. Bolivia _____		*e.*	puerto colombiano
6. jipijapa _____		*f.*	Chimborazo
7. Atacama _____		*g.*	El Callao
8. La Guaira _____		*h.*	lago navegable más alto del mundo
9. Lima _____		*i.*	estaño
10. Simón Bolívar _____		*j.*	ruinas incaicas
		k.	famosa playa chilena

EJERCICIO G   Escriba la palabra o expresión que complete correctamente cada frase.

1. La antigua capital de los incas fue _____.
   (Cuzco, Lima, Arequipa, La Paz)

2. Valparaíso es el puerto principal de _____.
   (Bolivia, el Ecuador, Chile, el Perú)

3. El país nombrado en honor del Libertador es _____.
   (Chile, el Perú, Venezuela, Bolivia)

4. La capital que Pizarro nombró en honor de un día de fiesta es _____.
   (Quito, Caracas, Bogotá, Lima)

5. La capital de Chile es _____.
   (Viña del Mar, Santiago, El Callao, Barranquilla)

6. El país andino que tiene costas en dos mares es _____.
   (Venezuela, Chile, Colombia, el Ecuador)

7. El Río Orinoco se halla en _____.
   (el Perú, Venezuela, el Ecuador, Bolivia)

8. El país con la capital más alta del mundo es _____.
   (Chile, Bolivia, Colombia, el Ecuador)

9. La yerba mate es un producto importante de _____.
   (Chile, Bolivia, el Perú, el Paraguay)

10. El puerto principal del Ecuador es _____.
    (Guayaquil, Cartagena, La Guaira, Valparaíso)

Civilizaciones indias

Antes de la llegada de los españoles, florecieron varias civilizaciones en el Nuevo Mundo. La más avanzada fue la de **los mayas**, que floreció del
5 siglo III al XVI. Los mayas estaban establecidos en el territorio que hoy comprende la península de Yucatán, Belice, Guatemala y partes de Honduras y El Salvador. La civilización maya logró un desarrollo increíble en la arquitectura, la astronomía
10 y las matemáticas. Hoy en día, en lugares como Chichén-Itzá y Uxmal, podemos admirar las ruinas de sus templos, tumbas, esculturas y murales. Los mayas tenían su calendario y habían logrado calcular con mucha precisión la duración del año
15 solar. Fueron, además, los únicos indios de América que desarrollaron una forma avanzada de escritura. Después de la conquista española, indios educados tradujeron al español muchos de los mitos, historias y leyendas mayas. Esos libros se consideran las
20 primeras manifestaciones de literatura latinoamericana.

Los aztecas desarrollaron su imperio en México durante el siglo XV. Su capital, Tenochtitlán, se encontraba en el lugar que hoy ocupa la
25 Ciudad de México. Los aztecas construyeron ciudades tan grandes como las de la Europa de la época. La religión dominaba todos los aspectos de su vida diaria. Construyeron enormes templos en forma de pirámides, donde celebraban ceremonias reli-
30 giosas que incluían sacrificios humanos. Muchas veces iban a la guerra sólo con el propósito de tomar prisioneros para sus sacrificios. Las esculturas aztecas son muy detalladas, y la más famosa es la gran piedra calendario circular, que representa la
35 superficie del sol.

Los incas desarrollaron un imperio en los Andes, que se extendió desde lo que es hoy el Ecuador hasta el centro de Chile, incluyendo partes de Bolivia y la Argentina. El centro de la
40 civilización estaba en el Perú. Su éxito se debió a su fuerte y estructurado sistema político y social. Además, tenían un ejército muy bien organizado y un sistema de caminos magnífico que comunicaba todos los puntos del imperio con la capital, Cuzco.

Allí construyeron grandes palacios, templos y edi- 45
ficios del gobierno. Tenían un emperador que, según la leyenda, descendía de los dioses. Todas las tierras le pertenecían al estado. Nunca desarrollaron la escritura, pero tenían un sistema especial de escribir y contar: hacían nudos en cuerdas de 50
varios colores y tamaños, formando un «quipu». Indios especializados sabían de memoria el significado de cada quipu. Usaban la llama y la alpaca, que les servían para el transporte y los proveían de carne para la alimentación y lana para la vesti- 55
menta. La lengua de los incas, el quechua, se habla todavía en el Perú y zonas de Bolivia, el Ecuador y el norte de Chile.

Hubo también otras civilizaciones menores: **los caribes,** en las Antillas, eran una tribu gue- 60
rrera que fue prácticamente exterminada por los primeros conquistadores. **Los chibchas** vivían en la región andina de Colombia y eran expertos artesanos; trabajaban muy bien el oro, y muchos de sus productos pueden admirarse hoy día en el 65
Museo del Oro en Bogotá. **Los guaraníes** eran de la región del Paraguay, y su lengua; el guaraní, se habla todavía en ese país casi tanto como el español. **Los araucanos** vivían originalmente en la costa de Chile, pero se fueron hacia la Argentina 70
cuando llegaron los españoles. Son famosos porque lucharon fuertemente contra los españoles y sólo fueron finalmente derrotados en el siglo XIX.

Descubrimiento, exploración y conquista
75

Cristóbal Colón fue el primero de los grandes descubridores y es conocido hoy como «el descubridor de América». Hizo cuatro viajes al Nuevo Mundo, pero nunca llegó a tocar el continente 80
norteamericano. Descubrió varias islas de las Antillas, las costas de América del Sur (cerca del Orinoco) y parte de la América Central. La fecha de su primer descubrimiento (el 12 de octubre) se celebra en todo el mundo hispano como el «Día 85
de la Raza».

---

50 **hacer un nudo** to tie a knot

Colón fundó en 1492 la primera colonia europea en el Nuevo Mundo, el Fuerte de Navidad, en lo que hoy es la isla de Santo Domingo. El siglo siguiente fue una época de conquista, colonización
5   y expansión. Entre los conquistadores más famosos, figuran los siguientes:

Juan Ponce de León, quien estableció una colonia española en Puerto Rico en 1508. En 1513, buscando la Fuente de la Juventud, des-
10   cubrió la Florida.

Vasco Núñez de Balboa, quien atravesó el istmo de Panamá y descubrió el Océano Pacífico en 1513, dándole el nombre de Mar del Sur.

Fernando de Magallanes, un navegante por-
15   tugués que emprendió el primer viaje alrededor del mundo. Fue una empresa heroica, completada por **Juan Sebastián Elcano,** español, al morir Magallanes en las Islas Filipinas.

Hernán Cortés, quien fue, tal vez, el más
20   famoso de los conquistadores. Partió de Cuba hacia el continente en 1518 y llegó en 1519 a la capital del imperio azteca, poniendo fin a la autoridad del emperador Moctezuma. En 1521 logró derrotar definitivamente a los aztecas y fue nombrado
25   gobernador de la Nueva España por Carlos V. Desde México organizó varias expediciones hacia Honduras y California.

Francisco Pizarro, quien acompañó a Balboa en su descubrimiento del Pacífico. En 1531 salió
30   de Panamá hacia el sur y llegó hasta las tierras del imperio inca en 1532. Allí derrotó al último emperador inca, Atahualpa. Fundó la ciudad de Lima en 1535, llamándola «Ciudad de los Reyes».

Francisco Vásquez de Coronado, quien
35   salió de México en busca de las fabulosas «siete ciudades de Cíbola», exploró gran parte de lo que es hoy el sudoeste de los Estados Unidos y descubrió el Gran Cañón.

Álvar Núñez Cabeza de Vaca, quien ex-
40   ploró gran parte de la Florida, Misisipi y el norte de México. Años más tarde fue nombrado gobernador de la provincia de la Plata y exploró la región del Chaco.

Pedro de Valdivia, quien estuvo en el Perú
45   con Pizarro y luego conquistó Chile, luchando contra los araucanos. Fundó la ciudad de Santiago de Chile en 1541 y fue nombrado gobernador de la nueva provincia.

Junto con los conquistadores, llegaron también
50   muchos misioneros al Nuevo Mundo. El más conocido de todos es **Bartolomé de Las Casas.**

Fue llamado el «apóstol de las Indias» o el «protector de los indios» porque, desde su llegada a América en 1502, se dedicó a luchar en favor de los indios. Éstos estaban siendo destruidos por los duros tra-   55
bajos a que eran sometidos y por la crueldad de los conquistadores. Escribió dos obras muy famosas, en las que cuenta la historia y pormenores de la conquista.

En nuestro país es muy conocido **Fray Junípero**   60
Serra, un evangelizador y colonizador del siglo XVIII. Fundó una serie de misiones en California, entre ellas las de San Diego, Los Ángeles y San Francisco.

Administración de las colonias   65

Todas las colonias se consideraban posesiones del rey. En 1509 se creó en España el Consejo de Indias, una organización encargada de dirigir la administración y economía del Nuevo Mundo. Las colonias estaban divididas en cuatro territorios ad-   70
ministrativos, llamados virreinatos: (1) el de Nueva España, que incluía México, Centroamérica, parte de lo que es hoy los Estados Unidos y las Antillas; (2) el del Perú, que incluía el Perú y Chile; (3) el de Nueva Granada, que incluía el Ecuador, Colom-   75
bia, Panamá y Venezuela; y (4) el del Río de la Plata, que incluía la Argentina, Bolivia, el Paraguay, el Uruguay y parte del Brasil. Estos virreinatos estaban gobernados por virreyes, nombrados directamente por el rey español.   80

La intención de la corona española era doble: (1) civilizar a los indios, convirtiéndolos a la religión católica; y (2) explotar las riquezas de las colonias para beneficio único de España.

El período colonial duró más o menos tres si-   85
glos. La población de las colonias estaba dividida en cuatro clases: (1) los españoles, que gobernaban y gozaban de todos los privilegios; (2) los criollos (de origen español, pero nacidos en las colonias), que estaban muy bien económicamente pero no   90
podían gobernar; (3) los mestizos (mezcla de español e indio o negro), que no tenían ni categoría social ni derechos políticos; y (4) los indios y los esclavos negros.

La independencia   95

A principios del siglo XIX, las ideas revolucionarias de la época fueron propagadas por los criollos ricos en las colonias. Además de la injusticia social

---

35   **en busca de** in search of

y política y de las restricciones económicas impuestas por España, tres sucesos históricos influenciaron la rebelión de las colonias: (1) la independencia de los Estados Unidos: (2) el espíritu de la Revolución Francesa; y (3) la invasión de España por las fuerzas de Napoleón.

El más importante de los precursores de la independencia fue el venezolano **Francisco Miranda.** Luchó en la guerra de independencia de los Estados Unidos y en la Revolución Francesa. En 1806 organizó, desde Nueva York, una expedición contra Venezuela que fracasó. Cuatro años más tarde, se unió a Simón Bolívar, a cuyo lado luchó hasta 1812. Fue tomado prisionero por los españoles y murió en una cárcel de Cádiz en 1816.

Tres de las revoluciones en las colonias estallaron en distintas partes en el mismo año, 1810. Los movimientos revolucionarios se pueden dividir en cuatro:

MÉXICO

El padre **Miguel Hidalgo,** cura del pueblo de Dolores (Guanajuato), inició la revolución mexicana el 16 de septiembre de 1810, con el famoso «Grito de Dolores». Al frente de un improvisado ejército de indios, logró varias victorias. Unos meses más tarde, en 1811, fue capturado y fusilado.

José María Morelos, también sacerdote, se unió al movimiento de liberación de Hidalgo. Después de varias batallas, reunió el primer Congreso Nacional Mexicano en 1813. En 1815 cayó prisionero y fue fusilado.

Agustín de Iturbide luchó en un principio al lado de los españoles, pero después se unió a los revolucionarios. En 1821 formuló el famoso Plan de Iguala, que reconocía a México como una monarquía constitucional, independiente de España. En 1822, un movimiento popular lo proclamó emperador, con el nombre de Agustín I. Pero una revolución republicana, encabezada por el general **Santa Ana,** lo obligó a abdicar. Iturbide murió fusilado en 1824, después de haber regresado al país y haber tratado de apoderarse del gobierno. Por la Constitución de 1824, México se constituyó en República Federal.

NUEVA GRANADA
(Norte de Sudamérica)

El venezolano **Simón Bolívar,** llamado el Libertador, es la figura dominante de la independencia de casi toda Sudamérica. Fue a la vez militar brillante, gran estadista, escritor y orador. Comenzó su larga lucha en 1810 y con las victorias de Boyac' (Colombia, 1819), Carabobo (Venezuela, 1821) y

Pichincha (Ecuador, 1822), aseguró la independencia de toda esa región. En 1822 se formó de esos territorios la República de la Gran Colombia, que duró hasta 1829. Bolívar fue su primer presidente. Pero sus sueños de una América unida no se realizaron. Murió enfermo y decepcionado en Santa Marta, Colombia, en 1830.

Antonio José de Sucre, también venezolano, combatió al lado de Miranda. Luego fue el principal lugarteniente de Bolívar. Bajo su mando se ganaron las batallas de Pichincha y Ayacucho, lo que le ganó el título de Gran Mariscal. Fue presidente de la nueva república de Bolivia de 1826 a 1828.

EL PERÚ Y EL RÍO DE LA PLATA
(Sur de Sudamérica)

El argentino **José de San Martín,** el «santo de la espada», hizo para el sur lo que Bolívar hizo para el norte. Declarada la independencia de la Argentina en 1816, San Martin organizó el Ejército de los Andes, con la ayuda del chileno **Bernardo O'Higgins,** para luchar por la independencia de Chile. Derrotaron a los españoles en las batallas de Chacabuco (1817) y Maipú (1818). Ésta última aseguró la independencia del norte y centro del país. En el sur, la lucha continuó hasta 1824. O'Higgins fue el primer presidente de la nueva república de Chile.

En 1820, San Martín emprendió la liberación del Perú. En julio de 1821 entró en Lima. Desde allí envió ayuda a Sucre para la batalla de Pichincha. En 1822, San Martín y Bolívar se entrevistaron en Guayaquil. A raíz de esta conferencia, San Martín entregó el mando militar a Bolívar, y se retiró de la lucha y del gobierno. La libertad del Perú fue asegurada finalmente por Sucre en la batalla de Ayacucho (1824).

CUBA

Durante la época de las grandes revoluciones, Cuba se mantuvo más o menos leal a España. Pero hacia el año 1845, comenzaron varios movimientos de independencia. En 1868, **Carlos Manuel de Céspedes** dio el «Grito de Cuba Libre», que inició una guerra de diez años. Desde entonces hasta 1895, Cuba se preparó para la independencia. **José Martí**, poeta, escritor y patriota cubano, fue el espíritu de ese movimiento. En Nueva York, en 1892, fundó el Partido Revolucionario Cubano, que trató de unificar todas las tendencias revolucionarias, y ordenó el levantamiento contra los españoles. Martí murió en 1895, en una invasión a la isla.

Más adelante, en 1898, a raíz de la guerra entre España y los Estados Unidos, éstos ocuparon Cuba, Puerto Rico y las Filipinas. Cuba se constituyó en república en 1901, pero la Enmienda Platt dio
5   derecho a los Estados Unidos a intervenir en la isla hasta 1934.

Desde la independencia hasta nuestros días

La independencia trajo consigo graves problemas
10 políticos, económicos y sociales, algunos de los cuales todavía existen hoy. Cada país hispanoamericano siguió su curso, y existen grandes diferencias entre ellos. Pero el sistema administrativo, económico y social heredado de los españoles afectó su
15 desarrollo y les dio rasgos comunes.

La historia que siguió a la Independencia está llena de crisis económicas, rebeliones políticas e injusticia social. Durante la primera mitad y parte de la segunda mitad del siglo XX los países no se
20 industrializaron, y muchos dependían de economías basadas en la exportación de un solo producto. Además, la mayoría de los recursos naturales eran explotados por compañías extranjeras, que sólo estaban interesadas en sacar la materia prima.
25 Las tierras estaban en manos de unos pocos terratenientes ricos, y una gran parte del resto de la población vivía en la miseria. La Iglesia Católica y los militares tenían mucho poder político y económico.
30 El primer cambio notable lo trajo la Revolución Mexicana, a partir de 1911. En 1917 se escribió una nueva constitución, que todavía está en vigor. Ésta reconocía los derechos de los trabajadores, reducía la influencia de la Iglesia y se man-
35 tenía fiel a los principios democráticos. Los gobiernos que siguieron organizaron una reforma agraria para darles tierra a los campesinos y nacionalizaron la industria del petróleo. Hacia 1950, México comenzó un programa de desarrollo in-
40 dustrial que sigue constante hasta nuestros días, con crisis económicas más o menos fuertes a lo largo de estos últimos años.

La mayoría de los países hispanoamericanos fueron gobernados por militares o dictadores du-
45 rante muchos años. Esto impidió el desarrollo de una sociedad democrática y libre y retrasó el cre-

cimiento económico e industrial. Por ejemplo, en Guatemala después de 36 años de guerrillas y de una gran variedad de gobiernos militares, se firmó en 1996 un tratado de paz terminando con las
50 guerrillas. En 1992 concluyó en el Salvador una guerra civil que duró 12 años. Fue entonces que se produjeron reformas políticas y militares. En el Uruguay rebeldes y militares estuvieron al mando del país hasta 1985, año en que el poder del pueblo
55 fue restaurado.

En Cuba y Nicaragua hubo revoluciones que trajeron cambios radicales. En ambos países se luchó contra dictaduras corruptas, pero el resultado ha sido otro tipo de gobierno absoluto y otro
60 tipo de problemas. Cuba es el único país del hemisferio occidental que se ha declarado comunista y lo sigue siendo hasta principios de nuestro siglo XXI.

Las guerrillas sandinistas marxistas gobernaron
65 durante los años 80 en Nicaragua hasta que se dieron elecciones libres en 1990.

La República Dominicana tuvo un gobierno dictatorial durante treinta años, que terminó en 1996 con elecciones democráticas. En la Argentina
70 también hubo un período de autoritarismo y el país no se convirtió en democrático hasta 1983. Después de 35 años de un gobierno dictatorial y militar, el Paraguay logró elecciones libres y populares en 1989. Chile no vio su democracia hasta
75 1990 después de un régimen militar dictatorial que duró casi veinte años. Bolivia y Perú ambos alcanzaron un gobierno democrático en 1980 después de varias de luchas militares.

Venezuela goza de una democracia desde 1959
80 con gobiernos más o menos estables. Aunque las guerrillas revolucionarias siguen atacando en Colombia, éstas no tienen la fuerza suficiente para derrotar al actual gobierno democrático. Costa Rica es de los pocos países hispanoamericanos que
85 ha gozado y sigue gozando de un desarrollo democrático estable y es por eso que tiene uno de los más altos niveles de vida de Hispanoamérica. Puerto Rico, al formar parte de los EE.UU., tiene un gobierno popular y una economía industria-
90 lizada y dinámica.

Después de la Segunda Guerra mundial, Hispanoamérica comenzó a ganar importancia en el mundo. Su población creció rápidamente, se encontraron vastos depósitos de petróleo y gas na-
95

---

22 **los recursos naturales** natural resources
24 **la materia prima** raw material
32 **estar en vigor** to be in effect

tural, y los países comenzaron a industrializarse. Internamente, las ciudades crecieron y comenzaron a atraer aún más población. Surgieron nuevos problemas administrativos y sociales. Se tuvo que invertir mucho dinero en transporte, construcción, salud pública y educación. Surgieron también nuevas fuerzas políticas: la mujer ganó el voto, creció la clase obrera, los sindicatos tomaron fuerza y muchos sacerdotes jóvenes comenzaron a criticar abiertamente la injusticia económica y social. Aumentó el comercio con los nuevos países independientes de Asia y África, y los países hispanoamericanos comenzaron a tratar de cooperar entre sí.

Relaciones interamericanas

En 1826 Simón Bolívar dio el primer paso hacia la unidad del hemisferio occidental. Invitó a representantes de todos los países del Nuevo Mundo a reunirse en Panamá. Aunque sólo cuatro naciones enviaron delegados, puede decirse que la Conferencia de Panamá no fue un fracaso. El ideal de Bolívar, de unir las Américas, tuvo sus comienzos allí.

En los años siguientes, el movimiento cobró fuerzas y creció. La Primera Conferencia Internacional de los Estados Americanos tuvo lugar en Washington, D.C. en 1889–1890. El propósito era el de mantener la paz en el hemisferio y mejorar las relaciones comerciales entre los países. En la conferencia de Buenos Aires de 1910, se creó la Unión Panamericana. El propósito de esta organización era el de establecer estrechas relaciones económicas y culturales entre las 21 naciones americanas.

En 1948 tuvo lugar, en Bogotá, la novena Conferencia Panamericana. La alianza fue reorganizada y recibió el nombre de Organización de los Estados Americanos (O.E.A.). La Unión Panamericana sería su secretaría permanente hasta 1970, año en que fue reorganizada bajo el nombre de Secretaría General. La O.E.A. es un organismo regional dentro del cuadro de las Naciones Unidas. Sus objetivos son varios: mantener la paz entre sus miembros, ayudarse mutuamente en caso de agresión y trabajar por el desarrollo cultural, social y económico de los estados miembros.

A principios de este siglo, la política de los Estados Unidos con respecto a Latinoamérica había creado malos sentimientos en esas naciones. Durante la presidencia de Franklin D. Roosevelt, el país trató de mejorar sus relaciones con Latinoamérica, iniciando un nuevo programa económico y político llamado «la Política del Buen Vecino».

En la Segunda Guerra Mundial, muchos países hispanoamericanos mostraron su fe en la democracia y su amistad con los Estados Unidos, declarando la guerra a nuestros enemigos, enviando tropas al frente y proveyendo de materias primas a los Aliados.

En 1961, el presidente John F. Kennedy inició el programa de la Alianza Para el Progreso, a raíz de la Revolución Cubana y su influencia en Hispanoamérica. El propósito de la Alianza Para el Progreso era el de ofrecer ayuda financiera y técnica para mejorar la vivienda, educación y servicios públicos en los países latinoamericanos. Para recibir ayuda, esos países debían iniciar reformas agrarias y cambios en sus sistemas tributarios. El programa no tuvo el éxito esperado y ha sido reemplazado por otros métodos de ayuda económica.

Al comienzo del siglo XXI, la mayoría de los países hispanoamericanos tienen gobiernos democráticos. A pesar del desarrollo comercial, económico e industrial que han experimentado en los últimos años, todos ellos siguen teniendo retos sociales, políticos y económicos por solucionar.

El aumento de la población y del desempleo, los salarios relativamente bajos y el deterioro de las zonas agrícolas debido a fuertes cambios climáticos han obligado a la gente a emigrar al extranjero o las grandes urbes, que se han convertido en ciudades superpobladas. Las condiciones de vida y los servicios son, en muchos casos, precarios. Hay disturbios sociales, criminalidad, contaminación del agua y del aire, y zonas muy pobres y poco accesibles.

La corrupción de ciertas administraciones políticas, los conflictos internos y fronterizos, y los escándalos financieros y bancarios han hecho estancar la economía y han impedido la modernización de sectores públicos y privados. La deuda interna y externa ha aumentado en muchos países al igual que la inflación, devaluando, así pues, la moneda y provocando la salida del capital.

A finales del siglo XX y principios del siglo actual las relaciones interamericanas se han estrechado. Una prueba de ello es el Mercosur, alianza

---

8 **la clase obrera** working class
24 **cobrar fuerzas** to gather strength

68 **el sistema tributario** tax system

de un mercado común entre Brasil, Argentina, Uruguay y Paraguay que surgió en 1991. Se estableció el libre comercio, una unión aduanera y un mercado común de transacciones de servicios, competencias y formas laborales. Además, EE.UU. formó el Tratado de Libre Comercio con México en 1994, con America Central en 2002 y con Chile en 2004. El Tratado de Libre Comercio de EE.UU. con los países andinos está en proceso de negociación. EE.UU. ha respaldado los gobiernos democráticos de Hispanoamérica, la seguridad ciudadana, el crecimiento económico y los mercados libres. El Tratado de Libre Comercio favorece las relaciones comerciales, las inversiones, las condiciones laborales y la integración entre los países, dando en definitiva una mayor estabilidad política y económica.

EJERCICIO A   Escriba la palabra o expresión que complete correctamente cada frase.

1. El primer navegante que dio la vuelta al mundo fue _____.

(Cabeza de Vaca, Elcano, Colón, Balboa)

2. Los indios que no fueron derrotados hasta el siglo XIX fueron los _____.

(incas, caribes, aztecas, araucanos)

3. El rey azteca derrotado por Cortés se llamaba _____.

(Tenochtitlán, Moctezuma, Cabeza de Vaca, Atahualpa)

4. Todas las colonias se consideraban posesiones _____.

(de los indios, del descubridor, del rey, de los dioses)

5. La ciudad de Santiago fue fundada por _____.

(Valdivia, Cabeza de Vaca, Cortés, Colón)

6. El imperio incaico fue conquistado por _____.

(Pizarro, Cortés, Valdivia, Colón)

7. Las colonias españolas eran gobernadas por _____.

(piratas, misioneros, virreyes, reyes indios)

8. Los indios de Centroamérica de cultura más avanzada eran los _____.

(toltecas, aztecas, guaraníes, mayas)

9. La Ciudad de México está hoy donde antes estaba situada la ciudad de _____.

(Tenochtitlán, Chichén-Itzá, Cíbola, Santiago)

10. La Florida fue descubierta por _____.

(Coronado, Ponce de León, Cabeza de Vaca, Balboa)

EJERCICIO B	Escriba la letra que indique la relación correcta con cada expresión de la columna de la izquierda.

1. Ponce de León   _____

2. Fuerte de Navidad   _____

3. Coronado   _____

4. Tenochtitlán   _____

5. Balboa   _____

6. Chichén-Itzá   _____

7. Junípero Serra   _____

8. Bartolomé de las Casas   _____

9. Cuzco   _____

10. Valdivia   _____

a. capital azteca

b. araucanos

c. apóstol de las Indias

d. siete ciudades de Cíbola

e. misiones en California

f. la Florida

g. Mar del Sur

h. ciudad maya

i. Santo Domingo

j. capital incaica

k. rey azteca

EJERCICIO C	Complete correctamente las frases siguientes.

1. En 1910, en Buenos Aires, se creó _____.

2. Después de una entrevista entre San Martín y Bolívar, el mando militar fue entregado a _____.

3. El Plan de Iguala estableció en México una _____.

4. El famoso «Grito de Dolores» fue dado por _____.

5. La libertad del Perú fue asegurada en la batalla de _____.

6. El único país del hemisferio que se ha declarado comunista es _____.

7. El primer paso hacia la unidad del hemisferio fue dado por _____.

8. El precursor más importante de la lucha por la independencia fue _____.

9. Hoy en día la mayoría de los países hispanoamericanos tienen gobiernos más o menos _____.

10. El patriota cubano que fue el espíritu del movimiento de la independencia fue _____.

EJERCICIO D   Escriba la letra que indique la relación correcta con cada expresión de la columna de la izquierda.

1. Bolívar _____
2. Martí _____
3. Unión Panamericana _____
4. San Martín _____
5. Kennedy _____
6. Hidalgo _____
7. Roosevelt _____
8. O'Higgins _____
9. Agustín _____
10. Sucre _____

a. Chile
b. Ayacucho
c. Grito de Dolores
d. el Libertador
e. Cuba
f. santo de la espada
g. O.E.A.
h. Política del Buen Vecino
i. Iturbide
j. la Alianza para el Progreso
k. Boyacá

EJERCICIO E   Complete correctamente las frases siguientes.

1. Cortés fue gobernador de México, cuyo nombre entonces era _____.

2. Los _____ son personas de origen español nacidas en la América Hispana.

3. La gran piedra, calendario circular que representa la superficie del sol fue hecha por los _____.

4. Los incas habían establecido su capital en _____.

5. Fray Junípero Serra estableció _____ en California.

6. Los dos héroes principales de la guerra sudamericana de independencia fueron Bolívar en el norte y _____ en el sur.

7. En tiempos de Cortés, los _____ dominaron la mayor parte de México.

8. La región de Bolivia, la Argentina, el Uruguay y el Paraguay se llamaba el virreinato de _____.

9. Ponce de León, buscando la Fuente de la Juventud, descubrió _____.

10. La gran época de la colonización española fue el siglo _____.

11. Santiago, capital de Chile, fue fundada por _____.

12. En vez de escribir, los incas usaban _____.

13. El primer conquistador que atravesó el istmo de Panamá fue _____.

14. Colón estableció la primera colonia del Nuevo Mundo en la isla de _____.

15. Los indios guerreros de las Antillas se llamaban los _____ .

16. Los araucanos vivieron en el _____ de Sudamérica.

17. Chichén-Itzá fue la ciudad principal de los _____ .

18. Las colonias fueron administradas por el Consejo de _____ .

19. El misionero que luchó más que ningún otro en favor de los indios se llamaba _____ .

20. Uno de los sucesos históricos que influyó en la rebelión de las colonias fue _____ .

21. El Gran Cañón fue descubierto por _____ .

22. En la guerra contra los Estados Unidos, España perdió las Islas Filipinas, Cuba y _____ .

23. El rey inca ejecutado por Pizarro fue _____ .

24. Tres de las revoluciones contra España estallaron en el año de _____ .

25. O'Higgins fue el primer presidente de _____ .

Chapter 36
La Literatura de Hispanoamérica

De los orígenes a la independencia

Hispanoamérica tiene una literatura rica y abundante, cuyos orígenes se encuentran en los llamados cronistas de Indias. Éstos fueron historiadores españoles que vinieron al Nuevo Mundo y registraron los sucesos de la conquista. Uno de los grandes soldados y cronistas de la época fue **Bernal Díaz del Castillo** (1492–1581). Fue compañero de Hernán Cortés y describió la conquista de México en su célebre «Historia verdadera de los sucesos de la conquista de la Nueva España».

Alonso de Ercilla (1533–1594) escribió uno de los mejores ejemplos de poesía épica del Renacimiento. Su famoso poema épico «La araucana» trata de las guerras entre los conquistadores españoles y los indios araucanos de Chile. A pesar del carácter autobiográfico de la obra y de que Ercilla era un soldado español, los héroes del poema son dos caciques araucanos, Caupolicán y Lautaro. El poeta muestra su admiración y simpatía por el valor y el heroísmo de los indígenas. «La araucana» sirvió de modelo para otros poemas épicos de la época y se considera el primer gran poema nacional chileno.

La cumbre de la poesía lírica americana de la época colonial está representada por la poetisa **Sor Juana Inés de la Cruz** (1651–1695). A esta monja mexicana se le llamó «la décima musa» o «el fénix de México». Los temas de sus versos son el pesimismo, la angustia y la vanidad de la vida. En ellos se nota su temperamento apasionado y su gusto por los contrastes y los juegos de conceptos.

José Joaquín Fernández de Lisardi (1776–1827) se distingue como el primer novelista de Hispanoamérica y el escritor más influyente de México en el siglo XIX. Fue conocido con el seudónimo «el Pensador Mexicano», nombre de uno de los siete periódicos que fundó. Su obra maestra, «El periquillo sarniento», es una novela picaresca que describe de manera realista la sociedad mexicana en vísperas de la independencia.

El venezolano **Andrés Bello** (1781–1865) se distinguió como abogado, educador, crítico literario, poeta, ensayista, periodista y filólogo. Pasó muchos años en Inglaterra, donde fundó tres revistas para dar a conocer la cultura de América. Después fue a Chile, donde escribió el «Código civil» del nuevo país y fundó la Universidad de Chile. Es el autor de una gramática que todavía se considera una de las mejores y más completas de la lengua castellana.

Simón Bolívar (1783–1830) representa la cumbre del pensamiento político de la época. Reveló una visión extraordinaria en sus documentos, como en la llamada «Carta de Jamaica», en la que revisa la situación política y social de Hispanoamérica y defiende la formación de una América unificada en una gran federación.

El siglo XIX

El siglo XIX se caracterizó en Hispanoamérica como el siglo de las revoluciones y de la independencia. Estos movimientos políticos se reflejan en la literatura que se produjo.

El argentino **Domingo Faustino Sarmiento** (1811–1888) fue embajador de su país en los Estados Unidos y presidente de la república de 1868 a 1874. Su obra maestra, «Facundo o civilización y barbarie», es un ensayo político y sociológico sobre las causas de la dictadura, el caudillismo y la barbarie de la pampa.

La época trágica de la dictadura de Juan Manuel de Rosas en la Argentina, fue descrita en la novela «Amalia» del escritor y poeta romántico **José Mármol** (1817–1871). Esta obra describe el terror que reinaba en Buenos Aires en la época y pinta vívidamente al tirano y su familia. Se considera la primera novela política de Hispanoamérica.

El mejor representante del costumbrismo hispanoamericano es el peruano **Ricardo Palma** (1833–1919). Creó un género llamado «tradiciones», narraciones con base histórica que mezclan lo real y lo imaginario con humorismo e ironía. Escribió miles de «Tradiciones peruanas» que cubren toda la historia del Perú, desde los incas hasta los primeros años del siglo XX. Tiene mérito también porque incorporó a su español las

---

32 **tener gusto por** to have a liking (an eye) for
42 **en vísperas de** on the eve of

47 **dar a conocer** to introduce
71 **el caudillismo** system of government by a political boss

expresiones y palabras nuevas surgidas en Hispanoamérica.

José Hernández (1834–1886) representa la
llamada poesía gauchesca, un género de poesía que
5 describe tipos y costumbres regionales. Su obra
«Martín Fierro» se considera el poema más famoso
de Hispanoamérica. El héroe de esta obra argentina es un gaucho que canta su propia historia,
describiendo al mismo tiempo todos los personajes
10 que habitan la pampa.

Una de las novelas más populares del siglo XIX
fue escrita por el colombiano **Jorge Isaacs** (1837–
1895). «María» es una obra sumamente sentimental, con descripciones exquisitas del paisaje del
15 valle donde nació su autor.

Florencio Sánchez (1875–1910) se considera
el mejor dramaturgo del siglo XIX. Este uruguayo
estableció las bases para el renacimiento del teatro
realista hispanoamericano del siglo XX. Sus obras
20 presentan la realidad de los problemas humanos
dentro de una sociedad a la que critica fuertemente. Entre ellas está «La gringa», un drama que
trata de los conflictos entre los criollos y los inmi-
grantes.

25 El siglo XIX dio también muchos poetas
románticos de fama internacional, entre los que se
distinguen dos cubanos y un colombiano. **José
María Heredia** (1803–1839) está considerado
como el primer romántico de la lengua española.
30 Su vida fue también un retrato del héroe romántico: tuvo que vivir en el exilio por sus ideas liberales, fue rebelde, sufrió y murió joven, pobre y
tuberculoso. Su poema «Niágara», inspirado en las
cataratas, es su obra más famosa.

35 La cubana **Gertrudis Gómez de Avellaneda**
(1814–1873) está considerada hoy día como una
de las mejores poetisas de la lengua española. Su
poesía está llena de confesiones, y sus temas constantes son el amor, el arte y Dios. Escribió además
40 seis novelas y una docena de tragedias al gusto de
la época.

Rafael Pombo (1833–1912) es el poeta más
completo que ha dado Colombia. Escribió poesía
reflexiva y filosófica y tenía además un talento es-
45 pecial para la poesía popular y la humorística. Es
importante porque enriqueció la literatura infantil
y tradujo al español muchos de los poetas ingleses
y norteamericanos, antiguos y contemporáneos.

Hacia fines del siglo XIX apareció un nuevo
movimiento literario, el Modernismo, en reacción 50
a la falta de originalidad del realismo y al senti-
mentalismo excesivo del romanticismo. El modernismo ponía énfasis en los sentimientos de
todos los hombres, expresados elegantemente a
través de nuevas imágenes. Este movimiento fue 55
más importante en la poesía que en la prosa y
duró hasta bien entrado el siglo XX. Una multitud de poetas, españoles e hispanoamericanos,
que lograron renombre internacional, fueron
modernistas. 60

El cubano **José Martí** (1853–1895), además de
ser uno de los precursores del Modernismo, fue un
hombre de grandes inquietudes morales, metafísi-
cas y políticas, que luchó y murió por la independencia de su país. Vivió en la ciudad de Nueva York 65
desde 1881 hasta el año de su muerte. Durante esa
época escribió sus poemas más famosos, los «Versos
sencillos», de los cuales se tomó la letra para la canción popular «Guantanamera».

Manuel Gutiérrez Nájera (1859–1895), de 70
México, es uno de los mejores representantes de la
transición del Romanticismo al Modernismo.
Escribió poesías y prosa llenas de dulzura y gracia,
cuyos temas son la tristeza, el dolor, la búsqueda de
Dios y el misterio de la vida. Publicó dos colec- 75
ciones importantes de cuentos, «Cuentos de color
de humo» y «Cuentos frágiles».

Rubén Darío (1867–1916), poeta nicara-
güense, fue el padre indiscutible del modernismo y
tuvo gran influencia no sólo en Hispanoamérica, 80
sino también en España. Viajó muchísimo durante
toda su vida, llegando a casi todos los países de
América y de Europa. Sus obras más importantes
son «Cantos de vida y esperanza» y «Prosas pro-
fanas». Ruben Darío fue muy popular entre los los 85
jóvenes de principios del siglo XX.

El ensayista más célebre de Hispanoamérica y
el que más influyó sobre la juventud a principios
de este siglo, fue el uruguayo **José Enrique Rodó**
(1872–1917). En su obra más conocida, «Ariel», un 90
maestro habla con sus estudiantes sobre la necesidad de tener ideales desinteresados, de desarrollar
el sentimiento de lo bello y lo moral y sobre los
peligros de las civilizaciones avanzadas y del espíritu de utilitarismo reflejado por los Estados 95
Unidos.

---

49 **hacia fines de** toward the end of
68 **la letra** lyrics
88 **a principios de** at the beginning of

El siglo XX

LA POESÍA

El auge de la poesía hispanoamericana continuó en el siglo XX, en el que se encuentran poetas y poetisas de fama mundial.

Luis Palés Matos (1893–1959), de Puerto Rico, cultivó la poesía llamada «negra o afroantillana», de profunda raíz popular. En su obra poética ofrece una visión del mundo y el folklore negros, usando metáforas, ritmos y sonidos de gran sensualismo. Su poema más conocido es «Danza negra», en el que centra su atención en la expresión musical negra que tanta influencia ha tenido en el mundo.

El poeta cubano **Nicolás Guillén** (1902–1989) es otro gran representante de la poesía afroantillana. Escribió poemas siguiendo el ritmo sensual del «son», uno de los bailes típicos de Cuba. Pero además su poesía es una protesta de tipo económico-social, presentada como un lamento de las clases oprimidas. Entre sus poemas más famosos están «Sóngoro cosongo», «Tú no sabe inglé», «Velorio de Papá Montero» y «No sé por qué piensas tú».

La obra del poeta peruano **César Vallejo** (1892–1938) no es muy extensa, pero le ganó fama internacional. Tiene como tema básico el sufrimiento del Hombre, tanto en su sentido individual como colectivo, por el solo hecho de haber nacido. Es uno de los poetas más hondos y humanos de la literatura en lengua española. «Poemas humanos» figura entre sus obras más conocidas.

El chileno **Pablo Neruda** (1904–1973) es sin duda el poeta hispanoamericano de más fama en el mundo entero, y no sólo por haber recibido el Premio Nobel de Literatura en 1971. Comenzó a escribir bajo la influencia del Modernismo, pero luego encontró su forma y materia propias. Neruda, seudónimo de Ricardo Neftalí Reyes, recorrió el mundo entero como diplomático de su país. Sus colecciones de poesías más importantes han sido traducidas a más de treinta idiomas. Éstas incluyen «Odas elementales», «Veinte poemas de amor y una canción desesperada», «Residencia en la tierra» y «El canto general».

El poeta y ensayista mexicano **Octavio Paz** (1914–1998) fue diplomático de su país en la India, estudió un tiempo en los Estados Unidos y ha vivido en Suiza y Francia. Su poesía muestra esa combinación de filosofía oriental, cultura occidental y mexicanidad que la hace universal. Sus temas constantes son la soledad, la falta de comunicación entre los hombres y la búsqueda del ser. Sus ensayos principales son «El laberinto de la soledad» y «El arco y la lira», y entre sus colecciones de poesías se encuentran «Libertad bajo palabra» y «Viento entero». Ganó el Premio Nobel de Literatura de 1990.

La mujer se ha destacado como escritora en la obra poética hispanoamericana. Quizás la más conocida de las poetisas es la chilena **Gabriela Mistral** (1889–1957), quien ganó el Premio Nobel de Literatura en 1945. Fue maestra durante casi veinte años y luego siguió trabajando por la educación como representante diplomática de su país. Los últimos años de su vida los pasó de consulesa en Nueva York. Su obra más importante es una colección de poesías que se titula «Desolación», que refleja su humanismo, su sensibilidad y su ternura.

La argentina **Alfonsina Storni** (1892–1938) fue lo que hoy llamaríamos una feminista. Era una mujer de ideas liberales, que luchó contra los prejuicios sociales por más libertad para la mujer. Su obra poética trata de la condición de la mujer y de lo que significa ser mujer en un mundo masculino. Ésta incluye «La inquietud del rosal», «El dulce daño», «Ocre» y «Mundo de siete pozos».

Julia de Burgos (1916–1953), de Puerto Rico, escribió una poesía amorosa muy intensa y llena de dolor, como «Canción de la verdad sencilla». Pero también escribió una poesía nacionalista en la que recuerda momentos dramáticos para América, como «23 de septiembre» e «Himno de sangre a Trujillo».

El amor romántico, representado en un tono menos exaltado, más coqueto e íntimo, se presenta en la obra poética de la uruguaya **Juana de Ibarbourou** (1895–1979). Esta poetisa ha sido llamada «Juana de América» desde 1929, a raíz de un homenaje ofrecido por su país, en el que participaron escritores y poetas hispanoamericanos famosos. Sus poemas más conocidos incluyen «Las lenguas de diamante», y «Raíz salvaje», «La rosa de los vientos» y «Perdida».

---

3 **el auge** period of prosperity
29 **por el solo hecho de** for the only reason that, just because
40 **recorrer el mundo** to travel around the world

EL TEATRO

El teatro hispanoamericano comenzó a surgir realmente después de la Segunda Guerra Mundial. Anteriormente era un teatro regional, interesado en los problemas políticos, económicos y sociales de un lugar determinado. La nueva generación ha tratado de crear un teatro de intereses más universales.

Uno de los más distinguidos dramaturgos fue el mexicano **Rodolfo Usigli** (1905–1979). Su teatro hace un análisis crítico de la idiosincrasia nacional mexicana. Sus obras más famosas son «El gesticulador» y «Corona de sombra».

Carlos Solórzano (1922–   ), guatemalteco-mexicano, es uno de los autores y críticos que más han contribuido a la renovación del teatro hispanoamericano. Entre sus obras figuran «La muerte hizo la luz», «Doña Beatriz», «Las manos de Dios», «El hechicero» y «Los fantoches».

Sebastián Salazar Bondy (1924–1965) fue un dramaturgo peruano en cuyas obras se manifiestan sus dotes de observador, su facilidad para manejar complejidades psicológicas y su dominio del lenguaje popular. Entre sus obras principales están «Algo quiere morir», «El fabricante de deudas», «Todo queda en casa» y «No hay isla feliz».

Emilio Carballido (1925–   ), el dramaturgo mexicano más conocido de su generación, es autor de más de setenta y cinco obras dramáticas. Dos tendencias fundamentales en su obra dramática son la realista y la fantástica. Sus dramas incluyen «El día en que se soltaron los leones», «La zona intermedia», «La danza que sueña la tortuga» y «Te juro Juana, que tengo ganas».

El chileno **Egon Wolff** (1926–2003) es un dramaturgo que muestra su conocimiento del teatro por la construcción y desenvolvimiento de sus temas. Entre sus obras más destacadas se encuentran "Los invasores", "Alamos en la azotea", "Flores de papel", y "Mi mamá me mima."

Osvaldo Dragún (1929–1999) ha logrado crear obras de sabor muy argentino, combinando temas trascendentales con un ambiente cotidiano. Entre sus dramas más importantes figuran «Historias para ser contadas», «Jardín del infierno» y «Y nos dijeron que éramos inmortales».

Jorge Díaz (1930–   ) nació en la Argentina, pero es ciudadano chileno. Es el dramaturgo hispanoamericano que más se ha relacionado con el teatro del absurdo. En sus últimas obras, sin embargo, se nota una tendencia hacia un teatro más comprometido política y socialmente. «El cepillo de dientes» se considera una de las mejores obras humorísticas del repertorio hispanoamericano. Sus otras obras incluyen «Requiem para un girasol» y «Topografía de un desnudo».

LA NARRATIVA

La literatura narrativa hispanoamericana del siglo XX tiene representantes con renombre internacional. Los autores contemporáneos van más allá de la preocupación por problemas políticos y sociales regionales y han logrado una dimensión universal. La novela, en especial, tuvo un gran resurgimiento a partir de los años cincuenta.

Mariano Azuela (1873–1952) es un novelista mexicano que describe las luchas sangrientas de la Revolución Mexicana. Su obra más famosa, «Los de abajo», fue escrita mientras el autor le servía de médico al ejército de Pancho Villa en 1915.

Horacio Quiroga (1878–1937), del Uruguay, debe su puesto en la literatura a sus excelentes cuentos cortos, los mejores de los cuales tratan de temas de horror, crueldad y muerte. Sus colecciones más conocidas son «Los desterrados», «Más allá» y «Cuentos de amor, de locura y de muerte».

Hugo Wast (1883–1962) es el seudónimo de Gustavo Martínez Zuviría, uno de los novelistas argentinos más populares y más traducidos. Escribió sobre los problemas sociales y económicos de la gente de las ciudades y los pueblos de la Argentina de su época. Entre sus novelas más conocidas están «Flor de durazno», «La casa de los cuervos» y «Desierto de piedra».

Rómulo Gallegos (1884–1969) vivió muchos años en el exilio por sus ideas políticas y fue, por muy corto tiempo, presidente de su patria, Venezuela. Se le considera el mejor novelista de su país. Su obra más célebre, «Doña Bárbara», describe la vida de los llaneros venezolanos, llevando a la vez el mensaje que la tiranía no es indestructible.

El mejor novelista de la literatura gauchesca fue el argentino **Ricardo Güiraldes** (1886–1927). En su novela «Don Segundo Sombra», describió con gran realismo la vida y las costumbres de los gauchos.

Martín Luis Guzmán (1887–1976) fue coronel del ejército de Pancho Villa y describió sus memorias de la Revolución Mexicana en su obra «El águila y la serpiente»; estos animales forman

---

60 **ir más allá de** to go beyond
64 **a partir de** from (some specified time)

el símbolo que aparece en la bandera mexicana. Vivió muchos años exilado en la ciudad de Nueva York.

El colombiano **José Eustasio Rivera** (1889–1928) escribió «La vorágine», considerada la novela por excelencia sobre la selva tropical. Es una novela de aventuras y de crítica social, que describe muy vívidamente la vida trágica de los caucheros en la selva del Amazonas.

El escritor argentino **Jorge Luis Borges** (1899–1986) es conocido mundialmente como poeta, cuentista y ensayista. Sus obras reflejan su conocimiento profundo de la expresión verbal, su habilidad analítica, su gran cultura universal, su maravillosa imaginación creadora y su experiencia de lo regional argentino. Entre sus colecciones de cuentos figuran «Ficciones», «El aleph» e «Historia universal de la infamia». Su ensayo más conocido es «Historia de la eternidad», en el que trata del tema del paso del tiempo que angustia a los hombres. En 1955 se quedó ciego y desde entonces tuvo que dictar sus escritos.

Las obras del guatemalteco **Miguel Ángel Asturias** (1899–1974) mezclan el misticismo de la cultura maya con la crítica político-social. Los diálogos de sus novelas reflejan la lengua popular hablada por el pueblo centroamericano. Su trilogía de novelas «Viento fuerte», «El Papa verde» y «Los ojos de los enterrados», describe la explotación de los indios por las grandes compañías yanquis en las zonas bananeras. Recibió el Premio Nobel de Literatura de 1967 por novelas como «El señor presidente» y «Hombres de maíz».

El ecuatoriano **Jorge Icaza** (1906–1978) expuso la explotación del indio en su novela «Huasipungo». Ésta logró fama universal y ha sido traducida a catorce idiomas. Su obra literaria incluye otras novelas, comedias y libros de cuentos. En lenguaje muy directo y realista, presenta tipos básicos de su país y la lucha entre los pobres y sus opresores.

El peruano **Ciro Alegría** (1909–1967), como Icaza, se considera representante de la llamada novela indigenista. Describió los problemas de la vida de los indios de su país en su novela «El mundo es ancho y ajeno», considerada como su obra maestra.

Pocos narradores hispanoamericanos han gozado de tanto prestigio internacional como el cubano **Alejo Carpentier** (1904–1980). Fue autor de la primera historia de la música afro-cubana y de la primera novela afro-cubana, «Ecue-Yamba-O». Pero además escribió otras novelas llenas de encanto y de magia, en las que muestra sus grandes conocimientos de la música, el folklore, la historia y la antropología, ampliando su concepto de «lo maravilloso americano». Entre sus novelas más conocidas y traducidas están «El acoso», «El reino de este mundo» y «El siglo de las luces».

Ernesto Sábato (1911–   ), ensayista y novelista argentino, debe su éxito internacional a dos novelas de tipo metafísico, «El túnel» y «Sobre héroes y tumbas». Ambas tocan cuestiones fundamentales que angustian al hombre contemporáneo. También ha escrito sobre el sentido de la actividad literaria. Entre sus obras más recientes está una recopilación de sus «Ensayos».

Las novelas y cuentos del argentino **Julio Cortázar** (1914–1984) revelan una intensa preocupación por la relación entre la realidad y la fantasía y por la condición absurda del hombre moderno. Entre sus obras más conocidas está «Rayuela», una novela cuya estructura fragmentada refleja la incoherencia de la vida y de la cultura contemporáneas.

La obra literaria del mexicano **Juan Rulfo** (1918–1986) presenta una voz y una visión tan profundas de su país, que ya forma parte de la herencia de la literatura hispanoamericana. Es conocido por una colección de sus cuentos más célebres, «El llano en llamas», y por su novela «Pedro Páramo», en la que todos los personajes son fantasmas de un pasado cercano pero olvidado. Jugando con el espacio y el tiempo, utilizando imágenes muy intensas y un lenguaje muy directo, Rulfo logra comunicar la aterradora experiencia del sufrimiento, el dolor, el hambre, la muerte y la lucha del hombre contra un medio estéril.

El chileno **José Donoso** (1924–1996) es otro escritor que ha contribuido a la renovación de la novela hispanoamericana con sus obras «Este domingo», «El lugar sin límites» y «El obsceno pájaro de la noche». En ellas presenta una visión intensa y crítica de la burguesía de su país. De hecho, sus obras exploran las diferentes clases sociales y reflejan, en particular, la decadencia de la clase social más alta de su país. Su narrativa es profunda y clara.

---

6   **por excelencia** preeminently, par excellence
8   **el cauchero** worker in a rubber plantation, person who searches for rubber trees

El escritor colombiano **Gabriel García Márquez** (1928–   ) recibió el Premio Nobel de Literatura de 1982. Entre sus obras más conocidas se hallan «Los funerales de la Mamá Grande», que es una colección de cuentos, «La hojarasca» y «El coronel no tiene quien le escriba». Su novela más célebre es «Cien años de soledad», en la que conviven lo real con lo imaginario. Esta obra se sitúa en un pueblo imaginario llamado Macondo, que representa la realidad de muchos pueblos hispanoamericanos. Sus personajes centrales aparecen en otras obras del autor y llegan a cobrar vida propia. Otras de sus obras más conocidas son «Crónica de una muerte anunciada», «El amor en los tiempos del cólera», «El general en su laberinto» y «Vivir para contarla».

Un autor mexicano de mucho renombre internacional es **Carlos Fuentes** (1929–   ). Sus obras utilizan técnicas del cine y del realismo mágico: alegorías, mitos, monólogos interiores y fragmentación del tiempo lógico. Entre las más conocidas están «La muerte de Artemio Cruz», «Cambio de piel» y «La cabeza de la hidra». A finales del siglo XX recibió importantes premios literarios entre los que cabe mencionar el Premio Cervantes y el Premio Príncipe de Asturias. Sus obras más recientes son «Los años con Laura Díaz», «Instinto de Inés» y «La silla del águila».

Guillermo Cabrera Infante (1929–2005) fue un escritor cubano que vivió en el exilio en Inglaterra desde 1966, y está considerado como uno de los grandes innovadores de la novela. Una de sus obras más conocidas, «Tres tristes tigres», se ha llevado varios premios literarios internacionales. Otra de sus obras importantes es «La Habana para un infante difunto», que es autobiográfica.

El novelista argentino **Manuel Puig** (1932–1990) es otro escritor conocido internacionalmente, cuyos libros han sido traducidos a la mayoría de los idiomas modernos. Sus novelas más importantes son «Boquitas pintadas», «La traición de Rita Hayworth» y «El beso de la mujer araña». Esta última estuvo prohibida por muchos años en la Argentina; de ella se filmó una película, co-producción internacional, que tuvo mucho éxito.

El novelista peruano que ha logrado mayor fama internacional es **Mario Vargas Llosa** (1936–   ). Muestra preocupación social y humana en todas sus obras, tratando de representar la violencia y la lucha por la vida en distintos niveles sociales de su país. Entre sus novelas más famosas están «La ciudad y los perros», «La casa verde», «Conversación en la catedral» y «La guerra del fin del mundo».

Vargas Llosa ha recibido numerosos premios a lo largo de su carrera literaria. Tiene ciudadanía española desde 1993 y es actualmente miembro de la Real Academia Española. Escribió sus memorias en la novela "El pez en el agua."

Isabel Allende (1942–   ) es chilena afincada en los Estados Unidos. Aunque fue periodista de profesión, es ahora la novelista latinoamericana más leída en el mundo. Sus novelas han sido traducidas a más de 25 lenguas y a menudo encabezan las listas de best-sellers. Su narrativa, fantástica y entretenida, cuenta de una manera profunda y minuciosa historias de familias y las relaciones entre los seres humanos. Entre sus novelas hay que destacar «La casa de los espíritus», «Eva Luna»,«Cuentos de Eva Luna», «El plan infinito», «Paula», «Afrodita: Cuentos, recetas y otros afrodisíacos» y «La hija de la fortuna».

Rigoberta Menchú (1959–   ) es guatemalteca y recibió el Premio Nobel de la Paz en 1992. Pertenece al grupo étnico maya-quiché. Su libro «Me llamo Rigoberta Menchú», del género testimonial y autobiográfico, fue traducido a más de 12 idiomas y relata las atrocidades que el pueblo maya sufrió durante los gobiernos militares de los años 80. Otro libro suyo es «Rigoberta: la nieta de los mayas.» Éste fue escrito con la colaboración del escritor guatemalteco Dante Liano y el periodista italiano Gianni Miná.

Augusto Monterroso (1921–2003) es de familia guatemalteca pero nació en Honduras. Es probablemente el cuentista guatemalteco más famoso del siglo XX y uno de los más reconocidos mundialmente. Ha recibido numerosos premios a lo largo de su carrera literaria. Entre sus obras más conocidas se encuentran «Lo demás es silencio», «Los buscadores de oro», «La oveja negra y demás fábulas» y «La palabra mágica».

---

12 **cobrar vida propia** to acquire a life of its own

EJERCICIO A | Escriba la letra que indique la relación correcta con cada expresión de la columna de la izquierda.

1. Sor Juana Inés de la Cruz _____
2. Bernal Díaz del Castillo _____
3. «Carta de Jamaica» _____
4. Ricardo Güiraldes _____
5. «El cepillo de dientes» _____
6. Ciro Alegría _____
7. «Cuentos de color de humo» _____
8. «Tradiciones peruanas» _____
9. Gabriel García Márquez _____
10. «El Aleph» _____

a. Ricardo Palma
b. la «décima musa»
c. la conquista de México
d. Manuel Gutiérrez Nájera
e. Jorge Luis Borges
f. «La vorágine»
g. «Cien años de soledad»
h. «Don Segundo Sombra»
i. «El mundo es ancho y ajeno»
j. Jorge Díaz
k. «Los de abajo»
l. Bolívar

EJERCICIO B | Complete cada una de las frases siguientes, escribiendo el título de la obra o el nombre del autor.

1. El gran poema épico de los gauchos es _____.
2. «El beso de la mujer araña» fue escrita por _____.
3. «Doña Bárbara» fue escrita por _____.
4. El erudito venezolano que escribió una gramática famosa fue _____.
5. «Facundo», un estudio sobre los gauchos, fue escrito por _____.
6. La novela que describe la vida de los caucheros en la selva es _____.
7. Rodó escribió un libro de ensayos llamado _____.
8. «Ficciones» es una colección de cuentos de _____.
9. «Cantos de vida y esperanza» es una importante colección de poesías de _____.
10. Juan Rulfo es conocido por dos obras tituladas _____.
11. «Tres tristes tigres» es una novela de _____.
12. Macondo es el pueblo donde se sitúa la acción de _____.
13. Dos de las novelas famosas de Vargas Llosa son _____.
14. La novela cuya estructura fragmentada refleja la incoherencia de la vida, se titula _____.

15. «Cambio de piel» fue escrita por _____.

EJERCICIO C   **¿Cierto o falso? Indique si cada frase es cierta o falsa. Si es falsa, cámbiela para que sea cierta.**

1. «El Pensador Mexicano» es el seudónimo de Bernal Díaz del Castillo.

_____

2. «La araucana» es un poema lírico.

_____

3. Andrés Bello es el autor de una gramática de la lengua castellana.

_____

4. La obra «Facundo» trata de los gauchos y la barbarie de la pampa.

_____

5. «Amalia» es una novela que se sitúa durante la dictadura de Trujillo en Santo Domingo.

_____

6. Una novela que describe la vida de los caucheros en la selva del Amazonas es «Martín Fierro».

_____

7. El Modernismo fue un movimiento literario de reacción contra el Clasicismo.

_____

8. José Martí se distinguió por ser el padre del Modernismo.

_____

9. La canción «Guantanamera» se basa en la obra poética «Cantos de vida y esperanza» de Rubén Darío.

_____

10. Dos novelistas mexicanos que describen las luchas sangrientas de la Revolución de 1910 son Mariano Azuela y Martín Luis Guzmán.

_____

11. Uno de los mejores cuentistas de Hispanoamérica fue César Vallejo.

_____

12. La vida de los llaneros venezolanos fue descrita en una novela de Ricardo Güiraldes.

_____

13. «El mundo es ancho y ajeno» es una novela en la que se describen los problemas de los indios de México.

_____

14. El escritor que expuso la explotación de los indios en las zonas bananeras fue Jorge Luis Borges.

_____

15. García Márquez, Asturias, Neruda y Gabriela Mistral ganaron el Premio Nobel de Literatura.

_____

16. «Pedro Páramo» es una novela que critica la burguesía de Chile.

_____

17. Dos poetas que tratan temas afro-antillanos en su poesía son Luis Palés Matos y Octavio Paz.

_____

18. La poetisa hispanoamericana ganadora de un premio prestigioso fue Alfonsina Storni.

_____

19. El primer romántico de la lengua española fue Rafael Pombo.

_____

20. Egon Wolff es el dramaturgo que más se ha relacionado con el teatro del absurdo.

_____

EJERCICIO D **Subraye la expresión que mejor complete cada una de las frases siguientes.**

1. El padre del modernismo fue

(a) Hugo Wast (b) Martín Luis Guzmán (c) Alonso de Ercilla (d) Rubén Darío

2. El primer novelista de Hispanoamérica fue

(a) José Mármol (b) Jorge Isaacs (c) Fernández de Lisardi (d) Florencio Sánchez

3. Una obra que trata de la conquista de Chile es

(a) «El periquillo sarniento» (b) «Cantos de vida y esperanza»

(c) «La araucana» (d) «Cuentos de color de humo»

4. Bernal Díaz del Castillo escribió acerca de la conquista de

(a) Cuba (b) México (c) la Argentina (d) el Perú

5. La «décima musa» fue

(a) Sor Juana Inés de la Cruz (b) Gertrudis Gómez de Avellaneda

(c) Gabriela Mistral (d) Juana de Ibarbourou

6. Un dramaturgo importante de la América del Sur fue

(a) Rafael Pombo (b) José Enrique Rodó

(c) Florencio Sánchez (d) Manuel Gutiérrez Nájera

7. Las «Tradiciones peruanas» fueron escritas por

(a) Ricardo Palma (b) José Eustasio Rivera (c) Ciro Alegría (d) Horacio Quiroga

8. Domingo Faustino Sarmiento

(a) fue presidente de la Argentina (b) murió por la independencia de Cuba

(c) escribió novelas sobre la revolución mexicana (d) nació en Nicaragua

9. Uno de los mejores cuentistas de Hispanoamérica fue

(a) Pablo Neruda   (b) Gutiérrez Nájera   (c) Alonso de Ercilla   (d) Horacio Quiroga

10. Rómulo Gallegos, además de ser novelista, fue presidente de

(a) México   (b) Colombia   (c) Venezuela   (d) la Argentina

11. La poetisa que recibió el honor de ser llamada «de América» fue

(a) Gabriela Mistral   (b) Alfonsina Storni   (c) Juana de Ibarbourou   (d) Julia de Burgos

12. El poeta chileno que recibió el Premio Nobel de Literatura fue

(a) Pablo Neruda   (b) Gabriel García Márquez

(c) Miguel Ángel Asturias   (d) Juan Ramón Jiménez

13. En las novelas de José Donoso el lector ve

(a) la explotación de los indios   (b) a la burguesía chilena

(c) los horrores de una guerra   (d) una caricatura del gran capitalista yanqui

14. La poetisa que luchó contra prejuicios sociales por la libertad de la mujer fue

(a) Gabriela Mistral   (b) Julia de Burgos   (c) Juana de Ibarbourou   (d) Alfonsina Storni

15. El dramaturgo mexicano más conocido de su generación fue

(a) Carlos Solórzano   (b) Rodolfo Usigli   (c) Emilio Carballido   (d) Osvaldo Dragún

Chapter 37
El Arte y la Música de Hispanoamérica

El arte

Cuando llegaron los conquistadores a Hispanoamérica, a principios del siglo XV, encontraron un arte muy rico desarrollado por los indios. El arte
5 precolombino, es decir, el arte de antes de la llegada de Cristóbal Colón, representa el desarrollo increíble de las culturas indígenas en la arquitectura, la escultura, los murales y la joyería. Hicieron esculturas para sus pirámides y construyeron pala-
10 cios, templos y edificios de gobierno, decorados con figuras de sus dioses. Elaboraron los metales preciosos como el oro y la plata y usaron piedras preciosas para adornar su joyería. Produjeron objetos de barro y de cerámica, que servían tanto de
15 adorno y decoración como para el uso diario.

Hoy en día se pueden ver las ruinas de las pirámides, los templos y demás estructuras al visitar lugares como Chichén-Itzá y Uxmal (México, los mayas), la ciudad de México (los aztecas) y Cuzco
20 y Machu Picchu (el Perú, los incas). También se exhibe el arte precolombino en los museos de muchos países, entre ellos el Museo de Antropología de la Ciudad de México, el Museo Arqueológico y el Museo del Oro de Lima y el Museo del Oro de
25 Bogotá. Éste último tiene la colección más grande del mundo de objetos de oro precolombinos.

Los españoles trajeron al Nuevo Mundo el estilo de arte que estaba de moda en el siglo XVI. Éste era de tipo religioso, por lo general, y sirvió
30 para la conversión de los indios al catolicismo. Tanto la pintura como la arquitectura que se desarrollaron en Hispanoamérica se parecían mucho a las de España. Por eso se ven ejemplos de la arquitectura románica, gótica, neoclásica y barroca o
35 churrigueresca en las catedrales, las iglesias y los edificios que se construyeron en los países hispanoamericanos. Hoy día a este estilo se le llama «estilo colonial»; es decir, del estilo de la época en que el país era colonia de España. Las ciudades de
40 Taxco y Guanajuato en México, Lima en el Perú y Cartagena en Colombia, entre otras, son ricos ejemplos del arte que floreció en Hispanoamérica durante la época colonial.

No fue sino hasta el siglo XX que Hispano-
45 américa produjo pintores de renombre internacional. Muchos de ellos representaron en su obra sus raíces indígenas y lo histórico, político y social de su país. Fueron los pintores y muralistas mexicanos los que empezaron a rechazar la dominación
50 cultural europea y utilizaron la pintura como instrumento de protesta social, cultivando sus rasgos característicos.

El más conocido de los pintores mexicanos es **Diego Rivera** (1886–1957). En la primera parte
55 de su vida pintó bajo la influencia del Cubismo y Postimpresionismo europeos. Hacia los años veinte comenzó a desarrollar su estilo vigoroso y se dedicó a la pintura mural, en la cual representó temas políticos y sociales. Sus murales adornan muchos
60 edificios públicos por toda la república de México; el más gigantesco de todos es una historia épica del país que adorna el Palacio Nacional de la Ciudad de México.

El muralista mexicano **José Clemente Orozco**
65 (1883–1949) defendió la causa de la Revolución Mexicana y muchos de sus cuadros representan escenas de esa revolución. Pintó además los frescos del Palacio de Bellas Artes de la Ciudad de México. Durante los varios años que vivió en los
70 Estados Unidos, pintó una serie de frescos importantes en Dartmouth College.

El mexicano **David Alfaro Siqueiros** (1896–1974) ha sido el defensor más prominente del arte como expresión de ideología política en la se-
75 gunda mitad del siglo XX. Estuvo preso muchas veces por sus ideas políticas. En sus cuadros y murales llenos de colores vivos, el realismo está mezclado con lo fantástico, y las figuras muestran sus emociones con gran fuerza. En 1932 Siqueiros or-
80 ganizó el Taller Experimental de la Ciudad de Nueva York, en el que estudiaron pintores como Jackson Pollock.

Carlos Mérida (1891–1984), pintor guatemalteco de tendencias abstractas que supo plasmar con orgullo y gran musicalidad sus raíces indígenas.
85 **Rufino Tamayo** (1899–1991) fue un pintor mexicano de gran renombre. Sus cuadros, algunos

---

16 **hoy (en) día** nowadays
28 **estar de moda** to be in fashion

74 **la segunda mitad** the second half
75 **estar preso** to be imprisoned

452

de ellos semi-abstractos, han captado en colores vivos las alegrías y tragedias de su país. Ganó varios premios internacionales de pintura, y sus murales adornan lugares como el Palacio Nacional de Bellas Artes y el Museo de Antropología de la Ciudad de México y el edificio de la UNESCO en París.

Miguel Covarrubias (1904–1957), también de México, fue famoso tanto en su país como en los Estados Unidos como pintor de caricaturas de personas célebres. Ilustró muchos libros y revistas que muestran su interés por el estudio de diversos tipos raciales.

Frida Khalo (1907–1954) pintora mexicana y tercera esposa de Diego Rivera. La pasión y el inconformismo la llevaron a plasmar una realidad llena de sufrimiento y de constante transformación.

Lo pintoresco de la vida de los gauchos ha sido representado en los cuadros del pintor impresionista argentino **Cesáreo Bernaldo de Quirós** (1879–1969). Sus numerosos cuadros constituyen un recuerdo importante de la vida de la pampa.

El pintor peruano **José Sabogal** (1888–1956) representó en sus cuadros la cultura indígena de su país. Vio el porvenir de su patria en la civilización de los mestizos.

Wifredo Lam (1902–1982) fue un pintor cubano influido por el surrealismo. En su obra se ven elementos imaginarios y fantasmagóricos de los sueños junto con elementos afro-cubanos. Uno de sus cuadros más famosos, «La jungla», está en la entrada del Museo de Arte Moderno de la ciudad de Nueva York.

En las últimas décadas han surgido varios pintores hispanoamericanos que poco a poco han logrado renombre, cuyos cuadros han sido exhibidos y adquiridos por galerías y museos en los Estados Unidos y en Europa. Entre ellos pueden mencionarse el argentino **Emilio Pettoruti** (1892–1971), pintor cúbista; el chileno **Roberto Matta** (1911–2002), de tendencia abstracta y surrealista; el ecuatoriano **Oswaldo Guayasamín** (1919–1999), de tendencia cubista; el colombiano **Alejandro Obregón** (1920–1992), de tendencia abstracta; **Rómulo Macció** (1931-   ), pintor vanguardista argentino; el colombiano **Fernando Botero** (1932–   ) de tendencia expresionista figurativa; y el surrealista peruano **Gerardo Chávez** (1937–   ).

La música

Gran parte de la música hispanoamericana está basada en temas folklóricos e indígenas, y hay mucha variedad en la música tradicional y popular de los diversos países y de las diferentes regiones dentro de un país. En la región del Caribe (Puerto Rico, Cuba, la República Dominicana y las costas de Colombia y Venezuela), la música es por lo general alegre, con influencia de ritmos africanos. Por el contrario, las canciones indígenas de los Andes, como el yaraví, son casi siempre lentas y tristes. Entre estos dos extremos hay una enorme variedad de ritmos, por ejemplo el corrido mexicano, descendiente directo de los romances españoles; el candombe uruguayo, ritmo de sus carnavales; el joropo venezolano, música de los llaneros; los valses peruanos, ecuatorianos y argentinos, de descendencia europea; las canciones guaraníes del Paraguay y el tango argentino. En este siglo además ha surgido una nueva versión del jazz norteamericano, llamada jazz afro-cubano, donde se han incorporado ritmos e instrumentos de la música afro-cubana.

Otros ritmos musicales que han pegado y siguen pegando en toda Hipanoamérica en los últimos años son: el son cubano, el jazz latino, la salsa y el merengue, los boleros, la música pop y el rock.

Instrumentos musicales

La guitarra española es también muy popular en Hispanoamérica, pero además hay otros instrumentos musicales importantes que han sido heredados de las culturas indígenas o adaptados de otros traídos por los españoles o por los negros de África. Ejemplos de estos instrumentos son el cuatro (una especie de guitarra con sólo cuatro cuerdas), la marimba (un instrumento parecido al xilófono), el bongó (un tambor de origen africano), el güiro (hecho de un fruto seco parecido a la calabaza y que se toca con un palito), la quena (una flauta heredada de los incas), las maracas (calabazas secas con piedrecitas o granos de maíz adentro) y las claves (dos palitos de madera dura que se usan para marcar el ritmo). Músicas folklóricas tan diversas como la del Estado de Veracruz en México, y la de los guaraníes del Paraguay, usan versiones del arpa europea moderna del siglo XVI.

---

58 **por el contrario** on the contrary

El baile

Los bailes tradicionales de Hispanoamérica son tan ricos y variados como su música y en muchos casos forman una unidad íntima con ella. Así, mu-
5 chos de los ritmos mencionados en la sección de la música, como el corrido, el tango, el joropo, el merengue y la salsa son también bailes. Están además, entre muchos otros, el bambuco colombiano, la zamacueca (o cueca) chilena, la milonga
10 argentina y uruguaya, la plena puertorriqueña y el jarabe tapatío mexicano. Hoy en día, gracias a los esfuerzos de varios grupos folklóricos que se han formado en muchos países, como el Ballet Folklórico de México, estas tradiciones se han estudiado
15 más a fondo para conservarlas. El repertorio de estas compañías artísticas, que incluye danzas nacionales y regionales de diversos orígenes, ha sobrepasado las fronteras hispanoamericanas y es conocido en otros países del mundo.
20   Dentro del área de la música bailable popular, ritmos como la conga, la rumba, el mambo y el chachachá cubanos, la guaracha y la salsa puertorriqueñas y cubanas, el merengue y la bachata dominicanos y la cumbia y el ballenato colombianos.
25 Muchos de ellos tienen su origen en bailes folklóricos.

Compositores, cantantes e instrumentistas

En el área de la música clásica hay dos composi-
30 tores hispanoamericanos conocidos internacionalmente. **Carlos Chávez** (1899–1978), mexicano, fue también un famoso director de orquesta y fundó la Orquesta Sinfónica de México y la Sinfónica Nacional. Su música mezcla elementos
35 de ritmos indígenas con las técnicas de la música moderna. Un ciclo de conferencias que dictó en la Universidad de Harvard, fue publicado bajo el título «Pensamiento musical». Entre sus obras más famosas están el ballet «El fuego nuevo» y la
40 «Sinfonía india».

Alberto Ginastera (1916–1983), argentino, fue compositor moderno de óperas, ballets, sinfonías y conciertos, en los que utilizó elementos musicales regionales y nacionales. Dos de sus obras
45 más conocidas son la ópera «Bomarzo» y la «Cantata para América mágica».

En el área de la música más popular hay por lo menos cuatro nombres importantes. El mexicano

Manuel Ponce (1882–1948) inició el movi-
50 miento nacionalista de la música de su país, cultivando temas nativos. Compuso numerosas obras para orquesta como «Balada mexicana» y «Chapultepec», pero su fama se debe a canciones de inmensa popularidad como «Estrellita». El com-
55 positor y director de orquesta cubano **Gonzalo Roig** (1890–1972) fue autor de muchas zarzuelas, la más conocida de las cuales es «Cecilia Valdés», y de popularísimas canciones como «Quiéreme mucho». **Ernesto Lecuona** (1896–1963), cubano,
60 compuso la «Rapsodia negra» para piano y orquesta, y canciones muy famosas como «Siboney» y «Malagueña». El mexicano **Agustín Lara** (1897–1970) debe su fama a canciones tan conocidas como «María Bonita» y «Granada»; ésta última
65 ha sido favorita en el repertorio de tenores de habla hispana.

De Hispanoamérica también han salido varios cantantes e instrumentistas que han ganado fama en el extranjero. Entre ellos están el tenor de ópera chileno **Ramón Vinay**, el barítono puerto-
70 rriqueño **Justino Díaz,** la gran cantante peruana **Yma Sumac,** el cantante y compositor argentino **Atahualpa Yupanqui,** y el famoso pianista chileno **Claudio Arrau,** intérprete de música clásica.

En los últimos años la música popular hispana
75 ha alcanzado mucha fama, no sólo en Hispanoamérica sino en el mundo entero. Por ejemplo, Latinoamérica ha dado importantes cantantes de boleros o música melódica y romántica. Entre ellos hay que mencionar al venezolano **José Luis**
80 **Rodríguez (El Puma)**, los mexicanos **Marco Antonio Muñiz** y **Luis Miguel** y los cubanos **Oswaldo Farrés**, **Antonio Machín**, **La Lupe**, **Celia Cruz** y **Gloria Estefan**. Además, la música pop latina actual la encabezan los cantantes puer-
85 torriqueños **Ricky Martin** y **Jennifer López**, la colombiana **Shakira** y los puertorriqueños **Chayanne** y **Marc Anthony**. El jazz latino lo forman, entre otros, los puertorriqueños **Ray Barreto** y **Eddie Palmieri**. El son cubano está representado
90 por el grupo *Buena Vista Social Club* formado por **Ibrahim Ferrer**, **Compay Segundo** y **Eliades Ochoa**, el grupo *La Vieja Trova Santiaguera* y el cantante **Pablo Milanés**.

Entre los cantantes de salsa más populares hay
95 que citar a **Rubén Blades**, **Los Van Van** y **Manolín y el Médico de la Salsa**. **Juan Luis Guerra** y **Johnny Ventura**, ambos dominicanos, son los cantantes de merengue y bachata más

---

15 **más a fondo** more thoroughly   69 **en el extranjero** abroad

conocidos internacionalmente. La rumba y el ballenato colombianos son cantados por figuras como **Carlos Vives** y **Amparo Sandino**. El rock latino, encabezado por los mexicanos, lo representan el grupo *Maná* y el guitarrista **Carlos Santana**.

Tres actores mexicanos que lograron gran exito en películas norteamericanas y dentro de su propio país fueron **Pedro Armendáriz, Dolores del Río** y el cómico **Cantinflas,** seudónimo de **Mario Moreno**.

| EJERCICIO A | Escriba la letra que indique la relación correcta con cada expresión de la columna de la izquierda. |

1. Rufino Tamayo _____

2. Bernaldo de Quirós _____

3. marimba _____

4. Manuel Ponce _____

5. Covarrubias _____

6. Pedro Armendáriz _____

7. Agustín Lara _____

8. Siqueiros _____

9. Carlos Chávez _____

10. Sabogal _____

a. «Estrellita»

b. «Sinfonía india»

c. películas norteamericanas

d. Granada

e. pintor peruano

f. pintor mexicano semi-abstracto

g. caricaturas

h. xilofón

i. gauchos

j. canción mexicana

k. pintura mural de ideología política

| EJERCICIO B | ¿Cierto o falso? Indique si cada frase es cierta o falsa. Si es falsa, cámbiela para que sea cierta. |

1. Los indígenas de Hispanoamérica no dejaron ninguna huella de su civilización.

_____

2. El arte precolombino se refiere al arte después de la llegada de Cristóbal Colón.

_____

3. Las pirámides y los templos de los indígenas muestran su increíble desarrollo en la arquitectura.

_____

4. El arte de Hispanoamérica en la época colonial se parecía al arte de España.

_____

5. Acapulco es un rico ejemplo del arte colonial.

_____

6. En el siglo XIX, Hispanoamérica produjo pintores de fama mundial.

_____

7. Diego Rivera se dedicó a la pintura mural.

_____

8. Rivera, Orozco y Siqueiros representan problemas políticos y sociales en su obra artística.

_____

9. Covarrubias vio el porvenir de su patria en la civilización de los mestizos.

_____

10. Cesáreo Bernaldo de Quirós pintó escenas de la lucha por la independencia de Venezuela.

_____

11. Antonio Machín y Celia Cruz fueron dos importantes cantantes de rock.

_____

12. El iniciador del movimiento nacionalista de la música mexicana fue Agustín Lara.

_____

13. Las composiciones musicales «Siboney» y «Malagueña» se deben a Carlos Chávez.

_____

14. Claudio Arrau fue un famoso tenor chileno.

_____

15. Frida Kahlo fue una famosa actriz mexicana.

_____

16. Dolores del Río era conocida en Norteamérica por sus bellas pinturas.

_____

17. El güiro y las maracas son instrumentos musicales hechos de madera.

_____

18. Un instrumento que produce sonidos melancólicos es la marimba.

_____

19. El jarabe tapatío es un baile regional de México.

_____

20. La cueca es un baile típico cubano.

_____

EJERCICIO C   **Subraye la palabra o expresión que complete correctamente cada frase.**

1. El tango es un baile   (a) argentino   (b) venezolano   (c) chileno   (d) mexicano

2. Un famoso cantante mexicano es   (a) Carlos Vives   (b) Ibrahim Ferrer   (c) Marc Anthony (d) Luis Miguel

3. Claudio Arrau fue un (a) compositor cubano (b) pianista chileno (c) actor mexicano (d) pintor cubano

4. (a) La guitarra (b) La quena (c) El güiro (d) El yaraví es una flauta incaica.

5. Un famoso muralista mexicano fue (a) Ernesto Lecuona (b) José Sabogal (c) Pedro Armendáriz (d) Diego Rivera

6. «Siboney» es una obra musical de (a) Agustín Lara (b) Carlos Chávez (c) Manuel Ponce (d) Ernesto Lecuona

7. Cartagena es (a) un mural famoso (b) una ciudad colonial (c) una canción mexicana (d) una cantante de ópera

8. La zamacueca y el joropo son (a) composiciones musicales clásicas (b) canciones revolucionarias (c) danzas indígenas (d) bailes típicos

9. Un famoso compositor argentino fue (a) Alberto Ginastera (b) Claudio Arrau (c) Miguel Covarrubias (d) José Sabogal

10. Un famoso pintor mexicano fue (a) Bernaldo de Quirós (b) José Clemente Orozco (c) Ramón Vinay (d) Wifredo Lam

EJERCICIO D Complete correctamente cada frase.

1. Un baile típico de Puerto Rico es _____.

2. _____ fue un famoso cantante chileno de ópera.

3. El _____ es una canción triste de los Andes.

4. El _____ es un baile típico de México.

5. _____ pintó los murales del Palacio Nacional de México.

6. _____ es un instrumento muy popular en todo el mundo hispano.

7. _____, músico cubano, compuso «Malagueña».

8. _____ son dos palitos que se emplean para marcar el ritmo.

9. _____, del Perú, fue una de las mejores cantantes del mundo.

10. _____, pintor peruano, describió en sus cuadros la cultura indígena de su país.

11. _____, cantante puertorriqueña, interpreta canciones de la última onda.

12. _____ se parece mucho al xilófono.

13. _____ son calabazas secas con granos de maíz adentro.

14. _____ se usa en la música folklórica de Veracruz y el Paraguay.

15. _____ fue una actriz mexicana de fama internacional.

Chapter 38

Costumbres Hispanoamericanas

Las costumbres y tradiciones hispanoamericanas reflejan la influencia española e indígena sobre todo, y en ciertos lugares también la influencia negra (especialmente en la música y los bailes).

Días de fiesta

5 La religión católica ha tenido un papel muy importante en la historia y en la vida diaria. Por eso muchas fiestas religiosas se han convertido en fiestas nacionales. Hay unas que son celebradas en to10 dos los países y otras que son típicas de cada país. Las Navidades, por ejemplo, se celebran de una forma u otra en todas partes. En México empiezan con las «posadas», que consisten en visitas a los vecinos durante los nueve días anteriores a la Noche15 buena. En la fiesta que sigue a las posadas, la gente baila alrededor de una piñata (una olla de barro vivamente decorada, que contiene dulces y regalos). Después rompen la piñata y cogen los dulces. En otros países se celebra más al estilo español, con 20 misas (especialmente la Misa de Gallo), aguinaldos y una gran cena.

Otras fiestas religiosas católicas como la Semana Santa y el Día de Todos los Santos (el primero de noviembre) se celebran en casi todos los países.

25 Por supuesto que el primero de enero es un día de fiesta. La noche anterior en muchos pueblos la gente sale a bailar por las calles. Hay grupos que llevan muñecos con figuras de viejos para enterrarlos, enterrando así el año viejo.

30 En todos los países hay ferias o carnavales que son más o menos famosos. Durante varios días hay música, bailes y desfiles de comparsas, ya sea en las calles o en salones de fiesta. En países donde aún existe la tradición (por ejemplo, México y 35 Colombia), hay también corridas de toros.

Cada país tiene su fiesta nacional, o Día de la Independencia, que conmemora la fecha en que logró finalmente la independencia de España. Por ejemplo, en México es el 16 de septiembre; en 40 Guatemala, Honduras, El Salvador, Nicaragua y Costa Rica es el 15 de septiembre; en Chile es el 18 de septiembre; en el Paraguay es el 14 de mayo; en Venezuela es el 5 de julio; en Colombia es el 20 de julio; en el Perú es el 28 de julio; en Bolivia es el 6 de agosto; en el Ecuador es el 10 de agosto; y 45 en Panamá es el 3 de noviembre.

En otros países se celebra como fiesta nacional el Día de la Independencia pero no de España, sino de otras invasiones. Así pues, en la República Dominicana se celebra el 27 de febrero, fecha de la 50 independencia de Haití; en el Uruguay es el 25 de agosto, fecha de la independencia de Brasil; en Cuba se celebran tres fiestas nacionales: el 10 de diciembre, fecha de la independencia española, el 20 de mayo, fecha de la independencia de EE.UU. 55 y el 26 de julio, el Día de la Revolución. En Puerto Rico hay dos fiestas nacionales, el 4 de julio, que es el día en que se celebra la Independencia de EE.UU. y el 25 de julio, Día de la Constitución. En Argentina sólo se celebra una 60 fiesta nacional que es el 25 de mayo, Día de la Revolución, contra los españoles.

Luego hay dos días que se celebran en toda Hispanoamérica: el primero de mayo, que es el Día del Trabajo, y el 12 de octubre, llamado el Día de la 65 Raza, que conmemora el descubrimiento de América.

Comidas y bebidas

En general, las comidas representan una mezcla de lo español y lo indígena, y sus ingredientes princi70 pales son el maíz, el frijol, el plátano, la carne y la papa (hay lugares en los Andes donde existen más de 30 variedades de papas).

Casi todos los países tienen su versión del tamal, y en muchos ésta cambia según la región. 75 Básicamente es una masa de maíz fresco molido o de harina de maíz que se cuece al vapor dentro de una hoja de maíz o de plátano. Puede rellenarse con pollo, cerdo carne de res, legumbres, garbanzos, etc. 80

---

2 **sobre todo** above all, especially

14 **anteriores a** preceding

22 **Semana Santa** Holy Week (week preceding Easter Sunday)

32 **el desfile de comparsas** masquerade parade

77 **cocer al vapor** to steam

Los frijoles (llamados habichuelas en varios países) se comen en diversos platos típicos. Los frijoles negros son muy populares en el Caribe y en Venezuela. Preparados con arroz, se llaman en Cuba «moros y cristianos». Los frijoles pintos o colorados se preparan refritos en México, y en potajes con jamón o carne y papas en otros países.

De las harinas del maíz y de la yuca se hacen diversas tortas y pasteles que reemplazan al pan en muchas comidas: tortillas en México, arepas en Colombia, Venezuela y la República Dominicana, cazabe en Cuba.

La empanada (una especie de pastel relleno con carne o pescado y otros ingredientes) es de origen gallego, pero se transformó en el Nuevo Mundo y tomó aspecto diferente en cada país. No es lo mismo la empanada argentina que la chilena, o la cubana que la panameña o la colombiana, aunque todas tienen el mismo nombre.

En la Argentina y en el Uruguay un churrasco es una combinación de carnes y órganos de la vaca que se adoban y se asan a las brasas.

En nuestro país son más conocidas las comidas del norte de México, como las enchiladas (tortillas enrolladas, rellenas de carne, pollo o queso y cubiertas de salsa), los tacos y el chile con carne. La forma de preparar estas comidas también varía de Tejas a California o Nuevo México.

Las bebidas alcohólicas más populares de Hispanoamérica son el ron, que se produce en los países del Caribe y el norte de Sudamérica; el tequila, que se destila del maguey en México; y el aguardiente obtenido de la destilación de la caña de azúcar.

En ciertos países como la Argentina, el Paraguay y Bolivia, se toma mate, una especie de té que se prepara de la yerba mate. Típicamente se toma en una calabaza por medio de un tubito llamado bombilla.

En Hispanoamérica se preparan también muchos jugos de frutas tropicales y se toma café (solo o mezclado con leche hervida) y chocolate (mucho más espeso que en nuestro país).

Tipos tradicionales

En varias regiones de Hispanoamérica se ven aún tipos tradicionales. En los grandes llanos donde se cría ganado y el medio de transporte principal es el caballo, se encuentran los vaqueros. Se llaman llaneros en Venezuela y Colombia y gauchos en la Argentina y el Uruguay.

El charro, vestido con su traje tradicional, es el jinete típico mexicano. La muchacha que lo acompaña se llama china poblana. Su vestido típico consiste en una falda ancha y larga de color rojo o verde y una blusa blanca (los colores de la bandera mexicana).

Los mariachis son grupos de músicos y cantantes callejeros que tocan la música mariachi de Jalisco, estado del oeste de México.

Trajes típicos

Uno de los artículos de vestido más típicos de Hispanoamérica es una especie de capa con abertura en el centro (para meter la cabeza), de la cual existen muchas variedades regionales. Se llama poncho en el centro y sur de Sudamérica y ruana en el norte.

El sarape es una especie de manta de colores vivos, hecha de lana o de algodón, que lleva el mexicano en los hombros.

La mayoría de los trajes femeninos consisten en blusas blancas y faldas largas y anchas de diversos colores, con franjas o cintas alrededor. De calzado usan alpargatas (especie de sandalia de tela gruesa y suela de soga que trajeron los españoles) y, en México, huaraches (también una especie de sandalia).

El sombrero más típico es una versión del sombrero de jipijapa, hecho a mano.

Unidad monetaria

La unidad monetaria de Argentina, Colombia, Cuba, Chile, la República Dominicana, México y el Uruguay se llama el peso. Sin embargo, los pesos de esos países no tienen el mismo valor. Así pues hablamos del peso argentino, el peso colombiano, el peso cubano, el peso chileno, el peso dominicano, el peso mexicano y el peso uruguayo. En los otros países circulan las monedas siguientes: en Bolivia, el boliviano; en Costa Rica, el colon; en Guatemala, el quetzal; en Honduras, el lempira; en Nicaragua, el córdoba; en Panamá, el balboa y el dólar norteamericano; en el Paraguay, el guaraní; en el Perú, el nuevo sol; en Venezuela, el bolívar; y Puerto Rico, el Salvador y el Ecuador tienen hoy el dólar norteamericano.

---

75 **sombrero de jipijapa** straw hat (Panama hat)
76 **hecho a mano** hand made

EJERCICIO A	Escriba la letra que indique la relación correcta con cada expresión de la columna de la izquierda.

1. lempira _____
2. las posadas _____
3. el 16 de septiembre _____
4. yerba mate _____
5. china poblana _____
6. 12 de octubre _____
7. enchilada _____
8. piñata _____
9. jipijapa _____
10. mariachi _____

a. sombrero
b. tortilla
c. Día de la Raza
d. Día de la Independencia de México
e. unidad monetaria
f. sarape
g. olla llena de dulces
h. té
i. charro
j. Navidad
k. cantante

EJERCICIO B	¿Cierto o falso? Indique si cada frase es cierta o falsa. Si es falsa, cámbiela para que sea cierta.

1. En México se celebran las posadas durante los ocho días anteriores a la Navidad.

2. Los gauchos son de los llanos de Venezuela y Colombia.

3. El tequila es una bebida intoxicante.

4. El Día del Trabajo se celebra el primero de abril.

5. Los mariachis son músicos mexicanos.

6. Los huaraches se llevan en las manos.

7. El aguardiente es una especie de té hecho de yerba.

8. La china poblana es la compañera del llanero.

9. Los gauchos viven en la pampa argentina.

10. El peso es la unidad monetaria de la Argentina.

_____

11. El 16 de septiembre es el Día de la Independencia de Venezuela.

_____

12. La unidad monetaria de Colombia es el bolívar.

_____

13. El Día de la Raza se celebra el dos de octubre.

_____

14. El maíz es un ingrediente básico de la comida hispanoamericana.

_____

15. El sarape es una manta usada por los bolivianos.

_____

EJERCICIO C	**En cada grupo, subraye la palabra que se relacione más directamente con el país.**

1. Venezuela: charro, bolívar, gaucho

2. el Perú: lempira, peso, nuevo sol

3. México: tacos, yerba mate, gaucho

4. Guatemala: mariachi, balboa, quetzal

5. la Argentina: gaucho, jipijapa, sarape

6. Honduras: guaraní, taco, lempira

7. México: china poblana, lempira, colón

8. el Paraguay: tamal, yerba mate, tequila

9. Bolivia: bolívar, córdoba, boliviano

10. Costa Rica: mariachi, llanero, colón

EJERCICIO D	**Identifique cada palabra, clasificándola como bebida, comida, moneda, tipo o traje.**

1. churrasco _____

2. empanada _____

3. mate _____

4. llanero _____

5. poncho _____

6. tequila _____

7. gaucho _____

8. nuevo sol _____

9. enchilada _____

10. charro _____

11. guaraní _____

12. tamal _____

13. balboa _____

14. lempira _____

15. huarache _____

Part Seven

Comprehensive Testing:
Speaking, Listening, Reading, Writing

MÉXICO

REPÚBLICA
DOMINICANA
PUERTO RICO
CUBA
HONDURAS
NICARAGUA
GUATEMALA
EL SALVADOR
COSTA RICA
PANAMÁ
VENEZUELA
COLOMBIA
ECUADOR
PERÚ
BOLIVIA
PARAGUAY
CHILE
URUGUAY
ARGENTINA

ESPAÑA
Islas Baleares
Islas Canarias

RATING AND SCORING FOR THE SPEAKING SECTION

Rating and Scoring: The rating procedures described below provide for a maximum of ten credits for the performance of each task. Each utterance is worth a maximum of two points and is rated on the basis of comprehensibility, appropriateness, and the characteristics listed in column 1 below. An utterance is any spoken statement that helps to accomplish the stated task.

Comprehensibility is determined by considering whether the utterance would be understood by a literate native speaker of Spanish who knows no English but is used to speaking with non-native speakers.

Appropriateness is determined on the basis of the utterance's contribution to the completion of the task to be performed.

2 POINTS	1 POINT	0 POINTS

Utterance is
• comprehensible
and
• appropriate
and
• strongly characterized by the following:
  • initiates and/or sustains and/or advances the conversation
  • uses common verb tense forms including past, present, and future
  • uses accurate structure
  • is articulated comprehensibly
  • uses a variety of vocabulary which may expand or clarify meaning
  • is extended discourse (may contain more than one short discrete utterance)
  • uses culturally correct gestures, social conventions and/or idiomatic expressions
	Utterance is
	• comprehensible
	and
	• appropriate
	but
	• a single, short, discrete utterance consisting of limited vocabulary/ structures
	   —or—
	• contains little or no evidence of the characteristics listed in column 1
		Utterance is
		• incomprehensible
		and/or
		• inappropriate
		
		Disregard if it is a
		• Yes/No response
		• Socializing device
		• Restatement of all or essential parts of what the teacher said
		• Proper noun(s) in isolation

[1] SPEAKING: ORAL INTERPERSONAL COMMUNICATION TASKS

Directions: The speaking test consists of communication tasks to be performed by a student with his/her teacher. Each task is a simulated conversation in which the student always plays the role of himself/herself and the teacher assumes the specific role indicated in the task. The tasks may involve one or more of the four communication functions: socializing, providing and obtaining information, expressing personal feelings or opinions, and getting others to adopt a course of action.

You will perform a total of two tasks. Each task consists of a brief statement in English to indicate the purpose and setting of the communication, the role of the teacher, and the person who is to initiate the conversation. Each task should be completed in six interactions between the student and the teacher. These interactions are called utterances.

[2] LISTENING COMPREHENSION

a. Questions in English

Directions: For each question, you will hear some background information in English once. Then you will hear a passage in Spanish twice and a question in English once. After you have heard the question, the teacher will pause while you read the question and the four suggested responses. Choose the best suggested answer and circle its letter. Base your answer on the content of the passage only.

1. What is being sold in the flea market?

   a. Well-known paintings by Picasso.

   b. Soap that is artfully wrapped.

   c. Items that make expensive gifts.

   d. Special detergents for colored clothing.

2. What does this advertisement suggest?

   a. The importance of consolidating one's debt.

   b. The need for lower interest rates on loans.

   c. Buying stocks while the market is solid.

   d. Saving money with certificates of deposit.

3. How did this young man learn his trade?

   a. He went to a special school.

   b. He bought a mechanic's shop.

   c. He was trained in the army.

   d. His friends taught him in one day.

4. What is the cause of this problem?

   a. Excessive traffic on this highway.

   b. Repairs being made to the bridges.

   c. Malfunctioning of the traffic signals.

   d. A strike by the bridge workers.

5. What will take place at the Unihotel?

    a.   A school reunion.

    b.   A fashion show.

    c.   A children's show.

    d.   A pep rally.

b. **Questions in Spanish**

Directions: For each question, you will hear some background information in English once. Then you will hear a passage in Spanish twice and a question in Spanish once. After you have heard the question, the teacher will pause while you read the question and the four suggested responses. Choose the best suggested answer and circle its letter. Base your answer on the content of the passage only.

1. ¿Quiénes deben aprovecharse de este anuncio?

    a.   Los que coleccionan pintura europea.

    b.   Los que pintan al estilo español.

    c.   Los que quieren vender arte de siglos pasados.

    d.   Los que conocen el arte de siglos pasados.

2. ¿Para quiénes es esta fiesta?

    a.   Para los deportistas.

    b.   Para los estudiantes del colegio.

    c.   Para los maestros del colegio.

    d.   Para los niños de los profesores del colegio.

3. ¿Qué ha causado esta preocupación?

    a.   La escasez de pollo en los mercados.

    b.   El precio elevado del pollo.

    c.   Un informe erróneo del Ministerio de Economía.

    d.   La falta de interés en el pollo como alimento.

4. ¿De qué se queja esta persona?

    a.   De las promesas no cumplidas de los candidatos.

    b.   De las aspiraciones de los candidatos.

    c.   De los candidatos hispanos que no se expresan bien.

    d.   De los candidatos que no representan al público hispano.

5. ¿Qué explica este anuncio?

    a.   Los servicios públicos han sufrido.

    b.   La policía interrumpió las llamadas telefónicas.

    c.   Lima tiene líneas de teléfono.

    d.   Hay ciertas partes del país sin servicio de teléfonos.

6. ¿Cuál es el propósito de esta exhibición?

  a. Enseñar maneras de conservar energía y ahorrar dinero.

  b. Vender nuevos aparatos eléctricos.

  c. Aumentar el consumo de la electricidad.

  d   Ahorrar trabajo en el Centro de Conservación.

7. ¿Qué desea hacer el Banco Nacional?

  a. Limitar los préstamos que pueden pedir los clientes.

  b. Ofrecer servicios más amplios a sus clientes.

  c. Disminuir los intereses que deben pagar los clientes.

  d. Vender carros de último modelo a los clientes.

8. ¿Qué pasa durante el recorrido de este tren?

  a. Ponen una película en el tren.

  b. Los viajeros pueden dejarse llevar por su imaginación.

  c. Se descubren sucesos misteriosos.

  d. Se viaja por el oriente.

9. ¿Cómo son estos sellos?

  a. Todos tienen una escena navideña tradicional.

  b. Sacan el mismo sello año tras año.

  c. Captan las figuras navideñas más populares.

  d. Hay una gran variedad de dibujos y de temas.

10. ¿Por qué llamó la madre al número indicado en el folleto?

  a. A su hijo le era difícil completar el rompecabezas.

  b. Faltaban piezas del rompecabezas.

  c. Quería oír una voz electrónica.

  d. Su hijo se sentía muy frustrado.

[3] READING COMPREHENSION

a. Directions: After each of the following passages there are five questions or incomplete statements. For each, choose the word or expression that best answers the question or completes the statement according to the meaning of the passage and circle its number.

1. Dicen que la necesidad es la madre de la invención. El refrán tiene algo de verdad pero el hecho de inventar es también producto de la naturaleza inquisitiva del ser humano y el deseo eterno de crear una trampa para ratones mejor.

  Los parques de atracciones son lugares en que se nota ese deseo de superar y sobrepasar las maneras de entretenimiento tradicionales tanto para los jóvenes como para los mayores. Entre las famosas atracciones que se encuentran en estos parques es la montaña rusa. Esta invención se basa en la ingeniosa creación de la joven emperatriz Catalina La Grande de Rusia. Para liberarse del aburrimiento y aprovechar el efecto deslizador del hielo en las tierras congeladas rusas, ella se metía en un cajón de madera y se descolgaba por la ladera de una montaña a gran velocidad.

La montaña rusa, como la llamamos hoy en día, consiste en un trencito que corre por unos carriles de subidas y bajadas que parece de lo más inofensivo, pero al ponerlo en marcha dan ganas a los pasajeros en los trencitos de levantarse y salir corriendo. Los avances de la tecnología y el afán de los inventores han provocado que descubran modos más atrevidos de divertir y asustar a las personas a la vez. Los pasajeros toman asiento en los trencitos y al bajar las barras de seguridad los pasajeros quedan herméticamente embarcados. Al mismo tiempo se oye una voz por altoparlante explicando unas reglas básicas de seguridad y una advertencia en tono grave que esto no es apto para cardíacos.

Ya es demasiado tarde. No hay remedio ni tiempo de llorar. Los pasajeros están por comenzar los dos minutos y medio más intensos que el parque pueda ofrecerles en materia de atracciones mecánicas.

El trencito se pone en marcha despacio . . . muy despacio comienza su ascenso a una altura de 25 metros. Y sin poder parpadear se siente una caída rápida y repetina que verdaderamente inspira el temor y el vértigo mientras les saca el aire de los pulmones a los pasajeros. Se siente que el trencito empieza a descolgarse en caída libre, a la buena gana de la gravedad, con una velocidad promedio de 90 kilómetros por ahora. Se ladea y vibra como bestia que pide pista para entrar a un primer giro de 360 grados, donde todos quedan de cabeza, los hombres cierran los ojos, las mujeres gritan, los valientes sudan y ni siquiera el más intrépido se atreve a soltarse de las manos porque en seguida viene la otra vuelta, más brava que la anterior, dando la impresión de que todos quedarán colgando. El aparato sigue su marcha y sus pasajeros sienten que han sobrevivido después de ver el mundo al revés. ¡Qué sensación! ¡Qué maravilla! ¡Qué terror! Y cuando el trencito se para y los pasajeros salen y pisan la tierra de nuevo, unos quieren volver a repetir la sensación porque creen que han dejado su alma en alguna de las caídas repetinas del aparato y deben recuperarla.

1. (a) Según la selección, ¿cuál es el propósito de los parques de atracciones?

1. Inspirar la creación de nuevas invenciones.
2. Proveer actividades de entretenimiento menos tradicionales.
3. Atraer a los menos valientes en sus momentos de ocio.
4. Ofrecer diversiones educativas al público.

(b) La invención de la montaña rusa se debe a

1. un dibujo sofisticado de la emperatriz Catalina La Grande.
2. una improvisación de una joven hace muchos años.
3. la imaginación de unos científicos rusos.
4. la necesidad de entretener al público.

(c) Antes de empezar su recorrido el público recibe

1. un chaleco de salvavidas.
2. consejos para no ofender a los otros pasajeros.
3. una explicación de la ruta del trencito.
4. instrucciones para proteger su seguridad.

(d) ¿Qué les asombra más a los pasajeros?

   1. La marcha lenta con que empieza su ascenso.

   2. Estar en posición cabeza abajo.

   3. La corta duración de la atracción.

   4. Tener que callarse durante el recorrido.

(e) ¿Por qué unos pasajeros vuelven a subir en el aparato?

   1. Quieren sobrepasar el nivel de terror que sintieron la primera vez.

   2. Tienen necesidad de comprobar lo intrépido que son.

   3. Desean recobrar algo que creen que perdieron la primera vez.

   4. Necesitan hacerlo para reponer el equilibrio.

2. «¿Qué quieres ser cuando seas grande?» No hay niño ni niña que no ha tenido que contestar esta pregunta de un tío, un primo o conocido de la familia. Aun los padres mismos les hacen esta pregunta. Lo que ha cambiado son las respuestas que dan los niños. Ya no son solamente las respuestas corrientes como policía, bombero, vaquero o maestro, sino hacen referencias a otras profesiones muy sofisticadas incluyendo la de astronauta.

   Las personas que quieren acercarse a las estrellas deben superar todos los límites. Unos requisitos básicos incluyen ser un atleta hábil para cualquier deporte, ser de temperamento calmado y no debe asustarse de nada. También debe estar dispuesto a arriesgarlo todo, inclusive la salud. Para ser astronauta la persona debe estar decidida, en un cien por ciento a seguir esta profesión y ninguna otra. Prepararse para ir al espacio es un proceso largo que dura de 10 a 20 años. Antes del entrenamiento, los aspirantes deben pasar duras pruebas de selección. En los años tempranos de la preparación para ser astronauta, el requisito básico era estar preparado físicamente. Esto ha cambiado porque a base de unas investigaciones que se han llevado a cabo los músculos no son necesarios ahora porque cuando uno está en gravedad cero no los usan y hasta se atrofían. Por medio de esos estudios averiguaron que tampoco importaba la edad ni el sexo de los candidatos y los que eran menos atléticos solían ser mejores astronautas. Lo más importante es que deben ser personas saludables, calmadas en una situación de pánico o de vida o muerte. Esto quiere decir que saben improvisar en el momento y pensar por sí mismos sin tener que consultar con nadie. Además deben ser buenos comunicadores para poder comunicar claramente sus iniciativas a su equipo que está en la Tierra. La mayoría de los seleccionados son ex pilotos de las Fuerzas Armadas de los Estados Unidos que conocen cómo trabajar en distintas gravedades y reaccionar instantáneamente en situaciones difíciles.

   La ciencia y la tecnología han creado más oportunidades profesionales para la juventud actual. Y la exploración del espacio seguirá ofreciendo más opciones en el mundo del trabajo. Aunque no se puede comparar el número de astronautas con el número de médicos o abogados que salen de las universidades, existen muchas nuevas oportunidades para los que tienen interés en la tecnología y el mundo científico, tanto en la Tierra como en el espacio.

1. (a) ¿Cuál es el tema de la pregunta que más se les hace a los niños?

   1. Su deporte favorito.

   2. Su postre predilecto.

   3. Sus planes para el futuro.

   4. Sus mejores amigos.

(b) ¿Cómo deben ser los que quieren ser astronautas?

    1. Fieles a su intención.

    2. De inteligencia extraordinaria.

    3. Inquisitivos y sensibles.

    4. De personalidad indecisa.

(c) ¿En qué se basan los cambios que han hecho en el perfil de los astronautas?

    1. Nuevas leyes de seguridad nacional.

    2. Investigaciones a lo largo de los años.

    3. Cambios en el propósito del programa de espacio.

    4. Falta de candidatos para el entrenamiento.

(d) La mayor parte de los candidatos astronautas seleccionados han venido de

    1. la vida militar

    2. otros países

    3. los laboratorios científicos

    4. universidades prestigiosas

(e) ¿A qué se debe el gran surtido de profesiones que existe hoy en día?

    1. Ideas inventivas de las personas.

    2. Estudios de los sociólogos.

    3. Énfasis en la igualdad de los sexos.

    4. Avances en el mundo científico y tecnológico.

b. Directions: Below each of the following selections, there is a question in English based on it. For each, choose the response that best answers the question or completes the statement according to the meaning of the selection. Circle the letter of your choice.

> La nueva colección «Cuéntame un cuento», reúne en cada volumen tres o cuatro cuentos populares con ilustraciones a todo color. En el libro dedicado a los cuentos de brujas hay una variedad de cuentos muy famosos. Éstos, junto con las divertidas y coloridas ilustraciones, constituyen un buen libro para una biblioteca infantil. Ya está disponible en su librería favorita.

1. What type of books does this collection contain?

  a. Science fiction.

  b. Mysteries.

  c. Children's stories.

  d. Famous cartoons.

ADVERTENCIA
Se hace saber que la libreta de cheques del
BANCO BOSTON, Suc. ONCE, impresa y
numerada para la cuenta corriente de RADIO
VICTORIA INFORMÁTICA S.A., cheques
Nros. 1.501.981 al 1.502.030, por haber sido
extraviada en blanco, NO TIENE NINGÚN
VALOR.

2. What is the purpose of this notice?

   a. To offer a reward for a lost checkbook.

   b. To cancel a book of blank checks.

   c. To close a checking account

   d. To claim a checkbook that was found.

Si Ud. piensa irse de vacaciones y dejar la casa sola, es necesario
que tome ciertas precauciones para que los ladrones crean que
la casa está ocupada. Por ejemplo, cancele la entrega del
periódico; baje el tono del timbre del teléfono; use un aparato
para encender y apagar las luces automáticamente a diario y
pídale a un vecino de confianza que le cuide la casa.

3. When should these suggestions be followed?

   a. When you will be away for an extended period of time.

   b. When you meet with your neighbors.

   c. When you expect guests at your home.

   d. After giving a big party at your home.

¿Qué desea Ud. hacer?
¿aumentar espacio a su casa?
¿modernizar la cocina o el baño?
¿crear armarios bien organizados?

Ofrecemos trabajo limpio, profesional y garantizado a un precio
al alcance de su bolsillo.

Llámenos al 1–800-CASAMIA para pedir un catálogo gratis o
hacer una cita para obtener más información.

O visítenos en www.casamia.com para aprender más sobre
nuestros servicios y entrar en nuestra sala de exhibición virtual.

4. What does this advertisement offer?

   a. home renovations

   b. mortgage refinancing

   c. interior decorating

   d. rental properties

> Como todos los domingos, en la última página encontrará el lector nuestra sección de anuncios, destinada especialmente a aquellas personas que buscan trabajo. Junto a informaciones y comentarios a cargo de nuestro equipo especializado en asuntos económicos, publicamos anuncios específicos de «Ofertas de empleo», además de los que aparecen en sus secciones correspondientes en las páginas de Anuncios Clasificados.

5. To which section of the paper does this notice refer the reader?

   a. The comics.

   b. The stock market.

   c. The theater and the movies.

   d. The want ads.

> Señores,
>
> Soy un lector habitual de su revista desde sus inicios. Me permito saludarlos y agradecerles por poner al alcance de la comunidad los avances en la ciencia, la tecnología y demás disciplinas del ámbito humano. También agradezco y los felicito por dar a personas que no manejamos un léxico técnico en ciencia la oportunidad de leer fácilmente diversos temas. Al revisar mi colección descubrí que me faltan algunos ejemplares, quizá porque los presté a mis estudiantes porque considero que mi labor como docente que soy es también lograr que otros aprendan más allá del salón de clases. Quisiera saber la manera más eficaz para obtener de nuevo los que me faltan. Saludos.

6. What problem does this reader identify?

   a. Understanding scientific articles.

   b. Maintaining the price of the magazine.

   c. Obtaining missing issues of the magazine.

   d. Teaching today's students.

c. **Directions:** After each of the following passages, there are five questions or incomplete statements in English. For each, choose the word or expression that best answers the question or completes the statement according to the meaning of the passage. Circle the number of your choice.

1. No es raro que personas que han pasado toda su vida en un solo lugar no conozcan las riquezas que están a unos pasos de la puerta de su casa. Estas riquezas pueden incluir sitios históricos e interesantes o parques naturales de mucha belleza. Quizás por falta de tiempo, la gente pasa estos lugares diariamente sin pensar en investigarlos más a fondo. Y cuando llegan a conocerlos, se quedan sorprendidos de lo que han perdido por tanto tiempo.

   Generalmente las escuelas toman la iniciativa en enseñarles a los estudiantes todo lo que está a su alcance en su barrio o ciudad. Es una manera efectiva de inspirar el orgullo y el patriotismo y enseñar la ciencia del gobierno civil en la que los jóvenes pueden aprender a lo vivo la historia, la ciencia y otras materias.

   La Sierra de Guadarrama, que está al norte de Madrid, les ofrece muchas oportunidades a los jóvenes de conocer la fauna y la flora que existen allí. Por medio de una iniciativa promovida por la Comunidad de Madrid y la empresa de ferrocarriles nacionales Renfe, se ha puesto en servicio un Tren de la Naturaleza. Aunque esta campaña se dirige a los estudiantes de entre 10 y 16 años durante mayo, junio y octubre, el resto del público puede disfrutar del servicio los viernes y sábados no festivos entre julio y la primera mitad de septiembre.

   Unas 60.000 personas han viajado en este ferrocarril desde su puesta en marcha en 1991. Pero el ferrocarril data de 1923, cuando el Rey Alfonso XIII inauguró la línea que empezaba su recorrido en Cercedilla y llegaba hasta Navacerrada. Cuarenta años después, el itinerario se amplió hasta la estación del Puerto de los Cotos, que hoy en día es el destino final del tren.

   Esta iniciativa tiene un doble carácter, recreativo y educativo. Por medio de ella se trata de incular a los estudiantes y a los madrileños en general, el amor y el respeto a la naturaleza. Para lograr estos propósitos, la excursión comienza en un antiguo vagón en la estación con la proyección de un audiovisual por el cual los estudiantes toman contacto con la fauna y la flora que van a ver a lo largo del recorrido. Unos sesenta minutos después los estudiantes abordan el tren de la Naturaleza y empiezan un recorrido que dura unos cuarenta minutos que les permitirá contemplar los bellos paisajes de la sierra desde una perspectiva de movimiento. Lo curioso es que al llegar a la estación final nunca saben qué clase de tiempo encontrarán. De un día que amaneció soleado y de clima templado en Madrid pueden llegar a un lugar cubierto de nieve y de temperatura fría. De esta manera aprenden también cómo otros factores como la elevación puede afectar el clima de un sitio.

   La excursión es un hermoso paseo repleto de diversas actividades educativas y recreativas que provee la oportunidad a los viajeros a respirar, unos por primera vez, el aire limpio y puro de montaña a pesar de que lo tienen a unos pasos de la puerta de su casa o a un corto viaje en tren.

   1. (a) What astonished many people?

      1. The time needed to find lost objects.

      2. The treasures of local museums.

      3. The close proximity of interesting sites.

      4. The need to explore new places.

      (b) One of the reasons schools generally include field trips is that it

      1. provides for active learning by the students.

      2. is required by law.

      3. enriches required subjects.

      4. breaks the monotony of the classroom.

(c) What is the purpose of the Tren de la Naturaleza?

1. To familiarize students with public transportation.

2. To enable students to carry out experiments.

3. To teach good conservation practices.

4. To focus on climatic variations.

(d) Puerto de los Cotos is

1. the station where an introductory film is presented.

2. the most distant station on this railway line.

3. the station that was inaugurated by King Alfonso XIII.

4. the oldest station on the route.

(e) Why is the Tren de la Naturaleza an important addition to the students' education?

1. It provides new experiences for many students.

2. It is an intergenerational learning activity.

3. It appeals to the interests of different age groups.

4. It improves student-teacher relations and school spirit.

2. Cada año con la llegada de la primavera se nota un gran cambio en la apariencia de las ciudades y pueblos. Es como si un artista hubiera salpicado su paleta de colores por todos los parques y calles con el florecimiento de una gran variedad de flores, acompañado de sus aromas perfumadas que son como brisas fragantes y placenteras que llenan la atmósfera. Y cada lugar tiene su fragancia distinta e individual de acuerdo con las flores que brotan de los árboles y retoños que abundan en la región.

Las flores han sido usadas terapéuticamente desde el comienzo de la historia porque combinan dos atributos importantes, el colorido y la fragancia, que son capaces de generar efectos inmediatos en el estado de ánimo de las personas. Sólo en los polos no crecen las flores por el frío que caracteriza su clima. Pero aun en las partes más áridas de la tierra como en los desiertos hay bellísimas flores. La hermosura de las flores ha conquistado todos los medios, tanto acuáticos como terrestres.

Las flores parecen ser como la manifestación artística de la naturaleza. El diseño de su forma, colorido y fragancia depende del lugar donde se encuentran. Cada nación se identifica con alguna flor que la represente. El sakura es la flor del cerezo que se asocia con el Japón. Todos los años se organiza un festival en el Japón que dura varios días y festeja la apertura de las flores y significa la llegada de la primavera. Los japoneses interpretan esta flor como la representación de la fugacidad de la vida, una vida efímera cuya belleza se extingue en un suspiro. Los aztecas veneraban la flor de la cactácea por las mismas razones. El tulipán es la flor de Holanda, la dalia es la de México y la orquídea es la de Costa Rica.

La flor nacional de Inglaterra es la rosa. La adoptaron como emblema durante el período de guerras civiles que empezaron en 1455. Se conoce como la Guerra de las Rosas que fue un enfrentamiento entre dos casas reales, la de Lancaster y la de York. Ambas casas usaban la insignia de una rosa: Lancaster una rosa roja, York una rosa blanca. El conflicto duró treinta años y lo ganó los Lancaster. Después, el futuro rey, Enrique VII, se casó con Elizabeth de York y las dos rosas se fundieron para formar la de Tudor, una rosa roja con centro blanco.

En la América del Sur las flores exhiben también su importancia como símbolo de cada nación. Existen muchas leyendas que han sido transmitidas de generación en generación por los indígenas que cuentan el origen de una flor como símbolo del país. Es interesante notar también que cada uno de los cincuenta estados de los Estados Unidos de América ha identificado una flor como símbolo del estado.

Las flores tienen un lenguaje propio y es importante saberlo porque no es siempre un lenguaje universal. Por su belleza y fragancia los ramos son siempre bien recibidos, pero conviene conocer previamente las claves ocultas del lenguaje de las flores. En cada cultura hay una flor según la ocasión y cada flor tiene un significado propio y expresa un sentimiento diferente. Por ejemplo, las rosas rojas representan el amor, las violetas significan confianza ciega, las anémonas representan el abandono. Aunque regalar flores es una antigua costumbre, es imprescindible saber escoger la flor apropiada para cada ocasión para evitar una situación de mal entendimiento cultural.

2. (a) Which description of the arrival of spring is best supported by the selection?

1. Flowers give cities and towns a colorful appearance.
2. Artists hold paint splattering festivals in public parks.
3. The effect of poor ecology is very evident.
4. Trees are cut to conform to local standards.

(b) Why are flowers used therapeutically?

1. They are abundant and easily accessible.
2. They help people in barren regions of the earth.
3. Their color and fragrance provide a sense of well-being.
4. Their use is restricted to trained professionals.

(c) The use of a national flower by countries is a reflection of their

1. security
2. identity
3. importance
4. power

(d) What was the ultimate result of the War of the Roses?

1. The continuance of the House of Lancaster.
2. The selection of a new head of state.
3. The modification of the royal house's flower.
4. The country's loss of self-esteem.

(e) Why is it important to know the language of flowers?

1. Flowers are used as universal symbols of emotion.
2. They facilitate communication.
3. People appreciate receiving flowers.
4. The symbolic meaning of flowers varies from culture to culture.

[4] WRITING

WRITING RUBRIC

DIMENSION	RESPONSE			
	4	**3**	**2**	**1**
PURPOSE/TASK	Accomplishes the task; includes **many** details that are clearly connected to the development of the task, but there may be some minor irrelevancies.	Accomplishes the task; includes **some** details that are generally connected to the development of the task, but there may be some irrelevancies.	Accomplishes the task; includes a **few** details, some of which may be only **loosely connected** to the task. There are many irrelevancies.	Attempts to accomplish the task; makes some reference to it but provides few or no supporting details.
ORGANIZATION The extent to which the response exhibits direction, shape and coherence.	Exhibits a logical and coherent sequence throughout; provides a clear sense of a beginning, middle and end. Makes smooth transitions between ideas.	Exhibits a logical sequence; provides a beginning, middle and end.	Attempts to provide a logical sequence and/or the beginning or ending is abrupt or unclear.	Exhibits little order; provides a series of separate sentences and/or disconnected ideas.
VOCABULARY	Includes a **wide variety** of vocabulary that expands the topic, but there may be minor inaccuracies.	Includes a **variety** of vocabulary related to the topic, but there may be minor inaccuracies.	Includes **basic** vocabulary; some vocabulary may be inaccurate or unrelated to the topic.	Includes **limited** vocabulary and/or most vocabulary is inaccurate or unrelated to the topic.
STRUCTURES/ CONVENTIONS • Subject/verb agreement • Tense • Noun/ adjective agreement • Correct word order • Spelling/ diacritical marks	Demonstrates **a high degree** of control of advanced level structure/conventions: • subject/verb agreement • present, past, future ideas expressed as appropriate • noun/adjective agreement • correct word order • spelling/diacritical marks **Errors do not hinder overall comprehensibility of the passage.**	Demonstrates **some** control of advanced level structure/ conventions: • subject/verb agreement • present, past, future ideas expressed as appropriate • noun/adjective agreement • correct word order • spelling/diacritical marks **Errors do not hinder overall comprehensibility of the passage.**	Demonstrates **some** control of advanced level structures/ conventions. **Errors do hinder overall comprehensibility and/or there are numerous elementary level errors.** —or— Demonstrates **a high degree** of control but uses only **elementary level** structures/ conventions.	Demonstrates **little** control of elementary or advanced structures/ conventions: • subject/verb agreement • present, past, future ideas expressed as appropriate • noun/adjective agreement • correct word order • spelling/diacritical marks **Errors impede overall comprehensibility of passage.**
WORD COUNT	—	—	Uses 100 or more comprehensible words in Spanish that contribute to the development of the task.	Uses 50–99 or more comprehensible words in Spanish that contribute to the development of the task.

a. Directions: Write your answer entirely in Spanish and include a minimum of 100 words. Place names and brand names written in Spanish count as one word. Contractions are also counted as one word. Salutations and closings, as well as commonly used abbreviations in Spanish, are included in the word count. Numbers, unless written as words, and names of people are not counted as words.

You must satisfy the purpose of the task. Be sure to organize your response and to include a beginning, middle, and ending. The sentence structure and/or expressions used should be connected logically and should demonstrate a wide range of vocabulary with minimal repetition.

1. During a shopping trip you were helped by a very (in)efficient and (dis)courteous salesperson. Write a formal letter to the store in which you bring this to their attention. Include in your letter the date, salutation, and closing. You may wish to include the purpose of the letter; the name of the salesperson; when this took place; what the person did; why you wish to commend (report) this salesperson; how you feel about what happened.

2. You have placed an order with a mail order company and have not yet received the merchandise. Write a letter to the company in which you bring this to their attention. Include the date, salutation, and closing. You may wish to include the nature of the problem; the date you placed the order; what you ordered; how you placed the order; the means of payment; what you would like them to do about the matter.

_____
_____
_____
_____
_____
_____
_____
_____
_____
_____

3. You have just returned from a visit to San Juan and realize that you forgot one of your possessions in your hotel room. Write a letter to the management in which you request their assistance in locating the item. Include the date, salutation, and closing. You may wish to include the nature of the problem; the article you left behind; a description of the item; the room you occupied; where you may have left it; how it can be returned to you.

_____
_____
_____
_____
_____
_____
_____
_____
_____
_____
_____
_____

4. Your local school is sponsoring a summer program in foreign languages in which the students speak only Spanish. They are looking for students to assist the teachers in the program. Write a letter to the director of the program in which you may wish to include your interest in the program: the reason for you interest, your qualifications, your special skills, your proficiency in Spanish, and your desire for an interview. Be sure to include the date, salutation, and closing.

_____

_____

_____

_____

_____

_____

_____

_____

_____

_____

_____

_____

_____

5. You wish to give a friend a duplicate of the watch that your parents gave you last year but you have not been able to locate it in any of the local stores. Write a letter to the manufacturer of the watch in which you request their assistance in helping you to obtain a similar watch. Include in your letter the date, salutation, and closing. You may wish to include the nature of the problem; a description of the watch; where your watch was purchased; how long you have had it; its cost; your request for information concerning where you can obtain it.

_____

_____

_____

_____

_____

_____

_____

_____

_____

_____

_____

_____

_____

_____

6. You are planning a trip to Lima during the coming summer. Write a letter to the tourist office requesting information. Be sure to include the date, salutation, and closing. You may wish to include the purpose of the letter; your plans; the dates of your trip; your special interests; your request for pertinent information, including the availability of hotel rooms and special trips for students.

_____

_____

_____

_____

_____

_____

_____

_____

_____

_____

_____

_____

b. Directions: In Spanish, write a story about the situations shown in the pictures below. It must be a story relating to the picture, **not** a description of the picture. Do **not** write a dialogue. The story must contain a minimum of 100 words. The sentence structure and/or vocabulary should be connected logically and should demonstrate a wide range of vocabulary with minimal repetition.

1. _____
_____
_____
_____
_____
_____
_____
_____
_____
_____
_____
_____
_____
_____
_____
_____
_____
_____
_____
_____

2. _____

_____

_____

_____

_____

_____

_____

_____

_____

_____

_____

_____

_____

_____

_____

_____

_____

_____

_____

_____

_____

3. _____

_____

_____

_____

_____

_____

_____

_____

_____

_____

_____

_____

_____

_____

_____

_____

_____

_____

_____

_____

_____

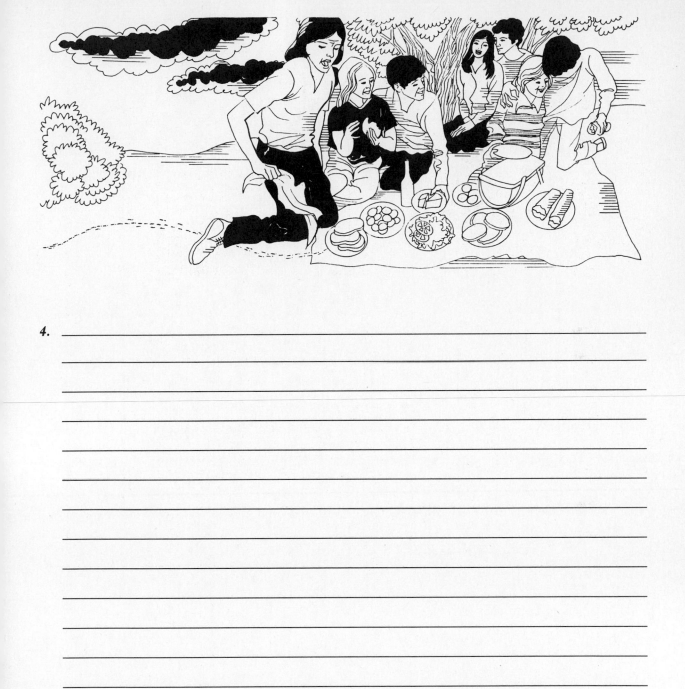

4. _____
_____
_____
_____
_____
_____
_____
_____
_____
_____
_____
_____
_____
_____
_____
_____
_____
_____
_____
_____
_____

Appendix

[1] REGULAR VERBS

a. Simple Tenses

INFINITIVE	usar	beber	subir
GERUND	usando	bebiendo	subiendo
PAST PARTICIPLE	usado	bebido	subido

INDICATIVE

PRESENT	uso	usamos	bebo	bebemos	subo	subimos
	usas	usáis	bebes	bebéis	subes	subís
	usa	usan	bebe	beben	sube	suben
IMPERFECT	usaba	usábamos	bebía	bebíamos	subía	subíamos
	usabas	usabais	bebías	bebíais	subías	subíais
	usaba	usaban	bebía	bebían	subía	subían
PRETERIT	usé	usamos	bebí	bebimos	subí	subimos
	usaste	usasteis	bebiste	bebisteis	subiste	subisteis
	usó	usaron	bebió	bebieron	subió	subieron
FUTURE	usaré	usaremos	beberé	beberemos	subiré	subiremos
	usarás	usaréis	beberás	beberéis	subirás	subiréis
	usará	usarán	beberá	beberán	subirá	subirán
CONDITIONAL	usaría	usaríamos	bebería	beberíamos	subiría	subiríamos
	usarías	usaríais	beberías	beberíais	subirías	subiríais
	usaría	usarían	bebería	beberían	subiría	subirían

COMMANDS

usa (tú)	bebe (tú)	sube (tú)
no uses (tú)	no bebas (tú)	no subas (tú)
usad (vosotros)	bebed (vosotros)	subid (vosotros)
no uséis (vosotros)	no bebáis (vosotros)	no subáis (vosotros)
use (Ud.)	beba (Ud.)	suba (Ud.)
usen (Uds.)	beban (Uds.)	suban (Uds.)
usemos (nosotros)	bebamos (nosotros)	subamos (nosotros)

SUBJUNCTIVE

PRESENT	use	usemos	beba	bebamos	suba	subamos
	uses	uséis	bebas	bebáis	subas	subáis
	use	usen	beba	beban	suba	suban
IMPERFECT	usara	usáramos	bebiera	bebiéramos	subiera	subiéramos
(-ra form)	usaras	usarais	bebieras	bebierais	subieras	subierais
	usara	usaran	bebiera	bebieran	subiera	subieran
IMPERFECT	usase	usásemos	bebiese	bebiésemos	subiese	subiésemos
(-se form)	usases	usaseis	bebieses	bebieseis	subieses	subieseis
	usase	usasen	bebiese	bebiesen	subiese	subiesen

b. Compound Tenses

INDICATIVE

PRESENT PERFECT

he	hemos			
has	habéis	usado	bebido	subido
ha	han			

PLUPERFECT

había	habíamos			
habías	habíais	usado	bebido	subido
había	habían			

PRETERIT PERFECT

hube	hubimos			
hubiste	hubisteis	usado	bebido	subido
hubo	hubieron			

FUTURE PERFECT

habré	habremos			
habrás	habréis	usado	bebido	subido
habrá	habrán			

CONDITIONAL PERFECT

habría	habríamos			
habrías	habríais	usado	bebido	subido
habría	habrían			

PERFECT INFINITIVE

haber	usado	bebido	subido

PERFECT PARTICIPLE

habiendo	usado	bebido	subido

SUBJUNCTIVE

PRESENT PERFECT

haya	hayamos			
hayas	hayáis	usado	bebido	subido
haya	hayan			

PLUPERFECT (-ra form)

hubiera	hubiéramos			
hubieras	hubierais	usado	bebido	subido
hubiera	hubieran			

PLUPERFECT (-se form)

hubiese	hubiésemos			
hubieses	hubieseis	usado	bebido	subido
hubiese	hubiesen			

[2] STEM-CHANGING VERBS

a. Infinitive in -ar

	pensar (e to **ie)**		**mostrar (o** to **ue)**		**jugar (u** to **ue)**	

INDICATIVE

PRESENT	pienso	pensamos	muestro	mostramos	juego	jugamos
	piensas	pensáis	muestras	mostráis	juegas	jugáis
	piensa	piensan	muestra	muestran	juega	juegan

SUBJUNCTIVE

PRESENT	piense	pensemos	muestre	mostremos	juegue	juguemos
	pienses	penséis	muestres	mostréis	juegues	juguéis
	piense	piensen	muestre	muestren	juegue	jueguen

b. Infinitive in -er

	perder (e to **ie)**		**volver (o** to **ue)**	

INDICATIVE

PRESENT	pierdo	perdemos	vuelvo	volvemos
	pierdes	perdéis	vuelves	volvéis
	pierde	pierden	vuelve	vuelven

SUBJUNCTIVE

PRESENT	pierda	perdamos	vuelva	volvamos
	pierdas	perdáis	vuelvas	volváis
	pierda	pierdan	vuelva	vuelvan

c. Infinitive in -ir

	pedir (e to **i, i)**		**sentir (e** to **ie, i)**		**dormir (o** to **ue, u)**	

INDICATIVE

PRESENT	pido	pedimos	siento	sentimos	duermo	dormimos
	pides	pedís	sientes	sentís	duermes	dormís
	pide	piden	siente	sienten	duerme	duermen
PRETERIT	pedí	pedimos	sentí	sentimos	dormí	dormimos
	pediste	pedisteis	sentiste	sentisteis	dormiste	dormisteis
	pidió	pidieron	sintió	sintieron	durmió	durmieron

SUBJUNCTIVE

PRESENT	pida	pidamos	sienta	sintamos	duerma	durmamos
	pidas	pidáis	sientas	sintáis	duermas	durmáis
	pida	pidan	sienta	sientan	duerma	duerman
IMPERFECT (-ra form)	pidiera	pidiéramos	sintiera	sintiéramos	durmiera	durmiéramos
	pidieras	pidierais	sintieras	sintierais	durmieras	durmierais
	pidiera	pidieran	sintiera	sintieran	durmiera	durmieran
IMPERFECT (-se form)	pidiese	pidiésemos	sintiese	sintiésemos	durmiese	durmiésemos
	pidieses	pidieseis	sintieses	sintieseis	durmieses	durmieseis
	pidiese	pidiesen	sintiese	sintiesen	durmiese	durmiesen
GERUND	pidiendo		sintiendo		durmiendo	

d. Infinitives in **-uir** (except **-guir**)

huir (y)

INDICATIVE

PRESENT   huyo, huyes, huye, huimos, huís, huyen
PRETERIT   huí, huiste, huyó, huimos, huisteis, huyeron

SUBJUNCTIVE

PRESENT   huya, huyas, huyamos, huyáis, huyan
IMPERFECT   huyera, huyeras, huyera, huyéramos, huyerais, huyeran
                 huyese, huyeses, huyese, huyésemos, huyeseis, huyesen
GERUNDIO   huyendo

e. Infinitives in **-iar** and **-uar**

enviar (i to í)   **actuar (u to ú)**

INDICATIVE

PRESENT	envío	enviamos	actúo	actuamos
	envías	enviáis	actúas	actuáis
	envía	envían	actúa	actúan

SUBJUNCTIVE

PRESENT	envíe	enviemos	actúe	actuemos
	envíes	enviéis	actúes	actuéis
	envíe	envíen	actúe	actúen

[3] SPELLING-CHANGING VERBS

a. Infinitives in **-cer** or **-cir**

convencer (c to z)   **conocer** (c to zc)

INDICATIVE

PRESENT	convenzo	convencemos	conozco	conocemos
	convences	convencéis	conoces	conocéis
	convence	convencen	conoce	conocen

SUBJUNCTIVE

PRESENT	convenza	convenzamos	conozca	conozcamos
	convenzas	convenzáis	conozcas	conozcáis
	convenza	convenzan	conozca	conozcan

b. Infinitives in **-ger** or **-gir**

dirigir (g to j)

INDICATIVE

PRESENT   dirijo, diriges, dirige, dirigimos, dirigís, dirigen

SUBJUNCTIVE

PRESENT   dirija, dirijas, dirija, dirijamos, dirijáis, dirijan

c. Infinitives in -guir

distinguir (gu to g)

INDICATIVE

PRESENT   distingo, distingues, distingue, distinguimos, distinguís, distinguen

SUBJUNCTIVE

PRESENT   distinga, distingas, distinga, distingamos, distingáis, distingan

d. Infinitives in -eer

leer (i to y)

INDICATIVE

PRETERIT   leí, leíste, leyó, leímos, leísteis, leyeron

SUBJUNCTIVE

IMPERFECT   leyera, leyeras, leyera, leyéramos, leyerais, leyeran
                leyese, leyeses, leyese, leyésemos, leyeseis, leyesen

GERUNDIO   leyendo
PAST PARTICIPLE   leído

e. Infinitives in -car, -gar, and -zar

sacar (c to qu)   **pager (g to gu)**   **gozar (z to c)**

INDICATIVE

PRETERIT	saqué	sacamos	pagué	pagamos	gocé	gozamos
	sacaste	sacasteis	pagaste	pagasteis	gozaste	gozasteis
	sacó	sacaron	pagó	pagaron	gozó	gozaron

SUBJUNCTIVE

PRESENT	saque	saquemos	pague	paguemos	goce	gocemos
	saques	saquéis	pagues	paguéis	goces	gocéis
	saque	saquen	pague	paguen	goce	gocen

[4] IRREGULAR VERBS

NOTE: Only the tenses containing irregular forms are given.

andar

PRETERIT: **anduve, anduviste, anduvo, anduvimos, anduvisteis, anduvieron**
IMPERFECT SUBJUNCTIVE: **anduviera, anduvieras, anduviera, anduviéramos, anduvierais, anduvieran**
           anduviese, anduvieses, anduviese, anduviésemos, anduvieseis, anduviesen

caber

PRESENT INDICATIVE: **quepo,** cabes, cabe, cabemos, cabéis, caben

PRETERIT: **cupe, cupiste, cupo, cupimos, cupisteis, cupieron**
FUTURE: **cabré, cabrás, cabrá, cabremos, cabréis, cabrán**
CONDITIONAL: **cabría, cabrías, cabría, cabríamos, cabríais, cabrían**
PRESENT SUBJUNCTIVE: **quepa, quepas, quepa, quepamos, quepáis, quepan**
IMPERFECT SUBJUNCTIVE: **cupiera, cupieras, cupiera, cupiéramos, cupierais, cupieran**
cupiese, cupieses, cupiese, cupiésemos, cupieseis, cupiesen

caer

PRESENT INDICATIVE: **caigo**, caes, cae, caemos, caéis, caen
PRETERIT: caí **caíste, cayó, caímos, caísteis, cayeron**
PRESENT SUBJUNCTIVE: **caiga, caigas, caiga, caigamos, caigáis, caigan**
IMPERFECT SUBJUNCTIVE: **cayera, cayeras, cayera, cayéramos, cayerais, cayeran**
cayese, cayeses, cayese, cayésemos, cayeseis, cayesen
GERUNDIO: **cayendo**
PAST PARTICIPLE: **caído**

conducir (and verbs ending in –ducir)

PRESENT INDICATIVE: **conduzco**, conduces, conduce, conducimos, conducís, conducen
PRETERIT: **conduje, condujiste, condujo, condujimos, condujisteis, condujeron**
PRESENT SUBJUNCTIVE: **conduzca, conduzcas, conduzca, conduzcamos, conduzcáis, conduzcan**
IMPERFECT SUBJUNCTIVE: **condujera, condujeras, condujera, condujéramos, condujerais, condujeran**
condujese, condujeses, condujese, condujésemos, condujeseis, condujesen

dar

PRESENT INDICATIVE: **doy**, das, da, damos, dais, dan
PRETERIT: **di, diste, dio, dimos, disteis, dieron**
PRESENT SUBJUNCTIVE: **dé**, des, **dé**, demos, deis, den
IMPERFECT SUBJUNCTIVE: **diera, dieras, diera, diéramos, dierais, dieran**
diese, dieses, diese, diésemos, dieseis, diesen

decir

PRESENT INDICATIVE: **digo, dices, dice**, decimos, decís, **dicen**
PRETERIT: **dije, dijiste, dijo, dijimos, dijisteis, dijeron**
FUTURE: **diré, dirás, dirá, diremos, diríamos, diríais, dirían**
CONDITIONAL: **diría, dirías, diría, diríamos, diríais, dirían**
PRESENT SUBJUNCTIVE: **diga, digas, diga, digamos, digáis, digan**
IMPERFECT SUBJUNCTIVE: **dijera, dijeras, dijera, dijéramos, dijerais, dijeran**
dijese, dijeses, dijese, dijésemos, dijeseis, dijesen
GERUNDIO: **diciendo**
PAST PARTICIPLE: **dicho**
COMMAND: **di** (tú)

estar

PRESENT INDICATIVE: **estoy, estás, está**, estamos, estáis, **están**
PRETERIT: **estuve, estuviste, estuvo, estuvimos, estuvisteis, estuvieron**
PRESENT SUBJUNCTIVE: **esté, estés, esté**, estemos, estéis, **estén**
IMPERFECT SUBJUNCTIVE: **estuviera, estuvieras, estuviera, estuviéramos, estuvierais, estuvieran**
estuviese, estuvieses, estuviese, estuviésemos, estuvieseis, estuviesen

haber

PRESENT INDICATIVE: **he, has, ha, hemos,** habéis, **han**
PRETERIT: **hube, hubiste, hubo, hubimos, hubisteis, hubieron**
FUTURE: **habré, habrás, habrá, habremos, habréis, habrán**
CONDITIONAL: **habría, habrías, habría, habríamos, habríais, habrían**
IMPERFECT SUBJUNCTIVE: **hubiera, hubieras, hubiera, hubiéramos, hubierais, hubieran**
        hubiese, hubieses, hubiese, hubiésemos, hubieseis, hubiesen

hacer

PRESENT INDICATIVE: **hago,** haces, hace, hacemos, hacéis, hacen
PRETERIT: **hice, hiciste, hizo, hicimos, hicisteis, hicieron**
FUTURE: **haré, harás, hará, haremos, haréis, harán**
CONDITIONAL: **haría, harías, haría, haríamos, haríais, harían**
PRESENT SUBJUNCTIVE: **haga, hagas, haga, hagamos, hagáis, hagan**
IMPERFECT SUBJUNCTIVE: **hiciera, hicieras, hiciera, hiciéramos, hicierais, hicieran**
        hiciese, hicieses, hiciese, hiciésemos, hicieseis, hiciesen
PAST PARTICIPLE: **hecho**
COMMAND: **haz** (tú)

ir

PRESENT INDICATIVE: **voy, vas, va, vamos, vais, van**
IMPERFECT INDICATIVE: **iba, ibas, iba, íbamos, ibais, iban**
PRETERIT: **fui, fuiste, fue, fuimos, fuisteis, fueron**
PRESENT SUBJUNCTIVE: **vaya, vayas, vaya, vayamos, vayáis, vayan**
IMPERFECT SUBJUNCTIVE: **fuera, fueras, fuera, fuéramos, fuerais, fueran**
        fuese, fueses, fuese, fuésemos, fueseis, fuesen
GERUNDIO: **yendo**
COMMAND: **ve** (tú)

oír

PRESENT INDICATIVE: **oigo, oyes, oye,** oímos, oís, **oyen**
PRETERIT: oí, oíste, **oyó,** oímos, oísteis, **oyeron**
PRESENT SUBJUNCTIVE: **oiga, oigas, oiga, oigamos, oigáis, oigan**
IMPERFECT SUBJUNCTIVE: **oyera, oyeras, oyera, oyéramos, oyerais, oyeran**
        oyese, oyeses, oyese, oyésemos, oyeseis, oyesen
PAST PARTICIPLE: **oído**
GERUNDIO: **oyendo**

poder

PRESENT INDICATIVE: **puedo, puedes, puede,** podemos, podéis, **pueden**
PRETERIT: **pude, pudiste, pudo, pudimos, pudisteis, pudieron**
FUTURE: **podré, podrás, podrá, podremos, podréis, podrán**
CONDITIONAL: **podría, podrías, podría, podríamos, podríais, podrían**
PRESENT SUBJUNCTIVE: **pueda, puedas, pueda,** podamos, podáis, **puedan**
IMPERFECT SUBJUNCTIVE: **pudiera, pudieras, pudiera, pudiéramos, pudierais, pudieran**
        pudiese, pudieses, pudiese, pudiésemos, pudieseis, pudiesen
GERUNDIO: **pudiendo**

poner

PRESENT INDICATIVE: **pongo,** pones, pone, ponemos, ponéis, ponen
PRETERIT: **puse, pusiste, puso, pusimos, pusisteis, pusieron**
FUTURE: **pondré, pondrás, pondrá, pondremos, pondréis, pondrán**
CONDITIONAL: **pondría, pondrías, pondría, pondríamos, pondríais, pondrían**

PRESENT SUBJUNCTIVE: **ponga, pongas, ponga, pongamos, pongáis, pongan**
IMPERFECT SUBJUNCTIVE: **pusiera, pusieras, pusiera, pusiéramos, pusierais, pusieran
pusiese, pusieses, pusiese, pusiésemos, pusieseis, pusiesen**
PAST PARTICIPLE: **puesto**
COMMAND: **pon** (tú)

querer

PRESENT INDICATIVE: **quiero, quieres, quiere,** queremos, queréis, **quieren**
PRETERIT: **quise, quisiste, quiso, quisimos, quisisteis, quisieron**
FUTURE: **querré, querrás, querrá, querremos, querréis, querrán**
CONDITIONAL: **querría, querrías, querría, querríamos, querríais, querrían**
PRESENT SUBJUNCTIVE: **quiera, quieras, quiera,** queramos, queráis, **quieran**
IMPERFECT SUBJUNCTIVE: **quisiera, quisieras, quisiera, quisiéramos, quisierais, quisieran
quisiese, quisieses, quisiese, quisiésemos, quisieseis, quisiesen**

saber

PRESENT INDICATIVE: **sé,** sabes, sabe, sabemos, sabéis, saben
PRETERIT: **supe, supiste, supo, supimos, supisteis, supieron**
FUTURE: **sabré, sabrás, sabrá, sabremos, sabréis, sabrán**
CONDITIONAL: **sabría, sabrías, sabría, sabríamos, sabríais, sabrían**
PRESENT SUBJUNCTIVE: **sepa, sepas, sepa, sepamos, sepáis, sepan**
IMPERFECT SUBJUNCTIVE: **supiera, supieras, supiera, supiéramos, supierais, supieran
supiese, supieses, supiese, supiésemos, supieseis, supiesen**

salir

PRESENT INDICATIVE: **salgo,** sales, sale, salimos, salís, salen
FUTURE: **saldré, saldrás, saldrá, saldremos, saldréis, saldrán**
CONDITIONAL: **saldría, saldrías, saldría, saldríamos, saldríais, saldrían**
PRESENT SUBJUNCTIVE: **salga, salgas, salga, salgamos, salgáis, salgan**
COMMAND: **sal** (tú)

ser

PRESENT INDICATIVE: **soy, eres, es, somos, sois, son**
IMPERFECT INDICATIVE: **era, eras, era, éramos, erais, eran**
PRETERIT: **fui, fuiste, fue, fuimos, fuisteis, fueron**
PRESENT SUBJUNCTIVE: **sea, seas, sea, seamos, seáis, sean**
IMPERFECT SUBJUNCTIVE: **fuera, fueras, fuera, fuéramos, fuerais, fueran
fuese, fueses, fuese, fuésemos, fueseis, fuesen**
COMMAND: **sé** (tú)

tener

PRESENT INDICATIVE: **tengo, tienes, tiene,** tenemos, tenéis, **tienen**
PRETERIT: **tuve, tuviste, tuvo, tuvimos, tuvisteis, tuvieron**
FUTURE: **tendré, tendrás, tendrá, tendremos, tendréis, tendrán**
CONDITIONAL: **tendría, tendrías, tendría, tendríamos, tendríais, tendrían**
PRESENT SUBJUNCTIVE: **tenga, tengas, tenga, tengamos, tengáis, tengan**
IMPERFECT SUBJUNCTIVE: **tuviera, tuvieras, tuviera, tuviéramos, tuvierais, tuvieran
tuviese, tuvieses, tuviese, tuviésemos, tuvieseis, tuviesen**
COMMAND: **ten** (tú)

traer

PRESENT INDICATIVE: **traigo,** traes, trae, traemos, traéis, traen
PRETERIT: **traje, trajiste, trajo, trajimos, trajisteis, trajeron**
PRESENT SUBJUNCTIVE: **traiga, traigas, traiga, traigamos, traigáis, traigan**

IMPERFECT SUBJUNCTIVE: **trajera, trajeras, trajera, trajéramos, trajerais, trajeran**
trajese, trajeses, trajese, trajésemos, trajeseis, trajesen

GERUNDIO: **trayendo**
PAST PARTICIPLE: **traído**

valer

PRESENT INDICATIVE: **valgo,** vales, vale, valemos, valéis, valen
FUTURE: **valdré, valdrás, valdrá, valdremos, valdréis, valdrán**
CONDITIONAL: **valdría, valdrías, valdría, valdríamos, valdríais, valdrían**
PRESENT SUBJUNCTIVE: **valga, valgas, valga, valgamos, valgáis, valgan**

venir

PRESENT INDICATIVE: **vengo, vienes, viene,** venimos, venís, **vienen**
PRETERIT: **vine, viniste, vino, vinimos, vinisteis, vinieron**
FUTURE: **vendré, vendrás, vendrá, vendremos, vendréis, vendrán**
CONDITIONAL: **vendría, vendrías, vendría, vendríamos, vendríais, vendrían**
PRESENT SUBJUNCTIVE: **venga, vengas, venga, vengamos, vengáis, vengan**
IMPERFECT SUBJUNCTIVE: **viniera, vinieras, viniera, viniéramos, vinierais, vinieran**
viniese, vinieses, viniese, viniésemos, vinieseis, viniesen

GERUNDIO: **viniendo**
COMMAND: **ven** (tú)

ver

PRESENT INDICATIVE: **veo,** ves, ve, vemos, veis, ven
IMPERFECT INDICATIVE: **veía, veías, veía, veíamos, veíais, veían**
PRETERIT: **vi,** viste, **vio,** vimos, visteis, vieron
PRESENT SUBJUNCTIVE: **vea, veas, vea, veamos, veáis, vean**
PAST PARTICIPLE: **visto**

[5] PUNCTUATION

Spanish punctuation, though similar to English, has the following major differences:

(a) The comma is not used before **y, e, o, u,** and **ni** in a series.

El viento, la lluvia y el frío causaron *The wind, the rain, and the cold*
daños al techo. *damaged the roof.*

(b) In Spanish, questions have an inverted question mark **¿** at the beginning and a
normal one at the end.

¿Qué estás haciendo? *What are you doing?*

(c) In Spanish, exclamatory sentences have an inverted exclamation mark (**¡**) at the
beginning and a normal one at the end.

¡Qué calor hace! *How hot it is!*

(d) In decimals, Spanish uses a comma where English uses a period.

7,5 (siete coma cinco) *7.5 (seven point five)*

(e) Spanish final quotation marks, contrary to English, precede the comma or period.

Cervantes es el autor de «**Don** *Cervantes is the author of "Don*
Quijote». *Quixote."*

[6] SYLLABICATION

Spanish words are generally divided at the end of a line according to units of sound.

(a) A syllable normally begins with a consonant. The division is made before the consonant.

de/cir   pre/ci/so   a/me/ri/ca/no   re/pe/tir

(b) **ch, ll,** and **rr** are never divided.

ca/**rr**o   ca/**ll**a/do   he/**ch**o

(c) If two or more consonants are combined, the division is made before the last consonant, except in the combinations **bl, br, cl, cr, pl, pr,** and **tr.**

trans/por/te   des/cu/bier/to   con/ti/nuar   al/ha/ja

But:

ha/**bl**ar   a/**br**ir   des/**cr**i/bir   a/**pr**en/der   des/**tr**o/zar

(d) Compound words, including words with prefixes and suffixes, may be divided by components or by syllables.

sur/a/me/ri/ca/no   *or*   **su**/ra/me/ri/ca/no

mal/es/tar   *or*   **ma**/les/tar

Spanish-English Vocabulary

The Spanish–English Vocabulary is intended to be complete for the contexts of this book. Basic terms usually taught in first-level courses and some obvious cognates are not included.

Nouns are listed in the singular. The gender of nouns is indicated as follows:

> *m.* = masculine
> *f.* = feminine
> *m. & f.* = masculine and feminine

Irregular plurals are given in full:

> **tapiz** *m.* (*pl.* **tapices**)

Adjectives are listed in the masculine form.

Verbs with spelling changes, stem-changing verbs, and irregular verbs are identified by the type of change in parentheses after the verb: **conocer (zc); tener** (*irr.*). Refer to the Appendix for sample conjugations.

abarcar (qu) to take in, include, encompass; to comprise

abertura *f.* opening; hole

abismo *m.* abyss, gulf

abogado *m.*, **abogada** *f.* lawyer

aborrecer (zc) to hate, loathe

abrazar (c) to embrace, hug

abrochar to fasten

aburrido bored; boring

aburrir to bore; **aburrirse** to get bored, be bored

acabar to finish; **acabar de** to have just

acampar to camp

aceite *m.* oil; **aceite de oliva** olive oil

aceituna *f.* olive

acerca de about

acercarse (qu) (a) to approach

acero *m.* steel

acertar (ie) to hit the mark, guess right

acompañar to accompany

aconsejar to advise

acontecimiento *m.* happening, event

acordarse (ue) (de) to remember

acostar (ue) to put to bed; **acostarse** to go to bed, lie down

acostumbrarse (a) to accustom oneself, get used to

actual current; present

actuar (ú) to act

acuático aquatic; **el esquí acuático** water skiing

acudir (a) to go or come to

acuerdo *m.* agreement; **estar de acuerdo (con)** to agree (with), be in agreement (with); **ponerse de acuerdo** to come to an agreement

adelantar to move forward, advance

adivinar to guess

adobar to prepare, dress; to season

adorno *m.* decoration

adquirir (ie) to acquire

aduana *f.* customs

advertencia *f.* warning

advertir (ie) to notify, warn

aeromozo *m.*, **aeromoza** *f.* flight attendant

afecto *m.* affection

afeitarse to shave

aficionado *m.*, **aficionada** *f.* fan, devotee; **teatro de aficionados** *m.* amateur theater

afligirse (j) to grieve

afrontar to confront; to face up to

afuera outside; **afueras** *f. pl.* outskirts

agitado agitated; upset; excited

agitar to stir up, rouse, excite

agradar to be pleased with; to please

agradecer (zc) to thank

agregar to add

aguafuerte *m.* etching

aguantar to bear, endure

aguardiente *m.* alcoholic beverage

aguinaldo *m.* bonus; Christmas gift

ahogarse (gu) to drown

ahorrar to save

aire *m.* air; **al aire libre** in the open air, outdoors

aislado isolated

ajedrez *m.* chess

ajeno somebody else's; alien, foreign

ajo *m.* garlic

alabar to praise

alargar (gu) to lengthen, elongate

alcalde *m.* mayor

alcanzar (c) to reach, catch up with

alcázar *m.* fortress; royal palace

alcoba *f.* bedroom

aldea *f.* village

alegrarse (de) to be glad, rejoice

alegría *f.* happiness

alemán German

alfiler *m.* pin

alfombra *f.* carpet

algodón *m.* (*pl.* **algodones**) cotton

alguien someone

alguno some

alma *f.* (**el alma**) soul

almacén *m.* (*pl.* **almacenes**) department store

almendra *f.* almond

almohada *f.* pillow

almorzar (ue, c) to eat (have) lunch

almuerzo *m.* lunch

alojamiento *m.* lodgings

alojar(se) to lodge; to be lodged, stay

alquilar to rent

alquiler *m.* rent

alrededor de around

altiplanicie *f.* high plateau

altura *f.* height

alzar (c) to raise (up), lift

ama *f.* (**el ama**) mistress, lady of the house; **ama de llaves** housekeeper

amanecer (zc) to dawn; *m.* dawn; **al amanecer** at dawn

amargura *f.* bitterness

amarrar to tie, fasten

ambos both

amenazador threatening

amenazar (c) to threaten

amistad *f.* friendship; *pl.* friends

amo *m.* master

analfabetismo *m.* illiteracy

anciano old; *m.* old man

ancho wide

anchura *f.* width; breath

andar (*irr.*) to walk, go

andén *m.* (*pl.* **andenes**) platform

angosto narrow

angustia *f.* anguish, distress

anillo *m.* ring

animado lively

animar to cheer up; to stimulate

anoche last night

anochecer *m.* nightfall, dusk; **al anochecer** at nightfall

anónimo anonymous

ante before, in the presence of

anteojos *m. pl.* eyeglasses

anterior previous, preceding

antes (de) before

antiguo old, ancient; former; old-time

antipático disagreeable, unpleasant

anuncio *m.* announcement; advertisement

añadir to add

aparecer (zc) to appear

apatía *f.* apathy

apenarse to grieve, distress oneself

apenas hardly, scarcely

aplicado studious, industrious

apoyo *m.* support

apresurarse to hurry

apretar (ie) to tighten; to be tight; to clasp

aprovecharse (de) to take advantage (of)

apuntar to note down, take a note of

apunte *m.* note, memorandum

archivar to file

archivo *m.* file

arder to burn

arena *f.* sand

arete *m.* earring

armario *m.* closet, wardrobe

arquitectura *f.* architecture

arrancar (qu) to root out, pull out; to snatch

arreglar to arrange; **arreglar la cama** to make the bed

arrepentirse (ie) (de) to repent, regret

arroz *m.* (*pl.* **arroces**) rice

arrugado wrinkled

arruinar to ruin

artesano *m.* craftsman

ascendencia *f.* ancestry, descent, origin

ascender (ie) to ascend; to promote

ascensor *m.* elevator

asegurar to assure

asequible within reach; available

así so, thus, in this way; **así que** as soon as

asilo *m.* asylum; **asilo de ancianos** old age home

asistir (a) to attend

asombrarse to be astonished, amazed

aspiradora *f.* vacuum cleaner; **pasar la aspiradora** to vacuum

aspirar (a) to aspire (to)

asunto *m.* matter, subject

asustado frightened

asustarse to be frightened, get scared; to get alarmed

atacar (qu) to attack

atención *f.* (*pl.* **atenciones**) attention; **prestar atención** to pay attention, to listen to

atender (ie) to wait on; to look after

atentamente attentively; thoughtfully; **le saluda atentamente** yours faithfully

aterrador frightening, terrifying

aterrizar (c) to land

atraer (*irr.*) to attract

atrapar to trap; to catch

atravesar (ie) to cross, pass through

atreverse (a) to dare

atrevido daring, bold; disrespectful, insolent

auge *m.* acme, period of prosperity

aumentar to increase

aún still, even

aunque although, even though, even if

auricular *m.* receiver, earpiece

avanzar (c) to advance

ave *f.* (**el ave**) bird

averiguar (ü) to find out, ascertain

aviso *m.* notice, warning

ayuda *f.* help, assistance

ayudante *m. & f.* assistant, helper

ayuno *m.* fasting

azafrán *m.* (*pl.* **azafranes**) saffron

azúcar *m.* sugar

azufre *m.* sulphur

azulejo *m.* tile

bajar (de) to lower; to take down; to reduce; to turn down; to get off; to go down

bajo short
baloncesto *m.* basketball
bandera *f.* flag
banquero *m.* banker
bañar to bathe; **bañarse** to take a bath
barato cheap, inexpensive
barco *m.* boat; ship
barrer to sweep
barro *m.* clay; mud
bastante enough, sufficient
bastar to be enough, suffice
basura *f.* garbage
bata *f.* robe
baúl *m.* trunk
belleza *f.* beauty
beréber Berber
billete *m.* ticket; banknote, bill
bizcocho *m.* biscuit; sponge cake
blando soft
boda *f.* wedding
boleto *m.* ticket
boliche *m.* bowling; bowling alley
bolsa *f.* bag; sack
bolso *m.* bag, purse
bollo *m.* roll, bun
bombero *m.* fireman; **cuartel de bomberos** *m.* firehouse (station)
bombilla *f.* light bulb; small tube for drinking mate
bondadoso kind
bosque *m.* woods, forest
bostezar (c) to yawn
bota *f.* boot
boticario *m.* pharmacist, druggist
botones *m.* (*pl.* **botones**) bellman
bóveda *f.* dome
bravo angry
breve brief
brillar to shine
broma *f.* joke; prank
bruja *f.* witch
burguesía *f.* bourgeoisie
burlarse (de) to make fun of
burlón mocking
busca *f.* search; **en busca de** in search of
buscar (qu) to look for
búsqueda *f.* search
butaca *f.* armchair

buzón *m.* (*pl.* **buzones**) mailbox

caber (irr.) to fit; to be room for
cabo *m.* end; **llevar a cabo** to carry out, carry through
cabra *f.* goat
cacique *m.* Indian chief
cadena *f.* chain
caer (irr.) to fall; **caerse** to fall down
caja *f.* box
cajero *m.*, **cajera** *f.* cashier
calabaza *f.* gourd, pumpkin
calcetín *m.* (*pl.* **calcetines**) sock
calentura *f.* fever
calidad *f.* quality
calificación *f.* (*pl.* **calificaciones**) grade, mark
calificar (qu) to grade
calumnia *f.* slander
calzar (c) (footwear) to put on, to wear; to take or wear a certain shoe size
callarse to become silent, stop talking
cámara *f.* camera; chamber; **pintor de cámara** *m.* court painter
camarera *f.* chambermaid; waitress
cambiar to change
cambio *m.* change; exchange; exchange rate; **en cambio** on the other hand
campamento *m.* camp
campana *f.* bell
campaña *f.* campaign
campeonato *m.* championship
campesino *m.*, **campesina** *f.* peasant
campo *m.* country, countryside
canasta *f.* basket
cancha *f.* court; **cancha de tenis** tennis court
cansado tired; **estar cansado** to be tired
cantante *m. & f.* singer
cantidad *f.* quantity
capítulo *m.* chapter
caprichoso whimsical; wilful
cara *f.* face; **cara a cara** face to face

carbón *m.* (*pl.* **carbones**) coal
carcajada *f.* loud laugh; **reír a carcajadas** to laugh heartily, roar with laughter
cárcel *f.* jail
carecer (zc) de to lack, be in need of
cargado laden
cargar (gu) to load; to carry
caridad *f.* charity
carnicería *f.* butcher shop
caro expensive; dear
carpintero *m.* carpenter
carrera *f.* race; career
carretera *f.* road
carril *m.* lane
cartaginés Carthaginian
cartel *m.* poster
cartera *f.* wallet, pocketbook; handbag, purse
casarse (con) to marry
caseta *f.* booth
casi almost
caso *m.* case, event; **hacer caso a** to heed, mind; **hacer caso de** to pay attention to
castañuelas *f. pl.* castanets
castigar (gu) to punish
castigo *m.* punishment
castillo *m.* castle
casualidad *f.* chance; coincidence; **por casualidad** by chance
cataratas *f. pl.* waterfall, falls
catre *m.* cot
caucho *m.* rubber
causa *f.* cause, motive; **a causa de** because of, on account of
cautivo captive
cebolla *f.* onion
cegar (gu) to blind
célebre famous
celoso jealous
celta Celt
cena *f.* supper, dinner
centro *m.* center; downtown
ceñir (i) to encircle, surround; to fasten around one's waist
cepillar(se) to brush (oneself)
cepillo *m.* brush
cercano near, close; nearby
cereza *f.* cherry
certidumbre *f.* certainty
cerviz *f.* nape of the neck

cesar to cease, stop
césped *m.* lawn, grass
cesta *f.* basket
chal *m.* shawl
chaqueta *f.* jacket
charlar to chat
chico small; *m.* boy, **chica** *f.* girl
chimenea *f.* fireplace
chiste *m.* joke
chistoso funny
chocar(se) (qu) con to crash into, collide with
ciego blind; *m.* blind man
cielo *m.* sky
ciencia *f.* science
científico *m.*, **científica** *f.* scientist
cine *m.* movie theater, movies
cinta *f.* tape; ribbon
cinturón *m.* (*pl.* **cinturones**) belt
circo *m.* circus
cirujano *m.*, **cirujana** *f.* surgeon
cita *f.* appointment; date
ciudadano *m.*, **ciudadana** *f.* citizen
clima *m.* climate
cobrar to charge; to collect; to acquire; **cobrar fuerzas** to gather strength
cobre *m.* copper
cocer (ue, z) to cook
cocinar to cook, do the cooking
cochero *m.* driver, coachman
cofre *m.* chest; case (for jewels)
coger (j) to seize, grasp, catch, take
cohete *m.* rocket
cola *f.* line; tail
coleccionar to collect
colgar (ue, gu) to hang (up)
colilla *f.* (cigarette) butt
colocar (qu) to place, put; to arrange; to place (in a job)
colorado red; **ponerse colorado** to blush
comedia *f.* play, comedy
comedor *m.* dining room
comentar to comment on; to discuss, gossip about
comenzar (ie) to begin, start
comestible *m.* foodstuff; **comestibles** *m. pl.* foods; groceries
como as; **¡cómo no!** certainly!, of course!

cómodo comfortable
compañía *f.* company
compartir to share
competencia *f.* competition
complejo complex
componer (irr.) to compose; to repair
compra *f.* purchase; **ir de compras** to go shopping
comprador *m.* buyer
comprender to include; to understand
comprometido engaged; committed
compromiso *m.* commitment; engagement; obligation
común common
concluir (y) to conclude, finish
concurso *m.* contest
condenar to sentence, condemn
condesa *f.* countess
condiscípulo *m.*, **condiscípula** *f.* classmate
conducir (irr.) to conduct, lead; to drive
conductor *m.* driver
confesar (ie) to confess
confianza *f.* trust; **de confianza** reliable, trustworthy
confiar (í) en to rely on; to confide in
confín *m.* (*pl.* **confines**) boundary
conforme a consistent with; in accordance with; **estar conforme** to agree
congelar to freeze
congreso *m.* convention; conference
conmover (ue) to stir, move, affect
conocer (zc) to know, be acquainted with; **dar a conocer** to introduce, to present
conocido known; *m.* acquaintance; **conocido como** known as
conseguir (i, g) to get, obtain; to succeed in
consejero *m.* counselor
consejo *m.* advice
consentir (ie) to consent; to allow; to pamper, spoil

consiguiente resulting; **por consiguiente** therefore, and so
consistir en to consist of; to be made of
constituir (y) to constitute, make up
construir (y) to construct; to build
consultorio *m.* doctor's office
consumo *m.* consumption
contado: al contado for cash
contar (ue) to count; to tell
contener (irr.) to contain
contra against
contradecir (irr.) to contradict
contrario *m.* contrary; **por el contrario** on the contrary
contribuir (y) to contribute
convencer (z) to convince
convenir (irr.) **en** to agree about (to, that); **convenir con** to agree with
convertir (ie) to convert; **convertirse** to be converted; to turn (into); to become
convidar to invite
convivir to live together, coexist
copa *f.* glass
cordillera *f.* mountain range
coro *m.* chorus
corona *f.* crown
corregir (i, j) to correct
correo *m.* mail; post office; **echar al correo** to mail
corrida *f.* run, dash; **corrida de toros** bullfight
corrido running; fluent, continuous
corriente current; **estar al corriente** to be informed, be aware
cortar to cut
corte *f.* court; *pl.* Spanish parliament
cortejar to court, woo
cortés courteous, polite
cortesía *f.* courtesy
cortina *f.* curtain
cosecha *f.* harvest
coser to sew
costar (ue) to cost
costumbre *f.* custom, habit
creador creative

crecer (zc) to grow
creer (y) to believe; to think
cría *f.* breeding
criado *m.*, **criada** *f.* servant
criollo *m.*, **criolla** *f.* Creole
cruz *f.* (*pl.* **cruces**) cross
cruzar (c) to cross
cuadra *f.* (street) block
cuadro *m.* painting, picture; frame
cualquier any
cuando when; **cuando quiera** whenever
cuanto all that, whatever; **¿cuánto?** how much?; **¡cuánto!** how!; **en cuanto** as soon as
cuaresma *f.* Lent
cuartel *m.* barracks
cuarto fourth; quarter; *m.* room
cubrir to cover
cuclillas: **en cuclillas** squatting
cuchillo *m.* knife
cuenta *f.* bill, check
cuentista *m. & f.* storywriter
cuenta *f.* account; bill; **cuenta corriente** current account
cuento *m.* story
cuerda *f.* rope, cord; string; **dar cuerda a un reloj** to wind a clock/watch
cuero *m.* leather
cueva *f.* cave
cuidado *m.* care; **tener cuidado** to be careful; **perder cuidado** not to worry
cuidadoso careful
cuidar to take care of, look after
culpa *f.* blame; fault; **echar la culpa** to blame; **tener la culpa de** to be to blame for; **Ud. tiene la culpa** it's your fault
cumbre *f.* top; mountain top; pinnacle
cumplir to fulfill; to do one's duty; **cumplir con la palabra** to keep one's word
cuna *f.* cradle
cura *f.* cure; *m.* priest
curiosidad *f.* curiosity
curioso curious; odd
cuyo whose

dado given
dama *f.* lady; **damas** *f. pl.* checkers
dañar to damage, hurt; **dañarse** to get damaged; to spoil, go bad
daño *m.* hurt; **hacer(se) daño** to hurt (oneself)
dar (*irr.*) to give; **dar a** to face
debajo de under
deber ought to, must; to owe
debido a due to
débil weak
decadencia *f.* decline
décimo tenth
decir (*irr.*) to say; **querer decir** to mean
declamar to recite
declaración *f.* (*pl.* **declaraciones**) statement; explanation
decorado *m.* scenery, set
dedicar (qu) to dedicate; to devote
defectuoso defective
defender (ie) to defend
delgado thin
dejar to leave out; to leave; to allow
demás: lo demás the rest; **los (las) demás** the others
demasiado too much; excessively; too
dentro de within
dependiente *m. & f.* clerk, salesperson
deportivo sports; sporting
derecha *f.* right hand; right side; **a la derecha** to the right
derecho straight
derrotado defeated
derrotar to defeat
derrumbar to knock down
desaparecer (zc) to disappear
desarrollar to develop
desarrollo *m.* development
desayunarse to have (eat) breakfast
descansar to rest
descanso *m.* rest, break
descolgar (ue, gu) to take down
desconocer (zc) not to know, be ignorant of
descortés discourteous, impolite
descubierto discovered

descubrir to discover
desde from; since; **desde hace** for + length of time
desembocar (qu) en to flow into, empty into
desenvolvimiento *m.* unfolding, development
desesperar to despair, lose hope
desfilar to parade, march past
desfile *m.* parade
desgraciadamente unfortunately
deshacer (*irr.*) to undo; to destroy
deslizarse (c) to slip, slide; glide
desmayarse to faint
despacio slowly
despacho *m.* office; study
despedirse (i) (de) to say goodbye (to), take leave (of)
despertador *m.* alarm clock
despertar(se) (ie) to awaken, wake up
después afterwards, later; **después de** after
destacado outstanding, distinguished
destacarse (qu) to distinguish oneself; to stand out
destruir (y) to destroy
desván *m.* (*pl.* **desvanes**) attic
detalle *m.* detail
detener (*irr.*) to detain; to hold up, delay; to stop
detrás (de) behind
devolver (ue) to return, give back
día *m.* day; **todos los días** everyday, daily; **hoy (en) día** nowadays
dibujante *m. & f.* sketcher
dibujo *m.* drawing, sketch
dictadura *f.* dictatorship
dictar (una sentencia) to pass, pronounce (judgement)
dieta *f.* diet
dios *m.* god; idol
dirigir (j) to direct
disculparse to excuse oneself; to apologize
diseñador *m.*, **diseñadora** *f.* designer
diseño *m.* design
disfraz *m.* (*pl.* **disfraces**) disguise; mask
disfrutar to enjoy

disparo *m.* shot

disponer (*irr.*) to dispose;
disponer de to have at one's
disposal; **disponerse a** to get
ready to

distinguir (g) to distinguish

distraído distracted;
absentminded

distribuir (y) to distribute

diversión *f.* (*pl.* **diversiones**)
amusement, entertainment

divertirse (ie) to enjoy oneself,
have a good time

doblar to fold (up, over); to turn,
go round

docena *f.* dozen

doler (ue) to hurt, ache, pain

dolor *m.* pain, ache

domicilio *m.* home; **servicio a
domicilio** home-delivery
service

dominio *m.* control; supremacy

dondequiera wherever

dormitorio *m.* bedroom

dramaturgo *m.* playwright

dudar to doubt

dueño *m.*, **dueña** *f.* owner

dulce *m.* sweet, candy

dulcería *f.* candy store

dulzura *f.* sweetness; gentleness

durar to last, go on for

echar to throw; to throw out,
dismiss, expel; to put in, add;
echar(se) a to start to + *inf.*

edad *f.* age; period

educar (qu) to educate; to train

eficaz effective; efficient

ejemplar exemplary, model

ejercer (z) to exert; (*power*) to
exercise, wield; (*profession*) to
practice

ejército *m.* army

elaborar to work on

elegir (i, j) to elect; to choose

embajador *m.*, **embajadora** *f.*
ambassador

embarcarse (qu) to embark, go
on board

embargo: sin embargo still,
however, nonetheless

embestida *f.* charge

emisora *f.* radio station

emocionante exciting, thrilling;
moving, touching

empeñarse en to insist on; to
persist in; to be determined to

emperador *m.* emperor

emperatriz *f.* (*pl.* **emperatrices**)
empress

empezar (ie) to begin, start

empleado *m.*, **empleada** *f.*
employee

emplear to employ; to use

emprender to undertake; to
embark on

empresa *f.* undertaking; enterprise

enamorado *m.*, **enamorada** *f.*
lover, beloved; **estar
enamorado** to be in love

encaje *m.* lace

encantador charming,
enchanting, delightful

encarcelado imprisoned, jailed

encargar (gu) to entrust; to put
in charge; (*goods*) to order;
encargarse de to take charge
of; to see about, attend to

encender (ie) to light; to ignite

encerrar (ie) to lock in; to
contain; **encerrarse** to shut
(lock) oneself

encima de above, on top of

encogerse (j) to shrink;
encogerse de hombros to
shrug

encontrar (ue) to find; to meet,
run into

encuesta *f.* survey; inquiry

energía *f.* energy; power; vigor,
drive

enfadarse to get angry, get
annoyed

enfermedad *f.* sickness, illness

enfermera *f.*, **enfermero** *m.*
nurse

enfermo sick, ill; *m.*, **enferma** *f.*
sick person; patient

enfrente de opposite, in front of

engañar(se) to deceive (oneself)

enlace *m.* link

enojar to anger; to upset; **enojarse**
to get angry, lose one's temper

enojo *m.* anger; annoyance

enriquecer (zc) to enrich;
enriquecerse to get rich; to
prosper

entablar (*conversation*) to start,
strike up

enterarse de to find out about,
to learn

enterrar (ie) to bury

entonces then; **en aquel
entonces** at that time

entrada *f.* entrance; admission;
(*theater, etc.*) ticket

entregar (gu) to deliver; to hand
over; to give up, surrender;
entregarse a to devote onself
to

entretener (*irr.*) to entertain,
amuse

entrevista *f.* interview

entrevistar to interview

enviar (í) to send; **enviar por** to
send for, fetch

envidiar to envy

envidioso envious, jealous

envolver (ue) to wrap (up)

época *f.* epoch, age; time, period

equipo *m.* team; outfit, gear

equivocarse (qu) to be
mistaken, make a mistake

erudito learned, scholarly

escalera *f.* staircase, stairs; ladder

escaparse to escape; to elope

escasez *f.* (*pl.* **escaseces**) scarcity,
shortage

escenario *m.* stage

escenografía *f.* scenery

escoger (j) to choose, select

escolar school; scholastic

esconder to hide

escrito *m.* writing; **por escrito**
in writing

escritor *m.*, **escritora** *f.* writer

escritorio *m.* desk

escritura *f.* writing

escuchar to listen to; to pay
attention to

escudero *m.* squire

escultor *m.*, **escultora** *f.* sculptor

esfuerzo *m.* effort

esmeralda *f.* emerald

eso that; **a eso de** at about; **por
eso** therefore, and so

espada *f.* sword

especie *f.* species; kind

esperar to wait for; to hope; to
expect

espeso thick

espiar (í) to spy
esquí *m.* (*pl.* **esquís**) ski; skiing
esquiar (í) to ski
esquina *f.* corner
establecer(se) (zc) to establish (oneself); to settle
estación *f.* (*pl.* **estaciones**) season; station
estacionar(se) to park
estadio *m.* stadium
estado *m.* state, condition
estallar to break out; to burst, explode
estante *m.* shelf
estaño *m.* tin
estatua *f.* statue
estilizar (c) to stylize
estilo *m.* style; manner, fashion
estío *m.* summer
estirarse to stretch
estrecharse to become closer
estrecho *m.* strait
estremecerse (zc) to shudder
estreno *m.* first use; first performance
excelencia *f.* excellence; **por excelencia** preeminently, par excellence
exigir (j) to demand, require
éxito *m.* success; **tener éxito** to be successful
experimentar to experience, go through; to suffer
exponer (irr.) to expose, exhibit; to expand, set forth
expulsar to expel
extensión *f.* (*pl.* **extensiones**) area
extinguir (g) to extinguish, put out
extranjero foreign; **al extranjero, en el extranjero** abroad
extrañar to miss; to feel the lack of
extraño strange, odd

fábrica *f.* factory
fabricar (qu) to make, manufacture
facultad *f.* faculty; school (of a university)
falda *f.* skirt

falta *f.* fault, mistake
faltar to be lacking, be wanting; to be missing, be absent from
fama *f.* fame; reputation
fantasma *m.* ghost
fantasmagórico phantasmagoric
fascinar to fascinate; to captivate
fe *f.* faith
felicitar to congratulate
feliz happy
felpa *f.* plush
fenicio Phoenician
feria *f.* fair; weekly market
feroz fierce
ferretería *f.* hardware store
ferrocarril *m.* railroad
fiarse (í) de to trust
fideo *m.* noodle
fiebre *f.* fever
fiel faithful
figurarse to figure, imagine; to suppose
fijarse (en) to stare (at); to notice, pay attention
filólogo *m.* philologist
filoso sharp
fin *m.* end; **fin de semana** *m.* weekend; **hacia fines de** toward the end of
fingir (j) to pretend, feign
firmar to sign
flan *m.* custard
florecer (zc) to flourish
florero *m.* vase; florist
folleto *m.* pamphlet; brochure
fomentar to promote, encourage, foster
fondo *m.* bottom; **a fondo** thoroughly; **fondos** *m. pl.* funds
foro *m.* upstage area
fortaleza *f.* fortress, stronghold
foto *f.* picture, photo; **sacar fotos** to take pictures
fracasar to fail; to fall through
fracaso *m.* failure
francés French
frecuencia *f.* frequency; **con frecuencia** frequently, often
frente *f.* forehead; **frente a** opposite, facing, in front of; **de frente** forward
fresa *f.* strawberry
fresco fresh; cool

fríjol, frijol *m.* bean
frontera *f.* border, frontier; boundary
frontón *m.* (*pl.* **frontones**) ball court
fuego *m.* fire
fuera outside; **fuera de** outside of; in addition to, besides; **estar fuera de sí** to be beside onself
fuerte strong
fuerza *f.* strength, force; **a fuerza de** by dint of; **cobrar fuerzas** to gather strength
fumar to smoke
función *f.* (*pl.* **funciones**) performance, show
fundar to found; to establish
fusilar to shoot, execute

gafas *f. pl.* eyeglasses
gaita *f.* bagpipe
galletita *f.* cookie
gana *f.* desire, will; **de buena gana** willingly, gladly; **de mala gana** reluctantly, grudgingly
ganadería *f.* cattle raising
ganado *m.* cattle
ganar to win; to earn; **ganarse la vida** to earn (make) a living
ganga *f.* bargain
garbanzo *m.* chickpea
garganta *f.* throat
gastar to spend
gemelo *m.* twin
gemir (i) to groan, moan
género *m.* genre; kind, sort
gente *f.* people
gerente *m. & f.* manager, director
gigante giant
gigantesco gigantic
gimnasio *m.* gym
girar to turn, revolve
gitano *m.*, **gitana** *f.* gypsy
globo *m.* balloon
gobernador *m.*, **gobernadora** *f.* governor
gobernar (ie) to govern
gobierno *m.* government
goma *f.* rubber; gum; **goma de borrar** eraser
gorra *f.* cap
gota *f.* drop
gozar (c) to enjoy

grabado *m.* engraving, print
grabadora *f.* recorder
grabar to record; to engrave
graduarse (ú) to graduate
granja *f.* farm
grano *m.* seed; grain
griego Greek
grito *m.* cry, scream; shout
grueso thick; bulky
gruñir to growl, grunt
guapo good-looking; (*man*) handsome; (*girl*) pretty, attractive
guardar to keep, hold on to; to put away; to keep safe; to preserve; **guardar cama** to stay in bed
guardia *f.* guard
guerra *f.* war
guerrero warlike
guía *m. & f.* guide; *f.* guidebook
guiar (í) to guide
guisado *m.* stew
guisante *m.* pea
gusto *m.* pleasure; taste; **dar gusto a** to please; **tener gusto por** to have a liking (an eye) for

haba *f.* (**el haba**) bean
hábil skillful; able, capable
hablador talkative
hacer (*irr.*) to do; to make; **hacer de** to act as, play the part of; **hacerse** + noun to become; **hacer saber** to inform
hacia towards
hacha *f.* (**el hacha**) ax
hamaca *f.* hammock
harina *f.* flour
hasta until; as far as; up to
hazaña *f.* deed, feat, exploit
hecho *m.* act; fact; **por el solo hecho de** just because
helar (ie) to freeze
heredado inherited
herido wounded
hermoso beautiful
hervir (ie, i) to boil
hielo *m.* ice
hierba *f.* grass
hierro *m.* iron
historia *f.* history; story
historiador *m.* historian
hoja *f.* leaf

hombro *m.* shoulder; **encogerse de hombros** to shrug
hondo deep
horario *m.* schedule; timetable
huelga *f.* strike
huerta *f.* orchard
huésped *m.*, **huéspeda** *f.* guest
huir (y) to flee
humedad *f.* humidity
humilde humble

ibero Iberian
identidad *f.* identity
iglesia *f.* church
igual equal; the same; **igualmente** the same to you; likewise
ilustre illustrious, famous
impedir (i) to prevent; to obstruct, hinder
impermeable *m.* raincoat
imponer (*irr.*) to impose
importar to matter, be important
importe *m.* amount; cost
impreso printed
imprimir to print
impuesto *m.* tax
incluir (y) to include; to enclose
inconformista nonconformist
indeciso indecisive; hesitant
indicar (qu) to indicate; to suggest
indígena indigenous, native; *m. & f.* Indian, native
indio *m.*, **india** *f.* Indian
influir (y) to influence, have influence
informes *m. pl.* references
ingeniero *m.*, **ingeniera** *f.* engineer
iniciar to initiate
inmigración *f.* (*pl.* **inmigraciones**) immigration
inolvidable unforgettable
inscribir(se) to register, enroll
intercambio *m.* exchange
inundar(se) to flood
inútil useless
invitado *m.*, **invitada** *f.* guest
inyección *f.* (*pl.* **inyecciones**) injection, shot; **poner(se) una inyección** to give (oneself) an injection

ir (*irr.*) to go; **ir más allá de** to go beyond
ira *f.* anger, rage
isla *f.* island
izquierdo left; **a la izquierda** to the left

jamás never, not ever
jamón *m.* (*pl.* **jamones**) ham
jarabe *m.* cough syrup
jardín *m.* (*pl.* **jardines**) garden
jardinero *m.*, **jardinera** *f.* gardener
jarro *m.* jug, pitcher
jefatura *f.* headquarters
jefe *m.*, **jefa** *f.* chief, boss
jinete *m.* horseman
joyería *f.* jewelry
judío *m.*, **judía** *f.* Jew
juez *m.* (*pl.* **jueces**) judge
jugador *m.*, **jugadora** *f.* player
jugar (ue, gu) to play
juguetería *f.* toy store
juguetón playful
juicio *m.* judgement
juntar to join, unite
junto together; **junto a** next to, close to
jurado *m.* jury; panel
juventud *f.* youth

lado *m.* side; **al lado de** beside
ladrillo *m.* brick
ladrón *m.* (*pl.* **ladrones**), **ladrona** *f.* thief
lago *m.* lake
lamentar to be sorry about, regret
lana *f.* wool
lanzar (c) to throw
largo long; **a lo largo de** along, alongside; throughout
lástima *f.* pity, shame
lastimar(se) to hurt (oneself)
laúd *m.* lute
lavandería *f.* laundry
lavaplatos *m.* (*pl.* **lavaplatos**) dishwasher
leal loyal
lectura *f.* reading
lechería *f.* dairy store
lechuga *f.* lettuce

legumbre *f.* vegetable
lejano distant
lejos (de) far (from)
lenguaje *m.* language; speech
lento slow
leña *f.* firewood
leño *m.* log
letra *f.* lyrics
letrero *m.* sign; poster
ley *f.* law
leyenda *f.* legend
libertad *f.* freedom, liberty
libra *f.* pound
libre free
librería *f.* bookstore
libreta *f.* notebook
lidiar (bull) to fight
ligero quick, rapid; light
limitar (con) to border on, be
  adjacent to
limosna *f.* alms, charity; **pedir
  limosna** to beg
limpiar to clean
limpio clean, neat
linterna *f.* lantern; flashlight
lío *m.* mess; fuss
listo ready; **estar listo** to be ready;
  ser listo to be clever, smart
llamada *f.* call
llanero *m.* plainsman
llano flat, level
llanura *f.* plain
llave *f.* key; faucet
llegada *f.* arrival
llegar (gu) to arrive; **llegar a ser**
  to become; **llegar a** + *inf.* to
  manage to, to succeed in
llenar to fill
lleno (de) full; filled with
llevar to carry, take; to wear
localidad *f.* ticket
locutor *m.*, **locutora** *f.*
  announcer; newscaster
lodo *m.* mud
lograr to achieve, attain;
  lograr + *inf.* to succeed in,
  manage to
lona *f.* canvas
lotería *f.* lottery
loza *f.* dishes, china
lucha *f.* fight, struggle; conflict
luchar to fight, struggle
luego then, next; afterwards;
  presently

lugar *m.* place; **tener lugar** to
  take place
lugarteniente *m.* lieutenant,
  deputy
lujoso luxurious
luna *f.* moon
luz *f.* (*pl.* **luces**) light

madera *f.* wood
madrileño of Madrid
madrugada *f.* dawn, daybreak
madrugar (gu) to get up early,
  be an early riser
maestría *f.* mastery; skill, expertise
maíz *m.* (*pl.* **maíces**) corn
maleta *f.* suitcase
manco one-armed, one-handed
mancha *f.* stain, spot
manchar to stain, dirty, soil
mandar to send; to order
mando *m.* command
manejar to drive; to manage; to
  handle
manera *f.* way, manner; **de
  manera que** so that
manga *f.* sleeve
manta *f.* blanket
mantel *m.* tablecloth
mantener (*irr.*) to maintain,
  support
mantequilla *f.* butter
manto *m.* cloak, mantle
manzana *f.* apple
manzano *m.* apple tree
mañanitas *f. pl.* Mexican
  birthday song
máquina *f.* machine; **escribir a
  máquina** to type
marca *f.* brand, make
marcar (qu) to mark; (*telephone*)
  to dial; **el tono de marcar**
  dial tone
marcharse to leave, go away
marido *m.* husband
marisco *m.* shellfish
marrón brown; maroon
Marruecos Morocco
mascar (qu) to chew
máscara *f.* mask
masticar (qu) to chew
materia *f.* subject; matter
materno maternal

matricularse to enroll, register
mayor older; greater, larger
mayoría *f.* majority
media *f.* stocking; sock
médico *m.*, **médica** *f.* doctor
medio half; means; **por medio
  de** by means of, through
mediodía *m.* noon; **al mediodía**
  at noon
medir (i) to measure
mejorar to improve
melocotón *m.* (*pl.* **melocotones**)
  peach
menester *m.* need; **es menester**
  it is necessary
menor younger; minor
menos less; **echar de menos** to
  miss
mentir (ie) to lie
mentira *f.* lie
menudo tiny, minute; **a menudo**
  often, frequently
merecer (zc) to deserve, be
  worthy of
merienda *f.* afternoon snack
mermelada *f.* jam, jelly
mesero *m.* waiter
meter to put in; to fit in
metro *m.* meter; subway
mezcla *f.* mixture
mezclar to mix
mezquita *f.* mosque
mientras while; **mientras tanto**
  meanwhile
milagro *m.* miracle
milla *f.* mile
miseria *f.* poverty, destitution;
  una miseria a tiny amount, a
  mere pittance
mismo same; himself
misterio *m.* mystery
mitad *f.* half; middle
mito *m.* myth
mochila *f.* knapsack
moda *f.* style, fashion;
  de moda fashionable, in
  fashion
modismo *m.* idiom
modo mean, way; **de modo que**
  so that
mojarse to get wet
molido ground, crushed
moneda *f.* coin; currency
monja *f.* nun

montaña f. mountain; **montaña rusa** f. roller coaster
montañoso mountainous
montar to mount; **montar a caballo** to go horseback riding
monte m. mountain
morado purple, violet
morder (ue) to bite
morir(se) (ue) to die, pass away
mostrador m. counter
mostrar (ue) to show; **mostrarse** to appear
mover (ue) to move
mozo m. waiter
muchedumbre f. crowd
mudarse to move (house)
mudo mute
mueble m. piece of furniture; **muebles** m. pl. furniture
muela f. tooth, molar
muerte f. death
muerto dead
multa f. fine, penalty
multar to fine
multitud f. multitude, crowd
mundial world; worldwide
mundo m. world; **todo el mundo** everybody
muñeca f. doll; wrist
musulmán Moslem

nacer (zc) to be born
nacimiento m. birth
nada nothing; **de nada** you're welcome
nadador m., **nadadora** f. swimmer
nadar to swim
nadie no one, nobody
naipe m. playing card
naranja m. orange
natación f. swimming
naturaleza f. nature
nave f. vessel, ship
navegante m. navigator, sailor
Navidad f. Christmas
neblina f. fog
necesitado needy
necesitar to need
negar (ie, gu) to deny; **negarse a** to refuse to
negocio m. business
nieta f. granddaughter

nieto m. grandson
ninguno none, not any
niñera f. nursemaid, nanny
nivel m. level
noche f. night; **esta noche** tonight; **por la noche** at night
nombrar to name; to appoint
nombre m. name; **nombre de pila** first name; **nombre y apellido** full name
nota f. grade; note
noticia f. news item; **noticias** f. pl. news; information
noticiero m. newscast
novedad f. novelty; **sin novedad** as usual
noveno ninth
novia f. girlfriend, fiancée, bride
novio m. boyfriend, fiancé, bridegroom
nube f. cloud
nublado cloudy
nudo m. knot; **hacer un nudo** to tie a knot
nuevo new; **de nuevo** again
nunca never

obedecer (zc) to obey
obligar (gu) to force, compel
obra f. work
obrero working; m., **obrera** f. worker
obstante: no obstante notwithstanding, nevertheless
obtener (irr.) to obtain, get
occidental western
octavo eighth
ocupado busy; occupied, taken; **estar ocupado** to be busy
ocurrir to happen, take place, occur
odiado hated
oeste m. west
ofrecer (zc) to offer
oír to hear; **oír decir que** to hear that; **oír hablar de** to hear about, of
¡ojalá que... ! I wish (hope) that . . . , If only . . . !
oler (hue) to smell
oliva f. olive; **aceite de oliva** m. olive oil
olivar m. olive grove

olvidar to forget
olla f. pot; **olla de barro** earthenware pot
onda f. wave; **de última onda** currently most popular
oponerse (a) (irr.) to be opposed to; to object to
oprimido oppressed
oprimir to press; to oppress
opuesto opposite
oración f. (pl. **oraciones**) sentence
orgulloso proud
oriental eastern
orilla f. shore; **a orillas de** on the banks of
oro m. gold
oscuridad f. darkness
oscuro dark
otomano Ottoman
otorgar to grant; to award
oveja f. sheep

paisaje m. landscape
paja f. straw
pájaro m. bird
pajita f. drinking straw
pálido pale
palito m. small stick
palma f. palm tree
panadería f. bakery
pandereta f. tambourine
pantano m. swamp
pañuelo m. handkerchief
papa f. potato
papel m. paper; role, part; **hacer el papel de** to play the role of
papelería f. stationery store
paquete m. package
par m. pair
parada f. stop
parado: estar parado to be stopped, be standing (up)
paraguas m. (pl. **paraguas**) umbrella
parecer (zc) to seem; **parecerse (a)** to resemble
parecido similar
pareja f. couple
pariente m. relative
párrafo m. paragraph
partidario m., **partidaria** f. supporter, follower

partido *m.* game, match; (*politics*) party

partir to start; to depart; **a partir de** from (some specified time)

pasado past; **el sábado pasado** last Saturday

pasajero *m.*, **pasajera** *f.* passenger

pasar to pass; to pass on; to cross; (*time*) to spend

pasatiempo *m.* hobby

pasearse to stroll, take a walk

paseo *m.* stroll; outing

pasillo *m.* aisle

paso *m.* step

pastel *m.* cake

paterno paternal

patinar to skate

patria *f.* native land, fatherland, mother country

patrón *m.* (*pl.* **patrones**), **patrona** *f.* boss, master

patrulla *f.* patrol

pavor *m.* dread, terror

payaso *m.* clown

pedazo *m.* piece; **hacer pedazos** to break (tear) to pieces

pedir (i) to ask for, request; **pedir prestado** to borrow

pegar (gu) to stick (on, up); to glue; to hit, strike, beat

peinar(se) to comb (one's hair)

pelear to fight; to come to blows

película *f.* film, movie

peligroso dangerous

peluquería *f.* hairdresser's, barber shop

peluquero *m.*, **peluquera** *f.* hairdresser

pena *f.* grief, sorrow; penalty; **valer la pena** to be worthwhile

pensamiento *m.* thought

pensar (ie) to think; **pensar + inf.** to intend to; **pensar de** to have an opinion of; **pensar en** to think about, of

pensativo thoughtful, pensive

peor worse

pera *f.* pear

perder (ie) to lose; **echarse a perder** to be spoiled; **perder cuidado** not to worry; **perder de vista** to lose sight of

peregrino *m.*, **peregrina** *f.* pilgrim

perezoso lazy

periodista *m. & f.* journalist

permanecer (zc) to remain, stay

permiso *m.* permission; **con permiso** excuse me; **pedir permiso** to ask for permission

perseguir (i, g) to pursue; to persecute

personaje *m.* (*literature*) character

personalidad *f.* personality

pertenecer (zc) to belong

pesa *f.* weight; dumbbell

pesado heavy

pesar to weigh; *m.* regret; sorrow; **a pesar de** in spite of

pesca *f.* fishing

pescado *m.* fish

pescador *m.* fisherman

pescar (qu) to fish

petróleo *m.* oil, petroleum

pez *m.* (*pl.* **peces**) fish

picante spicy, hot

pícaro mischievous; sly; *m.* rogue, rascal

pico *m.* peak, summit

pie *m.* foot; **estar de pie** to be standing; **a pie** on foot

piedra *f.* stone

piel *f.* skin; leather; fur

pierna *f.* leg

píldora *f.* pill

pintar to paint

pinto spotted

pintor *m.*, **pintora** *f.* painter

pintoresco picturesque

piña *f.* pineapple

pisar to step on

piscina *f.* swimming pool

piso *m.* floor

pista *f.* clue

placer (zc) to be pleased; *m.* pleasure, joy

planchar to iron, press

plano flat, level

plata *f.* silver

plátano *m.* banana

platino *m.* platinum

playa *f.* beach

plaza *f.* plaza, square; **la plaza mayor** the main square

plomo *m.* lead

población *f.* (*pl.* **poblaciones**) population

pobre poor

poco little; **hace poco** a short time ago

poder (*irr.*) to be able to, can, may; *m.* power

poesía *f.* poetry; short poem

poeta *m.*, **poetisa** *f.* poet

policía *f.* police force; *m.* policeman

policíaco police; **novela policíaca** *f.* detective story

polvo *m.* dust

poner (*irr.*) to put; to place; **poner la mesa** to set the table; **ponerse** to put oneself; to put on; **ponerse + adj.** to become, turn; **ponerse a + inf.** to begin to, set about

pordiosero *m.*, **pordiosera** *f.* beggar

pormenor *m.* detail, particular

portarse to behave; **portarse mal** to misbehave

portero *m.* doorman; porter

porvenir *m.* future

poseer (y) to possess, own

potable drinkable

potaje *m.* stew

potencia *f.* power

precio *m.* price

precioso precious; lovely

preciso necessary, essential; **es preciso** it is necessary

precursor *m.*, **precursora** *f.* forerunner

preferir (ie, i) to prefer

prejuicio *m.* prejudice

premio *m.* prize

prenda *f.* garment, article of clothing

preocupado worried

preocuparse to worry

preparar to prepare, get ready

preparativo *m.* preparation

preparatoria *f.* preparatory school

presenciar to be present at; to witness

presidir to preside at (over)

preso imprisoned; *m.* prisoner

préstamo *m.* loan

prestar to lend, loan

presumir to show off; to be conceited

pretender to try to, attempt

prevenir a to warn, forewarn
primaria *f.* elementary school
primo *m.*, **prima** *f.* cousin
principio *m.* beginning; **a principios de** at the beginning of
prisa *f.* hurry, haste; **de prisa** quickly; **estar de prisa** to be in a hurry
probar (ue) to prove; to try; **probarse** to try on
producir (*irr.*) to produce; to bring about
prometer to promise
pronosticar (qu) to predict, forecast
pronóstico *m.* forecast
pronto soon; **tan pronto como** as soon as
propietario *m.*, **propietaria** *f.* owner
propina *f.* tip
propio own, of one's own
proponer (*irr.*) to propose
propósito *m.* purpose
proseguir (i, g) to proceed with, continue
protagonista *m. & f.* main character
proteger (j) to protect
próximo next
prueba *f.* test
publicar (qu) to publish
publicidad *f.* publicity
público *m.* public; audience
pueblo *m.* town
puente *m.* bridge
puerco *m.* pig, pork
puerto *m.* port
puesto *m.* place; position; job; **puesto que** since, as
pulga *f.* flea; **mercado de las pulgas** *m.* flea market
punto *m.* point; **en punto** sharp
pureza *f.* purity

quebrar (ie) to break, smash
quedar(se) to remain; to have (be) left; (*place*) to be; **quedarse con** to keep, hold on to; **quedar en que** to agree that
quehacer *m.* chore

quejarse (de) to complain (about)
quemar to burn (up)
querer (*irr.*) to want, wish, love; **querer decir** to mean
querido dear
queso *m.* cheese
quienquiera whoever
química *f.* chemistry
quinto fifth
quitar(se) to remove, take off
quizás perhaps

rábano *m.* radish
radicar (qu) to be situated (in a place); **radicarse en** to settle
raíz *f.* (*pl.* **raíces**) root; **a raíz de** as a result of
ramo *m.* (*of flowers*) bunch
rana *f.* frog
rápido fast
raqueta *f.* racquet
rasgo *m.* characteristic, trait
rato *m.* while, (short) time; **pasar un buen rato** to have a good time
raza *f.* race
razón *f.* (*pl.* **razones**) reason; right; **tener razón** to be right; **no tener razón** to be wrong
reaccionar to react
real real; royal
realizar (c) to achieve; to fulfill
rebajado reduced
rebozo *m.* wrap, shawl
recado *m.* message; errand
receta *f.* recipe; prescription
recetar to prescribe
recibir to receive
recoger (j) to gather; to pick up
reconocer (zc) to recognize
recordar (ue) to remember
recorrer to travel, tour; **recorrer el mundo** to travel around the world
recorrido *m.* journey, run
recuerdo *m.* remembrance, souvenir; memory; **recuerdos** *m. pl.* regards, best wishes
recursos *m. pl.* resources
rechazar (c) to reject
red *f.* net
redondo round

reducir (*irr.*) to reduce
referir (ie) to recount; to refer
refrendar to endorse
refresco *m.* cool drink, soft drink
refrito refried
regado irrigated
regalar to give (away), present
regalo *m.* gift, present
regar (ie, gu) to water; to strew (in all directions)
regencia *f.* regency
regla *f.* rule; ruler
regresar to return
rehusar to refuse
reina *f.* queen
reinado *m.* reign
reino *m.* kingdom
reírse (í) de to laugh at
reja *f.* grating, grille
relámpago *m.* lightning
relato *m.* story, tale
rellenar to stuff, fill
relleno filled, stuffed
remar to row
remendar (ie) to patch, mend
Renacimiento *m.* Renaissance
rendir (i) to produce, yield; **rendirse** to surrender
renglón *m.* (*pl.* **renglones**) line (of writing)
renombre *m.* renown, fame
renovación *f.* (*pl.* **renovaciones**) renovation; renewal
renovar (ue) to renew; to restore, redecorate
reñir (i) to quarrel; to scold
reparar to repair; **reparar en** to observe, notice
repartir to distribute; to divide up
repente *m.* sudden movement; **de repente** suddenly; unexpectedly
repentino sudden; unexpected
replicar (qu) to answer back, argue
represa *f.* dam
res *f.* animal, beast; **carne de res** *f.* beef
resfriarse (í) to catch (a) cold
resfrío *m.* cold
resolver (ue) to resolve; to solve
respirar to breathe
restos *m. pl.* remains

retratar to portray
retrato *m.* portrait
reunión *f.* (*pl.* **reuniones**) meeting, gathering; social gathering
reunirse to reunite; to join together, gather
rezar (c) to pray
riego *m.* irrigation
rincón *m.* (*pl.* **rincones**) (inside) corner
riqueza *f.* wealth, riches
risa *f.* laugh; **causar risa a** to make (someone) laugh
risueño smiling; cheerful
robo *m.* theft, robbery
rodear to surround; **estar rodeado de** to be surrounded by
rodilla *f.* knee; **de rodillas** kneeling
rogar (ue, gu) to beg, plead for
rompecabezas *m.* (*pl.* **rompecabezas**) puzzle
romper to break; to tear up
roto broken
ruido *m.* noise
rumor *m.* murmur; buzz; confused noise
ruso Russian

saber (*irr.*) to know; **saber de** to know about, be aware of; **hacer saber** to inform
sabio *m.*, **sabia** *f.* learned person; scholar
sabor *m.* taste, flavor
sabroso delicious, tasty
sacar (qu) to take out
sacerdote *m.* priest
saco *m.* jacket
sacrificar (qu) to sacrifice
sacudir to shake; **sacudir el polvo** to dust
sagrado sacred
sala *f.* living room; (*concerts, etc.*) hall, house
salchicha *m.* frankfurter; sausage
salida *f.* exit; departure
salir (*irr.*) to come out; to go out, leave; (*sun*) to rise
saltar to jump
salto *m.* jump, leap; waterfall

salud *f.* health
saludable healthy; beneficial
saludar to greet
saludo *m.* greeting; *m. pl.* (*in letter*) greetings, regards
salvavidas *m.* (*pl.* **salvavidas**) life guard
salvo safe; **sano y salvo** safe and sound
sandía *f.* watermelon
sangriento bloody
sano healthy, fit
santo saint
satisfacer (*irr.*) to satisfy
secadora *f.* dryer
seco dry
secundaria *f.* high school
seda *f.* silk
sede *f.* headquarters; seat
seguido continuous; **seguidos** consecutive; **en seguida** at once, right away
seguir (i, g) to continue; to follow
según according to
seguridad *f.* security; safety
seguro safe; secure; certain; sure; *m.* insurance
selva *f.* forest; jungle
sello *m.* stamp
semáforo *m.* traffic light; **correr un semáforo** to run through a traffic light
sembrar (ie) to seed, sow
semejante similar
semejanza *f.* similarity, resemblance
sencillez *f.* simplicity
sentido *m.* sense; meaning
sentir (ie, i) to feel; to regret, feel sorry; **sentirse** to feel
señal *f.* sign
señorial lordly, majestic, stately
séptimo seventh
serpentina *f.* paper streamer
servilleta *f.* napkin
servir (i) to serve
sexto sixth
sien *f.* temple
siglo *m.* century
significado *m.* meaning
significar (qu) to mean
siguiente following; next
sillón *m.* (*pl.* **sillones**) chair

simpático likeable, pleasant, nice
sindicato *m.* union
sino *m.* fate, destiny
siquiera at least; even if; **ni siquiera** not even
sirena *f.* siren
sitio *m.* place; site; siege
sobrar to be left over, be more than enough
sobre *m.* envelope
sobre on; over, above; about
sobrenatural supernatural
sobrenombre *m.* nickname
sobrepasar to surpass, exceed
sobretodo *m.* overcoat
sobrevivir to survive
sobrio sober; moderate, restrained
socio *m.*, **socia** *f.* partner; member
soga *f.* rope
soldado *m.* soldier
soledad *f.* loneliness; solitude
soler (ue) + inf. to be in the habit of, to usually
solicitud *f.* application
solo alone
soltar (ue) to let go of; to turn loose
sombra *f.* shade
sombrero *m.* hat; **sombrero de jipijapa** straw (Panama) hat
sometido subjected
sonar (ue) to sound
sonreír(se) (í) to smile
soñar (ue) con to dream of
sopa *f.* soup
soplar to blow
sordo deaf
sorprenderse de to be surprised (amazed) at
sorpresa *f.* surprise
sostener (irr.) to sustain; to support
sótano *m.* basement, cellar
subir to raise; to go up; to climb
subrayado underlined
suceder to happen; to succeed, follow
suceso *m.* event, happening
sucio dirty
sueldo *m.* salary
suelo *m.* ground; floor
sueño *m.* dream; sleep
sufrimiento *m.* suffering; misery

sugerencia *f.* suggestion
superficie *f.* surface
suplicar (qu) to beg for, implore
suprimir to suppress
supuesto supposed; assumed;
  ¡por supuesto! of course!,
  naturally!
sur *m.* south
surgir (j) to arise, emerge
suspirar to sigh
suspiro *m.* sigh
sustituir (y) to substitute, replace

tabaco *m.* tobacco; cigar
tabla *f.* plank, board; shelf
talla *f.* (*of clothes*) size
taller *m.* workshop
tamaño *m.* size
tambor *m.* drum
tampoco neither, not either
tapa *f.* lid; cover; snack (*taken with drinks*)
tapiz *m.* (*pl.* **tapices**) tapestry
taquilla *f.* box office
tardanza *f.* delay
tardar to be long; to be late; to delay; to be slow to
tarde late; *f.* afternoon, evening;
  por la tarde in the afternoon
  (evening); **hacerse tarde** to be
  getting late
tarea *f.* assignment; chore
tarjeta *f.* card; **tarjeta postal** postcard
techo *m.* roof
tela *f.* cloth, fabric
telefonear to telephone
telefonista *m.& f.* (telephone) operator
teléfono *m.* telephone; **por teléfono** by phone
televisor *m.* television set
tema *m.* theme; topic
temblar (ie) to tremble, shake; to shiver
temer to fear, be afraid of
templado temperate
tenedor *m.* fork
tener (*irr.*) to have; **tener que** + inf. to have to; **tener por** + adj. to consider (someone) to be
terminar to end, finish
ternura *f.* tenderness

terrateniente *m.& f.* landowner
terraza *f.* terrace; balcony
terremoto *m.* earthquake
terreno *m.* terrain; land
tertulia *f.* regular informal gathering; group, circle
tesoro *m.* treasure
testigo *m.& f.* witness
tiempo *m.* time; weather; **a tiempo** on time
tienda *f.* store
tiento *m.* feeling, touch
tigre *m.* tiger
tijera *f.* scissors
tinto dyed; **vino tinto** *m.* red wine
tipo *m.* type, kind
título *m.* title
toalla *f.* towel
tocadiscos *m.* (*pl.* **tocadiscos**) record player
tocar (qu) to touch; (*music*) to play; **tocarle a uno** to be one's turn
todavía still, yet
todo all; **todos** everyone; **sobre todo** especially, above all
tontería *f.* foolishness; *f. pl.* nonsense
torcer (ue, z) to twist; to bend; to turn
torero *m.* bullfighter
tormenta *f.* storm
toronja *f.* grapefruit
torre *f.* tower
torta *f.* cake
tos *f.* cough
trabajador *m.*, **trabajadora** *f.* worker
traducir (*irr.*) to translate
traer (*irr.*) to bring; to carry; to take
traje *m.* suit; **traje de luces** bullfighter's costume
tranquilo tranquil; peaceful; calm
tranvía *m.* streetcar
tras after
tratar to treat; **tratar de** + inf. to try to; **tratarse de** to concern, be a question of
través: **a través de** through; across
travesura *f.* prank
trigo *m.* wheat

tristeza *f.* sadness
tronar (ue) to thunder
tropezar (ie, c) to stumble, trip; **tropezarse con** to run into
trozo *m.* fragment; passage, section; **trozos escogidos** selections
trueno *m.* thunder
tumba *f.* tomb, grave
tuna *f.* student music group

único only; unique
unidad *f.* unit; unity
unido close; united
útil useful
uva *f.* grape

vaca *f.* cow
vacilar to hesitate
vacío *m.* emptiness; void
valer (*irr.*) to be worth; to cost; **valer la pena** to be worthwhile
valioso valuable
valor *m.* value, worth; courage
vanguardia *f.* vanguard; **pintor de vanguardia** *m.* ultramodern painter
vapor *m.* steam
vaquero *m.* cowboy
variar (í) to vary, alter
variedad *f.* variety
varios several
vaso *m.* glass
vecino *m.*, **vecina** *f.* neighbor
vela *f.* candle
veleta *f.* weather vane
veloz swift, quick, fast
vencer (z) to conquer; to defeat; to overcome
vendedor *m.*, **vendedora** *f.* salesperson
vengar (gu) to avenge
veraz truthful
verdad *f.* truth
verdura *f.* green vegetable
vestimenta *f.* clothing
vestuario *m.* wardrobe, costumes; dressing room
vez *f.* (*pl.* **veces**) time; **a veces** sometimes; **a la vez** at the same time; **tal vez** perhaps

vicio *m.* vice
vid *f.* vine
vidrio *m.* glass
viento *m.* wind
vigilar to watch (over); to guard
vigor *m.* vigor; **en vigor** in force, applicable
villancico *m.* (Christmas) carol
vino, *m.* wine
virreinato *m.* viceroyship
virrey *m.* viceroy
visigodo Visigoth

víspera *f.* eve, day before; **en vísperas de** on the eve of
vista *f.* sight; **perder de vista** to lose sight of
viuda *f.* widow
viudo *m.* widower
vivo alive; lively
volante flying
volar (ue) to fly
volcar (ue, qu) to overturn
volver (ue) to return, come (go) back; **volver a** + inf. to... again;

volver en sí to regain consciousness; **volverse** + adj. to become
voz *f.* (*pl.* **voces**) voice
vuelo *m.* flight
vuelta *f.* turn; **dar vuelta** to turn; **estar de vuelta** to be back

zapatería *f.* shoe store
zarzuela *f.* Spanish musical comedy

able hábil, capaz; **to be able to** poder + *inf.*

about acerca de; **at about** a eso de; **to be about to** estar para + *inf.*, estar a punto de + *inf.*

absent ausente

accompany acompañar

according to según

accustom acostumbrar; **to be accustomed to** acostumbrar + *inf.*, tener la costumbre de

ache dolor *m.*

across a través (de); por

act actuar (ú)

advice consejo *m.*

afraid: to be afraid temer, tener miedo

after después de, después (de) que, tras

afternoon tarde *f.*; **in the afternoon** por la tarde

again de nuevo; otra vez; volver (ue) a + *inf.*

agree to convenir (*irr.*) en; **to agree with** estar conforme (con); estar de acuerdo (con)

agreement acuerdo *m.*; **to come to (reach) an agreement** ponerse de acuerdo

air aire *m.*; **in the open air** al aire libre

allow dejar, permitir

almost casi

alone solo; a solas

already ya

although aunque

always siempre

ambitious ambicioso

among entre

amount cantidad *f.*

amusement diversión *f.* (*pl.* diversiones); **amusement park** parque de diversiones *m.*, parque de atracciones *m.*

angry enojado; **to become (get) angry** enojarse, enfadarse

anniversary aniversario *m.*

announcement anuncio *m.*

annoy molestar

anxiously con ansiedad, ansiosamente

apparently al parecer, por lo visto

appear aparecer (zc)

apple manzana *f.*

application solicitud *f.*

approach acercarse (qu) a

around alrededor de

ashamed avergonzado; **to be ashamed of** avergonzarse (üe, c)

ask preguntar; **to ask for** pedir (i)

asleep: to fall asleep dormirse (ue), quedarse dormido

assignment tarea *f.*, deberes *m. pl.*

astonish asombrar; **to be astonished** asombrarse de

attack atacar (qu)

attend (*be present at*) asistir a; **to attend school** ir a la escuela (al colegio, a la universidad), seguir estudios en

attention atención *f.* (*pl.* atenciones); **to pay attention** poner (prestar) atención

audience público *m.*

aunt tía *f.*

away: to go away irse (*irr.*), marcharse

back atrás; **to be back** estar de vuelta

ball pelota *f.*

bargain ganga *f.*

bank banco *m.*

banker banquero *m.*

bark ladrar

baseball béisbol *m.*

basement sótano *m.*

bath baño *m.*; **to take a bath** bañarse

bathe bañar(se)

bathing suit traje de baño *m.*

beach playa *f.*

beauty belleza *f.*, hermosura *f.*

because porque; **because of** a causa de

become hacerse (*irr.*); llegar (gu) a ser; ponerse (*irr.*) + adj.

bed cama *f.*; **to go to bed** acostarse (ue); **to stay in bed** (*sick*) guardar cama

bedroom alcoba *f.*, dormitorio *m.*

before antes de, antes (de) que; (*in the presence of*) ante

beg rogar (ue, gu), suplicar

begin comenzar (ie), empezar (ie), principiar; ponerse a + *inf.*; echarse a + *inf.*

beginning principio *m.*; **at the beginning of** a principios de

behave (oneself) portarse bien

believe creer (y)

belt cinturón *m.* (*pl.* cinturones)

beside junto a, al lado de; **beside oneself** fuera de sí

better mejor; **it is better** es mejor, más vale

between entre

bird pájaro *m.*

birth nacimiento *m.*

birthday cumpleaños *m.* (*pl.* cumpleaños)

blame culpar, echar la culpa

bone hueso *m.*

booth caseta *f.*, cabina *f.*; **telephone booth** caseta de teléfono *f.*, cabina telefónica *f.*

bored aburrido; **to get (become) bored** aburrirse

born: to be born nacer (zc)

boss jefe *m.*, jefa *f.*, patrón *m.* (*pl.* patrones), patrona *f.*

bother molestar

break romper, quebrar (ie); **to break in pieces** hacer pedazos

breakfast desayuno *m.*; **to eat (have) breakfast** desayunarse

bright claro, luciente
bring traer (*irr.*); **to bring back** (*return*) devolver (ue)
broken roto
brother-in-law cuñado *m.*
build construir (y)
bury enterrar (ie)
bus autobús *m.* (*pl.* autobuses), bus *m.*; **bus stop** parada de autobuses (de buses) *f.*
businessman negociante *m.&f.*, comerciante *m.&f.*
busy ocupado

cage jaula *f.*
call llamada *f.*; **to call** llamar; **telephone call** llamada telefónica *f.*
camp campamento *m.*
candidate candidato *m.*, candidata *f.*
capable capaz
captain capitán *m.* (*pl.* capitanes)
care cuidado *m.*; **I don't care** me es igual, no me importa; **to take care of** cuidar (a, de)
careful cuidadoso; **carefully** con cuidado, con cautela, cuidadosamente
carry llevar; traer (*irr.*); acarrear; cargar (gu)
catalogue catálogo *m.*
catastrophe catástrofe *f.*
cent centavo *m.*
century siglo *m.*
certain cierto
chair silla *f.*
change cambio *m.*; **to change** cambiar
charge cobrar; **to take charge of** encargarse (gu) de
check cheque *m.*; **traveler's checks** cheques de viajero
choose escoger (j), elegir (i, g)
classmate condiscípulo *m.*, condiscípula *f.*, compañero de clase *m.*, compañera de clase *f.*
clean limpiar; limpio
climate clima *m.*
close (*nearby*) cerca, cercano (a)
closet armario *m.*
clothes (clothing) ropa *f.*

comb peine *m.*; peinar; **to comb one's hair** peinarse
come venir (*irr.*); **to come out** salir (*irr.*) de; **to come to** volver (ue) en sí; **to come upon** dar con, tropezar (ie, c) con
company compañía *f.*, empresa *f.*
complain (of) quejarse (de)
complaint queja *f.*
complete terminar, acabar, completar; completo
composer compositor *m.*, compositora *f.*
consent (to) consentir (ie) en
consider dar (*irr.*) por; tener (*irr.*) por; considerar
contest concurso *m.*
cool fresco; **to be cool** hacer fresco
copy copia *f.*
cost costar (ue)
count contar (ue)
courageous valiente
course: of course por supuesto, desde luego
cousin primo *m.*, prima *f.*
crazy loco
credit crédito *m.*
crew tripulación *f.* (*pl.* tripulaciones)
criminal delincuente *m.&f.*
cross cruzar (c), atravesar (ie)
cry llorar
cup taza *f.*
curiously con curiosidad
curtain cortina *f.*
custom costumbre *f.*
customer cliente *m.&f.*

danger peligro *m.*
dangerous peligroso
dare (to) atreverse (a)
date fecha *f.*; compromiso *m.*
day día *m.*; **the day after tomorrow** pasado mañana; **by day** de día; **every day** todos los días; **some day** algún día; **the next day** el (al) día siguiente; **this very day** hoy mismo

daybreak amanecer *m.*; **at daybreak** al amanecer
dear querido
deceive engañar; **to be deceived** engañarse
delay (in) tardar (en); **without delay** cuanto antes
delicious delicioso, rico
demand exigir (j)
deny negar (ie, gu)
depart partir, salir (*irr.*)
department departamento *m.*; **department store** almacén *m.* (*pl.* almacenes)
descend bajar, descender (ie)
deserve merecer (zc)
desk escritorio *m.*
destination destino *m.*
destroy destruir (y); acabar con
different distinto, diferente
diligently diligentemente
dining room comedor *m.*
dinner cena *f.*; **to have dinner** cenar
dirty sucio
disappear desaparecer (zc)
dish plato *m.*
distance distancia *f.*; **in the distance** a lo lejos
distinguish distinguir (g); **to distinguish oneself** destacarse (gu)
do hacer (*irr.*); **to have nothing to do with** no tener nada que ver con
doubt duda *f.*; **there is no doubt** no cabe duda, sin duda
doubtful dudoso
draw dibujar
dream sueño *m.*; **to dream of** soñar (ue) con
drink bebida *f.*; **to drink** beber, tomar
drive conducir (*irr.*), manejar
drop dejar caer (*irr.*)
drown (oneself) ahogar(se) (gu)
drugstore botica *f.*, farmacia *f.*
dry seco
during durante
dust polvo *m.*; **to dust** sacudir el polvo, limpiar; **to be dusty** haber (*irr.*) polvo

early temprano; con tiempo, con anticipación
earn ganar
earring arete *m.*, zarcillo *m.*
effort esfuerzo *m.*
elect elegir (i, j)
electrical eléctrico
elevator ascensor *m.*
elope fugarse (gu), escaparse
embrace abrazar (c), dar un abrazo
employ emplear
employee empleado *m.*, empleada *f.*
empty vacío
end fin *m.*; **to end** terminar; **at the end of** a fines de; al cabo de; **to end by** acabar por; **not hear the end of** no olvidarse fácilmente (pronto) de
enjoy gozar (c) (de), disfrutar (de); **to enjoy oneself** divertirse (ie), pasarlo bien
enjoyable agradable
enough bastante; **to be enough** bastar
enroll inscribirse; matricularse
enthusiasm entusiasmo *m.*; **enthusiastically** con entusiasmo
entire todo; entero
equal igual
escape escaparse
estimate calcular
even: even though aunque; **not even** ni siquiera
evening noche *f.*; **in the evening** por la noche; **every evening** todas las noches
every todos los, todas las; **everybody, everyone** todos, todo el mundo; **everyone else** todos los demás; **everything** todo; **every where** en (por) todas partes
except excepto, con excepción de
exchange cambio *m.*; intercambio *m.*; **to exchange** cambiar (por); **exchange student** estudiante de intercambio *m. & f.*; **exchange rate** (tipo de) cambio *m.*
expensive caro

explain explicar (qu)
eyeglasses anteojos *m. pl.*, gafas *f. pl.*

face cara *f.*, rostro *m.*; **to face** dar (*irr.*) a
fact hecho *m.*; **as a matter of fact** de hecho, en realidad
fail fracasar; **to fail to** dejar de + inf.
failure fracaso *m.*
faint desmayarse
fall caída *f.*; **to fall** caer (*irr.*); **to fall down** caerse
far, far away lejos (de)
fear miedo *m.*; **to fear** temer, tener miedo
feel sentir(se) (ie, i); **to feel like** tener ganas de
fence cerca *f.*, valla *f.*
few pocos; **a few** algunos, unos cuantos, varios
film película *f.*
finally al fin, por fin, finalmente
find encontrar (ue), hallar; **to find out** enterarse (de)
finish terminar, acabar
fire fuego *m.*
fireman bombero *m.*
fireplace chimenea *f.*
firm firme; **to be firm** mostrarse (ue) decidido
fit caber (*irr.*)
fix arreglar, componer (*irr.*)
flame llama *f.*
flee huir (y)
flood inundar; inundación *f.* (*pl.* inundaciones)
floor piso *m.*
fog neblina *f.*; **to be foggy** haber neblina
follow seguir (i, g)
following siguiente
foot pie *m.*; **on foot** a pie
for para, por; **as for** en cuanto a
forbid prohibir
foreign extranjero
forget olvidar, olvidarse de
former (the) aquél, aquélla, aquéllos, aquéllas
fortunately afortunadamente
freeze helar (ie); **to freeze over** helarse

frequently con frecuencia, a menudo, frecuentemente
frighten asustar; **to be frightened** asustarse, tener miedo
front de frente; **in front of** enfrente de, delante de, ante
full lleno
funny chistoso; **the funny thing** lo curioso
furious furioso
furniture muebles *m. pl.*

garbage basura *f.*; **garbage collector** basurero *m.*
garden jardín *m.* (*pl.* jardines)
gather recoger (j)
generally por lo general, por lo común, generalmente
German alemán
get obtener (*irr.*); conseguir (i, g); recibir
gift regalo *m.*
glove guante *m.*
go ir (*irr.*), andar (*irr.*); **to go out** salir (*irr.*)
grade nota *f.*, calificación *f.*; (*pl.* calificaciones); clase *f.*; grado *m.*
graduate graduarse (ú) (de)
granddaughter nieta *f.*
grandparents abuelos *m. pl.*
grandson nieto *m.*
greet saludar
guest invitado *m.*, invitada *f.*; huésped *m.*
guide guía *m. & f.*; **travel guide** guía turístico (de turismo) *m. & f.*
guidebook guía *f.*
guy chico *m.*

hair pelo *m.*, cabello *m.*; **to comb one's hair** peinarse
hand mano *f.*; **to hand over** entregar (gu); **on the other hand** en cambio; **to shake hands** darse la mano
hang (up) colgar (ue, gu)
happen pasar, ocurrir, suceder; **to happen to** por casualidad, acertar (ie) a + *inf.*

have tener (*irr.*); haber (*irr.*); **to have just** acabar de + *inf.*; **to have to** tener que + *inf.*

hear oír (*irr.*); **to hear from** tener noticias, recibir carta (respuesta) de; **to hear of (about)** oír hablar de

help ayuda *f.*; **to help** ayudar; **it cannot be helped** no hay remedio, no tiene remedio

hit golpear; (*target*) dar en

hope esperar

however sin embargo, no obstante

hunger hambre *f.* (el hambre); **to be hungry** tener hambre

hurry darse prisa, apresurarse

hurt doler (ue); hacer (*irr.*) daño (a); **to hurt oneself** hacerse daño

ice hielo *m.*

ice cream helado *m.*

if si; **as if** como si

ill enfermo

illness enfermedad *f.*

imagine imaginarse

immediately en seguida, de inmediato, inmediatamente

inch pulgada *f.*

increase aumentar

inexpensive barato

influence influencia *f.*; **to have influence on** influir (y), afectar

inn posada *f.*

instead of en vez de, en lugar de

intend to pensar (ie) + *inf.*

interest interés *m.* (*pl.* intereses); **to interest** interesar; **to be interested in** interesarse en (por)

invention invento *m.*

itinerary itinerario *m.*

job empleo *m.*, trabajo *m.*, puesto *m.*

joy alegría *f.*

jump saltar, brincar (qu), dar saltos

just solamente; precisamente; **to have just** acabar de + *inf.*

keep guardar; quedarse con; **to keep on** seguir (i, g)

kitchen cocina *f.*

know saber (*irr.*); conocer (zc); **to know about** saber de, estar enterado de, tener conocimiento de; **to know how** saber; **to get to know** (llegar a) conocer

lack carecer (zc) de; **to be lacking** faltar, hacer falta

lady dama *f.*, señora *f.*, señorita *f.*; **young lady** señorita *f.*

lake lago *m.*

last último; **to last** durar; **last** (*month, year*) (el mes, el año) pasado

late tarde; **to be getting late** hacerse tarde; **later** más tarde, después

latter (the) éste, ésta, éstos, éstas

least menos; menor, más pequeño; **at least** a lo (al) menos, por lo menos

leave salir (*irr.*) (de), irse (*irr.*); dejar; **to take leave of** despedirse (i) de

left izquierdo; **to the left** a la izquierda

left: to have left (*remaining*) quedarle a uno

lend prestar

less menos

let dejar

liberty libertad *f.*

library biblioteca *f.*

light luz *f.* (*pl.* luces); **to light** encender (ie)

lightning (bolt) relámpago *m.*

like gustarle (a uno); **to feel like** tener ganas de

line línea *f.*; cola *f.*

listen (to) escuchar; prestar atención

liveliness animación *f.*; energía *f.*

loan préstamo *m.*; **to loan** prestar

locate encontrar (ue), localizar (c)

lock encerrar (ie)

long largo; **a long time** mucho tiempo; **how long** ¿cuánto tiempo?; **longer** más (tiempo); **no longer** ya no

look (at) mirar; **to look for** buscar (qu)

lose perder (ie); **to get lost** perderse

loss pérdida *f.*

lot: a lot mucho

lottery lotería *f.*

love encantarle; amar, querer (*irr.*); **to be in love (with)** estar enamorado (de); **to fall in love (with)** enamorarse (de)

lucky afortunado; **to be lucky** tener suerte

luggage equipaje *m.*

lunch almuerzo *m.*; **to have (eat) lunch** almorzar (ue, c)

luxurious lujoso

magazine revista *f.*

mail echar al correo

maintain mantener (*irr.*)

man hombre *m.*; **old man** viejo *m.*

manager gerente *m. & f.*

manufacture fabricar (qu)

marry casarse (con); **to get married** casarse (con)

matter asunto *m.*; **to matter** importar; **as a matter of fact** de hecho, en realidad; en efecto; **no matter how** por + *adj.* + que + *subj.*

meanwhile mientras tanto

measure medir (i)

meat carne *f.*

meet encontrarse (ue) con; reunirse; conocer (zc)

memory recuerdo *m.*; memoria *f.*

message recado *m.*, mensaje *m.*

milk leche *f.*

minute minuto *m.*

miss echar de menos

mistake error *m.*, falta *f.*; **to be mistaken** equivocarse (qu); **to make a mistake** cometer un error

more más; **more and more** cada vez más

morning mañana *f.*; **in the morning** por la mañana

movies cine *m.*

much mucho; **how much** ¿cuánto?; **so much** tanto; **too much** demasiado; **to be too much** sobrar

mud lodo *m*.; **to be muddy** haber lodo

multiplied by por

must deber de, tener (*irr.*) que; **one must** hay que + *inf.*

near cerca de; **nearby** cercano

necessary necesario, preciso

need necesidad *f*.; **to need** necesitar, hacerle falta (a uno), faltarle (a uno)

nephew sobrino *m*.

nervous nervioso

never nunca, jamás

nevertheless sin embargo, no obstante

new nuevo; **nothing new** sin novedad

news noticia *f*.; noticias *f. pl.*

newspaper periódico *m*., diario *m*.

next próximo, entrante; siguiente; junto a, al lado de; **the next day** el (al) día siguiente

niece sobrina *f*.

night noche *f*.; **at night** de noche; **last night** anoche; **tonight** esta noche

nightfall anochecer *m*.; **at nightfall** al anochecer

noise ruido *m*.

none ninguno

now ahora; **from now on** de hoy en adelante; **not now** ahora no; **right now** ahora mismo; **nowadays** hoy día, actualmente

nowhere en ninguna parte

numerous numeroso; muchos

obey obedecer (zc)

occur ocurrir, suceder, acontecer (zc), pasar

offer ofrecer (zc)

office oficina *f*., despacho *m*.

often a menudo; muchas veces

oil aceite *m*.; **suntan oil** aceite bronceador *m*.

old viejo; **oldest** el (la) mayor, los (las) mayores

only solamente; **if only!** ¡ojalá!

orchestra orquesta *f*.

order (*command*) orden *f*. (*pl.* órdenes); **to order** ordenar, mandar; pedir (i)

other otro; **otherwise** de otro modo

owe deber

owner dueño *m*., dueña *f*.

paint pintar

pair par *m*.

paper ensayo *m*.; papel *m*., documento *m*.

park parque *m*.; **to park** estacionar; **amusement park** parque de diversiones

participate participar, tomar parte (en)

partner socio *m*., socia *f*.

passenger pasajero *m*., pasajera *f*.

passport pasaporte *m*.

pay (for) pagar (gu) (por)

perhaps tal vez, quizás

permit permitir, dejar; admitir

pick escoger (j), elegir (i, j); **to pick up** recoger (j)

picture fotografía *f*.; cuadro *m*.; (*movie*) película *f*.; **to take a picture** sacar (qu) una foto

piece pedazo *m*.; **piece of furniture** mueble *m*.; **to break in pieces** hacer pedazos

pity lástima *f*.; **it is a pity** es lástima

place lugar *m*., sitio *m*.; **to place** colocar (qu), poner (*irr.*); **to take place** tener lugar

plan plan *m*.; **to plan** planear

plate plato *m*.

play comedia *f*.; obra dramática *f*.; **to play** (*music*) tocar (qu); (*game*) jugar (ue, gu); (*a role*) hacer el papel de

pleasant agradable

please por favor; **to please** gustar, agradar

poem poesía *f*., poema *m*.

politician político *m*., política *f*.

population población *f*. (*pl.* poblaciones)

port puerto *m*.

poster cartel *m*.

pound libra *f*.

prefer preferir (ie)

prepare preparar

pretend fingir (j); pretender

previous anterior

price precio *m*.

pride orgullo *m*.

prince príncipe *m*.

princess princesa *f*.

principal director *m*., directora *f*.

prize premio *m*.; **first prize** (*lottery*) premio gordo *m*.

prohibit prohibir

project proyecto *m*.

promise promesa *f*.; **to promise** prometer

protect proteger (j)

provided that con tal que, siempre que

pursue perseguir (i, g)

put poner (*irr.*); **to put on** ponerse; **to put in** meter; **to put out** apagar (gu)

pyramid pirámide *f*.

quality calidad *f*.

question pregunta *f*.; **to be a question of** tratarse de

quickly rápidamente; pronto

quiet tranquilo; **to become quiet** callarse

quite bastante

race carrera *f*.; raza *f*.

railroad ferrocarril *m*.

rain lluvia *f*.; **to rain** llover (ue)

raise aumentar; levantar; alzar (c)

rate tipo *m*.; **exchange rate** (tipo de) cambio *m*.

ray rayo *m*.

reach llegar (gu) a, alcanzar (c)

ready listo; disponible; **to get ready to** disponerse (*irr.*) a

reality realidad *f*.

realize darse cuenta de

really de veras

receive recibir; admitir; aprobar (ue)

recommend recomendar (ie)

record disco *m*.

refuse negarse (ie, gu) a, rehusar
regard respecto *m.*; **in regard to** en cuanto a, con respecto a;
regards (*greeting*) recuerdos *m. pl.*
rehearsal ensayo *m.*
rehearse ensayar
relate contar (ue), relatar
relative pariente *m.*
relax descansar; **relaxed** descansado, relajado
remember recordar (ue), acordarse (ue) de
remove quitar
rent alquiler *m.*; **to rent** alquilar
repair reparar, componer (*irr.*)
request pedir (i)
respect respetar; **respected** respetado, estimado
responsibility responsabilidad *f.*
rest descanso *m.*; **to rest** descansar
retire jubilarse
return volver (ue), regresar; (*give back*) devolver (ue)
right derecho *m.*; **at (to) the right** a la derecha; **to be right** tener razón; **it will be all right** saldrá bien, se arreglará
river río *m.*
role papel *m.*; **to play a role** hacer un papel
room cuarto *m.*, habitación *f.* (*pl.* habitaciones); sitio *m.*, espacio *m.*; **to be room for** caber
routine rutina *f.*
rule regla *f.*; **to rule** gobernar (ie)
run correr
rush apresurarse

sacrifice sacrificio *m.*; **to sacrifice** sacrificar(se) (qu)
sad triste
sadness tristeza *f.*
safe seguro; **safe and sound** sano y salvo
same mismo; **at the same time** a la vez
scene escena *f.*
schedule horario *m.*
scream grito *m.*; **to scream** gritar, dar voces
script guión *m.* (*pl.* guiones)

seat asiento *m.*; **seated** sentado
seem parecer (zc)
seldom rara vez
sell vender
send mandar, enviar (í)
serve servir (i); **to serve as** servir de
set juego *m.*; **to set** (*the sun*) ponerse (*irr.*); **to set the table** poner la mesa
several varios
shame vergüenza *f.*
share compartir
shelf estante *m.*
shine brillar
ship barco *m.*, buque *m.*
shopkeeper tendero *m.*, tendera *f.*
short corto; **shortly** dentro de poco
show mostrar (ue), enseñar
shy tímido
side lado *m.*
sidewalk acera *f.*
similar parecido, semejante
since desde; puesto que, ya que
sit sentar (ie); **to sit down** sentarse
skillfully con habilidad, hábilmente
skit sátira *f.*, parodia *f.*
sleepy soñoliento; **to be sleepy** tener sueño
sleigh trineo *m.*
smart inteligente
smash hacer pedazos
smile sonrisa *f.*; **to smile** sonreír (í)
smoke humo *m.*; **to smoke** fumar
snow nieve *f.*; **to snow** nevar (ie)
so tan; **so that** de modo (manera) que
soap jabón *m.* (*pl.* jabones)
some alguno, algún; **someone** alguien; **something** algo; **sometimes** a veces
soon pronto; **as soon as** así que, tan pronto como, en cuanto
sorry ¡perdón!; **to be sorry** sentirlo (ie)
south sur *m.*
souvenir recuerdo *m.*

spend (*time*) pasar; (*money*) gastar
spite despecho *m.*; **in spite of** a pesar de
stage escenario *m.*, tablas *f. pl.*
stain mancha *f.*; **to stain** manchar
stamp estampilla *f.*, sello *m.*
stand (up) levantarse; **standing** de pie, parado
start empezar (ie), comenzar (ie); echarse a
stay quedar(se), permanecer (zc); **to stay in bed** (*ill*) guardar cama
stereo estéreo *m.*
still todavía, aún
stomach estómago *m.*; **stomach ache** dolor de estómago *m.*
stop parar (se); dejar de + *inf.*; **bus stop** parada *f.*
store tienda *f.*
storm tormenta *f.*
strange extraño, raro
strict estricto
stroll dar una vuelta, dar un paseo, pasearse
strong fuerte
student alumno *m.*, alumna *f.*, estudiante *m. & f.*; **exchange student** estudiante de intercambio *m. & f.*
studies estudios *m. pl.*
succeed (in) lograr + *inf.*
success éxito *m.*; **to be successful** tener éxito
such tal
suddenly de repente, de pronto
sugar azúcar *m.*
suit traje *m.*; **bathing suit** traje de baño *m.*
suitcase maleta *f.*
sunrise salida del sol *f.*
support apoyo *m.*; **to support** apoyar, mantener (*irr.*)
surprise sorpresa *f.*; **to surprise** sorprender; **to be surprised** asombrarse (de)
swim nadar

table mesa *f.*; **to set the table** poner la mesa
tablecloth mantel *m.*

take tomar; llevar; **to take off** quitarse; (*plane*) despegar (gu); salir (*irr.*); **to take out** sacar (qu)

telegraph telégrafo *m.*

telephone teléfono *m.*; **on the telephone** por teléfono

tell decir (*irr.*)

tent tienda *f.*

textbook libro de texto *m.*

thank dar las gracias, agradecer (zc)

theater teatro *m.*

then luego; entonces

therefore por consiguiente, por eso

thing cosa *f.*; **it's a good thing that** menos mal que

think pensar (ie); **to think of** pensar en; **to think about** (*consider*) considerar, pensar en

thirst sed *f.*; **to be thirsty** tener sed

threaten (to) amenazar (c) (con)

through por; a través de

throw echar, tirar, arrojar

ticket billete *m.*, boleto *m*; **round-trip ticket** billete de ida y vuelta

tight apretado; **to be tight** apretar (ie)

time tiempo *m.*; (*hour*) hora *f.*; (*in a series*) vez *f.* (*pl.* veces); **on time** a tiempo; **from time to time** de vez en cuando; **to have a good time** divertirse (ie), pasar un buen rato; **for a long time** durante mucho tiempo, por largo rato

tired cansado; **to become tired** cansarse

together junto

tomorrow mañana; **the day after tomorrow** pasado mañana

ton tonelada *f.*

tonight esta noche

too demasiado, muy; (*also*) también

tool herramienta *f.*

tour excursión *f.* (*pl.* excursiones)

town pueblo *m.*

toy juguete *m.*

travel viajar

tray bandeja *f.*

trip viaje *m.*; **to take a trip** hacer un viaje; **round trip** viaje de ida y vuelta

trophy trofeo *m.*

try (to) tratar (de + *inf.*), intentar; **to try on** probar(se) (ue)

twice dos veces

twist torcer (ue, z)

umbrella paraguas *m.* (*pl.* paraguas)

uncle tío *m.*

unfortunately por desgracia, desgraciadamente, desafortunadamente

university universidad *f.*

unless a menos que

until hasta

up arriba; **up and down** de un lado para otro

use usar; **I used to go** iba, solía ir, acostumbraba ir

usually por lo común, por lo general, generalmente

vase florero *m.*, jarrón *m.* (*pl.* jarrones)

vegetable legumbre *f.*, verdura *f.*

visit visitar

wait (for) esperar

waiter mesero *m.*, mozo *m.*; camarero *m.*

want desear, querer (*irr.*)

war guerra *f.*

warm caliente; **to warm oneself** calentarse (ie); **to be warm** (*weather*) hacer calor; (*person*) tener calor

warn avisar, advertir (ie), prevenir (*irr.*)

wash lavar(se)

waste (*time*) perder (ie)

watch reloj *m.*; **to watch** mirar, reparar en

way camino *m.*; manera *f.*; **to get one's way** salirse con la suya

wealth riqueza *f.*

wedding boda *f.*

weekend fin de semana *m.*

welcome bienvenido; **you're welcome** de nada, no hay de qué

wet mojado; **to get wet** mojarse

wheat trigo *m.*

whenever cuando quiera (que)

wherever dondequiera (que)

while mientras (que); **a little while ago** hace poco; **in a little while** dentro de poco

whistle silbar

whoever quien(es) quiera

wide ancho

wife esposa *f.*, mujer *f.*, señora *f.*

win ganar; **winning** (*number*) premiado

wind viento *m.*; **to be windy** hacer viento

wind (*a watch*) dar cuerda (a un reloj)

wish (for) desear, anhelar

with con; **with me** conmigo; **with you** contigo, con Ud., con Uds.; **with him(self)** consigo

within dentro de

without sin, sin que

wood madera *f.*; **wooden** de madera

word palabra *f.*; **to keep one's word** cumplir con la palabra

work trabajar; funcionar

worry preocupación *f.* (*pl.* preocupaciones); **to be worried** estar preocupado; **not to worry** perder (ie) cuidado, no preocuparse

worse peor; **worst** el (la) peor, los (las) peores

write escribir; **written** escrito; **in writing** por escrito

yet todavía; **not yet** todavía no

young joven; **younger** menor; **youngest** el (la) menor, los (las) menores

Index